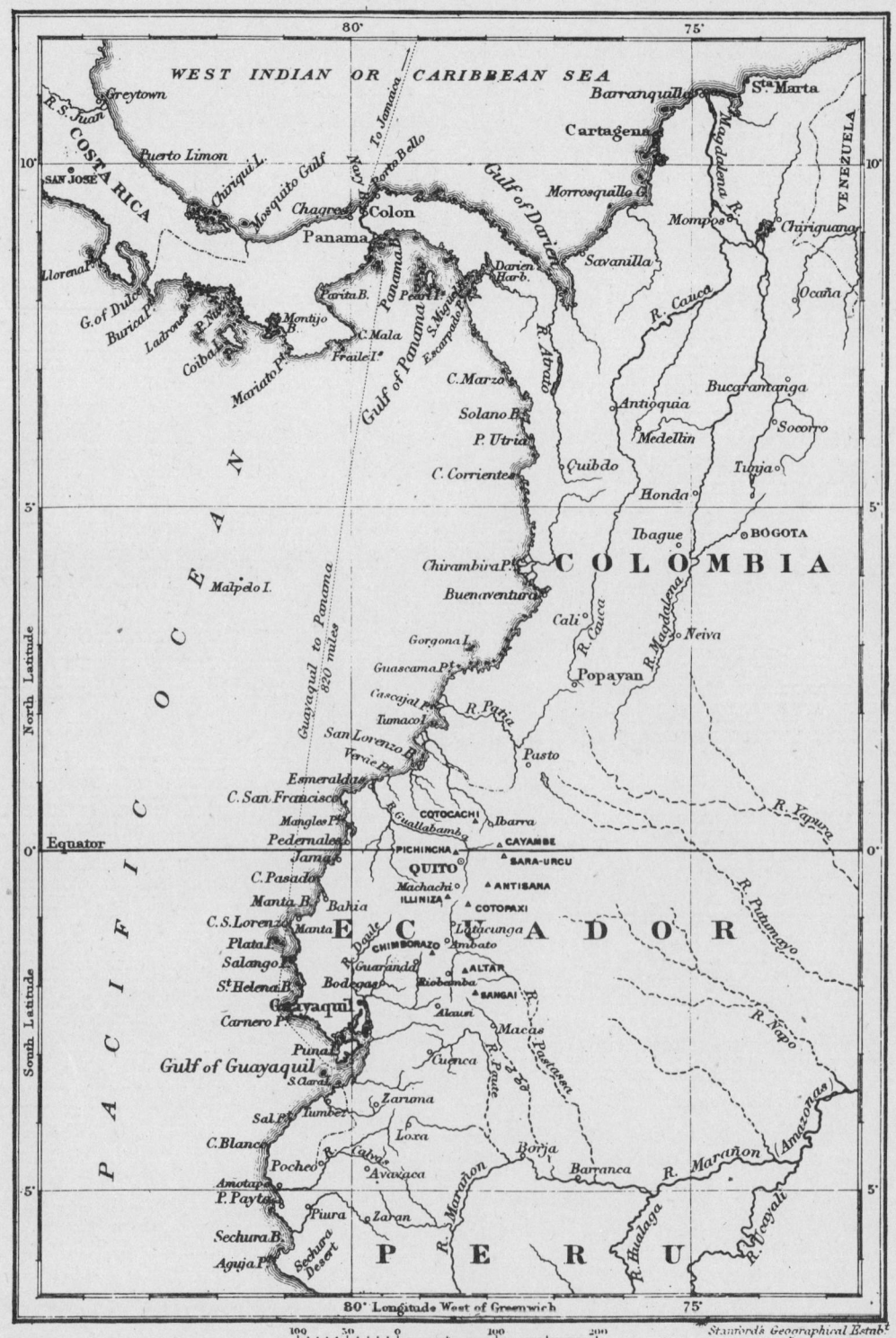

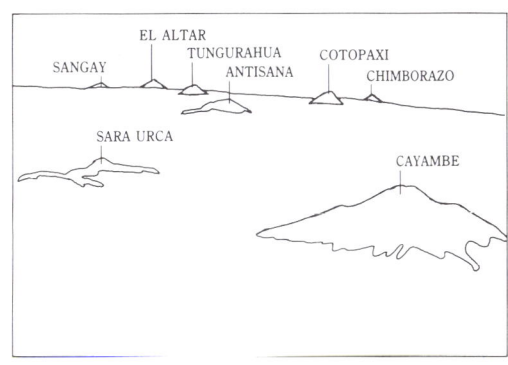

The Ecuadorean snowpeaks from 30,000 feet elevation, just north of the Equator. This photograph, taken from the bombardier's sight of an airplane, may be the only existing shot of all the important peaks on a clear day.

TRAVELS AMONGST THE GREAT ANDES OF THE EQUATOR

"THE WHIRLING SNOW MOCKED OUR EFFORTS."

TRAVELS AMONGST THE GREAT ANDES OF THE EQUATOR

EDWARD WHYMPER

A NEW EDITION
WITH INTRODUCTION
AND PHOTOGRAPHS BY

LOREN McINTYRE

GIBBS M. SMITH, INC.
PEREGRINE SMITH BOOKS
SALT LAKE CITY

This is a Peregrine Smith Book

Introduction copyright © 1987 by Gibbs M. Smith, Inc.

Photographs copyright © 1987 by Loren McIntyre

All rights reserved. No part of this book may be reproduced without written permission from the publisher, with the exception of short passages for review purposes

Published 1987 by Gibbs M. Smith, Inc., P.O. Box 667, Layton, Utah 84041

Front cover: *Cotopaxi (Ecuador)* by Loren McIntyre

Cover design by J. Scott Knudsen

Printed and bound in the United States of America

91 90 89 88 87   5 4 3 2 1

FIRST EDITION

Library of Congress Cataloging-in-Publication Data

    Whymper, Edward, 1840-1911.
    Travels amongst the great Andes of the equator.
    Includes index.
    1. Andes Region—Description and travel.
2. Ecuador—Description and travel.
3. Mountaineering—Andes Region. 4. Whymper, Edward, 1840-1911—Journeys—Andes Region.
5. Whymper, Edward, 1840-1911—
Journeys—Ecuador.
I. McIntyre, Loren, 1917-   . II. Title.
F3741.A6W6   1987   918'.0439   87-16215
ISBN 0-87905-281-3

INTRODUCTION TO THE
1987 EDITION

At nightfall on 15 August 1966, as I was lying belly-down in my sleeping bag reading *Travels Amongst the Great Andes of the Equator,* I felt Cotopaxi groan and shudder as if alive. One of those small earthquakes that precede a volcanic eruption? Or just the daily slippage of a glacier down this enormous pile of lava and ash that Edward Whymper's superstitious Alpine guide called an "animal?"

My candle guttered for lack of oxygen though I was still far below Cotopaxi's summit. Conscious of the icecaps poised a vertical mile above my tent, I turned to Whymper's account of an eruption of lava[1] from Cotopaxi's crater in 1877:

"The weight must be reckoned by hundreds of millions of tons, its heat at thousands of degrees Fahrenheit, and when it . . . fell in cascades upon the surrounding slopes of snow, ice, and glacier, much of it must have . . . bounded downwards in furious leaps, ploughing up the mountain like cannon-shot. Portions of the glaciers, uncemented from their attachments by the enormous augmentation of heat, slipped away. . . ."

He reported how floods swept down both sides of the Continental Divide, sluicing farmhouses and mule trains into the Pacific Ocean on one side and the Amazon Basin on the other.

"When I passed this way," noted Whymper three years later, "I found the country a wilderness." He scaled soft ash to Cotopaxi's summit and pitched his tent. His thermometer registered 13° F—the lowest reading of his entire equatorial journey. Soon he smelled burning rubber and found that the temperature of cinders under the tent floor was 110° F. He stayed the night above 19,000 feet to prove that conditioned humans could survive awhile at that height.[2]

The slopes cooled, and thousands of snowfalls later I clawed up mas-

INTRODUCTION TO THE 1987 EDITION

sive new glaciers to reach the ice-free crater, a third of a mile across and still steaming. From the top, on that rare clear day, I sighted a dozen solitary snow peaks, nearly all of them volcanoes.

Eleven of the peaks were climbed during the first half of 1880 by Whymper, a Londoner, and his two Italian companions, Jean-Antoine Carrel and a nephew, Louis Carrel. Eight were first ascents. The Europeans deemed most of the remaining peaks over 13,000 feet (they number nearly forty) to be "contemptible." Whymper lost several weeks to a "stomach gone all wrong," a disablement that stiill afflicts travelers to the hinterlands of Ecuador. And Louis Carrel was laid up for two months after freezing his feet on Chimborazo during their first and highest climb.

The summit of Chimborazo was Whymper's major goal. He was prepared to devote all his time in Ecuador to Chimborazo alone to observe physiological effects of low atmospheric pressure. He also planned to study highland flora and fauna, and he brought eleven barometers to measure altitudes of mountains.

Whymper did not own up to his chief motivation: a zest for high adventure. It enlivens page after page of his *Travels*. He was driven by an urge to find ways, however dangerous and difficult, to climb impressive peaks. He enjoyed setting foot on a mountaintop—especially if he was the first to do so. He liked to set records in an age when record-setting was not the rage that it is today.

Whymper termed the experience "sport" in an earlier book, his classic *Scrambles Amongst the Alps*. He wrote *Scrambles* when he was concerned less with demonstrating erudition than extolling the manly virtues of mountaineering. "Caution and perseverance gain the day—the height is reached!" it concludes, "and those beneath cry, 'Incredible; 'tis superhuman!' "

Most people view scaling dangerous heights as unnecessarily risky, if not downright peculiar. So some climbers, as they grow older, try to upstage their aberration with a show of higher purpose. But after such theatrics, and after adding a log to the fire and opening a bottle, they usually reveal a mania for mountains far more intimate than any affair with a microscope or petri dish.

INTRODUCTION TO THE 1987 EDITION

This syndrome can be traced back to naturalist Alexander von Humboldt's attempt to climb Chimborazo in 1802, when that mountain was thought be the world's tallest. The climb was the high point of a five-year scientific sojourn in the New World by the father of modern geography, and the feat helped him to achieve international renown. Learning thirty years later that British surveyors of the Himalayas had reached greater elevations, Humboldt the climber felt let down: "All my life I have imagined that of all mortals I was the one who had risen highest in the world—I mean on the slopes of Chimborazo!"

In a way he had: the earth's equatorial bulge raises Chimborazo's summit higher than any mountain—nearly two miles higher than Everest's—when measured from the center of the globe.

One of Edward Whymper's reasons for casting his expedition to Ecuador in a scientific mold was to gain the support of officialdom in a land where no one would believe climbing was sport. But Ecuadoreans were not about to be taken in by the "science" ploy. They knew the Europeans were really looking for treasure. Ever since the Spanish conquest of the Incas in the 1500s legend has held that loot lies buried in the mountains. In 1966, when I came down from Cotopaxi, rural authorities demanded to know whether I had found the treasure that climbers keep seeking.

In 1880 their predecessors put the same question to Whymper's porters, who replied, "The Doctor, dressed like a king, went from one place to another, looking about; but after a time Señor Juan and Señor Luis seemed afraid of him, for they tied him up with a rope." "Enough of this; tell us, did they find treasure?" "We think they did. They went down on their hands and knees searching for it, and they wrapped what they took in paper and brought it away." "Was it gold?" "We do not know, but it was very heavy." The royal attire was Whymper's Ulster coat over a dressing-gown. His crown was a Dundee whaling-cap. The treasures were mineral samples.

Another reason for Whymper's insistence that he climbed for scientific reasons is that he was still burdened by the bitter aftermath of his conquest of the Matterhorn in 1865. That triumph ended in a tragedy that brought Whymper notoriety and "held up the tide of mountaineering for fully

INTRODUCTION TO THE 1987 EDITION

half a generation," according to one alpine club president. Four of Whymper's companions perished on the way down from the summit. One was a famous guide, another an English lord.

The accident took the joy out of "scrambles" that Whymper had begun at age twenty when he journeyed to the Alps in 1860 to sketch major peaks. During the next four years he made several first ascents in the Alps.

Eight times Whymper attacked the Matterhorn without achieving the summit of that awesome pinnacle. Other climbers were trying to get there first. The best of them was an Italian guide from the village of Valtournanche who had often embraced the mountain but had never gotten on top of it. He was Jean-Antoine Carrel, who was sometimes hired by Whymper and who long afterwards would become Whymper's "chief of staff" in Ecuador.

By 10 July 1865 Whymper had climbed 100,000 vertical feet in eighteen days and was ready to tackle the Matterhorn, with Carrel as guide, by the hitherto "impossible" northeast ridge where he had discovered that the tilt of the strata afforded better footholds. But on the 11th, Carrel stole a march on Whymper by heading without him up the southern face of the Matterhorn, bound for the summit with six of the best Italian guides.

Whymper chose not to linger "as a foolish lover" at the foot of the Matterhorn. He combined forces with three other Englishmen and their guides and raced up the northeast ridge on the 13th and 14th.

"At 1.40 p.m. the world was at our feet, and the Matterhorn was conquered." It was a splendid day. The seven climbers built a cairn and shouted at the defeated Italian party, still 1,200 feet below.

But on the way down, the inexperienced middle man on the rope fell and knocked three others off the cliff. The rope broke, saving Whymper and two guides. The others plunged 4,000 feet onto Matterhorn Glacier.

Three days later Jean-Antoine Carrel reached the summit from the more difficult Italian side.

Chastened by the Matterhorn's "terrible vengeance" and by critics unable to share his enthusiasm for mountain climbing, Whymper turned in 1867 from the many-peopled Alps to the vacant ice of Greenland. But a survey in 1872 convinced him that crossing the icecap was beyond his means.

INTRODUCTION TO THE 1987 EDITION

Colonial politics thwarted a Himalayan project in 1874. Then the War of the Pacific in 1879, involving Chile, Peru, and Bolivia, put an end to his preparations to climb the highest peaks in the Andes. "I turned to the Republic of Ecuador, the most lofty remaining country which was available." He brought along Jean-Antoine Carrel, then fifty-two, and his nephew Louis Carrel, twenty-six.

Edward Whymper at forty was a more sober man than the exuberant author of *Scrambles*. Few Ecuadoreans appeared to him to be as "upright, brave, and true" as his Alpine friends of yore. A fastidious fellow, he detested untrustworthy hirelings and filthy lodgings, "though, after all, a muddy ditch is not the worst of beds—one soon becomes attached to it."

He had utmost confidence in himself and Jean-Antoine, although he regarded the famous guide as a bit of a bumpkin and laughed at his superstitions. Jean-Antoine's cure for all ailments from dysentery to anoxia was red wine. "Especially when heated and beaten up with raw eggs . . . at the Eve of St. John, when the moon is full, for women who are in family way; providing it is drunk whilst looking over the left shoulder. . . ."

In Ecuador, while Whymper abstained from "high gymnastics" in the interest of science, the Carrels grew tired of being mere porters. "They pined for work more in harmony with the old traditions; for something with dash and go,—the sallying forth in the dead of the night with rope and axe, to slay a giant; returning at dusk, with shouts and rejoicing, bringing its head in a haversack. I sacrificed a day to meet their wishes, and told them to select a peak, just as one may give a sugar-plum to a fractious child to keep it quiet."

The Carrels got more headhunting than they could handle at the second camp on Chimborazo, about 16,000 feet high, and Whymper got a flying start at studying the pathology of oxygen deprivation. All three of the experienced alpinists turned belly-up with AMS (Acute Mountain Sickness), also termed soroche in English, Spanish, and Quechua—the Inca tongue. They suffered splitting headaches, fever, and "found it impossible to sustain life without every now and then giving spasmodic gulps," like fish out of water. They could not eat, but "wished to smoke, and found that our

INTRODUCTION TO THE 1987 EDITION

pipes almost refused to burn, for they, like ourselves, wanted more oxygen."

Whymper was mystified that a companion, Mr. Perring, "a rather debilitated man [who] could scarcely walk on a flat road without desiring to sit down," was not distressed by the altitude.[3] To the contrary; Perring nursed the fallen veterans for two or three days.

They followed Alexander von Humboldt's 1802 route to a cliff so steep that Whymper declared, "Thus far and no farther a man may go who is not a mountaineer." His barometer read 18,400 feet. The place was about as high as Humboldt and his three ill-equipped companions could have climbed, although Humboldt had asserted that "According to the barometric formula given by LePlace, we had now reached an elevation of 19,286 English feet." Whymper did not accuse that most famous scientist of the nineteenth century of exaggerating the height, but he did marvel politely at "the divine speed" of Humboldt's descent: 3,686 feet in one hour.[4]

I photographed the route from both surface and air while writing a book about Humboldt's sojourn in the New World. My guide was Marco Cruz, an Ecuadorean who has climbed on five continents. Marco first scaled Chimborazo at fourteen, with his father, and has returned to the 20,702-foot summit more than fifty times. At Humboldt's approximate high point, both my excellent altimeters as well as Marco's registered 18,200 feet—a bit loftier than one-half sea-level pressure.[5]

Working north from Chimborazo, the three Europeans scaled ten more of Ecuador's highest mountains between 1 February and 30 June 1880. One historic first ascent, up the steep twin peaks of Illiniza, belonged to the Carrels alone. On two other Illiniza attempts, Whymper stopped short of risking a fall from steep friable rock, glazed with ice and concealed in cloud.

Similar dangers kept the team from assailing the spires of El Altar, once the highest mountain in Ecuador. Indian legend tells of the stupendous eruption of Capac Urca—Almighty Mountain—that laid darkness on the highlands centuries ago. Its cone exploded and left an enormous caldera rimmed with a crescent of peaks. Seeing the mountain as a great cathedral, Spaniards named it The Altar. They called the northern rim The Canon and the eastern The Tabernacle. The southern spires, at 17,457 feet the loftiest rim,

INTRODUCTION TO THE 1987 EDITION

they named The Bishop.

Whymper did not go near Sangay, Ecuador's sixth highest peak, a symmetrical cone south of El Altar that fires salvos of lava projectiles so lethal that the Matterhorn's bounding rockfalls are confetti by comparison. Seldom-seen Sangay is almost always blanketed with clouds that swirl up from the Amazon Basin. Whymper sighted it only once, while climbing Chimborazo, and described huge jets of steam that shot skyward at twenty-two miles a minute. For hundreds of years Sangay has been ejecting lava and ash continually and therefore may be higher than the 17,159 feet long listed as its altitude.

One splendid morning I approached the summit in a small plane to marvel at Sangay's ongoing spectacle of fire and ice. Rivers of lava sizzled through fresh snowfalls. Out of the crater floor burst molten blobs of lava that whizzed hundreds of feet above my plane, froze into contorted black stones, and arched back down to pockmark the snow.

More passive perils, crevasses, endangered the expedition on all four of the largest snowpeaks, Chimborazo, Cotopaxi, Cayambe, and Antisana. Whymper saw crevasses on Antisana half a mile long, two hundred and fifty feet deep, and eighty feet across. He fell into a hidden one seventy feet deep when a snow bridge collapsed, and dangled for anxious minutes between sheer ice walls on a taut rope held by Louis Carrel on one side of the crevasse and Jean-Antoine on the other. This time a good rope saved him, whereas on the Matterhorn it was the failure of a bad rope that saved Whymper's life. Although Whymper was apparently unruffled by the fall, he did write later of Jean-Antoine's complaint that "his blood had been turned sour by the crevasse episode. This dangerous malady, however, yielded to the benign influence of the universal remedy. . . ."

One insidious glacier flows from the 18,996-foot summit of Cayambe south across the Equator. It is not very steep and seems to offer an easy route to the top, yet it is riddled with crevasses concealed under smooth layers of snow. The three Europeans climbed it from the southern hemisphere into the northern, from autumn into spring, and back again the same day.

INTRODUCTION TO THE 1987 EDITION

Upon arrival in Ecuador, Edward Whymper and the Carrels had climbed from the sea to the summit of the country in three quick weeks. Now the Englishman decided to exit the Andes in the same grand manner that he had entered: via Chimborazo.

On their second ascent of Chimborazo the climbers felt little of the acute mountain sickness which had felled them during their first venture into the virgin heights six months earlier. Weather was good enough to let them witness an eruption of Cotopaxi, sixty miles to the north. Dense clouds of ash drifted overhead, staining the sun green. The sky turned the color of blood, of tarnished copper, of polished brass.

In 1966, while reading Whymper's *Travels* on the slopes of Cotopaxi, I had wondered whether the great volcano might someday blow itself to smithereens, leaving only a jagged-edged caldera like El Altar's. Whymper's concept of Cotopaxi's geologic future was more gentle. He imagined that "the great cone which has so often trembled with subterranean thunders" will simply become extinct. "Its crater will disappear," he wrote, "and over its rugged floor and its extinguished fires, soft snowflakes will rear a majestic dome loftier than Chimborazo."

Loren McIntyre

---

[1] The eruption was sudden and lasted only an hour. Perhaps it was not lava but an outpouring of incandescent pyroclasts.

[2] Whymper was unaware that four hundred years earlier Inca priests had built shrines as high as 22,000 feet on fifty or more Andean volcanoes from southern Peru to central Chile. Their summits are cold but—because of slight precipitation—almost free of snow. At an open sulfur pit on the summit of Aucanquilcha Volcano, 20,262 feet, in northern Chile, I have watched miners pound rocks all day at a greater height than Cotopaxi.

[3] Such anomalies had already been reported by Dr. Conrad Meyer-Ahrens of Leipzig in 1854, as related in a fascinating handbook about the history and physiology of man and altitude: *Going Higher,* by Charles S. Houston, M.D. (Boston: Little, Brown & Co., 1987).

[4] Whymper's swiftest descents in Ecuador were hardly half as fast. He constantly clocked himself. His idea of a good rate of climb was 800 feet an hour. On the level at 10,000 feet elevation his walking speed was twelve minutes a mile in hobnailed mountain boots. His sea-level norm was eleven minutes.

[5] 380 Hg = 5500 meters = 18,045 feet.

INTRODUCTION TO THE 1987 EDITION

ECUADOREAN PEAKS IN ORDER OF ELEVATION

NAME	HEIGHT	CLIMBED	FIRST ASCENT
Chimborazo	20,702	Yes	Yes
Cotopaxi	19,347	Yes	No
Cayambe	18,996	Yes	Yes
Antisana	18,714	Yes	Yes
El Altar	17,457	No	
Sangay	17,159	No	
Illiniza	16,800?	Carrels only	Yes
Carihuairazo	16,750?	Yes	Yes
Tungurahua	16,700?	No	
Sincholagua	16,360?	Yes	Yes
Cotacachi	16,290?	Yes	Yes
Quilindana	16,130?	No	
Pichincha	15,728?	Yes	No
Corazon	15,700?	Yes	No
Ruminahui	15,600?	No	
Sara Urca	15,500?	Yes	Yes

INTRODUCTION.

It will be within the knowledge of most of those who take up this book that it has long been much debated whether human life can be sustained at great altitudes above the level of the sea in such a manner as will permit of the accomplishment of useful work.[1]

The most opposite statements and opinions have been advanced concerning this matter. The extremes range from saying that fatal results may occur, and have occurred, from some obscure cause, at comparatively moderate elevations, down to that no effects whatever have been experienced at the greatest heights which have been attained. Allegations of the latter class may be set aside for the present, for the evidence is overwhelming that, from 14,000 feet above the level of the sea and upwards, serious inconveniences have occurred; that prostration (amounting in the more extreme cases to incapacitation) has been experienced; and that, in some instances, perhaps, even death has resulted through some cause which operates at great elevations.

This evidence has come from all parts of the world, and has accumulated during several centuries. It has been afforded, independently, by multitudes of persons of diverse conditions — by cultured men of science down to illiterate peasants, the latter of whom cannot have heard of experiences beyond their own; and, although the testimony often differs in detail, it agrees in the

[1] In saying this, it is not meant that there is any doubt as to the *possibility* of the *existence* of life at great elevations, for aeronauts have several times shewn, since the commencement of this century, that life *may* exist, for short periods, at heights exceeding any as yet discovered upon the earth.

INTRODUCTION.

general, leading features. Nausea and vomiting; headaches of most severe character; feverishness; hemorrhages; lassitude, depression and weakness, and an indescribable feeling of illness, have been repeatedly mentioned as occurring at great elevations, and have only been cured by descending into lower zones. To these maladies the term mountain-sickness is now commonly applied.

It is very generally admitted that mountain-sickness should be attributed to the diminished atmospheric pressure (or, as it is termed, to the rarefaction of the air) which is experienced as one goes upward. Yet, in various parts of the world, the notion is, and has long been entertained, that it is due to local causes, such, for example, as noxious exhalations from vegetation. Some support to this notion seems to be found in the fact that whilst the greatest heights in Europe (15-16,000 feet) are annually ascended by throngs of persons without perceptible inconvenience, multitudes of others in Asia and America suffer acutely at lower elevations (14-15,000 feet); and it would therefore seem that there are influences at work on the latter continents which do not operate in Europe. The apparent discordance is explicable without having recourse to local influences, which could not be deemed sufficient to account for the effects in general, even if they might be entertained in particular instances. Whilst the assumed causes are local, the observed effects are world-wide; and no cause would be adequate to account for the effects except one operating in every clime and at all times.

But, although it is very generally admitted that the evils which have been enumerated are due to diminished atmospheric pressure, many persons are unconvinced that such is the true explanation, especially those who are accustomed to travel amongst the mountains of Europe; and it is pointed out, apparently with force, that the whole of the symptoms can be produced by other causes, and that aeronauts have sometimes attained higher elevations than have ever been reached on the earth, and have scarcely been affected at all. It is argued that some persons are predisposed to nausea,

INTRODUCTION.

that others are liable to bleeding at the nose, or habitually suffer from headache, and that this accounts for much which has been laid to rarefaction of the air; and further, it is said, or conjectured, that the fatigues inseparable from travel in mountain-regions account for more: in short, that mountain-sickness is to be attributed to the frailties of human nature, or to the imperfections of individual constitutions, and is considered as a sign, or indication, of weakness or incompetency.

It is undeniable that there is some truth in these observations, and it can scarcely be doubted that effects which have been produced by fatigue have often, wrongly, been attributed to rarefaction of the air, and that effects which have been produced by rarefaction of the air have often been assigned to fatigue. The immunity from unpleasant symptoms which has sometimes been enjoyed by aeronauts, even when bounding in a few minutes to enormous elevations,[1] has tended to foster scepticism; and has appeared to support the opinion that fatigue and personal imperfections have had much to do with mountain-sickness, and not to accord with the view that it is produced by diminished pressure—otherwise, why should these persons, transported without effort to superior elevations in the air, have escaped, whilst others, at much inferior ones upon the earth, suffer?

It is scarcely necessary to occupy these pages with a mass of

---

[1] The following data are taken from the *Reports* of Mr. J. Glaisher, F.R.S., to the British Association for the Advancement of Science, 1862-3—

Date.	Time.	Barometer.	Diff. of Time.	Diff. of Pressure.
July 17, 1862	9.43 A.M.	29·193	44 min.	14·55 inches.
,, ,,	10.27 ,,	14·637		
Sept. 5, ,,	1.3 P.M.	29·17	33 ,,	14·62 ,,
,, ,,	1.36 ,,	14·55		
April 18, ,,	1.17 ,,	29·66	32 ,,	14·85 ,,
,, ,,	1.49 ,,	14·81		

Starting from the level of the sea, the height attained in each case was about 19,000 feet, without injurious effects being felt. I am not aware that any one, *upon the earth*, has ever experienced a natural difference of pressure of fourteen and a half inches in less than four or five *days*.

INTRODUCTION.

extracts in support of the foregoing statements. Those who desire to pursue the matter in detail may usefully turn to the very comprehensive summary in *La Pression Barométrique*, by M. Paul Bert,[1] where 156 pages are devoted to experiences in high places, 25 more to aeronauts, and 120 more to theories. Evidence of a nature similar to that which is quoted by M. Bert continues to accumulate, and is often, apparently, of a contradictory character. For example, since returning from the journey which is described in the following pages, three writers upon Mexico[2] have mentioned that breathing is affected in that city by the 'rarefied atmosphere,' although the altitude in question is less than 8000 feet above the sea; while on the other hand, quite recently (in speaking of the Southern Andes up to heights 13,800 feet above the sea), Dr. A. Plagemann says, "with regard to the effects of rarefied air on the body at high elevations, neither he nor his companions suffered at all."[3] Still more divergent is the statement by Mr. W. W. Graham that he reached nearly the height of 24,000 feet in the Himalayas, and that "neither in this nor in any other ascent did he feel any inconvenience in breathing other than the ordinary panting inseparable from any great muscular exertion."[4]

This unique experience has met with little credence in India.

[1] G. Masson, Paris, 1878. This work has received the highest honours in France. The experiments made by M. Bert upon himself at low pressures, although extremely interesting, left off sooner than could have been desired. In the first of the two experiments which I quote in the Appendix to this volume, he submitted himself to an artificial diminution of pressure somewhat greater than that which is experienced at the summit of Chimborazo, and in the second one to about the pressure which would be enjoyed on the top of Mount Everest. But this was done for only a brief space of time. The first experiment extended over only sixty-six minutes and the second one over eighty-nine minutes; and, as soon as any ill effects commenced to manifest themselves, M. Bert refreshed himself with oxygen. The experiments shewed that oxygen may exercise a beneficial influence.

[2] See *A Trip to Mexico*, by H. C. R. Becher, Toronto, 1880, p. 73; *Mexico To-Day*, by T. U. Brocklehurst, London, 1883, p. 28; and *Winter in the Slant of the Sun*, in *Good Words*, 1887, p. 245, by the Bishop of Rochester.

[3] *Proceedings of the Royal Geographical Society*, April 1887, p. 249.

[4] *Proc. Royal Geog. Soc.*, August 1884, p. 434.

INTRODUCTION.

It is, however, a certain fact that all individuals are not equally affected by diminished pressure, and that instances have occurred at such heights as 14–15,000 feet in which some persons have suffered whilst others have escaped, though the latter have not been exempt upon mounting to greater altitudes. But whilst this must be admitted; and also the probability that the effects of fatigue have often been wrongly interpreted; and, further, that personal frailties are frequently manifested upon mountain ascents, or at great elevations, there is a large residuum which cannot be explained away; and any one examining the matter can hardly fail to arrive at the conclusion that mountain-sickness is a world-wide reality.

This subject, long since, appeared to me to be worthy of investigation for its own sake, more particularly for ascertaining the heights at which effects begin to manifest themselves; the symptoms; and whether the effects are permanent. It seemed certain that, sooner or later, every one must be affected by diminished pressure, but the manner in which it would operate was uncertain, and whether its effects would be felt permanently at any given elevation was unknown. Those who have been affected by mountain-sickness have always desired to be rid of the infliction, and have descended to lower levels at the earliest opportunity. Hence it had not been ascertained whether cures might be effected on the spot; or, to put the matter in another way, whether one can become habituated to low pressures. The remarks which have fallen from those who are most entitled to attention have not been of an encouraging nature, and it may be inferred from their general tenor that as the cause is constant and permanent so will the effects be constant and permanent.

De Saussure, after finding himself through weakness, and difficulty in breathing, unable to make during a four and a half hours' stay on the summit of Mont Blanc the experiments which he had repeatedly performed in less than three hours at the level of the

INTRODUCTION.

sea, said he thought it probable that they would *never* be made at the higher station.[1]

Darwin, who visited the Portillo Pass in the Chilian Andes, although but slightly affected there (at 13–14,000 feet), said, "certainly the exertion of walking was extreme, and the respiration became deep and laborious. It is incomprehensible to me how Humboldt and others were able to ascend to the elevation of 19,000 feet."[2]

The Schlagintweits attained great heights in Asia, and made some remarks that are more to the point than any others which I am able to quote, although they do not go much into detail. In the second volume of their *Results of a Scientific Mission to India and High Asia*,[3] p. 484, they say, "As to the beneficial effect of acclimatisation, we can speak from our own personal experience." [By this expression, I understand them to say that they became somewhat habituated to low pressures.] But they add, in continuation, "what might have been the consequence had we prolonged our stay in these lofty regions it is impossible to say, the probability, however, being that a longer sojourn would have told severely upon our health." This is said in connection with an attempt that they made to ascend Ibi Gamin (Kamet), on Aug. 19, 1855, upon which occasion they reached the height of 22,230 feet.[4] In a Report by them which was published at Madras in 1855 (and was reprinted at Calcutta) there is this further information :— "At two o'clock at last it had become absolutely impossible to go

---

[1] "Quoique je ne perdisse pas un seul moment, je ne pus faire dans ces 4 heures & demie toutes les expériences que j'ai fréquemment achevées en moins de 3 heures au bord de la mer."—*Voyages dans les Alpes*, vol. iv, p. 148.

"Je conservois l'espérance bien fondée d'achever, sur le Col-du-Géant, ce que je n'avois pas fait, & que vraisemblablement l'on ne fera jamais sur le Mont-Blanc."—*Id.* § 2023, p. 215.

[2] *Narrative of the Surveying Voyages of His Majesty's Ships Adventure and Beagle*, vol. iii, p. 393.   [3] London and Leipzig, 1862.

[4] The height was deduced from observations of mercurial barometer, and it is the greatest as yet attained upon the earth which has been determined by observations on the spot.

INTRODUCTION.

any higher; two of our people who had got sick had remained behind, *and we all the rest felt exceedingly tired and exhausted, as we certainly never were in our life.* . . . We had got much used to the influence of height, especially during our Thibetan journey, but up there not one escaped unhurt; we all felt headache."

To attain results which might be of a more or less conclusive character, it appeared to me that it would be necessary to eliminate the complications arising from fatigue, privations, cold, and insufficiency or unsuitability of food; that the persons concerned should have been previously accustomed to mountain work; that the heights to be dealt with ought to be in excess of those at which it had been generally admitted serious inconveniences had occurred; and that preparations should be made for a prolonged sojourn at such elevations.

The Himalayas and their allied ranges offered the best field for research, and in 1874 I projected a scheme which would have taken me in the first instances on to the very ground where others had been placed *hors de combat*, and from these positions I proposed to carry exploration and research up to the highest attainable limits. But, just at the time when it was possible to start, our rulers entered upon the construction of a 'scientific frontier' for India, and rendered that region unsuitable for scientific investigations. I was recommended by experienced Anglo-Indians to defer my visit, and I followed their advice. Equally debarred, by the unhappy dissensions between Chili, Peru, and Bolivia, from travel amongst the highest of the Andes, I turned to the Republic of Ecuador, the most lofty remaining country which was accessible.

As the main object of the journey was to observe the effects of low pressure, and to attain the greatest possible height in order to experience it, Chimborazo naturally claimed the first attention, on account of its absolute elevation above the sea;[1] and I proposed to

[1] Its height, according to Humboldt, is 21,425 feet. See *Recueil d'observations astronomiques, d'opérations trigonométriques, et de mesures barométriques*, par Alexandre de Humboldt, Paris, 1810, vol. i, p. lxxiii (introd.).

INTRODUCTION.

encamp upon this mountain, at gradually increasing heights, with the ultimate aim of reaching the summit. But as there was no certainty that this could be done, and a possibility, at least, that the results of the investigations might be of a negative character, various other objects were kept in view, principal amongst them being the determination of the altitudes and of the relative positions of the chief mountains of Ecuador, the comparison of boiling-point observations and of aneroids against the mercurial barometer, and collecting in Botany and Zoology at great heights. I concerned myself neither with commerce or politics, nor with the natives and their curious ways; and there are, besides, many interesting topics which might be dwelt upon that find no place in this volume. The Ecuadorian Loan, for example, is a capital subject, and a few pages might well be devoted to a matter in which the public takes so much interest, and from which it derives so little.

Having only my own very small means to depend upon, my staff was necessarily upon the most modest scale. Three assistants were indispensable, and these I proposed to draw from the mountain-guides of Europe. My old guide, Jean-Antoine Carrel, of Val Tournanche,[1] accepted my proposals, and two others also agreed to go but withdrew from their engagements shortly before the date for departure, and placed me in a great difficulty. After vainly endeavouring to obtain the services of some of the best-known men, I was obliged to instruct Carrel to bring any one he could. His cousin Louis (with whom I was already acquainted) came, but no one else could be procured at so short notice, and a third man had to be picked up in Ecuador, and proved, naturally, of no service when a knowledge of mountain-craft was wanted.

It was not advisable to attempt to travel in Ecuador without recognition, and I sought the good offices of the then President of the Alpine Club in this matter. I cannot acknowledge too warmly the cordial co-operation of Mr. Charles Edward Mathews, and the

---

[1] For the antecedents of J.-A. Carrel, see *Scrambles amongst the Alps*, J. Murray, 1871.

INTRODUCTION.

personal trouble he took that my wishes might be efficiently represented in the right quarters. Through his instrumentality, I was put in communication with the Ecuadorian Consul-General in Great Britain (Mr. Edmund Heuer of Manchester), and subsequently received from His Excellency the President of the Republic assurance that I should be heartily welcome in his country; and, upon application at the Foreign Office, Lord Salisbury was pleased to direct Her Majesty's representatives at Guayaquil and Quito to afford every assistance in their power — an instruction which they interpreted sympathetically. Upon the introduction of Mr. Mathews, George Dixon, Esq., M.P. for Birmingham, rendered most valuable service by undertaking to send out in advance and to place in secure hands at Guaranda and Quito a quantity of my heavy baggage.

Through my old friend Mr. Douglas Freshfield, the Caucasian explorer, the projected journey became known to Freiherr von Thielmann, who had recently ridden through Colombia and Ecuador,[1] and he most kindly met me at Ostend, to give the benefit of his experiences; and from this accomplished diplomatist-traveller it was communicated to Dr. Alphons Stübel, of Dresden, who with rare liberality presented me with a copy of the unpublished altitudes in Ecuador[2] which had been deduced from the observations made by him in 1871–73 in conjunction with Dr. W. Reiss. Many other equally friendly services were performed both by friends and strangers, especially by the fraternity of mountain-travellers, and amongst the very last communications which reached me, just before departure, came a cheering *bon voyage* from the veteran Boussingault, who forty-eight years earlier had himself endeavoured to ascend Chimborazo.

Similar good fortune continued on the outward voyage. My sincere thanks are due to the agents of the Royal Mail Steam Packet Company, and to the Acting-Consuls at Colon and Panama,

---

[1] And made the ascent of Cotopaxi.
[2] *Alturas tomadas en la Republica del Ecuador*, Quito, 1873.

INTRODUCTION.

for their undeserved attentions, and particularly to the Right Hon. H. C. Childers (at that time chairman of the Royal Mail Steam Packet Company), who most courteously granted me the use of one of his cabins in order that work might be carried on uninterruptedly. Upon arrival at Guayaquil we were at once received into the house of Mr. George Chambers, H.B.M.'s Consul, and were treated with genuine hospitality.

It is now my duty to acknowledge in the most prominent manner the invaluable services which were rendered throughout the journey by the cousins Carrel. Travellers are not always fortunate in their assistants, and, occasionally, even fall out with them. Under circumstances which were frequently trying, our party, although exceedingly small, was always closely united. The imperturbable good temper of the one man, and the grim humour of the other, were sources of continual satisfaction. I trusted my person, property, and interests to their care with perfect confidence, and they proved worthy of the trust, and equal to every demand which was made upon them.

We travelled through Ecuador unarmed, except with passports which were never exhibited, and with a number of letters of introduction which for the most part were not presented; adopting a policy of non-intervention in all that did not concern us, and rigidly respecting the customs of the country, even when we could not agree with them: and traversed that unsettled Republic without molestation, trusting more to our wits than to our credentials, and believing that a jest may conquer where force will fail, that a *bon-mot* is often better than a passport.

CONTENTS.

CHAPTER I.
FROM LONDON TO GUARANDA.

ECUADORIAN POLITENESS—GUAYAQUIL—ENGAGE AN INTERPRETER—THE RAINY SEASON—SOME SNAKE STORIES—RIVER GUAYAS AND ITS TRIBUTARIES—ARRIVE AT BODEGAS DE BABAHOYO—INDECOROUS BEHAVIOUR OF OUR MULES—ALL ALIVE AT LA MONA—"THE ROYAL ROAD"—A TROPICAL JUNGLE—ASCENT OF THE OUTER ANDES—TAMBO LOMA (THE HOTEL ON THE HILL)—SUMMIT OF THE OUTER RANGE—THE PACIFIC RANGE OF ECUADOR—DESCENT INTO THE VALLEY OF THE RIVER CHIMBO—ARRIVAL AT GUARANDA—MAPS BY LA CONDAMINE AND DON PEDRO MALDONADO—ROUTE MAP AND MAP OF CHIMBORAZO . Pages 1-18

CHAPTER II.
FROM GUARANDA TO THE FIRST CAMP ON CHIMBORAZO.

A CANDID MAN—INVISIBILITY OF CHIMBORAZO—THE GREAT ARENAL—VISIT TO TORTORILLAS—THE AUTHORITIES OF GUARANDA—TREASURES!—FIRST VIEW OF CHIMBORAZO—DISCOVERY OF ITS TWO SUMMITS—MAGNITUDE OF ITS GLACIERS—DISCUSSION OF ROUTE—THE SOUTH-WEST RIDGE—THE CARRELS START TO SELECT A CAMPING-PLACE—PRINCIPAL OBJECT OF THE JOURNEY—HUMBOLDT'S ATTEMPT TO ASCEND CHIMBORAZO IN 1802—BOUSSINGAULT'S ATTEMPTS IN 1831—DIVINE SPEED—DISILLUSIONIZED—COMPARISONS OF THE BAROMETERS—A HOPE DISSIPATED—EXECUTED INSTANTANEOUSLY—RETURN OF THE CARRELS—MORE THAN 19,000 FEET HIGH "BY ANEROID"—A PARTING BENEDICTION—ARRIVAL AT THE FIRST CAMP ON CHIMBORAZO . . . 19-40

CHAPTER III.
THE FIRST ASCENT OF CHIMBORAZO.

INGRATITUDE—ROUTE UP THE VALLON DE CARREL—ON MOUNTAIN-SICKNESS—PLAN OF OPERATIONS—THE COMMISSARIAT—ARRIVAL AT THE SECOND CAMP—*HORS DE COMBAT*—CHLORATE OF POTASH—THE MERITS OF RED WINE—PERRING DISTINGUISHES HIMSELF—SYMPTOMS OF MOUNTAIN-SICKNESS—LIFE AT LOW PRESSURES—REASONS WHY MERCURIAL BAROMETERS ARE BROKEN—PRECAUTIONS—STRANGE BEHAVIOUR OF THE ANEROIDS—DESCRIPTION OF THE SOUTH-

CONTENTS.

WEST RIDGE—EXPLORATION BY THE CARRELS—MORE THAN 19,000 FEET HIGH BY MERCURIAL BAROMETER—ESTABLISHMENT OF THE THIRD CAMP—THE OX-CHEEK OF CHICAGO—A LIBELLOUS STATEMENT—DESERTION OF THE INDIANS—ARRIVAL AND FLIGHT OF THE GUARD—"THE BONES OF SOME RUMINANT"—ASSAULT OF THE BREACH—DISCOMFITED—SECOND ATTACK—PASSAGE OF THE BREACH—ARRIVAL ON THE SUMMIT OF CHIMBORAZO—ITS HEIGHT—DISCORDANT OBSERVATIONS—SANGAI IN ERUPTION—THE SOUTHERN WALLS—AN ICE-AVALANCHE—THE RETREAT . . . . . Pages 41-80

CHAPTER IV.

FROM CHUQUIPOQUIO TO AMBATO, LATACUNGA AND MACHACHI.

FROST-BITTEN—PERRING IS DESPATCHED TO AMBATO—AN ARISTOCRATIC INN-KEEPER—DESCRIPTION OF THE TAMBO OF CHUQUIPOQUIO—OUR APPETITES FAIL—HEIGHT OF THE BAROMETER ON CHIMBORAZO—WEATHER ON CHIMBORAZO—THE BASIN OF RIOBAMBA—DIMENSIONS OF CHIMBORAZO—RETURN OF PERRING WITH THE LITTER—THE ROBBER OF CHUQUIPOQUIO—THE HIGHWAY TO QUITO—MEASUREMENT ON THE ROAD—DOCTORED AT AMBATO—VISITS AND VISITORS—THE DRY SHERRY OF AMBATO—WAGNER'S "ASCENT" OF CHIMBORAZO—MARKET-DAY—THE PUMICE OF AMBATO—WE CAPTURE A "BISHOP"—TUNGURAGUA—THE BASIN OF AMBATO—LATACUNGA—OCCUPATIONS OF THE LADIES—ARRIVAL AT MACHACHI—"IT IS ONLY THE *GRINGOS*" 81-99

CHAPTER V.

ON AN ASCENT OF CORAZON, AND WALKS IN THE LANES OF MACHACHI.

A TRUTHFUL INN-KEEPER—LIFE IN THE INTERIOR—MY YOUNG FRIENDS AT MACHACHI—GREAT BEDS OF VOLCANIC DUSTS—THE BASIN OF MACHACHI—WE SEE A DEAD DONKEY AND MEET A SCORPION—LA CONDAMINE'S ASCENT OF CORAZON—DESCRIPTION OF THE SUMMIT—ON "RANGE IN ALTITUDE"—ENTOMOLOGY AT GREAT HEIGHTS—HUMBOLDT'S YELLOW BUTTERFLY—A ZOOLOGIST'S PARADISE—WALKS IN THE LANES OF MACHACHI—ANTONIO RACINES INTRODUCES ME TO AN *AMPHIPOD*—THE DOGS OF MACHACHI . . . 100-119

CHAPTER VI.

ON COTOPAXI AND ILLINIZA.

THE PROJECT—LOUIS BECOMES CONVALESCENT—WE GO TO THE FARM OF ROSARIO—COTOPAXI—ANGLES OF ITS SLOPES—ITS POSITION AND ERUPTIONS—ERUPTIONS IN 1877—DARKNESS CAUSED BY CLOUDS OF EJECTED ASH—LAVA BOILS OVER THE RIM OF THE CRATER—THE FLOODS THAT ENSUE—FIRST ASCENT OF COTO-

CONTENTS.

PAXI BY DR. W. REISS—OTHER ASCENTS—ON ILLINIZA—PERPETUAL MISTS—WE ENCAMP AT 15,207 FEET—GLACIERS ON ILLINIZA—TUFTED SNOW-CORNICES—DEFEATED—WEATHER IN THE INTERIOR OF ECUADOR . . Pages 120-135

CHAPTER VII.
THE ASCENT OF COTOPAXI, AND A NIGHT ON THE SUMMIT.

START FOR COTOPAXI BY FREIHERR VON THIELMANN'S ROUTE—PEDREGAL—ABUNDANCE OF BEETLES ON THE PLAIN OF LIMPIOPONGO—*COLPODES*—BOMBS THROWN OUT BY COTOPAXI—WE CAMP AT 15,130 FEET—CULINARY TROUBLES—THE YANASACHE LAVA AND ITS SURROUNDINGS—ON VOLCANIC "ASH," DUSTS, SANDS, AND LAPILLI—THE INSINUATING NATURE OF VOLCANIC DUST—DESCRIPTIONS BY PROF. T. G. BONNEY—THE WORSHIP OF THE CROSS—NATIVE ATTIRE—SHOES OF STRING—PREPARATIONS FOR THE ASCENT—FLORA OF THE CONE—THE START—CUMULUS CLOUD SEEN 23,000 FEET HIGH—GLACIERS ON COTOPAXI—ARRIVE AT THE TERMINAL SLOPE OF ASH—THE PREVALENT WINDS—REACH THE EDGE OF THE CRATER AND GO PARTLY ROUND IT—ENCAMP AT 19,500 FEET—WARMTH OF THE CONE—COLDNESS OF THE AIR—A NIGHT ON THE SUMMIT—ARE WE "HABITUATED"?—INSPECTION OF THE CRATER BY NIGHT—PERIODICAL STEAM-BLASTS—DESCRIPTION OF THE CRATER—"THERE WAS FIRE BELOW"—A GREAT SAFETY-VALVE—THE HEIGHT OF COTOPAXI—DESCENT TO PEDREGAL—SOME MORE "TREASURES"! 136-156

CHAPTER VIII.
THE FIRST ASCENT OF SINCHOLAGUA.

A SEVERELY SCIENTIFIC ASCENT—THE OLD STYLE—GIANTS WANTED—SINCHOLAGUA—CROSS THE RIO PITA—DECEITFUL GROUND—WARM SPRINGS—MANNER OF APPROACH TO THE SUMMIT—BEATEN BACK—THUNDER AND LIGHTNING—STEEPNESS OF THE IMMEDIATE SUMMIT—DEPARTURE FROM MACHACHI AND ARRIVAL AT QUITO 157-166

CHAPTER IX.
ON QUITO AND THE QUITONIANS.

THE BASIN OF QUITO—POPULATION OF THE CITY—*QUEBRADAS*—WATER AND WATER-CARRIERS—THE PANECILLO—MANNERS AND CUSTOMS AT QUITO—A TRUCULENT INNKEEPER—ON HEAD-GEAR AND HATS—INTERVIEW WITH THE PRESIDENT—HOW GENERAL VEINTEMILLA CAME INTO POWER—HISTORY—GARCIA MORENO—DEMONSTRATIONS—A PROMISING PEOPLE—MAÑANA—ECUADORIAN BONDS—INDIANS AT QUITO—PRICES IN ECUADOR—OPENINGS FOR COMMERCIAL ENTERPRIZE—ON BANKS AND MONEY—AN EASY WAY OF EARNING A DIVIDEND 167-183

CONTENTS.

CHAPTER X.
THE FIRST ASCENT OF ANTISANA.

THE BASIN OF CHILLO—AGUIRRE'S METEOROLOGICAL OBSERVATIONS IN THE *COMPTES RENDUS*—A CHAMPION MUD-HOLE—THE HACIENDA OF PIÑANTURA—RENCONTRE WITH SEÑOR REBOLLEDO — THE GREAT LAVA-STREAM OF ANTISANILLA — ARRIVAL AT THE HACIENDA OF ANTISANA—THE CLOUDINESS OF ANTISANA—BEATEN ON OUR FIRST ATTEMPT AT AN ASCENT—ON SNOW-BLINDNESS—START AGAIN, AND CAMP AT 15,984 FEET ABOVE THE LEVEL OF THE SEA—ENORMOUS CREVASSES—"I FEAR AN AVALANCHE"—ARRIVAL ON THE SUMMIT—HIGH TEMPERATURES—THE HEIGHT OF ANTISANA—CRATERS AND CREVASSES—THE FLORA OF ANTISANA — ON CONDORS AND FLIGHTS OF THE IMAGINATION—THE RANGE IN ALTITUDE OF THE CONDOR—A GREAT, SOLEMN ASSEMBLY—THE COTTON FACTORY AT CHILLO—RETURN TO QUITO . . Pages 184-206

CHAPTER XI.
UPON AN ASCENT OF PICHINCHA.

A CURE FOR SOUR BLOOD—REMINISCENCES OF CHICAGO—THE ROUTE TO PICHINCHA—ITS TWO SUMMITS, RUCU- AND GUAGUA—*ENSILLADAS*—A TAME CRATER—NATURE OF THE HIGHEST POINT — RECURRING SPECIES — HUMMING-BIRDS — SALT FISH FOR DINNER 207-216

CHAPTER XII.
THE FIRST ASCENT OF CAYAMBE.

THE ROAD TO THE NORTH—CAYAMBE—CROSS THE GREAT QUEBRADA OF GUALLABAMBA—ECCENTRICITIES OF THE ANEROIDS—A FIGHT FOR THE CHAMPIONSHIP—SPORT IN ECUADOR—A POTATO BED — START FOR THE ASCENT OF CAYAMBE—MENACED BY A CONDOR — DISAPPEARANCE OF JEAN-ANTOINE AND ITS CONSEQUENCES — INDIAN HOSPITALITY — INGRATITUDE — CAMP ON CAYAMBE AT 14,762 FEET—THE POINTE JARRIN AND THE ESPINOSA GLACIER — ASCENT OF CAYAMBE (19,186 FEET)—OUR FASTEST ASCENDING RATE—SARA-URCU—COLD QUARTERS 217-237

CHAPTER XIII.
THE FIRST ASCENT OF SARA-URCU.

LIFE AT LA DORMIDA (11,805 FEET) — EXPERIENCES OF GONZALO PIZARRO — THE TREASURES OF SARA-URCU — A CAMP IN A SWAMP — WATER-PARTING ON THE EQUATOR — THE *CHUSQUEA ARISTATA* OF MUNRO — CORREDOR MACHAI (THE HUNTER'S REFUGE)—THE FATE OF THE BARK HUNTERS—TICKLED—INCESSANT RAINS—THE CHIEF OF THE STAFF IS ATTACKED IN THE REAR—A GLIMPSE OF SARA-URCU — TURNING AN ENEMY TO ACCOUNT — ARRIVAL ON THE SUMMIT—THE HEIGHT OF SARA-URCU—A SUPER-SATURATED PLACE—HUMBOLDT'S FIRE-PROOF FISH—WHO SHALL DECIDE WHEN DOCTORS DISAGREE? 238-255

CONTENTS.

CHAPTER XIV.
ON THE PROVINCE OF IMBABURA, AND THE FIRST ASCENT OF COTOCACHI.

IN QUEST OF ANTIQUITIES — DISCOVERY OF AN OLD INDIAN KETTLE ! — THE PROVINCE OF IMBABURA — GO TO COTOCACHI AND MAKE FRIENDS WITH THE PRIEST — THE LATEST THING IN QUEBRADAS — UPHEAVAL OR SUBSIDENCE ? — THE ASCENT OF COTOCACHI — THE WHIRLING SNOW MOCKS OUR EFFORTS — ON THE SUMMIT OF COTOCACHI (16,301 FEET) — SUNDAY SPORTS — THE *TUMULI* OF HUTANTAQUI — DESTRUCTION OF IBARRA — GO TO CARRANQUI — EVIDENCES OF A "STONE AGE" — STARS IN STONE — ARE THEY WEAPONS OR SYMBOLS ? — TYPICAL STONE IMPLEMENTS — HOUSEHOLD GODS — SCARCITY OF OBJECTS IN METAL — OLD INDIAN POTTERY — MUSICAL WHISTLES — "VASE-BUSTS" — THE CONTENTS OF A GRAVE — A SMASH ON MOJANDA — RETURN TO QUITO . . . Pages 256-286

CHAPTER XV.
A VISIT TO THE PYRAMIDS OF QUITO.

JEAN-ANTOINE AND LOUIS ASCEND ILLINIZA — THE BASE-LINE OF THE FRENCH ACADEMICIANS — ERECTION OF THE PYRAMIDS OF QUITO — FUSS OVER THE INSCRIPTIONS — DESTRUCTION OF THE PYRAMIDS — DISCOVERY OF LA CONDAMINE'S INSCRIBED STONE — THE MODERN PYRAMIDS — SELLING OFF — "NO TRUST GIVEN" — POPULATION OF ECUADOR — ENGAGE FRANCISCO JAVIER CAMPAÑA — FINAL DEPARTURE FROM QUITO 287-295

CHAPTER XVI.
UPON A WALK ON THE QUITO ROAD, AND A JOURNEY TO ALTAR.

ANOTHER ATTEMPT ON ILLINIZA — DAVID'S PET LLAMA — REPULSED — RATES ON ILLINIZA — A WALK ON THE QUITO ROAD — THE POLITICAL TAILOR — THE MASTER OF CANDELARIA — AT CAMP IN THE VALLEY OF COLLANES (12,540 FEET) — DESCRIPTION OF ALTAR — RETREAT — A NIGHT AT PENIPE — HABITS OF THE ECUADORIAN MULE 296-309

CHAPTER XVII.
THE FIRST ASCENT OF CARIHUAIRAZO.

WE RETURN TO THE CHARGE — AN HONEST INDIAN — CAMP NEAR THE HIGH ROAD AND MEASUREMENT FOR "A SCALE" — HIGHWAY ROBBERS — A THREATENED ATTACK — QUICKSANDS — CAMP ON CARIHUAIRAZO (13,377 FEET) — PEDRO DE PENIPE — SARA-URCU TACTICS — ON THE SUMMIT OF CARIHUAIRAZO (16,515 FEET) — AN INSULAR FLORA — A CRATER WANTED — JOY TURNED INTO MOURNING — OUR DOG BECOMES SNOW-BLIND — CROSS ABRASPUNGO (14,480 FEET) — A GREAT LAVA-STREAM — FOURTH CAMP ON CHIMBORAZO (14,359 FEET) — MONSIEUR DECEIVES HIMSELF ! 310-319

CONTENTS.

CHAPTER XVIII.
ON THE SECOND ASCENT OF CHIMBORAZO.

CHIMBORAZO FROM THE NORTH-NORTH-WEST — THE FIFTH CAMP (15,811 FEET) — PEDRO DECLINES AN ASCENT — AN ERUPTION OF COTOPAXI — CROSS THE GLACIER DE STÜBEL AND SEE THE PACIFIC — A GREEN SUN — DIRECTION OF THE WIND REGISTERED — A FALL OF VOLCANIC DUST ON THE TOP OF CHIMBORAZO REGISTERS THE HEIGHT OF THE BAROMETER — THE GREATEST HEIGHT AT WHICH PHOTOGRAPHY HAS BEEN PRACTISED — A CALCULATION — TWENTY-FIVE THOUSAND PARTICLES TO A GRAIN! — CAUSE OF THIS ERUPTION — REDUCTION IN THE HEIGHT OF CHIMBORAZO — THE RATE OF THE SECOND ASCENT — ON A BAROMETRIC LEVEL — GREAT ARENALS — THE FLORA OF CHIMBORAZO — COMPLETE THE MEASUREMENT FOR "A SCALE" . . . . Pages 320-334

CHAPTER XIX.
UPON SOME RESULTS OF THE JOURNEY.

CONFIGURATION OF THE ANDES OF ECUADOR — PARALLEL CORDILLERAS — THE WALLS OF CHIMBORAZO — HUMBOLDT'S TRIANGLE — ALTITUDES OF THE GREAT ANDES OF THE EQUATOR — TEMPERATURES ON SUMMITS — ON THE SNOW-LINE AND GLACIERS — BOTANICAL RESULTS — ZOOLOGICAL RESULTS — UPON OUR EXPERIENCES AT LOW PRESSURES 335-384

CHAPTER XX.
RETURN TO GUAYAQUIL—CONCLUSION.

A PUBLIC DUTY — DEATH IN THE NIGHT — REMAINS OF A COMBAT — DESCENT THROUGH THE FOREST — THE LAST CAMP — THE BRIDGE OF CHIMBO AND THE ECUADORIAN RAILWAY — YOUR EXCELLENCY HAS FORGOTTEN TO PAY FOR THE PINE-APPLES! — DEPARTURE FROM GUAYAQUIL 385-392

APPENDIX.

		PAGE
A.	ALTITUDES DETERMINED IN ECUADOR	395
B.	THE RANGE OF THE BAROMETER IN ECUADOR	402
C.	COMPARISONS OF THE ANEROID AGAINST THE MERCURIAL BAROMETER	405
D.	UPON BOILING-POINT OBSERVATIONS	417
E.	TEMPERATURES IN ECUADOR	421
F.	UPON BODY TEMPERATURE	425
G.	HUMBOLDT'S ATTEMPT TO ASCEND CHIMBORAZO	428
H.	BOUSSINGAULT'S ATTEMPTS TO ASCEND CHIMBORAZO	431
I.	DECLARATION OF FRANCISCO J. CAMPAÑA	435
J.	EXPERIMENTS BY M. PAUL BERT	437

LIST OF ILLUSTRATIONS.

The drawings were made by
F. Barnard, A. Corbould, F. Dadd, W. L. Jones, W. E. Lapworth, W. H. Overend,
P. Skelton, E. Wagner, E. Wilson, Joseph Wolf, and Others ;
and were Engraved on Wood by Edward Whymper.

FULL PAGE ILLUSTRATIONS.

1. "The whirling snow mocked our efforts" (see Chap. XIV.) *Frontispiece.*
2. Chimborazo, from the slopes above Guaranda . *To face page* 24
3. Chimborazo, from a little above the third camp . ,, 64
4. "We were then twenty thousand feet high" . . ,, 68
5. Ice-cliffs under the summits of Chimborazo . ,, 76
6. Carried on the litter into Ambato . . . ,, 90
7. Cotopaxi (19,613 feet), from the Hacienda of S. Rosario ,, 124
8. Part of the interior of the crater of Cotopaxi . ,, 147
9. Part of the exterior of the crater of Cotopaxi . ,, 150
10. Antisana (19,335 feet), seen from the Hacienda . ,, 190
11. "They dashed in amongst them and threw their lassos" ,, 205
12. The second camp on Pichincha (14,992 feet) . . ,, 209
13. "They prowled around us at night, and left their footprints in the snow" . . . . . ,, 229
14. At camp on the Equator, at Corredor Machai . . ,, 242
15. Some typical Stone Implements collected in Ecuador . ,, 271
16. Examples of old Indian Pottery collected by the Author ,, 279
17. "It rolled over and over down the slope" . . ,, 285
18. "The sky was dark with the clouds of ash" . . ,, 326
19. The Southern Walls of Chimborazo . . . ,, 337
20. Selections from the bedroom collection at Guayaquil ,, 391

IN THE TEXT.

PAGE
1. On the way to Bodegas 1
2. A young person of Guayaquil 4
3. A house at Bodegas 5
4. At La Mona 7
5. A collector 9
6. Native house at Guaranda 18
7. Crossing the Great Arenal 19
8. Portrait of Alexander von Humboldt 28
9. The chief of the police 37

LIST OF ILLUSTRATIONS.

		PAGE
10.	The populace at Guaranda	39
11.	One of our arrieros	40
12.	Aiguilles on Chimborazo	41
13.	The second camp on Chimborazo (16,664 feet)	48
14.	Manner of packing the barometers	54
15.	The right and the wrong kind of stand	55
16.	Method of suspension	56
17.	The third camp on Chimborazo (17,285 feet)	60
18.	"Lower it would not go"	69
19.	Sangai in eruption	74
20.	The head of the expedition	80
21.	A ragamuffin at Chuquipoquio	81
22.	Back of the tambo of Chuquipoquio	85
23.	The entrance to the tambo	88
24.	Señor Juan Guerrero Duprat	92
25.	A pumice filter at Ambato	95
26.	A "Bishop" of Ambato	96
27.	One of my young friends	100
28.	Ecuadorian spur	102
29.	Carved drinking-cup	102
30.	Ecuadorian riding-whip	103
31.	Section in the lane at Machachi	104
32.	Machachi and Corazon	108
33.	Dressed rocks found on Corazon	110
34.	Indian reed-pipes	119
35.	Snow-cornices	120
36.	Cotopaxi in eruption in 1743	128
37.	An Academician observing the barometer	135
38.	A bomb from Cotopaxi	136
39.	Cotopaxi from the first camp	137
40.	An alpargata	143
41.	The first camp on Cotopaxi (15,139 feet)	144
42.	Position of the tent on the summit of Cotopaxi	149
43.	"There was fire below"	151
44.	Plan of the crater of Cotopaxi	152
45.	Indian crucifix	156
46.	The bells of Pedregal	157
47.	Sincholagua, from near Pedregal	161
48.	The summit of Sincholagua	163
49.	At Pedregal	165
50.	Entrance to the Hacienda, Pedregal	166
51.	Ecuadorienne earrings	167

LIST OF ILLUSTRATIONS.

		PAGE
52.	THE OLD WATER-CARRIER AT QUITO	169
53.	A LADY OF QUITO	171
54.	PORTRAIT OF GARCIA MORENO	174
55.	ECUADORIAN HAND-MADE LACE	179
56.	BEETLE-WING EARRING	183
57.	THE HACIENDA OF ANTISANA	184
58.	OUR BEST NOCTURNAL COLLECTOR	200
59.	DIAGRAM TO ILLUSTRATE FLIGHT OF THE CONDOR	203
60.	SNOW-SPECTACLES	206
61.	PICHINCHA, FROM MACHACHI	207
62.	ON THE ROAD	216
63.	CHAMPIONS	217
64.	INGRATITUDE	228
65.	CAYAMBE (19,186 FEET) FROM THE WEST	233
66.	CHARMS?	237
67.	LA DORMIDA DE MAYORAZZO	238
68.	A HIND-LEG OF A SPIDER FROM CORREDOR MACHAI	243
69.	SARA-URCU, FROM CORREDOR MACHAI	247
70.	TURNING AN ENEMY TO ACCOUNT	248
71.	FOUNTAIN ON THE PLAZA AT CARRANQUI	256
72.	"*THIS* IS *VERY* OLD, SEÑOR!"	257
73.	LANCE-POINT FOUND AT QUITO	258
74.	COTOCACHI, FROM CARRANQUI	263
75.	STARS IN STONE	269
76.	SOME UNUSUAL FORMS OF STONE IMPLEMENTS	273
77.	TOOL-SHARPENERS?	274
78.	MAIZE-HEADS IN STONE	275
79.	HEADS IN STONE, FROM RIOBAMBA	276
80.	THE HEAD OF AN OLD INDIAN SILVER PIN	277
81.	SIX-RAYED STAR IN BRONZE	277
82.	BRONZE HATCHETS FROM CUENCA	278
83.	ORDINARY FORMS OF OLD INDIAN POTTERY	278
84.	SOME OF THE LESS COMMON FORMS	279
85.	ORNAMENTATION OF POTTERY	280
86.	INDIAN MUSICAL WHISTLES	281
87.	THE DON POT	282
88.	DOUBLE-HEADED JAR OR VASE	283
89.	THE CONTENTS OF A GRAVE	284
90.	THE INCA VASE	285
91.	THE MONEY-BOX	286
92.	LA CONDAMINE'S INSCRIBED STONE	287
93.	PLAN, SECTION, AND ELEVATION OF THE PYRAMIDS OF QUITO	289

LIST OF ILLUSTRATIONS.

		PAGE
94.	THE PYRAMID OF OYAMBARO, IN 1880	292
95.	A STAMPEDE	296
96.	AT CAMP IN THE VALLEY OF COLLANES	305
97.	THE BRIDGE OF PENIPE	308
98.	A THREATENED ATTACK	310
99.	PLAN OF CAMP	312
100.	CARIHUAIRAZO, FROM THE SOUTH	317
101.	THE FOURTH CAMP ON CHIMBORAZO (14,359 FEET)	318
102.	CHIMBORAZO, FROM THE NORTH-NORTH-WEST	320
103.	COMMENCEMENT OF THE ERUPTION OF COTOPAXI, JULY 3, 1880	323
104.	A PHASMA FROM LA DORMIDA, CAYAMBE	335
105.	HUMBOLDT'S TRIANGLE	340
106.	JEAN-ANTOINE AND THE BABIES	344
107.	FORCEPS OF AN EARWIG FROM CAYAMBE	354
108.	EARWIG FROM 13,353 FEET ON CHIMBORAZO	355
109.	*PIERIS XANTHODICE*, LUCAS	357
110.	A MOTH FROM 12,000 FEET ON PICHINCHA	358
111.	MOTHS FROM 14,500 FEET ON COTOCACHI, AND SUMMIT OF PICHINCHA	359
112.	*HYALELLA INERMIS*, S. I. SMITH	361
113.	*COLIAS ALTICOLA*, GODMAN & SALVIN	364
114.	*COLIAS DIMERA*, DOUBL. & HEW.	364
115.	A TROPICAL DREAM	385
116.	"WE CAME AGAIN INTO THE LAND OF BUTTERFLIES"	388
117.	CERTIFICATES OF EXAMINATION OF BAROMETER NO. 558	397
118.	CHIMBORAZO, FROM GUAYAQUIL	442

MAPS, ETC.

1. GENERAL MAP OF ECUADOR, COLOMBIA, &C . . . Verso of front endsheet.
2. PLAN OF QUITO, AFTER FATHER J. B. MENTEN . . . Following page 167.
3. MAP OF THE PROVINCE OF QUITO, BY DON PEDRO MALDONADO   Endsheets.
4. ROUTE MAP TO ILLUSTRATE "TRAVELS AMONGST THE GREAT ANDES."   Foldout.

ERRATA.

At page 12, note 1, "Villavicensio" should read "Villavicencio."
 "   " 112, note 1, "Chap. XII," should read "Chap. XIX."
 "   " 114, note 1, "Chapters VI, XIII, and XV." should read "Chapters VI, XIII, and XIX."

TRAVELS AMONGST
THE GREAT ANDES
OF THE EQUATOR

ON THE WAY TO BODEGAS.

CHAPTER I.

WE landed at Guayaquil on December 9, 1879, after an uneventful voyage across the Atlantic, and an unexpected detention upon the Isthmus of Panama.[1] Our ship had scarcely anchored before a Custom House officer sought me out, to deliver an ornate speech; which commenced, according to the manner of the country, with declarations that he himself, his property, and other things besides were mine, and terminated with the welcome intelligence that he had been ordered to pass my baggage without examination, and free of duty.

Guayaquil is the chief port of the Republic of the Equator (Ecuador), and is second in population only to the capital, Quito.[2] In 1879, it was a very busy place. The war between

[1] See *The Contemporary Review*, March, 1889.

[2] It appeared to me to have about 28,000 inhabitants. No census has, I believe, yet been taken in Ecuador. All statements in regard to the population are to be received with caution.

Peru and Chili caused a large accession of trade, and filled it with a horde of refugees. Lodgings were scarcely to be had for money, and services were difficult to procure. Life seemed too easy for the lower orders at this place. At very trifling expense they can breakfast on chocolate, dine on bananas and cocoa-nut, and fall back at night on pine-apples. Lodging is not a difficulty with *them*, and dress is almost superfluous in a climate so equably warm. The elders go about in very light attire, and the young people appear in the streets in the earliest *mode* of Eden. Workmen set an exorbitant value on their services, and the very labourers expected to be paid at the rate of little English Bishops.

Not much was wanting to perfect our arrangements. Our principal need was a third man, as interpreter and general assistant, and it was supplied by Mr. Perring, an Englishman who had lived many years in Ecuador, and had frequently acted as Government courier between Guayaquil and Quito. This matter settled, there was time to look about, and I betook myself daily to the highest accessible ground—a hill at the northern end of the town—to endeavour to get a view of the Andes, and especially of Chimborazo.

Up to this time we had scarcely had a glimpse of the Andes. On the first half of the voyage from Panama our course was at too great a distance from the coast; and, on approaching the Equator, although the nearer parts of the outer ranges could be discerned, their tops were in cloud, and the great snow-peaks were invisible. Several Captains of the Mail Steamers, who had long experience, said that they had only seen Chimborazo from the Pacific Ocean on three or four occasions in the course of thirteen or fourteen years; and Mr. Chambers told me that the mountain was not commonly seen at Guayaquil more than once or twice a month.

I proposed to make my way to Chimborazo by the ordinary route to Quito, *viâ* Bodegas and Guaranda. From Guayaquil to Bodegas one takes the steamer, up the Guayas, and for the rest of the way transit is effected by horses, mules, or donkeys. As the rainy season was about to commence, and would impede or almost stop traffic whilst it lasted, there was an unusual demand for baggage animals, and it was expedient to arrange beforehand, to avoid detention at Bodegas. So we remained at Guayaquil, until information arrived that our train was ready.

Whilst waiting for news from Bodegas, I prowled about the outskirts of the town in search of snakes, being desirous of acquiring the handsome and venomous "Coral" which had not hitherto been acclimatized in Europe.[1] I did not see a live snake of any sort or description whilst at Guayaquil. It was the end of the dry season, and they had gone out of town for a time; but I understood from Mr. Chambers that he had many Coral snakes on his property, and could spare a few without inconvenience, and he promised to have a living specimen ready against our return to Guayaquil.[2]

[1] A few years ago, a French traveller—Mons. André—made an endeavour to introduce it from Colombia. His specimen arrived alive at Lille, where the French douaniers, suspecting contraband, insisted upon opening the box in which it was secured. The snake immediately made its appearance, to take a look around, and the douaniers retired. It then walked out, and disappeared, and was heard of no more. This, according to M. André, was the first attempt to introduce the Coral snake into Europe. See *Le Tour du Monde*, vol. 35, p. 182, Paris, 1878.

[2] Unfortunately, when that time came, they were too shy and could not be caught. Mr. Chambers was good enough to despatch another equally venomous reptile after me, to soothe my disappointment. The following sad story, however, came to hand instead of the snake.

It seems that it was shipped in a box by one of the Mail Steamers, and, being regarded with suspicion, was placed in a boat hanging from the davits. In the course of the voyage, about a dozen little snakes made their *début*, and, after crawling through a small knot-hole in the box, wriggled along the davits, and thence on to the deck. In the morning, when passengers came out to exercise, they found snakes already in possession. Quartermasters were set to clear them out, but one little snake managed to bite the second officer, and caused his arm to swell so much that he had to be taken on shore at Panama and be put in hospital. No one would venture to approach the box with the parent snake. The plug was knocked out of the bottom of the boat and it was

On December 13 we received advice that our animals were ready, and left Guayaquil the same afternoon on board the river-steamer *Quito*, with a large and very miscellaneous freight,[1] and arrived about midnight at Bodegas. Opposite to Guayaquil the Guayas is a noble river, more than a mile and a quarter across, with good depth of water. It is joined just above the town by its principal tributary, the River Daule, and beyond the junction, though remaining fully a mile wide, it becomes shallow. At a distance of about thirteen miles N.N.E. of Guayaquil it receives the waters of another important tributary, the River Yaguachi, a stream which is formed by the union of the Chimbo and Chanchan. In their upper courses, these rivers are only mountain torrents—

A YOUNG PERSON OF GUAYAQUIL.

---

lowered into the sea. The box floated away and drifted on to Flamenco I., off Panama, where some residents fired through and through it until the snake was killed. Mr. Chambers subsequently received a special request not to ship any more passengers *of that class*.

[1] The war in Peru caused an exodus of Italian organs from Lima, and thirty refugee instruments landed at Guayaquil just before our arrival. Four of these were on board the *Quito*, concentrated on the fore part of the upper deck, each playing a different tune. The Ecuadorians enjoyed the babel, but the alligators in the river seemed more sensitive. They came up and stared with open mouths, and plunged down again immediately, out of hearing.

The Guayas and its tributaries are full of alligators. On a trip up the river in July, 1880, I saw a large sandbank completely covered by a horde of them, lying peaceably alongside each other. The natives do not seem to be troubled by their proximity, though it is admitted they do occasionally chew incautious children.

the Chimbo being the more important of the two, and taking the drainage of the whole of the eastern slopes of the Pacific Range of Ecuador, and of the western slopes of the great block of mountains to the south of Chimborazo. Above the junction of the Yaguachi the Guayas becomes narrower, though it still remains quite 2000 feet across for some miles above Zamborondon. It then branches out into the flat land in numerous canal-like ramifications, and by the time Bodegas is reached dwindles down to insignificant dimensions.

Although we had approached more closely to the Andes we still saw nothing of them. On the lower reaches of the river this was not to be wondered at, for the land was being cleared by firing, prior to the advent of the rains, and clouds of smoke rose thousands of feet in the air, obscuring everything, except the banks close at hand. At Bodegas we got beyond this; the sun shone brilliantly, but not a sign of a mountain could be seen, though I shortly found that we were less than thirty-five miles from summits 14-15,000 feet above the sea. Chimborazo, I was told, could be seen from Bodegas, and bore from that place N.E. by E., or thereabouts.

The town of Bodegas de Babahoyo (called for brevity Bodegas) contains about 2000 inhabitants. It is the *entrepôt* of Quito, where goods are temporarily stored, and where a number of agents dwell whose business it is to receive goods from the steamers and to arrange for their transit into the interior. In the rainy season, the river rises here from

A HOUSE AT BODEGAS.

30 to 35 feet, and, overflowing its banks, turns the country into a vast lake. Hence many of the houses in this district are built on piles or posts. The area over which the floods extend is indicated by the houses that are constructed in this manner.

We left Bodegas at 1.20 p.m. on December 14, and crossing by a bridge to the right bank of the river commenced the journey over some open, flat, sandy ground. All went comfortably for a time. Jean-Antoine Carrel headed the caravan, mounted,[1] carrying one of the mercurial barometers and some other instruments; I followed, similarly equipped; then came the baggage animals, and the muleteers (arrieros) with Louis and Perring brought up the rear. Just one hour after the start, when we were jogging quietly along, the leading mule suddenly became possessed by ten thousand devils, and rushed hither and thither, throwing its heels high in the air; and succeeding in loosening its load, which turned round under its belly, it then commenced a series of violent fore and aft movements with its hoofs, to try to pulverize my photographic camera, and the other things which it carried.

In course of time we got to regard such episodes as a part of the daily routine. The most outrageous performers were generally the animals with the lightest loads; and, unless their extravagancies were promptly checked, their example became contagious, and the whole troop scattered, some galloping away, while the rest engaged themselves in madly battering their loads with the intention of dislodging them. A load on the Quito road usually weighs more than 300 lbs., and we probably committed a mistake in giving our beasts too little to carry in the low country.[2]

[1] In order to travel quickly, a considerable part of my baggage was sent out in advance, and was placed in secure hands at Guaranda and Quito. I am much indebted to Mr. Theakston, a forwarding agent at Bodegas, for his attentions there and at other places.

[2] All my cases were made with a view to transit by mules, and none weighed more than 75 lbs. Two of these and a few small articles were allotted to each

We made a short march on the first day, and stopped about 4 p.m. at the little, straggling village La Mona. Our house stood on posts, and like most others in this neighbourhood was built of bamboo, and was thatched with leaves. We passed the night, according to the custom of the country, in string hammocks, which were slung on the verandah on the first floor. Sleep was enlivened by superabundant animal life. Bats flapped

AT LA MONA.

our faces, and thousands of insects swarmed down upon the candles, while scuttling things of all sorts ranged the floor and invaded our boots.

A change was made in our arrangements next day. From this time onwards, Jean-Antoine took charge of both the mercurial barometers, to leave me free to attend to the details of

animal. Thus our loads seldom weighed more than 160 lbs., and this was as much as was good at great elevations. I saw many donkeys on the Quito road carrying eight dozens of wine or beer in four cases. Such loads cannot have weighed less than 280 lbs.

the caravan whilst passing along "the Royal Road." This is the title which has been given for many generations to the route from Bodegas to Guaranda. Although republican Ecuadorians have done much levelling, and amongst other things have abolished titles of nobility, they have omitted to level their roads, and cling with curious tenacity to the pompous title of this primitive track. In the matter of mud it did not come up to expectations. It was not so pre-eminently filthy as to be entitled to precedence over all other roads in this country; though it certainly was, in some parts, what Ecuadorians call 'savoury.' The mud is compounded of decaying animal and vegetable matter, churned up with earth, and the product is a greasy and captivating slime. The interesting series of ridges—termed *camellones*—crossing the track at right angles to its course, are generally considered by travellers to have been originated by the regular tread of animals.[1] Typical examples have a furrow of liquid mud upon each side of a ridge of slippery soil, with a difference of level of two feet or more between the top of the ridge and the bottom of the furrows; and man and beast struggle over the one and wallow in the others upon this *grande route* to the interior.

The traffic at this time was considerable both upwards and downwards, and the loads were often very miscellaneous in character. Champagne assorted with iron bedsteads seemed to travel well, while sheets of corrugated iron laid flat across the backs of donkeys gave rise to much bad language in narrow places. Coming down from the interior, on their way to the coast, we met numerous teams, often twenty or thirty in a troop, bringing huge bales of quinine bark, accompanied by gangs of unkempt

[1] Though they are maintained and deepened by the tread of animals, it is questionable if they were originated by them. Upon some new road which was being made to the south of Otovalo, I noticed furrows being *dug*, and there were already amongst them (without the assistance of traffic) many first-class puddles, which promised to make this, in a short time, a worthy continuation of "the Royal Road."

Indians, who humbly doffed their hats as they passed by. All day long, in front or behind, there could be heard a subdued murmur of snortings, braying, smashing, and objurgation: and from time to time, at fresh bends in the road, another caravan would appear,—horned cattle doing duty as well as horses, asses, and mules—the exclamations and whip-cracking became louder,

A COLLECTOR.

and we could distinguish the cries of the arrieros — their 'Burros!' and 'Burras!' 'Mula ha has,' and 'Cholos,' mingled with many 'Lados!' and expressions which will not bear translation.

For most of the way from Bodegas to Savaneta the Royal road was just such a beaten track as may be seen on many English commons. Next it led through shady jungle, and after Playas was passed it began to rise, jungle gradually changed to forest, and the road became damp, dirty, and confined. When a gleam of sunlight pierced the interlaced branches, we could see the great *Morphos* sailing in security amongst the hooks and spines of the tropical vegetation, and *epiphytals* thriving in gloom on stagnant air. But we could not tarry, for the rains had already commenced, and every one advised us to press on.[1]

The second night found us at Muñapamba, a regular stopping-place, 1337 feet above the sea, where a hut, called a Tambo, was surrounded by a motley throng of beasts, and bipeds who were practising the revolting habit that is referred to more particularly in Chapter IV.; and we passed an uneasy night in the open air upon plank beds, which were the only couches known at this establishment.

At 7 a.m., on Dec. 16, we left the tambo, and crossed to the right bank of a little stream, called the S. Jorge River. The Andes were still invisible, although we were actually upon their lower slopes. Everything was enveloped in mist, and a few

[1] In consequence of having been detained for ten days upon the Isthmus of Panama, we only just escaped the coast wet season. The intention to collect *en route* was abandoned, as we were constantly warned by persons we met on the road that rain was falling heavily on the mountains.

Amongst the few species secured on the first day's journey, there have been found an undescribed Ant (*Camponotus*), a Bug (*Pnohirmus*), and two Beetles (*Epitragus* and *Prionocalus*). These are described and figured in the Supplementary Appendix which is published simultaneously with this volume.

The *Prionocalus* that is described by Mr. H. W. Bates under the name *P. trigonodes* was picked up close to La Mona. It is one of the larger of known beetles, and being the finest we got during the day I looked at it attentively while putting it into alcohol. It gathered its limbs together, and appeared to expire almost instantaneously, without a struggle. The same happened with nearly everything that was obtained in Ecuador, with lizards, frogs, fish, etc., as well as with insects.

The genus *Prionocalus* was founded by Adam White upon specimens received from Mexico. It has also been found in Peru, and some years ago Mr. Waterhouse described a fine species from Ecuador (locality unknown, but supposed to have been on the eastern or Amazonian side of the Andes) under the name *P. Buckleyi*, from specimens collected by the late Mr. Buckley. I obtained *P. Buckleyi* at the height of about 4000 feet on the Royal road, and subsequently, through a collector, a third species of the genus, which was taken at the height of about 6000 feet, in the country to the west of Quito.

hundred yards was the most one could see in any direction. The path rose more steeply and continuously than upon passes which are commonly traversed by mules in the Alps, and degenerated as we ascended. It became a mere rut, hollowed out on the face of the mountain, without provision for drainage, and was left entirely to take care of itself. Earth that fell on to it from the banks at the side was trodden into the general filth. If pools accumulated, there they remained. Animals dying *en route* were left to rot, and were not removed. We passed two disabled mules, stuck fast, abandoned to their fate.

In two hours from Muñapamba we arrived at the village of Balsabamba, and after a brief halt continued the steep ascent; soon after noon entering the zone where rain had been falling during the last eight days, and then every one pressed forward to seek the nearest shelter, at Tambo Loma. Whilst toiling up the greasy zigzags, we were overtaken by a genial man, made up of straps and buckles, who was riding extra-post to Quito, and were guided by him across the quagmire that surrounded the "Hotel on the Hill" to the principal apartment, a windowless den about nine feet square and six feet high. There was neither bed nor bedding, food nor firing at this place.[1] We slept on our packing-cases.

On the morning of the 17th we quitted Tambo Loma soon after daybreak, piloted by the friendly courier. The muleteers said that the road was nearly impassable, and during a rise of 3000 feet we found it a morass, a sea of mud, into which our animals sank up to their knees or deeper. At length, when a little less than 10,000 feet above the level of the sea, we gradually topped the mists, and obtained our first view in the Andes.

[1] An Ecuadorian tambo is meant to give shelter to drovers and mule-drivers. These classes commonly carry food with them, for economy, and are content to sleep in pig-styes. The tambo meets their requirements, and seldom contains accommodation or food for the few others who travel in Ecuador. At La Mona we put up at a private house. Savaneta, Playas, Muñapamba, and Balsabamba are recognized stopping-places, and have tambos.

In a dim way, we could make out the buttress on which Tambo Loma was placed; but, although overlooking the mists, we could see neither the tambo, nor Muñapamba at the bottom of the valley, the flat land, the Pacific, nor anything to the west except mist,—light and thin above, dense and black below. Towards the east it was nearly clear. A few hundred feet above us, our road led to a gap, or pass in the mountains. We made at once for this place, and in a few minutes left the steaming Pacific slopes behind, and passed, as it were, into another world. The view from this place was a revelation.

From Bodegas until our arrival at this spot we had not been able to see as much as a mile in any direction. We passed through forest; the track constantly rose; the barometers told us we were getting high; but in what direction our road would lead, whether it would keep to the east, north-east, or south-east, was not known. From the existing maps of Ecuador[1] it did not appear that any important mountains intervened between Guaranda and the coast, and until this moment I had supposed that the western slopes of Chimborazo led continuously towards the Pacific. For the best authority upon this particular district, Mr. Richard Spruce, says, "On the western side" (of Chimborazo) "I can find no positive break from the summit down to the plain. There is no intervening salient peak, and no ridge whose origin may not be traced to the peak of Chim-

---

[1] Namely, the map by Don Pedro Maldonado, the map in La Condamine's *Voyage*, and the map accompanying the work *Geografia de la Republica del Ecuador*, by Manuel Villavicensio, New York, 1858. In the portion of the Maldonado map that I have reproduced (which is placed at the end of this volume), it will be seen there is no suggestion of an important range of mountains to the immediate west of Chimborazo and the valley of the R. Chimbo, and in several places, notably just north of the words R. Yaguachi, the map suggests flat, forest-covered land. On the map of La Condamine this district has evidently been copied from Maldonado, and some of the hill-work given by the latter authority is abolished, making the land appear flatter still; and in the Villavicensio map this process is still further carried out, and there appears to be nothing except unimportant hills between Guayaquil and Chimborazo.

borazo."[1] In this matter he is, however, incorrect. It is more convenient to give at this point all that need be said on the subject than to recur to it again.

The place where our road crossed the mountains was a true pass, leading through a gap, from the head of one valley on the western to another on the eastern side of a large and important range of mountains. Two small huts on its summit were termed Tambo Gobierno.[2] I read the two mercurial barometers here at 10 a.m., and there was a nearly corresponding (11 a.m.) observation by Mr. Chambers at Guayaquil, and from these observations it appears that the height of Tambo Gobierno is 10,417 feet. A short distance from us, both to the north and to the south, there were points from 1000 to 1500 feet higher; and to the north, I found subsequently, the general elevation of the range increased, and that there were a number of summits 13–14,000 feet above the level of the sea, — some, I believe, closely approaching the height of 15,000 feet. The general elevation diminishes when proceeding southwards, though it remains considerable to its furthest extremity, where the River Chimbo, suddenly changing from a nearly north and south course to an east and west one, skirts its base. At this end, the slopes rise abruptly from a few hundred feet above the level of the sea to 7–8000 feet, and are magnificently wooded.

On December 19 and 26, when proceeding from Guaranda to Chimborazo, I had unclouded views of the eastern side of this range; and from December 27 to January 12, whilst encamped upon Chimborazo, I commanded and looked down upon the eastern side of the whole of the northern part of it. In the following July, whilst making the circuit of Chimborazo, I saw that that mountain was everywhere well separated from the

[1] See page 7 of his *Report on the expedition to procure seeds and plants of the Cinchona succirubra, or Red Bark Tree*, London, 1861.

[2] They contained accommodation for neither man nor beast, and nothing edible except one very shrivelled, old Indian woman.

range on its west; and subsequently, after skirting the great block of mountains to the south of Chimborazo, I came upon the range again at the Bridge of Chimbo, passed around its southern extremity, and saw its western slopes at that end dying out in the neighbourhood of Barraganetal. They also extend as far as Muñapamba. Its northern extremity, and north-western slopes, I have not seen at all. The range has, however, an ascertained length from north to south of 65 miles, and is in breadth 18 to 20 miles—that is to say, it is at least twice the length and breadth of the range of Mont Blanc.

The range is bounded on the east by the valley of the River Chimbo, and the course of this valley is well seen in the neighbourhood of Guaranda. To the north of that town it opens out into a very large basin, which receives the whole of the drainage of the western side of Chimborazo. South of Guaranda, the valley for a long distance runs north and south. At Guaranda the river is 8530 feet, and at Chimbo (formerly called the Bridge of Chimbo), according to the Railway authorities, it is 1130 feet above the level of the sea. These facts sufficiently show that Chimborazo itself, and the great *massif* of which it is the culminating point, are separated by a large and profound valley from the range of which I have spoken; and, as this range is not yet known by any distinctive appellation, I propose to call it the Pacific Range of Ecuador.[1]

At Tambo Gobierno we passed as it were into another world. The slopes of the Pacific Range were densely wooded right up to their crests on the side facing the Ocean, while their eastern ones were almost absolutely bare of vegetation. In a few hundred yards the track lost its royal character, and on the other side of the ridge became as dry as the Sahara. A good, made road down a steep lateral valley led us through the

[1] The stream near Chimbo marked Agua Clara on my map, is a mountain torrent gushing out of the southernmost extremity of the Pacific Range, and now supplies Guayaquil with water.

village of S. Miguel to the larger one of S. José, where we halted for food; and we then pushed on in advance of our caravan, arriving just before nightfall at the small town of Guaranda, the place which I intended to use as a base for attack upon Chimborazo.[1]

NOTE UPON THE MAPS OF ECUADOR.

Most modern maps of Ecuador are based upon those of M. de la Condamine and Don Pedro Maldonado. The former of these, on a scale of about nineteen geographical miles to an inch, was published in 1751, at Paris, in the work Journal du voyage fait par ordre du roi à l'Équateur, servant d'introduction historique a la mesure des trois premiers degrés du méridien, and was entitled Carte de la Province de Quito au Perou, dressée sur les Observations astronomiques, Mesures géographiques, Journaux de route et Mémoires de Mr de la Condamine, et sur ceux de Don Pedro Maldonado. Par Mr d'Anville de l'Acad. Imperiale de Petersbourg.

---

[1] I give below our times between the several places which have been mentioned. A single horseman, or a pedestrian, would not occupy so long, more especially if proceeding in the reverse direction. Bodegas to La Mona, 2 hours 40 min.; La Mona to Savaneta, 2 hs.; Savaneta to Playas, 2 hs.; Playas to Muñapamba, 4 hs.; Muñapamba to Balsabamba, 2 hs.; Balsabamba to Tambo Loma, 3 hs. 30 min.; Tambo Loma to Tambo Gobierno, 2 hs. 45 min.; Tambo Gobierno to S. José de Chimbo, 2 hs. 30 min.; and thence to Guaranda, 3 hours.

The following shade temperatures were observed, in the open air:—

Dec. 14.	La Mona	83°	Faht.	at 8 p.m.
,, 15.	do.	72°	,,	,, 4 a.m.
,, ,,	do.	74°	,,	,, 7 ,,
,, ,,	Playas	78·5	,,	,, noon.
,, 16.	Muñapamba (1337 feet)	70°	,,	,, 6.45 a.m.
,, ,,	Tambo Loma (6850 ,,)	62·5	,,	,, 7 p.m.
,, 17.	do.	59·5	,,	,, 4 a.m.
,, ,,	do.	60°	,,	,, 5.30 a.m.
,, ,,	Tambo Gobierno (10,417 feet)	60°	,,	,, 10 a.m.
,, ,,	S. José de Chimbo (8200 ,,)	65°	,,	,, 1.45 p.m.

The latter map, in four sheets, on a scale of about twelve geographical miles to an inch, extending from 2° N. Lat. to 6° S. Lat., was published in Paris in 1750, under the title Carta de la Provincia de Quito y de sus adjacentes. Obra posthuma de Don Pedro Maldonado, Gentilhombre de la Camara de S. Mag. y Governador de la Prov. de Esmeraldas. Hecha sobre las Observaciones Astronomicas y Geograficas de los Academicos Reales de las Ciencias de Paris y de las Guardias Mar. de Cadiz y tambien de los RR. PP. Missioneros de Maynas. En que la Costa desde la Boca de Esmeraldas hasta Tumaco con la Derrota de Quito al Marañon, por una senda de à pie de Baños à Canelos, y el curso de los Rios Bobonaça y Pastaça van delineados sobre las proprias demarcaciones del difunto Autor. Sacada à luz por orden, y à expensas de su Magestad. M.DCCL.

These two maps were constructed from the same material, and (although differing in some matters of detail) are nearly identical. In M. de la Condamine's *Journal du Voyage* frequent reference is made to Maldonado (see vol. 1, pp. 110, 141-2, and 208-210) and to his share in the production of these maps. In general, the central portion of the region which is represented is based upon the work of the Academicians, whilst the remainder is largely due to Maldonado. Two different classes of work, of very different degrees of value, have been embodied; namely (1) triangulation of the most precise character, starting from a long and carefully-measured base, checked by a base of verification; and (2) surveys of the rougher kinds, made by the less accurate methods.

La Condamine says that Maldonado was a "créole du Pérou." He was for some time Governor of the district of Esmeraldas, and devoted himself to discovering a more direct road to Quito from the Pacific than that *viâ* Guayaquil, which was then, as it is still, the route in general use. He succeeded in doing so, and concurrently made extensive topographical observations. Afterwards, in company with La Condamine, he descended the

Amazons, and assisted in the survey of that river, and then proceeded to Europe to introduce his new way from Panama to Quito to notice in Spain. He went to Paris to superintend the production of his map; and, after other travels, came to London, and died there of fever on Nov. 17, 1748, aged about forty years. He had been elected a Corresponding Member of the French Academy of Sciences, and at the time of his death was about to be proposed at the Royal Society.

In constructing the Route Map which accompanies and illustrates this volume I have put the maps of La Condamine and Maldonado entirely on one side, and have commenced afresh. I have used the Latitudes of La Condamine for Quito and Riobamba, and have adopted 79° 52′ 27″ W. as the Longitude of Guayaquil. The details have been filled in from my own observations (principally angles taken with a transit theodolite) except such courses of rivers as are given in dotted lines. Many of my names will not be found in earlier maps, and in the positions both of towns and mountains I frequently differ from my predecessors. As nearly every town, village or inn is given on the route from Guayaquil to Quito, this route map may be found of some service by persons travelling between the coast and the capital.

The Map of Chimborazo has been constructed from my own observations by Mr. Turnbull under Mr. Bolton's direction at Stanford's Geographical Establishment. Its scale depends upon a measurement made on the Quito road, between Chuquipoquio and Mocha.

The Plan of the Glacier de Débris on Chimborazo has been constructed by myself from my own observations, and its scale depends upon a base of 600 feet which I measured below our Second Camp, upon the western side of the glacier.

I have thought it desirable for the further illustration of my narrative, and for comparison, to give in fac-simile the central portion of the Maldonado map. This has been reproduced from the copy in the Map Room of the British Museum. The road by which the Governor of Esmeraldas hoped to benefit his country (*camino nueve de Quito*) will be seen indicated in the neighbourhood of the Equator, leading from Nono to the Rio Blanco (a branch of the R. Esmeraldas). It has never come into general use. Mr. Stevenson was deputed in 1809 to re-examine it, and he reported favourably (see *Historical and descriptive narrative of twenty years' residence in South America*, by W. B. Stevenson, Lond., 1829, vol. 2, pp. 355-7, etc.); but down to the present time the circuitous route *viâ* Guayaquil has been preferred.

NATIVE HOUSE AT GUARANDA.

CROSSING THE GREAT ARENAL.

CHAPTER II.

FROM GUARANDA TO THE FIRST CAMP ON CHIMBORAZO.

THE town of Guaranda seemed very lifeless, although it had about 2000 inhabitants, and I ventured to remark to an assistant at the inn[1] that it appeared dull, meaning that there was an absence of trade and traffic. "It is, your Excellency," said the dirty waiter, "it is deplorably dull; but to-night some choice spirits will come in, *and will kick up a delightful row.*" His master remains in my recollection as a person of unusual candour. There had been some difficulties over an account that he had presented to the representative of a foreign power just before our arrival, but he tendered no paltry excuses, and roundly declared that Consuls, Ministers, *and all that sort of thing* must

[1] At this place there was an inn, where meals could be had. The beds were objectionable, and the apartments were filthy. We passed the night in the open gallery on our packing-cases, and on Dec. 18 transferred ourselves to a house which I engaged during our stay.

pay double,—a fact which members of the diplomatic service will do well to remember when they pass his way.

Guaranda had been fixed upon as headquarters for a time because it was reported to be nearer to Chimborazo than any other town or village. The road to Quito leads through it, and passes over the southern extremity of the mountain, across a plain called "the Great Arenal." The highest point of this was commonly estimated to be about 14,000 feet above the level of the sea. We were therefore assured of being able to transport our baggage to that elevation without calling upon the natives to do anything unusual. How much higher we should be able to utilize them depended upon the nature of the lower slopes; and as we had no information about them, and did not know how far we were from the mountain, we set out at 4.30 a.m. on the 19th to reconnoitre.

It will seem almost incredible that we should have approached so closely to Chimborazo without obtaining a glimpse of it. Prescott says[1] it affords a magnificent prospect to the mariner on the Pacific Ocean. It was invisible from the Pacific, and also at Guayaquil, at Bodegas, Tambo Gobierno, and Guaranda, though at all those places we were informed that it might, could, or should be seen; and upon the 19th, if we had not been aware that we actually touched its lower slopes, we might have gone past it without entertaining a suspicion that we were underneath a mountain of first-class magnitude, notably loftier than anything in its vicinity.

Upon leaving Guaranda there was a sharp descent to the River Chimbo, which was crossed by a bridge 360 feet below the level of the town, and the road then mounted by a pretty regular incline along the slopes on the eastern side of the valley, and gradually bore away from the river. At 5.35 a.m. it was light enough to see comfortably, and by 6.30 we were nearly 11,000 feet above the sea. At this elevation we made a short

---

[1] *History of the Conquest of Peru*, Book I., chap. i.

halt to look at the mountains to the west. Many of the nearer ones were considerably higher than our position, and as we rose fresh tops kept coming into view, shewing the extent and importance of this hitherto ignored Pacific Range.[1]

The first part of the road to the Arenal was a fairly good mountain-path, left, as elsewhere, to take care of itself. Higher up it became slimy, and our pace was reduced, especially amongst some first-class *camellones* near the top of the pass. On the last two hundred feet the track disappeared, and every one followed the way that seemed best over the steep, sandy slope. The immediate summit was a rounded ridge of sand, and when this was crossed the Great Arenal came into sight, sloping at first very slightly and afterwards more abruptly towards the north-east, and stretching uninterruptedly to the base of Chimborazo.

Under the guidance of our arriero we made for the Tambo of Tortorillas (12,828),[2] the only place of refuge between Guaranda and Chimborazo except a wooden shed at the place marked Ensillada. The tambo was too filthy to enter,[3] and we went a few hundred yards aside, and sitting on a grassy knoll looked towards our mountain. Clouds hung about the whole of the upper part, and we could not anywhere see up to the snow-line.

---

[1] Between 11,000 and 12,500 feet the vegetation on the banks by the roadside was rather unusually attractive. I collected an *Eryngium*; several species of *Gaultheria* (*Gaultheria* near *conferta*, Benth., *G. Pichinchensis*, Benth., and another); *Bidens humilis*, H.B.K. (widely distributed in Ecuador); *Draba grandiflora*, Hook. and Arn.; *Hypericum* (*Brathys*) *strutheolæfolium*, Juss.; *Castilleia fissifolia*, L.; *Chætagaster stricta*, D.C.; a *Calceolaria*, a *Geranium*, etc. etc.

The Botanical Collections made on this journey have been worked out at the Botanical Department of the British Museum under the personal direction of Mr. Wm. Carruthers, F.R.S., to whom I offer my best thanks for his attentions and courtesy.

[2] This place, as well as all others mentioned, will be found upon the large map accompanying this volume.

[3] It was composed of one room, which was kitchen and everything else. One of the foulest tambos in Ecuador—the courtyard a sea of mud. Obtained potato soup, bread, and chocolate here.

The buttresses in the immediate vicinity of Tortorillas were very steep, and came to sudden terminations on the sandy plain. The *vallons*, however, between them were moderately inclined, and we heard that mules frequently went up one of them to fetch ice, which was cut for sale in Guayaquil. It was clear that we should be able to take natives about 2000 feet above Tortorillas, or to about 15,000 feet above the sea,—how much higher could not be said.

Having learnt this, and obtained a notion of the position of Chimborazo, we returned in the course of the evening to Guaranda,[1] and on the next day, the mountain still remaining invisible, made the acquaintance of the very thin upper crust of the town, which was composed of the official termed the 'Jefo-politico,' the Commissary of Police, and the Priest; and discovered on the other side of our courtyard a pretty Spanish girl, with lustrous black eyes, who captivated the Carrels—by peeling their potatoes.

The Jefo-politico, Señor Don Dario Montenegro, Lieut.-Col. in the Ecuadorian army, and Señor Don J. Pazmiño, Commissary of Police, made themselves agreeable. We exchanged visits, and I found that they knew more about my intentions than I did myself. A few days later they gave me another call, evidently with something upon their minds, though I could not perceive what was the object of the interview. At length the principal official thus addressed me. "Señor, we understand perfectly, that in an affair like yours, it is *necessary* to dissemble,—a little;

[1] Whilst returning, I was overcome with dizziness, feverishness, and intense headache, and had to be supported by two of my people part of the way. Owing to this, we occupied as long in returning as in ascending. I took 30 grains of sulphate of quinine in the course of the night, and was covered up with a mountain of blankets, and in the morning became all right again.

Left Guaranda 4.30 a.m. Stopped 20 min. *en route*. Arrived at the top of the Great Arenal 10.35 a.m., and at Tortorillas 11.45 a.m. Left Tortorillas 1 p.m., and arrived at Guaranda 8.30 p.m. I estimate the distance to Tortorillas and back at 35 miles.

At 6 a.m. the shade temp. in the open air was 45° Faht. At 7.45 a.m., 49°; at 10.35 a m. (summit of Arenal), 52°; and at Tortorillas, at mid-day, 56°·5.

and you, doubtless, do quite right to say that you intend to ascend Chimborazo,— a thing that everybody knows is perfectly impossible. *We* know very well what is your object! You wish to discover the TREASURES which are buried in Chimborazo, and, no doubt, there is *much* treasure buried there; and we hope you will discover it; but we hope, when you have discovered it, you will not forget *us*." "Gentlemen," I said, "I shall be delighted to remember you, but in respect to the other matter — the treasure — I venture to suggest that you shall pay half the expenses of the expedition, and take half the treasure we discover." Upon hearing this, they drew long faces, and went away. Shortly afterwards, there came an empty person of Riobamba, with his mouth full of a story of priceless riches buried between Chimborazo and Carihuairazo; to discover which should be *my* aim for *his* advantage; and to him I said, " Lead us there, and we will share the spoil!" But he made no answer, and went away, and we saw his face no more.[1]

On Dec. 21, we obtained our first view of Chimborazo. Instruments had been kept in readiness; a place of observation to the north of and somewhat higher than the town had been selected, and we hurried to it to make the most of the opportunity. Two things instantly arrested attention. One of these was that Chimborazo had *two* summits — twin, snowy domes — apparently, nearly equally elevated. The other was that the whole of that part of the mountain which was seen from Guaranda was nearly covered with glaciers.

All the writers who have referred to Chimborazo from personal knowledge, notably Humboldt and Boussingault, have spoken of 'the summit,' never of summits; and in a well-known passage in *Asie Centrale*, which has been embodied in many geographical works, Humboldt expressly declares that he saw no glaciers in Ecuador. "I have seen nothing in the tropics,"

---

[1] At almost every place we visited in Ecuador persons introduced themselves with stories of buried treasures.

he says, "neither in Quito,[1] nor in Mexico, resembling the Swiss glaciers"; and he quotes a confirmatory passage from Boussingault, in which the latter says that *he* is only acquainted with *one* glacier in Ecuador, upon the mountain Tunguragua —"c'est le seul glacier que j'aie vu en Amérique entre les tropiques." Yet I saw Chimborazo crowned by glacier, and streaming with glaciers. They departed in all directions from a plateau on the top, almost covering the mountain.[2]

The question then arose, Which of these two summits is the higher, and the real top of Chimborazo? and in the discussion that followed it appeared that we all inclined to the opinion that the right-hand or more eastern and more distant one, although apparently lower, was actually loftier than the left-hand or more westerly one. Upon bringing the theodolite to bear upon it, I found that it (the eastern summit) was depressed 2' 30" below the other.

We then debated the manner of approach to the eastern summit. Assuming it to be the higher of the two, how was it to be attained? The natural course would have been from the south-east.[3] This side of the mountain, however, was never perfectly free from clouds. It was steep, and so far as we could see, it was almost completely covered by glacier. We could distinguish multitudes of crevasses—the essential and distinctive feature of glaciers; and great schrunds which are the outward and visible signs of the dislocation of these icy masses in their passage across unusually irregular ground. Over these

---

[1] In this passage, Humboldt means the viceroyalty of Quito (embracing the whole of Ecuador), not the City of Quito. I give the passage at length in Chapter XIX.

[2] The view facing p. 24 is from a photograph which was taken a few days later. For the purposes of our discussion I sketched the mountain.

[3] The reader will be able to follow me upon the accompanying plate. The tambo of Tortorillas lies to the right, beyond the range of the engraving. The Great Arenal is behind the distant ridge, which stretches from one side to the other. The lowest part seen of Chimborazo is more than 16,000 feet above the sea.

CHIMBORAZO, FROM THE SLOPES ABOVE GUARANDA.

slopes and schrunds, clouds came and went ceaselessly. We cherished the idea that we were unfortunate in the weather, and that presently they would be dissipated. It took time to learn that they were a great and permanent feature of the mountain, due to the condensation of damp air coming from the Amazonian region.

A direct approach to the eastern summit from the side of Guaranda could not be contemplated for a moment; for the glaciers streaming from the two domes fell over cliffs, and above nearly perpendicular precipices of rock there rose perpendicular walls of ice, which broke away as the glaciers progressed, and rolled into a basin, of which we only saw the head. We could trace the grooves and scorings on the slopes below made by falling bodies, and knew that we could not venture there.

Underneath the western summit, and leading nearly southwest, there appeared to be a ridge coming down to the Arenal, and to the west of this there was another basin, filled with rather tumultuous glacier. This was succeeded by another ridge, bearing on its crest a number of sharp pinnacles of rock. We could only conjecture what came behind this. The view was terminated on the extreme left by a very long snow-slope, which seemed to be remarkably free from impediments, and appeared to stretch continuously almost from the snow-line up to the western dome. This ridge was a considerable distance away, and we could not learn whether it was possible to reach its inferior end. Choice of route was narrowed to it and the south-west ridge, and I gave a casting vote in favour of the latter, being largely influenced in arriving at this decision by the supposition that it was in this direction Humboldt and Boussingault made their memorable attempts to ascend the mountain.

There was one point upon this ridge (hereafter referred to as the south-west ridge of Chimborazo) which, in our united opinion, was likely to present difficulties.[1] If this place could be passed, I reckoned that we should be able to reach the top of the mountain. A route could be traced through the great crevasses by bearing to the west, and I proposed to work round the western summit, to get between the two domes, and then to strike right and left.

Jean-Antoine and Louis were eager for an immediate start, but I refused to break up headquarters at Guaranda until we were assured that we could reach the south-west ridge by way of the Arenal. There was a long interval about which we knew nothing, and I despatched them at 2 p.m. on the 21st to endeavour to connect the lowest part that was visible from Guaranda with the highest ground that we had seen from the Arenal; and instructed them, in the event of this appearing a promising direction, to select a fit place for camping, if possible, at about 16,000 feet — that being the greatest height up to which it was probable we should be able to force natives and mules.[2] This was a mission they were thoroughly competent to execute, and they left me at Guaranda to carry on work in which they could have rendered very little assistance.

It is stated in the Introduction that the main object of this journey was to observe the effects of low pressures; that, to experience them, it was necessary to get to great elevations; and that, in order to discriminate between the effects which might properly be attributed to low pressures and those which might be due to fatigue, it was necessary to eliminate the latter. To accomplish this, it was obviously better to have dealings with mountains easy of access than with those involving high gymnastics, and Chimborazo had seemed especially favourable for

---

[1] It will be explained at a later point why we considered this might be a critical place.

[2] They took Aneroid F with them, in order that I might be able to form an idea of the height they reached, and I set the pointer in the movable rim to let them know when they had attained the desired elevation.

these investigations on account of the apparent facility with which previous travellers had attained great heights upon its slopes.

I had relied implicitly upon the accounts of Humboldt and Boussingault, and accepted without reserve their statements that they had in 1802 and 1831 respectively reached the heights of 19,286 and 19,698 feet. There were matters in their relations that I did not understand; particularly, the divine speed with which they descended. Yet I was more disposed to imagine that they had incorrectly noted the times which had been occupied than that there was any considerable mistake in the determination of their altitudes; for both were provided with mercurial barometers, and had had much experience in the use of these instruments in the field. It was natural to conclude that the work must be simple if these travellers, unacquainted with the art of mountaineering, and unprovided with professional assistance, could reach so great elevations with such facility, and descend at such a prodigious rate.

Alexander von Humboldt was in his 33rd year at the time that he made his attempt to ascend Chimborazo. He had enjoyed three years of continuous travel in South America, he was inured to the peculiarities of the climate, and he had the companionship of his friends Bonpland and Carlos Montufar—a son of the Marquis de Selvalegre, one of the most important personages of the district. They were all young men, and, selecting a favourable moment for the enterprize, they made their expedition under advantageous conditions. There are frequent allusions to Chimborazo throughout the works of Humboldt, and he evidently was profoundly impressed by his experiences. Towards the close of his long life, and at an age when men do not speak lightly, he declared that he still considered it was the grandest mountain in the world.

Notwithstanding the frequent references to this occasion which are made in the works of Humboldt, I am unable to tell from his own writings where he actually went.[1] He does not give courses, or bearings, or such indications as enable one to identify with certainty the positions to which he refers. He states that upon June 23, 1802, he reached the height of

19,286 feet by 1 p.m., and that this was greater than he "had dared hope for. In many places the ridge was not wider than

---

[1] See *Vues dans les Cordillères*, pp. 104-7; *Aspects of Nature*; *Kleinere Schriften*; *Recueil d'Observations Astronomiques*, etc. etc. I think it better to adopt as authoritative the account which is given in Karl Bruhns' *Life of Humboldt* (8vo, Lond., 1873, vol. 1, pp. 311-315) than to attempt to construct a narrative from these diverse relations. His biographer must be assumed to be fully acquainted with all that has been written on the subject.

from eight to ten inches. To our left a precipice covered with snow. . . . On the right was a fearful abyss. . . . The rock became more friable and the ascent increasingly difficult and dangerous. We were obliged to use both hands and feet. We advanced all the more slowly, as every place that seemed insecure had first to be tested." These are some of the expressions used in regard to places which were passed over in the earlier part of the day. Higher up, "one after another all began to feel indisposed, and experienced a feeling of nausea accompanied by giddiness. . . . Blood exuded from the lips and gums." At last they were stopped by a ravine "some 400 feet deep and 60 feet wide, which presented an insurmountable barrier. We could see clearly that the ridge on which we stood continued in the same direction on the other side of the ravine. . . . There was no means of getting round the cleft. . . . The softness of the snowy mass prohibited such an attempt." This was the turning-point. Its height was determined by observation of mercurial barometer at 19,286 feet. They remained there but a short time, and when about half-way down encountered a violent hail-storm, which a little later was succeeded by snow. The flakes fell so thickly that the ridge was covered several inches deep. He says that they left their highest point a little after 1 p.m., and at a few minutes after 2 reached the place where they had left their mules (at 15,600 feet), that is to say, he claims to have descended 3686 feet *in one hour!*[1]

Joseph-Dieudonné Boussingault was in his 29th year when he attempted to ascend Chimborazo in 1831, and had been living for several years in elevated regions in the neighbourhood of the Equator. He was accompanied by an American (Col. Hall) and a Negro. On Dec. 14, they went to "the farm of Chimborazo,[2] which he said was at an elevation of 3800 mètres

---

[1] See Appendix G at the end of this volume, where the relation from Karl Bruhns is given in full.

[2] This, I conjecture, is the place now called Chuquipoquio.

(12,467 feet), and at 7 a.m. on the 15th, under the guidance of an Indian, followed a rivulet enclosed between walls of rock, "whose waters descend from the glacier;[1] but very soon," he says, "we quitted this fissure, in order to direct our steps towards Mocha.[2] We rose very gradually, and our mules walked with difficulty through the débris of rock. The slope then became very rapid, the ground was unstable, and the mules stopped almost at every step. They no longer obeyed the spur. The breathing of the animals was hurried and panting. We were then at an elevation of 4808 mètres (15,774 feet)." They left the mules at this height, and "began to ascend a ridge which abutted on a very elevated point of the glacier. It was mid-day. We went up slowly; and as we got higher on the snow the difficulty of breathing and walking became more and more felt; but we easily regained our strength by stopping at every eight or ten steps. As we went on, we felt extreme fatigue from the want of consistency in the snowy soil, which gave way continually under our feet, and in which we sank sometimes up to the waist. We were soon convinced of the impossibility of proceeding. We went to rest on a block of trachyte, at an elevation of 5115 mètres (16,781 feet). Thus, after much fatigue, we had only risen 307 mètres (1007 feet) higher than the place whence we had set out. At 6 o'clock we were back at the farm."

They determined to make another attempt. "The weather had been splendid, and Chimborazo had never appeared so magnificent. We resolved," he says, "to try to ascend the steep side, that is to say, by the slope facing the Arenal. We knew that it was upon this side M. de Humboldt had ascended, and we had been shewn at Riobamba the point he had reached, but it was

[1] It is curious to note that Boussingault here refers to a glacier, although elsewhere he says that he has seen only *one* glacier in the Tropics, upon the mountain Tunguragua.

[2] From this it appears that they made for the easternmost glacier of Chimborazo, which is marked K upon my map.

impossible to obtain precise information about the route which he had followed to get there." They set out at 7 a.m. on Dec. 16, for the Arenal,[1] and by 9 o'clock had got to a height of 4335 mètres (14,223 feet), and stopped for breakfast. At 10.45 a.m., they left their mules at a height of 4945 mètres (16,224 feet), that is to say, they had got them 2000 feet upwards in an hour and three-quarters, including the time occupied by breakfast and reading the barometer. At 12.45 they were at a height of 5680 mètres (18,636 feet), or had mounted 2412 feet more in two hours, including the stoppages necessary for further observations of the barometer and the formation of a geological collection, notwithstanding that they had to pause every six or eight steps to get breath. Here they halted for rest, and again read the barometer, yet at 1.45 p.m. they had reached a height of 6004 mètres (19,698 feet), although upon this section they "were obliged to stop every two or three steps" to get breath, and even to sit down. They commenced to descend about 3 p.m., and at 4.45 arrived again at the height of 4335 mètres (14,223 feet), that is to say, descended 5475 feet in an hour and three-quarters. Boussingault says the descent was wearisome (pénible). It seems, however, to have been rather lively. His average rate throughout the whole of the descent was 52 feet *per minute,* over slopes on which a thin coating of snow lay over ice, where step-cutting was necessary; over a 'mauvais pas,' and a 'nappe de glace,' where 'a slip would have been fatal'; and *talus,* 'quite im-

[1] Boussingault, like Humboldt, gives neither courses nor bearings. He appears to have followed the ordinary track round the mountain, and must have arrived at the Arenal by passing through the place called Tortorillas. The speed with which he now travels is remarkable, and is very much faster than the rates quoted for his first attempt.

He evidently intended to follow the route taken by Humboldt; and presumably he did so, as nothing subsequently is said to the contrary. I endeavoured in 1879 to learn more particulars from M. Boussingault about the route he followed. He informed me that he could not at that distance of time (forty-eight years) remember anything more than he had published. Boussingault died in 1887, aged 85.

practicable for mules.'[1] But he was beaten by Humboldt, who descended 3686 feet in sixty minutes, or at an average rate of *sixty-one feet per minute*, down a ridge which in many places was not wider than from eight to ten inches, with friable rock which had to be climbed; where every loose place had first to be tested, and from the insecurity of the footing greater caution was necessary than during the ascent—the last part of the way being through a storm which covered the ridge with several inches of snow. This is a divine rate for men encumbered with mercurial barometers, and laden with geological collections.

I had not imagined that we should equal these extraordinary rates of speed. I did not, and do not, understand how they were accomplished.[2] It had seemed to me probable that the times which were occupied were incorrectly noted. My perplexities were increased when I saw Chimborazo from Guaranda, and studied the mountain in connection with the narratives of these two famous travellers. I was roughly disillusionized. Accepting its height as 21,425 feet, a fair notion could be formed where 19,500 feet would come; and it was evident that no one could stand at that elevation, at any part of the mountain, without having glaciers in front, behind, and upon each side, and that no one could gain that elevation without, also, *passing over* glacier.

It now seemed probable that the altitudes had also been incorrectly determined, and I began to take more interest in the elevation of Chimborazo. The height of this mountain has

[1] For the full account, from which these quotations are made, see Appendix H, at the end of this volume. The title of the original is *Ascension au Chimborazo, exécuté le 16 décembre, 1831, par M. Boussingault*.

[2] When writing *Scrambles amongst the Alps*, I tabulated a large number of ascents of the principal Alpine peaks to obtain a notion of the average rate of progression of mountaineers in general; and found that 1000 feet per hour, taking the *mean* of ascent and descent, was a respectable rate, including halts. That is to say, ten hours would be a fair allowance for the ascent and descent of 5000 feet involving work of moderate difficulty. This, however, had reference to unencumbered men, and to mountain work less than 16,000 feet above the sea.

undergone vicissitudes. Sometimes it has been greater and sometimes smaller.[1] Humboldt says (in *Aspects of Nature*, vol. 1, p. 96) that until 1820 it was still regarded as "the highest summit on the surface of the earth."[2] It looked very large from Guaranda. The snowy part that was visible (and this was only a fraction of the whole) extended nearly over a point of the compass (ten degrees and a half). We were more than twice the distance from it that the Brévent is from Mont Blanc, yet at that distance its crevasses and schrunds appeared larger and more formidable than the crevasses on Mont Blanc which can be seen from the Brévent. It was clear that an ascent was not to be effected without labour. The route that I proposed to take seemed the easiest if not the only way by which it could be ascended on the side of the Arenal.

While the Carrels were away prospecting, I gave attention to the barometers, for measurement of atmospheric pressure was the first consideration, as this was at the bottom of all the work which was to be undertaken. I took to Ecuador two mountain mercurial barometers of the Fortin pattern,[3] as well as boiling-point thermometers and aneroids. Although the employment of aneroids, and the boiling-water method are recommended in works of authority[4] for the determination of differences of pressure, I

---

[1] Juan and Ulloa made it 21,615 feet; La Condamine, 20,592 feet; Humboldt, 21,425 feet; and Reiss and Stübel, 20,703 feet.

[2] This teaching seems to have prevailed at a later date, for in the first and second editions of E. Barrett Browning's *Aurora Leigh*, published in 1856-7, the following passage occurs:—

> "I learnt the royal genealogies
> Of Oviedo, the internal laws
> Of the Burmese empire, . . . by how many feet
> Mount Chimborazo outsoars Himmeleh."

[3] And left a third one (Kew pattern) with Mr. Chambers for simultaneous comparisons at Guayaquil.

[4] See *Hints to Travellers*, sixth edition, pp. 89, 305, 309, etc.

felt that observations made by them would not command confidence; but as the transport of mercurial barometers is a ticklish matter, and they seldom survive prolonged use, I carried boiling-point thermometers and aneroids as a reserve in case of accident, and took every opportunity to compare the indications of the three kinds of instruments, to instruct myself how far they agreed when used in the field.

All the instruments arrived at Guaranda in safety.[1] From London to Bodegas they had been in my own charge, and I then handed the two Fortins over to Jean-Antoine, who, to ensure the safety of these delicate instruments, walked the greater part of the way from Bodegas to Guaranda. From the unceasing attention that they required, the barometers were nicknamed "the babies," and many children would be fortunate indeed if they were tended with the loving care which he bestowed upon those mercurial infants.

The two Fortin barometers were verified before departure at Kew Observatory,[2] and were hung alongside each other at Guaranda. The mean of the readings of these two barometers, reduced to 32° Faht., was the standard to which all the other observations were referred.

The boiling-point thermometers were in two series (150°—185°, and 180°—215°), in order to have each degree a good length; and a number of experimental comparisons were made with them, upon which a few general observations are offered in Appendix D.

Seven aneroids were taken to the interior of Ecuador.[3] All of these were made for the journey, and they were frequently

[1] Except one aneroid, which was either lost or stolen. During our halt at S. José de Chimbo, an Ecuadorian who heard that I carried aneroids was very urgent to buy one. I shewed him mine, and on arrival at Guaranda found that one of them had disappeared. A reward was offered for its recovery, without result.

[2] A facsimile of the Certificate of Verification of No. 558 is given in Appendix C.

[3] And an eighth was left with Mr. Chambers at Guayaquil, as a reserve in case of accident to the mercurial barometer.

tested before departure under the air-pump, and compared with the Makers' Standard, as well as compared with my own standards which had been, as I have said, verified at Kew. The prime reason for carrying so many aneroids was the apprehension that, despite the care which was taken of the mercurial barometers, I might be suddenly deprived of them by some unhappy smash; and, having a number, the occasion was favourable for comparing the actual working of the two classes of barometers.

Whilst aneroids are much recommended by some persons, by others they are much condemned. Though it is common to hear them spoken of as unreliable it is certain that differences of pressure can be determined by them with marvellous accuracy. When I sought for information or instruction how and why they were unreliable I obtained no satisfaction, and I was unable to learn that any one had ever taken the trouble to compare the actual working in the field of aneroids against the mercurial barometer at low pressures.[1] The recommendations in favour of aneroids have been made, it is to be presumed, on the *assumption* that they *do* read against the mercurial barometer with the same degree of accuracy when employed in the field as they do when tested against it under the air-pump.

This seemed to be a fit subject for investigation, and I entered upon the enquiry without prepossessions either for or against aneroids, cherishing the hope that the *means* of several would closely accord with the mercurial barometer,—a hope that I entertained because these instruments seemed to be pretty equally divided between those which had a tendency to read too high and those which had a tendency to read too low. The idea was that the plus errors of some might or would balance the minus errors of others.

This hope was speedily dissipated. I found that my aneroids did *not* read against the mercurial barometer when used in the

[1] I do not ignore Mr. Glaisher's comparisons in balloon. See Appendix A, § 18.

field with the same accuracy, or in the same manner, as they had done when tested under the air-pump, and that their behaviour was perplexing. Upon leaving Guayaquil (just above the level of the sea), one of the seven read *higher* than the mercurial barometer, and the six others all read lower than it, though not to a large extent. The mean of the readings of the whole of the aneroids was 0·055 of an inch *lower* than the mercurials, and the seven instruments differed amongst each other to the extent of 0·346 of an inch. It was to be expected that they would continue to differ amongst each other, and that the greatest difference would increase, as this is what is commonly found to occur in most assemblages of aneroids. The object of comparison in the field was to determine whether increase of the differences amongst the aneroids would affect the mean error of the whole when compared with the mercurial barometer; that is to say, would the mean error of the aneroids remain 0·055 of an inch, or would it become materially altered?

It became apparent at an early stage of the journey that the means of the aneroids shewed larger and larger departures from the mercurial barometer. After a little time, each individual instrument indicated *lower* pressures than the mercurial barometer.[1] By the time we arrived at Guaranda the mean error of the aneroids had increased from −0·055 to −0·520 of an inch, and it augmented daily.[2] In the course of the narrative I shall point out from time to time the exceedingly serious errors which would have been fallen into in determination of altitudes if I had been obliged to rely upon aneroids alone.[3]

When the weather was favourable I took out the camera,

[1] Aneroid D, the one which read *higher* than the mercurials at Guayaquil, by the time we arrived at Tambo Gobierno had a minus error of 0·359 of an inch.

[2] See Appendix C, § 5, and the tables showing the constant growth of the "greatest difference," and the "mean error of aneroids."

[3] Those who desire to pursue this subject are referred to the pamphlet *How to use the Aneroid Barometer*, which is published simultaneously with this volume.

and photographed Chimborazo, and the Spanish girl with the lustrous eyes, and other objects of interest; which came to the ears of the Authorities, and then *they* wished to be photographed, along with their progeny. It was difficult to refuse, but I grudged a plate on them alone, and sent out Mr. Perring to pick up subjects with a stronger local flavour, to include in the group; and, with an excess of zeal, he pounced down upon the first person he came across, an old Indian woman, and drove her before him into the courtyard. She came in crying and screeching, clasping her hands, and appealing to the Almighty to save her from my cruelty. "What have I done," she shrieked, "that I should be seized and brought here to be killed? Señor Patron! spare my life! What have I done to be treated thus?"—a speech which drew a roar of laughter from the others, who were waiting to be executed.[1]

The Carrels returned, very tired, at 8.45 a.m. on Dec. 23, bringing a good report. To shew the height they had attained, they had placed the pointer attached to the movable rim of the aneroid against 15·370 inches. They had traversed the ground intervening between the Arenal and the

THE CHIEF OF THE POLICE.

ridge I proposed to follow, and Jean-Antoine had selected a camping-place upon it; but they thought that we should be unable to reach this spot comfortably, with a laden team, in one day from Guaranda, and spoke emphatically of the fatigue they had experienced in pounding up a sandy *vallon* leading to it. They had accordingly selected another and lower camping-place

[1] It was explained afterwards that her fright was due to the Chief of the Police, whose office was in our courtyard. Perring was supposed by her to be one of his myrmidons.

on the northern side of the Arenal, at the base of the mountain, and proposed that on the first day we should not try to go farther.

The needle of Aneroid **F** pointed to 15·370 inches when the Carrels were at the place that they selected for the higher camp, and as the corresponding figures on the "scale of feet" were 19,122 they could have fairly claimed to have reached that height "*by aneroid.*" I estimated that they had only got about as high as 16,450 feet. The Aneroid **F**, at all stages of the journey, read *lower* than the mercurial barometers. At Guayaquil its error was −0·172; at Muñapamba it was −0·208; at Tambo Gobierno it was −0·629; and, upon arrival at Guaranda, −0·708 of an inch.[1] Its error constantly increased. When they left Guaranda on Dec. 21 it amounted to −0·890 of an inch, and on their return upon the 23rd it had risen to −1·080 inches. I assumed that the error was *regularly* increasing, and that when they reached their highest point, soon after mid-day on the 22nd, it amounted to *one inch*. In that case, the true barometric reading would be 16·370 inches.

The figures corresponding with 16·370 inches upon the "scale of feet" were 17,400, but from this amount I subtracted 950 feet, for the following reason. Aneroid **F** (like a great part of the aneroids which are in use) had its zero, or level of the sea, at 31 inches, and made 30 inches correspond with a height of 894 feet above the sea.[2] I assumed that atmospheric pressure at the level of the sea on Dec. 22 was a little less than 30 inches,[3] and deducted 950 feet accordingly. This

[1] It should not be supposed that this was due to bad graduation. I had seen this aneroid, like all the others when tested under the air-pump, accord inch by inch with the attached mercurial barometer.

[2] See *How to use the Aneroid Barometer*, pp. 56-7.

[3] This could be assumed with some probability, as the variations in atmospheric pressure are small in Ecuador. See Appendix B.

Upon return to Guayaquil, I found that Mr. Chambers had recorded 29·957 inches (merc. bar. reduced to 32°) as the reading at 11 a.m. on Dec. 22.

CHAP. II.   *WE START FOR CHIMBORAZO.*   39

reduced the height of the place they had selected for the second camp to 16,450 feet, and up to that spot, they said, animals might be taken.

We now thought that there was nothing to hinder us from starting on the 24th, but upon discussing matters with the arrieros it appeared that our departure must be postponed, as they would not be absent from Guaranda on Christmas Day. At 9.45 a.m. on the 26th our troop of fourteen animals (ten for baggage and four for riding) filed out of the yard,[1] followed by three arrieros and two Indians who were employed to carry some long poles which were wanted for signals and other uses. The Priest blessed me and mine, and all that we had. The Chief of the Police, dressed in his best, came to see us off;

THE POPULACE AT GUARANDA.

while the populace of Guaranda sat on a wall and regarded us with stolidity.

The Indians were supplied by the Authorities, and proved an undesirable contingent. They lagged behind under various pretences, with the obvious intention of bolting, and would speedily have disappeared had not somebody kept in the rear to prevent their escape.[2] One of them, an exceptionally sulky

[1] The price demanded for baggage or riding animals in Ecuador was generally very moderate. On this occasion it was a *peso* (equal to about 2s. 8d.) per day and forage.

[2] They were paid in advance, according to the custom of the country, and had to be provided with shoes. Although natives of all sorts were continually

and stubborn fellow, carried his poles in such a manner that they struck everything we passed, and by these and other antics delayed us so considerably that we occupied seven hours in getting to the Arenal. After crossing its summit, we left the usual Quito track (which passes by Tortorillas) on our right, and under the leading of Jean-Antoine steered a nearly north-north-easterly course over the upper and level portion of the great plain. The sun was approaching the horizon, and threw immensely long shadows upon the luminous sand. Carrel guided us to the spot he had selected, just at the mouth of a *vallon* leading directly towards the western summit.[1] We camped under a moonlit sky by the side of a tiny stream. The night was still and cold, and at meal-time we all—mountaineers, arrieros, and Indians—sat together round a blazing fire in the centre of the encampment. The temperature fell unexpectedly low. The minimum thermometer registered 21° Faht., and our little brook became a mass of solid ice. The remains of the soup in the cooking utensils were frozen up, cruelly hard,—but it was harder still to find in the morning that the Indians and five of the mules had disappeared.

ONE OF OUR ARRIEROS.

met with trudging bare-footed along the roads, whenever one was hired he found himself unable to walk without shoes, and that he had none.

[1] Left Guaranda 9.45 a.m.; arrived at Ensillada 1.50 p.m. Halted 45 min. Arrived at summit of Arenal 4.45 p.m.; and at Camp 1 (14,375 feet) at 5.50 p.m.

AIGUILLES ON CHIMBORAZO.

CHAPTER III.

THE FIRST ASCENT OF CHIMBORAZO.

THE temperature in the night was unexpectedly low for so moderate an elevation as that of the first camp. Only a week before, at Tortorillas, we had experienced 56°.5 at mid-day, and I scarcely anticipated that the freezing-point would be touched at the height of 14,000 feet in the neighbourhood of the Equator.[1] This sharp frost caused me to observe the nocturnal minima at our subsequent camps, and, from the table that is given in Appendix E, it will be seen that the minimum of the night of Dec. 26 was below the average. It occurred upon an exceptionally fine night, with a clear sky.

[1] The only information I possessed upon temperatures of any sort at considerable elevations in Ecuador was that published by Boussingault in the *Comptes Rendus*, in 1879, vol. lxxxviii, p. 1241. This relates to the Hacienda of Antisana (13,306 feet), and is referred to more particularly in my chapter upon Antisana.

The disappearance of the mules and Indians was a more serious matter. The arrieros could afford to take it coolly, as the hire of their animals had been paid in advance. Deprived of seven backs, two journeys became necessary to the second camp, and the best arrangement I could make was to despatch Jean-Antoine in charge of the caravan, whilst Louis and I waited below at the foot of the *vallon*, ostensibly to finish work there, but really to prevent any more desertions.

Jean-Antoine went away at 10 a.m. on the 27th, with eight laden mules, the three arrieros and Perring. He was to remain above, to commence the establishment of the camp, and to send the team back as soon as it could be unloaded. One mule was retained below, for this beast seemed to be oppressed with such a load of melancholy (which I attributed to sore ribs) that I had not the heart to send it higher. Louis was well employed in collecting firewood, and in transferring surplus stores up the *vallon* to a depôt; whilst I, after finishing my proper work, went aside, and stripped for a real good wash before going to regions where ablutions were unknown. Presently there was a noise, and I became aware that the mule had broken loose and was frisking about. The animal rejoiced in freedom, and, intoxicated by success, went as near to standing upon its head as a mule can go. Its behaviour seemed to me supremely ungrateful, and I went for that animal. It ran away; but it was handicapped, for it had a long halter, which trailed along the sandy plain, whilst I ran unimpeded, and gained on it at every stride. When I seized the halter it was I who was captured. The wretched beast dragged me unmercifully over the sandy soil until Louis came to my assistance, and we then towed it in triumph back to camp.

On the side of the Great Arenal three *vallons* lead up into Chimborazo.[1] One of these, narrow at its mouth and broader above, is bounded at its upper extremity by the glacier which

---

[1] See the map of Chimborazo inset on the large general map.

is marked **G** upon my map. This one we naturally termed the Vallon de Tortorillas. The next towards the west—the Vallon de Débris—leads to the glacier marked **F**. The third, still farther to the west, was that up which our caravan had gone. I called this the Vallon de Carrel. The Great Arenal stretches along the base of the ridges that divide these little valleys.[1] In the vicinity of Tortorillas its soil is grassy, and affords pasturage to sheep and cattle; but vegetation becomes more and more sparse as one proceeds towards the west, and ultimately it almost entirely disappears. The soil in the centre of the plain is composed of fragments of lava—much of it scoriaceous; they presently become smaller and more equal in size, and on the west of the plain the surface is composed of what can only be called fine sand, which drifts in this direction. This is partly volcanic dust, and probably is partly derived from attrition of the larger fragments. Much of the matter was no doubt ejected by Chimborazo, but it is certainly to some extent supplemented by the volcanic dust which is constantly floating about the country, and is borne by the prevalent winds towards the south-west.

This sandy soil was very loose, and toilsome to ascend even upon moderate gradients. Hence I was surprised that our caravan returned soon after 1 p.m., having occupied only a little more than three hours in going to and returning from the second camp. After allowing the animals a rest, they were reloaded with as much as was good for them, and the remainder of the provisions and stores were left in depôt at the entrance of the Vallon de Carrel. At this point I must stop to explain more particularly the manner in which it was proposed to conduct our operations.

Neither of the two Carrels, nor I myself, had ever experienced the least symptom of mountain-sickness. None of us,

---

[1] These *vallons* cannot be seen in the view facing p. 24. They are hidden by the ridge that stretches across the engraving.

however, prior to this journey had been 16,000 feet high; and, probably, had never sustained so low a pressure as 17 inches. I had at various times been in the company of persons who said they were affected by 'rarefaction of the air,' and who were unable to proceed; but their symptoms, so far as I observed them, might have been produced by fatigue and unfamiliarity with mountaineering, and were not of the more acute kind. Although I attached little importance to such cases as had come under my own personal observation, I had never felt disposed to question the *reality* of mountain-sickness; and on the contrary had frequently maintained that it is reasonable to expect some effects should be produced upon men who experience much lower atmospheric pressures than those to which they are accustomed; and that it is much more remarkable to find that, *apparently*, no effects of a detrimental kind are caused on many persons who ascend to the height of 14-15,000 feet (or, say, sustain a pressure of seventeen and a half inches), than it is to learn that others have suffered at slightly lower pressures. The thing that seemed most puzzling was that, at the greatest heights I had reached, instead of appearing to suffer any injurious effects, the effects seemed positively beneficial; and from this I thought it was not unlikely that we should be able to reach much more considerable heights, and to sustain considerably lower pressures, without being adversely affected.

Some of my friends, however, who had been as high as 17-18,000 feet, competent mountaineers, and men who could speak without exaggeration, told me that they had not been at all comfortable at such elevations. It seemed certain that sooner or later we should suffer like the rest of the world, but I proposed to put off the evil day as long as possible; to mount gradually and leisurely, by small stages, so that there should be no abrupt transition; and to get to the lowest attainable pressures (the greatest heights) by the simplest means that could be devised, and by the easiest routes that could be found, in order that extreme exertion and fatigue should take no part in anything that might happen. This will explain why we proceeded so deliberately. Should it be found necessary, I was prepared to devote the whole of the time that I could remain in Ecuador to Chimborazo alone. I did not see fit either before our departure from Europe, or at any period of the journey, to communicate the nature of my objects to my assistants, or what was likely to befall them. At starting, they were only aware that we should proceed to South America, and that they would be employed in mountain work, at great elevations.

As it would be impossible to retain natives at our higher camps, and we ourselves might be detained at them by bad weather or from other causes even for weeks at a time, it was necessary to be well provided with food; and as it could not be expected that we should be able to obtain on the spot provisions which would keep for a length of time, I concluded, before leaving Europe, that to work with certainty we must make ourselves entirely independent of the resources of the country in the matter of the food which would be consumed at the greatest heights. A large quantity of the most portable and most condensed provisions accordingly went out for our use.[1]

These provisions were packed in boxes measuring $28\frac{3}{4} \times 11\frac{1}{4} \times 10\frac{3}{4}$ inches, weighing about 72 lbs. apiece. Each of these boxes contained three tin cases, measuring $9\frac{3}{4} \times 9 \times 8\frac{3}{4}$ inches, and each tin case held food for four men for one day. The tins, being thoroughly soldered down, could be left exposed in the worst weather, or dipped in water without taking harm. The contents comprised nearly everything that was requisite except water and firing. A great saving of time was effected in the field by

[1] By persons having commercial relations with Ecuador, it was considered very absurd to take food to that country. I was told before departure that everything one could possibly want could be obtained there. It is indeed true that nearly everything *may* be obtained in Ecuador. It is also true that we often had great difficulty in obtaining *anything*. My surplus stores were sold to advantage. Medicines and other things brought high prices.

arranging the food in this manner, and it relieved me from the necessity of continual calculations, and from apprehensions that some of the minor requisites might be forgotten.[1]

For a thousand feet above the first camp, our reladen caravan progressed at a fair pace, and then (pressure being about 17·250 inches) straggling commenced. My own mule reached the head of the *vallon* (about 16,000 feet above the sea) without shewing signs of exhaustion. It then struck work, and I dismounted. So far, the bed of the *vallon* was loose, sandy soil, with little vegetation. Our course then turned to the right, that is towards the east, up the western slopes of the south-west ridge of Chimborazo, and led by steeper gradients over firm ground, covered

---

[1] Each tin case contained:—Ox-cheek, 2 lbs.; Mutton, 2 lbs.; Beef, 2 lbs.; Potted ham, one tin; Liebig's extract, 2 ozs., in tin; Preserved soup, 2 pint tins; Cocoa and milk, one tin; Condensed milk, one tin; Sugar, 4 ozs.; Mustard, 1 oz.; Salt, 2 ozs.; Pepper, 1 oz.; Biscuits, about 2 lbs., in tin; Lemonade powder, in tin; Seidlitz powders, in tin; 3 pills; small bottle of Chlorodyne; Black-currant and cayenne lozenges, 2 ozs.; Muscatelles, 12 ozs.; Tea, 3 ozs. These quantities were found sufficient, or more than enough, with the exception of sugar. Irrespective of things which were bought already tinned, more than 2000 tins were soldered down.

The interstices between the circular tins were filled in with candles, in tin tubes, and the smaller spaces were taken up with bead-necklaces and various articles for presents, and the whole contents were jammed tight with cotton wool, tow and paper. Mustard, pepper, salt and other small articles were taken in glass bottles fitted into tin tubes. All the glass bottles were subsequently used for the preservation of natural history specimens. There was no waste, and, in consequence of the care which was taken in packing, not a single bottle was broken, and nothing whatever was spoiled or even injured by damp.

The boxes were of the best deal, planed smooth, with rounded edges and corners, and were double-varnished. The lids were screwed down, and the screws worked into metal cups, so that the lids should not be overscrewed. Many of these cases came back in serviceable condition.

Except when installed at great heights, the food that was arranged in this manner was treated as reserved stock. At Guaranda, and other places where they could be obtained, we laid in *fresh* provisions.

A list of the rest of the outfit will be found in *Hints to Travellers*, fifth edition, pp. 284-288. The preparation of it occupied almost as much time as the performance of the journey.

with shattered blocks of lava fallen from the *arête* above.[1] I patted and coaxed my animal on for a few yards, and then it stopped again. It clearly found difficulty in supporting its own weight. By continued encouragement, it was induced to advance a few steps at a time; but the halts became more frequent, and, impatient of delay, I pushed on, and left it to pursue its course by itself. Looking back, to see how the rest were progressing, I found that they were scattered over about half-a-mile, and that all the animals were in difficulties, though none carried more than one hundred and sixty pounds.

Carrel had selected a position for the second camp with much judgment, at the foot of a wall of lava, which perfectly protected the tent on one side. The place was easy of access, and the highest point to which mules could be taken; with snow-beds in its vicinity that would yield water, and ground round about it upon which we could exercise. The baggage animals struggled upwards one by one, and by 5.30 p.m. all had arrived.[2] The barometer stood at this place at sixteen inches and a half.

We were all in high spirits. The weather had been fine, and the move had been successfully effected. It was arranged that one of the arrieros, F—— by name, should sleep at Tortorillas, and come up daily to learn what was needed; and all the rest of the troop were sent back to Guaranda. They left us very gladly; for although we had succeeded in establishing our camp at the selected spot, it had only been done by great exertions on the part of my people and their beasts. The mules were forced up to the last yard they could go, and staggering under their burdens (which were scarcely more than half the weight they were accustomed to carry), stopped repeatedly, and by their trembling, falling on their knees, and by their general behaviour, shewed

[1] Upon any mule pass in the Alps, this would have been considered quite ordinary, and easy ground.

[2] The average time they took in coming from the first to the second camp was two hours.

that they had been driven to the verge of exhaustion. When we others arrived at the second camp, we ourselves were in good condition,—which was to be expected, as we had ridden most of the way; but in about an hour I found myself lying on my back, along with both the Carrels, placed *hors de combat*, and incapable of making the least exertion. We knew that the enemy was upon us, and that we were experiencing our first attack of mountain-sickness.

THE SECOND CAMP ON CHIMBORAZO (16,664 FEET).

We were feverish, had intense headaches, and were unable to satisfy our desire for air, except by breathing with open mouths. This naturally parched the throat, and produced a craving for drink, which we were unable to satisfy,—partly from the difficulty in obtaining it, and partly from trouble in swallowing it. When we got enough, we could only sip, and not to save our lives could we have taken a quarter of a pint at a draught. Before a mouthful was down, we were obliged to breathe and gasp again, until our throats were as dry as ever. Besides having our normal rate of breathing largely accelerated, we found it impossible to sustain life without every now and then giving spasmodic gulps, just like fishes when taken out of water. Of course there was no inclination to eat; but we wished to smoke, and found that our pipes almost refused to burn, for they, like ourselves, wanted more oxygen.

This condition of affairs lasted all night, and all the next day, and I then managed to pluck up spirit enough to get out some chlorate of potash, which by the advice of Dr. W. Marcet, had been brought in case of need. Chlorate of potash was, I believe, first used in mountain travel by Dr. Henderson, in the Karakorum range, and it was subsequently employed on Sir Douglas Forsyth's Mission to Yarkund in 1873-4, apparently with good effect.[1] Before my departure, Dr. Marcet (with whom I had been in communication) urged me to experiment, with a view of confirming

[1] The surgeon to this expedition states that he distributed little bottles of it amongst the members of the embassy, and says that, from his own experience, he "can testify to its value in mitigating the distressing symptoms produced by a continued deprivation of the natural quantity of oxygen in the atmosphere. The large proportion of oxygen contained in the salt probably supplies to the blood what in these regions it fails to derive from the air, and thus restores through the stomach what the lungs lose. Whatever the explanation of its action, however, there is no doubt of its efficacy in relieving the dreadful nausea and headache produced by the circulation of an inefficiently oxygenated blood."—*Kashmir and Kashgar*, by H. W. Bellew, C.S.I.

I have been informed by members of this expedition that they ate, or munched, dry chlorate of potash.

these experiences. Ten grains to a wine glass of water was the proportion he recommended,—the dose to be repeated every two or three hours, if necessary. It appeared to me to operate beneficially, though it must be admitted that it was not easy to determine, as one *might* have recovered just as well without taking it at all. At all events, after taking it, the intensity of the symptoms diminished, there were fewer gaspings, and in some degree a feeling of relief.

Louis Carrel also submitted himself to experiment, and seemed to derive benefit; but Jean-Antoine sturdily refused to take any 'doctor's stuff,' which he regarded as an insult to intelligence. For all human ills, for every complaint, from dysentery to want of air, there was, in his opinion, but one remedy; and that was Wine; most efficacious always if taken hot, more especially if a little spice and sugar were added to it.

The stories that he related respecting the virtues of Red wine would be enough to fill a book. The wine must be Red— "White wine," he used to say dogmatically, "is bad, it cuts the legs." Most of these legends I cannot remember, but there was one which it was impossible to forget, commencing thus. "Red wine when heated and beaten up with raw eggs is good for many complaints—particularly at the Eve of St. John, when the moon is at the full, for women who are in the family way; provided it is drunk whilst looking over the left shoulder, and"—I never heard the end of that story, because I laughed too soon.

His opinions upon things in general were often very original, and I learned much whilst in his company; amongst the rest, that, for the cure of headache, nothing better can be mentioned than keeping the head *warm* and the feet *cold*. It is only fair to say that he practised what he preached. I can remember no more curious sight than that of this middle-aged man, lying nearly obscured under a pile of ponchos, with his head bound up in a wonderful arrangement of handkerchiefs, vainly attempting to smoke a short pipe whilst gasping like a choking cod-fish, his naked feet sticking out from underneath his blankets when the temperature in the tent was much below the freezing-point.

Strange to relate, Mr. Perring did not appear to be affected at all. Except for him we should have fared badly. He kept the fire going — no easy task, for the fire appeared to suffer from the want of air just like ourselves, and required such incessant blowing that I shall consider for the future a pair of bellows an indispensable item in a mountaineer's equipment. Mr. Perring behaved on this occasion in an exemplary manner. He melted snow, and brought us drink, and attended to our wants in general, and did not seem any worse at the second camp than at Guaranda. Yet he was a rather debilitated man, and was distinctly less robust than ourselves. He could scarcely walk on a flat road without desiring to sit down, or traverse a hundred yards on a mountain side without being obliged to rest.

It is natural to enquire how can one account for this man of enfeebled constitution being unaffected, when three others, who were all more or less accustomed to high elevations (low pressures), were rendered, for a time, completely incapable? It seems possible to afford a tolerably adequate explanation, but it is better to reserve all comments upon our experiences until the conclusion of the journey, and to proceed now with the narrative.

I was taken aback at this early admonition, for I expected to have been able to sustain a lower pressure without being adversely affected. Our symptoms did not differ in any material point from those which have already been recorded by persons deserving of credence, and, so far, the experience was not unexpected; but they appeared earlier than was anticipated, and, when I got into a condition to think, I was greatly surprised at the suddenness with which we were overtaken, and at the fact that we succumbed nearly simultaneously. It is scarcely exaggeration to say that in one hour we were all right, and that in the next we were all wrong. Two out of the three had already visited the place without being attacked.

The symptoms come under the three heads, headache, disturbance of the natural manner of respiration, and feverishness. Headache with all three of us was intense, and rendered us almost frantic or crazy. Before 6 p.m. on Dec. 27, we had, I believe, been entirely free from headache in Ecuador. My own continued acute until the 30th, and then it disappeared gradually. With Louis it did not last quite so long, and Jean-Antoine got better sooner than his cousin. When it was at its maximum we all seemed to be about equally afflicted. The interference with our natural manner of respiration was even more troublesome. At 6 p.m. we could move about, talk, or eat and drink freely, while at 8 p.m. and throughout the night of the 27th, eating would have been impossible, and to talk or drink was difficult. We could only gasp ejaculations, or a few words at a time, and efforts at conversation were cut short by irrepressible, spasmodic gulps; while, during the whole time, respiration was effected through open mouths, the ordinary amount of air taken in through the nostrils being found inadequate. We were all feverish, but no observations were made until 1 p.m. on the 28th, when my own temperature was found to be 100°·4 Faht.[1] It was no doubt considerably higher in the previous night.[2] On this head, nothing can be said in regard to the Carrels; for, though they spoke of feverishness, they positively declined both then and at all times to have their temperatures taken.

It will be understood from what has just been said that our 'incapacity' was neither due to exhaustion or to deficiency of bodily strength, nor was owing to inability to cope with mountaineering difficulties or to weakness from want of food,[3] but was caused by the whole of our attention being taken up in efforts to

[1] See Appendix F for the manner of observation. At Guaranda on Dec. 23 my temperature was 98°·2; and at 10.30 a.m. on the 27th it was 98°·4.

[2] This was a cold night. The minimum thermometer was fixed in position before we were incapacitated, and so I know that temperature on the night of the 27th again fell to 21° Faht.

[3] The attack immediately followed a meal.

get air; and my two assistants, spontaneously and without any questioning or prompting on my part, attributed the condition in which we found ourselves to the 'rarity of the air' at our second camp. There is evidence of my own inability to perform my regular work in the blanks in my journals at this date, and further evidence of the reality of the attack in the fact that we could not smoke. Two out of the three were habitual consumers of tobacco, and had become slaves to this vice to such an extent that they smoked conscientiously upon every opportunity. When such persons put aside their beloved pipes there is certainly something wrong. All three found smoking too laborious, and ceased their efforts in a sort of despair. But it should not be understood, from anything which may have been said, that I discussed the subject with the Carrels, for I considered it best to leave them in ignorance of the fact that they were the subjects of a scientific enquiry.

There was a perceptible improvement in their condition on the night of Dec. 28, though little in my own. On the 29th they were eager to be off exploring, and I sent them away at 7.50 a.m., instructing them to continue the ascent of the south-west ridge; to look out for a higher camping-place; and not to endeavour to reach a great elevation. Owing to my lifeless condition, I should only have hampered their movements by accompanying them, and while they were away I turned my attention again to the barometers.

The two mercurial barometers arrived safely at the second camp. One of them (No. 550) was stowed away in a cleft in the rocks, and the other (No. 558) was alone used on Chimborazo. It may be of some service to travellers to mention the precautions which were taken in regard to these instruments.

There are two principal reasons why so many mercurial barometers are broken in the field. 1. Because they are insufficiently protected when in transit; and 2. because a bad method of suspension is employed when they are being observed. Mountain barometers are usually sent out by their makers in a zinc-lined leather case (similar to that shewn in the annexed figure), and are carried slung by straps across the shoulder, the large ends uppermost,—that is to say, with cisterns reversed. These cases may give enough protection if the instruments are carried along a road, or over easy ground, but they do not afford sufficient to withstand the shocks, jolts, and accidents of travel. Sometimes the case is actually crushed in upon the tube, and in other instances the tube is broken by concussion, although the case may not be injured. Each of the ordinary cases of my barometers was again enclosed in a wooden box, with deal sides and oak ends, and was padded all around with a quantity of tow to deaden concussion. They were always carried on the back, *upright*, with the large ends uppermost, and were kept in position by knapsack straps. Although they were treated with the utmost care, they had to sustain many accidental knocks and jars, and upon several occasions Jean-Antoine had to hastily throw himself off his beast, as best he could, to avoid an utter smash.[1]

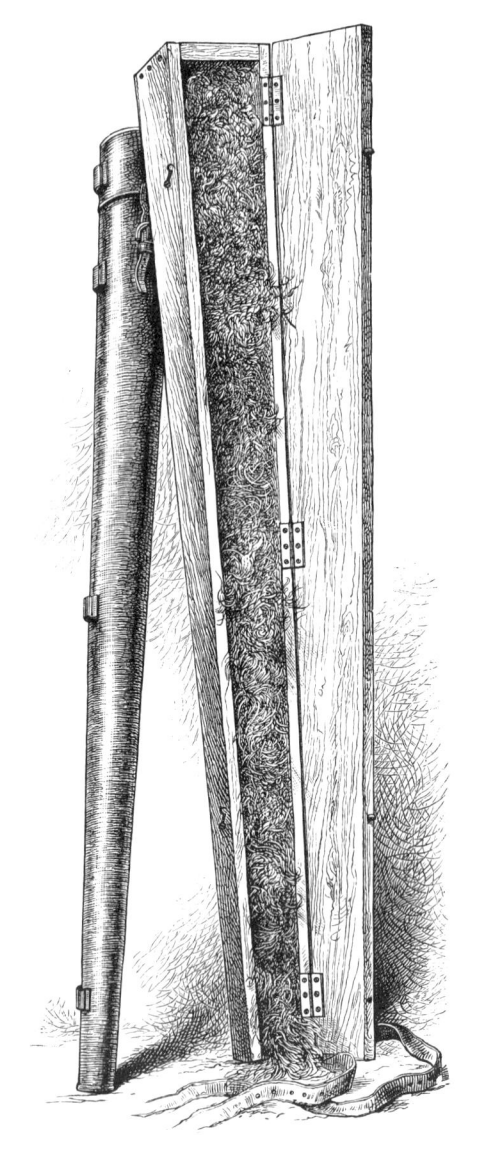

---

[1] Each barometer in its case, as supplied by the maker, weighed 6 lbs. Each additional wooden case weighed 6½ lbs. more.

CHAP. III. *METHOD OF SUSPENSION.* 55

The stand usually supplied by instrument makers (see FIG. 1) is one of the worst that can be devised for use out of doors. It is bad because the base (D E F) of the pyramid formed by the tripod is not large enough in proportion to its height; because the point of suspension (A) of the barometer (B C) is much too low; because the legs (A D, A E, A F) of the tripod are fixed in a rigid position, and cannot be set in or out to accommodate the irregularities of the ground; and upon snow it is nearly *useless* because these thin metal legs sink in to or beyond the cistern (C) before a sufficient foundation can be obtained. A moderate breeze puts the barometer in movement (though it should be perfectly at rest for a good observation) and a slight knock may make it oscillate from G to H. If the cistern should swing as far as X the stand will overturn, and the barometer almost certainly will be destroyed.

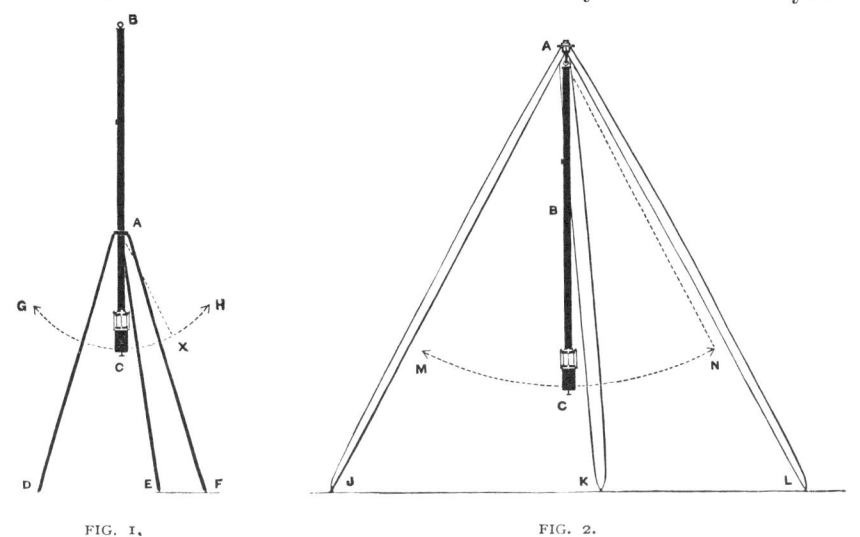

FIG. 1.   FIG. 2.

I discarded the usual method of suspension, and hung the barometers from the stands belonging to the theodolite (A J K L, FIG. 2). The stability of these stands is infinitely greater than that of the form usually employed; their legs can be set in and out to meet the requirements of each occasion; and, when hung in the manner shewn in the diagram, barometers have little tendency to swing to and fro. No shock that is likely to occur will make the cisterns move from M to N—though, if they did so, the stands would not be overturned. The actual method of suspension at A, Fig. 2, is a device of my own, and is shewn in the accompanying engraving, which renders description unnecessary. To set out a theodolite stand and hang a barometer in position upon this catch is an affair of a few seconds, while if the ordinary stand is employed minutes are occupied in the operation.

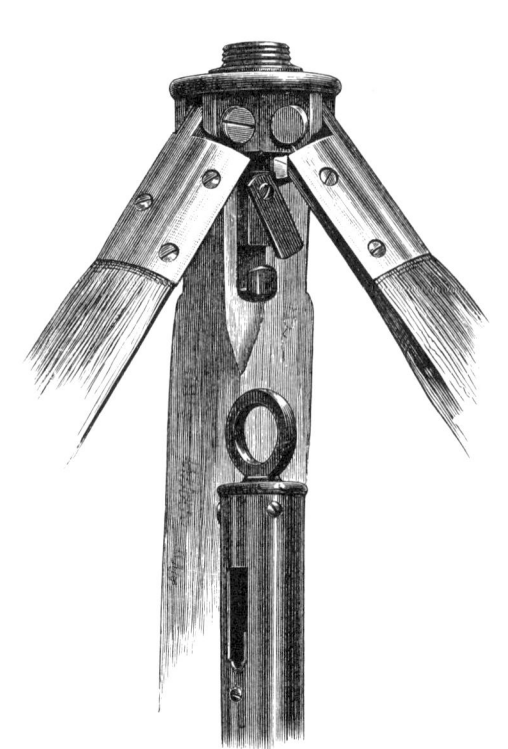

The mercurial barometer read 16·476 inches at 11 a.m. on Dec. 28, 16·488 inches on the 29th, and 16·480 on the 30th. Mr. Chambers, at Guayaquil, made simultaneous observations on the 28th and 29th, and found no change in pressure on the latter day. But while the mercurials were demonstrating the remarkable stability of the barometer in Ecuador the aneroids showed *lower* pressures on each successive day.

Place of Observation.	Barometer.	Dec. 28, 1879. 11 a.m. inches.	Dec. 29 1879. 11 a.m. inches.	Dec. 30, 1879. 11 a.m. inches.
Second Camp	Merc. Bar. No. 558 (corrected)	16·476	16·488	16·480
Guayaquil	do. No. 554 (do.)	29·910	29·910	...
Second Camp	Means of six Aneroids	15·643	15·611	15·577
Do.	Errors of means of Aneroids	−0·833	−0·877	−0·903
Do.	Aneroid F	15·300	15·300	15·280
Do.	Error of Aneroid F	−1·176	−1·188	−1·200

At the last reference to Aneroid F (p. 38) its error amounted to −1·080 of an inch. At the first camp on Chimborazo it was increased to −1·152 of an inch, and from the above record it will be seen that it still augmented daily.

Thus, while the mercurial barometer shewed a slight *increase* in pressure, the whole of the aneroids, on the other hand, indicated pressure *diminishing*.[1] If I had depended upon the latter instruments, atmospheric pressure in Ecuador, instead of appearing, as it is, remarkably steady,[2] would have seemed liable to large fluctuations, and very erroneous suppositions might have been based upon these observations; or if the altitude of the second camp had been deduced from the means of the six aneroids it would have come out about 1500 feet too high, through adopting a pressure for the upper station nine-tenths of an inch lower than the truth.

The behaviour of these aneroids was so anomalous and perplexing that I felt greatly inclined to read them no more; and it was only the apprehension of disaster to the mercurials that induced me to continue to occupy my time in recording observations which appeared perfectly worthless. From subsequent experiments in the workshop[3] it has been found that their behaviour is neither exceptional nor unintelligible; but when we were upon Chimborazo it puzzled me exceedingly, and I rushed to the conclusion that I had not been well served, and that my aneroids were emphatically a bad lot.

Our camp was situated on the southern side of a rather conspicuous gap in the ridge, and a large rectangular mass of lava against which the tent was placed made a good landmark, which was rendered still more apparent by one of our long poles that was fixed up as a signal. Below us, our ridge spread out considerably as it approached the Arenal, and above us it led for a long distance towards the western dome.

On our right or east, looking towards the summits, there was

---

[1] See *How to use the Aneroid Barometer*, p. 35, § 40.   [2] See Appendix B.
[3] *How to use the Aneroid Barometer*, pp. 15-34.

a basin occupied by a glacier (the Glacier de Débris, about which I shall speak more particularly presently) terminating in a *vallon* leading down to the Arenal. On the farther or eastern side of this glacier there was another ridge that carried, opposite to our camp, a rather prominent secondary peak, which we dubbed — from its situation and from a fancied resemblance to the Mont Blanc aiguille — the Aiguille du Midi. This, and another smaller one that we called the Aiguille du Géant, being higher than our station, shut out much of the vista to the east. The ridge of which they formed part did not extend to so great a height as our own. It became lost amid the snow and scattered rocks shewn upon the right of the view facing p. 24, and over its higher extremity, in the early morning, we could occasionally see some of the tumultuous glacier which covers a great part of the eastern side of Chimborazo, with its numerous crevasses and gigantic schrunds. Over these slopes and schrunds clouds gathered ceaselessly, tantalizing us when they were whirled aloft and torn into shreds, only to be replaced in a few seconds by equally impenetrable mists manufactured from invisible vapours.

On the left or west of our ridge there was the Vallon de Carrel, up which we had come; and at the head of this there was glacier E (Glacier de Thielmann) of my map, that has its origin in the crown of the western dome. The farther or northern side of this glacier was bounded by a long and serrated ridge which terminated the view in that direction.

Above the camp, rising 500 feet higher at an angle of about 35°, our ridge was covered with disintegrated lava mingled with patches of sand; a stony waste, easy enough to traverse,— Mr. Perring, indeed, could ascend or descend it by himself. Up to this elevation (nearly 17,200 feet) Chimborazo could be ascended in the month of January without touching snow! The crest or *arête* of the ridge then rose for some distance at a less abrupt angle, and was occupied by jagged blocks or pinnacles of lava which concealed its continuation in the rear. Except by looking

Tidewater shores of the Guayas River near Guayaquil, looking about the same as they did in Whymper's time.

Aerial of the wet forest which Whymper penetrated to begin his climb into the Andes.

Aerial of the red cliffs described in detail by Whymper and illustrated on pages 64, 76, 320, and 337.

The Whymper Glacier on the northern face which he pioneered and climbed directly to the summit on his second ascent. It is the classic route to the top of Chimborazo.

The eastern side of Chimborazo. Whymper did not climb this side; his approach was from the other side of the mountain, towards the right.

at the ridge in full front from Guaranda, I did not know what was behind. The Carrels had disappeared amongst the craggy lavas, and as I had selected this as the line of ascent, and could not see a practicable route either to the right or left, I awaited the return of my assistants with some anxiety. Night had almost set in before they were descried coming down the slope that rose from the camp, and it was quite dark when they arrived at the tent, almost breathless, scarcely able to keep on their legs, staggering under their own weight! They threw themselves down and went to sleep without either eating or drinking, and I did not hear their report until the next day.

Misled by the time that had been occupied, they believed they had reached a very great height. [I found subsequently that they had got to about 19,300 feet above the sea.] "The thing is certain," said Jean-Antoine joyously, by which he meant Chimborazo could be ascended. However that might be, their condition, and the length of time they had been absent, led me to the conclusion that our present location was not high enough as a starting-point, and that another move upwards must be made, though they said that there was no other place at which we could properly encamp.

On the morning of the 30th Jean-Antoine was crippled by inflammation of the eyes, and had to submit to be doctored with a solution of sulphate of zinc, but his cousin was sufficiently revived in the afternoon to be sent with Perring down to the depôt to fetch the tent which was to be advanced to the third camp. They returned at nightfall, having found it as much as they could carry, though it weighed only 35 lbs., a load which the athletic Louis would have thought a trifle at lower elevations (higher pressures). The minimum at our camp this night was 20°·5 Faht.

On the 31st, the Carrels and I (each carrying a few small things) went up the ridge to select a camping-place; and, finding that no protection could be obtained at a higher point, decided to plant ourselves amongst the broken lava, close to the crest of the ridge, on its eastern side, at a height of 17,285 feet (merc. bar. at 1 p.m. read 16·081 inches). The position was a bad and exposed one, and it was a troublesome matter to clear space sufficient even for our small tent. That done, we returned to the second camp, and shortly afterwards our arriero-courier arrived, convoying three Indians who had been sent by the authorities at Guaranda, in response to my application, to replace the others who had bolted. After feeding them well, to give them a little confidence, they were at once despatched, under the care of the Carrels, carrying baggage to the third camp.

THIRD CAMP ON CHIMBORAZO.

The arriero (F——) also brought intelligence that the depôt had been broken into and robbed, and I accordingly sent him back to watch the stores, and Perring to Guaranda, with a written request to the Jefo-politico to supply a guard for the baggage so long as we remained on the mountain. When the Indians returned at the end of the afternoon particular pains were taken to keep them in a good humour. They were well fed and petted, provided with wraps, had shelter rigged up for them, and a good fire made. Yet I fully expected they would desert us, and was quite surprised in the morning to find that they were remaining. The minimum temperature in this night was again 20°.5 Faht.

It will be inferred from the last paragraphs that we were now in a somewhat better condition. The more disagreeable symptoms of our mountain-sickness had disappeared, the gaspings had ceased, and headache had nearly gone. Still, although improving, we found ourselves comparatively lifeless and feeble, with a strong disposition to sit down when we ought to have been moving, and there was plenty at that time to keep us moving —mainly owing to the unpleasant discovery that some of our tinned meat had gone bad.

I had invested in a quantity of ox-cheek, and one tin of it had been placed in each case. Upon opening the very first case it was noticed that the ends of the ox-cheek tin were *convex*, and knowing what this meant, I had it thrown away at once. With one after another we found the same and acted similarly; but at last, upon opening another case, a most appalling stench rushed out, and we found that the ox-cheek had burst its bonds, and had not only become putrid itself, but had corroded the other tins and ruined almost the whole of the food in the case. It then became necessary to examine each case seriatim, to know exactly how we were off for food, and the end of the matter was we found ourselves obliged to hurl over the cliffs a mass of provisions which had cost endless trouble to prepare.[1]

[1] I promised the manufacturer of that horrible stuff an advertisement upon my return, but I am deprived of the pleasure of fulfilling my promise. I am advised that it might be considered libellous to publish the name of a person who has sold putrid meat, and I much regret that it cannot be given the publicity that he deserves. He caused much loss and severe labour. The whole of the provision cases had to be opened and his goods ejected. In instances where the ox-cheek had burst, its stench rendered it necessary to scrape and cleanse all

On January 1, 1880, leaving the Carrels to continue this repulsive work, I went down to inspect the depôt, where F—— was remaining as watchman, and took the three Indians to collect firewood, as our stock was getting low. The majority of the boxes were too solid to be broken open, and pilfering I found had been confined to a wine case (from which six bottles were abstracted) and to a flimsy trunk belonging to Perring. Having despatched the Indians upwards with their loads of wood, I followed them leisurely, searching in the Vallon de Carrel for treasures that had no attractions for the authorities at Guaranda.[1] The Indians saw their opportunity, and upon return to camp I discovered that they had dropped their loads and brought up no wood whatever; and, having stealthily picked up their little bundles of belongings under the very noses of the Carrels, had vanished, like the others.

The labour of porterage was again thrown upon Jean-Antoine and Louis, who bore their burdens cheerfully, and started off at an early hour on Jan. 2 with a couple of loads to the third camp. About 10 a.m. Perring made his appearance, accompanied by two persons in uniform, carrying rifles, and a muleteer and boy with a load of wood. I recognised 'the guard,' but desired

the other packages in the case several times with soap and water, and to rub them bright with sand, before we could venture to open them. When opened, we found that the stench had often penetrated the joints of the tins, and rendered their contents unfit for consumption. The worst part of the business, however, was the prejudice that it caused against the rest of the tinned food, all of which was found to be unexceptionable, unless it had been defiled by the ox-cheek. Some of my followers flatly refused to touch any of it.

Messrs. Crosse and Blackwell did *not* supply the ox-cheek and did supply some of the rest; and, as one would expect, their goods were found satisfactory. Their preserved soups, in particular, were excellent for our purposes.

[1] In this *vallon* I found *roches moutonnées* several miles lower than the existing Glacier de Thielmann; and I obtained in it most of the insects and plants which are enumerated in Chapters V. and XVIII. At a little less than 15,000 feet above the sea I found a solitary fern (*Polypodium pycnolepis*, Kze.). This is the greatest height at which a representative of this family was obtained on the journey.

an introduction to the others, and found that Mr. Perring had suspected that F—— was the thief, and had thoughtfully engaged a fresh arriero as courier, before arresting our late one, who was now a prisoner and on his way to Guaranda in charge of two of my guards;[1] whilst the other pair had taken the earliest opportunity to wait upon me, not to pay their respects, but to state that unless they were paid eightpence each per day, *punctually every day,* they would take themselves off. I assured them that it would give us the greatest pleasure to see one of them every day, punctually, at the third camp, to receive the four eightpences, and appointed Mr. Perring paymaster; but they took themselves off, I neither know when nor where, and relieved us from all trouble on their account, except the settlement of a bill from the authorities at Guaranda for services which had not been rendered.

They did not, however, depart from the second camp until we had shewn them the way to the third one. Their unexpected visit was too good an opportunity to be lost. I impressed every one to assist in the move, and at the end of the afternoon we had got three weeks' provisions at the upper station. The second camp was then left to take care of itself, with the tent standing, and a good supply of food and firing alongside. A line of communication was now fairly established. However bad the weather, we could always retreat upon the second camp, and from it to the depôt near the first one, scarcely more than two hours from Tortorillas, where we could communicate with Guaranda; and the word was given the same afternoon that Chimborazo was to be assaulted on the next morning.

At 5.35 a.m.[2] on Jan. 3, we left the tent, and, scrambling

[1] This was done without my approval or knowledge. There did not seem to be any evidence against this man; and, if there had been, we could not have obtained his conviction without the witnesses which were necessary (according to Mr. Perring) to satisfy the law of Ecuador.

[2] There was seldom light enough for travelling over unfamiliar ground earlier than 5.30 a.m.

through the shattered lava behind it, crossed the *arête* and emerged on the western side of the ridge. There was then the view before us that is given on the opposite page. The western dome, which had been hidden during part of the ascent, again became conspicuous; crowning wall-like cliffs of lava, that grew more and more imposing as we advanced. As regards the western summit, there are two series of these cliffs—the upper ones immediately underneath the dome, surmounted by sheer precipices of ice, and the lower ones at the end of a spur thrown out towards the south-west. These lower cliffs are neither so extensive nor as perpendicular as the upper ones,[1] and they are crowned by snow, not by glacier. Our ridge led up to their base, and at the junction there was a want of continuity rather than a distinct breach in the walls.[2] This was the spot which, when examining the mountain on Dec. 21, at a distance of sixteen miles, we had unanimously regarded as the critical point, so far as an ascent was concerned (see pp. 25, 26).

Up to this place the course was straightforward. In the immediate foreground, and extending upwards for 500 or 600 feet, large beds of snow in good condition covered the ridge. The pinnacle or aiguille near at hand was upon the *arête* or crest of it, and the two others shewn in the engraving upon p. 41 were higher up on the right hand or eastern side. The ridge itself appears to be fundamentally an old flow of lava. Rock specimens which were taken *in situ* at various elevations, though differing to some extent in external appearance, are nearly identical in composition,[3] and I have no doubt that several, at least, of the other principal

---

[1] They are seen in the view facing p. 24, which is taken from almost precisely the same direction as that facing this page, though at a much lower level.

[2] Marked Z on the *Sketch plan of part of the Southern side of Chimborazo*.

[3] "This rock (from the second camp, *in situ*) is a dullish lavender-grey colour, with crystals of glassy felspars up to about ·1 inch long, and some minute blackish specks, which weather rather a reddish colour. I think it very probable that a little sanidine is present among the felspars. The rock is a variety of the hypersthéniferous augite-andesites.

CHIMBORAZO, FROM A LITTLE ABOVE THE THIRD CAMP.

ridges of this mountain were originally lava-streams. Their normal appearance has been largely modified; much is covered up by snow, the exposed portions have been greatly decomposed and eroded, and lie almost buried underneath their own ruins.

After these convenient snow-beds were traversed our ridge steepened — both as regards its *arête*, and the angles of the slopes on each side; and became in part covered by pure ice, and partly by ice mingled with small stones and grit. When this conglomerate was hard frozen, it enabled us to ascend without step-cutting; but the débris often reposed uncemented on the surface, and rendered caution as well as hard labour necessary. I found here, scattered over about fifty feet, rather numerous fragments of partly fossilized bones. Sir Richard Owen, to whom they were submitted, pronounced them to be "the bones of some ruminant." The unhappy ruminant most likely did not come there voluntarily, and I conjecture that it was conveyed to this lofty spot, either entire or in part, by a condor or some other bird of prey, to be devoured at leisure.

At 7.30 a.m. we arrived at the foot of the lower series of the Southern Walls of Chimborazo, and the termination of the

"The specimen taken near the third camp, and representing the rock which prevails throughout the ridge by which the first ascent was made, is a rock macroscopically related to the one last described, but is a little redder in colour, more vesicular in structure, and with slightly larger crystals of felspar (up to about ¼th inch diameter). So far as the base and its included microliths are concerned, there is little to add to the preceding description, except that a dusty ferrite is rather abundant, as the colour of the rock would lead us to expect, the larger crystals of felspar do not materially differ from those already described, hypersthene is abundant, undoubted augite being rare, and there are two or three small crystals of a strongly dichroic hornblende. Also one or two crystals of what appears to be an iron mica. The predominance of hypersthene entitles this to the name of a hypersthene-andesite."—Prof. T. G. Bonney, F.R.S., *Proc. Royal Soc.*, No. 232, June 19, 1884.

The whole of the rocks collected upon this journey were submitted to Professor Bonney, by whom they were described in the *Proceedings of the Royal Society* in a series of five papers (Jan. 31–Nov. 27, 1884). Prof. Bonney has also favoured me with the summary which will be found at pp. 140-143 of the *Supplementary Appendix* to this volume.

south-west ridge. Then the axes went to work, and the cliffs resounded with the strokes of the two powerful cousins, who lost no time in exploration, as they had already passed this place on Dec. 29. The breach in the walls (for so it must be termed from want of a better expression) rose at an angle exceeding 50°, and here, for the same reason as upon the *arête* we had quitted, snow could not accumulate to any depth, and the major part of the daily fall slid away in streams, or tiny avalanches, down to the less abrupt slopes beneath; while the residue, dissolved and refrozen, glazed the projecting rocks, and filled their interstices with solid ice. Thus far and no farther a man may go who is not a mountaineer. To our party it caused only a temporary check, for the work was enchanting to the Carrels after the uncongenial labour in which they had been employed, and during a short time we made good progress — then, all at once, we were brought to a halt. Wind had been rising during the last half-hour, and now commenced to blow furiously. It was certain we could not reach the summit on that day; so, getting down as quickly as possible, and depositing the instruments and baggage in crannies in the cliffs after reading the barometer,[1] we fled for refuge to the tent, holding ourselves, however, in readiness to start again on the next morning.

Under the small further diminution in pressure which was

---

[1] At 8 a.m. on Jan. 3, the air temperature in the shade was 22°·5 Faht., and at the same time the mercurial barometer (corrected for temperature) read 15·276 inches.

I ascended again to this place on Jan. 6 to obtain an observation at 11 a.m. On this occasion the air temperature in the shade was 49°·5 Faht., and the mercurial barometer (reduced to 32°) read 15·298 inches. There was a simultaneous observation by Mr. Chambers at Guayaquil. The height adopted (18,528 feet) is the mean of the altitudes deduced from the observations made upon these two days.

The difference of level between the third camp and the foot of the lower series of the Southern Walls of Chimborazo amounts to 1243 feet. We occupied 115 minutes in ascending and 30 minutes in descending that amount. The descent was effected at the rate of 41 feet per minute, *and we could not have gone much faster*. This rate may be compared with those mentioned upon pp. 31, 32, which it is stated were maintained over courses three or four times as long.

experienced this day (seven-tenths of an inch), no very marked effects ensued. The most noticeable points were the lassitude with which we were pervaded, and the readiness with which we sat down. Atmospheric pressure varied little at the third camp. At 6 p.m., on Jan. 2, the mercurial barometer (red. to 32°) read 15·992 inches, and at 5 a.m., on Jan. 3, 15·974 inches; but the aneroids continued to lose upon the mercurial, and their mean error on Jan. 4-5 had risen to $-0·974$ of an inch, from $-0·903$ in. when they were last compared at the second camp (see p. 56). Two were already nearly out of range; another couple were out of order; and two others alone remained serviceable for yet lower pressures.

We again started from the third camp on Jan. 4, at 5.40 a.m. The morning was fine and nearly cloudless, and profiting by the track made on the previous day we proceeded at first at a fair rate and finished the escalade of "the breach" at about eight o'clock. Then bearing away to the left,[1] at first over snow and then over snow-covered glacier, we mounted in zigzags, to ease the ascent. The great schrunds at the head of the Glacier de Thielmann were easily avoided; the smaller crevasses were not troublesome; and the snow was in good order, though requiring steps to be cut in it. Jean-Antoine Carrel led, and my orders to him at starting were that we were to go slowly — the rest was left to his discretion. I noticed, at this stage, that his paces got shorter and shorter, until at last the toe of one step almost touched the heel of the previous one. At about 10 a.m., at a height of 19,400 feet, we passed the highest exposed rocks, which were scoriaceous lava, apparently in consolidated beds,[2] and for

[1] Our track at this part of the ascent is shewn in dotted line upon the view facing p. 24.

[2] Exposed in patches, about twelve feet long, projecting a few feet above the snow. The Carrels got nearly as far as these rocks upon December 29.

"A slightly scoriaceous lava, rough to the touch, almost purple-black in colour, with numerous very minute specks of a glassy felspar. Except that the base is rendered rather more opaque by disseminated opacite, it does not differ materially from several already described. There are the usual crystals of felspar, one or two

some distance farther we continued to progress at a reasonable rate, having fine weather and a good deal of sunshine.

At about 11 a.m. we fancied we saw the Pacific, above the clouds which covered the whole of the intervening flat country; and shortly afterwards commenced to enter the plateau which is at the top of the mountain, having by this time made half the circuit of the western dome. We were then twenty thousand feet high, and the summits seemed within our grasp. We could see both,—one towards our right, and the other a little farther away on our left, with a hollow plateau about a third of a mile across between them. We reckoned that in another hour we could get to the top of either; and, not knowing which of the two was the higher, we made for the nearer. But at this point the condition of affairs completely changed. The sky became overclouded, the wind rose, and we entered upon a tract of exceedingly soft snow, which could not be traversed in the ordinary way. The leading man went in up to his neck, almost out of sight, and had to be hauled out by those behind. Imagining that we had got into a labyrinth of crevasses, we beat about right and left to try to extricate ourselves; and, after discovering that it was everywhere alike, we found the only possible way of proceeding was to flog every yard of it down, and then to crawl over it on all fours; and, even then, one or another was frequently submerged, and almost disappeared.[1]

Needless to say, time flew rapidly. When we had been at this sort of work for three hours, without having accomplished half the remaining distance, I halted the men, pointed out the gravity of our situation, and asked them which they preferred, to turn or to go on. They talked together in patois, and then Jean-Antoine

being much rounded and very full of dull glassy enclosures; there is a fair amount of augite, but no well-characterised hypersthene; so that the rock may be named an augite-andesite."—Prof. T. G. Bonney, *Proc. Royal Soc.*, June 19, 1884.

[1] Louis Carrel could not touch bottom with a twelve-foot pole that he was carrying. It would have continued to descend by its own weight if he had left hold of it.

"WE WERE THEN TWENTY THOUSAND FEET HIGH."

said, "When you tell us to turn we will go back; until then we will go on." I said, "Go on," although by no means feeling sure it would not be best to say "Go back." In another hour and a half we got to the foot of the western summit, and, as the slopes steepened, the snow became firmer again. We arrived on the top of it about a quarter to four in the afternoon, and then had the mortification of finding that it was the lower of the two. There was no help for it; we had to descend to the plateau, to resume the flogging, wading, and floundering, and to make for the highest point, and there again, when we got on to the dome, the snow was reasonably firm, and we arrived upon the summit of Chimborazo standing upright like men, instead of grovelling, as we had been doing for the previous five hours, like beasts of the field.

The wind blew hard from the north-east, and drove the light snow before it viciously. We were hungry, wet, numbed, and wretched, laden with instruments which could not be used. With much trouble the mercurial barometer was set up; one man grasped the tripod to keep it firm, while the other stood to windward holding up a poncho to give a little protection. The

"LOWER IT WOULD NOT GO."

mercury fell to 14·100 inches,[1] with a temperature of 21° Faht., and lower it would not go. *The two aneroids* (D and E) *read 13·050 and 12·900 inches respectively.* By the time the barometer was in its case again, it was twenty minutes past five. Planting our pole with its flag of serge on the very apex of the dome, we turned to depart, enveloped in driving clouds which entirely concealed the surrounding country.

Scarcely an hour and a quarter of daylight remained, and we fled across the plateau. There is much difference between ascending and descending soft snow, and in the trough or groove which had already been made we moved down with comparative facility. Still it took nearly an hour to extricate ourselves, and we then ran,—ran for our lives, for our arrival at camp that night depended upon passing "the breach" before darkness set in. We just gained it as daylight was vanishing, and night fell before it was left behind; a night so dark that we could neither see our feet nor tell, except by touch, whether we were on rock or snow. Then we caught sight of the camp fire, twelve hundred feet below, and heard the shouts of the disconsolate Perring, who was left behind as camp-keeper, and stumbled blindly down the ridge, getting to the tent soon after 9 p.m., having been out nearly sixteen hours, and on foot the whole time.

The reduction in pressure we experienced upon Jan. 4 amounted to nearly two inches (16·000 to 14·100 inches),—a considerably larger diminution than had occurred while mounting from the first to the second camp on Dec. 27 (17·900 to 16·500 inches). Yet on the former day we were entirely free from the afflictions of the latter one. There was neither feverishness, headache, gasping, nor the nausea, vomitings, and hemorrhages of which others have spoken. The only effect of which I was conscious, or could trace in my companions, was lassitude or want of vivacity. Our rate on this day was

---

[1] This is the original reading, uncorrected for temperature.

deplorable. Nearly sixteen hours were occupied in ascending and descending 3200 feet. There was a marked diminution in pace the higher we ascended, and although this, to some extent, was owing to the nature of the snow (the softness of which according to the Carrels was unprecedented in their experience) it seemed probable that it was not entirely due to it; and I proposed to test this on another occasion by sweeping round and avoiding the hollow part of the plateau, where the soft snow alone occurred.

The eyes of my mountaineers were inflamed.[1] Louis did not shew to advantage on this day, and I thought it noteworthy that he, the youngest, biggest, and not the least powerful of the three, manifested more signs of fatigue than men who were fourteen and twenty-six years older. Whilst descending, he took the lead, and walked irregularly — sometimes blundering or staggering forwards, and then suddenly checking his pace abruptly. Jean-Antoine, on the contrary, walked well, and descended with a steady, uniform stride (though encumbered with his twelve-pound baby), in admirable style for a man of fifty-two. There was little difference in our condition on the morning of the 5th. Louis mentioned that his toes were frost-bitten,[2] and so were the tips of my own fingers, through turning the milled heads of the cistern and vernier screws of the barometer with ungloved hands.

The reading of the mercurial barometer upon the summit was half an inch higher than I expected; and, from the rough computation which I made on the spot, upon the assumption that the simultaneous height of the barometer at Guayaquil was a little below 30 inches and that the temperature of the air there was 75° Faht., the height of Chimborazo came out 20,608

[1] On the 4th of Jan. I used a knitted woollen head-piece (with a linen mask as well during part of the time), and wore neutral-tint spectacles throughout the day. The Carrels incautiously uncovered their eyes occasionally, and suffered accordingly.

[2] He was indebted to this through going without gaiters. The snow on the summit was wet as well as soft, and he got his feet wet.

feet,[1] or 817 feet *lower* than the determination of Humboldt. Although I had no doubt of the accuracy of my readings,[2] I thought it was desirable to repeat them, if possible at 11 a.m., for the sake of combination with Mr. Chambers' observations at that hour.

Two aneroids (D and E) were taken to the summit, and when read against the mercurial they shewed a considerable increase in their errors upon those which were observed at the third camp —

    Error of D at last comparison at the third camp was − 0·724 inch.
    Do.   E   do.   do.   − 0.774 „
    Do.   D upon the summit of Chimborazo .   . − 1·060 „
    Do.   E   do.   do   .   . − 1·210 „

The actual readings on the summit of these two aneroids were (D) 13·050 inches, and (E) 12·900 inches.[3] The mean of the readings (12·975 inches), thus, was no less than 1·135 inches *lower* than the reading of the mercurial barometer (corrected for temperature); and if the altitude of Chimborazo had been deduced from this mean, in combination with Mr. Chambers' observations at Guayaquil, the height of the mountain would have come out more than a thousand feet *greater* than the determination of Humboldt!

I considered that it was desirable to ascend Chimborazo again, to see whether we could improve our route, to learn whether our deplorable rate at the upper part was due to the softness of the snow or was to be attributed to diminution in atmospheric pressure; and to remain a longer time on the summit to repeat the observations of the barometer, and to obtain a

---

[1] Upon being re-computed by Mr. Ellis (after the Guayaquil observations were known), this was reduced to 20,545 feet.

[2] The mercurial barometer was set up directly we reached the summit, but the reading was not entered until it was found that the mercury of the instrument had taken up the temperature of the air.

[3] These aneroids were graduated to 13 inches.

round of angles,—for it was obvious that this commanding position covered an immense range. It was consequently understood that another ascent was to be made, as soon as the conditions became favourable.

The weather on Jan. 5 was cold and windy, and much sleet fell. The arriero-courier came up with a sheep,[1] and went down to "the authorities" with a cordial invitation to pay us a visit, as I wished to see how far they were fitted to occupy higher positions than their comparatively obscure ones at Guaranda. Jean-Antoine and Perring descended to the second camp for firewood, and Louis remained nearly all day in the tent, engaged in household affairs.

The view from our eyrie was more extensive towards the east and south than that seen from the second camp. Over the ridge on the opposite side of the Glacier de Débris we obtained an occasional glimpse of Sangai, an active volcano which seems to be known only by name.[2] In Ecuador it is reputed to be formidable, and when we were established at Guaranda we frequently heard noises which were attributed to it by the natives.[3] It appeared to be distant from us about forty miles, and its rather symmetrical cone rose well above the intervening ranges. There were large snow-beds near its summit, but the apex of the cone was black, and was doubtless covered with fine volcanic ash. The saying is current that eruptions of Sangai are to be apprehended when Cotopaxi becomes tranquil, and the

[1] The animal was driven up to the second camp.

[2] I am not acquainted with any information about it in print, except the brief references to it by Mr. Spruce in the *Journal* of the Royal Geographical Society for 1861, nor aware that the base of its cone has been reached. Messrs. Reiss and Stübel in their *Alturas* give 17,464 feet as its height.

[3] On Dec. 20-21 the noises resembled reports of volleys of musketry at the distance of half a mile or so. On these and upon other days the sounds were heard only between 7 and 9 a.m. They were not accompanied by any vibration, and the natives paid no regard to them. The name of this mountain has not been introduced upon the large map, as I was unable to fix its position.

opinion seemed to prevail that the two mountains act as safety-valves to each other.

Upon the few occasions that we saw it (though scarcely any smoke issued from the crater), there were outrushes of steam at intervals of twenty to thirty minutes[1] which shot up with

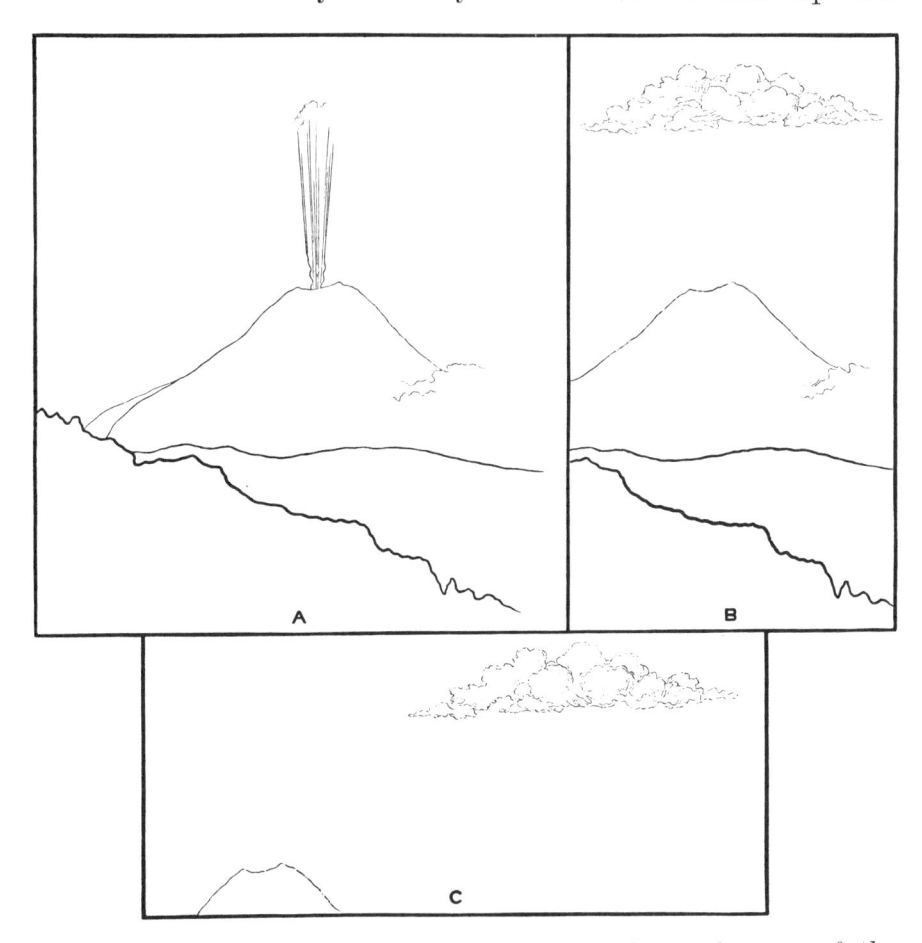

immense rapidity five or six thousand feet above the top of the mountain. They then spread out into mushroom-like clouds, which were drifted by the wind towards the south. The annexed diagram shews three phases (A, B, C) of these eruptions. In A, the nearly invisible jet is being projected. In B, the eruption has

[1] Similar ejections of steam, on a smaller scale, were also observed upon Cotopaxi. See Chapter VII.

ceased, and the steam-cloud has formed; and, in C, this cloud is being carried to leeward, and is melting away. Sometimes these clouds drifted ten or twelve miles before they were dissipated, and as a rule they had quite disappeared before a fresh outburst created a new one.

Three points of interest in connection with these outbursts of steam may be mentioned. 1. The rapidity of the ejection. This can be estimated with some probability, as our position was nearly on a level with the summit of Sangai, and was favourably situated for observation. The part of the cone within sight was about 4000 feet high; the jets rose to about once and a half this height, in less than three seconds, and they were consequently projected in the air at the rate of about *twenty-two miles per minute*. 2. The cloud formed by the steam took the shape of ordinary cumulus, rudely flat below, and piled up above. This was repeated time after time. 3. The drift of these clouds southwards demonstrated the existence of a current of air, 22–23,000 feet above the sea, directed from north to south. From our small number of observations, it would be rash to conclude that this current is a permanent one, although from subsequent experiences it would appear that it exists during a considerable portion of the year.

The 6th of January commenced with fine weather, and I went again with the Carrels to the foot of the Southern Walls. This time we ascended the 1243 feet in 88 minutes. The lower cliffs (marked D on the sketch plan of Chimborazo) are not so lofty, or as perpendicular as the upper series, and (if provided with ice-axes) one can traverse the slopes underneath them without much trouble, though they are steep and have many streaks or sheets of ice caused by the refreezing of the water which trickles off the rocks. There is evidence that a certain amount of liquefaction goes on even at the top of Chimborazo (notwithstanding the low mean temperature that prevails there) in the enormous icicles which depend from the lower surfaces of the coronal glacier. Some were fully one hundred and fifty feet long.

I found at this place, on rocks *in situ* at the base of the cliffs, patches of the lichen *Lecanora subfusca*, L., spread over a considerable area. This was the highest point at which any lichen was obtained upon Chimborazo, or during our journey amongst the Great Andes of the Equator; and, so far as I can learn, it (18,500 feet) is the greatest elevation at which anything appertaining to the vegetable kingdom has been found in either of the Americas.[1] Another lichen of the genus *Gyrophora* was in quantities in the vicinity of the third camp (17,200 – 17,300 feet).

Standing at the foot of the Southern Walls,[2] I was more puzzled than before to understand how my predecessors could have attained the elevations of 19,286 and 19,698 feet. According to my rough computation, the height of this place was about 18,400 feet above the level of the sea.[3] This, it seems to me, was the spot at which Humboldt and Boussingault stopped. The latter traveller, in the account reprinted in Appendix H, says that his (second) attempt was made by way of the Arenal. This limits his route to the three *vallons* which have been already mentioned. He states that he got his mules to a height of 4935 metres (16,224 feet), and this indicates that he followed the same *vallon* as ourselves, for he could not have got them nearly so high either in the Vallon de Débris or in that of Tortorillas. He then speaks of following an *arête*, and his account agrees with the *arête* of the south-west ridge; and if his narrative is to be taken in a literal sense he must

---

[1] There are in the Botanical Department of the British Museum some specimens of a moss of the genus *Orthotrichum*, collected by the Col. Hall who accompanied Boussingault upon his attempts to ascend Chimborazo, which are said to have come from a height of 18,800 feet, and to be the last trace of vegetation. I obtained species of this genus upon the summit of Corazon (15,871), but did not meet with it upon Chimborazo, or see mosses growing anywhere upon that mountain higher than 16,700 feet.

It follows from what is said about the elevation attained by Col. Hall and Boussingault that I cannot suppose these specimens actually came from so great a height.

[2] A detailed sketch of a portion of them accompanies Chapter XIX.

[3] In recomputation, this has been increased to 18,528 feet.

ICE-CLIFFS UNDER THE SUMMITS OF CHIMBORAZO.

PHOTOGRAPHED AT 18,500 FEET.

"THIS, IT SEEMS TO ME, WAS THE SPOT AT WHICH HUMBOLDT AND BOUSSINGAULT STOPPED."

have stopped at the foot of the Southern Walls, at or about the place marked F upon the illustration in Chapter XIX., and by a little cross on the plate facing p. 24, for his description agrees with that place and cannot apply to any other.[1] I am unable to explain how he found that this place was elevated 19,698 feet above the sea; still less do I understand, if he stood at this spot, having the Glacier de Débris on his right, and the Glacier de Thielmann on his left, and magnificent sections of glacier crowning the Upper Walls, immediately above him, how it was he declared that he had seen no glaciers upon Chimborazo!

There is less certainty that Humboldt arrived at this spot. It is impossible to determine from his own narrative where he actually went. Boussingault says he knew that Humboldt made his attempt upon the side of the Arenal; and, inasmuch as the route we followed is the only way by which the elevation of 18,500 feet can be reached with reasonable facility on that side, it seems not impossible that he also got as far as the foot of the Southern Walls;[2] and, if he arrived there, this also would be the place at which his progress would be arrested. Go farther he could not, for the four hundred and fifty feet[3] of broken rock and intermingled ice in the breach form an insurmountable barrier to the uninitiated.

The view from this position is one of the most striking upon the mountain. It commands the ridge up which we made our way, and embraces the whole length of the Glacier de Débris, the

---

[1] "Nous nous trouvions au pied d'un prisme de trachyte dont la base supérieure, recouverte d'une coupole de neige, forme le sommet du Chimborazo. . . . De toutes parts nous étions environnés de précipices. . . . La couleur foncée de la roche contrastait de la manière la plus tranchée avec la blancheur éblouissante de la neige. De longues stalagmites de glace paraissaient suspendues sur nos têtes."

[2] There are, however, several reasons why this is dubious. In *Aspects of Nature*, vol. 2, p. 34, he states that his highest point was "on the *eastern* declivity of the Chimborazo." By no stretch of the imagination can "the side of the Arenal" be made the eastern side of the mountain. In Karl Bruhns' *Life* it is said that progress was stopped by "a ravine, some 400 feet deep, and 60 feet wide," and there is no such ravine or cleft upon the south-west ridge.

[3] We measured the breach with a line on Jan. 6.

vallon below, and in the far distance a little peep of the Arenal road, where by the aid of glasses the passing mule-trains bound from the capital to the coast could be discerned, and condors sailing to and fro watching unguarded flocks and herds.

The inferior portion of the Glacier de Débris lies below the line of perpetual snow, blackened and obscured with fragments of lavas of every hue and shape, broken from places inaccessible to the hammer; but its upper half, sprinkled by the daily falls, grows purer as it rises, and terminates in a steeply-sloping basin, closed by the *cirque* of cliffs of the Southern Walls, crowned by a vertical section of ice (E) which shews the thickness of the glacier at the summit of Chimborazo.

Whilst waiting at the point marked A on the Plan, ready to snatch a view of the opposite walls should an opening occur in the mists, a portion of the projecting ice-cliffs near the summit broke away, and some thousands of tons dropped hundreds of feet without touching anything, falling into the amphitheatre with a noise which fairly made us quiver; and then, shattered into millions of fragments, danced down the converging slopes to the upper basin, and marched onwards, covering the entire glacier; continuing to roll, grind against, and even to clamber over each other, until nearly opposite the second camp,—driving a cloud of icy spray nearly a mile farther. In this way the Glacier de Débris is fed and maintained.

Shortly afterwards, following its usual custom, the weather deteriorated. High wind and a severe thunderstorm made us scamper to the tent for shelter, leaving the instruments, as before, stowed away in fissures in the cliffs. Next morning, my Chief of the Staff enquired what we were going to do, and whether the instruments should be brought down. I said, "No, we have not finished our work." He then attempted to dissuade me from another ascent, arguing that the weather was bad, and that it would be useless, and so forth. It came out gradually that he himself positively refused to go up again, or even to stop where we were. I reminded him of the labour which had been incurred in establishing our camps, and pointed out the severe loss that would occur if they were broken up. He assented to all that I said, and simply took up the position that *he* would not ascend Chimborazo again. Louis did not join in the discussion,—the older man spoke for both. Upon asking for a reason, he said that he considered the length of time we were at so great a height was injurious to his health; that he had pains all over his body, and was afflicted with dysentery. After spending much time in argument, and finding that he could not be brought into a different frame of mind, I despatched Perring to Guaranda to bring up mules for the retreat.[1]

To tell the truth, I did not think much of the ailments he mentioned, for he appeared to be in very good preservation; and I concluded that he was tired of the monotony of his life, and unfavourably contrasted the tameness of our proceedings with the dashing exploits to which he had been accustomed. From this point of view a good deal might have been said. The cousins had been employed on Chimborazo more as beasts of burden than as mountaineers, in weather which for continuous badness was the worst we had known, in occupations that brought them no compensation for the hardships they endured; and I did not feel inclined to judge them too harshly, though intensely chagrined at their sudden collapse, and at being compelled to descend when our work was not half finished.

During the time Mr. Perring was absent, all the baggage was concentrated below; and on the 10th, when the team arrived, it was speedily loaded, and despatched to the tambo of Chuquipoquio, on the east side of Chimborazo. Perring necessarily accompanied the caravan as interpreter, and I remained alone at the second camp; for I refused to leave until some of my projects were accomplished, amongst these the most

---

[1] This day (Jan. 7) we went up to recover the instruments, and got to the foot of the Southern Walls in eighty-five minutes.

important being the observation of angles for the construction of a plan of our surroundings. Before they left, a base line, 600 feet long, was measured from near the second camp to the position marked STATION 3 on the sketch plan of part of the southern side of Chimborazo, and poles were erected as signals on the centre of the Glacier de Débris and at other places. But the mists that had prevailed prevented angles being observed at these positions, and until they were obtained I proposed to stop. Perring was directed to return on the afternoon of the 11th with a sufficient number of beasts for the transport of the remaining baggage, and then the little procession passed out of sight, with Jean-Antoine as rear-guard, lingering as if after all reluctant to go, turning to wave an adieu, calling out, "Take care of yourself, Monsieur, take care!"

In this singular position I remained two days longer. At 4 p.m. on the 12th I turned my back on the second camp, and, going gently on foot, arrived at 10.45 at the tambo of Chuquipoquio. The great gate of the massive portal was opened somewhat tardily, for all were asleep and the place was in darkness, and I went to bed about 1 a.m., not in the least knowing what the next move would be.

THE HEAD OF THE EXPEDITION.

A RAGAMUFFIN AT CHUQUIPOQUIO.

CHAPTER IV.

FROM CHUQUIPOQUIO TO AMBATO, LATACUNGA AND MACHACHI.

EARLY on the next morning, the mystery was solved. Louis was found to be a cripple, quite unable to walk, through his feet having been severely frost-bitten. They were frightfully swollen, blistered and discoloured. Jean-Antoine, however, was restored; his dysentery having yielded to frequent internal applications of hot wine and cognac.

It appeared that they were somewhat shamefaced about these frost-bitten feet, and when they found that serious mischief had been done they were half afraid to confess it, expecting that a storm would be raised by this result of their negligence.[1] It

[1] Louis Carrel did not wear gaiters on Jan. 4, and as his shoes were of the ill-fitting kind usually worn by Alpine peasants, snow worked down into them, and his feet got wet. Both men were in fault. It was a part of their contract that they were to bring gaiters, and it was the business of Jean-Antoine to see that everything requisite was provided.

was not a time for scolding. I saw now why Louis had blundered and floundered about during the descent. The poor man was in a very bad way, and the first thing was to find some one who understood the proper treatment for him, as his case was beyond our abilities.

It so happened that shortly after my arrival the proprietor of Chuquipoquio came up from Riobamba, and from him we learned that there was at the town of Ambato, about twenty-two miles away, a medical man who had a good reputation; and on the 14th Perring was despatched to that place to procure lodgings and to bring back the means of transporting the cripples — for there were two of us. I was also in need of a doctor through having acquired in Ecuador a complaint which rendered riding impossible, and obliged me to walk with circumspection.

Señor Chiriboga, the proprietor of the tambo, was the son of a gentleman of Riobamba, who was said to be the representative of one of the oldest families in Ecuador, and would have been, if titles had not been abolished, Marquis de Chimborazo. The possible Marquis was a man of middle age, with an intelligent head, and he came up "to do us honour, to supply our needs, to watch over and care for us" — so he said. He fell on my neck and kissed me, and begged that I would write an account of our ascent, "to enrich the Archives of Riobamba." I took this request seriously, but he became invisible until just before we left his house, and I forgot his existence except when my eye lighted upon the neglected document, which was to have enriched the archives of his native town.

Chuquipoquio is situated towards the eastern end of Chimborazo. There is no village. The establishment is partly tambo and partly farm, and like most of the *Haciendas* in the interior of Ecuador is surrounded by high walls, and has a half-fortified appearance. The courtyard in front was entered through a massive portal, with strong gates, which were generally kept locked and bolted, and the buildings on the opposite side were of one story, in the hut style of architecture. Two or three ragamuffins were attached to the place, which was managed by a very dirty Indian, styled the major-domo, who was assisted by an equally dirty wife.

This was the only house of entertainment between Ambato and Guaranda (for the miserable tambos at Tortorillas and Mocha count for nothing), and it had things all its own way. A bottle of Bass cost four shillings, and other articles were in proportion. But our greatest grievance was that we could scarcely get anything at any price. Though there were cows, milk was doled out by spoonfuls; there were fowls that "belonged to some one else" and never laid eggs; there was famine as regards bread, and meat was not to be thought of. So we had to fall back upon our reserved stock to save ourselves from starvation.

Examination of the stock shewed that we had eaten less than usual while upon Chimborazo; though, owing to the complications introduced by the putrid ox-cheek, one could not tell to what extent. Upon speaking of this as an unexpected circumstance to Jean-Antoine, he surprised me by saying that they (that is to say, Alpine peasants generally) noticed the same thing when they were upon mountain expeditions in the Alps. I should have thought the reverse was the case, and that the appetites of guides left nothing to be desired, except a wish that they might be diminished.[1]

In the mornings, when every one cleared out of the tambo, some going north and others south, the courtyard which had resounded with the pawing of restless beasts became as still as death, and I turned to my journals. I found that my residence upon Chimborazo had extended over seventeen days. One night was passed at 14,375 feet, ten more at 16,664 feet, and six others at 17,285 feet above the sea, and this is perhaps the greatest length of time that any one has remained continuously at such

---

[1] It should, however, be noted that we do not know how much the Alpine peasant consumes when he is *at home*.

elevations.[1] In these days, besides ascending to the summit, I went three times as high as 18,528 feet. Or, the case may be stated in the following way. In the period intervening between 4.45 p.m. on Dec. 27 and 4 p.m. on Jan. 12 I did not experience a higher pressure than 16·500 inches, except during the few hours on Jan. 1 when I descended to inspect the depôt. For six consecutive days, namely, from 4 p.m. on Jan. 2 to the same hour on Jan. 8, pressure was never higher than sixteen inches; and in these six days, on three occasions, the barometer was observed to be standing below 15·300 inches, and on one other day to be as low as 14·100 inches.[2]

In these seventeen days we had experienced the reality of mountain-sickness, and found that we were not exempt from it at a pressure of sixteen and a half inches; that in course of time the more acute symptoms disappeared, as we became habituated to that pressure, and that we were able to sustain a slight further diminution without their recurrence. There was no certainty

---

[1] The nearest parallel of which I am aware is to be found in the experiences of some of the officers of Sir Douglas Forsyth's Mission to Yarkund. See the Geographical Report of Capt. (now Col.) H. Trotter, R.E., in *Report of a Mission to Yarkund in 1873, under command of Sir T. D. Forsyth, K.C.S.I., C.B.;* 4to, Calcutta, 1875.

[2] During the whole of this time, there was not one really fine day. As a rule, the weather at daybreak on Chimborazo was reasonably good at our level, and the two summits were cloudless, or nearly so. Clouds at that time, however, always existed beneath us, commencing at about 13–14,000 feet, and extending how low I cannot say. Hill-tops of greater elevation than this were commonly clear. By 8 a.m., or thereabouts, clouds commenced to form over the eastern side of the mountain; and, gradually extending upwards, generally shut out the summits by 10 a.m. There were thunderstorms on the south side of Chimborazo on every day from Dec. 28 to Jan. 12 inclusive, and some were extremely violent. These seldom occurred before mid-day. Snow fell around us every day, on an average, to the extent perhaps of three inches per day. The snow was commonly wet, and in small flakes. Dry, powdery snow did not occur. Hail fell, but not in great quantities or in pellets of large size. The extreme temperatures noted at the camps were 72°·5 Faht. at 11 a.m., in the tent at the second camp on Jan. 9, and 17° Faht., the minimum of the night of Jan. 5, at the third camp.

When Whymper's party neared two miles above sea level, they began to encounter clouds, and complained that although they were now up in the Andes, they hadn't seen any mountains.

Aerial approaching Chimborazo from the north side, looking south. Whymper climbed from the high western *arenal* (the plain of ashes and cinders under clouds off to the right) up to the base of the red cliffs, at the right side of the peak. Then he crossed to the left, to the bottom of the smooth (apparently, though full of hidden crevasses) glacier leading to the summit, and climbed directly up and south to the first and lower rounded summit, then south across deep snow to the southern higher summit.

The lower and easier part of the route to Chimborazo's summit. The grade does not look very steep from this angle, an illusion resulting from pointing the camera upwards. The tough part is climbing around to the left of the red cliffs and then up Whymper Glacier to the summit. At the foot of the cliffs, ahead, is where Whymper and the Carrels collapsed with AMS (Acute Mountain Sickness). Whymper said his purpose for the expedition was to study the effects of low pressure. He had a richer opportunity than he expected.

Ecuadorean climber Marco Cruz on the *Aiguilles*, the spires which Whymper illustrates on pages 41 and 64. This shows that McIntyre followed Whymper's route up Chimborazo, the same route climbed by Alexander von Humboldt on his unsuccessful attempt much earlier in the century.

that they would not reappear if we remained continuously at yet lower pressures, and I had proposed to test this by stopping on the summit for some length of time. The unfortunate *dénouement* which had just occurred necessitated an entire recasting of my plans, and whilst groaning inwardly under their enforced abandonment a scheme came into my head from the execution of which it seemed possible to derive some consolation.

BACK OF THE TAMBO OF CHUQUIPOQUIO.

This idea it was discreet to keep secret until the right time arrived for divulging it, and I proposed to exercise the same reticence now.

The tambo of Chuquipoquio is built upon the lower, eastern slopes of Chimborazo, which extend almost uninterruptedly down to Riobamba. This town is on flat ground, at the bottom of a huge basin. Carihuairazo, Chimborazo and its continuations bound it upon the west; and on the south it is enclosed by a transverse range (upon which the village of Nanti is situated), that stretches across, and in a manner may be said to connect the Range of Chimborazo with that which culminates on the eastern side of the basin in the mountain Altar. The drainage of this basin, which from crest to crest is about thirty miles across, is collected into one stream of insignificant dimensions—the River Chambo—near the Bridge of Penipe, and, after sweeping round the base of Tunguragua, falls into the River Pastassa.

Ecuador in this latitude, commencing from the west, has first lowlands extending from the coast as far inland as the villages of Catarama and Ventanas; then comes the Pacific Range, rising 14,000 feet and upwards in elevation;[1] next the basin occupied by numerous small valleys that converge towards the head of the River Chimbo (9–10,000), succeeded by the Range of Chimborazo; and this is followed by the basin of Riobamba, bounded on its opposite side by the Range of Altar, which sends out spurs many miles yet farther towards the east.[2]

The Range of Chimborazo includes Chimborazo itself, Carihuairazo on its north-east (extending almost as far as the town of Ambato), and a great block of mountains on its south[3] which nearly fills the blank space on the Route Map that is embraced between the River Chimbo and my track from Riobamba past Guamote to Chimbo. The mountain proper, even without these continuations, covers an amount of ground equal to or greater than some of the principal *ranges* of the Alps. From the pass of Abraspungo to the Great Arenal it measures nearly ten miles, all the intervening space being higher than 14,000 feet above the sea; while from south-east to north-west, reckoning only the part which is above 9000 feet, it is nearly thirty miles across.

Chimborazo as seen from Chuquipoquio has no resemblance to a cone. Its summit appears to be formed of a ridge,[4] the upper part of which is everywhere buried beneath snow-covered glacier. Below this, along a large part of its southern side, there

[1] From the second camp on Chimborazo (16,664 feet) the highest visible point of the Pacific Range was depressed only 2° 20′.

[2] Part of this information was obtained on a later visit to this district.

[3] The highest of these mountains closely approach but do not enter the line of perpetual snow.

[4] This deceptive appearance is the result of foreshortening. Chuquipoquio is too close to the summit to let its proportions be seen properly. The mountain is viewed to much greater advantage from Riobamba. The second (*i.e.* the western) summit of Chimborazo cannot be seen from Chuquipoquio, and the highest point is concealed at Tortorillas.

are many precipitous cliffs, that sometimes completely sever the glaciers on the apparent summit ridge from the secondary ones below. The glacier J of my map (Glacier de Chuquipoquio) is an example. This and the Glacier de Moreno are conspicuous at the tambo, and several others which are laid down upon the map are also more or less seen from it. Between their inferior extremities and Chuquipoquio there are several transverse ridges, which are hilly rather than mountainous in character;[1] and on the eastern side of the tambo the slopes become still more gentle, and finally die out a little distance short of Riobamba.

Perring returned on the evening of the 16th, bringing thirteen mules, eight wild-looking Indians, and two persons in uniform who had been sent by the Governor of Ambato as a 'guard of honour.' He said that no vehicle of any kind could be procured, and that the Indians had come to carry me upon a litter. In the early morning they began to construct it, first of all having to make ropes to bind it together; and they

[1] On Jan. 15, Jean-Antoine and I walked across the eastern end of Chimborazo, and turned the corner about a mile from the base of the Glacier de Moreno. We continued round the northern side at a level of about 14,000 feet until we were due south of the summits of Carihuairazo, then dropped down into the valley which occupies the depression between the two mountains, and descended it as far as the high road, and so came back to our starting-point. Our track is not given upon the map.

In the course of this walk, we found a *Calceolaria* (*C. rosmarinifolia*, Lam.) in abundance near Chuquipoquio; and several species of *Gentiana*, of *Lupinus* and *Cerastium*, a *Valeriana*, a *Vaccinium* and a *Ranunculus* (*R. Peruvianus*, Pers.) growing between 12,000 and 14,000 feet. The grasses upon the slopes were principally Poas, Fescues, and Deyeuxias. When about 13,800 feet high we caught sight of a large white spot about a mile off, and found it was an isolated patch of a splendid grass (*Gynerium argenteum*, Nees) growing eight to nine feet high, by the side of a little stream. A few days later we discovered the same species two thousand feet lower, near Mocha, but these were the only localities where it was noticed. A little below 14,000 feet, on the north-east side of the mountain, at the foot of some cliffs, facing the north, I was attracted from a long distance by the flowers of some Currant bushes (*Ribes glandulosum*, R. & P.). This is the greatest elevation at which an example of that Order was obtained in Ecuador.

THE ENTRANCE TO THE TAMBO.

accomplished the job in their own fashion pretty quickly, covering the framework of poles with a superstructure of ponchos. Louis was hoisted into the saddle with his feet well bandaged in lint and made up into bundles, and by nine o'clock we were ready to leave.

But it was easier to get into the Tambo of Chuquipoquio than out of it. The bill had to be settled, and it could not be obtained, and in the meantime the caravan was kept locked up in the courtyard. When the bill came, its portentous total made me examine the items. It commenced by charging for each individual thing supplied at a meal. Bread was put down at two shillings for a few slices; half a pint of milk was entered at half-a-crown, and coffee at three shillings and twopence; and after this "the meal" was charged for over again, at a price which was quite adequate irrespective of the previous entries. A number of things were put down that had not been supplied, and the total was made to amount to considerably more than the proper addition of the items. These matters were explained through Perring to the major-domo, who took the account away, and kept us locked up.

After waiting more than an hour it came out that Señor Chiriboga, our worthy host (who had travelled all the way from Riobamba "to supply our needs, to watch over and care for us"), was stowed away in a remote corner of the establishment, and had been there during the whole of our stay — in bed. I found the possible Marquis stretched out in a miserable den, in an advanced state of intoxication, with a bottle of spirits and a wine-glass on a chair by his side. He was made to understand that there might be trouble if he continued to detain my people, and after some parleying they were set free. I then wasted a half-hour in discussion with the drunken man, who evaded answers, and, sometimes addressing me as 'Your Excellency' and sometimes as 'Doctor,' kept on saying it was 'all right,' and that his servant would see to it; while the wretched slave (who had no doubt acted under orders) declared that he had followed instructions. "Right, your Excellency," said the landlord, "quite right, my servant will see to it." "You hear what your master says, — you are to do what is right." "My master told me to make out the bill in that way," replied the major-domo. "You hear what your servant says, Señor Chiriboga." "Quite right, Doctor — take a drink; yes, it is all right, my servant will do what is right." The keys might have been obtained by force, but such a procedure would most likely have given rise to prejudicial rumours. Of the two evils I thought it was best to be swindled. I paid the entire amount, under protest, and was then unlocked and joined my people, who had halted about a mile away, wondering at our non-appearance.

The road that we took to Ambato is almost the only one

in the interior of Ecuador. It was constructed by order of Garcia Morena, a former President of the Republic, and it is in more senses than one the highway to Quito. It commences at Chuquipoquio, where the traveller to his surprise suddenly drops from a trail or mule-path on to a road broad enough for four or five vehicles to be driven abreast. It has slightly falling gradients on leaving the tambo, and it then rises as it passes over the Paramo of Sanancajas—a stretch of bleak moorland forming part of the lower eastern slopes of Carihuairazo. It then descends almost continuously to Ambato, bending round and avoiding the village of Mocha, through which the old track to Quito passes.

In the following June-July I measured by direct measurement the distance by the road between Chuquipoquio and the place marked by an asterisk on the Map of Chimborazo, and found it was 35,670 feet. When crossing the paramo it is perfectly straight for two and a half miles, and this part and many other sections of it are paved with round, knobbly stones which are distressing alike to man and beast. They are found so painful to traverse, that horsemen, baggage-animals, and pedestrians decline to use the road when it is paved in this manner, and go by preference into the little ditches on each side, or even take to the wild moorland, where there is much less risk of dislocating the ankles. The paved parts of the road are rapidly becoming covered with grass.[1]

After crossing the Paramo of Sanancajas we descended into the basin of Ambato. The litter, carried at the head of the

[1] I concur in the following remarks by Mr. Church. "Its great width appears to me to be an error. I doubt if any part of it is used by five carts or carriages per day. It is almost entirely used as a mule-track, for which it serves abundantly well; but the neglect of the Government to keep this excellent road in repair is fast turning it into nothing but a mule-track. A year or two more, under its present neglect, will make it impassable for carriages. . . . There are no plans in the Government Offices of the cart-road, and the Government tells me that none exist."—Page 49 of a *Report* by Mr. George Earl Church to Mr. Blaine. Washington, Feb. 15, 1883.

CARRIED ON THE LITTER INTO AMBATO.

caravan, escorted by the guards, seemed to be conveying some malefactor to prison; but the oddity of the sight excited no attention, and the natives passed by stolid, or apathetic, as usual. On arrival at the town,[1] we went straight to the house of His Excellency Señor Juan Guerrero Duprat, Minister for Foreign Affairs, who had agreed to let a suite of his principal apartments for four shillings a day! and on the morrow sent for the doctor who had been recommended, Dr. Abel Barona, a gentleman who left a pleasant recollection through skilful attention combined with moderation in charges.[2] In a few days he set me up; and promised Louis that in a week he would be able to get about,—a good-natured fiction that did not deceive any of us. Though the swelling was soon reduced, the flesh parted in large gashes, and until these were healed he could not make serious attempts at walking.

At the earliest opportunity, I paid a visit to the Governor. The poor man was afflicted with the mumps, or some kindred complaint, and had his jaws tied up with a coloured handkerchief; and, as he also wore a floral dressing-gown, his appearance was rather decorative. He rose from a sort of divan, and bowed very slowly and profoundly, with an obvious eye to effect. But he was very courteous, and we soon got talking about the possible Marquis. The Governor said that every one was robbed at Chuquipoquio, and that a week seldom passed without complaints coming to his ears. He suggested bringing an action against Señor Chiriboga at Riobamba, and when I enquired whether it was not the fact that he was very well connected, and that it was *possible* the result might be unfortunate, he

[1] Left Chuquipoquio at 11.15 a.m., and arrived at Mocha at 2.45 p.m. Halted until 4, and arrived at Ambato at 9 p.m. From the reasons mentioned in the text, we travelled slowly. I found the litter a very suitable and pleasant method of conveyance. The Indians shambled or jog-trotted almost the entire distance, without shewing signs of fatigue.

[2] These details are given as a set-off to our experiences at Chuquipoquio. The treatment at that place was quite exceptional.

replied "it is *possible*, it *is possible*" with an emphasis and look that shewed we understood each other.

SEÑOR JUAN GUERRERO DUPRAT.

A number of persons honoured us with visits whilst we were at Ambato, for it soon got noised abroad that "the *gringos*" had arrived. Besides the usual individuals with visions of gold mines and dreams of buried treasure, there was a General whose sole impediment to opening up a new route to the Amazons was the immediate want of fifty pounds. As this happened to be the exact sum for which I felt a pressing need, we did not do much business together. Following him came a gentleman who seemed to think that we lacked occupation. Although he spoke English fluently, there was a certain want of sequence in his remarks which made me fancy that he was an escaped lunatic. He kindly put his observations into writing in order that they might be studied at leisure, and I am thus enabled to present some of his suggestions in his own words.[1]

In the course of his explorations, my Chief of the Staff discovered a compatriot, who was engaged in the manufacture

[1] The following is the opening paragraph of the document he sent me. "The Government of the Equator have the desire to erect a piramid in the point of

of Dry Sherry. Jean-Antoine's account of the process was a little deficient in lucidity, but as he made it quite clear that Plaster of Paris largely entered into it, and that the juice of the grape did not come in at all, I took good care to avoid the Dry Sherry of Ambato. Paolo Oberti, the ingenious manufacturer of this beverage, had accompanied Dr. Wagner upon his "ascent" of Chimborazo, and voluntarily made the declaration which is given below.[1]

Ambato contains, I imagine, about 5000 inhabitants, yet for six days in the week it wears the lifeless aspect common to all the towns of the interior. On Mondays troops of people pour in from the surrounding villages, for the most part mounted (as no person who has the least respect for himself goes on foot), the cavaliers accompanied by their dames, riding the same beast, astride,—perched in front of their lords, or else behind, holding on to their waists; while the despised peons trudge barefooted through the dust, driving mules or asses bringing rolls of matting, baskets of cackling fowls, or sacks of maize, potatoes and other farm-produce, for sale at the market in the great Plaza.

intercession of the Equator with the Meridian, and you may aid to fix it. With this purpose it would be well to profit of the works of Bouguer and Lacondamine, and in order that I may be well understood will put in Spanish language, that you may do a good translation into the english, speaking in Quito with the sage Dr. Menthem (a german) the director of astronomical observatory, besides the inscriptions will put in latin language, because theirs authors themselves have put in that tongue."

[1] [Translation.] "On the occasion that Paul Oberti accompanied Dr. Maurice Wagner to make an ascent of Chimborazo, on the occidental side, about the end of 1858 or the beginning of 1859, the Doctor was attacked with intermittent fever, and he likewise met with insurmountable difficulties which prevented him from reaching the top of Chimborazo. He was only able to reach the line of perpetual snow.

"It is to be understood that the said ascent was made on the opposite side of the Arenal. They slept in the sheep-pen nearest to the mountain of Chimborazo, belonging to the farm of Santa Rosa.

PABLO OBERTI.

"Ambato, Jan. 21, 1880."

Some previous writer has justly said that this place seems like an oasis in a desert. The hills in its immediate vicinity are mostly bare, monotonous ridges covered with volcanic dust, which is set in movement by the slightest breath of air. These surface dusts are a heterogeneous assemblage, to some extent derived from the fundamental soil, and partly by drift from other localities, or by fresh depositions from the most recent eruptions of the yet active volcanoes of the Republic. A little way below the surface one comes to a vast deposit of pumice, not in blocks or lumps that would be termed pumice-stone, but in fragments which have been ejected during some terrific convulsion, or period of eruptions. The town of Ambato is built on this deposit.[1] The comparative coarseness of the fragments seems to indicate that the place of eruption was not far distant. The largest ones may measure a quarter of an inch in diameter, and weigh as much as $\frac{1}{3}$ to $\frac{1}{4}$ of a grain. They more commonly weigh about thirty to a grain, and range in size from ·05 to ·1 of an inch in diameter.

Pumice in lumps or masses no doubt exists in large quantities in the interior of Ecuador, though I saw little of it. The largest pieces I found *in situ* were upon the summit ridge of the highest point of Pichincha, and these were scarcely a foot in diameter. Natural blocks of it are sometimes hollowed out and employed as filters, and there was one of these in daily use in the house of Señor Duprat.

In the course of our journey, this pumiceous dust was met with again, overlain by other dusts which had been ejected during

---

[1] It has been examined microscopically by Prof. T. G. Bonney and Miss Catherine A. Raisin, who have favoured me with the following report. "The material is mainly a colourless, vesicular pumice. Much of it is quite clear, but many of the fragments have entangled within them some small microliths, and also plates of a pale greenish mica, which occurs occasionally in small clearly-defined crystals, shewing pseudo-hexagonal form (·02 mm. to ·01 mm. diameter). Some of the mica has a yellowish or brownish colour. Small spheroidal blebs occur within the pumice, brownish and granular, which appear to be a deposit coloured by oxide of iron."

subsequent eruptions. At the town of Machachi, more than fifty miles away, it was found ten feet below the surface, covered by three beds of volcanic ash which amounted in the aggregate to 52 inches in thickness, of an entirely different nature, each having a strongly marked character of its own. The pumice here is in extremely minute fragments. It is rare to find amongst it one as much as $\frac{1}{50}$ of an inch in diameter. The majority are much smaller, and many thousands go to a grain. From the critical examination to which it has been subjected, there is no doubt that the pumice at Machachi was ejected at the same period as that at Ambato; and from having superimposed upon it other vast beds of ash, from eruptions which occurred beyond the range of history, one may conclude that it is amongst the older of the more recent volcanic products of Ecuador. It is the invariable rule with volcanic dusts that the grosser particles settle first; and, as the finest ones are found much to the north of Ambato, it would appear that the dominant winds, at the time the dust was blown into the air, were directed from south to north.

A PUMICE FILTER AT AMBATO.

There were some pleasant walks on the western side of the

town amongst which we sauntered for recreation. One day, Jean-Antoine and I came upon a tame llama, browsing by the side of a lane. It was the first my companion had seen, and he approached the animal to stroke its nose; but alas, when he was within a couple of yards, the gentle creature reared its pretty head and spat in his face. Carrel was greatly affronted, and to soothe his ruffled feelings I proposed a walk in the garden of the Minister for Foreign Affairs, a shady retreat on the right bank of the little river that flows through the town. Presently we saw a Bishop amongst the bushes. His Lordship was dressed in orange and black, and had very hairy legs. We did not, however, at that time know it was a Bishop, or we should have been more discreet. Jean-Antoine unceremoniously clapped him on the back, then gave a great yell, and the Bishop flew away. I conjecture that Ambato has been unfortunate in its episcopal rulers, for nothing can well be more stinging than the charges of this insect.

A "BISHOP" OF AMBATO.

Though Louis began to improve, it was evident that a long time would elapse before we could count upon his assistance, and we others had to consider what we should do with ourselves. Tunguragua was the nearest large mountain to Ambato, and this had been already investigated by Messrs. Reiss and Stübel.[1] Altar and Sangai were too far away. After many con-

[1] Some account of Tunguragua is given in the little pamphlet by Dr. Stübel entitled *Carta del Dr. Alfonso Stübel a S. E. el Presidente de la Republica, sobre sus viajes a las montañas Chimborazo, Altar, y en especial sobre sus ascensiones al Tunguragua y Cotopaxi.* Quito, 1873.

Tunguragua does not keep in a state of continual activity like Cotopaxi and Sangai, though it is by no means an extinct volcano. It broke out into violent

sultations it was determined to shift head-quarters to Machachi where Jean-Antoine and I could find occupation until the disabled man had recovered. On Jan. 24 we marched to Latacunga, and on the 25th to Machachi; as usual, with a train of mules, for no vehicle—not even a bullock-cart—could be obtained at Ambato.[1]

The basin of Ambato, which we traversed on the 24th, is bounded on the south by a spur thrown out from Carihuairazo in the direction of Tunguragua; on the west by low mountains for which I heard no distinctive name; and on the east by an important block, containing lofty summits, that are known under the general appellation of the mountains of Llanganati.[2] On approaching Latacunga the slopes draw in from each side, and form the northern boundary of the basin, and after passing the town they again retire, and circle round what may be termed the basin of Latacunga, which is bounded and enclosed on the north by the Tiupullo ridge. The River Cutuchi drains the basin of Latacunga, and has not a deep bed. After passing the town, until near Baños, this same river is called the Patate, and throughout the greater part of its course flows through a deep and striking ravine, a portion of which is well seen from the village of Yambo. The River Pastassa is formed by the junction of the Patate and the River Chambo, coming from the basin of Riobamba.

The town of Ambato is at the lowest point of the road (8600 feet), which rises gently almost all the way to Latacunga

eruption on Jan. 12, 1886, and, I am informed by Mr. Chambers, did much damage. Ash from this outburst fell at Guayaquil.

[1] At this time an omnibus ran from Ambato to Quito once a week, leaving at mid-day on Tuesdays, and arriving at its destination about 4 p.m. on Wednesdays. The seats had been engaged in advance, and we were thus unable to make use of it. This was the only coach of any sort running in the interior of Ecuador.

[2] The importance of the mountains of Llanganati will not be apprehended by any one passing along the Quito road. Their outlying portions, which are alone seen, do not suggest the rugged and complicated ranges that are in the rear. The complete exploration of this district alone would afford a traveller good occupation for several years.

(9140), a place with perhaps 5000 inhabitants, built on rather flat ground, dangerously near to a stream that is liable to sudden swellings when Cotopaxi is in eruption. We went by advice to the little hotel of Pompeyo Baquero,—the best kept house we entered in Ecuador. Everything was clean, and the place was free from fleas, a fact which was the more welcome because Ambato was densely populated with these wild animals. In the apartments we had just quitted there were more fleas per square yard than I have known anywhere. When rays of sunlight streamed in through the windows, a sort of haze was seen extending about a foot above the floor, caused by myriads of them leaping to and fro.

The favourable impression which was created by the propriety of Baquero's hotel was utterly destroyed by what we saw upon leaving this town. At the door of every house on the sunny side of the street leading to the bridge, the ladies of Latacunga were basking in the warmth. Mothers had their children reposing in their laps, and daughters seemed to be caressing their parents. To the non-observant they would have formed sweet pictures of parental and filial affection. A glance was enough to see that all this assemblage were engaged in eating the vermin which they picked out of each other's hair. According to the old historians, this habit was established in the country before the Spanish conquest. It is practised now by the hybrid Ecuadorian race as much as by the pure Indians. There were more than two dozen groups on one side of this single street engaged in this revolting occupation, which they carried on without shame in the most public manner. Though I shook the dust of this town off my feet, it was impossible to forget the Ladies of Latacunga, for the same disgusting sight was forced upon our attention throughout the whole of the interior.

Upon leaving the town, under the guidance of Mr. Perring, we took the road on the right bank (western side) of the Cutuchi. This part of the Moreno road was erased during the eruptions of Cotopaxi in 1877, and no doubt it will be swept away again, as it is very slightly higher than the ordinary level of the river. Scarcely a person was seen between Latacunga and Callo, for the arrieros (who form almost the whole of the travelling population of the country) prefer the *old* road on the left bank (eastern side), as this is more elevated above the stream, and has contiguous rising ground to which they can escape in case of inundation. The two roads reunite just to the north of Callo,— one of the bladder-like hills, common in Ecuador, that are termed 'panecillos.' Here one commences the ascent of the Tiupullo ridge (a sort of connecting link between Illiniza and Rumiñahui), and rising in serpentine bends reaches the height of 11,559 feet;[1] and then, after passing a gently undulating tract which may almost be compared with the Surrey highlands, descends by somewhat abrupt zigzags into the basin of Machachi. Daylight had gone when we entered upon the longest piece of straight road in Ecuador, and it seemed interminable in the darkness. When we arrived at the village every one had fastened up for the night and gone to bed. Pleadings for admittance were unheeded, so the effect of whip-handles and hob-nailed boots was tried. Presently a husband and wife were heard in consultation. "My dear," said the masculine voice, "it's robbers; *you* had better go to the door." It was opened very reluctantly by a dishevelled female, who found it was "only the *gringos*," and at length the way into the courtyard was unbarred, and admitted us to the tambo kept by Antonio Racines, who became our host for several weeks.

[1] This is the height of the summit of the road. The highest points upon this ridge are three small peaks called Chaupi, which can be seen from long distances. The view from the top of the Tiupullo ridge is one of the most extensive in Ecuador. It embraces Tunguragua and Chimborazo on the south; Illiniza, Cotopaxi, and Rumiñahui close at hand; and extends as far north as Cotocachi (distant seventy-five miles). The city of Quito cannot, however, be seen from it.

ONE OF MY YOUNG FRIENDS.

CHAPTER V.

ON AN ASCENT OF CORAZON, AND WALKS IN THE LANES OF MACHACHI.

CERTAIN circumstances led me to say in the morning, "Señor Racines, now tell me, upon your word of honour as a gentleman, Are there fleas in this house?" There was just a fractional hesitation, and then the tambo-keeper answered with the air of a man who spoke the truth, "Señor, upon my word of honour, *there are.*" The information had been confirmed beforehand. It was decided to have a general clear out, and Jean-Antoine, to his credit, became chief housemaid. The contents of our apartments were taken into the gallery of the courtyard, and were scrubbed, brushed, beaten or shaken, much to the wonder of the natives. The news spread, and soon the *patio* was filled with a troop of sallow urchins, grinning from ear to ear. "These *gringos* are very odd," they said. "See! that is the *Senor patron*. Look!"—pointing to Jean-Antoine—"that is Señor Juan. What a fine beard!"

In these operations Louis could not be of much service, as he needed absolute repose. His time was principally employed in the study of a coarsely-coloured print of the Immaculate Conception, and in watching a little girl in blue, at the general shop on the opposite side of the road, who alternated the sale of rolls with the occupation of the Ladies of Latacunga. When he began to hobble about, and could sit in a chair on our little balcony, life became more interesting to him; for his eye could sweep over the whole of the great basin of Machachi, and trace the Quito road from Tambillo to the Tiupullo ridge, with the passing herds of cattle; or see, right in front, the daily thunder-clouds gather round the cliffs of Rumiñahui and Pasochoa, and, in the vista between the two, the needle-crest of Sincholagua, or, on rare occasions, the noble, snow-clad mass of Antisana.

From our windows on the upper floor of the tambo, all that passed on the road came under our inspection. In the early morning cattle were shifted from one place to another, and sometimes a wild bull went along, in charge of mounted men, lassoed fore and aft; a horseman in the front towing it by the horns, and two others each with a separate fastening in the rear, ready to check its pace if it became too frisky, or to give it a touch with their lances if it needed stimulus.

As day advanced, arrieros with their teams made their appearance, and they constituted the greater part of the passers-by. Though travelling for the sake of viewing their country is a thing unpractised by Ecuadorians, we saw occasionally some one a little out of the common, going perhaps on a visit to a neighbouring farm, and such a person was generally worth examination. When got up correctly, he wears a so-called Panama hat, a straw hat which will roll up and can be put in the pocket, and may cost anything between ten shillings and ten pounds.[1] To take care of this precious article he puts on a white outer casing, but as this would get spoiled by rain he

[1] The lowest price I heard quoted in Quito was nine shillings.

covers it with oilskin, so that he has three hats one on top of the other. To protect his eyes he ought to use a pair of blue goggles. Outside, he displays a poncho of superior quality, and underneath it there are several of a coarser kind.¹ What he may wear in the way of trousers cannot be said, for they are covered up by buskins made from the skin of some wild animal, and his feet are nearly invisible. If seen, one most likely observes that his toes are peeping through his shoes. But for all deficiencies thereabouts he makes up in the heel, by his spurs, which are gigantic. The annexed figure represents what is considered a moderate thing in spurs.² If he is properly fitted out, he carries at the button-hole a carved drinking-cup, and at his side a tremendous sheath-knife, or *macheta*, an article that is supposed to be necessary for clearing away branches. A person of distinction will be strong in his whip, which will have a wrought-iron handle, as it is found that that description does not break so readily on the head of a mule as a wooden one, and he will carry a guitar at his saddle-bow. Such a person, according to the phrase

¹ The ponchos in most general use were coarse woollen ones, measuring 52 × 52 inches. They cost seven or eight shillings apiece, and seemed usually to be made locally. There was a poncho-maker nearly opposite to us at Machachi. In Quito and to the north, cotton ponchos are frequently worn. They are both lighter and cheaper.

² The rowels sometimes measure five inches across.

of the country, is 'a great cavalier,' and if he is decently mounted he may aspire to marry any woman in the land.

In the evening, when traffic ceased, the youth of the *faubourg* turned out for the only pastime they enjoyed, which consisted in whacking a huge ball in the air by clubs fastened around their wrists. The Christian names of the children of this place were of the fanciful kind common in Ecuador. Fidelity might be seen playing with Conception, or Incarnation running after Immortality. They became useful as collectors, and angled for reptiles which they would not dare to touch, and brought them in alive, dangling from cotton nooses at the end of sticks.[1] "What," my young friends timidly enquired of the dusky Indian youth who was nominal waiter and actual slave at the tambo, "does the Señor Doctor do with all these things?" and, when it was heard that they were collected with a view to the future, the rumour was circulated that we lived on lizards and frogs, and were thought more odd than before.

Machachi reposes upon a series of strata of volcanic ash or dust which must have been emitted during eruptions incomparably more severe than any that are recorded. The sections which can be seen by the sides of the lanes shew this very clearly. In one that was exposed in the road nearly opposite to the tambo, leading to the village proper, the surface soil which was under cultivation was about six feet deep, composed of a miscellaneous assemblage of volcanic débris. This was followed by a horizontal stratum of the finest ash, ten inches thick, almost as soft to the touch as cotton-wool. It was perfectly uniform in character throughout; composed of infinitesimal fragments,

---

[1] Nothing would induce Ecuadorians—either whites or Indians—to touch lizards, and they were almost equally afraid to handle frogs.

and may properly be termed an impalpable powder. It is found to be principally made up of felspar and hornblende, with some pumice and a small admixture of mica and magnetic particles.[1] Underneath it comes a dark and comparatively coarse basaltic (?) ash, two feet and a half thick; and this is succeeded by a finer ash of the same nature, one foot deep. In these two strata, three feet and a half thick, pumice occurs only in small quantities. Underneath them, extending how deep I do not know, there is a fine and brilliantly white dust of a totally distinct character from all above it. This mainly consists of pumice, and closely approximates in its constitution to the coarser ash which was found at Ambato (see pp. 94–5).[2] These four beds are

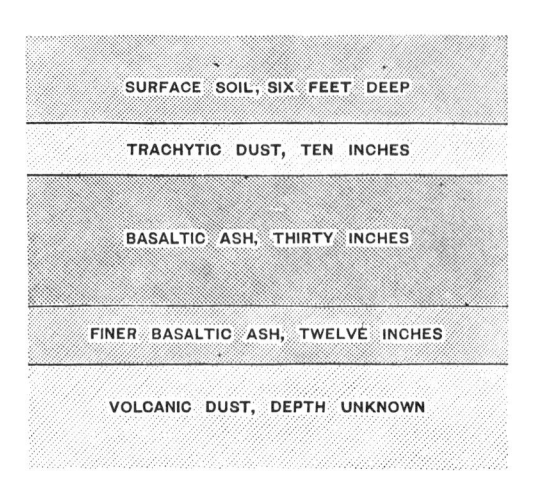

```
SURFACE SOIL, SIX FEET DEEP
TRACHYTIC DUST, TEN INCHES
BASALTIC ASH, THIRTY INCHES
FINER BASALTIC ASH, TWELVE INCHES
VOLCANIC DUST, DEPTH UNKNOWN
```

[1] Prof. T. G. Bonney and Miss Raisin say: "It consists largely of mineral fragments, which are often of broken crystalline form. The coarser vary from ·05 to ·15 mm. in length, the finer may average from ·01 to ·02 mm. Pumice is present, some of it enclosing fairly large crystals. The minerals in the ash are chiefly felspar (some being contained within the pumice) and green pyroxene, so far as could be ascertained, hornblende. A few largish chips of brown mica occur, and some black opaque grains, probably an iron oxide. The finest dust seems to consist chiefly of felspar and of pumice."

[2] Almost the sole point of difference between them is that the Ambato deposit contains a considerable percentage of rocky fragments. This is better seen in bulk than in microscopic samples.

"The lowest stratum at Machachi consists mainly of clear, colourless vesicular pumice, which includes greenish mica, some in minute hexagonal plates. This ash is very like that from Ambato" (described on p. 94), "but is rather clearer, having fewer of the microlithic aggregations, and it contains more numerous grains of a clear felspar, mostly in angular chips. Brown or greenish spheroids occur, which are probably similar to those of Ambato; they are very regular in form, sometimes shewing rounded holes or granular structure, and they rather mimic the appearance of casts of organisms."—Prof. T. G. Bonney and Miss C. A. Raisin.

divided from one another almost as sharply as in the section upon p. 104, and each evidently belongs either to a single eruption, or period of eruptions.

Machachi is situated[1] towards the bottom of a basin measuring about twenty-one miles from north to south and eleven from east to west, which is bounded on the north by the Tambillo ridge (a modest eminence connecting the lower slopes of Atacatzo with the Puengasi ridge), on the south by the Tiupullo ridge, on the east by Rumiñahui and Pasochoa, and on the west by the north-eastern slopes of Illiniza, Corazon, and the south-eastern slopes of Atacatzo. The elevation of this area is greater than the basins of Latacunga or Riobamba, and with the exception of its north-east corner it is everywhere more than 10,000 feet above the sea. The drainage of the basin is collected into a small stream called the Rio Grande,[2] which passes to the east of the Puengasi ridge, and ultimately falls into the Pacific at Esmeraldas. The high road to Quito[3] runs very directly across the bottom of this basin, falling slightly the whole way from south to north, as far as the little cluster of houses called Tambillo, where the ascent of the ridge of the same name commences; and, when this is passed, the basin of Quito is entered, and the road again falls continuously towards the capital.

Illiniza, Corazon, Atacatzo, Pasochoa, and Rumiñahui stand

[1] The tambo and a long line of straggling houses are upon the high road, but the town (or village) proper of Machachi is about three-quarters of a mile to the east. The entire population amounts perhaps to 2500 persons.

[2] Where we crossed it on our way to Pedregal it was not more than two feet deep and fifty across. It was frequently remarked that the volume of water in the streams was exceedingly small, considering the areas drained by them. This is no doubt due to the soil being greatly fissured. In December, I walked across the Chimbo at Guaranda from stone to stone without wetting my feet. The bridge seemed dangerously low, but I was informed by the authorities that it was never in risk of being carried away, although the rainfall there, as well as in the interior generally, was considerable.

[3] In Jan., Feb., and June I measured 22,385 feet where it runs across the plain. The measurement extended from the most northern house of Machachi to the fine bridge of Jambeli, the largest structure of its kind I saw in Ecuador.

around the rim of the basin of Machachi. The imposing figures which are given upon my map as their elevations above the level of the sea may lead some to suppose that this mountain panorama must be exceptionally fine. From more than one reason this is not the case. It should be understood that in the heart of the Ecuadorian Andes there are no such rugged *chains* as are considered Alpine.[1] The character of much of the interior is hilly rather than mountainous. There are long stretches of barren soil, for which the term moorland is the nearest English equivalent; and large, flat or slightly undulating areas which may not improperly be called plains.[2] The elevation of this land is about 9000 feet above the sea, and out of (or from and above) it the mountains rise which have a world-wide reputation; and in considering them it is necessary, in order to form a just conception of their absolute magnitude, and of their relative importance as compared with well-known peaks in the Alps and elsewhere, to apply a constant deduction of 8-9000 feet to the heights which they are stated to rise above the sea-level. This is not all. The lower slopes of most of the mountains of the interior are unusually long, and rise at very moderate inclinations,[3] and the amount of precipitous ground is less in proportion to the total height than is commonly the case elsewhere. By reason of this, it is possible to take beasts of burden to the great heights that are mentioned throughout this volume. From my mountaineer's point of view some of these peaks 13,000 feet and upwards in elevation were contemptible, for to all appearance, by exercising a little ingenuity, one could ride to their summits on the back of a mule or donkey.[4]

[1] The only exception to this general statement may perhaps be found in the mountains of Llanganati.

[2] Such as the plains of Riobamba, Machachi, and Tumbaco.

[3] This applies only to the *interior*. The western (or outer) slopes of the Pacific Range of Ecuador would be accounted steep by any one.

[4] This was the case with Pasochoa (13,961) and Atacatzo (14,892). We actually took a donkey above 14,000 feet on Pichincha.

Illiniza was obviously the loftiest of the several mountains which have been enumerated, and I sent Jean-Antoine on Jan. 29–30 to reconnoitre it; but as he reported that it was nearly inaccessible from the north we turned our attentions to Corazon, at first ludicrously under-estimating its distance. We went out late one day, expecting to reach the top and come back again, and did not even get to the foot of the actual peak. This, however, was a red-letter day—we saw a dead donkey, under a hedge about 1500 feet above Machachi; and a few hundred feet higher met a scorpion who was coming downhill.[1]

Corazon was ascended a century and a half ago by La Condamine and Bouguer. The former says expressly (at p. 58 of vol. 1 of his *Journal du Voyage*) that they made the expedition upon July 20, 1738.[2] In the prosecution of their work, they encamped twenty-eight days somewhere upon the mountain (doubtless upon its eastern side), but there are no precise indications of the route which was taken by them, nor could any information be obtained at Machachi, though a certain Ecuadorian

---

[1] It has been identified as *Brotheas subnitens*, Gervais, by Prof. E. Ray Lankester.

Scorpions were very seldom seen in the open, though they were abundant at Machachi, and could be found almost everywhere by turning over stones. At Quito, too, they were numerous in old walls. But, throughout the entire journey, at all our upper camps we did not discover a single one, and they could hardly have been overlooked, as the ground was always levelled for the establishment of the tents. It is probable, therefore, that 12,000 feet is about the upper limit of the range of the scorpion in Ecuador.

[2] "Un vent froid et piquant nous couvrit en peu de temps de verglas : il nous fallut en plusieurs endroits gravir contre le rocher, en nous aidant des pieds et des mains : enfin nous atteignîmes le sommet. . . . Ce sommet étoit élevé de 250 toises au dessus de notre signal, et surpassoit de 40 le *Pic de Pitchincha*, où nous avions campé l'année précédente ; aussi le mercure étoit-il plus bas d'environ deux lignes au *Coraçon* : il s'y soûtenoit à 15 pouces 10 lignes. Personne n'a vû le baromètre si bas dans l'air libre ; et vraisemblablement personne n'a monté à une plus grande hauteur : nous étions 2470 toises au dessus du niveau de la mer."

In *Histoire de l'Academie Royale des Sciences* (année 1746), Paris, 1751, in a list of the highest mountains of 'the Province of Quito,' this mountain is entered "El Coraçon, la plus grande hauteur où l'on ait monté."

named Lorenzo vowed that he had been to the top. This man was engaged to act as our guide.[1]

The mountain Corazon has received its name from a resemblance it is supposed to have to a heart. It is a prominent object from Machachi, placed almost exactly midway between Atacatzo and Illiniza. Its slopes extend to the outlying village of Aloasi,

MACHACHI AND CORAZON.

and after rising gently and then abruptly lead one to easy grass land, which continues uninterruptedly to the foot of a cliff about 800 feet high, that is found at the top of the mountain. With trouble, one might ride, upon the eastern side, to within a thousand feet of the summit. On some days the mountain was almost covered with snow down to 14,500 feet, and on others no snow whatever was seen on any part of it.

[1] Local guidance is useful over the lower slopes, as they contain large earthquake fissures (*quebradas*) which are occasionally quite impassable.

Lorenzo led us to a place a long way to the south of the summit, and then evidently came to the end of his knowledge. On his 'ascent' he had gone as far as one can go with the hands in the pockets, and had stopped when it was necessary to take them out.[1] We continued in the same direction to see what the western side was like, and presently put on the rope. Our guide was the first to be tied up, and, though he said little, his face expressed a good deal. Possibly he supposed that he had been inveigled to this lonely spot to be sacrificed on the cairn of stones put together by Jean-Antoine, which bore a suspicious resemblance to an altar.

The western side of the highest part of Corazon, like the eastern side, is formed of a great cliff. Snow gullies run up into it, and one of these, towards the south end of the ridge, seemed to promise easy access to the summit. We had only progressed a few yards on this *couloir* when the clatter and buzz of falling stones was heard, which flew down at a tremendous pace, quite invisible as they passed by. We retired under cover of some rocks to read the barometer,[2] and then returned to the south end of the peak, skirted the base of the eastern cliff, worked round to the north side, and ascended by the ridge that descends towards Atacatzo.[3]

[1] This man, however, was a good fellow; cheerful and willing, and an excellent pedestrian.

[2] The original unreduced reading at 8.45 a.m. was 17·383 inches, temp. 37° Faht.

[3] Lorenzo remained below, trying to dry his trousers. We started from Machachi at midnight on Feb. 1, reached the summit at noon on Feb. 2, left it at 3.10 p.m., and, rejoining our guide, continued towards Machachi until we struck the route taken on Jan. 27; and then, as it was getting dusk and the ground was not familiar to our man, thought it better to bear away to the south, and return by the route which was taken in the morning. We got back to Machachi at 7.45 p.m.

The route on this day was unnecessarily circuitous, and is not given on the map. The ascent of Corazon can be made most easily by taking the line we followed on Jan. 27, as far as we went, and completing it in the same way as upon Feb. 2. The track on the map combines portions of the routes of these two days.

The upper part of Corazon is a great wall, roughly flat on the top, which is, I believe, a dyke — a mass of lava that has welled up through a fissure. At its highest, it is nearly level over a length of 250 feet, and is only a few yards across from east to west.[1] At 1.15 p.m., on the highest point, the mercurial barometer read 16·974 inches, at a temperature of 43° Faht. The height deduced (15,871 feet) is slightly greater than that assigned to the mountain by La Condamine (2470 toises), and by Reiss and Stübel (4816 mètres). The extreme difference between the three measurements amounts to seventy-five feet.

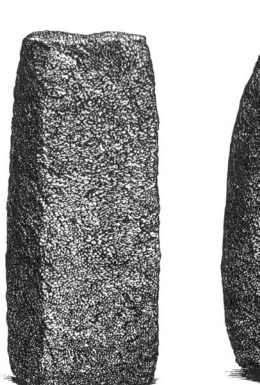

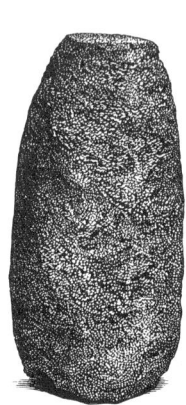

DRESSED ROCKS FOUND ON CORAZON.

There was on the summit an indication of a previous ascent in two dressed fragments of rock, about nine inches long, which caught the eye directly we arrived. They were a black, scoriaceous lava, similar to the highest rock obtained on Chimborazo, and subsequently on various parts of the cone of Cotopaxi. I saw no natural fragments of it on Corazon, and therefore conclude that these dressed pieces must have been transported some distance by the

---

[1] Though the summit was free from snow, and there was none on the eastern side, there was much in gullies on the western side, and we fancied there might be considerable beds or even a glacier below. Viewed from the west this mountain would be considered to be within the snow-line.

The theodolite was brought up, in the hope that angles might be obtained. We were surrounded by mists nearly the whole time — sometimes not being able to see the length of the summit ridge. For a few seconds there was an opening which gave a superb view of Cotopaxi, whitened by new snow, rising above the dark cliffs of Ruminahui, and behind it the mountains that lie to the east of the basin of Ambato. This was the only glimpse I had of the mountains of Llanganati, and from this casual glance I think an explorer of that region will find plenty of occupation, for the mountains are close and steep, and the region seems complicated. There was much snow upon the highest points.

person or persons who deposited them on the spot where they were found.[1]

The rock of the summit is described by Prof. Bonney as an augite-andesite,[2] and closely resembles examples from several of the mountains which will be referred to in later chapters. Its natural colour is a slaty-grey, but this is only apparent in newly-broken, unweathered fragments. Surfaces which are exposed to the atmosphere become a dull red (approximating to indian red), and this colouring doubtless arises from the rusting of the iron that is present in these lavas.[3]

The summit ridge was by no means exclusively rocky. The scoriaceous surfaces, by decay, had been converted into soil, and in the earth so formed there was quite a little flora. I collected five lichens and as many mosses, three Drabas, a Lycopodium, a Werneria, and an Arenaria. These were growing upon the very apex of the mountain, and from their abundance and vigorous condition it was clear that most if not all of the species might have attained a considerably greater elevation if there had been higher ground in the vicinity.[4]

From amongst this vegetation, I disinterred an earthworm,

---

[1] On return to Machachi, no one could throw light on the matter. The objects appeared to have been on the summit for years; yet (though they were not freshly dressed) they did not appear to be a century and a half old. One can hardly suppose that La Condamine and Bouguer indulged in this frivolity. To have trimmed these specimens with such regularity would have occupied a considerable length of time. They weigh eight pounds.

[2] *Proc. Royal Soc.*, June 19, 1884, and *Supp. App.*, p. 142.

[3] The volcanic dusts referred to on pp. 125, 141 are only this rock in a finely-divided state. If some of it is placed upon a sheet of paper and a magnet is moved about underneath, it will appear to dance. The particles of iron can be drawn off and separated from the rocky ones by means of the magnet.

[4] *Alectoria divergens*, Ach., *Gyrophora* sp., *Neuropogon melaxanthus*, Nyl., *Parmelia* sp., *Stereocaulon* sp.; *Andreæa striata*, Mitt., *Bartramia aristata*, Mitt., *B. Potosica*, Mont., *Cryptodium lutescens*, Jaeg., *Orthotrichum* sp.; *Lycopodium Saururus*, L.; *Draba imbricata*, C. A. Mey., *D. obovata*, Benth., and *another (not determined); *Arenaria dicranoides*, H.B.K. Those marked with an asterisk were abundant.

a beetle, a bug, and some spiders. Several species of flies were seen on the ridge, but I only succeeded in capturing one. The earthworm was about an inch long, and in an immature condition. Prof. W. B. Benham has referred it to the genus *Rhinodrilus* of Perrier, and thinks it is probably the same species that was subsequently found upon Cayambe, which he names *R. Ecuadoriensis*.[1] Few earthworms were seen at great elevations in Ecuador, and the summit of Corazon was much the highest point at which one was obtained. The beetle is found by Mr. Bates to belong to the genus *Colpodes*, and is described by him at p. 20 of the *Supplementary Appendix* (*C. diopsis*). It was also taken on Pichincha.

The scantiness of the collection on the summit of Corazon is to be attributed to the hailstorms which occurred while we were there. Rain, sleet, hail, or snow often impeded or completely put a stop to this description of work. When the atmospheric conditions were favourable something was always obtained, wherever we went; and at the greatest heights I laid hands upon everything that was seen, either animal or vegetable, anticipating that the zoological side, at least, would yield much new to science.[2] Whether this should or should not prove to be the case, the occasions afforded opportunities of contributing to the knowledge of the range of species in altitude. The results, so far as they have been worked out, are presented in the *Supplementary Appendix*, and in the Tables in Chapter XIX. the representatives of the various Orders are enumerated which were obtained at the most considerable elevations.

By the expression *range in altitude* I mean the difference in level of the highest and lowest points at which any particular

[1] See Chapter XII. This is the fourth species that has been found of the genus *Rhinodrilus*. The three others came from Venezuela, Surinam, and Demerara.

[2] The Botany of the interior of Ecuador had been investigated by the late Prof. William Jameson, who resided many years at Quito, and made excursions in its neighbourhood. For some time he held two appointments in the capital. Being a Professor of Botany, he was made, very appropriately, Master of the Mint.

species may be found.[1] If one should be obtained or observed at the level of the sea and also at 10,000 feet above it, its observed range in altitude would be 10,000 feet. Most things, either animal or vegetable, have a much more limited range than this, yet there are some which attain or even exceed it.

Insects in the Great Andes of the Equator range higher than birds. At the greatest heights they were found less upon the surface than *in* the soil, sometimes living amongst stones imbedded in ice, in such situations and numbers as to preclude the idea that they were stragglers. Small in size, and unattractive in appearance, they have hitherto been entirely overlooked. Though some species were obtained at a greater elevation above the sea than I observed the Condor, their range in altitude appears to be small. They were found at these high situations and nowhere else, though the same species sometimes recurred at *similar* elevations upon widely-separated mountains.

Few persons have concerned themselves, in any part of the world, with entomology at great altitudes. Such remarks as have been made upon it have generally had reference to the stray individuals that are termed stragglers, which, generally being wind-borne, and found upon the surface, are those which most readily catch the eye. Thus Humboldt (who ignores[2] what may be termed the residential population) says, in *Aspects of Nature*, vol. 2, pp. 33–4 :—

"Even butterflies are found at sea at great distances from the coast, being carried there by the force of the wind when storms come off the land. *In the same involuntary manner insects are transported into the upper regions of the atmosphere, 16,000 or 19,000 feet above the plains.* The heated crust of the earth occasions an ascending vertical current of air, by which

---

[1] Some persons may attach the same meaning to the expression *vertical range*. I venture to think that term is not felicitous. Comparatively few things can be said to have any vertical range, and many have none.

[2] The *Zoology* of Humboldt and Bonpland's *Voyage* contains only about a dozen species of insects for which localities in Ecuador are mentioned, and not one of these appears to have come from a greater elevation than ten thousand feet.

light bodies are borne upwards. . . . When Bonpland, Carlos Montufar and myself reached, on the 23rd of June, 1802, on the eastern declivity of the Chimborazo the height of 19,286 English feet, we saw winged insects fluttering around us. We could see that they were Dipteras, but . . . it was impossible to catch the insects. . . . The insects were flying at a height of about 18,225 feet. . . . Somewhat lower down, at about 2600 toises (16,680 feet), also therefore within the line of perpetual snow, Bonpland had seen yellow butterflies flying very near the ground."

The aim and intention of this passage is to shew that insects are transported involuntarily to great altitudes, and this unquestionably often occurs. Most persons who have travelled in mountainous regions have found, at one or another time, in very elevated situations (sometimes on snow or glacier), insects which, from their known habits and habitats, cannot have domiciled themselves on the spot;[1] and their actual transportation in quantities, in ascending currents of air, has occasionally been witnessed. But it would be erroneous to assume that insect-life in the neighbourhood of the snow-line in Equatorial America is *limited* to stragglers, or that they form a considerable percentage of it. The upper zones of the Great Andes have a residential population,[2] and I shall endeavour to shew, at a later point, that the 'yellow butterfly,' which Humboldt uses to give point to his remarks, probably comes within the category of 'permanent residents'; and, if it does, it is not a happy example of a wind-borne straggler.

At first, the dimensions of the great basin of Machachi were underrated or unappreciated. Objects which were supposed to be a mile distant sometimes proved to be two or three miles away. Woods looked like clumps of bushes, and impassable ravines appeared mere ditches. When we became better acquainted with it, the bare, almost naked-looking plain was found to

[1] Examples are given in Chapters VI., XIII., and XV.

[2] In the *Supp. App.* there will be found 98 species of insects which were taken at 10,000 feet and upwards. Of these, 15 are known, 71 are new to science, and 12 are not identified.

contain unsuspected dells and nooks decorated with ferns,[1] and hidden lanes, wandering in concealed *quebradas,* gay with Salvias, Fuchsias, and Verbenas,[2] giving shelter to a countless population, varied in habits, different in natures, whose range was determined by light and shade, heat and cold, moisture and vegetation—many timid and shrinking from observation, seldom straying far from the spots that were home or habitation, where they must be sought to be found.

Pumas and deer ranged over the high, rugged ground; foxes, weasels, and opossums dwelt on the lower slopes; and down in the basin there was a Zoologist's paradise. Butterflies above, below, and around;[3] now here, now there, by many turns and twists displaying the brilliant tesselation of their under-sides. Some congregated in clusters on the banks of streams or in muddy places, while others sailed in companies over the open plain. Mayflies and Dragonflies danced in the sunlight; lizards[4] darted across the paths; and legions of spiders

[1] *Asplenium Trichomanes,* L.; *Cystopteris fragilis,* Bernh.; *Polypodium athyrioides,* Hook. (abundant); *P. angustifolium,* Sw.; *P. lucidum,* Bory; *P. murorum,* Hook.; and *P. plebejum,* Schlecht.

[2] The following were some of the more common plants in the hedges and ditches:—*Lepidium Humboldtii,* DC.; *Cassia tomentosa,* L.; *Rubus sp.;* *Fuchsia petiolaris,* Kth.; *Chuquiragua lancifolia,* H.B.K.; *Dalea Mutisii,* H.B.K.; *Solanum ochrophyllum,* Van Heurck?; *Alonsoa caulialata,* R. & P.; *Salvia vermicifolia,* H.B.K.; *Stachys elliptica,* H.B.K.; *Verbena prostrata,* Br.; *Bomarea Caldasiana,* Herb.; and *Cyperus melanostachyus,* H. & K. A very queer flowering-plant, resembling a mushroom, was also abundant at Machachi. It has been described in the *Journal of Botany,* June 1890, by Mr. E. G. Baker, who says, "in its floral characters it resembles *Helosis,* and in its rhizome *Corynœa;* it is therefore interesting as forming a connecting link between these two genera. This will make the third species of *Helosis,* the others being *H. Guyanensis,* Rich., and *H. Mexicana,* Lieb."

[3] We obtained a *Steroma;* three species of *Pedaliodes;* *Lymanopoda lœna,* Hew.; *L. tener,* Hew.; *Agraulis glycera,* Feld.; *Pyrameis huntera* (Fabr.); *P. carye* (Hübn.); *Junonia vellida* (Fabr.); *Lycœna koa,* Druce; *L. Andicola,* n.sp.; **Pieris xanthodice,* Lucas; *P. suadella,* Feld.; *Colias lesbia* (Fabr.); ** C. dimera,* Doubl. & Hew.; *Papilio Americus,* Kollar; *Pamphila phylœus* (Drury); and an *Ancyloxypha.* Those marked with an asterisk were very numerous.

[4] *Liocephalus trachycephalus* (A. Dum.).

pervaded the grass, many very beautiful — frosted-silver backs, or curious, like the saltigrades, who took a few steps and then gave a leap. There were crickets in infinite numbers; and flies innumerable, from slim daddy-long-legs to ponderous, black, hairy fellows known to science as *Dejeaniæ;* hymenopterous insects in profusion, including our old friend the Bishop of Ambato, in company with another formidable stinger, with chrome antennæ, called by the natives 'the Devil'; and occasional *Phasmas* (caballo de palo) crawling painfully about, like animated twigs.[1]

In the early morning it was generally fine, though seldom clear. The weather always degenerated as day advanced, and at noon the sun was scarcely ever seen. Soon afterwards gathering clouds proclaimed a coming storm. When the thunder-echoes ceased to roll between Corazon and Rumiñahui, Jean-Antoine and I used to turn out for our walks in the lanes of Machachi. The short equatorial day was nearly over. The hum of the bee and the chirping of the cricket had ceased, and the toilers in the fields had already retired. We met no one, and there were no sounds (except perhaps the distant notes of a reed-pipe played by some Indian lad wending his way homewards) until the frogs[2] began their music; and when this presently died away,

---

[1] The following Beetles, first obtained at Machachi, are described in the *Supp. App.*, pp. 8–65:—*Anisotarsus Bradytoïdes, Pelmatellus variipes, P. oxynodes, Pterostichus liodes, Colpodes alticola, Uroxys latesulcatus, Clavipalpus Whymperi, Barotheus Andinus,* **Baryxenus æquatorius,* and *Eurysthea angusticollis,* by Mr. H. W. Bates; *Philonthus Whymperi,* **P. divisus, Meloe sexguttatus,* and *Ananca debilis,* by Dr. D. Sharp; *Astylus bis-sexguttatus* (the most widely distributed beetle in the interior of Ecuador, found almost everywhere between 9000 and 13,500 feet) by the Rev. H. S. Gorham; and **Naupactus segnipes* by Mr. A. S. Olliff. Those marked by an asterisk were only found at Machachi. The rest were subsequently obtained elsewhere, at similar, or at slightly higher and lower elevations.

[2] *Phryniscus lævis,* Gthr.; *Hylodes unistrigatus,* Gthr.; and *Nototrema marsupiatum* (Dum. & Bibr.). The *Hylodes* (so-called 'tree-frogs') were taken on the ground.

an almost perfect stillness reigned — the air was scarcely disturbed by the noiseless flight of the gigantic moths, and the gentle twittering of the little birds making snug for their long night.

Our rooms became a museum, and sometimes almost a menagerie. Aided by a troop of willing helpers, never a day passed without acquiring things that had not been seen before;[1] for

> "The Almighty Maker has throughout
> Discriminated each from each, by strokes
> And touches of his hand, with so much art
> Diversified, that two were never found
> Twins at all points."

In these pursuits I was much assisted by the tambo-keeper, who interested himself in furthering our work. He introduced me to *Cyclopium cyclopum*, the only fish in the interior—a highbred fish, with a string of names that a Duke might envy;[2] and was the means of procuring the first *Amphipod* collected in Ecuador. "Señor Antonio," I said to him one day, "Mr. James Orton, M.A., Professor of Natural History in Vassar College, New York, observes[3] that the only crustacean found in the interior 'is a small cray-fish abounding in the filthy, stagnant waters about Quito.' Now couldn't you raise a crab or a shrimp, or something of that kind, for it is very sad to think that there are no crustaceans in Ecuador." The good man did not know whether I was speaking in jest or in earnest, so I set to work with my pencil to enlighten him, and invented forms which it

---

[1] One afternoon we made an excursion to a *panecillo* on Corazon, and beat the bushes into an old umbrella. So far as they are determined, everything obtained was new. The following species are included in the *Supplementary Appendix*. Coleoptera : — *Cercometes Andicola*, Olliff (p. 58); *Pandeletius argentatus*, Olliff (p. 62); *Aphthona Ecuadoriensis*, Jacoby (p. 85); and *Dibolia viridis*, Jacoby (p. 86). Rhynchota : — *Margus tibialis*, *Harmostes Corazonus*, *H. montivagus*, *Dionyza variegata*, and *Lygus excelsus* (pp. 113-4). Most of these species were obtained only at this locality.

[2] See *Supp. App.*, pp. 137-9.   [3] In *The American Naturalist*, 1872, p. 650.

would be difficult to assign to any existing genera. Antonio Racines still looked perplexed, as well he might; but at last his face brightened, and he held up a forefinger, and beckoned. "Come with me." He led me to a little ditch about half a mile outside the village, with stagnant water, and amongst the weeds I got my first crustacean, which has been identified by the Rev. T. R. R. Stebbing as *Hyalella inermis*, S. I. Smith.[1]

Thus the time passed quickly and pleasantly. Still, it must not be supposed that our lives were always as sweet as rose-water, for trouble sometimes arose through the want of that convenient, universal language which it is expected will prevail when the lion lies down with the lamb. Ecuadorians have their habits and customs, many of which we did not understand — nor did they understand ours. At Machachi it was customary for the natives to keep mongrel curs as guardians of their property; and these brutes, though somewhat respectful to cavaliers, looked upon a pedestrian as, presumably, a person of bad character, and did not understand that a man may wish to pluck a flower without desiring to steal a poncho.

The first time I took a solitary walk in the lanes of Machachi it was dark before I rejoined the main road; and upon entering the suburb that stretches a mile to the south of the tambo several of these curs rushed out and made for me. Others joined them, until at last there were about a dozen, from the size of a fox-hound downwards, snarling and snapping and making dashes at my shins and calves in a most uncivilized manner, and they got to the length of fastening on my clothes like hungry wolves. Upon remonstrating the next day with some of their owners at this rude treatment I was assured that it was quite a mistake to call the dogs savage — they were very good dogs, indeed (and this was said by way of commendation), their virtues were so well known that when any person in the neighbourhood was in want of a dog he would come to Machachi *to steal one*.

---

[1] A figure is given in Chapter XIX. See also *Supp. App.*, pp. 125-7.

For the future I went about armed with a bludgeon, as these guardians seemed quite capable of eating one up. If this had occurred, and their masters had been brought before a Jefo-politico, the defence would have been substantially the same as that which was made by a gentleman, living in a Midland county, whose two Pyrenean mastiffs, on meeting a curate riding on horseback, hunted him and pulled him down. Their owner assured the Bench that they were the gentlest creatures alive, but they were unaccustomed to see curates riding on horseback, and thought it was improper. The Machachi men would have said, "It is certainly to be deplored that there is nothing left of the Doctor except the buckles of his braces, but this is not the fault of the dogs, who are the best dogs in the World. The fact is, the Señor *would* go on foot, he would not ride on horseback, and the dogs did not understand it"; and there is no doubt that the defence would have been considered a good one.

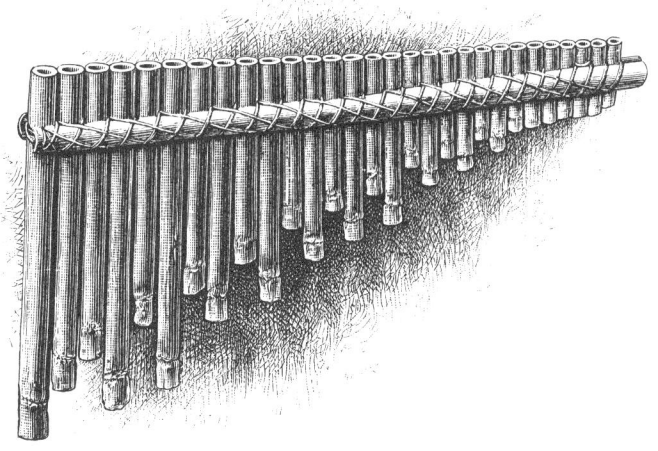

INDIAN REED-PIPES.

SNOW-CORNICES.

CHAPTER VI.

ON COTOPAXI AND ILLINIZA.

When I was detained, a very unwilling guest, in the inn at Chuquipoquio, kept by the possible Marquis, a project entered my head from the execution of which I promised myself some compensation for being obliged to quit Chimborazo prematurely. My vexation had been keen at being compelled to retreat from that mountain after so much labour had been expended in establishing our lofty camps; and although this was lessened when I learned the real cause of the defection of my assistants, and anger gave place to pity for the unfortunate sufferer, it did not alter the fact that we left before our work was finished, and that it was interrupted at an interesting point.

We had learned on Chimborazo that mountain-sickness was a reality. Although the more acute symptoms had disappeared, whilst remaining at low pressures, it was not certain that they would not reappear; still less that they would not recur if we remained continuously at a yet lower pressure than we had experienced at the third camp, namely, about 16 inches. To settle this matter, so far as it could be done in Ecuador, I had intended to ascend Chimborazo again, perhaps several times, and had even projected a residence on the snow plateau at its summit. This now could not be done. The stores and baggage which had cost so much time and trouble to take up had all been brought down again, the camps were broken up, and the information which was desired could only be obtained by beginning afresh in some other quarter.

All the other Great Andes of the Equator were believed to be lower than Chimborazo, and consequently we were not likely to add materially to what we had already learned concerning the effects of diminished atmospheric pressure by simple ascents and descents of them. Moreover, two of the loftiest — Antisana and Cayambe — were as yet unclimbed, and, even should we get up them, it was probable that we should be unable to remain on their summits. So my thoughts naturally turned to the great volcano Cotopaxi. It was reported that there was a large slope of ash at the apex of its terminal cone, and I proposed to encamp upon it, close to the top of the mountain. If this could be done, and if we should find that we could remain at this height (19,500 feet) for a length of time without suffering inconvenience from the low reigning pressure, it would substantially advance our information, and would give good grounds for hope that one might carry exploration elsewhere as high as 24,000 or 25,000 feet above the level of the sea; though it would still leave in uncertainty the possibility of attaining the very highest summits in the world. It is idle to suppose that men will ever reach the loftiest points on the globe, unless they are able to camp out at considerably greater elevations than twenty thousand feet.

The chance of having a nocturnal view of the interior of the crater, though a secondary, was a powerful attraction. Those who had hitherto ascended Cotopaxi had remained a very short time on the top, and had only obtained fragmentary views of the crater, and had given rather divergent accounts of it. Opportunities do not often occur of looking by night into the bowels of a first-rate, active volcano, and the idea of camping upon the apex of the cone grew upon me, the more I thought about it. By doing so, I proposed to kill two birds with one stone. The project could not be executed without the active co-operation of both the Carrels, and it was useless to mention it so long as the frost-bitten feet of Louis remained unhealed.

I therefore kept the scheme to myself until the times appeared favourable; and when Louis began to mend, and there was a prospect of his being able to get to work again, I broached the matter diplomatically and circuitously; and, concealing my principal motive, harped upon the secondary ones; spoke of the famous eruptions of Cotopaxi, referred to the discrepancies in the determinations of its height, to the uncertainty of the nature of its crater, the delights of being warm in camp, and the opportunity of having a peep into the subterranean world, and contrasted the dicta of various eminent authorities to shew how little volcanic knowledge had advanced, and spoke long without effect. At last, my Chief of the Staff said one day, in his own peculiar idiom, "You have raised within me a great desire to look into this animal," and I knew then that the matter was as good as settled, for the younger man seldom opposed the wishes of his imperious cousin.

When the gashes in the frost-bitten feet of Louis began to heal, and he could hobble about, preparations for our adventure were set agoing. To lessen risks, I divided the instruments; we studied economical methods of cooking; added to our wraps, and rehearsed generally; and then we recrossed the Tiupullo ridge [1] to the farm of Rosario, to get a profile view of the mount-

---

[1] Stopped for a time at the tambo of S. Aña, and inquired of the man who kept it if he had ever known stones thrown out by Cotopaxi as far as his place,

ain. At daybreak on the morning following our arrival (Feb. 8), the imposing mass of Cotopaxi became visible. The atmosphere of smoke and haze which is always hanging about it subdued its details without concealing its general contour, and produced an effect of stupendous size and enormous height. A large quantity of steam issuing from the crater was first of all borne towards us, then, as shewn in the engraving, was drifted to the south-west, and finally was carried northwards.

The farm of Rosario is nearly due west of Cotopaxi, distant about eighteen and a half miles, and its position is sufficiently elevated (10,356 feet) to enable one to judge the proportions of the mountain. I found that the general angles of the northern and southern slopes of the cone were rather *less* than 30°, and a week later, when due north of it, I observed that the eastern and western sides, though somewhat steeper, scarcely exceeded 32°.[1] These moderate angles confirmed the impression that this ascent could be made with facility, and that such troubles as might arise would be more due to too much wind, or to *want* of wind, and to the labour incident upon carrying a quantity of material to a great elevation, than to the nature of the ground which we should traverse.

Cotopaxi is an ideal volcano. It comports itself, volcanically speaking, in a regular and well-behaved manner. It is not one of the provoking sort — exploding in paroxysms and going to sleep directly afterwards. It is in a state of perpetual activity, and has been so ever since it has had a place in history. There are loftier mountains which have been volcanoes, and there are active volcanoes with larger craters, yielding greater quantities of lava, but the summit of Cotopaxi, so far as is

and he said he had. Asked as to the size of the largest, he picked up one about three inches in diameter.

[1] They have been stated by others to be 40° and upwards. In the view of Cotopaxi given in Humboldt's *Vues dans les Cordillères*, its northern and southern slopes are represented rising at an angle of 50°. This very misleading view has been copied into many other works.

known, has the greatest absolute elevation above the level of the sea of all volcanoes that are in working order.

It is situated about forty-three geographical miles south of the Equator and thirty geographical miles south-east of Quito. In the accompanying view from the farm of Rosario the summit of the mountain has an elevation of 9300 feet above the spectator, and between the edge of the plain in the middle distance and the foot of the cone there is a depression, occupied by the bed of the River Cutuchi. This river takes its rise at the western foot of Cotopaxi. The head waters of the Cutuchi are divided from the streams flowing to the north by a plain called Limpiopongo, the highest point of which is behind, and a little to the left, of the domed hill (Callo) shewn in the engraving. All the streams that descend from the northern side of Cotopaxi go to form the River Pita, which, after getting clear of the mountain Sincholagua, enters the basin of Chillo, and ultimately falls into the River Esmeraldas, and so into the Pacific Ocean. The streams which rise on the eastern side of Cotopaxi flow through unexplored country, but there is good reason for supposing that they fall into the River Napo. It is of little consequence what may happen in that direction. The Cutuchi and Pita, however, and the rivers into which they fall, traverse the heart of Ecuador, and all places that they pass are more or less unsafe, according to their levels, and their positions in relation to the rivers. Some of the more proximate places to Cotopaxi are in no hazard from its eruptions, whilst others, at much greater distances, are in constant danger from them. Thus, while the village of Machachi is secure, the town of Latacunga is in imminent peril. The nearest house to the crater—the tambo of S. Aña—is safe, though many buildings in the basin of Chillo[1] were erased by the floods which poured down at the last great eruption. This took place on June 26, 1877; and, as

---

[1] The basin of Chillo lies to the north of the mountain Sincholagua. The village is not marked on my map, as I was unable to fix its position.

COTOPAXI (19,613 FEET), FROM THE HACIENDA OF S. ROSARIO (10,356 FEET).

it is the best recorded one that has occurred, I propose to refer to it before proceeding with my narrative.

In the earlier part of 1877 a rather unusual degree of activity was manifested by Cotopaxi, and columns of smoke (composed of fine dust, which is commonly termed volcanic ash) rose sometimes a thousand feet above the cone, and at night the steam and smoke that issued was brilliantly illuminated by flames or incandescent matter within the crater. The dust was carried in this or that direction according to the prevailing winds, and much fell at Machachi and its neighbourhood.[1] No alarm seems to have been caused until June 25, when, soon after mid-day, an immense black column was projected about twice the height of the cone (say, 18,000 feet) in the air, and was accompanied by tremendous subterranean bellowing. This eruption was clearly seen from Quito and Latacunga, as the wind blew the ash towards the Pacific, and left the view of the mountain from north and south unobscured.[2] The summit glowed at night, but next morning its appearance was normal until 6.30 a.m., when another enormous column rose from the crater. This time the ejected matter first drifted due north, spreading out to the north-west and north-east, and subsequently was diffused by other winds all over the country. In Quito it began to be dusk about 8 a.m., and the darkness increased in intensity until mid-day, when it was like night. One man informed me that he wished to return home, but could not perceive his own door[3] when immediately opposite to

[1] Shewing a prevalence of south-east winds.

[2] The first intelligence of this eruption reached Europe through the ejected matter falling upon steamers passing between Panama and Guayaquil, at a distance of nearly two hundred miles from the mountain.

[3] The darkness was caused by the prodigious quantity of dust that was floating in the atmosphere. I found at Quito a person who had had the sagacity to spread out a sheet of paper to receive the particles as they settled, and I secured this collection. Some are as large as ·007 to ·008 of an inch in diameter, though many are much smaller. This dust has been described by Prof. Bonney in the *Proceedings of the Royal Society*, June, 1884.

it, and another said he could not see his hand when it was held close to his face.

At daybreak, on the 26th, the mountain could be clearly seen from places to the south of it, as the ash was blown *northwards,* and the eruption does not appear to have excited any particular alarm, or even attention.[1] Some inhabitants of Mulalo, however, were looking at the summit at 10 a.m., and all at once saw molten lava pouring through the gaps and notches in the lip of the crater, bubbling and smoking, so they described it, like the froth of a pot that suddenly boils over. The scene which then ensued upon the mountain was shut out from mortal eyes, for in a few minutes the whole of it was enveloped in smoke and steam, and became invisible; but out of the darkness a moaning noise arose, which grew into a roar, and a deluge of water, blocks of ice, mud and rock rushed down, sweeping away everything that lay in its course, and leaving a desert in its rear. It is estimated that it travelled as far as Latacunga at the rate of fifty miles an hour—and this is not impossible.[2]

The scene upon the cone in the moments following the outpouring of the lava through the jagged rim[3] of the crater must have surpassed anything that has been witnessed by man. Molten rock filled the crater to overflowing. Its rise was sudden, and its fall, perhaps, was equally abrupt. One may well pause to wonder at the power which could raise the quantity sufficient

[1] It must be remembered that the people living in its vicinity are accustomed to see it smoking and blowing off steam. The ejection of a column of ash to several times the ordinary height would not be enough to attract special attention.

[2] In three hours after passing Mulalo it destroyed a bridge at the foot of Tunguragua. The distance between these places is forty-five miles, or probably sixty miles following the windings of the rivers. This would give a mean rate of about twenty miles per hour. The flood going northwards reached Esmeraldas at 4 a.m. on the 27th. In a direct line that town is about one hundred and fifty miles from the crater, but it is more than double the distance by the circuitous route which was taken. This gives a mean rate of about seventeen miles per hour.

[3] This passage will be better understood by reference to the two views of exterior and interior portions of the crater that accompany Chapter VII.

to fill this vast arena, nineteen thousand feet above the level of the sea, even for a moment.[1] The weight must be reckoned by hundreds of millions of tons—its heat at thousands of degrees Fahrenheit, and when it emerged through the depressions of the rim, and fell in streams or cascades upon the surrounding slopes of snow, ice, and glacier, much of it must instantly have been blown into the air by sudden evolution of steam, and falling again upon the cone bounded downwards in furious leaps, ploughing up the mountain like cannon-shot. Portions of the glaciers, uncemented from their attachments by the enormous augmentation of heat, slipped away bodily, and, partly rolling, partly borne by the growing floods, arrived at the bottom a mass of shattered blocks.[2]

The flood which ultimately proceeded towards the south at first rushed away from Cotopaxi across the bed of the River Cutuchi up to the bend that the new road makes near Callo; and then, deflected by the rising ground, it turned towards Latacunga, rooted up the road, and swept away arrieros with their teams and everything upon it, erased houses, farms and factories, and destroyed every bridge in its course. When I passed this way, I found the country a wilderness.[3]

Many eruptions have occurred of this description, and upon

[1] The observation of the natives of Mulalo that it bubbled over suddenly in a number of places at once, and the immediate irruption of the floods *in all directions* are strong evidence. The opinion that the lava retreated as rapidly as it rose is entertained because the flood ceased in an hour or less, and a large quantity of ice near the summit remained unmelted.

[2] According to Dr. T. Wolf blocks of ice were carried eight to ten leagues from the mountain, and some of them remained for months after the eruption upon the plain of Latacunga, and left, as they melted, hillocks of rubbish three or four feet high, and several yards in diameter.

[3] The flood which went north, though equally formidable, did less damage to property. For a number of miles it traversed uninhabited country. The principal loss on this side was caused by the obliteration of the cotton factories at Chillo belonging to the Aguirre family. I was told by one of their workmen that some of the machinery was transported thirty miles, down into the ravine of Guallabamba. Messrs. Aguirre have now put up other mills on higher ground.

some occasions the mountain has belched forth flame as well as ashes. Several persons whom I examined on this point seemed to be able to discriminate between the appearance of fire-lit clouds

COTOPAXI IN ERUPTION IN 1743.

and of actual flame, and positively affirmed that they had seen flames rise above the lip of the crater, though not to a great height. La Condamine, in his *Journal du Voyage*, relates that in 1743–4 flames rose at least two thousand feet above the top of the mountain, and his associates Juan and Ulloa, in their

Voyage historique, give the quaint picture which I reproduce herewith.

There need be little wonder that there are so few exact accounts of the great eruptions of Cotopaxi. No one lives in close contiguity to the vent which is the natural channel of escape for the imprisoned and compressed gases that work the mischief, and thus the earlier admonitions of approaching eruptions often pass unnoticed; and when the mightier ones commence, every person within sight or hearing, knowing too well either from experience or from tradition the results which are likely to ensue, concerns himself more in safeguarding life and property than in philosophical considerations of the forces of nature.

Ecuadorians have left the investigation of their great volcano to strangers. A century and a half ago, La Condamine proposed to attempt its ascent, but had to abandon his project because no one would accompany him. Humboldt, at the beginning of the century, after entertaining the same idea, finally came to the conclusion that it was impossible to reach the brink of the crater. So far as I am aware, the first person to reach the summit was Dr. W. Reiss, of Berlin, on Nov. 27, 1872.[1] Starting from the village of Mulalo, with ten natives, he appears first to have travelled about north-east, and subsequently east-north-east. The same route was taken by Dr. A. Stübel, of Dresden, in March, 1873;[2] and, in September, 1877, the summit was reached by Dr. T. Wolf, a Jesuit long resident in Ecuador, who started from the same direction as the others,[3] but adopted a more northerly line of ascent, in consequence of finding that the route they had taken on the actual cone had been rendered impassable by the eruption

[1] See *Nature,* April 10, 1873. I was informed in Ecuador that an ascent had been made by a native of Latacunga, before Dr. Reiss, but I was unable to obtain any evidence that such had been the case.

[2] An account in Spanish was published at Quito by Dr. Stübel in the form of a letter to the President of the Republic of Ecuador (see note, p. 96), and also appeared in French in the *Bulletin de la Société de Géographie,* Paris, 1874.

[3] An account was published by him in Spanish, at Guayaquil.

of June 27. Lastly, in January, 1878, the summit was gained by Freiherr Max von Thielmann, who, starting from Machachi, passed through the hamlet of Pedregal to the mountain by the route shewn in dotted line upon my map, and completed the ascent by the same way as Dr. Wolf.[1]

The accounts of these gentlemen agree in general very well; though none of them saw to the bottom of the crater, and they differed amongst each other as to the height of the mountain and several matters of detail. By remaining a greater length of time in the field I hoped to clear up, or at least to bring more into harmony, various discrepancies; and in going to the mountain I proposed to follow the line taken by Von Thielmann, for, from a description which he was good enough to give me personally, it appeared to be more desirable than the way by Mulalo.

I brought a letter of introduction to the proprietor of the farm, and was received very courteously.[2] His house was the nearest one to Illiniza, and we came to it hoping to combine an ascent of that mountain with our inspection of Cotopaxi. No information in regard to Illiniza is in print, and this is not a matter for surprise, as it is almost perpetually shrouded in mist. Persons living in its neighbourhood say that it is seldom or never perfectly clear. At one or another time we were seventy-eight days in its vicinity, yet we did not see the whole of the mountain on any single occasion.[3] Only partial views were obtained, lasting a few

[1] See the *Alpine Journal*, Aug., 1878, pp. 45–47.

[2] There was the same uncleanliness about this hacienda that was remarked in most other places. My apartment had the appearance of not having been cleaned or even swept since the building was erected. The whole ceiling was covered with a dense black mass of house-flies clustered over one another to the depth of perhaps half an inch. I could not have imagined that such a spectacle was possible. There were also tens of thousands on the upper part of the walls.

Feeling something hard under the pillow I looked underneath, and found a prayer-book, a revolver, and a guitar. This was apparently the bedroom of the head of the establishment.

[3] In May and June, Louis Carrel stopped for five weeks at Machachi, and in this time only saw Illiniza twice.

minutes, and usually it was completely invisible. It happened that shortly before sunset on Feb. 7 a strong north-west wind set in and cleared the summit of clouds, and from this casual glance an ascent appeared to be a certainty.

This mountain is probably seventh in rank of the Great Andes of the Equator. It is slightly inferior in elevation to Sangai and is loftier than Carihuairazo. It has two peaks, or rather it is composed of two mountains that are grouped together, the more northern of which is the lower, and is called Little Illiniza.[1] The summits of both are sharp, and during the time of our stay in Ecuador they were completely covered by snow. The proprietor of the hacienda could give us no information as to the nature of the country to their west, and it is probable that for some distance, at least, it has never been seen by human eye. He was, however, well acquainted with the lower slopes of the mountain on the eastern side, and said that his people would be able to conduct us to a considerable height.

Upon leaving the hacienda on Feb. 8, under local guidance, our route was nearly north for four miles, partly over cultivated ground, rising gently most of the way; and it then turned sharply to the west, up a long spur thrown out from the main southern ridge of the mountain. The course up the spur was about N.W. by W. until we had reached the height of 14,700 feet, and then our local guides came to the end of their knowledge and our animals struck work. There were nine of them, and eight persons to drive, yet there was more difficulty in making them advance than on Chimborazo when moving from the first to the second camp.[2] As usual, none of their loads

[1] They have been measured by Messrs. Reiss and Stübel, who assign the heights 17,405 and 16,936 feet to them respectively. I think there is a greater difference in their elevation, and (for the reason stated in Chapter XVI.) that Little Illiniza is not so high as 16,936 feet.

[2] This probably arose from other causes besides diminution in pressure. The ground was steeper, and they had traversed a greater distance than on the other occasion.

exceeded 160 lbs. We pushed on for a few hundred feet higher, up steep slopes of volcanic sand, having a very vague idea of the situation of the summit, as we had been in clouds nearly all the day; and, upon arriving at some sufficiently flat ground, encamped at 15,207 feet, with sleet falling thickly. All the people (except the Carrels), along with the animals, were then sent back to the farm.

In course of time it was found that we had got close to the southern edge of a glacier on the eastern side of the peak, and that the upper 2200 feet or thereabouts of the mountain was composed of a large wall (which is possibly nothing more than a dyke), of no great thickness from east to west; having two principal ridges,—one descending from the summit towards the south-south-west, and the other north-north-east. The face fronting the east was almost entirely covered by glacier right up to the summit, and there was also a glacier, or more than one, on the western side.

Jean-Antoine and I started soon after daybreak on Feb. 9,[1] and made good progress over the glacier so long as it was at a moderate inclination; but in the course of an hour we found ourselves driven over to the western side of the mountain, and shortly afterwards were completely stopped in that direction by immense *séracs*. We then doubled back to the main ridge, and reached the crest of it, at a somewhat greater height than 16,000 feet, up some very steep gullies filled with snow. The huge *séracs* looming through the mist above us on the western side shewed clean walls of ice which I estimated were 200 feet high, lurching forwards as if ready to fall, separated by crevasses not less than twenty to twenty-five feet across. Nothing could be done on that side. The ridge was steep and broken; its rocks were much decomposed, externally of a chalky-white appearance, pervaded with veins and patches of lilacs and purples, and inter-

---

[1] Leaving Louis in charge of the camp. He came by his own desire, though still unable to walk.

spersed with numerous snow-beds overhanging one or the other side in cornices. The thickness of the mists hindered progress, and shortly before mid-day (being then about 17,000 feet above the sea) we were brought to a halt. The clouds drifted away for a few minutes, and we saw that although we might advance perhaps two hundred feet higher we should not be able to reach the summit.[1]

Two glaciers have their origin on the upper part of the southern ridge of Illiniza. That which goes westwards, almost from its commencement, is prodigiously steep, and is broken up into the cubical masses termed *séracs*. The other glacier, descending towards the east, though steep, is less torrential. The two were united on the crest of our ridge, and over some cleft in it there was a sheer, vertical wall of glacier-ice perhaps a hundred feet high. We could see no way of turning it, and there appeared no possibility of getting higher upon this side except by tunnelling. But if we had passed this obstacle we should not have reached the top of the mountain, for its extreme summit was garnished with a cornice of a novel and very embarrassing description.

In the illustration at the head of this chapter two types of snow-cornices are represented. That on the right of the engraving is common upon the crests of ridges near the summits of many Alpine peaks, and in other high ranges, including the Andes. The one upon the left I have seen only amongst the Great Andes of the Equator, and for the first time on the summit of Illiniza. We observed them again upon the *lower* peaks of Antisana, Cayambe, Cotocachi and elsewhere. The formation of snow-cornices of the more usual type is due to drift of the snow, and the icicles underneath them to the subsequent action of the sun; and the process of their manufacture, upon a small scale, can be observed upon the ridges of roofs during any severe snowstorm. The other type

[1] The top was seen only during these few minutes, and then became invisible until we left the mountain.

— the tufted cornice — is probably due to variability of winds, and the fringe of pendent icicles, all round, to the influence of a nearly vertical sun at noon. With the exception of Illiniza, they were not found at the very highest points of the mountains which have been mentioned, and we thanked our stars that it was not necessary to have dealings with them.

We descended eighty feet to read the barometer; made our way down the eastern face, and became mist-bewildered on the glacier near the camp. Our shouts were heard by Louis, who pluckily hobbled out some distance to guide us, and we then packed up, and awaited the return of our followers. They arrived at 4.30 p.m., and we quitted a mountain upon which, I do not attempt to disguise, we were fairly beaten.[1]

Our experiences upon Corazon and Illiniza began to open our eyes regarding weather at great elevations in Ecuador. Hitherto we had seen little of vertical suns, and regarded ourselves as the victims of circumstances, and looked daily for the setting in of a period of cloudless skies, with something like tropical warmth. On Illiniza we enjoyed thunderstorms, snow and hailstorms, sleet, drizzle and drenching showers, and scarcely saw the sun at all.[2]

---

[1] Started from the hacienda on Feb. 8 at 9.35 a.m., and arrived at camp 4 p.m. Left camp with Jean-Antoine at 6.30 a.m. on Feb. 9, and in five minutes took to the glacier. Reached highest point attained at 11.45, and got back to camp 3.45 p.m. Left camp 5 p.m., and arrived about 8.50 at the hacienda. Temperature in the shade was 36° Faht. at 5.45 a.m. at our camp, and 49·5 at mid-day, when 17,000 feet above the level of the sea.

[2] The conditions upon Illiniza were unfavourable for collecting. Out of the snow sludge around our camp I obtained only three mosses (*Racomitrium crispipilum*, Jaeg., *Splachnobryum Spruceanum*, C.M., and a *Webera*), and a short distance below our highest point found two others (*Breutelia subarcuata*, Schimp., and *Didymodon acutifolius*, Jaeg.).

At 16,500 feet, whilst descending, I captured a small bug, which has been referred by Mr. Distant to the genus *Emesa* (*Supp. App.*, p. 117). Though alive, it was evidently a wind-borne straggler, but it is noteworthy on account of this being the greatest elevation at which animal life was either obtained or observed. Its habitat was perhaps in the woods on the Panecillo of Corazon (see p. 117).

At Machachi we met Señor Lopez, an engineer of the Ecuadorian railway, who said that this weather was in no way exceptional, and would be found alike over all the higher ground, in any month. We resigned ourselves to the inevitable, and set to work perfecting preparations for a journey to Cotopaxi.

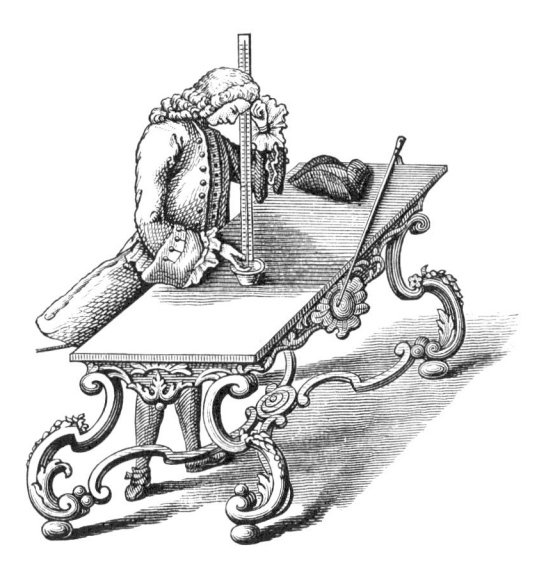

AN ACADEMICIAN OBSERVING THE BAROMETER.
(AFTER JUAN AND ULLOA.)

A BOMB FROM COTOPAXI.

CHAPTER VII.

THE ASCENT OF COTOPAXI, AND A NIGHT ON THE SUMMIT.

WE started from Machachi for Cotopaxi on February 14. The party consisted of Jean-Antoine and Louis, Mr. Perring, six natives of Machachi as porters, nine mules and three arrieros, and a couple of sheep—a pair of ungraceful and graceless animals, who displayed the utmost reluctance to go to the slaughter. They squatted on their haunches and refused to move, and when at last, after infinite persuasion, they were induced to get up, they ran between our legs and tried to upset us.

It was our intention to travel direct to Cotopaxi, but a violent storm drove us for refuge into Pedregal, a little hamlet composed of a farm and a cluster of cottages, situated on open ground, at the northern foot of Rumiñahui. The hacienda was surrounded by the customary high wall, with a huge portal at the entrance to the courtyard, and had a ruined chapel on the farther side, in which we took up our quarters, by invitation. At dusk the bells were tolled for prayer, and young and old, in twos and threes, came over the moorland to hold a service of their own, without the aid of priest.

In the morning of February 15 we pursued our way up the valley of the Rio Pita, over gently undulating land, which became

CHAP. VII.   *THE APPROACH TO COTOPAXI.*   137

more and more sterile and desolate as we approached the mountain, and presently entered on the plain of Limpiopongo, the divide of the waters of the Pita and Cutuchi — a nearly level expanse, several miles across. I found here, in great numbers, a rather large beetle belonging to the same tribe as our cock-

COTOPAXI FROM THE FIRST CAMP.

chafer, of a species which proves to be new to science, and appears to Mr. H. W. Bates so different from known forms as to warrant the erection of a new genus (*Leucopelæa*) for its reception.[1] *L. albescens* apparently tries to stand on its head. I saw multitudes of them in this interesting position; many more fallen on their backs kicking about, unable to regain their feet; and many others

[1] For description and figure see *Supplementary Appendix*, p. 30.

T

lying dead upon their backs.[1] Both upon the plain and some distance up the cone I found another nearly allied beetle (*Platycœlia nigricauda*), about an inch long, which also proves to be a new species;[2] but the *Colpodes*, that were so numerous at great heights upon the other Andes of the Equator, and the snouted *Curculios*, which were found in many places close up to the snow-line, were entirely absent here.[3]

Dotted over the plain and its surroundings, perched on the tops of hillocks, or on slopes where they could not have been transported by water, as far as four or five miles from the crater, there were many rounded masses of scoriaceous lava, from a few inches up to five or six feet in diameter, having the appearance of bombs thrown out during eruptions.[4] The plain, however, was not cut up, and appeared to have almost entirely escaped visitation by the floods that careered down the cone in 1877. This, no doubt, was due to the Yanasache lava[5] (the most prominent lava stream on this side) dividing the floods, and sending them away to the right and left. We steered for this lava, and, finding it too rugged for our mules, passed round its base (13,455 feet), and came to a valley filled with drifted ash, upon its farther or southern side, leading directly towards the summit. Easy enough to man, it proved very laborious ground for our team, and at

[1] Though they were standing head downwards, closer inspection might have shewn that they were emerging hindquarters first from the sandy soil. This beetle moved very sluggishly.   [2] *Supp. App.*, p. 30.

[3] Eighteen species of the genus *Colpodes* were obtained on the journey between the heights of 13,000 and 15,800 feet, out of which sixteen species are new to science. These are described by Mr. H. W. Bates in the *Supplementary Appendix*, pp. 13–22.

[4] Our natives scouted this idea, though familiar with the fact that Cotopaxi ejects myriads of fragments of smaller size, in such quantities as to turn day into night. The same incredulity was exhibited by the tambo-keeper at Machachi, and the man at S. Aña. They had never known anything more than two or three inches in diameter to be projected as far as their localities, and could not be got to believe that larger masses might fall closer to the mountain.

[5] I follow Von Thielmann in using this name. I did not hear it employed by the natives.

3.50 p.m., on arriving at a rude framework of poles at the height of 15,130 feet, we decided to camp, and sent all our animals back to Machachi — presently learning that we had unexpectedly hit on the place where Von Thielmann had stopped, by discovering a bottle containing his record.

It was not a very eligible locality, for two of the essentials of a good camping-place — wood and water — were wanting ; and one half of my forces went upwards in search of *snow*, whilst the others descended two thousand feet in quest of *scrub*, leaving me in charge of the camp, to act as cook, journalist, and cattle-tender. One of the sheep had already been killed, and some of the choicest cuts had been placed in our pots and kettles to be boiled, and I promised my people that when they returned they should have such a feed as would make up for days of semi-starvation. But when they were gone I began to think that I had promised too much, for the fire would not burn, and I had to lie flat on my stomach and blow hard to keep it alight at all. And then snow and hail began to fall, and I found my feet got uncomfortably cold while my head was exceedingly hot, and just at this time I heard *a noise*, and, looking up, perceived that the other sheep, which had not been turned into mutton, had escaped from its fastenings, and was hurrying down the slope. I gave chase and caught it, and talked to it about the wickedness of attempting to escape. The sheep certainly looked sheepish, but it would not return upwards without much persuasion, and when we got up again I found that the sheep that *had* been turned into mutton had turned over into the volcanic ash, and had nearly put out the fire. All the broth had descended among the ash, the fire was nearly extinguished, and the meat itself was covered in a most abominable way with a sort of gritty slime. Such nasty-looking stuff it has never been my lot to see, before or since ; and I almost blush to think of the devices which had to be employed to make it presentable. But all's well that ends well ! I came up to time, and my people were never the wiser, though

I *did* clean that meat with our blacking-brush, and wipe out the pots with a pocket-handkerchief.

Our camp was pitched upon and was surrounded by matter ejected from the volcano, to which the terms dust, sand, lapilli, and ash are usually given. The finest particles are termed dusts, coarser ones are called sand and lapilli. The term ash covers all three expressions, and in this sense I have used it elsewhere. It is, however, open to the double objection that it conveys no exact idea of either the dimensions or quality of the particles, and suggests a quite erroneous idea. In using the term ash (or ashes) we generally mean the residue of something which has perished by fire. Thus we speak of the ash of paper, tobacco, or coal; and, when this expression was first applied to matter ejected by volcanoes, those who employed it were no doubt under the impression that the particles which they so designated were actually the residue of something which had been consumed by fire. This idea would be fostered by the matter very commonly being of an ashy colour.[1] Close investigation of the materials shews that there is scarcely anything (or nothing) of the nature of ash amongst them. They are composed of rocky and mineral fragments. The rocky ones are often *angular* chips of lava, while felspar constitutes a large proportion of the glassy ones. Fragments of scoria (scum of lava) are common, and magnetic particles are always present in the Cotopaxi dusts.

It is a rather troublesome peculiarity of volcanic dust that it will penetrate anywhere. The extreme fineness of the more

[1] A number of the volcanic dusts I collected in Ecuador have this appearance when *seen in bulk*. Some incline towards slaty-grey, while others are of slightly warmer hues. Under very moderate magnifying power it is, however, seen that the particles are rather sharply divided into very light-coloured glassy fragments, and very dark rocky ones. The ashy colour is produced by the admixture of the two classes of atoms. Several of these Cotopaxi dusts have been examined microscopically by Prof. T. G. Bonney, F.R.S., and are described by him in the *Proceedings of the Royal Society*, June, 1884. Those who are desirous of pursuing this subject are referred to that paper.

minute particles permits it to get into places which might be deemed inaccessible. It floats in the air, travels round corners, and insinuates itself through cracks into sheltered places which cannot be reached by objects falling directly from the heavens, and when settled in them it is secure against disturbance by wind. Whatever falls upon open ground, on the contrary, is wafted hither and thither by the slightest breeze,[1] and thus the traces even of considerable eruptions are speedily confused with previous ones.[2] There was a good illustration of this in the immediate vicinity of our camp. In all the cavernous recesses of the scoria, and in other sheltered places, there was a thick deposit of a dust of a very marked granular character, in appearance, though not in constitution, quite unlike any other I obtained.[3] This had evidently, from the thickness of the deposit, been ejected during a somewhat severe eruption, and must have fallen everywhere. Though found in every hollow or protected place, it could not be identified anywhere else. Yet this was a rather coarse dust, the predominant particles weighing about two thousand to a grain, and the largest ones measuring ·04 of an inch

[1] Upon this account, travelling in the interior of Ecuador during dry weather is often exceedingly unpleasant. It is sometimes impossible to face the clouds of dust which are raised. With myriads of sharp, glassy and rocky fragments constantly drifting about, it is not surprising that eye complaints are common amongst the natives.

[2] This was the case with the dusts which were ejected during the great eruptions of 1877. By general consent, they fell most heavily around Machachi; and, according to Antonio Racines, covered everything to a depth of more than two inches, and obliged the inhabitants to drive their animals elsewhere for food. At the time of our stay, he could not point them out anywhere as a distinct stratum, as they had been dispersed by wind, or turned over in the course of agriculture.

[3] "A dust consisting of dark granules, mixed with light grey and reddish specks. The materials are rather coarse, the granules ranging from about ·01 to ·015 inch. The most abundant are minute lapilli of scoriaceous aspect, and dark colour, almost black; in less numbers are glassy whitish and reddish granules; with these occur fragments of felspar, augite, and hypersthene. Of the latter mineral there was a fairly perfect crystal about ·015 long. . . . The granular character of the dust readily distinguishes it from other examples."—Prof. T. G. Bonney.

in diameter. The atoms of the *finer* dusts may not be so much as a thousandth of an inch in diameter, or, as I shall relate in Chapter XVIII., weigh one twenty-five-thousandth part of a grain.

The night of February 15–16 passed away without excitement. There were occasional rumblings in the bowels of the mountain, and a few noises of a sharper sort, which sounded like slams of doors in an ordinary stone corridor. Snow fell for several hours, and in the morning the tent and packing-cases were laden with it, though it was rapidly disappearing on the cone. We found this usually happened.[1] Several inches of snow fell every day, but it remained only a short time, notwithstanding the temperature of the air, which was sometimes as low as 24° Faht. The warmth of the cone quickly liquefied it; the snow-water descended immediately into the porous soil, and the mountain steamed from head to foot. It is in this way the atmosphere of haze is produced to which I have already referred.

Our first business in the morning was to improve the shelter for our people, and to sort them off—for there were too many mouths to feed. The whole of the Machachi men were told they might go home, or stop, as they pleased; and that those who stopped should receive a silvered cross in addition to their pay.[2] "If I did not believe in *that*," said the oldest of the troop, Gregorio Albuja, "I would not have come here. I will stop with you"; and, taking the cross, which I held out, he pressed it reverently to his lips, and then passed it to his companions, who did the same. Two others agreed to stop, and the rest returned home.

Those who remained we now proceeded to dress up in accord-

[1] Snow fell on Cotopaxi, in February, quite 1000 feet lower than upon Chimborazo in January.

[2] I took to Ecuador a number of gilt and silvered crosses, and made use of them as rewards for special services. The worship of the cross was introduced into this country at the point of the sword, and has been developed by means of the whip. It is now firmly rooted there, amongst all classes. Even the Indians voluntarily make for themselves such rude crucifixes as that in the illustration upon p. 156.

ance with our ideas of propriety, for the ordinary native dress is as unsuited to mountaineering as can well be. It commences with a straw hat that generally blows away, and terminates with alpargatas (string shoes), which, although sufficient when marching along dusty roads, inadequately protect the feet when tramping

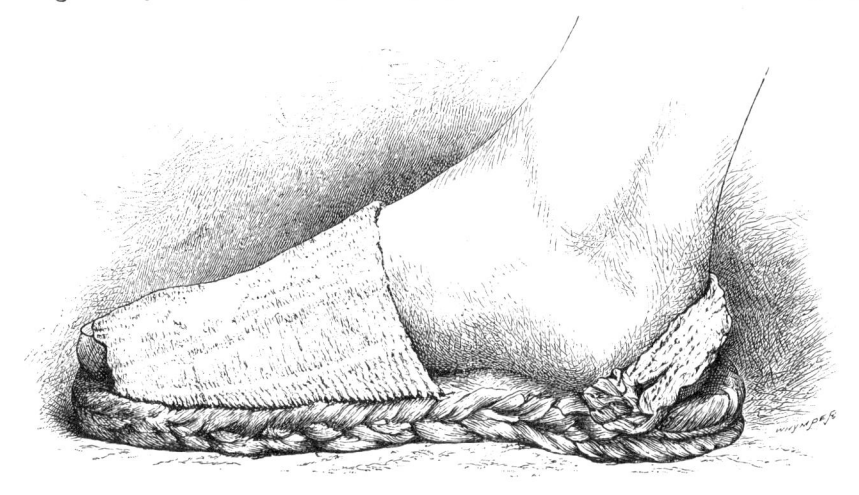

AN ALPARGATA.

over snow and rock. Having rigged them out in some of our surplus stores, I despatched them upwards under the direction of Jean-Antoine with a tent, and a quantity of rope, provisions, and etceteras, and they had a constant struggle with the elements. Both of the Ecuadorians broke down after a time, and the heavy part of the work, as usual, was performed by the Carrels. The weather was the worst. During most of the day it hailed or snowed, and in the rest there was fog or high wind, accompanied by much thunder and lightning.

The weather on February 17th strongly resembled that of the day before. At daybreak the temperature was 28° Faht., and in the previous night it had been three degrees lower. But upon this day we heard no noises proceeding from the interior of the cone, although they had been frequent during the 16th. At 7 a.m. the summit was visible for a few minutes, and was seen to be emitting vast clouds of steam continuously, which rolled up over the edge of the crater, and drifted away towards the north. Storms of hail were frequent; and both here, and when we were subsequently encamped at the summit, stray flashes of lightning occurred in uncomfortable if not in dangerous proximity — blazing out at unexpected times, and conveying the impression that the atmosphere was saturated with electricity.

When it was possible to work outside the tent we explored the neighbourhood, but our acquisitions here were less than upon any other mountain that we visited. The beetles already mentioned, and an ubiquitous frog (*Phryniscus lævis*, Gthr.) were the only things we saw appertaining to the animal kingdom. Round about and below our camp there were lichens upon the lava belonging to the genera *Stereocaulon* and *Lecanora*, and between 14,000 and 15,000 feet there was some quantity of a Valerian (*V. Bonplandiana*, Wedd.), a few stray plants of Gentian in flower (*G. foliosa*, H.B.K.), and two Composites (*Culcitium nivale?* and *Senecio humillimus*, Sz. Bip.).

CAMP ON COTOPAXI (15,139 FEET).

Above the camp I found nothing, either animal or vegetable, except some shabby patches of moss (at 15,350 feet), which has been dubiously identified as *Webera nutans*, Schimp. Everything besides growing in ash was covered with it, and presented a very dirty and unhappy appearance.

The preparations for a start to the summit were now completed. The tent below was left standing, well-provisioned, in case we had to make a precipitate retreat; and there was food enough near the top of the mountain for several days, should we be kept prisoners there. The morning of February 18 was unusually fine, and the upper part of the cone was free from clouds for several hours. I started off Jean-Antoine Carrel with two natives at 5.20 a.m. and followed with Louis at six, catching the others when they were about 17,000 feet above the sea. We had fine views of Sincholagua (16,365 feet), Antisana (19,335), and Cayambe (19,186), and spent time in examining these mountains with a telescope, with a view to ascending them.[1] Antisana bore N.E. by E., distant about 28 miles, and there was in its rear, and rising higher than it, a large pile of cumulus cloud, which I estimate cannot have been less than 23,000 feet above the level of the sea. This is the greatest elevation at which I have seen this description of cloud anywhere.

The ascent to Cotopaxi, by the route we followed, was a walk; and the direction that we took is best indicated by saying that we kept along the crest of the rather ill-defined ridge[2] which descends almost continuously from the summit towards the mountain Rumiñahui.[3] No climbing whatever was necessary. The

---

[1] Later on we ascended all three mountains. They were distant 12, 28, and 62 miles respectively.

[2] This ridge is the Yanasache lava. It appears to issue from a fissure in the cone between 18,000 and 19,000 feet above the sea. It was completely buried in snow at that height.

[3] The route we followed is seen in the view upon p. 137, taken from the lower camp. The view upon p. 144 was taken with the back to the summit of Cotopaxi, looking towards Rumiñahui.

lower camp was distant about 8600 feet from the nearest part of the crater, and in this distance we rose 4500 feet. Isolated snow-patches commenced at about 15,400 feet, and a little higher we were able to follow snow uninterruptedly right up to the slope upon which I proposed to encamp. In order to ensure regularity in the march, we tied up in line, a proceeding that our natives did not at all comprehend, and they wondered still more at the use of the axe in cutting steps in the snow, to facilitate progress. The most interesting feature I noticed upon this section of the mountain was the existence of glaciers upon the upper part of the cone. They occurred on each side of us, and in some places extended to within 500 feet of the top; but, through being much covered by ash, it was not possible to say exactly where they commenced or terminated, and for the same reason they were quite unrecognisable at a distance.

At 11 a.m. we arrived at the foot of the great slope of ash upon the western side of the summit, which leads right up to the edge of the crater, and we found this was the steepest and most laborious part of the ascent. I estimate it to be 750 feet high, and 1100 feet long. It was composed of the materials which are being daily, even hourly ejected[1] (mainly of particles weighing about 500 to a grain, with an admixture of angular fragments of lava up to a quarter of an inch in diameter), and it was piled up nearly to the maximum angle at which it would stand. I know experimentally that its materials will stand at

[1] The eruptions of Cotopaxi yield information respecting the prevailing winds of this region, and shew clearly that they by no means blow uniformly from the *east*, as some suppose. The slope of ash at the top of Cotopaxi, upon its western side, proves, however, the preponderance of easterly winds at that particular spot and elevation; and from the whole of my experiences in Ecuador I should say that in the interior generally, near the earth (at heights from 9000 to 10,000 feet) easterly winds predominate, and that north-westerly ones are as rare as in Great Britain. But winds blowing from the *true* east were almost equally scarce, though north-easterly and south-easterly ones were frequent. From greater elevations (say 20,000–40,000 feet above the sea) there was abundant evidence of the occurrence of powerful northerly and southerly winds, as well as easterly ones.

PART OF THE INTERIOR OF THE CRATER OF COTOPAXI.

FROM A PHOTOGRAPH TAKEN AT 19,500 FEET.

41°, but the face of the slope was not, I think, steeper than 37°.[1] We deposited our baggage at the foot of it until we had completed the ascent, and found that occasional streaks of ice gave some stability to the mass, which would otherwise have slipped down in large quantities at every step.

We hurried up this unstable slope as fast as we could go, and reached the western edge of the summit rim exactly at mid-day. The crater was nearly filled with smoke and steam, which drifted about and obscured the view. The opposite side could scarcely be perceived, and the bottom was quite concealed. As the vapours were wafted hither and thither, we gained a pretty good idea of the general shape of the crater, though as a whole it was not seen until night-time.

A few minutes after our arrival, a roar from the bottom told us that the "animal" (Carrel's term for the volcano) was alive. It had been settled beforehand that every man was to shift for himself if an eruption occurred, and that all our belongings were to be abandoned. When we heard the roar, there was an "it is time to be off" expression clearly written on all our faces; but before a word could be uttered we found ourselves enveloped only in a cloud of cool and quite unobjectionable steam, and we concluded to stop.

The establishment of the tent was the first consideration. It was unanimously decided that it was not advisable to camp at the top of the slope, close to the rim or lip of the crater, on account of wind and the liability to harm from lightning, and the more I examined the slope itself the less I liked it. It was naked, exposed, and slipped upon the slightest provocation. Jean-Antoine and I therefore set out on a tour to look for a better place, but after spending several hours in passing round about a quarter of the crater, without result, we returned to the others, and all hands set to work to endeavour to make a platform upon the ash. This proved to be a long and trouble-

[1] This is the angle represented in the section on p. 149.

some business. Unlike snow, it gained no coherence by being beaten or trampled down, and the more they raked to extend our platform the more slipped down from above. Ultimately it was made sufficiently secure by scooping channels in the portion of the slope which was above and tenderly pouring many tons upon the slope below, so as to strengthen the base. The tent-ropes were secured to large blocks of lava, which had to be brought from long distances and buried in the ash. For additional security four ropes were run out besides the usual ones, and we rigged up our long rope as a sort of handrail to the nearest convenient point of the rim of the crater, from which we were distant 250 feet. When this was done, the natives were sent back to the lower camp, and the Carrels and I remained alone.

We had scarcely completed our preparations when a violent squall arose, which threatened to carry the whole establishment away, and during an hour it was a great question whether our abode would weather the storm. The squall passed away as suddenly as it rose, and for the rest of our stay we were not much troubled by wind. While this was occurring there was another cause for alarm. A great smell of india-rubber commenced to arise, and on putting my hand to the floor of the tent I found that it was on the point of melting. On placing a maximum thermometer on the floor (at the point marked C in the annexed diagram), it rose until it indicated 110° Faht. As my feet did not feel at all warm I tried the temperature at the other side of the tent (at A) and found it was only 50°, and in the middle (at B) it was 72°·5. These temperatures were maintained during our stay on this spot. Outside, even during the daytime, the air was intensely cold;[1] and the minimum of

---

[1] This had been anticipated, and we suffered no inconvenience from cold. I sent up a large quantity of extra ponchos and wraps, and our wearing apparel was more than doubled. Besides my usual dress, I wore an extra flannel shirt, a thick woollen sweater, a down dressing-gown, and a huge Ulster coat over all.

the night of February 18, registered by a thermometer placed four feet above the ground and four feet from the tent on its windward side, was 13° Faht., which was the lowest temperature that was observed during the whole of the journey.

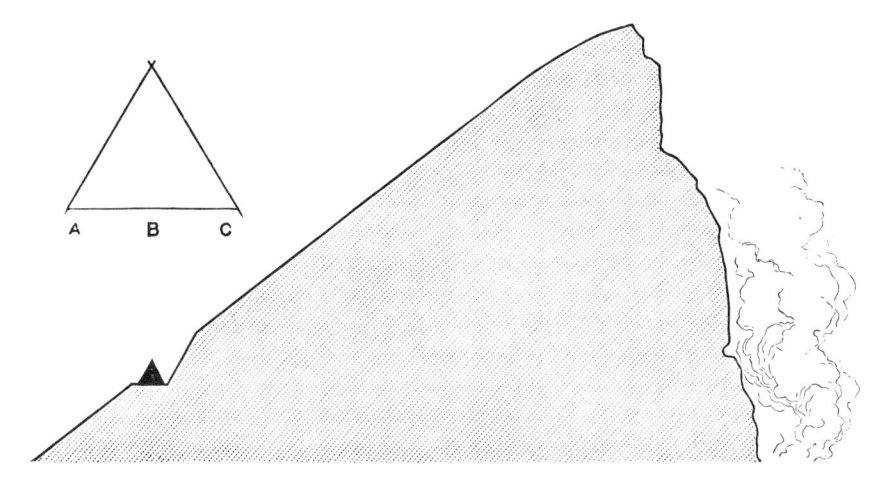

POSITION OF THE TENT ON THE SUMMIT OF COTOPAXI.

When daylight began to fail, we settled down in the tent, and it is now time to recur to the motive which had taken us to the summit of Cotopaxi. There were three principal questions to which I desired answers. 1. Shall we, upon again reaching the elevation, and experiencing the diminution in pressure which had rendered us incapable on Chimborazo, have a recurrence of our experiences upon that mountain? 2. Or, are we now habituated to a pressure of 16 inches? 3. If we are habituated to a pressure of 16 inches, shall we now be able to remain some length of time at a considerably lower pressure without being rendered incapable?

During the ascent I had watched my people with mingled feelings of curiosity and anxiety. Their pace was rather slow,[1]

My head was protected by a knitted woollen headpiece, crowned by a Dundee whaling-cap, with flaps.

[1] Between the first camp and the summit we rose at the rate of 700 feet per hour, which was a fair one for heavily-laden people. My own load weighed 23 lbs. All the others carried more than 30 lbs. apiece.

but it was steadily maintained. At one point, when between 18,000 and 19,000 feet above the level of the sea, they went up 360 steps without stopping. I noticed nothing unusual during the ascent, nor upon the summit, except the overpowering desire to sit down, which always mastered us when we were at great elevations (low pressures), and the disposition to breathe through open mouths. The collapse on Chimborazo had, however, occurred very suddenly. We were all right in one hour and all wrong in the next. It came upon us, so it seemed, without premonition. All at once, we found ourselves with intense headaches (not having had any before), gasping for air, and half asphyxiated. Hour after hour went by on the summit of Cotopaxi without anything of the kind happening again. Jean-Antoine refused to admit that he had any ailments; Louis acknowledged that he had a rather sharp headache, and I had a slight one. That was all, beyond the feeling of lassitude which, I repeat, always came over us at the greatest heights. On Chimborazo we had all been feverish. Even when recovering, my blood temperature was as high as 100°·4 with the air at 49°. On Cotopaxi it remained at 98°·2 both with higher and lower air temperatures. In short, during the twenty-six hours which we passed on the summit of Cotopaxi, from mid-day February 18, to 2 p.m. on the 19th, there was no recurrence of the more acute symptoms, and no perceptible effects were produced (beyond those which have been mentioned) by the low atmospheric pressure that we experienced.[1]

When night fairly set in we went up to view the interior of the crater. The atmosphere was cold and tranquil. We could hear the deadened roar of the steam-blasts as they escaped from time to time. Our long rope had been fixed both to guide in the darkness, and to lessen the chance of disturbing the equilibrium of the slope of ash. Grasping it, I made my way

[1] At 6.20 a.m., on Feb. 19, on the rim of the crater (above the tent), the mercurial barometer stood at 14·748 inches, with the air temperature at 21° Faht.

PART OF THE EXTERIOR OF THE CRATER OF COTOPAXI.

upwards, prepared for something dramatic, for a strong glow on the under sides of the steam-clouds shewed that there was fire below. Crawling and grovelling, as the lip was approached, I bent eagerly forward to peer into the unknown, with Carrel behind, gripping my legs.

The vapours no longer concealed any part of the vast crater, though they were there, drifting about, as before.

"THERE WAS FIRE BELOW."

We saw an amphitheatre 2300 feet in diameter from north to south, and 1650 feet across from east to west,[1] with a rugged and irregular crest, notched and cracked; surrounded by cliffs, by perpendicular and even overhanging precipices, mixed with steep slopes — some bearing snow, and others apparently encrusted with sulphur. Cavernous recesses belched forth smoke; the sides of

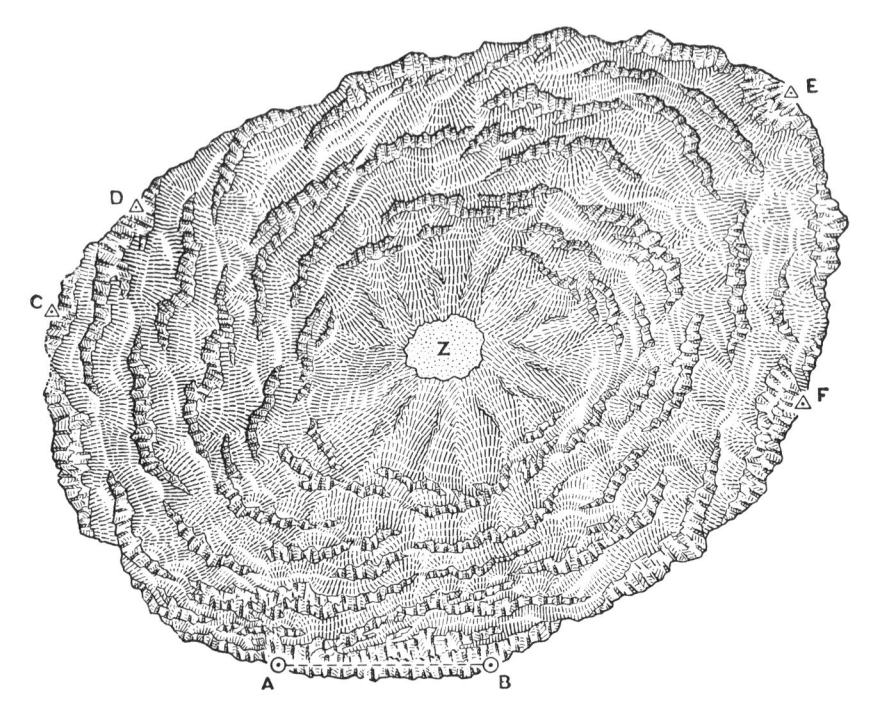

cracks and chasms no more than half-way down shone with ruddy light; and so it continued on all sides, right down to the bottom, precipice alternating with slope, and the fiery fissures becoming more numerous as the bottom was approached. At the bottom, probably twelve hundred feet below us, and towards the centre, there was a rudely circular spot, about one-tenth of the diameter of the crater, the pipe of the volcano, its channel

---

[1] The accompanying plan is made from measurements which were taken on the following morning. From A to B (600 feet) was measured by a line. Z represents the mouth of the pipe at the bottom of the crater. C was the lowest point in the lip or rim, and A, D, E, were the highest ones.

of communication with lower regions, filled with incandescent if not molten lava, glowing and burning; with flames travelling to and fro over its surface, and scintillations scattering as from a wood-fire; lighted by tongues of flickering flame which issued from the cracks in the surrounding slopes.

At intervals of about half an hour the volcano regularly blew off steam. It rose in jets with great violence from the bottom of the crater, and boiled over the lip, continually enveloping us. The noise on these occasions resembled that which we hear when a large ocean steamer is blowing off steam. It appeared to be pure, and we saw nothing thrown out, yet in the morning the tent was almost black with matter which had been ejected. These intermittent and violent escapes of (comparatively) small quantities of steam proceeded with considerable regularity during our stay on the summit, but I cannot suppose they are continually happening. They can scarcely have occurred when we saw the clouds of steam quietly simmering out of the crater from the Hacienda Rosario (see p. 123), or from our camp upon Feb. 17, and upon numerous other occasions. My predecessors on Cotopaxi do not speak of them. They were evidently of the same nature, though much inferior in force to those which we had seen emitted from Sangai a few weeks previously.

I do not feel able to frame an explanation which would account for these outbursts if it is assumed that fluid, molten lava filled the pipe. I conjecture that the lava in the pipe leading from the bottom of the crater, although intensely hot, was cooling and settling down, closing fissures and imprisoning steam that desired to escape, which presently acquired sufficient force to burst through the barriers and effect temporary relief. I imagine that the settling and closing-up process recommenced after each outburst, until some unusually violent explosion established what may be termed a free vent. The steam then welled out unimpeded, in the manner we so frequently observed. After such occasions, the internal pressure being diminished, I presume that the closing-up process went on with greater activity, and that the vent was sometimes entirely closed, causing the volcano to appear unusually tranquil.

Steam unquestionably plays a leading part in the operations of Cotopaxi, and sometimes the quantity that issues is enormous. One morning in the following April, when encamped, at the height of 14,760 feet, on Cayambe, at a distance of about sixty miles to the north-north-east, just after daybreak, we saw Cotopaxi pouring out a prodigious volume of steam, which boiled up a few hundred feet above the rim of its crater, and then, being caught by a south-westerly wind, was borne towards the north-east, almost up to Cayambe. The bottom of this cloud was about 5000 feet above us; it rose at least a mile high, and spread over a width of several miles; and, as it was travelling a little to the east of us, we had a perfect and unimpeded view of it. I estimate that on this occasion we saw a continuous body of *not less than sixty cubic miles* of cloud formed from steam. If this vast volume, instead of issuing from a free vent, had found its passage barred, itself imprisoned, Cotopaxi on that morning might have been effaced, and the whole continent might have quivered under an explosion rivalling or surpassing the mighty catastrophe at Krakatoa.

We were up again before daylight on the 19th, and then measured 600 feet on the western side of the crater, and took angles to gain an idea of its dimensions. I photographed it,[1] and made final observations of the mercurial barometer to determine its altitude. From the mean of the whole, its summit appears to be 19,613 feet above the sea. In 1872-3, Messrs. Reiss and Stübel (by angles taken from various barometrically measured bases) made its height 19,498 feet; and, by the same method, La Condamine, in the early part of last century, found that its height was 18,865 feet. As there is not much proba-

[1] The engraving facing p. 147 has been made from this photograph. The whole of the interior of the crater was surrounded by cliffs and slopes of the same character.

bility of considerable error in any of the determinations, it would seem that Cotopaxi has materially increased its elevation in the course of the last century and a half.

The time to descend had now arrived, and at 11.30 a.m. our Ecuadorians should have remounted to assist in carrying our baggage down again. The weather, however, was abominable, and they preferred to leave the work to us. After depositing our more bulky stores at the foot of the great slope of ash, we tramped down to the first camp. The feet of Louis were still in a very tender state, and he could not take part in racing; but Jean-Antoine and I went down as hard as we could, and descended the 4,300 feet in 110 minutes. Two days more elapsed before animals could be brought from Machachi for the retreat, and it was late on the 21st before we got clear of Cotopaxi. The night was dark, and the path invisible; but guided by the bells we gained the hamlet, and encamped once more in the chapel of Pedregal.

The rest of my Machachi men now returned home, and the authorities lost no time in interviewing them, for these poor noodles were possessed with the idea that we were in search of gold. "Tell us, what did they do?" Said my men, "The Doctor, dressed like a king, went from one place to another, looking about; but after a time Señor Juan and Señor Luis seemed afraid of him, for they tied him up with a rope." "Enough of this; tell us, did they find treasure?" "We think they did. They went down on their hands and knees searching for it, and they wrapped what they took in paper and brought it away." "Was it gold?" "We do not know, but it was very heavy." This, though true, was rather misleading. The "royal" attire which so impressed them consisted of the Ulster coat and dressing-gown underneath, crowned by the Dundee whaling-cap; and the "treasures" we carried away were samples of the jagged crest and débris of the terminal slope.

Cotopaxi shews no signs of approaching decrepitude, and for many centuries yet to come it may remain the highest active volcano in the world; or perchance the imprisoned forces may find an easier outlet, through barriers offering less resistance, and either Sangai, Tunguragua, or Pichincha may become the premier volcano of the Equator. Whilst the great cone which has so often trembled with subterranean thunders — buried beneath glaciers more extensive than those of Cayambe or Antisana — will echo with the crash of the ice-avalanche; its crater will disappear, and, over its rugged floor and its extinguished fires, soft snowflakes will rear a majestic dome loftier than Chimborazo.

INDIAN CRUCIFIX.

THE BELLS OF PEDREGAL.

CHAPTER VIII.

THE FIRST ASCENT OF SINCHOLAGUA.

DURING our stay at the summit of Cotopaxi, we had remained continuously for twenty-six hours at a lower pressure than had been experienced during any twenty-six consecutive hours on Chimborazo,[1] without having a recurrence of what I have ventured to term the *acute* symptoms of mountain-sickness; and this was satisfactory, as it indicated that we had become somewhat habituated to low pressures. It is material to observe that, although we were actively employed during much of the time, the work in which we were engaged did not tax our strength. It is by no means certain, if larger demands had been made upon it, that our condition would have remained equally sound.

The ascent of Cotopaxi, however, was considered severely scientific by my men. Prolonged residences in exalted situations were

[1] The highest reading of the mercurial barometer (reduced to 32° Faht.) at our camp (135 feet below the summit of Cotopaxi) was 14·808 inches, and the lowest was 14·761 inches. This (19,500 feet) was the most elevated position at which we encamped on the journey.

little to their taste. They pined for work more in harmony with the old traditions; for something with dash and go,—the sallying forth in the dead of the night with rope and axe, to slay a giant; returning at dusk, with shouts and rejoicing, bringing its head in a haversack. I sacrificed a day to meet their wishes, and told them to select a peak, just as one may give a sugar-plum to a fractious child to keep it quiet.

Giants were scarce in the neighbourhood of Pedregal. My men looked upon Pasochoa with a sort of contempt, and at Ruminahui with disfavour, as there were at least half-a-dozen ways up it; and their choice fell upon Sincholagua, an attenuated peak, appetizing to persons with a taste for Aiguilles, that had stared us in the face when we looked out of the window at Machachi,[1] which *might* be ascended in one way, and in one only. It may be described as forming a northern extension of the *massif* of Cotopaxi, and it stands to that mountain in much the same relation as Carihuairazo to Chimborazo.

In a section of Ecuador in this latitude, the ground (proceeding from west to east) falls continuously from the summit of Corazon [2] to the bed of the Rio Grande; then ascends, to cross a ridge connecting Pasochoa with Ruminahui, and descends, gently, through

[1] Its height according to Messrs. Reiss and Stübel is 16,365 feet (4988 mètres), and La Condamine 16,435 feet (2570 toises). It is probably the tenth in rank of the Great Andes of the Equator.

[2] I am unable to say anything about the country on the Pacific side of Corazon. We did not see it, and it is possible that for some distance to the west of this mountain it has never been seen by any one. No reliance can be placed upon that part of the Maldonado map.

Amongst the curious mistakes of detail in this map may be mentioned the insertion of the name of Ruminahui (Ruminaui) over the position actually occupied by Pasochoa, and the entire omission of the former mountain. On this map, nothing is made to intervene between Corazon and Cotopaxi. In La Condamine's map, Ruminahui occupies its proper position,—Pasochoa, however, is omitted.

Ruminahui (15,607 R. & S.) is a large and prominent mountain, though not one of the greatest of the Andes of the Equator. From north to south it extends over about twelve miles, and it fills the space between the eastern (right) bank of the Rio Grande, and our track from Pedregal to Cotopaxi.

Pedregal to the bed of the Rio Pita (about 11,300 feet). Sincholagua rises on the eastern side of this river, and forms the culminating point of a long ridge running northwards from Cotopaxi, which dies out in the basin of Chillo, and in a manner may be said to extend to the east and north-east until it meets the western slopes of Antisana.[1]

As Sincholagua promised to give full occupation for a day, it was arranged to ride as far as animals could be used; and we should have started before sunrise, only, when the right time came our mules were nowhere, or, speaking more correctly, they were everywhere, as the arrieros after carefully driving them into a yard where there was nothing to eat had left the entrance to it unclosed, and the animals very sensibly wandered out on the moorland, where they could browse.

We sallied forth on Feb. 23, at 7 a.m., and after returning a few miles over the Cotopaxi track turned sharply towards the east, directly towards our mountain; crossed the tiny Rio Pedregal and some moorish ground, and at 8.15 forded the Rio Pita.[2] The ravages of the great flood which descended from Cotopaxi on June 26, 1877, were fresh at that time, and it was clear that when it was at its highest this stream must have been about 1100 feet wide, and not less than fifty feet deep.[3] When we crossed this formidable river it had shrunk to a width of about two hundred feet, and was no more than three feet in depth.

Sincholagua rose abruptly on its right bank. The Carrels went to the front, and in a few minutes Louis became embogged

[1] Three weeks later, from the Hacienda of Antisanilla, I saw that the country between Antisana and Sincholagua might almost be termed table-land; having undulations, but no salient peaks, and an extreme elevation of 12–13,000 feet.

[2] I did not observe the height of this point. It was probably about the same as that of the Hacienda of Pedregal (11,629 feet).

[3] From the note at p. 126, it will be seen that the flood travelled the whole distance from Cotopaxi to Esmeraldas at about the rate of seventeen miles per hour. Owing to the steepness of the fall, the rate was no doubt much greater during the earlier part of its course, when it descended into the basin of Chillo, and erased the factories of the Aguirre family.

in some alluring and deceitful ground. In this country (and it may perhaps be said of the slopes of mountains in general) any spot that is especially verdant is sure to be swampy. In Ecuador, this is no doubt an indication that the earth in the immediate neighbourhood of such spots is *not* fissured; water is unable to drain away, and the soil becomes saturated.[1]

After all hands had extricated Louis and his beast from the morass, Cevallos (our principal arriero) took the lead. He was a capital horseman, and, unlike the majority of his class, had no objections to his animals going to great heights. We pushed on hard, and in two hours and a quarter rose three thousand feet,— half-way up coming suddenly upon three deer, gambolling about. These lower slopes, though steep, were easy to ride over, and up to 14,000 feet and higher were rather luxuriantly covered with grasses.

At about the height of 14,800 feet our animals could go no farther, and were left in charge of Cevallos. This spot was just above the clouds which are underneath the summit in the engraving on the opposite page. All the grass land was below, and we were confronted with crags, precipitous enough for any one, crowned by fields of snow and ice, the birthplace of a fine hanging-glacier which crept down almost perpendicular cliffs,

[1] The scarcity of rills and streams upon most of the Great Andes of the Equator was continually remarked, and we frequently had trouble in obtaining a supply of water. It seems not improbable that the surface drainage infiltrates to great depths, and supplies much of the steam that escapes from the active volcanoes. Little of it reappears on the surface in springs. The only warm spring of any size that I saw in the interior was near Machachi, about fifty yards from the west (left) bank of the Rio Grande, and about fifteen feet above that river. It bubbled up freely in a considerable volume in a pool, twelve by ten feet across, with a quantity of gas escaping. The temperature of this spring at mid-day was 69° Faht., and of the air 65°·25. It was *said* that in the early morning the temperature of the water was *higher*. It was scarcely necessary to investigate the accuracy of this statement. The air temperature in the morning was generally below 55° Faht.; and, if the warmth of the spring remained constant, the contrast between the two temperatures would be greater then than at mid-day. People come both to drink at and to bathe in this pool. Its taste was compared to Vichy water.

clasping the rocks with its fingers and arms.

We tied up, and steered north-east over some rugged ground. The manner of approach had been settled beforehand. The south side of Sincholagua was inaccessible; garnished with pin-

SINCHOLAGUA, FROM NEAR PEDREGAL.

nacles like the teeth of a saw, and terminated at the immediate summit by sheer precipice. The western side was equally unassailable, and the only way by which the top *might* be reached was from the north, along the snow *arête* at the crest of the mountain.

In two hours we rose more than another thousand feet, and (having turned sharply to the right and climbed the snow on the left of the engraving) passed under the cliffs of the minor (northern) peak. We were nearly sixteen thousand feet high, with a clear sky, and the summit not far off; men in good spirits, rather inclined to crow, and to vaunt the superiority of the old style, when — Heaven knows where it came from — a hailstorm sent us flying for protection to the cliffs, crouching in their fissures, covering our faces with our hands to save them from the half-inch stones which bounded and ricochetted in all directions, and smote the rocks with such fury that they dislodged or actually broke fragments from the higher ledges. Twice we left our refuge and were beaten back. These ice-balls were as unpleasant as a shower of bullets.

Then came a lull. Snow began to fall, at first mixed with the hail, and afterwards in large flakes, thickly. The hail ceased, and was succeeded by lightning. Emerging from our retreat, we traversed the glacier to a small island in its midst,[1] and stormed the slope banked-up against the wall which forms the summit ridge, and found the drifted snow along its crest surmounted a sheer precipice on the eastern side. The narrow way along the top led to the foot of the final peak. The route could not be mistaken, though the summit was invisible and our *arête*, rising at an increasing angle, disappeared in the thunderclouds.

Hitherto the flashes had only glanced occasionally through

---

[1] This was the fifth mountain in the neighbourhood of the Equator upon which we had already found glaciers. The others were Chimborazo, Carihuairazo, Illiniza and Cotopaxi.

the murky air, each followed by a single bang, which is all one hears when close to the point of discharge.[1] Around the peak they blazed away without intermission, several often occurring in a single instant. The whole air seemed to be saturated with electricity, and the thunder kept up an almost continuous roar.

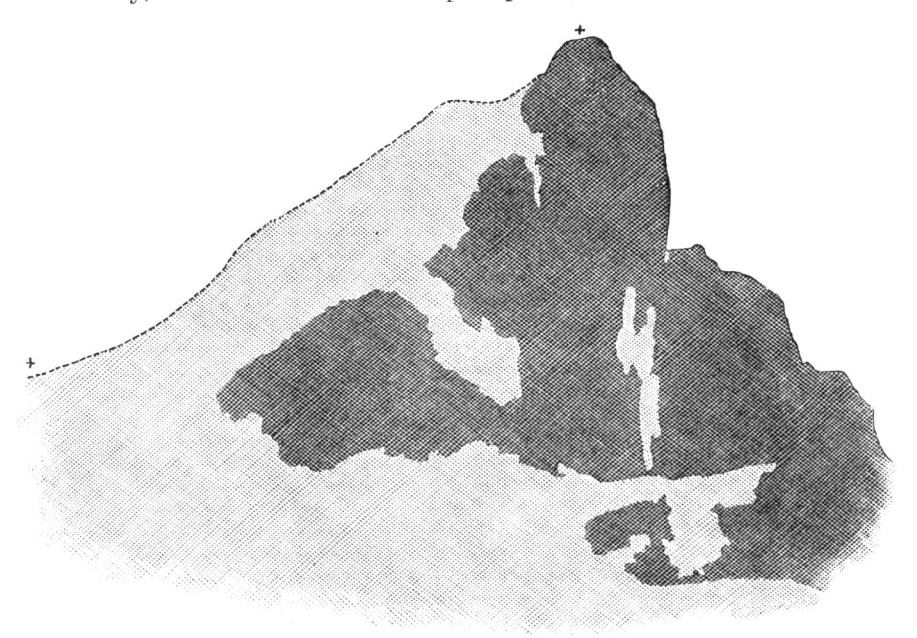

THE SUMMIT OF SINCHOLAGUA.

With ice-axes hissing ominously, and confined to the crest of the ridge by the abruptness of its sides, we gradually approached the summit. The last few yards were the steepest of all. The snow was reduced to a mere thread (too small to be shewn in the annexed engraving[2]), leaning against the rock, and it was marvellous that it stood firmly at such an angle. Steps at an ordinary distance apart could not be made. The leading man stretched forward to scrape away a small platform, flogged it

[1] See *Scrambles amongst the Alps*, pp. 172-4.

[2] Which gives an accurate sectional representation of the final peak from north to south. Our track is shewn by the dotted line, and the summit lies underneath the cross. From east to west the top of this mountain is much smaller than in the other direction.

down to make it cohere, then dashed his axe in as high as he could reach and hooked himself up, while number two drove in his baton as far as it would go to prevent the snow from breaking down.[1] In this manner we arrived at the summit. Its top was too small to get upon, and, by exception, was solid, unshattered rock right up to its very highest point. Jean-Antoine knocked off its head with his ice-axe whilst I operated a few feet below.

Having performed this important ceremony, we immediately descended, face inwards for the first part of the way, with lightning blazing all around as far as the end of the summit ridge. Then it ceased; we ran down to Cevallos, and, driving the beasts before us at a trot to the bottom of the slopes, recrossed the Rio Pita higher up than before, and pushed the pace hard all the way to Pedregal.[2] The giant was slain, and we returned, rejoicing, with its head[3] in a bag, though with little to shew besides, and nothing that need be mentioned except a sedge (a variety of *Carex Jamesoni*, Boott) which was obtained at the height of about 14,500 feet.

[1] Both here and in other places we should have been beaten if the snow had not been moist and tenacious. Dry, flour-like snow will not stand at such angles as were traversed at the top of Sincholagua.

[2] Left the summit at 2.30 p.m., and arrived at Pedregal 6.50 p.m. The time occupied on the ascent and descent (excluding halts) was 9 hs. 25 min. The mean of the ascending and descending rates was about one thousand feet per hour.

[3] "A compact dark-coloured rock, with a slightly rough fracture, containing numerous small crystals of whitish felspar, generally not exceeding ·1 inch in the longer diameter. Under the microscope, the ground-mass is seen to be a felted mass of minute elongated crystallites, probably felspar, and of specks of opacite; there is probably a residual glassy base, but so numerous are the crystallites that it is by no means easy to be sure. In this ground-mass are scattered larger crystals of plagioclastic felspar similar to those already described, augite, with probably some hypersthene and magnetite. The rock is thus an augite-andesite, probably hyperstheniferous."—Prof. T. G. Bonney, *Proc. Roy. Soc.*, Nov. 1884.

In the paper already cited in *Hist. de l'Acad. Roy. des Sciences*, Paris, 1751, La Condamine says :—"Sinchoulagoa, Volcan en 1660, communiquant avec Pitchincha." I do not know his authority for these statements. No semblance of a crater was seen on any part of it.

Louis now (after seven weeks' rest) was sufficiently restored for active exertion, and I proposed to make my way to Antisana. Being advised that it would be easiest to proceed *viâ* Quito, I decided to shift head-quarters to the Capital, and we returned to Machachi to make the necessary preparations. When the time came for departure, quite a little crowd assembled. We had entered the place strangers, our ways appeared odd to the natives, and we could not converse with freedom. But in course of time a good understanding had arisen. The language of kindness is understood everywhere. They had been useful to us, and we had not been unmindful of them; and now, when about to leave, all our young friends (with the little girl in blue), David and his wife, Gregorio, Lorenzo, the poncho-maker, and many others came together to say good-bye; while Antonio Racines, arrayed in his best, accompanied us several miles on the road, and took leave with many good wishes and profound salutations.

AT PEDREGAL.

On crossing the Tambillo ridge (10,090 feet) Quito made its appearance, looking very insignificant at the foot of Pichincha. Upon entering the city we went at once to the Hotel Giacometti, where rooms had been already secured by the good offices of the British Minister, Mr. F. Douglas Hamilton.

ENTRANCE TO THE HACIENDA, PEDREGAL.

ECUADORIENNE EARRINGS.

CHAPTER IX.

ON QUITO AND THE QUITONIANS.

THE Capital of the Republic of the Equator is situated at the bottom of the eastern slopes of Pichincha, close to where they abut against the Puengasi ridge; and between these two mountains the drainage of the area which may properly be termed the *basin* of Quito escapes, through a cleft, on to the Plain of Tumbaco. This basin extends from the city to the Tambillo ridge, and is bounded on the west by Atacatzo and part of Pichincha, and on the east by Puengasi. Previous writers have spoken of the *valley* of Quito; and (ignoring the natural lines of drainage which have been enumerated[1]) have even applied that term to the whole of the interior embraced between Riobamba and the Plain of Tumbaco. The only area to which this designation can properly be given is that which is indicated above; and even this, it seems to me, is more aptly called the *basin* of Quito.

The population of the city is commonly said to range from 60,000 to 80,000; but, from comparison of the spaces known to be covered by towns whose population has been ascertained, I

[1] See pp. 86, 97, and 105.

REFERENCES.

1. GOVERNMENT OFFICES.
2. GRAND PLAZA.
3. ARCHIEPISCOPAL PALACE.
4. THE CATHEDRAL.
5. THE JESUIT'S CHURCH.
6. GIACOMETTI'S HOTEL.
7. RESIDENCE OF THE CHILIAN MINISTER.
8. RESIDENCE OF THE BRITISH MINISTER.
9. PLAZA.
10. CHURCH OF S. ROQUE.
11. DO. S. MARCOS.
12. DO. S. BLAS.
13. DO. S. SEBASTIAN.
14. DO. STA. BARBARA.
15. DO. S. JUAN.
16. DO. DE LA RECOLLECCION DE LA MERCED.
17. DO. S. DIEGO.
18. POLYTECHNIC SCHOOL
19. THE OBSERVATORY.
20. PUBLIC GARDEN.
21. ESTABLISHMENT OF THE JESUITS.
22. SCHOOL OF THE CHRISTIAN BRETHREN.
23. PLAZA.
24. BRIDGE & ROAD TO MACHACHI & THE SOUTH.
25. ROAD TO THE NORTH.
26. SCHOOLS.
27. ROAD TO TUMBACO, PIFO, & PAPALLACTA.
28. CHURCH & CONVENT OF S. FRANCISCO.
29. DO. DO. LA MERCED.
30. DO. DO. S. AUGUSTIN.
31. DO. DO. S. DOMINGO.
32. CHURCH OF THE IMMACULATE CONCEPTION.
33. DO. DEL CARMEN ANTIGUO.
34. DO. DEL CARMEN MODERNO.
35. DO. OF STA. CLARA.
36. DO. DO. CATARINA.
37. HOSPITAL CHURCH.
38. HOSPITAL.
39. HOSPICE.
40. CHAPEL OF JERUSALEM.
41. QUEBRADA UNDER QUITO.
42. OPEN SPACE.
43. CONVENT.

QUITO

FROM A PLAN BY J. B. MENTEN

1875

Scale of English Feet

Road to the North   Road to Tumbaco

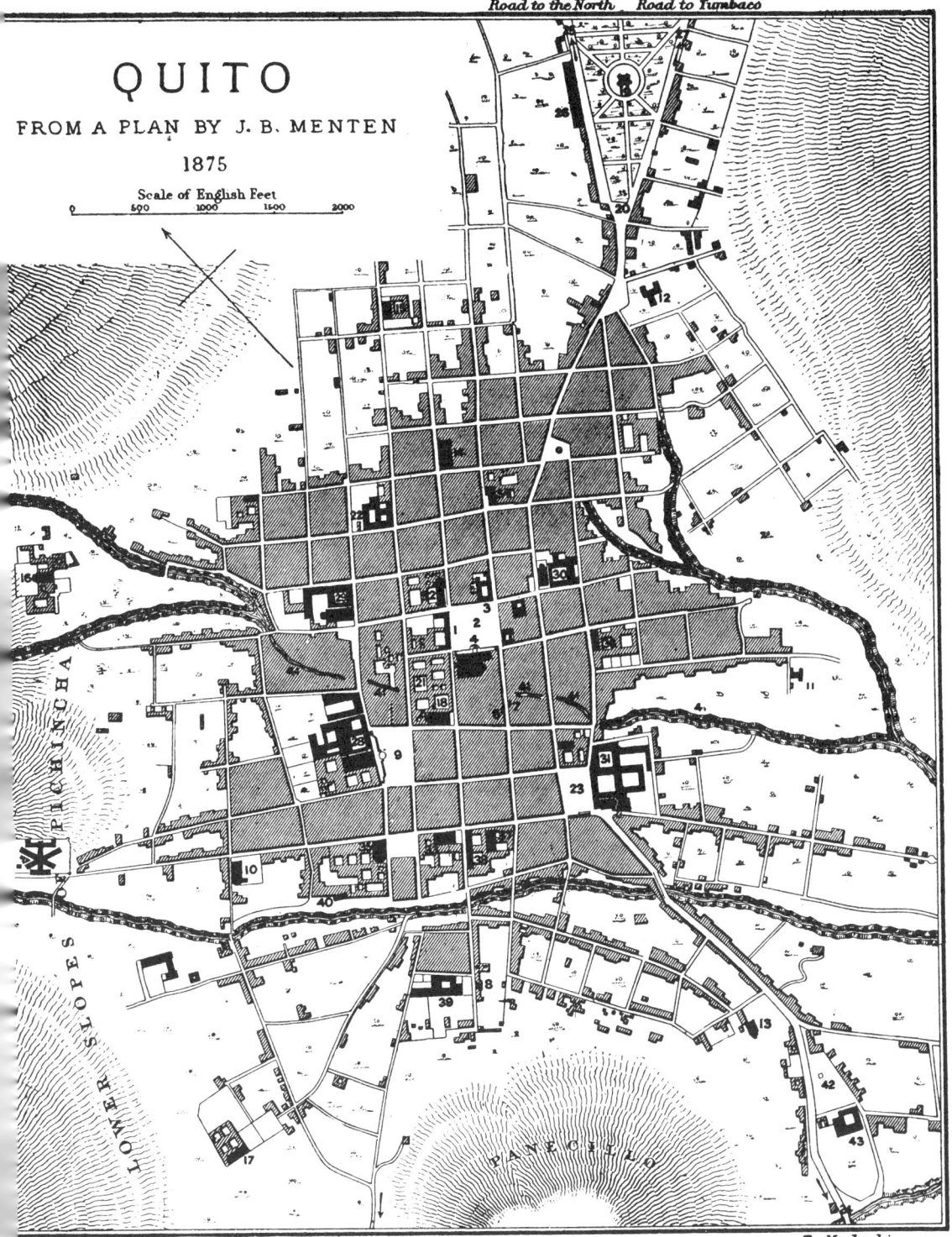

LOWER SLOPES OF PICHINCHA

PANECILLO

To Lloa & Pichincha   To Machachi

feel confident that the number of its inhabitants is far beneath the lower of these estimates.[1] The compact part of Quito does not cover a square mile; and, I think, at the most, the city proper cannot contain more than 30,000 persons. The total may, perhaps, amount to 34,000 or 35,000 if the suburbs which extend along the roads going north and south are included.

The northern is some hundreds of feet higher than the southern end of Quito.[2] Several ancient *quebradas* run through the heart of the city; and, as the whole of the ground upon which it stands is sloping, there is a natural drainage into these fissures. This fact, and the daily occurrence of sharp showers which cleanse the place, doubtless account for its freedom from bad smells, and immunity from pestilence. It had no proper supply of water. The populace depended upon the public fountains and their surrounding basins in the Plazas, which were contaminated with abominations. Very particular persons had two pennyworths of water brought every morning, several miles, in large pots;[3] but, judging from the limited number of water-carriers, the fastidious class formed a select minority of the population. There was one old water-carrier, with white hair and a pink face, who was a well-known figure in Quito. I offered to take his portrait, and told him that he should have a shilling if he stood quite still and only fourpence if he moved. "Señor," said the old fellow, "though several gentlemen have proposed to do the same, you are the first who has suggested any remuneration."

[1] Dr. W. Jameson says (*Journal of Royal Geog. Soc.*, 1861, p. 185): "On several occasions the Government has been desirous of ascertaining the actual number of inhabitants, but without arriving at a satisfactory result. The people became alarmed, from an idea that the formation of a census is a preliminary step towards the imposition of a tax." Mr. Church (in *Report* to Mr. Blaine, dated 1883) says the same.

[2] The accompanying Plan is after one made by Father J. B. Menten, S.J., who was Director of the Observatory in 1880. Corrections and additions have been introduced into it. The names of the streets have been changed since the original was made, and it would be useless to give them.

[3] A *medio* (equal to twopence) was the regular charge for a jar like that borne by the water-carrier I have engraved.

The best near view of the city is obtained from the top of a regularly formed Panecillo, which is just within the range of the Plan,[1] and from the same spot there is an admirable panorama of the Great Andes in the immediate neighbourhood of the Equator. Looking north, first comes Cotocachi (16,301), a rather sharp peak,

THE OLD WATER-CARRIER.

of pyramidal form, referred to in a later chapter; next, turning eastwards, there is Mojanda (14,083 R. & S.), which perhaps covers a greater space than any other mountain in Ecuador; then Cayambe (19,186), a grand, snow-clad extinct volcano lying just north

[1] The Panecillo is a recognized playground for the children of Quito. It was covered with grass and patches of dwarf shrubs. At the summit there was a quantity of moss of the genus *Macromitrium*, and abundance of the lichens *Physcia chrysophthalma*, D C., and *P. flavicans*, D C. Amongst this vegetation I collected about thirty species of spiders, beetles, etc., including those which are enumerated in the *Supplementary Appendix*, Preface, p. ix.

of the Equator; followed by Sincholagua, Cotopaxi, Pasochoa, Rumiñahui, the three hills of Chaupi on the Tiupullo ridge, Corazon, Atacatzo, and Pichincha.[1]

The majority of the dwellings in the city have only a ground-floor with one story above, and the streets mostly have a tame appearance from the small height of the houses and want of objects breaking the sky-line. Any one looking down upon these five hundred acres of flat, featureless roofs will appreciate the artistic value of chimney-pots. Quito has neither chimneys nor fireplaces. Its temperature is supposed to be sufficiently high to dispense with artificial warmth, and no provision is made for heating apartments. As a matter of fact, it *is* usually high enough for comfort,[2] though fires would be agreeable when it falls a degree or two lower than usual, for small variations are more felt in this equable climate than in places where the range in temperature is greater.

It is customary here, when a visitor takes off his hat upon entering a room, to beg him to put it on again; and, in the absence of permission, leave is generally requested. This, it is said, arises from apprehension that cold will be taken by remaining uncovered. The same persons, upon going out of doors, take off their hats to flashes of lightning, no matter whether rain is falling; and, when the streets are busy and lightning is abundant, a grotesque effect is produced by these salutations, which seem to be regarded a duty by well-behaved persons, and are performed as punctiliously as the homage which is paid to religious processions, when they are in sight.

Our hotel was nearly in the centre of the city. It was kept by a truculent Corsican, who habitually stuck his arms akimbo and frowned at his guests, as if ready to knock them down or eat off their heads. One day, at the *table d'hôte*, he fought a pitched

---

[1] I did not see Illiniza from the Panecillo, and am unable to say whether it is ever visible from it.

[2] For temperatures at Quito, see Appendix E.

Northwest side of Antisana, showing that it has an exploded crater.

The Illinizas (twin peaks) seen to the west, at dusk, from the Pan-American Highway.

These shattered glaciers show that the Illinizas are very difficult climbs. This peak was first climbed by the Carrels. Whymper made two attempts to climb it, and failed both times because he was surrounded by cloud and could see nothing, and the slopes and crags were sheathed with new ice.

Wheatfield in the Central Highlands between Chimborazo and Quito.

An irrigation technique at least a thousand years old.

Central Highlands village, which McIntyre calls "the most Inca-appearing village I have ever found."

A water-carrier reminiscent of Whymper's illustration on page 169.

Salasaca Indian dancers, near Ambato (see page 82).

Wild horses on the rocky plain called Pedregal at the foot of Cotopaxi.

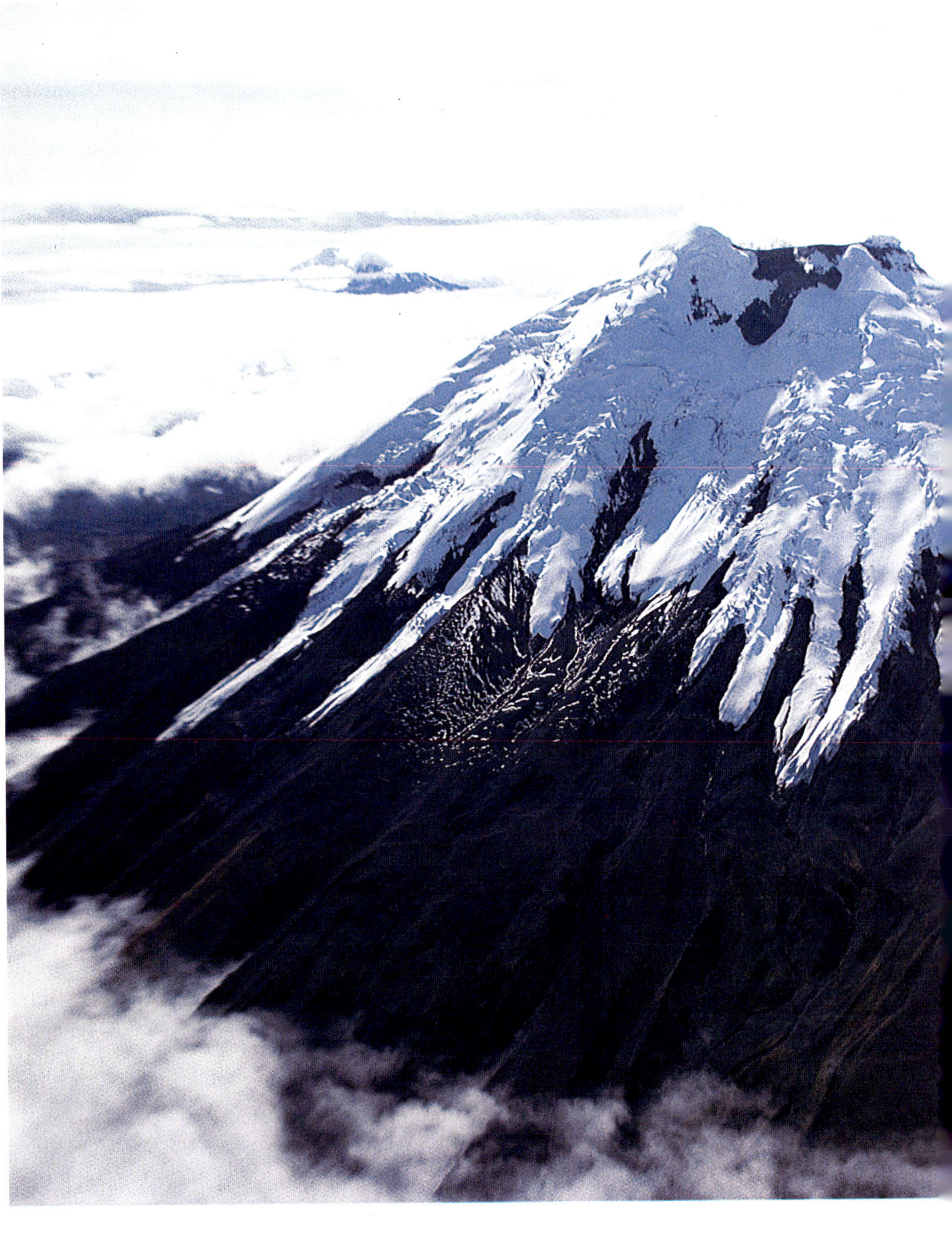

Loren McIntyre on Cotopaxi's glacier, late in the afternoon the day before his summit ascent.

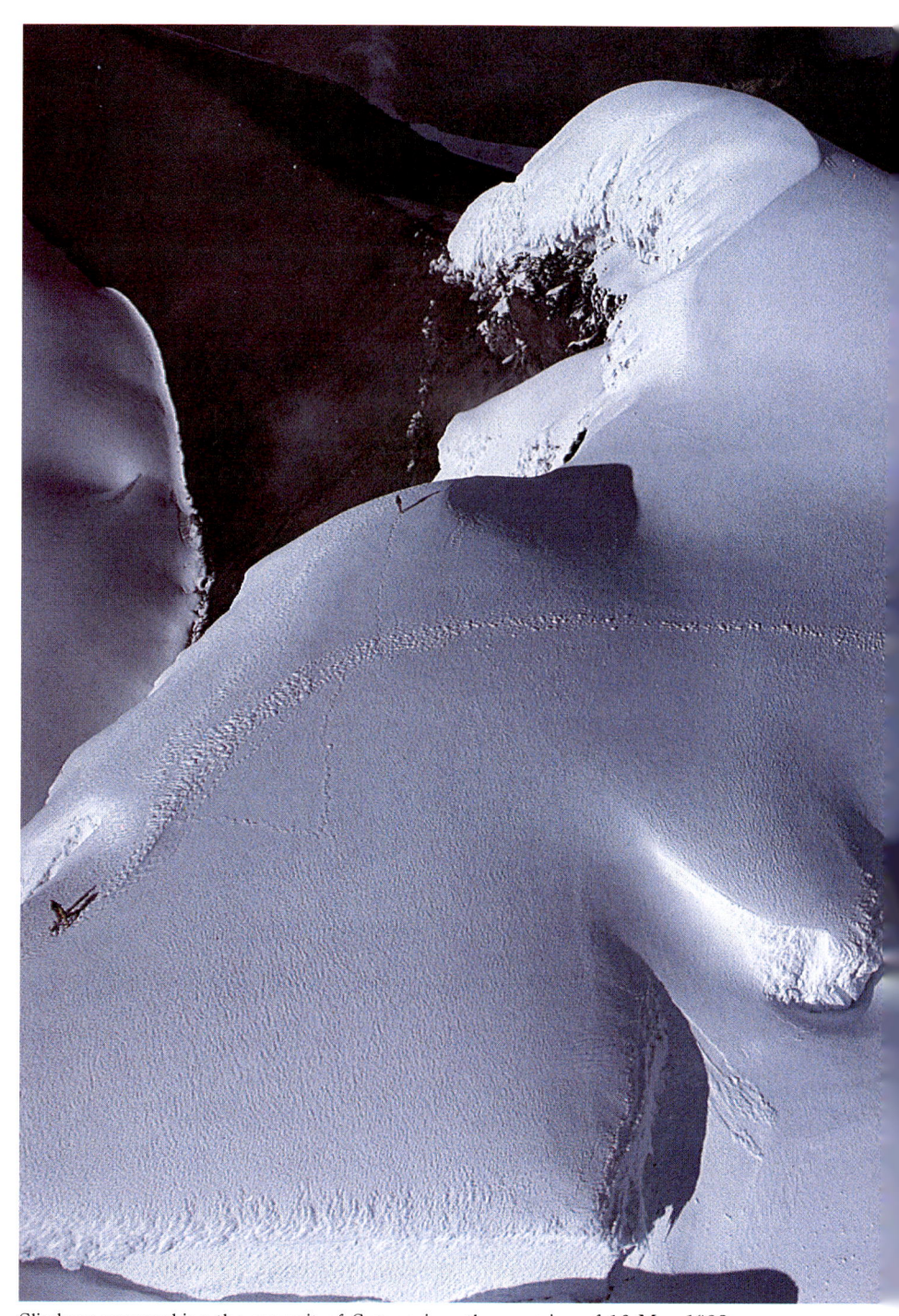

Climbers approaching the summit of Cotopaxi on the morning of 16 May 1982

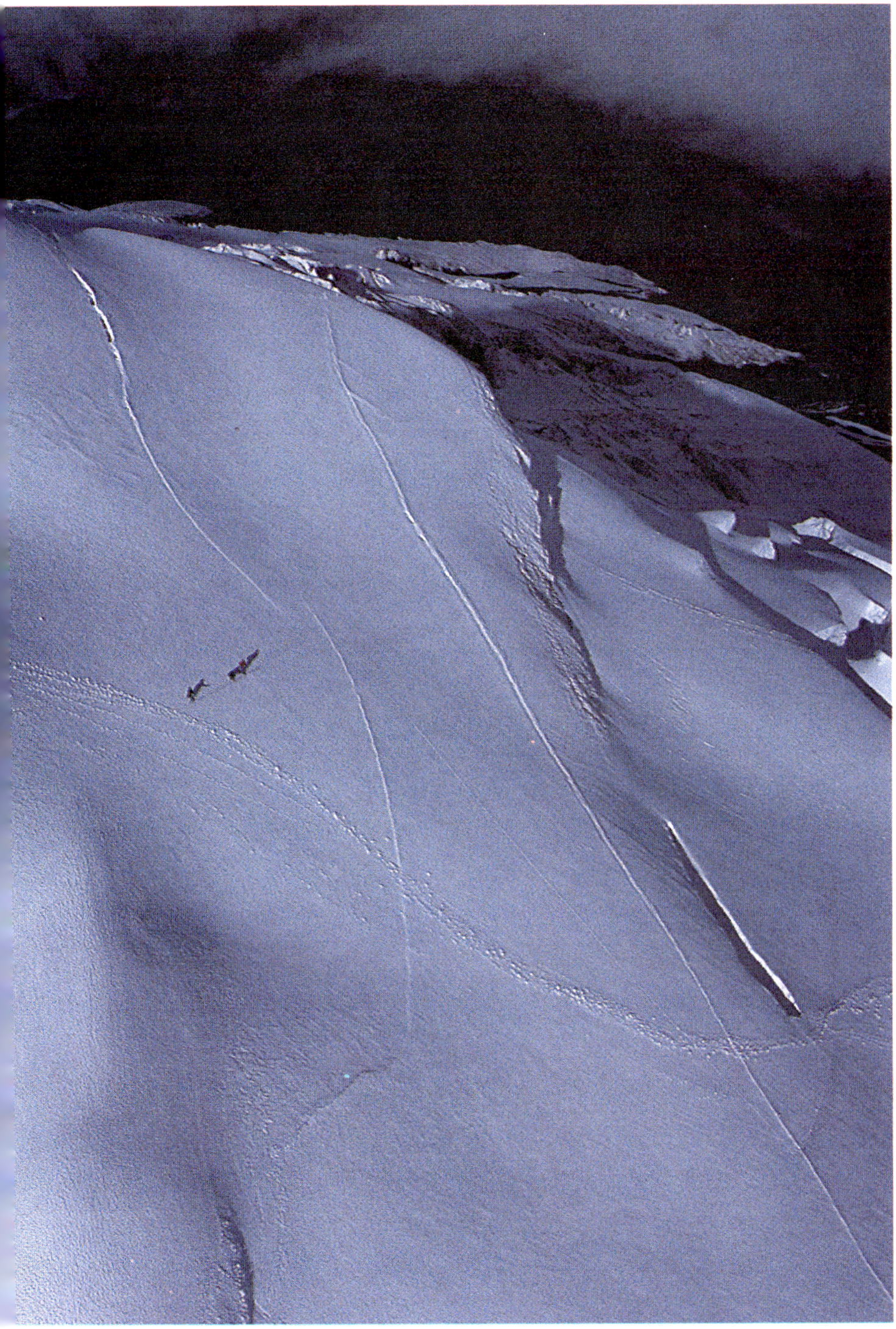

Cotopaxi's summit crater, 2300 feet by 1650 feet.

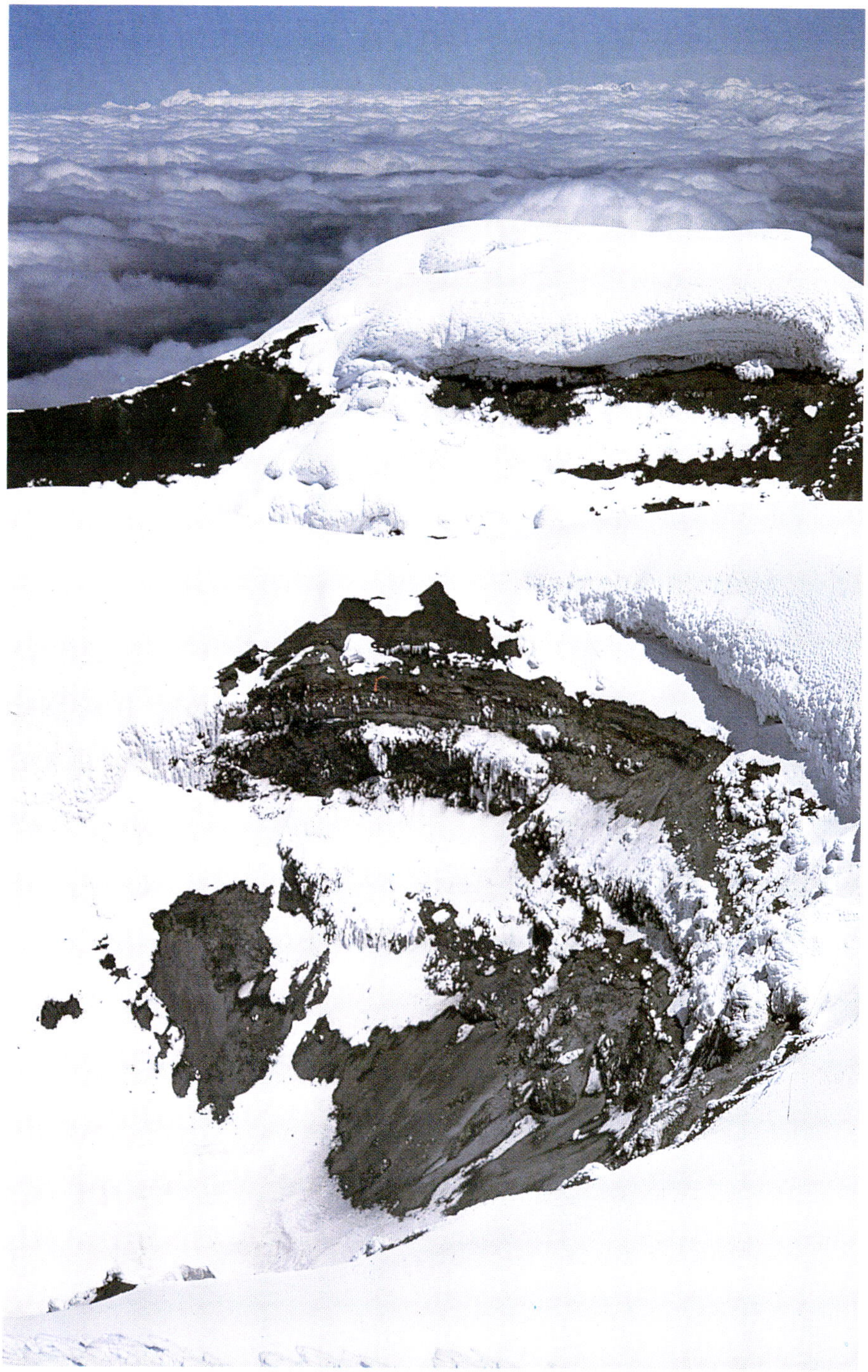

El Altar is an exploded volcano with a huge caldera which contained a glacier when Whymper went by. He did not climb any of the spires around the rim of the caldera.

Sangay in the jungle.

Looking north at Sangay's south face as McIntyre flies around the mountain.

Quito, in 1966, with Pichincha in background. This photograph illustrates that Quito is not in a valley, but is situated on a shelf on the east side of the volcano.

La Ronda, the most colonial street in Quito, preserved from a century before Whymper.

battle in his own *salle-à-manger*. Conversation turned upon the merits of the Napoleons, and Giacometti entertained strong opinions about them, which did not coincide with those of a young Frenchman who had served in the cavalry, and taken part in the combats around Metz. Presently, the gentlemen called each other liar and coward, and then all at once they jumped up and charged —Giacometti seizing a chair by its back and raising it with both hands to brain his guest, who, however, eluded the blow, and grappling with the *maître d'hôtel* soon had him sprawling on the floor, kicking and raving like a madman. Glasses and crockery flew about, and the result would have been very serious (for the china) had not two persons fallen upon the combatants and dragged them apart. No sooner was the innkeeper released than he snatched up a bottle, and again made towards the cuirassier to break it on his head, but they were parted, and dragged yelling from the room to finish the fray outside. The coarseness of their language would have done credit to Billingsgate. I could not see that it was in the least diminished by the low pressure reigning at Quito.

From my windows at the hotel I looked out on one of the principal streets, and had excellent opportunities of viewing the little peculiarities of the Quitonians. Here, as well as in other parts of South America, it is correct for ladies to cover up their features when walking abroad, but I found there was great laxity in this matter, and that the lower orders paid no attention to such proprieties. The straw hats of local manufacture were not fashionable. Men wore the black, chimney-pot hat of civilization, and I have a story to relate about something which befel a black hat in Quito.

A LADY OF QUITO.

Upon the day following our arrival, His Excellency the President of the Republic sent a very polite message through Mr. Hamilton, intimating his wish to see me. He received us without formality and with much cordiality, dismissing a visitor (who was, I believe, a Colonel in the Ecuadorian Army) to the farther end of the apartment. Out of regard to his time, after a little general conversation, we rose to go; but he insisted upon our remaining, and presently inquired if there was anything he could do for me. I answered that there was. At this, just a shade of displeasure appeared on his mobile features, though he kindly asked, "In what way?" I said that it would afford me gratification if he would permit his name to be connected with one of the Great Andes. "With the highest point of Chimborazo," I went on, "one cannot meddle. Its second peak has not been christened, and I ask permission to be allowed to associate your name with it."

The President now became interested in Chimborazo, and desired to know its height, and upon hearing it expressed surprise, saying, "I should have thought it was thirty thousand feet high, *at the least.*" " Pardon me, your Excellency," I replied, one *could* not have proposed to associate the name of *Veintemilla* with a peak *thirty* thousand feet high." He forgave this *impromptu* by asking for an account of the ascent, and Mr. Hamilton engrossed the General's attention with a graphic description of it. Presently, finding himself in want of a blackboard, and seeing nothing more like one than a black hat which was upon the table, he used it to illustrate the spiral ascent, and excited my admiration by the vigour and accuracy with which he traced our route, as he drove a deep furrow through the shining nap, to shew how we sank in the snow.

While this *tête-à-tête* was progressing, the President leaning forwards on his elbows, intently following Mr. Hamilton's discourse, I noticed a movement at the other end of the room; and, glancing round, found that the Colonel was writhing in agony. It was *his* hat, and he was on the point of exploding with suppressed rage at seeing his Sunday head-gear used as a black-board for 'that wretched gringo.' He glared and scowled and seemed ready to spring forward and assassinate all three of us. Mr. Hamilton was quite unconscious that he was raising a storm, but the President noticed my glance, and, turning his head, immediately perceived the state of affairs. His smile then caused our Minister to look, and to drop the hat instantly. With grim humour (which I fear made the Colonel go over to the Revolutionary party), the President requested Mr. Hamilton to continue, as he was much interested; and then by a few light touches, which fortunately went in the direction of the nap, the ascent was completed.

His Excellency General Ygnacio de Veintemilla came into power by a combination of stratagem and force, and went out fighting. It is difficult to procure information upon the modern history of this country; and, in default of a more authoritative source, I make the following extract from the *Catecismo de Geografia de la Republica del Ecuador*, by Juan Leon Mera, Quito, 1875, pp. 180-184.

"During the Presidency of Garcia Moreno," he says, "the nation entered upon a new life; order and economy were introduced into the national finances, part of the floating debt was redeemed; Brethren of the Christian Schools, Sisters of the Sacred Heart, and Jesuit Fathers were brought in to direct public instruction; and some important public works were begun, particularly the high road between Quito and Guayaquil. At the end of 1863, in the interior, a Liberal Revolution was suppressed. . . In 1864 another Revolution was discovered, and there were revolutionary movements in Manabi. . . In 1865 the Revolutionists of Guayaquil seized the steamer Guayas. The President made, personally, the necessary arrangements, and went after the enemy. Those ringleaders who fell into the hands of the conqueror were put to death. . . Peace being re-established, Jeronimo Carrion succeeded Moreno as President"; he resigned in 1867 and Javier Espinosa was elected, but (in 1868) "the effervescence of parties continued, people talked openly of a Liberal Revolution, the Conservative party saw their danger and hastened to make one by renominating Garcia Moreno on Jan. 16, 1869. The President resigned the same day, and the Revolution spread over the whole Republic. Meanwhile, a Revolution in Guayaquil broke out (Mar. 19) which was suppressed. . . In December of the same year a conspiracy was discovered in Quito, and a new Revolution in Cuenca was suppressed. Since that time order has been established and peace assured, and Ecuador continues on her path of material and moral progress under the shelter of Republican institutions, based on the catholic principles which she has determined to adopt."

This little book concludes by stating that Garcia Moreno was assassinated on August 6, 1875.[1] He was succeeded by Dr. Borrero, who recalled General Veintemilla from exile, and placed him in command at Guayaquil. The General advised his patron that he expected the occurrence of another Revolution, and requested the troops might be sent from Quito. Having obtained them, and denuded the Capital of soldiers, Veintemilla made the Revolution, and ejected Borrero. The new President had been in power about two years at the time of my visit, though not always in peaceful possession. At the end of 1877 some rebels from the north, joined by a number of Quitonians, compelled the General to intrench himself in the heart of the city. Presently the insurgents ran short of ammunition and the others sallied forth and defeated them. Four hundred were said to be killed in this affair. It was no secret in 1880 that plots were

GARCIA MORENO.

[1] He was brutally murdered on the Grand Plaza, in front of the Government Offices. Moreno is admitted to have been the strongest President of modern times. He deserved well of his country by the construction of the great road through the interior, and the introduction of compulsory education.

on foot to remove him, and the conspirators would have endeavoured to accomplish this at an earlier date if they had seen their way past his three thousand breechloaders.

The Clericals lost no opportunity of perambulating the streets with religious processions, and these were treated with respect. The President made counter-demonstrations with his troops, by parading them every day. I noticed that individual Priests walking about were treated with scant courtesy, and possibly on this account they appeared little in public. By his opponents, General Veintemilla was frequently termed the head of the irreligious party, from his want of harmony with the Church.[1] Under his rule, newly-arrived ecclesiastics were refused admittance to Ecuador,[2] and the Jesuits, though not expelled, went more or less into hiding. He was ultimately ejected in July, 1883, after six or eight months of revolution, and Caamaño was elected President. His term of office expired in 1888, and now Señor Antonio Flores rules the Republic.[3]

[1] The Church property, though somewhat despoiled, is still very extensive. The Cathedral, the Jesuits' Church, and the Church of the Immaculate Conception are the most important religious edifices. The latter was partly destroyed by fire while I was at Quito, on the night of March 25, 1880 (the night preceding Good Friday). At a time when the building was crowded, a candle on the High Altar tumbled over and set the surrounding decorations in a blaze. There was a panic amongst the congregation and several lives were lost.

[2] This was the fate of some who arrived at Guayaquil on the same steamer as myself. They were sent on board again, having been previously informed that there were too many of their profession already in the country and recommended to go to Lima. They could not have looked more unhappy if they had been told to go to Jericho.

[3] A President is practically Dictator. See the *Report* to Mr. Blaine by Mr. Church from which I have already quoted. He states that the Congress is composed of a Senate and House of Deputies, and that it assembles (usually for sixty days) *every second year*. The executive power is confided to the President, who is assisted by a Council of State. "The large majority of the Council are named by the President, and are his willing servants." According to Article 80 of the Constitution, the Council "may confer extraordinary powers" upon the President, and authorize him "to increase the army, dispose of the public funds, collect taxes in advance, impose forced loans, change the capital of the country, expatriate or imprison citizens, etc."

I feel it unnecessary to say much respecting the manners and customs of the Ecuadorians. They are a promising people. Mr. Hassaurek (who was for several years United States Minister-Resident at Quito) says[1] :—

> The "custom of making high-sounding promises is universal among Ecuadorians. . . If you make the acquaintance of one of them, he will overwhelm you with offers of his services. He will beseech you to 'count him as one of the number of your friends'; he will place his house, his haciendas, his horses at your disposal; he will ask you to treat him confidentially, and to speak to him frankly, whenever you should need anything that he can supply; he will protest his ardent desire to be your friend and to serve you in every possible manner. . . Should you really apply to them for any of the services so pompously proffered, you must expect, as a general rule, that they will find a well-sounding excuse for refusing."

Mr. Hassaurek seems inclined to consider these protestations as of no greater value than the words "your very humble and obedient servant" at the end of a letter, and as regards the majority of them his view is possibly correct. No one except an idiot would be disposed to treat them literally. The difficulty experienced by strangers is to discriminate between expressions which are simply flowery, and those which are meant to be substantial. On various occasions, houses, haciendas, and horses, were actually placed at my disposal, and gentlemen went out of their way to render valuable services and unexpected courtesies; and it would be exceedingly ungracious to ignore these disinterested actions, even though there were a large number of unredeemed pledges, and flowers which did not blossom into fruit. As regards these it is charitable to think with Mr. Church that "the enthusiastic kindness of their hearts frequently causes Ecuadorians to

[1] See *Four Years among Spanish-Americans*, by F. Hassaurek, New York, 1867. The descriptions in this work of the natives and their ways are generally accurate. In other matters, this author is often unreliable. At p. 119, he says, "For leagues round Quito *scorpions have never been heard of. . . Flies, even, are very rare. . . There are no lizards, or even bugs or beetles in the grass or on trees.*" These statements are untrue.

make promises small and great, which afterwards escape their memory or are beyond their ability to perform."

Amongst their other salient peculiarities one may point out that Punctuality, which is esteemed a virtue by some, they seem to consider a pernicious vice. Their inveterate habit of procrastination, and use of the word *mañana*, has been a theme upon which every one has written who has dealt with Ecuador. Nothing is to be done *to-day*. Everything is *promised* for *to-morrow*, and when the morrow arrives it will be promised for mañana again. The equality of the temperature, and the equality in the length of the days, and the presumption that to-morrow will be like to-day, in my opinion, have much to do with this. "It would be good for these people," said Jean-Antoine, "to have a winter." The Alpine peasant, well acquainted with its inconveniences and hardships, felt that upon the whole they acted beneficially by promoting habits of industry and forethought.

It is less possible to make allowances for their general disposition to disregard the sacredness of agreements, to repudiate contracts, and to advance ulterior claims. Following these practices, as a natural result, there is universal distrust and want of confidence. They do not think the same as other people about these matters; or, to put it in a different way, their code of honour is different from ours. In many countries it is considered complimentary to say "Sir, your Word is as good as your Bond"; but, for reasons which need not be pointed out, one is debarred from the use of that phrase in Ecuador. A foreigner at Quito, concerned in trade, who from many dealings with the Ecuadorians was able to speak with some authority, said to me, "I never consider a transaction terminated unless I give my customer a whipping." It appears that, in this country, the marks of the whip answer in the place of a receipt-stamp.

These observations apply solely to the white and to the hybrid population. The Indians have the same hospitable instincts as the Spanish-Americans, and I am inclined to characterize as their principal infirmity an extreme timidity, heightened by the general, and all-pervading distrust. The Indian population in Quito bore a larger proportion to the whites than in the towns we had already visited.[1] I am told that a number still remain of pure descent, whose ancestors have never contracted alliances with the conquerors. On the other hand, it is said that such a thing as a Spanish family of perfectly pure descent is not to be found in the country. For the most part the Indians lived in the suburbs. They flocked in every morning, and kept daily market with their baskets of wares on the three great plazas. I bought from them the examples of hand-made lace that are given on p. 179, which competes successfully with importations. It was remarked, too, that preference was shewn for the thread and calico made at Chillo, and for the coarse woollens produced at some local factories, over similar English manufactures, notwithstanding that the foreign goods could sometimes be obtained at lower rates than the native ones.

Prices in Ecuador generally ruled high, though there was a large difference in some matters between what was asked on the coast and in the interior. Labour at Guayaquil was absurdly dear, and rents were extravagant, while in the interior both were low. Foreign goods were expensive all over the country, and seldom sold for less than three or four times European prices.

A nominal quart bottle of Bass cost one and eightpence to two shillings at Guaranda, and two shillings at Ambato. At Latacunga it had risen to three shillings and fourpence, and that was the price at all places farther to the north.[2] They asked two shillings and threepence for a threepenny cake of soap at Ambato. A piece of sponge which might have been obtained for less than sixpence in England cost me a peso at Quito, and

[1] This continued as we progressed northwards. In Cotocachi, Otovalo, and the surrounding neighbourhood Indians largely outnumbered the whites.

[2] Bass' Ale was found all over Ecuador, and was highly appreciated there. At Quito, an enterprizing German was endeavouring to brew. Each of his pint bottles yielded about a gallon of froth and a tea-cup of beer.

ECUADORIAN HAND-MADE LACE.

three shillings and fourpence (ten reals) was the price at the Capital *per pound* for English salt. All glass and china was very dear there, partly through the large amount of breakage in transit, from bad packing.

Native productions were often by no means low in price. Meat (when it could be got) was cheap, and generally ranged from twopence-halfpenny to threepence per pound. In the north, fresh eggs could be bought for four a penny; while in Guayaquil, and in the more southern parts, one to two pesos apiece were demanded for miserable chickens. Spirits of wine cost me three shillings per pint at Guayaquil, and tenpence at Quito! At Otovalo, Cayambe, and other places, brown sugar and unroasted coffee were each tenpence per pound, though raised in the district. Common raisins cost three shillings, and camphor four shillings per pound in Quito.[1]

The high prices of foreign commodities were attributed to excessive duties and the expense of transit. Still, there appeared to be a good margin left, and I doubt if any one was satisfied with less than a hundred per cent. profit. Everywhere there appeared to be openings for commercial enterprize, either for retailers or for wholesale transactions, yet the country seemed to have little attraction to Englishmen, for at the time of my stay there were only three in Quito.[2] Personally, I should not advise any one to embark a single shilling in Ecuador. There are an unknown quantity of earthquakes and revolutions to be taken into account. A man may be rich in one day and wrecked the next. These possibilities invest trade in this region with the excitement of gambling, and the trader should also bear in mind that the repudiation of agreements and the non-fulfilment of contracts will often upset his calculations and blight his hopes.

These references to prices lead me to conclude this chapter

---

[1] Medicines and fancy goods were sold at larger differences from European prices. I could have sold my stock of sulphate of quinine for more than its weight in gold.

[2] Namely, Mr. Hamilton, British Minister-Resident; Mr. Jones, a shopkeeper; and Mr. Verity, an English mechanic out of employment. Of other foreigners there were about twenty-five French, a dozen Germans, and ten Italians, Danes and Swedes.

with a few words upon the money and the Banking institutions of Ecuador. At the time my journey was made, money was reckoned in *Pesos* and *Reals*.[1] Eight *Reals* made a *Peso*. The coins most frequently met with were the silver Peso, silver pieces worth one and two Reals, and half-Real pieces, termed *Medios*. There was a gold coinage not in circulation, and a silver quarter-Real which was seldom seen. In Guayaquil (and I believe on the coast generally) bronze coins were not current; though they were in general use in the interior, and were said to be legal tender as far south as Riobamba. At this time the English Sovereign was worth sixty Reals, and the Peso, therefore, was equal to two Shillings and eight Pence.

There were only two banks, namely, the Bank of Ecuador at Guayaquil, and the Bank of Quito at the Capital. Both of these institutions issued notes (down to the value of one Peso), which were accepted as readily as silver, at their full value, and were very convenient.[2]

I travelled in Ecuador by means of a Letter of Credit, entitling me to draw up to the amount of a sum which was deposited in a London Bank before the letter was issued. I drew something from the Bank of Ecuador, and received from that institution a fresh letter of credit to the Bank of Quito.

The amount taken from the Bank of Ecuador was principally in paper. For small payments it was necessary to have a considerable quantity of reals and medios, and these were handed over the counter in a closed bag. Upon being examined, it appeared that the arithmetic of the Bank differed from that in common use. Anyhow, the money was short by a serious

[1] I am informed that the *present* manner of reckoning money is based on the *hard* or ten real Dollar. The old *Peso* is no longer recognized. This hard dollar is called a *Sucre*, and is of the same nominal value as the Peruvian *Sol*, and the Chilian and Colombian Dollars.

[2] The notes of the Bank of Ecuador circulated everywhere. Those of the Bank of Quito were accepted in the interior generally, but were refused at Riobamba and at places more to the south.

amount; but, inasmuch as it was not counted before being taken away, it was useless to make reclamations.

When proceeding into the interior, these coins were often declined; for it appeared that the natives have a child-like desire to see the image and superscription, and absolutely refuse to take payment in coin that has got into the condition of an elderly British sixpence. It curiously happened that in about one half of the cash I received at Guayaquil one could not distinguish obverse from reverse. No one would accept it, and at Quito I sold it off as old metal, at less than half its nominal value, preferring to put up with the loss rather than be incommoded any longer by a bag of coin which would not pass. This is all I have to say at present concerning the Bank of Ecuador.

At Quito money was drawn when it was required, and before my departure I proposed to close accounts and to take the balance. The Bank Manager deducted about four pounds sterling for what he was pleased to term his 'advances.' I was unable to regard as 'advances' monies which were paid on account of a sum which had been deposited several months before, though he assured me that "it was their usual custom." Said I, "your custom is novel and interesting, and it shall be mentioned in a book that I intend to write upon my journey, as it is a thing that ought to be known," and supposed that this would be the end of the matter.

Shortly afterwards, however, the Bank Manager expressed a desire to see me, and tendered the money he had stopped, not, he said with some emphasis, because I was going to write a book, but because he thought "it would be more regular" to charge the amount to the Bank of Ecuador. I mentally contrasted "it is our usual custom" with "it would be more regular," and only remarked that perhaps the Bank of Ecuador would not take the same view; and upon return to Guayaquil my surmise proved to be correct, and I found that the Bank of Ecuador had snapped its fingers at its brother in the Capital.

This is all I have to observe about the Bank of Quito, except that it is said to be a flourishing institution, paying good dividends. The two Banks enjoy, I am told, the privilege of re-issuing their notes until they are worn out, and refuse payment of them when certain marks and numbers disappear. Though this manner of earning a dividend is exceedingly simple in operation and certain in results, and seems to be accepted by the people with perfect resignation, it is possible that it is one of the various causes which produce the universal mistrust of each other and of everybody that is exhibited throughout the country.

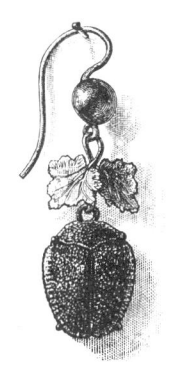

BEETLE-WING EARRING.

THE HACIENDA OF ANTISANA.

CHAPTER X.

THE FIRST ASCENT OF ANTISANA.

WE[1] left Quito for Antisana on March 4, the day following my interview with the President; and crossing the Puengasi ridge, descended into the basin of Chillo. This is another of those large (almost saucer-shaped) depressions which it seems to me are more appropriately termed *basins* than valleys. It is, however, often called the *valley* of Chillo, after a small village on its southern edge, where there is a cotton factory belonging to the Aguirre family.[2]

---

[1] To replace Mr. Perring, who left me at Quito, I engaged a Mr. Verity, an English mechanic who had recently terminated an engagement at the Chillo factory. He continued with me until the beginning of May, and I found his acquaintance with the country round Quito very useful.

[2] This is one of the old, noble families of Ecuador. Under the Republican levelling they were deprived of their title, Marquis de Selvalegre.

THE BASIN OF CHILLO.

This basin is bounded on the east by Antisana, which is one of the loftiest of the Equatorial Andes, and is amongst those that extend over a great space of ground. From east to west, that part of it which is 12,000 feet above the sea or higher, covers about twenty miles,[1] and from north to south it is not much less extensive. On the south, the basin is enclosed by Sincholagua; on the west, by Pasochoa and the Puengasi ridge; and on the north by the southern end of an important block of mountains (of which there is no indication on my map) called Guamani,[2] that extends right up to the Equator, and on the west almost touches the village of Pifo. The drainage of this basin, united with the Rio Pita (coming from Cotopaxi), and with the Rio Grande from the basin of Machachi, intersects the Plain of Tumbaco, and falls ultimately into the Rio de Guallabamba.

During our passage across the basin of Chillo, I did not at any time get a glimpse of a single one of these surrounding mountains; and seldom saw more than two or three miles in any direction, often not so much as a mile. I did not see a single feature from which bearings for positions could be obtained, and our track as far as the Hacienda of Antisanilla is accordingly laid down from dead reckoning. The bottom of this basin is considerably lower, and its temperature is appreciably higher than that of Quito.[3]

Shortly before my departure from Europe, Boussingault published in the *Comptes Rendus* of the French Academy of Sciences

---

[1] On the west, Antisana may be considered to extend as far as the Hacienda of Piñantura (10,308 R. & S.)

[2] The ramifications of Guamani, so far as I am aware, have never been explored. Nothing is known of its eastern side. In the month of April, I overlooked this region from the north, and found there were no peaks in it fairly within the snow-line.

[3] Though the land here was more under cultivation than the greater part of the country we had traversed, the inhabitants were miserably off for food. Potato soup was the only article of diet that could be relied upon. All our provisions were taken from Quito.

some Meteorological observations[1] which were said to have been made by Señor Carlos Aguirre, thirty-three years before, at the Hacienda of Antisana. These observations had a particular interest for me, for they gave information respecting the weather we were likely to experience at great heights in the neighbourhood of the Equator. It appeared from them that the elevated farm where they were made enjoyed a very equable temperature, and was abundantly provided with fogs. Temperature was highest in January and lowest in August, and the mean for the year (1846) was found to be 5°·18 C. (equal to a little more than 41° Faht.). In 375 days there were recorded 130 of fog, 122 rainy, 36 with snow, and only 34 on which the sky was visible.[2]

After crossing the Rio Pita,[3] the weather kept up its character, and black thunder-clouds gathered in all directions. Foreseeing the tempest, we hurried for shelter to a large farm, the Hacienda Colegio, and just escaped a tremendous downpour. The sudden irruption of a score of men and beasts was treated as a matter of course. We were received with the greatest urbanity, and on leaving at 4.45 on the following morning were provided with a guide as far as the small village of Pintac — midway between the

[1] *Détermination de la hauteur du mercure dans le baromètre sous l'équateur; amplitude des variations diurnes barométriques à diverses stations dans les Cordillères*, par M. Boussingault. *Comptes Rendus hebdomadaires des séances de l'Acad. des Sciences*, tome lxxxviii., No. 24.

[2] Upon my return (through a reference made by Dr. W. Reiss) I found that these observations had also appeared in the *Comptes Rendus* in 1851 (tome xxxii.) There are numerous discrepancies between these papers. In the one published in 1879 it is stated that the greatest observed diurnal variation of the barometer (in 1846) was 1·65 mm., on April 27; while in the other paper there is a record of 1·69 mm., on March 12, 1846. The mean annual temperature is said in vol. lxxxviii. to have been 5°·18 C., and in vol. xxxii. it is seen to have been 4°·86 C. It is desirable that some one should point out which of these two papers is to be considered authoritative.

[3] The Rio Pita was running very rapidly here. Our animals crossed it by swimming, and were carried down about a quarter of a mile before they came to land.

two places passing over some road that was several degrees worse than the Camino Real between Muñapamba and Tambo Gobierno, with mud two to three feet deep. I had been rebuked in Quito for objecting to that 'Royal' route, because our animals had sunk halfway up their flanks. Upon asking my monitor what *he* considered a bad road, he said, "A road is bad when the beasts tumble into mud-holes and vanish right out of sight." This nearly occurred at one place. Our narrow track (at this spot, a mere rut between two walls of earth) divided. On the right there was a steep and greasy passage, and on the left a pool, eight or ten feet across. My animal stopped on the brink, unwilling to proceed. Dismounting, I gave it a touch with the whip, it went head first into the slough, and emerged on the other side a miserable object, dripping with filth, which for a second had risen above its hindquarters. This mud-hole was about four feet deep, and was the finest we discovered in Ecuador.

On quitting Pintac, however, the track became better, and highly interesting; at some parts leading between deep, mossy banks laden with semi-tropical ferns and creepers, underneath branches and roots, and crossing sparkling streams — rare things in this country. After passing the large farm of Piñantura,[1] our ardour was damped by one of the afternoon deluges, and when this ceased we found our path ran roughly parallel to a great stream of lava, which descended from the clouds, and spread out into the valley of the Isco.

Whilst winding in and out of the bends, amongst the arched foliage, in advance of the others, I was surprised — not having met a soul in the course of the day — to see a grave and very unshaven man approaching, well mounted on a fast ambler; by dress, as well as by demeanour, evidently no common wayfarer. He drew rein, and there was scarcely time to wonder who was this distinguished stranger before another horseman cantered round the

---

[1] Insects were abundant here, and several novelties were secured whilst on the march. See *Supp. App.*, pp. 20 and 60.

farther corner, and another, and then they came by twos and threes, until I saw thirty or more, rising and falling over the undulating ground like buoyant ships on a breezy sea; jovial, wild-looking fellows, picturesquely attired in sombreros and with legs encased in hairy buskins, all riding powerful horses, and sitting like men born in the saddle. As they came up, they halted at a respectful distance behind their lord. I sent Verity forward to make enquiries; and then, after formally saluting, each party went its way.

I was not aware until the train had swept past that we had met Señor Rebolledo, the owner of Antisana, of the farms of Piñantura, Antisanilla, Antisana and all the intervening country, and other large estates; the proprietor of a princely domain, unlimited on the Amazonian side. If one enquired how far it extended, they answered, "As far as you can go to the East" —it had no boundaries in that direction.

They had been engaged in a grand stock-taking; and, as the cattle ranged over many miles and had to be driven in from long distances, the work was too much for the usual hands, and *major-domos* had been borrowed from the surrounding properties to assist in the operation. Judging from their hilarity, the census was satisfactory. Señor Rebolledo heard somehow that we were without cheese, and sent a quantity after us. A messenger came daily to the Hacienda of Antisana to learn our wants, and I had only to express a desire to have it satisfied. "Tell me," I said, when we were better acquainted, "why do you shower these civilities upon me?" and received no other answer than "I took to you from the first."

In a short time after passing this splendid troop, the track dipped down to cross the Isco rivulet, and we arrived at the Hacienda Antisanilla (12,342 feet), a small place built alongside the lava-stream of which I have spoken—rather densely populated by savage dogs, and by herdsmen who were not so refined in the matter of cleanliness as one might have wished. I could not trust myself upon the beds which they politely vacated (loose straw strewn over wooden bunks) and passed the night by preference on the top of a four-foot table.

The length of the lava-stream of Antisanilla can hardly be less than seven to eight miles. I clambered to the top, and got little reward, for the farther side, as well as its upper and lower extremities, were lost in mist. Its red colouring is probably superficial, and the nucleus of the mass, I conjecture, is a very dark and compact lava, specimens of which were broken out with some labour.[1] The surface was extremely rugged, and bore an amazing quantity of the lichen *Usnea florida*, Fries.

On the morning of March 6 we left for the Hacienda of Antisana, led by one of Señor Rebolledo's people, who dismounted from time to time, and lit the grass to shew the way to our laggards. The Hacienda was a barn-like building, occupying one side of a large enclosure for herding cattle; and had remained, I was told, unaltered since the visit of Humboldt. We took up quarters on the first floor, and kept constant watch from its little gallery for the appearance of Antisana, which had been completely invisible during the last few days. We should not, indeed, have had the slightest suspicion that we were in the neighbourhood of a mountain of the first rank, or a mountain of any kind, if the herdsmen had not told us the contrary.

In the course of the afternoon the mists opened lazily, and revealed bits here and there, and then drifted across and shut them out.[2] These occasional glimpses lasted only a few minutes

---

[1] "A black, sub-vitreous rock, containing small crystals of white felspar, whose diameter is commonly not more than 0·125 inch. The general aspect of the specimen shews it to be one of the darker varieties of andesite, a member of the group of rocks that have been variously named melaphyre, pitchstone-porphyrite, etc. . . . The rock on the whole agrees best with augite-andesite. Its specific gravity, determined by Mr. J. J. H. Teall, is 2·656."—Prof. T. G. Bonney, *Proc. Royal Soc.*, March 13, 1884.

[2] The view facing p. 190 has been constructed from several photographs which I took at this time. We did not see so much of the mountain at any single moment.

or seconds, and shewed that the mountain had not the simplicity of form that we had supposed. At such distances as it had previously been seen (25 to 30 miles) the minor details were indistinguishable, and the crest had seemed to be a long, uninterrupted, snowy ridge. It now became apparent that its structure was more complicated; and, if the mountain had been viewed for the first time from the Hacienda, we might have been in doubt as to the position of the highest point.[1]

From these fragmentary glimpses, I made out that the upper 3500 feet of Antisana were almost absolutely covered by snow and glacier, and that on an ascent we should not touch rock at all. The summit bore 50° E. of N. (magnetic) from the Hacienda, and the base of the nearest glacier had almost exactly the same bearing.[2] The main course of this ice-stream occupied the hollow in the centre of the view, and at its superior extremity was fissured by large and very long crevasses; higher still there were many compound fractures, and the summit of the mountain was protected by an enormous schrund, forming a moat, which was obviously impassable on the west and north. I proposed to make for the nearest glacier; and, after ascending the trough or hollow, to bear to the left with the view of reaching the summit from the south. Anticipating that nothing would be gained by waiting, I gave the order to march.

We started from the Hacienda of Antisana at 4.35 a.m., on March 7, and steering N.E. (under the guidance of some of the herdsmen, who had a perfect acquaintance with the lower slopes) got to the base of the glacier (15,295 feet) at 6.40; having lost some time by the disappearance of a certain impetuous person who could not brook local leaders.[3] Our animals were left here,

[1] The true summit of Antisana lies underneath the asterisk at the top of the engraving.

[2] This glacier is concealed by clouds in the engraving.

[3] Jean-Antoine always endeavoured to be in front, and on several occasions caused trouble by getting out of touch. He was cured of this habit by something that occurred on Cayambe.

ANTISANA, (19,335 FEET) SEEN FROM THE HACIENDA (13,306 FEET).

and we proceeded on foot, by moraine on the northern side (right bank) of the glacier, nearly seven hundred feet higher in forty minutes; and then, arriving at the termination of land, dismissed the natives, who up to this point had carried the baggage. The elevation of this place was 15,984 feet above the sea.

We roped up at once,[1] and took to the ice at 7.30 a.m. Only the first part of it was free from snow, and it was highly crevassed; but, as the fissures were small at the beginning, we were able to keep a direct course for about an hour, at this time passing alongside the serrated ridge that is shewn on the right of the engraving,[2] having the upper part of the mountain free from cloud. The glacier then steepened, and became broken up into *séracs* (nearly invisible from below) which required much cutting, and beating down to consolidate the snow-bridges leading from one to another. Some of these passages were very complicated, and extensive circuits had to be made to avoid the largest crevasses. At 10.30 a.m. the mists caught us up, and half an hour later we arrived at a prodigious schrund, not less than two hundred feet deep and some sixty feet wide. We wasted more than two hours in attempts to cross it, and I spoilt my eyes by vainly endeavouring to see into the invisible. At last it was found that we had run into a *cul-de-sac*, and had to retreat. At 1.20 p.m. we turned to descend,[3] and by 5.55 were back at the hacienda.

[1] Although not necessary to do so at this stage, it would have been at a later one. It conduced to regularity in the march.

To the advantages to be derived from the use of the rope in mountaineering which are set forth at pp. 372-377 of *Scrambles amongst the Alps* may be added that it tends to produce a better average rate of speed. The pace of a party is determined by that of its slowest member. When tied up, the rapid or impetuous ones cannot rush away, and the slow-coaches are urged on.

[2] The points on this ridge were decorated with tufted cornices. See p. 133.

[3] The place at which we turned back was 17,623 feet above the sea. It was found afterwards that we had borne too much to the right, and had been going away from the summit.

It appears from a passage in the *Comptes Rendus* (vol. lxxxviii., p. 1241)[1] that Boussingault was affected on Antisana by snow-blindness, and I had a similar unpleasant experience on the 7th of March. Though the harm was done between 11 a.m. and 1 p.m. (through uncovering the eyes to use my field-glass), it did not manifest itself for some hours later. In the course of the evening I became unable to see, and remained in that condition for twenty-four hours. Verity sat up through the night handing rags dipped in a solution of sulphate of zinc, changing them when they grew hot, and this occurred in a few minutes after each application.

The affection that is termed 'snow-blindness' is inflammation of the eyes. They become extraordinarily sensitive to light. The lids refuse to open; tears come freely, and coagulating round the lashes glue the lids fast. To apply a lotion effectively, the lids must be forced open, and the instant this is done the patient will imagine that red-hot needles are being driven through the eyes into the brain. The pain is acute, and sometimes makes strong men howl.[2]

Snow-blindness has long been known to Indians dwelling in the Andes. Acosta, writing three centuries ago, mentions a remedy that they applied, which reminds one of the raw beefsteaks used by prize-fighters.

---

[1] "Pendant mon ascension, je fus atteint subitement d'une ophthalmie des plus graves, causée par la réverbération des neiges. Obligé de retourner à Quito, je dus renoncer à continuer les observations que j'avais commencées à la métairie."

[2] Medical men recommend two or three grains of sulphate of zinc to an ounce of water. In practice, I find that the solution may be made stronger, with safety and benefit, and that six, eight or ten grains to the ounce is not too much to use. Although the inflammation may be reduced quickly, and the absolute inability to see may soon pass away, the eyes remain tender and weak for a long time (after a bad attack, even for weeks or months) and they are more liable to be affected than before, unless extra precautions are taken.

Puffing and cracking of the skin, and snow-blindness, can be avoided by keeping the face covered, and by using tinted snow-spectacles. My usual appearance at great elevations on this journey is shewn at p. 80.

"Comming," he says, "one night into a Tambo or Inne, being much afflicted with paine in mine eies, thinking they would fall out, the which dooth commonly happen in those partes, for that they passe thorow places covered with snow, which is the cause of this accident, being troubled with this paine, and out of patience, there came an Indian woman, which said to me, 'Father, lay this to thine eies, and thou shalt be cured.' It was a peece of the flesh of vicuñas, newly killed and all bloody. I vsed this medicine, and presently the paine ceased, and soone after went quite away."[1]

On the evening of March 8 I began to recover sight,[2] and planned another attempt to scale the misty mountain. I cherished great expectations of a boundless view on the eastern side, when looking down upon the basin of the Amazons — the largest forest-covered region in the world. The only two known ways out of Ecuador, through the Andes, to the great South American river, are those which lead through Papallacta[3] for the Napo route, and through Baños for the Pastassa. These places are about ninety miles apart, and nothing is known of the intervening country, or of that more north and south. The trails on these routes pass through forest. No distant vistas are possible, and our knowledge of the region has scarcely advanced since it was first made known, shortly after the Spanish Conquest.

I conjectured that the atmospheric conditions on Antisana strongly resembled those which prevailed on Chimborazo, where it had frequently been noticed, from our Second and Third Camps, that the clouds sank below 16,000 feet at the approach of night, and left the higher regions clear. With the return of day they again mounted, or were re-created, around the summits. The complicated ice-navigation near the top of Antisana could not

[1] Quoted from *The Natural and Moral History of the Indies*, by Father Joseph de Acosta (reprinted from the English translated edition of Edward Grimston, 1604, for the Hakluyt Society, 1880; vol. 1, pp. 287-8).

[2] The right eye remained painful for two months, and did not recover until return to Europe.

[3] Papallacta, according to Dr. M. Villavicensio, means 'country of potatoes.' It is the name of a small village, lying, I am told, about as far to the north of the summit of Antisana as the Hacienda of Antisanilla lies to the west of it.

be effected in a fog. It was necessary to see where we were going, and to arrive at this part at an early hour, before the mists had risen. It was therefore arranged to camp out, at the edge of the glacier, as high as natives could be taken.

On March 9, at 12.55 p.m., we started again; got the caravan to the foot of the moraine at 2.40, and all the baggage up to the camping-place (15,984 feet) by 4 p.m. Our natives with Verity then returned to the hacienda, leaving us at the extreme top of the moraine[1] on the right bank of the glacier, which forms a tail or lower prolongation of the basin in the centre of the engraving. A fierce hail-storm occurred while we were on the way, and snow fell heavily afterwards; yet the temperature did not descend so low as the freezing-point in the night, and at 4 a.m. on the 10th it stood at 40°·5 Faht.

The weather seemed very doubtful in the morning, and we delayed until daybreak, to see how it would develop. The Carrels and I got away at 5.38 a.m., and travelled quickly, through deriving considerable benefit from the track made on the 7th, which was well seen, although several inches of snow had recently fallen. At 7.30 a.m. clouds formed around the highest point of the mountain, and it remained invisible until the afternoon. At about 8 a.m., when approaching the summit ridge, we got into a labyrinth of crevasses, and had difficulty in finding a way amongst them. The chasms in the ice on the upper part of Antisana are of great

[1] The moraine on which we encamped contained samples of the upper rocks of Antisana that had come from various heights and directions. All were lavas,— some compact and others scoriaceous. Several of the more compact varieties are very handsome rocks when polished, in colour ranging from lavender-grey to purple-black. No rocks could be obtained higher than the camp. Such as were exposed were in inaccessible positions.

My collection has been examined by Prof. T. G. Bonney, and is described by him at length in the *Proceedings of the Royal Society*, Mar. 13, 1884. "The rocks which form the actual peak of Antisana," he says, "are augite-andesites, containing at any rate occasionally hypersthene, and to the same group belongs, though perhaps it is slightly more basic, the rock of the great lava-stream which has descended to Antisanilla."

size,—some, as much as half a mile long, two hundred and fifty feet deep, and sixty to eighty feet across. One of the larger ones was crossed by a snow-bridge; and, although tied widely apart, all of us were on the bridge at the same time. Above this the slopes steepened, and ominous cracking sounds occurred. All three exclaimed simultaneously, "I fear an avalanche."[1] But no snow-slip happened, and presently the gradients lessened, ceased, and the slopes fell away in front.[2] My cherished dream of a boundless view over the Amazonian basin was annihilated in that instant. Nothing could be seen through the mists that encircled the mountain. The snow still rose on our left, and we bent round to the north, and after a few hundred yards it fell away on that side. Then we bore north-west, west, south-west, south, south-east and round to north again, always keeping the rising snow against the left shoulder. At last we could perceive no tendency to rise or fall in any direction, and came upon a nearly level plain of snow, lost in mist on all sides. This was the summit.

It was still early in the day, and we reposed upon the snow, around the barometer, in air so calm that it could scarcely be said to blow from any quarter. At 10.20 a.m. the barometer

---

[1] I overruled Jean-Antoine on this occasion. He wished to take the slope transversely, and I insisted upon going straight up, holding the opinion that that course was less likely to disturb the equilibrium of the slope than by making a groove *across* it.

These cracking sounds are produced by snow on the lower parts of slopes slipping down and being divided from the snow above. Sometimes the fissures that are caused are nearly invisible (scarcely the eighth of an inch across) or they may be inches or feet wide. This depends upon the extent of the slip. If the snow above has got good hold it may remain immovable, notwithstanding the division; but, more usually, through being deprived of support, some of it slips down against the part which has already yielded, and the shock causes the face of the slope to peel off in an avalanche. See the impressive narrative by Mr. P. C. Gosset in the Appendix to *Scrambles amongst the Alps*.

[2] We struck the summit-ridge about half an inch to the right of the asterisk on the engraving.

(reduced to 32° Faht.) read 15·129 inches, with air temperature 53°·5, and at 11.20 a.m. (red. to 32° Faht.), 15·154 inches, air temp. 56° Faht. In the hour and forty minutes we remained on the top[1] temperature in the shade ranged from 44° to 60° Faht.,[2] though the highest temperature observed at the Hacienda during our stay there was only 49°. Thus, the *lowest* temperature experienced on the summit of Antisana (44°), more than 19,000 feet above the level of the sea, surrounded by ice and snow in every direction for several miles, was only 5° less than the *highest* temperature observed at the farm, six thousand feet lower. Such an occurrence is unprecedented in my experience.

Mr. Ellis, in calculating the height of Antisana, has employed, at my request, the means of the readings at 10.20 a.m., and 11.20 a.m., in conjunction with an 11 a.m. observation by Mr. Chambers at Guayaquil (merc. bar. red. to 32° Faht., 29·912 inches, with air temp. 80° Faht.), and his deduced altitude for the summit is 19,335 feet. If this determination and that subsequently made of Cayambe are correct, Antisana is the *third* in rank of the Great Andes of the Equator.[3]

---

[1] We arrived on the summit at 10 a.m., and left it at 11.40 a.m.

[2] March 10, 1880. Summit of Antisana (19,335 ft.) . 10.20 a.m. 53°·5 Faht.
   Do.   do.   . 10.30 ,,   50°·0 ,,
   Do.   do.   . 10.35 ,,   45°·0 ,,
   Do.   do.   . 10.45 ,,   45°·0 ,,
   Do.   do.   . 11.15 ,,   50°·0 ,,
   Do.   do.   . 11.20 ,,   56°·0 ,,

I used on this occasion the thermometer attached to the mercurial barometer; a mercurial maximum thermometer; a quick-acting plain mercurial thermometer; and a spirit minimum thermometer. The first-named of these was verified at Kew Observatory, and was re-compared upon return. I give in Appendix A a facsimile of the Kew certificate of verification.

At 10 a.m. on March 9 at the Hacienda of Antisana, temperature in the shade was 43°·5 Faht.; at 10 a.m. on March 11 it was 45°; and at 11.40 a.m., on the 6th, it was 48°.

[3] See my remarks on this subject in Appendix A. According to La Condamine and Reiss & Stübel, Antisana is the *fourth* in rank of the Great Andes of the Equator (La Condamine, 19,313; R. & S., 18,885 feet).

After we had descended a short distance the clouds cleared sufficiently to let it be seen that we had been on the top, and to shew that the snowy portion of the mountain extends for a long distance to the north-east. As there was still time to spare, we made a detour, in search of craters, to the curved ridge which connects the nearer peaks of Antisana with the more distant ones in the engraving; and looked down upon some exceedingly precipitous glacier on the other side. We saw no open crater, nor anything suggestive of one on any part of Antisana; though, on March 7, when arrested at the edge of the great crevasse, several puffs of strongly sulphurous vapour reached us. Dr. W. Reiss, however, says,[1] in the *Proceedings* of the Geographical Society of Berlin for 1880, that there is a crater, opening towards the east, filled with a glacier (from which a stream flows that is impregnated with sulphur), and I presume that he must refer to the glacier basin we saw beneath us.

An hour later we were at the bottom of the snow-slopes, with only about a mile of slightly descending and nearly flat glacier between ourselves and the tent,—having just discussed whether the rope should be taken off, to move with greater freedom, and decided against it, as we were so near home; striding along at our best pace, about fifteen feet apart, Louis in front and Jean-Antoine last, keeping step as we walked. In the twinkling of an eye the surface gave way, and I shot down, as it were through a trap-door, nearly pulling both men over; and in the next second found myself dangling between two varnished walls of glacier, which met seventy feet beneath.

The voices of the cousins were nearly inaudible, for the hole was no bigger than my body, and they could not venture to

[1] "Der Antisana umschliefst einen tiefen, nach Osten geöffneten Krater, in dessen Grunde die über die steilen Wände herabziehenden Schnee und Eismassen sich zu einem mächtigen Gletscher ansammeln. Dem Gletscher, dessen unteres Ende in 4216 m. Höhe liegt, entspringt der sauere, mit Schwefel geschwängerte Bach der *Quebrada 'Piedra Azufre,'* dessen Namen schon auf eine, wenn auch noch so geringe vulkanische Thätigkeit hinweist."

approach it. With slow and anxious pulls they hauled away, fearing that the rope would be severed by the glassy edges; but, before my head touched the bridge, more of the brittle structure yielded, and I went down again. This was repeated several times, and then Jean-Antoine, seeing that their efforts must be ineffectual so long as they were on opposite sides, leaped the chasm; and, with united pulls, the two cousins landed me with a jerk, through the frozen vault and its pendent icicles, on to the surface, poorer by a cap, though not otherwise the worse for the immersion.[1] In twenty minutes we arrived at the camp, where the others were already in waiting, and by 6.40 p.m. we were back at the Hacienda, having spent some time on the way in adding to our collections.[2]

The Hacienda of Antisana is reputed to be the highest farm in Ecuador, and it owes its existence to the grazing that is afforded by the surrounding slopes. The cattle seemed to find upon them quite sufficient pasturage, though the grasses in general were not so luxuriant as upon Chimborazo, and other places at

---

[1] It is usually considered unnecessary to be tied up when traversing glacier that is not covered by snow. This incident shews the contrary. After my extrication, we examined the crevasse, and found that it was several hundred feet long, and seven feet wide where I broke through. It differed from all others that we had ever seen in being bridged by *ice*. This was only an inch or two thick in the centre, though more substantial where it sprang from the walls of the crevasse. It could neither be detected by any 'droop' on the surface nor by 'sounding' in the usual manner. We had crossed it three times without being aware of its existence. Its formation was no doubt due to the peculiar meteorological conditions which prevail in the Andes of the Equator; and, as there was a strong probability that there were more of the same kind, we considered it advisable to use a double rope on subsequent traverses of Ecuadorian glaciers.

[2] The ascent of Antisana was effected at a better rate than usual, owing to the assistance derived from our old track. Leaving camp (15,984 feet) at 5.38 a.m., at 10 a.m. we were on the summit (19,335 feet). Including halts, this ascent was therefore made at the rate of 767 feet per hour. We started from the summit at 11.40 a.m., and were back at camp by 2.20 p.m. Including the loss of time from the detour and the crevasse incident, the descent was made at the rate of 1340 feet per hour.

FLORA OF ANTISANA.

greater heights than thirteen thousand feet. The flora here, whilst interesting from its characteristic Andean species, had few other attractions,— yet the flowers of *Gentiana foliosa*, H.B.K., were somewhat showy; the downy heads of *Culcitium* were not without a certain grace; and not far from the Hacienda, at about 14,000 feet, we found the elegant fern *Polypodium heteromorphum*, Hook. & Grev. This was, with one exception, the highest position at which we obtained ferns in Ecuador. The examples of the Orders which are mentioned in the footnote,[1] marked by asterisks, were found on the western slopes of Antisana at *greater* elevations than the same species were noticed elsewhere.[2]

[1] The following is a list of our gatherings upon Antisana. Lichens:— *Lecidea* sp., Antisanilla (12,342); *Neuropogon melaxanthus*, Nyl., at our camp (16,000); *Stereocaulon* sp., Antisanilla (12,342); *Stereocaulon* sp. at our camp (16,000); *Usnea florida*, Fries, Antisanilla (12,342). Fungi:— *Omphalia umbellifera*, Fr. (13,000); *Psilocybe* sp. (13,000), both from the slopes below the Hacienda of Antisana. Lycopodiaceæ:— *Lycopodium Saururus*, L. (15-16,000). Filices:— *Polypodium vulgare*, L., Antisanilla (12,342), and *P. rigidum*, Hook. & Grev., Antisanilla (12,342), both growing among hollows on the margin of the lava-stream close to the Hacienda; *P. heteromorphum*, Hook. & Grev., on the slopes above the Hacienda of Antisana (14,000). Gramineæ:— *Deyeuxia recta*, Bonpl. (13,300-15,000); *Deyeuxia* sp. (14,000); *Luzula alopecurus*, Desv. (14,000); *Poa* sp. (14,000); *Festuca mollis*, Kth. (14,000). Gentianaceæ:— *Gentiana foliosa*, H.B.K. (14-15,000); *G. rupicola*, H.B.K. (14-15,000); *G. sedifolia*, H.B.K. (14,500). Ericaceæ:— *Pernettia Pentlandii*, DC. (14-14,500); *Vaccinium penæoides*, H.B.K. (15-16,000). Compositæ:— *Achyrophorus*, near *setosus*, Wedd., at our camp (16,000); *Baccharis alpina*, H.B.K. (14-14,500); *Culcitium adscendens*, Kth. (14-15,000); *C. nivale*, Kth. (14-15,000); *C. reflexum*, Kth. (15-16,000); *Loricaria ferruginea*, Pers. (15-16,000); *Perezia pungens*, Less. (14,500); *Werneria* sp. (14,500); *Werneria densa*, Benth. (15-16,000). Leguminosæ:— *Astragalus geminiflorus*, H.B.K. (14-15,000); *Lupinus microphyllus*, Desv. (14,500); *Lupinus* sp. (14-15,000); *L. nubigenus*, H. & B. (15,000). Geraniaceæ:— *Geranium* sp. (14,500). Malvaceæ:— *Malvastrum phyllanthos*, Asa Gray (15-15,500); *M. Pichinchense*, Asa Gray (15-16,000); *Malvastrum* sp. (15,000). Carophyllaceæ:— *Cerastium* sp. (14-15,000). Cruciferæ:— *Draba obovata*, Benth. (14-15,000); *D. arctioides*, H.B.K. (15-16,000); *Draba* sp. (15-16,000); *D. imbricata*, C. A. Mey. (15-16,000). Ranunculaceæ:— *Ranunculus Peruvianus*, Pers. (14-15,000).

[2] For fuel at our camp on Antisana (and at the higher ones generally) we depended principally upon *Lycopodium Saururus*, L., and *Loricaria ferruginea*,

The Beetles that were obtained in the neighbourhood of the Hacienda were mostly new to us at the time.[1] Diptera were represented by about half a dozen species, and several hymenopterous insects (including *Ichneumonidæ*) attained their greatest altitude here. For the reception of a slender Bug that we captured, Mr. Distant has erected the genus *Neomiris*. Of Butterflies we saw only four species, three of which (*Lymanopoda tener*, Hew., *Lycæna koá*, Druce, and *Pieris xanthodice*, Lucas) are amongst the most common and most widely distributed in Ecuador; but the fourth, a small *Colias* taken in the immediate vicinity of our camp, had not been seen since we left Chimborazo.[2] As we sat in the quaint little gallery of the Hacienda after our return from Antisana, our poor, old, battered lantern again proved our best nocturnal collector, and attracted a numerous company of Moths, from which I secured seven species in about as many minutes.[3]

OUR BEST NOCTURNAL COLLECTOR.

On the next day we turned our attention to Condors. In

Pers. Drabas and Wernerias were abundant and came in usefully. It was, however, always difficult to obtain fuel, and a large part of the time of my assistants was usually occupied in collecting the quantity necessary for cooking. At the higher camps, we could never afford to have fires for the sake of warmth.

[1] Seven species were new to science, and are described in the *Supplementary Appendix*, namely, *Pterostichus (Agraphoderus) Antisanæ*, Bates (p. 10); *P. (Agraph.) liodes*, Bates (p. 11); *Colpodes megacephalus*, Bates (p. 13); *C. alticola*, Bates (p. 21); *Bembidium fulvocinctum*, Bates (p. 22); *Clavipalpus Antisanæ*, Bates (p. 27); and *Hilipus longicollis*, Olliff (p. 75). Several of these were discovered by my assistants, who worked zealously while I was incapacitated.

[2] Described as *Colias alticola* by Messrs. Godman & Salvin, *Supp. App.*, p. 107.

[3] Three belonging to the genera *Cidaria*, *Dariza*, and *Scordylia*, and four other very distinct species which have not yet been identified.

Aspects of Nature, vol. 2, p. 4, Humboldt says this bird often soared over his head "above all the summits of the Andes"; and at p. 41 of the same volume he observes, "It is a remarkable physiological phenomenon, that the same bird, which can fly in circles for hours in regions of the atmosphere so rarefied, should sometimes suddenly descend, as on the western declivity of the Volcano of Pichincha, to the sea-shore, thus passing rapidly through all gradations of climate." Mr. James Orton, late Professor of Natural History in Vassar College, improves upon this, and states that the Condor "can dart in an instant from the dome of Chimborazo to the sultry coast of the Pacific." The shores of that Ocean are nowhere less than one hundred and twenty miles from the mountain; and if my schoolboy readers will multiply sixty by sixty, and then by one hundred and twenty, they will find the rate (in miles) per hour, at which the Condor can fly, according to Professor Orton.[1] They will probably wonder at the keenness of eyesight which enabled him to trace this lightning rapidity; and will be disposed to enquire how he was advised of the arrival on the shores of that sultry coast of the particular Condor which started from the frigid dome. As these flights of the imagination may lead some to suppose that the Condor has a very great range in altitude on the Equator; that it habitually soars at extraordinary elevations; and that it flies with immense rapidity, I venture to give some of our own observations.

When we were upon Chimborazo, I was, at first, a little appre-

Between Antisanilla and Piñantura I also captured a species of *Opisogonia*; and, in the lower part of the Chillo basin, an *Agrotis*, *Eupyra regalis*, Her. Schf. (the most handsome moth I saw in the interior of Ecuador), *Sangala necyria*, Feld. & R., and *Scotosia dubiferata*, Walk.

[1] Professor Orton, along with four others, travelled from Guayaquil to Quito in 1867, and thence down the Amazons to Para; and subsequently wrote a book entitled *The Andes and the Amazon*. This journey "was made under the auspices of the Smithsonian Institution." The quotation is from p. 106 of the English edition, published by S. Low, Son and Marston, 1870.

hensive that we might attract the attention of these formidable birds. They were numerous round about the mountain. When the atmosphere permitted us to look below, we commonly saw a dozen on the wing at the same time. They were seen daily, and it was their ordinary and everyday habit to sail to and fro at a moderate elevation above the ground they were watching, where there were cattle and sheep. On no single occasion did we see a Condor rise so high as the Second Camp (16,660 feet), nor, I think, approach within a thousand feet of its level.

Condors were very numerous upon the lower slopes of Antisana. A score or more continually hovered over the pastures, keeping ordinarily about 1500 feet from the ground—an elevation which they have no doubt learned by experience is sufficient for practical purposes. They did not 'dart' upwards or downwards, but rose rather slowly; and, when they had attained their usual height, maintained themselves at it by nearly imperceptible movements of the wings, and floated, balancing themselves in the air, turning to this or that side, gradually descending; and then, by a few leisurely strokes, regained their former level; continuing to float and circle in this manner by the hour together.

We did not either when upon or in the neighbourhood of the summits of Chimborazo and Antisana, or near the summits of any other mountain, see a Condor in our vicinity upon a single occasion, and I think never observed one so high as 16,000 feet. I believe Humboldt to have been mistaken in supposing that he often saw the bird soaring above all the summits of the Andes. Any one, however skilled in judging distances, may be deceived in such a matter. In the accompanying diagram, let H stand for Hacienda; S for the summit of Antisana; the line WR indicate the level of our camp; and A, B, a pair of Condors, hovering over the lower slopes. An observer at H might naturally suppose the birds to be higher than the summit, though to another at W it would be apparent that they were below his level. While there may, possibly, be occasions when the Equatorial Condor departs from its usual routine, I think such instances must be rare; and that the upper limit of its habitual range cannot be higher than 16,000 feet.

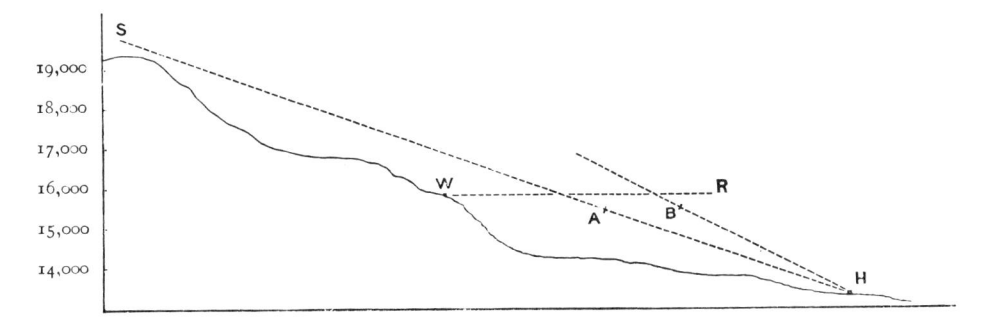

Though some of these birds were in captivity at Quito, we saw none at liberty so low as 9000 feet, and were unable to learn that they *ever* visited the sea. Mr. J. S. Wilson, who had lived for twenty-five years in Ecuador, and passed the greater part of that time upon the coast, told me that he had never known one to come down to the plains, or heard of such an occurrence. I imagine, therefore, that the Equatorial Condor very seldom descends to the Pacific. It seems, indeed, probable that it *never* does so. It is said that those which are despatched (in confinement) from the interior to the coast invariably die before reaching Guayaquil.[1] Yet it is an undoubted fact that Condors frequent the sea-shore in more southern parts of South America. Whether the same individual birds also soar to great heights, and are specifically the same as the Condor of the Equator, are questions that I am unable to answer. If there are no marked points of difference between them, it will be ascertained that this species has a range in altitude of about 16,000 feet (not in any one country, but spread over thirty degrees of latitude) and this is perhaps the greatest that is possessed by any bird.

On the few occasions upon which we were approached by Condors in a menacing manner, we became aware of their presence

[1] This happened to some which were sent by Baron Gabriel de Gunzburg from Quito to Guayaquil, while I was in Ecuador.

from their shadows being cast upon us by a nearly vertical sun. They never came near when the sun was concealed, and if they hovered in our neighbourhood they always kept the sun at their backs. This cannot be their invariable habit in a country where the sun is so often invisible, though possibly it is adopted whenever there is a chance, and the motive is obvious. The objects to be attacked are dazzled by the sun's rays, while the assailants are able to examine their brilliantly-lighted, intended victims at their ease, whose eyes are picked out at the earliest opportunity, and are thus rendered completely defenceless. The herdsmen on Antisana had lifelong familiarity with the Condor, and did not stand in awe of it. They told me that the bird was particularly addicted to old horse and young calf, and might, after feeding, be easily caught with the lasso. Señor Rebolledo said that it would be a mercy to slaughter some of his worn-out steeds, and one was killed and laid out in order that his people might display their dexterity.

We all descended to Antisanilla on the afternoon of March 11, and the baggage went on the next morning to Piñantura;[1] while I was taken to a neighbouring valley to see how wild cattle were captured, and after witnessing some clever horsemanship was led a mile or two towards the south. The slaughtered horse had been laid out on high ground, in a hollow surrounded by little knolls; and watchers, posted in concealment, counted the company as it assembled. A scout stopped us while still a mile away, saying that the feast had scarcely commenced, although eighteen Condors had arrived, and he kept us lying for several

[1] The following times were occupied between the places which have been named in this chapter. Quito to top of Puengasi ridge, 75 min.; thence to the commencement of the flat ground on the other side, 1 h. 55 min. There was a good made road so far. Hacienda Colegio to Pintac, 4 hours; Pintac to Hacienda of Piñantura, 2 h. 25 min.; Piñantura to Hacienda of Antisanilla, 4h. 15 min.; Antisanilla to Hacienda of Antisana, 3 h. 5 min. (without the baggage train). Hacienda of Antisana to Antisanilla, 2 h. 55 min. (with the baggage). Antisanilla to Piñantura, 2 h. 30 min. (without the baggage).

"THEY DASHED IN AMONGST THEM AND THREW THEIR LASSOS."

hours hidden in the grass, while this great, solemn assembly sat watching the dead horse. Our time being exhausted, we stalked up to within two hundred yards, and then mounted, without uttering a word, expecting every moment that we should be perceived. But the birds sat still as mutes, out of sight in the hollow; and we crept nearer, with the herdsmen leading, and on the signal being given they dashed in and threw their lassos, and all the eighteen Condors flew away,[1]—scared and hurriedly, yet without the lightning rapidity that is attributed to them by Professor Orton.

From Piñantura, I despatched the baggage to Quito in charge of the Carrels, and paid a visit to the cotton factory at Chillo, accompanied by Mr. Verity.[2] The mill was 193 feet long, in the form of the letter H,—the legs being one storey and the line joining them two storeys high. The interior was made up of four large rooms (card-room, spinning-room, weaving-room, etc.), each about 80 feet long and 24 feet wide. They were ginning their own cotton with gins made by Platt of Oldham, and producing calico and thread. Sixty hands were employed — entirely Indians — working sixty hours per week. Each family had a house rent-free, with about an acre and a half of ground attached, and all kept pigs and fowls, while some had as many as six or eight cows and oxen. The whole of the machinery came from Lancashire, and was being worked by a turbine. This

[1] This business was spoiled by want of attention to orders. The horse should have been killed on the 11th, and the job was put off until *mañana*. We found that the Condors had hardly eaten anything.

[2] I met Señor Carlos Aguirre at Chillo; and, congratulating him upon his valuable observations in the *Comptes Rendus*, expressed surprise that he should have isolated himself for so long a time, at such a dismal place, in the service of science. Señor Aguirre informed me that the observations were not made by himself, but by a young Ecuadorian whom he deputed to do the work.

Some weeks later, I paid another visit to Chillo, and was again unable to fix its position. It should come somewhere on my map between the words Pasochoa and Hac. Colegio. The height of Chillo, according to Humboldt, is 8576 feet above the level of the sea.

mill was in constant and profitable employment, scarcely able to keep pace with the demand for its productions. The yarn was all bought up direct by Indians and woven by them into ponchos. The excellent order and cleanliness of the establishment, with the contented aspect of the people, were a most agreeable surprise, and said much for its Manager, Mr. Daniel Slater, who was the only foreigner employed.

Daylight had long departed when we set out to recross the Puengasi ridge to the Capital. It was near midnight when we arrived at the hotel, and except for Verity's familiarity with the place there would have been some difficulty in finding it, for Quito is lighted very economically. The law is that every householder must put a lighted candle at dusk in front of his dwelling. The law does not concern itself with the length of the candle, and householders think that the fag-ends of tallow dips are best suited for the purpose. Hence, at an early hour of the night, the city is in total darkness.

SNOW-SPECTACLES.

PICHINCHA, FROM MACHACHI.

CHAPTER XI.

UPON AN ASCENT OF PICHINCHA.

On my return to Quito I found Jean-Antoine was indisposed. Externally, there did not seem to be much the matter with him. He said that his complaint was an *internal* one, and that his blood had been turned sour by the crevasse episode. This dangerous malady, however, yielded to the benign influence of the universal remedy (see p. 50), and in a short time he declared himself fit for active service.

There was something else, too, calculated to sour the temper. The stench of the putrid ox-cheek pervaded everything, and each day the Carrels took a load of foul tins down to the Machangara (a rivulet that runs through Quito) to try to rid them of the abominable odour by scouring them bright with sand; a very mean and menial occupation—almost as bad as carrying home washing for a Chinaman, which on the Pacific Coast is considered the lowest depth of degradation that can befall a human being.

Before proceeding to the north, we made an excursion to the top of Pichincha. So far as extent is concerned, this is an important mountain. The part of it that is 10,000 or more feet above the level of the sea is quite fifteen miles from North to South, and its summit rises 6000 feet above Quito. Yet there is little about it of a thoroughly mountainous character. It is composed principally of undulating, grassy slopes, over which one can ride higher than 14,000 feet. It is impossible to feel great respect for an eminence that can be climbed on donkey-back, and the truth is that the ascent of Pichincha is scarcely more arduous than that of the Eggischorn.

We left Quito on the 21st of March, at 7.55 a.m., with a team of seven animals and three arrieros; passed to the west of the Panecillo (by the road shewn on the Plan) through the village of Magdalena, and (leaving Chillogallo on the left [1]) commenced to mount the slopes of Pichincha; going at first over a small *col*, and descending on the village of Lloa, then ascending through meadows, followed by a considerable stretch of wood. In an unctuous rut between walls of earth, one of our mules floundered and fell with its legs doubled underneath; and our chief arriero —a Chillogallo man—after a few feeble efforts, would have abandoned it on the spot. Then we experienced the usual afternoon shower-bath, and, getting into the clouds, became perplexed as to our whereabouts. Camped at 4 p.m.[2] in sleet and drizzle, unable to see a hundred yards in any direction, and sent the animals and natives back to Lloa.

At night, when the atmosphere cleared, it was seen that we had camped about midway between the two peaks of Pichincha,

---

[1] The village of Chillogallo is principally occupied by arrieros. It is seldom possible to obtain horses or mules in Quito itself. If wanted, they have to be procured from Chillogallo.

[2] The height of this camp was 14,007 feet above the sea.

J.-A. CARREL   LOUIS CARREL   VERITY

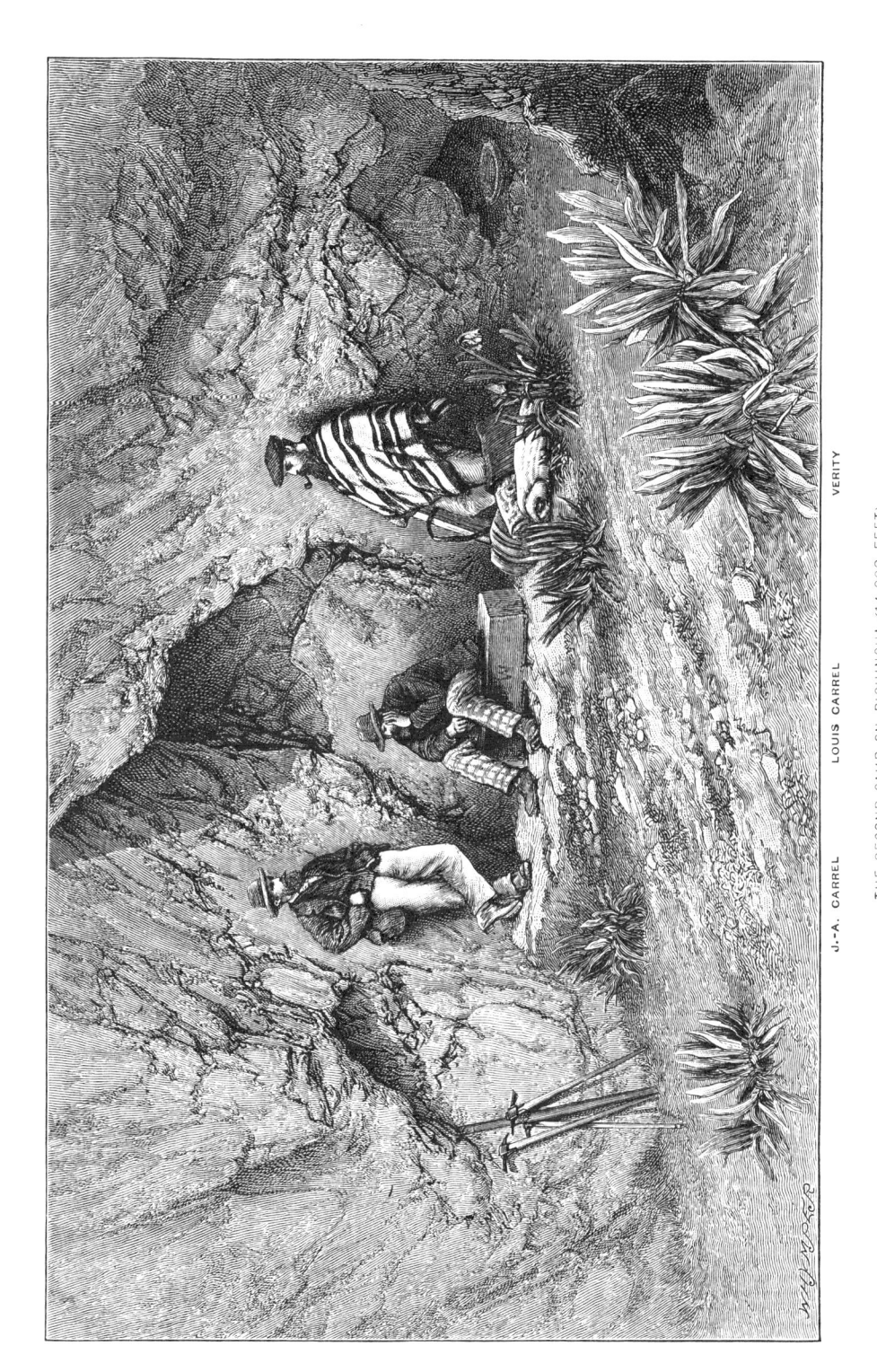

THE SECOND CAMP ON PICHINCHA (14,992 FEET).

which we conjectured were those that are called Guagua and Rucu.[1] Although there are numerous allusions in the works of previous writers to these summits and to the craters of Pichincha, and we had met various persons in Quito who claimed to have visited the *craters* (for it was said there were *several*), I was unable to tell from anything that had been said or heard what was the relative position of the summits,[2] or where the craters were located; and when these two peaks made their appearance we were not certain which of the two was the higher. The right hand or eastern one *appeared* to be the lower and the easier to ascend, and I sent Louis to tackle it, while Jean-Antoine and Verity went to pay their attentions to the other.

During their absence I mounted to the depression in the ridge connecting the two peaks, or *ensillada* as it is termed,[3] and found that on the other side it descended very steeply. So far as mist would permit one to see, this was the head of an ordinary mountain valley. I awaited the return of my people, and, as their reports agreed that the western peak was the higher, shifted our camp in the afternoon up to a sort of cave that had been discovered by Jean-Antoine,[4] a convenient place (where some cavities in the lava were protected by overhanging masses) roomy enough to let each one select a nook for himself; and my assistants, consequently, were able to snore *ad libitum*, without having their ribs poked with an ice-axe. From this refuge, which was just

---

[1] According to Dr. M. Villavicensio, Rucu-Pichincha means old Pichincha, and Guagua-Pichincha means young or child Pichincha. From this it would appear that, traditionally, the highest point is of less age than the lower one.

[2] Rucu is said to be the most eastern one. Besides these two peaks, others are sometimes referred to. I saw only two.

[3] There are many *ensilladas* in Ecuador. The term is the equivalent of 'saddle' as used in the Alps.

[4] By taking a more circuitous route, mules might have been brought to this place, 14,992 feet above the level of the sea. Three hundred feet above it I found the minute mushroom (*Cantharellus*) which has been described in the *Journal of Botany*, June 1890, by Messrs. Massee and Murray. This (15,300 feet) was the greatest height at which Fungi were obtained.

a thousand feet below the top of Guagua-Pichincha, there was an extensive prospect to the south and east. We saw the summits of Illiniza and Corazon rising immediately over that of Atacatzo;[1] and Cotopaxi and Antisana (each nearly forty miles away) by moonlight.[2] In the night I heard, at irregular intervals, roars (occurring apparently at no great distance) exactly corresponding to the noise made by the escapes of steam from the crater of Cotopaxi. The minimum temperature at night was 29° Faht.

On the next morning (March 23) all four of us followed Jean-Antoine's track, and upon striking the western ridge of Guagua I found there was a very precipitous fall on the other (or northern) side, where the crater, presumably, was located. We crossed this ridge, and after descending about four hundred feet saw that we were in the valley that I had looked down upon from the *ensillada*. While the upper part of it was rocky, precipitous, and bare, the slopes below were covered with a good deal of vegetation; amongst which there was neither smoke, steam, fissures, nor anything that one would expect to see at the bottom of the crater of a volcano which is said to have been recently in eruption. This however, no doubt, is *a* crater of Pichincha.[3] Its depth, reckoning from the highest point of the mountain, is probably not less than two thousand feet; its breadth is fully as much, and the length of the part we saw was at least a mile. It had none of the symmetry of the crater of Cotopaxi. The western extremity was clouded during the whole of our stay on the summit.

[1] The summits of the four mountains Illiniza, Corazon, Atacatzo, and Pichincha are nearly in a line; that is to say, a line drawn from the former to the latter passes almost exactly through the summits of the two others. From our second camp on Pichincha I found that the top of Corazon was 3°15′ more west than Atacatzo, and Illiniza was 3°45′ more west than Corazon.

[2] The large snow or glacier plateau on the north-east of Antisana appeared an important feature of that mountain, when seen from Pichincha.

[3] In a paper published at Chalons, in 1858, by the Society of Agriculture, Commerce, Arts and Sciences of the Department of the Marne, entitled *Ascencion du Pichincha*, M. Jules Remy refers to this valley when speaking of "the crater"; and he states that it leads to another one, farther to the west, from which it is

In the view placed at the head of this Chapter, Guagua-Pichincha is the little peak that is almost exactly in the centre of the engraving; and the other one, a quarter of an inch on its right, is that which was ascended by Louis Carrel. The bottom of the depression between the two is the *ensillada,* and it was here I had my first view of this crater-valley. Subsequently, by passing to the left and skirting the base of Guagua-Pichincha, the same valley was seen again. I think it is likely that others have acted similarly, and through not observing that they have looked down upon one and the same valley have made two craters out of one.

We then reascended to the *arête* of the ridge, and followed it until Jean-Antoine said that the top was reached. The rocks fell away in front, and there was no reason to doubt him; but, while the barometer was being unpacked, some crags, a long way above, loomed through the mist. "Carrel," I said, "if we are on the summit of Pichincha, *what is that?*" He was struck dumb for a time, and gasped "Why, I never saw that before!" We shut up the barometer, and went on, and in half an hour were really on the top of Pichincha. Nothing more need be said about the ascent than that it might be made alone, by any moderately active lad. The right way up the final peak is by the ridge leading to the west, and it is probable that this route has been taken before, for on the other sides, although not inaccessible, the last eight hundred feet are very steep.

I found that the summit of Guagua-Pichincha was a ridge of
separated by a wall of rock. This statement must be made on the strength of information, for a farther crater evidently was not *seen* by M. Remy.

His companion Mr. Brenchley went to the bottom of the crater-valley by rolling head over heels, happily, without taking harm; and set to work to examine 'a bed of sulphur and a fumarole' that had been seen from above. The following sentence contains the whole of the information that is given about them. "Il n'y a ni feu ni laves de formation récente."

This paper was kindly communicated to me by M. Remy after my return to Europe; and, having compared it with the several other accounts given of the craters of Pichincha, I have come to the conclusion that their authors were gifted with much imagination.

lava about one hundred and fifty paces long, mainly firm rock, though strewn with loose, decomposing blocks, amongst which there were a number of lumps of pumice, up to a foot or rather more in diameter.[1] Close to the very highest point (15,918 feet),[2]

[1] Professor Bonney says:—"In the rock from the summit of Guagua-Pichincha, the external surfaces have a slightly scoriaceous aspect; and, where the lichen-growth is chipped away, are of a dull grey to rusty-brown colour. The fractured faces shew the matrix to be of a dull, but not dark colour, in places slightly vesicular, the walls of the hollows being coated with a pellicle of iron rust. In the matrix are scattered pretty thickly whitish felspar crystals, not generally exceeding 0·2 inch in diameter, and granules of a black mineral, less than 0·125 inch in diameter. . . The rock is a hornblende-andesite."

The specimen "from the highest point of Rucu-Pichincha" (the peak ascended by Louis Carrel is presumably Rucu) "is a compact grey rock, containing scattered crystals of a glassy felspar up to about 0·2 inch in diameter, and smaller specks of a black pyroxenic mineral. . . Grains of magnetite occur. . . The matrix is often darkened by specks of kaolin and ferrite. . . The rock is a hyperstheniferous augite-andesite."—*Proc. Royal Soc.*, Jan. 31, 1884.

[2] At 11.15 a.m., on March 23, the Mercurial Barometer, reduced to 32° Faht., read 16·974 inches, with air temperature 46° Faht. The 11 a.m. reading at Guayaquil (reduced to 32°) was 29·882 inches, air temperature 80° Faht.

Messrs. Reiss and Stübel give the height of 15,706 feet (4787 mètres) for Guagua- and 15,542 feet (4737 mètres) for that of Rucu-Pichincha. These elevations were determined by △, not by barometrical observations on the summit. According to them, Guagua is the western and Rucu is the eastern summit.

La Condamine, at p. 33 of his *Journal du Voyage*, gives 2430 toises as the height of his "*station* on the highest point of Pichincha (*station sur le plus haut sommet de Pitchincha*)"; and at p. 56 of his *Mesure des trois premiers Degrés* he gives the same amount (2430 toises) as the height of the *eastern* summit. As the highest summit of Pichincha is the *western* one, I feel somewhat perplexed.

Humboldt makes various references in his works to Pichincha, and in such a way as to lead one to suppose that he had been upon the very highest point of the mountain. I feel unable to say whether he did attain the highest point. At p. 28 of the section entitled *Nivellement Barométrique* in his *Recueil d'Observations Astronomiques*, he gives 4854 mètres as the height of Rucu-Pichincha, "the most eastern of *three* rocky towers." This is equal to 15,925 English feet, which closely corresponds with the height I found for Guagua-Pichincha. He further puzzles me by a footnote, at the beginning of which he states that Pichincha has *four* principal summits, and speaks of a *fifth* one at the end; and he completes my bewilderment by saying that M. de la Condamine did *not* measure Rucu, although that gentleman gives 2430 toises as the height of the eastern summit, which all are agreed is Rucu-Pichincha.

a little pile of stones had evidently been put together by the hand of man. Snow-beds were somewhat numerous in fissures, yet the top of this mountain scarcely touches the snow-line.

The whole of the summit-ridge had an appearance of age, and bore a large quantity of lichens (*Gyrophora* sp., *Lecidea* sp., and *Neuropogon melaxanthus*, Nyl.); and within fifty feet of the extreme top there was a large plant, with thick, woolly leaves, and a nearly white, pendent, downy flower — I presume, a *Culcitium* — which was one of those that constantly attracted attention by recurrence at particular altitudes.[1] It made its appearance whenever we reached the height of 14,000 feet, and was never seen much lower. From its size and prominent characters it was not readily overlooked, and I cannot be far wrong in estimating that its range in altitude extends from about 13,500 to 16,000 feet above the level of the sea.

Twenty-one species of Beetles were collected upon Pichincha between the heights of 12,000–15,600 feet, belonging principally to the *Carabidæ*, *Otiorrhynchidæ*, and *Curculionidæ*. The whole are new to science. Some, like the *Astylus* described by Mr. Gorham, inhabit the interior of Ecuador generally, and attain here the upper limit of their range. Their delight is in leaves and branches, and they cease to be seen when arborescent vegetation is left below. Eight species were found *only* on Pichincha. The remainder were obtained on other mountains, either at similar, or at somewhat higher or lower elevations. Two of these (namely, *Helicorrhynchus vulsus*, Olliff, and *Macrops cœlorum*, Olliff)[2] were afterwards taken again, one hundred miles away, at 16,000 feet on Chimborazo.[3]

[1] It was found also within a few feet of the extreme top of Corazon (15,871 feet). The specimens that we attempted to preserve turned out badly, and were thrown away. Several clumps of it were growing round about our second camp, and are shewn in the engraving facing page 209.

[2] Figures of these are given in the *Supplementary Appendix* on the Plate facing page 60, and upon page 72.

[3] Examples of *recurring* species are mentioned in Chapter XIX.

The first competent naturalist who devotes his whole time to this mountain will reap a splendid harvest. After he has satiated himself with beetles and butterflies, he will be able to feast his eyes upon the ruby and emerald breasts, and cyanine tails, of the numerous humming-birds abounding upon it and in its neighbourhood, which include some of the most remarkable and beautiful forms that are known. The tiny *Soldado* (Mulsant's Wood-star) barely three inches long, and the not much larger *Prelado* (*Myrtis fannyæ*, Less.) affect the plain of Tumbaco; *Pterophanes Temmincki*, Boiss. (the largest Ecuadorian species, measuring nearly nine inches across its wings) is said to be limited to the foot of Corazon; *Petasophora anais*, Less., locally called 'the Royal Humming-bird,' is common in the basins of Quito and Chillo; and the long-tailed *Cynanthus* and *Lesbias* are diffused on the western side of the mountain generally. Not fewer than eight others, including the extraordinary 'Sword-bill' (*Docimastes ensiferus*, Boiss.),[1] and three 'Puff-legs,' are common on the mountain itself. There is reason to believe that, when more attention is paid to the habits and habitats of these birds, it will be found that several at least of the species which are said to be confined to particular localities will be discovered at other places at equivalent altitudes. Humming-birds in Ecuador are obtained through the Indians. Information as to localities is principally derived from them, and probably is frequently misunderstood. So far as it could be done, I procured the local names of the species which were obtained,[2] and have brought them together in the accompanying list, arranged according to the classification of the British Museum *Guide* to the Gould collection.

[1] In my specimen, the bill is three and a quarter inches long.

[2] I am greatly indebted to Dr. P. L. Sclater, F.R.S., for naming this collection. Several of the localities mentioned in the list, not visited by me (S. Domingo, Nanegal, Mindo, Canzacoto, Gualea and Nono), will be found on the Maldonado map. The valley of Chota (in the extreme north of Ecuador) is not given upon either map.

HUMMING-BIRDS ON PICHINCHA.

Scientific Name.	Common Name.	Locality.	Local Name.
EUTOXERES AQUILA, Bourc.	"SICKLE-BILLS"	S. Domingo de los Colorados	PICO CURVO.
PHAETHORNIS JARAQUI, Bourc.	"LONG-TAILED HERMITS"	Nanegal	PLATANERO NEGRO.
OREOTROCHILUS PICHINCHA, Bourc.	"HILL-STARS"	Cayambe, Antisana & Pichincha	PECHO BLANCO.
O. CHIMBORAZO, Delatt. & Bourc.	Do.	Chimborazo	ESTRELLA DE CHIMBORAZO.
PETASOPHORA ANAIS, Less.	"VIOLET-EARS"	Basins of Chillo and Quito	QUINDE REAL.
PANOPLITES JARDINII, Bourc.	"GREEN-BACKS"	Nanegal and Mindo	VICENTE.
PHLŒOLEMA ÆQUATORIALIS, Gould.	"LILAC-THROATS"	Canzacoto	CANZACOTO.
PTEROPHANES TEMMINCKI, Boiss.	"SAPPHIRE-WING"	Foot of Corazon	EL GRUESO.
DOCIMASTES ENSIFERUS, Boiss.	"SWORD-BILL"	Lloa, Pichincha	PICO LARGO.
HELIANTHEA LUTETIÆ, Delatt.	"STAR-FRONTLETS"	Do. do.	ALA BLANCA.
HELIANGELUS STROPHIANUS, Gould	"SUN-ANGELS"	Gualea and Pilalo	CRAVATA MALVA.
HELIOTRYPHA PARZUDAKII, Long. & Parz.	Do.	Puela (Colombia)	QUINDE DEL PUELA.
THALURANIA VERTICEPS, Gould	"WOOD-NYMPHS"	Gualea and Napo	LUIS FELIPE.
ACESTRURI MULSANTI, Bourc.	"MULSANT'S WOOD-STAR"	Plain of Tumbaco	SOLDADO.
MYRTIS FANNYÆ, Less.	"WOOD-STARS"	Do.	PRELADO.
LESBIA AMARYLLIS, Bourc.	"TRAIN-BEARERS"	Nono, Tumbaco, etc.	COLA LARGA.
CYNANTHUS CYANURUS, Steph.	Do.	Nanegal and West side generally	COLA AZUL.
RAMPHOMICRON HERRANI, Delatt.	"THORN-BILLS"	Pichincha	FINO.
R. MICRORHYNCHUM, Boiss.	Do.	Foot of Corazon, and Nono	OBISPO.
AGLÆACTIS ÆQUATORIALIS, Cab. & Heine	"SUN-BEAMS"	Slopes of Pichincha above Quito	
ERIOCNEMIS LUCIANI, Bourc.	"PUFF-LEGS"	Lloa, Pichincha	PALA BLANCA.
E. VESTITA, Less.	Do.	Tunguragua	
E. NIGRIVESTIS, Bourc.	Do.	Nono, and slopes of Pichincha	PICHINCHANO.
E. MOSQUERA, Bourc. & Delattr.	Do.	Pichincha	DORADO.
EUCEPHALA GRAYI, Delatt. & Bourc.	"SAPPHIRES"	Valley of Chota	CABEZA AZUL.
CHLOROSTILBON PUCHERANI, Bourc.	"GREENLETS"	Plain of Tumbaco	QUINDE MOSCA.

We got back to the second camp soon after mid-day; and, as there was no prospect of improvement in the weather, packed up and returned to Quito. It was now close upon Easter, and we could not leave again until Good Friday was over. Giacometti, on that day, at considerable trouble to himself, thoughtfully provided his guests with salt fish for dinner; and though this nauseous diet was eaten with meekness and resignation by all good Catholics, one of the boarders—a Yankee Jew—protested, in language which would have been rough in the Western States, against the subtraction of his customary pound of flesh as a fraud on his stomach, and against the substitute as an insult to his religion. The next day we left Quito by the road to the North, on our way to Cayambe, and did not return again to the Capital before the third of May.

ON THE ROAD.

CHAMPIONS.

CHAPTER XII.

THE FIRST ASCENT OF CAYAMBE.

Two roads lead out of the northern end of Quito. One, passing to the east of the Observatory, descends through a narrow gorge rather rapidly on to the Plain of Tumbaco, and is used by persons going to the village of the same name, to Pifo, or to Papallacta. The other, on the west of the Observatory, is the road to the North, and it was this one we took on the 27th of March, on our way to the great Equatorial mountain Cayambe.

I had seen Cayambe from the cone of Cotopaxi, and at Quito from the Panecillo, but these views were obtained at too great distances (62 and 43 miles respectively) to distinguish details; and enquiries were made at Quito to learn the names of inhabited places, contiguous to the mountain, where information might be procured as to the best manner of approaching it. From Señor Carlos Aguirre I heard that one of the properties belonging to his family, a large farm called Guachala, was situated on its southern outskirts, and he favoured me with a letter to his tenant. The village called Cayambe was the nearest place of any size to the mountain, and the only one where food was likely to be obtained.

The party on this journey consisted of the two Carrels, Verity, and the principal arriero (Cevallos) we had taken several times before; who was assisted by a second mule-driver of a jovial temperament, much given to strong waters, and by a very willing and pleasant-tempered native, David Beltran. These three men came from Machachi, and formed an excellent working team. Four beasts were taken for riding, and four others for baggage.

After proceeding a few miles from Quito, we quitted the main road,[1] and turned to the east, towards the Plain of Tumbaco, which was at a lower level, gently sloping towards the north. It was on the eastern side of this (upon what they called the Plain of Yarouqui) that La Condamine and his associates measured their famous base-line in Oct.–Nov., 1736; and the little pyramid of Carabourou, marking its northern end, caught the eye, a glittering speck of light, as we approached the edge of the great Ravine or *Quebrada*[2] of Guallabamba.[3]

This immense chasm forms a boundary to Mojanda (also called Yana-urcu), a mountain which is seldom referred to in geographical works, although it rises to the respectable elevation of 14,000 feet, and covers, perhaps, a greater area than any other individual mountain in Ecuador.[4] While for the most part its

---

[1] This road to the North is a fairly good *track*, not a metalled road.

[2] *Quebrada* is a word that is heard very often in Ecuador. A ditch is a quebrada, or an earthquake crack a few feet across, or a chasm more than 2000 feet deep, such as the great ravine of Guallabamba.

[3] Multitudes of lizards were seen in passing between Quito and Guallabamba. We secured several specimens of *Liocephalus trachycephalus* (A. Dum.), and there were I think at least two species that we failed to catch. Compare this with the passage quoted at p. 176 from Mr. Hassaurek.

[4] Its slopes on the south-west terminate at the Quebrada of Guallabamba, and on the north extend almost as far as the town of Otovalo.

slopes are not steep, the abruptness of its cliffs bordering the quebrada can hardly be exceeded; and there is nothing elsewhere in the neighbourhood of Equatorial America equalling the grandeur of this profound earthquake fissure.[1] Just where the ground commenced to fall steeply, I halted to examine the barometers, for the purpose of determining the depth of the ravine, and for reading the aneroids against the mercurial; as this was a favourable occasion for comparing the indications of the two classes of barometers.

No reference having been made to the aneroids since p. 72, it may be supposed that they were put aside, and were neglected. This was not the case. Systematic comparison of the barometers was part of my daily routine, though regarded almost as waste of time; for it was difficult to see what advantage could be derived from employing instruments which all read lower than the truth, and differed to a large extent one from another. The comparisons which were made since we left Chimborazo shewed that the index-errors of all the aneroids remained nearly constant at any given pressure; and had a tendency to augment while ascending (that is, with pressure diminishing) and to lessen whilst descending (pressure increasing).[2] At Quito, on the 20th of March, the mean error of the whole amounted to −1·009 inches; that is to say, the mean of the whole of the aneroids indicated a pressure more than an inch *too low* at Quito. If this mean had been employed for determination of altitude, in conjunction with the Guayaquil observations, it would have made the height of the Capital above the level of the sea about 1,400 feet in excess of the truth.

Although it appeared to me that these aneroids were worthless for determination of elevation above the level of the sea, I had already remarked that their indications often accorded

---

[1] A few remarks upon this and other quebradas are made in a later Chapter.

[2] See the Table at the end of Appendix C, giving the mean error of the aneroids.

extremely well with those of the mercurial barometer when observing differences of level, *when the observations were made quickly,* — that is to say, when only a short interval of time elapsed between the readings at the lower stations and the upper ones, or between the upper and lower ones, as the case might be. At the Ravine of Guallabamba I expected to descend about 3000 feet[1] in two hours, and looked forward with curiosity to see whether upon this large difference of level I should observe the same satisfactory accordance between the aneroids and the mercurial barometer as had previously been noted upon minor ones.

At the top of the descent, at mid-day, the reading of the mercurial barometer No. 558 (reduced to 32° Faht.) was 21·692 inches. The two aneroids I carried (marked A, B), at the same place and time, read 21·140 and 19·940 inches respectively. Aneroid A, thus, had an index-error of —0·552 inch, and B an index-error of —1·752 inches. At 2.30 p.m., on the bridge at the bottom of the ravine, the reading of the mercurial barometer (red. to 32° Faht.) was 23·929 inches; of Aneroid A, 23·400 inches; and of Aneroid B, 22·200 inches. The increase in the pressure shewn by the three barometers, therefore, was

Mercurial Barometer, No. 558	2·237 inches.
Aneroid A	2·260 ,,
Do. B	2·260 ,,

The result, although in one sense highly satisfactory, was puzzling; for here were two aneroids, one with an index-error of —0·552 of an inch, and the other with an error more than three times as large, each indicating *precisely* the same increase in pressure, and differing in the measurement from the mercurial barometer only to the extent of 0·023 of an inch (an error of a shade more than one per cent in the measurement).

---

[1] From my barometric observations, the depth of the ravine from the commencement of the descent to the top of the bridge amounted to 2834 feet. With the addition of the part below the bridge, the total depth is a little less than 3000 feet.

Or the matter may be put in the following way. When we were at the bottom of the ravine, and the mercurial barometer No. 558 read 23·929 inches, the barometer at Guayaquil was standing at 29·900 inches. The actual difference in the atmospheric pressure between the upper and lower station was therefore 5·971 inches. Aneroid B, however, at the bottom of the ravine, read 22·200 inches, and thus made it appear that there was a difference of pressure of 7·700 inches. The *error* therefore of B in a measurement of 5·971 inches was 1·729 inches, *or more than* 28 *per cent*. Yet this same instrument, it was seen just now, in a measurement of 2·237 inches, differed only to the extent of 0·023 of an inch from the mercurial barometer. Comparisons of this nature were continued, though no more are quoted in the course of my narrative. I returned to England, and remained for several years, entirely unable to understand this anomalous behaviour.[1]

We stopped for the night at the village of Guallabamba (7133 feet), a pleasant little place, with an agreeable temperature,[2] embowered in foliage, where we bought oranges shaken

[1] It appeared inexplicable to several of the leading instrument-makers and meteorologists under whose notice it was brought. The prominent manner in which it was referred to in a paper communicated to the Royal Geographical Society (see *Proc. Roy. Geog. Soc.*, 1881, p. 450) also failed to draw elucidations from any one.

I continued to investigate the matter; and, after working during several years in tabulating and comparing the original observations, subsequently occupied several years more in experiments in the workshop, with the results which will be found in the pamphlet entitled *How to use the Aneroid Barometer*. See also Appendix C.

As even a condensed summary of this investigation necessarily extends to considerable length, I have thought it best to issue it separately from, though simultaneously with the present volume.

[2] At 8 p.m., 67° Faht. Strangers seldom come here. The natives said it was two years since they had seen a *gringo*. The place was badly off for food. There was of course no meat. Bread only came once a week from Quito.

At the bottom of the Ravine of Guallabamba, at 2.30 p.m., temperature in the shade was 75°·5 Faht., and this was the highest we experienced in the shade anywhere in the interior of Ecuador.

from the trees at the rate of four a penny; and on the 28th left for Guachala, passing at mid-day the village of Cousobamba (about the same elevation as Quito), where there was *chicha*, but no water. The track wound through a large diversity of scenery, sometimes amongst woods, or dipping into quebradas, and this must be one of the grandest rides in the universe when the surrounding mountain panorama is visible. We arrived at Guachala,[1] however, without having had a single glimpse of Cayambe; and, finding that the tenant was absent, rode over the next morning to Cayambe village, in quest of information.

I brought a letter of introduction to the Jefo-politico, and learnt that he was on the plaza, engaged in an affair of importance. He was surrounded by a large part of the male population, crowding together, jostling and pushing each other to get a good view of the business which was being transacted. It was the concluding round of a cock-fight for the championship of Cayambe, and when it was over the Jefo-politico had leisure to attend to me. He promised that a guide should be provided; but, say what I would, the conversation invariably bore round

---

[1] In the garden at the back of this establishment, before breakfast on the 29th, I collected fourteen species of bugs and beetles, eleven of which prove to be new to science. The bushes were loaded with the *Astylus* described by Mr. Gorham (*Supp. App.*, pp. 52-3). Whilst engaged in this occupation, the sun came out (at 8 a.m.) brightly, and drove me into the house. This was the only occasion upon the whole journey that I felt the rays of the sun were dangerous. The people in general at Cayambe and Guachala seemed to me to have even lighter complexions than those at Quito, which implies that they do not feel the sun very often.

Between Guallabamba and Guachala I dismounted twice to secure fine beetles which were literally crossing our path, belonging to the *Dynastidæ*. One of these is a known species (*Heterogomphus Bourcieri*, Guerin); for the reception of the other, Mr. Bates has instituted the genus *Praogolofa* (*Supp. App.*, p. 34).

The following times were occupied in going from the capital to Guachala. Quito to the top of the Quebrada of Guallabamba, 4 hours 50. min.; descent to the bottom of the ravine (cutting the zigzags) 1 h. 35 min., those following the path took 2 hs. 30 min.; bridge to the village of Guallabamba, 70 minutes. Guallabamba to Cousobamba, 3 hs. 20 min.; thence to Guachala, 5 hours.

to cock-fighting, which in this region is considered the most rational and delightful of all sports. He expressed incredulity when told that in England it was only enjoyed by the lower orders, though he would have readily believed that the Lord Chancellor comes down every morning to the Law Courts with a fighting-cock under each arm. "You surprise me," said the Jefo-politico, "for all the best cocks come from England."

Three weeks later I passed two nights at this village, and found that to each pillar in the courtyard of my host's house a fighting-cock was tied. His champions passed their spare moments in attempts to carry on a desultory warfare; and, when night came, chased sleep away by screams of defiance. I growled to the schoolmaster that they disturbed the sacredness of midnight. "Oh," said he, "they always crow at the *even* hours"; and it was the fact that they raised their voices at twelve, two, and four, and let one, three, and five slip by unnoticed!

The Jefo-politico, Señor Antonio Jarrin de Espinosa, was the owner of Cayambe mountain, of five thousand head of cattle, and a man of large possessions; and when he invited us to quit comfortable quarters at Guachala, and to sleep at his Hacienda Chuarpongo, I anticipated we were going to enjoy a rather good time, in a country house, suitable for a person of his distinction. Chuarpongo was on the outskirts of Cayambe, and looked down upon the Equatorial village. The building was composed of little more than one room, which was filled with raw potatoes — if they had been cooked it would have been all right. Mashed potatoes would make a nice bed, being of a plastic and accommodating nature; but these raw potatoes of Chuarpongo were uncompromising, and left a strong impression on both mind and body.

I think it must be assumed, from the exceptional courtesy he shewed, Señor Espinosa was unaware that we had to repose upon beds of raw potatoes. The guide he provided was himself. He arrived at 4 a.m., on the 31st of March, at Chuarpongo, with two of his major-domos (and a third one from a neighbouring estate), accompanied by five fine deerhounds; and led us in the darkness a long way east-south-east, before beginning to approach the summit of our mountain.[1] At about 8 a.m., at a bend of 'the Monk's Valley,' they stopped to enquire where I wished to arrive, and upon indicating a rocky point, at the edge of the glaciers underneath the summit, they proceeded up the ridge dividing the Monk's Valley from another on its south-east.[2] At 10.15, on coming to the point where the heads of these two valleys met, we halted for a meal, with the sun shining brilliantly.

While resting on the grass, a great shadow suddenly appeared in our midst, and made us all alive. A Condor had dropped down, and was hovering with outstretched wings about five-and-twenty yards above. The deerhounds ran in, cowering with terror, and casting furtive glances at the huge bird, whilst pressing against us, trembling with fear. It was remarkable to see the fright that possessed these big dogs, when they were in perfect security amongst our large party. Shouts drove the assailant away, and presently we proceeded.[3]

The course now led up very steep ground, that formed a step to another valley above, and the passage of this part occupied some length of time, as the animals had to be unloaded. When all were got to the top, Jean-Antoine was missing,[4] nor

[1] Our courses during the remainder of this Chapter and for Chapter XIII. can be followed on the inset map of part of Cayambe that is given at the top of the large, general route map.

[2] On this part of the way we passed several Falcons. One, sitting on a rock about fifty feet off, would not fly away when shouted to.

[3] This bird had been seen hovering about for some time. It seemed to *drop* down upon us, and for an instant came within twenty yards.

The largest Ecuadorian Condor of which I have heard is said to have measured 10 feet 6 in. from tip to tip of the wings. Most of those we saw on Antisana and elsewhere would not I think have measured so much as nine feet.

[4] I had despatched him in advance (so that the barometer should not be imperilled by the floundering of the animals) with instructions to wait for us above.

could any one tell where he was. Halting the others, and handing all the things I usually carried over to Louis in order to move quickly, I scrambled a couple of hundred feet up the ridge on the northern side of the valley, and descried the Chief of the Staff about half-a-mile ahead, picking his way through some swampy ground.

Just then a deer galloped down the cliff; the hounds went off in hot pursuit, and holding us entranced by their splendid bounds down break-neck rocks gave the errant man a still longer start. When they came back, discomfited and panting, we went on, and for a time held parallel courses — the others down below on the flat floor of the valley, and I on the top of the ridge, so close that we could keep up conversation. Presently they got out of sight and hearing. I continued, however, to progress along the *arête*, intending to rejoin them when the cliffs between us became less precipitous.

At mid-day clouds formed about our neighbourhood. I had arrived close above the spot where we were to have encamped, but could not see twenty yards, or get a response to continual whistling and shouting. About this time I was joined by one of the hounds, who seemed to share my perplexity, and ran about in all directions, stopping to listen. I then bore round to the south, and finding no track concluded that the others must have passed over rock, and left no trace; so proceeded higher up, and doubled back, purposely selecting such ground as would allow a good track to be made on it. Presently we came to some bits of climbing which were too steep for the dog, and, whilst rendering him assistance, a few specks of snow commenced to fall. They quickly changed to flakes; in a few minutes there was a blinding snow-storm, and the track was completely obliterated. I continued to search for two hours more, and then considered it was time to attend to my own safety.

We were nearly 16,000 feet high; without compass or instruments, food, protection or the means of making a fire, for Louis had taken everything. We went down, regardless of direction, solely occupied with the view of getting to a lower level. Any valley on this side of the mountain, if followed to its extremity, would bring one on to the plain of Cayambe. At about 4 p.m., getting out of cloud-land, we came upon the head of an unknown valley, which was joined some distance off by another, each with its own little torrent. There was a slope of sand, perhaps eight hundred feet high, between us and the nearest stream, and leaving a track on it that could be seen a mile away I marched across to the right bank of the valley, but had to come back again, as my four-footed friend stopped howling on the bank, refusing to take to the water. I carried the big baby across in my arms. The streams were unfordable when united, and presently fell into a wall-sided ravine with impassable cliffs on the left bank. The opposite slopes, being fissured by earthquake-cracks, were nearly as impracticable; and we were forced to keep to the bottom, in morass, covered with reeds; and for two hours more I waded through slime, clutching the stems, not daring to leave go, lest I should be swallowed up.

It was nearly dark when we escaped from this horrible bog, and came upon steeply descending ground; where I descried a little thicket, the first semblance of shelter that had been seen. Preoccupied in finding a refuge of any sort, I did not at first notice that we had hit upon a lair, or sleeping-place, of some of the cattle who from time to time escape to the mountains from the tyranny of man. We had been warned to avoid them, as they pay no regard to anyone, and become savage and dangerous wild-beasts, with marvellous agility. The idea that several might bounce in, inclined to resent this unauthorized occupation of their brush-wood bed, gave something to think about through the eleven hours of darkness.

We left the lair at earliest dawn, and, after descending an abrupt step, found that the lower part of the valley was densely wooded. I spied the remains of a track, a very old one, evidently unused for a long time, overgrown and obliterated in many places, or closed by interlaced branches. The dog crept underneath without much trouble, and found the way instinctively; whilst I was driven to make long detours, and several times should have lost myself had not the sagacious animal stood on the track and waited, or come and led me back. Much sooner than I anticipated, sky became visible through openings in the branches, and about 7.30 a.m. we suddenly emerged on to the open; and at the foot of a grassy hill saw a little Indian hut, emitting blue smoke, curling upwards in front of the plain, with a man and woman outside busy at their morning work. I smelt breakfast, and pounced down on them like a hawk. "Have you locro?" "Yes, Señor." "Give me some locro" (said very peremptorily). "That I will, Señor" (said heartily), and he brought out a basonful at once, with another for the dog, and we all sat outside in the sunshine eating potato-soup together. They were an old, homely couple, unencumbered either by bashfulness or servility. He pressed us to take more, and came down the river's side until the outlying houses of the village were seen, and then with a polite salutation was about to take leave; but I detained him, and, pouring my loose money into his hand, left him in stupefied adoration, uncertain whether he had seen a vision or entertained a gringo.

When I reappeared soon after 9 a.m. on the 1st of April at the house of the Jefo-politico, a messenger was despatched to advise the others; and Señor Espinosa, Jean-Antoine, and Verity arrived in the course of the afternoon, with congratulations upon my safe return from this circular tour. The day was too far advanced to make another start for the camp. Having time on our hands, we wandered about the village, and formed the acquaintance of priest and schoolmaster; and discovered that one could buy two-pennyworth of bread at a time, and no more. If you want a larger quantity, you may buy another medioworth, and so on, but on no account will a shilling's worth be sold at once. Later on, attracted by the sound of music, we came upon a minstrel, with upcast eyes, appealing to his star. Then there was a flash, and a quickly following splash, for she suddenly appeared on the balcony to damp his ardour, according to the manner of the country; and made us go back, wondering at the ways of women,—resolved never to play a guitar under a first-floor at Cayambe.

Our mountain looked immense from the village, and we saw on the 2nd of April that, like Antisana, its upper 3–4000 feet was almost completely buried under snow and glacier. On the west, its slopes die out very gradually on the Plain of Cayambe,[1] and upon this side they do not become steep until one gets higher than 13,000 feet. On the south the angles are more abrupt, and upon its eastern side the mountain is precipitous. It was formerly supposed to be the only great mountain, anywhere in the world, immediately upon the Equator, and it has become improbable that a loftier one will ever be discovered exactly on the Line.

INGRATITUDE.

[1] The Plain of Cayambe is bounded by Cayambe, Imbabura, and Mojanda. Its drainage falls into the Rio de Guallabamba, and by the Esmeraldas into the Pacific.

"THEY PROWLED AROUND US AT NIGHT, AND LEFT THEIR FOOT-PRINTS IN THE SNOW."

Leaving Verity behind to continue buying two-pennyworths of bread until he had accumulated a sackful, I went up to the camp, and was received with open arms, as one risen from the dead. The ten men searched until they found my track, and divining my intentions had given me up for lost. They passed the night of the 31st of March in lamentations, for the White Valley down which I had made my way, Señor Espinosa told them, was pathless, inaccessible, and full of wild beasts. He said it was useless to attempt to follow, and the thing to do was to return to the village, to organize a search for my bones. Pumas, indeed, were rather numerous in this neighbourhood. A young horse belonging to Señor Espinosa had just been killed by one, and an Indian we passed reported that he had noticed another roving about. Yet we never saw any, although they prowled around us at night, and left their footprints in the snow.

The camp (14,762 feet) was established at the eastern end of an upper prolongation of the Monk's Valley, and was commanded on the north by the precipitous cliffs along which I had gone. On the east (that is to say, at the head of the valley) there was a ridge descending a little to the west of south from a secondary peak of Cayambe, and on the eastern side of this there was a large glacier — invisible alike from our camp and from the village — which my people had discovered during my absence. This glacier was one of the finest we found in Ecuador, having its birth in the snows at the upper part of the mountain, and a length of several miles after it streamed away from the central reservoir. The part nearest to the camp descended steeply, in what is termed an *ice-fall*. There were no moraines nor even stray rocks upon it, though there were two small, lateral moraines upon its western side, which shewed that rocks had risen above the ice in former times, and that the glacier had been larger.

Our course led alongside and partly over these moraines to the top of the secondary peak of which I have already spoken, that juts out from Cayambe like the Aiguille du Gouter on

Mont Blanc, and affords a perfect stand-point for studying the western side of the mountain. Its position is sufficiently indicated by saying that it is at the head of the Monk's Valley and the White Valley; and it cannot be mistaken if it is added that it lies south-west of the highest point of Cayambe, and is elevated 16,164 feet above the sea.[1]

The extreme top of this peak was flat, and the lava *in situ* was strewn with small pieces of pumice and a number of varieties of other lavas[2] (all, however, having a strong family resemblance to each other) which doubtless were morainic matter, and had been deposited there when the contiguous glacier rose to a higher level. Growing amongst them, there was a quantity of *Andreæa striata*, Mitt., a moss of unattractive character, which seemed to thrive in most exposed positions, and grew both on naked lavas, amongst snow, or in damp volcanic ash.[3]

---

[1] On April 3, at 11 a.m., the mercurial barometer No. 558 (reduced to 32° Faht.) read 16·924 inches, air temperature 55° Faht. The 11 a.m. reading at Guayaquil, reduced to 32° Faht., was 29·915 inches, air temp. 79° Faht.

[2] "The rocks of Cayambe are very uniform in character, and of the same general type as those of Chimborazo, Antisana (in part), and Pichincha (in part). They are andesites, but as they contain hornblende and augite, as well as mica, it is difficult to give them a distinctive name. . . Perhaps it is more appropriate to classify these rocks with the augite-andesites, using the word hornblendic as a qualifying epithet, except in the case of the second specimen described, which might perhaps be termed a mica-andesite."—*Proc. Royal Soc.*, June 19, 1884.

[3] It had been already collected around the Second Camp on Chimborazo, upon the summit of Corazon, and had been seen in the neighbourhood of the snow-line generally.

In the *Journal of the Royal Geographical Society* for 1861, at pp. 184-190, there is an account of a journey made by the late Dr. William Jameson, of Quito, to Cayambe in 1859. He visited the lower slopes of the northern side of the mountain. Botany was his principal object, and a list is given of seventy-eight species of plants that he collected between the height of 10,000 feet and the neighbourhood of the snow-line. In consequence of Dr. Jameson's labours, I did not devote any time to the flora of Cayambe.

The altitudes given in this paper are generally too high. For Cayambe village he quotes 9724 feet. According to my observations it is 9323 feet above the sea. Messrs. Reiss & Stübel say 9357 feet.

I called this peak the Pointe Jarrin, and the glacier the Espinosa Glacier, after their proprietor.

Cayambe culminates in three domes or bosses, all completely enveloped by snow-covered glacier. The only visible rock high up on the western side is a small cliff, about 800 feet below the northern of these three summits, which is capped by a vertical section of ice, similar to that shewn in the plate facing p. 76. From examination of this mountain at great distances, it was known that the central boss was the highest. It bore north-east from the Pointe Jarrin, and appeared to be more or less accessible, though decorated at its crest with overhanging cornices and surrounded by large crevasses. The course agreed upon was 20° East of North for the first part of the way over the lower glacier; with the intention of bearing round to the south, and steering directly for the summit, after having got clear of the fissures at the head of the ice-fall. To save time on the following day, I caused steps to be cut up the rounded slopes of the glacier where they pressed against the Pointe Jarrin, and in the course of the afternoon advanced food and instruments to the edge of the ice.

On the 4th of April we left the tent at 4.40 a.m., and walked by lantern-light as far as the top of the Pointe Jarrin. The morning was fine and clear, and the view at this time embraced almost all of the mountains which have hitherto been enumerated.[1] After traversing some flat and easy glacier, we

[1] On the 6th of April I again ascended the Pointe Jarrin, and was more fortunate than usual in getting angles for position. I observed the bearings on this occasion of Mojanda, Imbabura, Cotocachi, Pichincha, Atacatzo, Corazon, Illiniza, Cotopaxi, and Antisana. Ruminahui, Pasochoa, and Sincholagua were clouded, and Cayambe shut out the whole of the view to the east. The two peaks of Illiniza, 72 to 73 miles away, could be readily distinguished, and at this distance were 0° 45' apart. Antisana (more than 40 miles away) looked huge, and we again saw the large, snowy shoulder on its north-east. Below this, there was a wonderfully level ridge running out in the same direction, perhaps four or five miles farther. After that, the slopes appeared to descend towards the east with **great rapidity**.

became involved in a complicated maze of snow-covered crevasses at the head of the ice-fall of the Espinosa Glacier, which had to be threaded cautiously. This was followed by moderately-inclined slopes, and we then entered upon a large plain that took three-quarters of an hour of steady going to cross. This we called the Grand Plateau. Afterwards the slopes became steeper, with occasional large open crevasses and numerous concealed ones, and were rapid near the top, which was gained soon after 10 o'clock in the morning.

Early in the day mists began to form and gather beneath us, and we pushed on to endeavour to have a view from the summit. At 9.30 a.m., when quite a short distance below the highest point, we were well seen by a crowd assembled on the Plaza of the village; but in a few minutes more the clouds caught us up, and we did not get out of them until the close of the day.

The true summit of Cayambe is a ridge, running north and south, entirely covered by glacier. Its height (deduced from the mean of two readings of the mercurial barometer at 10.45 and 11 a.m.) is 19,186 feet, and this mountain is therefore the fourth in rank of the Great Andes of the Equator.[1] Of the other two summits the northern one is the higher, and it is well-nigh inaccessible, being almost surrounded by gigantic crevasses, and surmounted by tufted cornices. The central or true summit presented fewer difficulties, though it was not altogether easy of access. It was a stroke of good fortune to find a snow-bridge across the highest crevasse, just under the place where there was a break in the coronal cornice.

Glacier departs in all directions from the summit of Cayambe

---

[1] The mean of these two readings (reduced to 32° Faht.) was 14·983 inches. The 11 a.m. reading at Guayaquil (red. to 32° F.) was 29·915 inches, air temperature 79° Faht. At some future date it may perhaps appear that Cayambe is *third*, and that Antisana is the fourth in rank. There is, I imagine, a very slight difference in the elevation of these two mountains.

CAYAMBE (19,186 FEET), FROM THE WEST.

in a manner that is seldom seen on mountain-tops. From the huge schrunds that surrounded the three bosses of the summit-ridge, on *all* sides, I think that there are at no great depth beneath the surface several pinnacles like those which form the summits of Sincholagua and Illiniza. By persons who are familiar with glacier-clad eminences it will be apprehended without saying that a slight diminution in the thickness of the superincumbent ice may cause the apex of this mountain to become inaccessible.

During the 83 minutes we remained on the summit, temperature fluctuated between 32°–41° Faht. On arrival, the wind was light, without any very pronounced direction. It strengthened as day advanced, and soon after 11 a.m. blew in squalls from the east, and we retired. The upper part of this mountain was a regular battlefield for the winds. On several occasions in the succeeding fortnight, when encamped southwards, we saw their struggles for victory. If the east wind conquered, the whole mountain became invisible; but if, as happened sometimes, a north-west wind prevailed, then the western side, and even the rest, was seen.[1]

It being still early in the day, we diverged to the north to get some samples of the highest rocks;[2] and then followed our track literally, as the mists were dense,—proceeding very cautiously, 'sounding'[3] at almost every step in consequence of the increased softness of the snow, and grovelling on hands and knees across the rotten bridges. We returned to camp at 3.40 p.m.

So far as I am aware, no attempt has hitherto been made to bring together rates of speed which have been attained upon mountains. Probably, they are not often well ascertained; for persons engaged in mountain-travel, or in mountaineering, generally have their attention too much absorbed by inevitable details, or by the novelty of their surroundings, to observe and note with precision the times occupied, and the duration of halts. It was necessary to observe the rates we attained in order to form an opinion as to the effects of low pressures on the bodily powers; and, whenever it was practicable, our times were noted.[4]

Upon Cayambe we attained our fastest *ascending* rate. We left camp (14,762 feet) at 4.40 a.m., and arrived on the summit (19,186) at 10.12 a.m.; the only positive halt being one of ten or twelve minutes at the top of the Pointe Jarrin, to put on rope and gaiters. In 320 minutes of actual going we rose

---

[1] The east wind was damp, and comparatively warm. There was a notable difference in the height of the snow-line on different sides of the mountain. On the west, there was no permanent snow so low as 16,000 feet above the level of the sea.

[2] The rock (lava) of this cliff closely resembled that which had been taken lower down, and Prof. Bonney informs me that microscopic examination shews that the differences are only varietal. "Hornblende, iron-mica, and augite are present, the last being the less conspicuous constituent."

[3] Those who are acquainted with the technicalities of mountaineering are referred to *Scrambles amongst the Alps*, p. 375, where a figure is shewn in the act of 'sounding.'

[4] Several of our rates, which were well ascertained, are brought together in a tabular form in Chapter XIX.

4424 feet, or 13·85 feet per minute (= 831 feet per hour).[1] Some may say this is not a fast rate; or others may entertain a contrary opinion, and argue that the ascent must have been very easy to have permitted us to travel so quickly. It was no part of my aim to make or to break 'records'; and, personally, I have no objection to the adoption of either of these opinions.

Whether fast or slow, I remarked that both of the Carrels commenced to give indications of fatigue when we were about 18,000 feet high. Jean-Antoine was a man who always wished to be in front, and if he yielded up the lead voluntarily it was a sure sign that he was tired. In ascending the last twelve hundred feet, although the axes were little used and we seldom sank more than a foot in the snow, the men changed places, and took the lead alternately, perhaps a dozen times. Louis had no desire to retain it,—indeed, I think it may be said that neither of them *could* have held it for any length of time. Although these changes scarcely occupied a minute apiece, I found the little stoppages very convenient. Instead of hindering, they probably assisted progress; and it should be added, to the credit of the cousins, that this ascent was made without a fault. There was no retracing of steps, and doing work twice over. Due to this, our ascending rate, on that day, was better than the average.

We had now paid some attention to the first, second, third and fourth of the Great Andes of the Equator. There was no likelihood of finding their supremacy disputed; for my predecessors agreed that these mountains towered head and shoulders above all the rest, and they were in general agreement as to the order in which the others followed. According to La Condamine, and Reiss and Stübel, Altar, Sangai and Illiniza were next in rank.

[1] The descending rate is not known, on account of the detour. We left the summit at 11.35 a.m.; arrived on Pointe Jarrin at 2.40 p.m.; stopped thirty minutes, and then went down in another half-hour to the camp.

In the *Geografia de la Republica del Ecuador* of Dr. M. Villavicencio I had, however, lighted upon a reference to a mountain called Sara-urcu, which is not, I believe, mentioned either by La Condamine, Humboldt or Boussingault. Its height, according to Villavicencio, was 17,276 feet (6210 varas). As this closely approximated to the elevation assigned to Altar, Sangai and Illiniza, it seemed not impossible that the mountain might prove to be the fifth in rank; and before quitting the neighbourhood I proposed to hunt it down, being the more moved to do so because it was said to be situated well to the east, and might afford another chance of having a glimpse of the great, unknown Amazonian basin.

At Quito I was unable to procure any information as to the location of Sara-urcu. Few persons were acquainted with the name; but when Señor Espinosa heard me mention it he said that the mountain (and all the country to the east) belonged to *him*, and that he would indicate its direction. When we first started for Cayambe, Señor Espinosa did point out a vague something in the clouds which he said was Sara-urcu. We did not actually see the mountain until the 4th of April, and then it appeared only for a few seconds, just long enough to obtain an idea of its position. In those few seconds we saw that we should in all probability be able to ascend it, if its base could be reached.

Before leaving Cayambe, I sent Jean-Antoine with David in advance, to see if they could light upon another camping-place in the right direction; retaining Louis and Verity to assist in collecting. In the neighbourhood of the camp (that is to say, either a little above or below 15,000 feet above the level of the sea) we found the nine beetles that are mentioned below,[1]

[1] **Colpodes pustulosus*, Bates (*Supp. App.*, p. 14); **C. rotundiceps*, Bates (p. 15); **C. fusipalpis*, Bates (p. 17); *C. steno*, Bates (p. 20, with Figure); **Trechus* sp.; *Bembidium fulvocinctum*, Bates (p. 22); *Naupactus parvicollis*, Olliff (p. 67); **Listroderes inconspicuus*, Olliff (p. 69); and *Erirrhinus glaber*, Olliff (p. 76). Those marked by asterisks were found only on Cayambe.

including three species of *Colpodes* which were obtained only at this locality. We had already obtained members of this genus at great heights on several other mountains, and on Pichincha had been struck by the fact that they existed in considerable numbers amongst frozen soil. The two which have been named by Mr. Bates *C. megacephalus* and *C. Pichinchæ* came from Guagua-Pichincha, the former from the summit-ridge (at 15,600 feet), and the latter from the second camp (14,992 feet). In each case they were discovered whilst breaking out rock specimens, and were found in colonies, thriving amongst stones which were cemented together with ice. Some species of *Colpodes* come from more genial zones, but the larger part of those we obtained enjoyed life under very frigid conditions. The minima of the four nights Ap. 2 – Ap. 5 inclusive, were 27°, 31°, 24°·5, and 24° Faht. respectively, degrees of cold sufficient to hard freeze the surface of the soil; which, further, was usually covered with snow in the morning.

The scouts returned, bringing a good report; declaring that they had found *a regular palace* — an old Indian dwelling, *planted all round with shrubs* — which would permit the tents to be dispensed with; and we broke up camp on the 6th, to go to this wonderful place, expecting they had either dropped upon an edifice of prehistoric age, or on some relic of the dusky Incas.

CHARMS ?

LA DORMIDA DE MAYORAZZO.

CHAPTER XIII.

THE FIRST ASCENT OF SARA-URCU.

Upon leaving Cayambe on the 6th of April, we came down three thousand feet by a buttress or ridge running out towards the south-south-west, and then turned to the east; camping that night in the 'palace surrounded by shrubs'—the structure represented at the head of this chapter—which was called La Dormida (the sleeping-place) de Mayorazzo (11,805 feet), a good thing of its kind, though not very palatial; and at this lower level we got again into a warmer climate. In the daytime temperature was higher than 50° Faht., and the lowest minimum was well above freezing-point (38°·5).

La Dormida was a hut occasionally used by herdsmen when searching for strayed cattle, and was situated in a wood—almost a forest; surrounded by fallen and decayed trunks, laden with

CHAP. XIII. *GONZALO PIZARRO CROSSES THE ANDES.* 239

mosses[1] growing luxuriantly, thickly caked and interlaced upon the rotten bark. In the clearing around the edifice little birds hopped about fearlessly, and at night clouds of moths[2] sailed into the tent, attracted by the lights.

The valley in which La Dormida is situated forms the southern boundary of Cayambe; and at its head, two or three miles more to the east, there is the divide or water-parting of the streams flowing into the Pacific and Atlantic. The whole of the drainage of the eastern side of Cayambe goes into the Atlantic. Most of the streams flowing down its southern slopes, and all of those upon its west, fall into the Pacific.

Somewhere not far away, perhaps over this very ground, Gonzalo Pizarro, 'the most dexterous with the lance of any man that ever passed into the New World,' 'the most beloved man in all Peru,' crossed the Andes in 1540 (it is said) with 340 Spaniards, 4000 Indians, and about 4000 Swine, to look for 'the Land of Cinnamon'; on the memorable expedition which resulted in the discovery of the River Amazons by his lieutenant Orellana, and in the death of the greater part of the explorers.[3]

The exact route taken by Gonzalo Pizarro cannot I think be told with certainty from the relation of Garcilasso de la Vega.[4] It is, however, certain that he crossed and recrossed the

[1] *Thuidium delicatulum*, Lindb.; *Sematophyllum subscabrum*, Mitt.; *S. pungens*, Mitt.; *Didymodon*, near *acutifolius*, Jaeg.; *Porotrichum variabile*, Hampe; *Neckera Jamesoni*, Tayl.; *Lejeunia* sp.; *Aneura* sp.; and *Dicranum speciosum*, Hook. & Wils.

[2] *Eurimene excelsa*, var. (very numerous); *Halsidota suffusa*, H.S.; *Agrotis* sp.; *Epiolus sordilus*, H.S.; and others.

[3] See *The Royal Commentaries of Peru*, by Garcilasso de la Vega (translated by Sir Paul Rycaut), fol., Lond., 1688, pp. 601–7, 631–3.

[4] It is said that upon starting Pizarro went through 'the Province of Quixos, which lies North from *Quitu*'; that he returned to the north of his outward route; and that when he re-arrived in the interior some of the inhabitants of Quito went thirty leagues to succour him. Little dependence, I imagine, can be placed upon the figures. Inasmuch as the trail through Papallacta is the only known way across the Eastern Andes, at the present time, in the neighbourhood

Andes somewhere near the Equator; and that this valiant leader, and his picked band of hardy adventurers, found that to overcome the natural difficulties of the region was a harder task than the Conquest of Peru. "The most irresistible of all was Hunger, that grievous and cruel Enemy of Man and Beast, which hath been so fatal to both in that uninhabited Countrey."[1]

From what we could learn of the people of Cayambe (and this was very little) the natural difficulties of the neighbourhood had not been overstated. It was not of course for a moment believed that we were attracted here by any such ridiculously transparent motive as the determination of the elevation of a mountain. In their eyes there was another allurement. Saraurcu was said to contain boundless riches—much gold and silver —which, it was delicately hinted, we might perhaps discover. Upon arrival at La Dormida two men were found in waiting 'to assist' us. One of them—a very old Indian—being physically an infant, I sent back to his village. The other was a toughlooking half-breed, whom I called 'The Spy'; and in order that he might do that for which he was sent I despatched him, with

of the Equator, it seems probable that Gonzalo Pizarro went by that route. It is still customary for persons proceeding by it to go a few miles *to the north* on leaving Quito, though they speedily bear round to the *east*. The words Rio de los Quixos will be found on the Maldonado map, to the east of Antisana.

[1] "By reason of the continual Rains, and moisture of the Earth, their woollen Cloths and linen being always wet, became rotten, and dropped from their Bodies, so that from the highest to the lowest every Man was naked, and had no other covering than some few Leaves. . . So great, and so insupportable were the Miseries which *Gonzalo Piçarro* and his Companions endured for want of Food, that the four thousand *Indians* which attended him in this Discovery, perished with Famine. . . Likewise of the three hundred and forty *Spaniards* which entred on this Discovery, two hundred and ten dyed, besides the fifty which were carried away by *Orellana*. . . Their Swords they carried without Scabbards, all covered with rust, and they walked barefoot, and their Visages were become so black, dry and withered, that they scarce knew one the other; in which condition they came at length to the Frontiers of *Quitu*, where they kissed the Ground, and returned Thanks to Almighty God, who had delivered them out of so many and so imminent dangers."—*The Royal Commentaries of Peru*, p. 632.

most of the others, on the 7th, 8th, and 9th to explore in the direction of Sara-urcu.

At this time I was feverish, and found my internals going wrong, from the last few days' experiences; and remained in the hut under a pile of ponchos, directing operations. The scouts came back with bad reports. The animals, they said, could go no farther; there was an end to paths and trails, except occasional wild-beast tracks; there was nothing whatever to eat, and everything must be carried; there was no place to camp upon, the whole country was a dismal swamp; and everlasting rain was falling; so much so that, although they supposed they had been near to Sara-urcu, they were quite unable to be sure. On discussion, it was concluded that the tents must be left behind, as we were not strong enough to carry both them, the wraps and food. Hence it was indispensable to find a place which would afford some protection against weather, and wild-animals; and on the third day they reported an overhanging cliff which would answer sufficiently well. It was arranged that Cevallos should remain at La Dormida to care for his beasts, with the Jovial Man to go to and fro between the village and the hut transporting provisions, which were to be brought to the front by Verity and the Spy; while David acted as camp-keeper at the advanced post, and the Carrels and I pursued exploration.

April 10. *From La Dormida towards Corredor Machai.* We made a forward move, leaving Cevallos and his assistant at the hut to tend the animals and keep up communications; half of the rest going in advance, while the others including myself waited for some additional food from Cayambe village. This arrived late, and delayed us so much that we could not reach the next camping-place by nightfall, and had to stop in a swamp, on a spot where, if you stood still, you sank up to the knees in slime. This place was just on the divide, nearly 13,000 feet above the sea, and during the greater part of the eleven hours night sleet or rain fell, rendering it well-nigh impossible to keep up a fire out of the sodden materials. For me the men constructed a sort of floating bed, cutting down reeds, and crossing and recrossing them, piling them up until they no longer sank in the slime. For themselves they made smaller platforms of a similar description, and sat on their heels during the whole night, trying to keep up a fire.

April 11. *At Corredor Machai.* We advanced and rejoined the others, having to pass through country more difficult than any we had hitherto traversed. The land was entirely marshy, even where the slopes were considerable; and upon it there was growing a reedy grass to the height of eight to ten feet,[1] in such dense masses as to be nearly impenetrable. The machetas were found inadequate. It would have taken several weeks' labour of our whole party to have cleared a track over a single mile. The only way of getting through was by continually parting the reeds with the hands (as if swimming), and as they were exceedingly stiff they sprang back directly we let go, and shut us out from each other's sight. The edges of the leaves cut like razors, and in a short time our hands were streaming with blood, for we were compelled to grasp the stems to prevent ourselves from sinking into the boggy soil. On this day we crossed the divide, and the streams now flowed towards the Atlantic. *The whole country was like a saturated sponge.*

We joined the others in due course, under an overhanging cliff of silvery mica-slate,[2] which we afterwards found was known by the name of Corredor Machai, or the hunter's refuge. It

[1] This has been identified by Prof. D. Oliver with the *Chusquea aristata* of Munro,—a reedy grass which is only known to grow in this region.

[2] "A rather fine-grained micaceous gneiss. The slaty formation is evidently due to a rough cleavage traversing the rock, on the planes of which a silvery mica has been rather largely developed. . . The structure of the rock is perplexing; it must undoubtedly be classed with the crystalline schists, but I suspect that the very marked schistosity is a secondary development due to crushing."—Prof. T. G. Bonney, *Proc. Royal Soc.*, Nov. 27, 1884.

THE BEDROOM   THE KITCHEN

AT CAMP ON THE EQUATOR, AT CORREDOR MACHAI (12,779 FEET).

was almost the only spot where it was possible to camp, and it afforded good protection on one side, of which we were glad, as there were numerous tracks of bears, pumas and other wild-beasts about. The lurch forward of the cliff prevented rain falling directly upon us, unless it blew from the north-east; but everything burnable was dripping with moisture,[1] and the surrounding land was so wet that water oozed or even squirted out in jets when it was trodden upon. Corredor Machai was placed on the southern side of a small valley, descending north-west, with several depressions (passes?) at its head.

At mid-day despatched two men across the valley to advance provisions in the direction in which we supposed Sara-urcu was situated. It had not yet been seen, and our view was limited by the mists to the immediate surroundings. They returned with a human skull which they had picked up not far away. "I know that skull," said the Spy; "it belonged to a man who went out searching for quinine bark. There were twenty of them altogether, and four came back. This one laid down to sleep, a snow-storm came on, and he did not wake again."[2] Sent some of the people to bring up more food from La Dormida, and made the rest hew down reeds to construct 'one man bed-rooms.' Laid the reeds sloping against the foot of the cliff, leaving room enough behind to creep into. Many spiders about; some very ticklish. Examined one with a lens, and found out why.

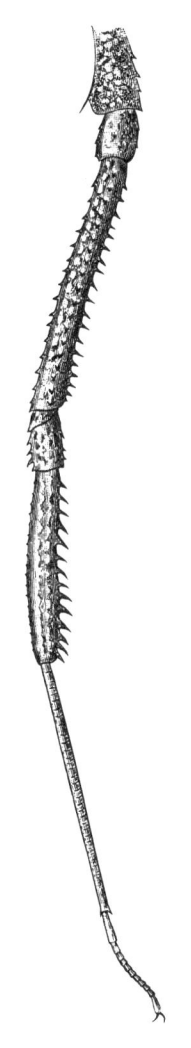

A HIND-LEG OF A SPIDER FROM CORREDOR MACHAI.

[1] We found paraffin oil of great use in *starting* fires when fuel was damp. It was employed here, and at all our high camps. A few pints of it were always carried.

[2] Searching for Chinchona trees, to strip them of their bark, is a favourite occupation in this country.

April 12. *Corredor Machai to Camp on Sara-urcu.* Advanced with the Carrels to the place where food was deposited yesterday, and left the others at Corredor Machai to keep up communications. Whilst descending to the bottom of our valley, saw a large bear walking along the other side, going straight ahead through the reeds as if they interposed no obstacle. Shouted to it, but it scarcely deigned to notice us, and only just turned its head aside for a moment, and went on into a thicket of scrub. Tracks of wild animals afforded assistance, as the reeds had often been trodden down. Passed several cattle lairs. The slopes here were as swampy as upon the other side.

Seldom saw two hundred yards in any direction on this day. Rain fell incessantly in a steady mizzle. Encamped in the afternoon against a bit of cliff with very slightly overhanging rock, at the height of 13,754 feet,[1] not knowing where we were, though believing we were close upon Sara-urcu. No fire possible. Minimum in night 35°; and, at 6 a.m. on the 13th, 36°·5 Faht.

April 13. *In Camp on Sara-urcu.* Made small excursions, to find out where we were. Discovered nothing, beyond a large glacier on the north, which we conjectured proceeded from our mountain. Sent the Carrels out in different directions exploring, and endeavoured to improve shelter. Built a low wall of clods and stones round the open side,—an addition which made the place as comfortable as an ordinary ditch on a winter's night.

Jean-Antoine came back hurriedly in the afternoon, looking behind him nervously. "Why, Carrel, man, what *is* the matter?" "Monsieur," said he, "just now I was over there, looking at the glacier to find a way down, when I heard a noise behind, and turning round saw two big bulls a few yards off, with their heads down, ready to pitch me over the precipice. I ran away up a rock, and they came after me; and one stood on one

---

[1] The Mercurial Barometer at 6 p.m. on April 12 (reduced to 32° Faht.) read 18·278 inches, air temperature 40° Faht. The simultaneous reading at Guayaquil (red. to 32°) was 29·917 inches, air temperature 78° Faht.

side, and the other on the other; and when I tried to escape on one side they both came there, and when I tried the other side they both went *there*, but at last I escaped, and here I am, quite out of breath." "Monsieur," he said, "on my word of honour, they were as fat as butter, and skipped about like chamois!"

April 14. *From Camp on Sara-urcu to Corredor Machai.* It rained all night. Temperature in our hole was 36°·75 Faht. at daybreak. This was a miserable place for protection against the weather. Nothing reasonably overhanging could be found. The loose stones, lying about, were either boulders too large to move, or too small to be of use. Shelter consisted solely of our three mackintosh ponchos, suspended from the Manilla rope. Large seams of massive quartz were a feature here. Nothing more golden was found than some glittering pyrites.

Rain continued without intermission. No one at Cayambe had spoken about these incessant rains. From the aspect of the country (so different from any other part of Ecuador), from the saturation of the hills, the innumerable small pools, streamlets and springs, I am convinced they are nearly perpetual. Being thoroughly sodden, and without the means of drying ourselves, we descended in the afternoon to Corredor Machai. Arrived drenched from the waist downwards.

Occasional glimpses of the country to the south (between Sara-urcu and Antisana) shewed that it contained a number of small ranges, without any single peak rising notably higher than the rest. Many were loftier than our station, and the highest are probably about 14,500 feet above the sea. No mountain was snow-covered, though there were numerous small patches of snow upon many of the peaks. I imagine that this district is entirely uninhabited.

Found five men who had come up with a letter to Verity from the Jefo-politico, saying that there was a strong report in the village that we were lost. Got rid of them as soon as possible, as they brought nothing, and ate up food we wanted. People grumbling, and wanting to return.

April 15. *At Corredor Machai.* Started Verity and David at 4 a.m. to hurry up provisions, as we are now reduced to biscuit and water. It continued to rain incessantly. This night while dozing in my den, I thought the stars had at last come out. Found that the light proceeded from a luminous beetle. Caught it, and put it into methylated spirit.[1]

> "Disputes have been, and still prevail,
> From whence his rays proceed,
> Some give that honour to his tail,
> And others to his head."

Or, at least, so says a Poet. Though this insect must have expired in a minute or two after immersion, it glowed for several hours; and gave enough light to tell the time by my watch, and to read the small writing in my Journal. The light was emitted from the two abdominal segments next above the lowest one. Min. temp. at night 39°·5 Faht.

April 16. *At Corredor Machai.* At mid-day temperature rose to 58° Faht.! In the afternoon, the Jovial Man and the Spy arrived with meat, bread, and other things just at the right time, and soon afterwards it left off raining. With the exception of about twelve hours in all, it has rained continuously from the night of the 10th until now. At 4 p.m. mists cleared away a little, and at 5 we saw Sara-urcu. Got its bearing and sketched it.[2] In a few minutes the mountain was invisible again. Arranged for a forced march to-morrow.

All the reeds round about our platform at the base of the cliff had been cut or beaten down, so that the view should not be impeded. The mountain appeared nearly in the place we

---

[1] Mr. Gorham identifies this insect as a male *Photinus longipennis* of Motschulsky, and says it is common in Colombia. I had previously obtained a female at La Dormida. See *Supp. App.*, p. 48.

[2] It was useless to try to photograph in this misty atmosphere. One could not work with the camera with the same certainty as with the pencil.

SARA-URCU, FROM CORREDOR MACHAI.

expected, on the northern side and at the head of the valley. Saw that it was surrounded by glaciers on the south. The summit *seemed* to be a sharp snow peak. This appearance we knew was delusive.

April 17. *Ascent of Sara-urcu.* Left Corredor Machai at 5.30 a.m. Foggy. Went as before across the valley, a little to the north of east. Rain fell 6 to 8 a.m. Passed camp on Sara-urcu at 8.55, picking up necessaries which had been left there in readiness. Then steered east; rounded the slopes of the ridge bounding the southern side of the large glacier proceeding from our mountain; passed the base of a small lateral glacier and took to the ice at 10.50 a.m. Put on the rope. Could not see a hundred yards in any direction. Steered east-south-east.

The summit of Sara-urcu bore almost exactly due east from Corredor Machai, and an east-south-east course was calculated to bring us right upon it. To return steering by compass was more dubious. We did not apprehend losing ourselves on land; nor upon snow and glacier, even in a fog, if our track was not obliterated. There was every probability that it would be quickly effaced; while it would be necessary, to escape from the glacier, to hit off the exact place where we took to it. It was by no means certain that we could do this, trusting to the compass alone; for it is very difficult to hold to one general course in a fog, when courses have to be changed every other minute, as they must necessarily be upon crevassed glacier.

To ensure our return, Louis therefore carried a quantity of four-foot lengths of the reed tops, to place as guide-marks on the glacier; and planted

TURNING AN ENEMY TO ACCOUNT.

another as soon as the last one he had fixed became dim. While this scarcely hindered progress, it allowed us to proceed with greater confidence. We rose steadily, crossing many crevasses; and when about 15,000 feet high suddenly emerged from the clouds, and found ourselves face to face with the pointed snow peak. Behind this, a wall of snow[1] led to the true top.

With out-turned toes we went cautiously along the crisp *arête*, sharp as a roof-top, and at 1.30 p.m. stood on the true summit of Sara-urcu; a shattered ridge of gneiss—wonder of wonders, blue sky above[2]—strewn with fragments of quartz, and micaschist similar to that at Corredor Machai,[3] without a trace of vegetation. The usual atmospheric conditions prevailed. Cayambe and all the rest was shut out by unfathomable, impenetrable mists, limiting the view to a few hundred yards around the summit, which was surrounded by glaciers on all sides.[4] Temperature rose and fell as puffs of steamy air came from the great cauldron on the east. The barometer stood at 17·230 inches,[5] and thus it was clear that Sara-urcu was *not* the fifth

[1] This is nearly concealed in the view upon p. 247.

[2] But no sunshine. The sun, I believe, was not seen by us from the 5th to the 20th of April.

[3] In the moraine at the margin of the ice where we first took to the glacier there was much ferruginous quartz, and iron pyrites, the origin perhaps of the rumoured treasures of Sara-urcu.

The rock *in situ* at the summit was "a rather fine-grained gneiss, containing quartz, felspar, dark mica, with probably a little chlorite and epidote. . . All the specimens brought from Sara-urcu are metamorphic rocks. They do not, indeed, belong to the earliest types, such as the coarse gneisses of the Hebrides, but still they are greatly altered."—Prof. T. G. Bonney, in *Proc. Royal Soc.*, Nov. 27, 1884.

[4] We could not at any time see the full length of the large glacier on the west of Sara-urcu, *or even across it*. It appeared to bend round towards the north. The glaciers on the south side of the mountain are small. There was another one, descending towards the north-east, which, so far as could be seen, was more considerable.

[5] On April 17, at 1.45 p.m., the Mercurial Barometer (reduced to 32° Faht.) read 17·230 inches, air temperature 46° Faht. The 11 a.m. and 6 p.m. observations

in rank of the Andes of the Equator, and indeed was less in height than several of the minor peaks which had been already ascended.

Surprised by darkness before we could arrive at Corredor Machai, another miserable night had to be passed at the upper station. On the 18th we descended, and took ourselves off as speedily as possible. After the reed, the chief Botanical feature of the valley in which the 'Hunter's refuge' was placed was the extraordinary manner in which the twigs and branches of such trees as were there were laden—almost stifled—with the lichen *Usnea barbata*, Fries. This lichen and the *Chusquea* were the two dominant species, and put nearly everything else out of sight. The flora here is probably extensive. Close to the rock there were Currant bushes in flower, a Fuchsia (*F. Loxensis*, H.B.K.) at the greatest height these plants were seen, and Ferns were numerous, although concealed.[1] But all the botanical treasures in Ecuador would not have enticed us to stop. We turned our backs on this super-saturated place with the greatest possible pleasure; passed the nights of the 18th and 19th at La Dormida, and on the 20th returned to Cayambe village, understanding better than when we left it why Gonzalo Pizarro *kissed the ground* when he stood again on *terra firma*.

Such information as I brought from Sara-urcu differs materi-

at Guayaquil (red. to 32° F.) were 29·912 and 29·859 inches, air temperatures, respectively, being 80° and 81° Faht. During our stay on the summit, temperature fluctuated between 43°·5—55° Faht.

Flies, evidently stragglers, of three distinct species were captured on the summit. Like the rest of the Diptera, they remain undescribed.

[1] The following were some of the more common species round about Corredor Machai. Lichens:—*Bæomyces imbricatus*, Hooker (abundant); *Parmelia Kamtschadalis*, Eschw.; *Sticta laciniata*, Ach. (abundant); *Sticta* sp.; and *Usnea barbata*, Fries (very abundant). Mosses:—*Breutelia* sp.; *Daltonia bilimbata*, Hampe; *Hypnum cupressiforme*, Linn., var.; *H. Schreberi*, Willd. (abundant); *Metzgeria clavæflora*, Spruce; *Mnium rostratum*, Schrad.; *Plagiochila* sp.; and *Rhizogonium mnioides*, Schimp. Ferns:—*Cheilanthes scariosa*, Kaulf.; *Hymenophyllum sericeum*, Sw.; and *Polypodium subsessile*, Baker.

ally from the statements made about that mountain by Villavicencio. He gives in his *Geografia* 6210 varas as its height;[1] upon his map, places it south of east of Quito and *south-south-west* of Cayambe (mountain), near Papallacta; he quotes from Velasco[2] to the effect that it was a volcano which formerly emitted fire, and he says it has latterly ejected ashes, producing consternation in the Capital, whence it is distant thirty-five miles.[3] I found that Sara-urcu is only 15,502 feet high, and is placed south-east by south of Cayambe (mountain); that it is not a volcano, and cannot have emitted fire and ejected ashes; and that it lies considerably to the *north* of east of Quito, at the distance of about forty-five English miles. Instead of being the fifth in altitude of the Great Andes of the Equator, it proved to be the lowest of all the snow-peaks, and considerably inferior in elevation to several which scarcely reach the snow-line.

Before we left Cayambe I pursued enquiries for *Cyclopium* (*Pimelodus*) *cyclopum*. In the first volume of the Zoology of Humboldt and Bonpland's Journey, a description,[4] and a figure drawn on the spot by Humboldt himself, of this fish are given, which is said (p. 23) to be the *only* one found in the 'Kingdom of Quito' at heights above 8752 feet (1400 toises). This statement is in itself somewhat remarkable, and the information which

[1]. Reckoning the vara at 2·782 English feet, 6210 varas are equal to 17,276 English feet. I am not aware what foundation he had for this statement. Possibly, he heard that the mountain bore large glaciers, and conjectured that its elevation must be near those of the other glacier-bearing Andes.

[2] I have not been able to find a reference to this mountain in Velasco.

[3] "Segun refiere el P. Velasco en su historia de Quito, este volcan ha arrojado llamas por dos veces; mas, en estos últimos años, ha arrojado gran cantidad de cenizas volcánicas, por Diciembre de 1843, i por el mismo mes, en 1856. La primera de estas erupciones duró dos dias, i puso en mucha consternacion á los habitantes de Quito, i á sus pueblos circumvecinos. La altura de esta montaña es de 6210 varas sobre el mar... Está situado á 35 millas E. de Quito."—*Geografia de la Republica del Ecuador*, por Manuel Villavicencio, 8vo, New York, 1858, pp. 52-53.

[4] Vol. i, pp. 21-25, Pl. 7. *Mémoire sur une nouvelle espèce de Pimélode, jetée par les volcans du Royaume de Quito.*

accompanies the description is extraordinary. Humboldt says that during minor eruptions of Cotopaxi, Tunguragua, and Sangai, and eruptions or convulsions of Imbabura and Carihuairazo, immense numbers — thousands — of these fish (which he calls *Pimelodus cyclopum*) are thrown out; that they are sometimes ejected from the craters at the summits of these mountains, and sometimes through fissures in their slopes; curious to say, "constantly at the elevation of 15,986–16,626 feet (2500 to 2600 toises) above the sea." He speaks of this as a regular occurrence in the case of the first three named mountains, and says that the pestilential odours which arise from the decay of these fish cause fevers, etcetera.

The most wonderful part of the story has yet to come. These fish, which are supposed to be ejected from the craters of fiery volcanoes 17,000 to 19,500 feet above the sea, or from fissures at heights of 16,000 to 16,600 feet, are said to reach the plains *alive*, after they have tumbled or have been washed all the way down the sides of the mountains. The distinguished traveller adds, cautiously, "this fact does not appear to me to be sufficiently vouched for"; but says, immediately afterwards, "What is certain is that, amongst the thousands of dead fish one sees come down from Cotopaxi there are very few sufficiently disfigured to let one believe that they have been exposed to great heat. This fact becomes more striking when we consider the soft flesh of these animals. . . It appeared very interesting for Natural History to verify the nature of these animals." For the rest let me refer the reader to the original, or to *Aspects of Nature*, vol. ii, p. 231, where the same story is given in different words.

It will, I think, be gathered from the original, that Humboldt did not himself see any of the fish which were said to have been 'ejected.' He identified them with the fish which are found in ponds, lakes, and streams throughout the interior of Ecuador, and it was one of these latter that he figured and described. He commits himself, however, to a belief in the story by the passage commencing "What is certain," and especially by the title of his paper (Memoir upon a new species of Pimelode *thrown out* by the Volcanoes of the Kingdom of Quito). In *Aspects of Nature* he says that these fish live in subterranean reservoirs in the Volcanoes. There seems no limit to the credulity of man. All these marvels have been frequently embodied in works treating upon Natural History, without protest.

I venture to point out that from 12,000 feet upwards the slopes of Cotopaxi are *uninhabited;* that the height of 16,000 to 16,600 feet is an altitude to which the natives of Ecuador *never go* under ordinary circumstances, still less would they be there during an eruption; and that no one can possibly affirm from personal knowledge that these fish have ever been thrown out from the crater, or from fissures at the height of 16,000 feet.

From 15,000 feet upwards the cone of Cotopaxi was found to be so warm as to quickly liquefy snow which fell upon it (see p. 142). At 19,500 feet the face of the slope was observed to have a temperature of 50° Faht., and at the depth of eight feet 110° Faht. (see p. 148). At this height, water boiled at 179°·1 Faht. It was clear that at a very moderate distance below the surface the boiling-point of water would be reached. A subterranean reservoir of quite small dimensions would necessarily be surrounded by rock at a temperature probably much exceeding the boiling-point of water.

As it is stated that the fish which are *supposed* to have been ejected from the crater, or to have been expelled from the subterranean reservoirs, were frequently alive, and had their flesh in good preservation, it appears to me there is stronger evidence against the notion that they dwell in subterranean reservoirs than in favour of it. Fish cannot emerge in this rough manner from boiling-water or from super-heated steam alive, and with their skins intact. Yet I do not like to abandon all belief in this pet story of childhood, as wonderful in its way as the history of Shadrach, Meshach, and Abednego. Possibly, after some eruptions and earthquakes large numbers of these fish *have* been found out of water, but this would not prove ejection by or from the volcanoes. Floods occasionally pour down the slopes of Cotopaxi, causing rivers to swell and to overflow their banks (see pages 127, 138, and 159); and it would be no marvel if during such inundations multitudes of fish were borne from their native haunts, and left stranded when the waters subsided. Also, during earthquakes, fissures opening in the earth may change the courses of streams; or might, by intersecting the beds of pools, drain them and leave shoals of fish high and dry, living and unscathed. In these possibilities there is, I imagine, the sub-stratum of truth upon which a mountain of fable has been raised.

In an indirect manner, the statement that *Pimelodus cyclopum* is the *only* fish found in the interior above 8750 feet has been questioned. Other travellers have brought home fish from this region, on several occasions, which have been described under various names. In a paper in the *American Naturalist* for 1871 (pp. 694–5), Dr. Putnam, however, advanced the opinion that the whole of these so-called different species should be referred to one, somewhat variable, species; and as the descriptions had been based upon a small number of examples I thought it was advisable to collect freely, in order that the matter might be re-investigated.

Machachi was the first place where enquiries were made, and I introduced the matter there to the tambo-keeper, who at once declared that *several* kinds of fish could be found in the neighbouring streams. "My good Antonio," said I, "if you will only shew me *two* kinds I will give you five pesos." This manner of approaching the subject commended itself to the landlord, and he soon brought examples; but, although there were differences amongst them, Antonio Racines did not earn the reward; for when they were placed side by side he was obliged to confess that they were all one kind. Yet he maintained to the last that other fish were to be found in the interior of Ecuador, and that they grew six, seven to eight inches long.

From the Machachi specimens I selected young and old, and those presenting most variety; and at Cayambe made friends with the schoolmaster, and induced him to send his scholars to scour the streams and ponds. Nothing could have suited the urchins better. *Pimelodus cyclopum* began to arrive from all points of the compass. They filled a bucket, and I had to cry "Stop!" Again I made a selection, and enquired "What shall we do with the rest?" "Eat them," said the Jefo-politico; and they were cooked and consumed, and were found not to be more nasty than other small fry composed principally of heads and tails. Here again slight differences could be noted, but no one could venture to say that there were two species. At Chillo, and Riobamba, I again procured a large number, with similar results.

Out of the many hundreds which passed through my hands, none exceeded four inches in length. Fifty-one were preserved, and submitted upon my return to the independent examination of the late Dr. F. Day, who coincided with the views expressed by Dr. Putnam, and therefore upheld the statement originally made by Humboldt.[1] *Pimelodus cyclopum* (proposed by Dr. Putnam to be called *Cyclopium cyclopum*) is found throughout the interior of Ecuador generally, from 8500 to 10,000 feet above the sea;[2] in streams flowing both into the Atlantic and Pacific; and in ponds, pools and lakes quite disconnected. It swims with a wriggly action; comes frequently to the surface to breathe; and often appears to be blind, or at least to see very imperfectly. It should be repeated, however, that a number of Ecuadorians stoutly maintained that there were other fish in the streams, as much as a foot in length; and I have no reason to doubt their sincerity, although they failed to produce examples.

[1] Dr. Day's remarks will be found in the *Supplementary Appendix*, pp. 137-9, accompanied by figures of this fish seen from above, below, and in profile.

[2] And perhaps much higher. I was unable to investigate the numerous ponds and pools on Antisana, the small lake at the foot of the cone of Cotopaxi, and the larger one upon Mojanda.

FOUNTAIN ON THE PLAZA AT CARRANQUI.

CHAPTER XIV.

ON THE PROVINCE OF IMBABURA, AND THE FIRST ASCENT OF COTOCACHI.

UPON the 21st of April we left Cayambe, and crossed the depression between Mojanda and Imbabura to the village of Otovalo;[1] having two objects in view—an ascent of Cotocachi, and collection of Antiquities in the district which has been in the past, and is still, the most densely populated in Ecuador.

I went to that country possessed with the notion that there must have been an Equatorial "Stone Age," though without positive information that stone implements could be found; or knowing whether during Incarial times weapons and implements of stone were in common use. Having nothing to shew, for a

[1] There was a fair track all the way, and from the Lake of St. Pablo to Otovalo there was a respectable road.

long time there were no results. If one talked of the Incas the natives enquired with surprise "Who were they?" and they seemed equally unacquainted with the works of their (probably) much more remote ancestors. So we fell back upon asking for *old things*, and then came shabby umbrella tops, battered scissors, and broken pottery — objects which were rejected because they were not nearly old enough. At length we seemed to have struck oil. One night, when at supper, the door was stealthily opened; and a rough head peeped round, peering out of a dilapidated poncho that concealed a bulky object. "You have something to shew?" "Yes, Señor." "Is it old?" "That it is"; and, tossing aside his ragged garment, he displayed his treasure, saying, triumphantly, "*this* is *very* old, Señor!"

At Machachi, by persistent enquiries, Perring at last discovered a battered stone axe, and thus getting a start, through having something to shew, we picked up others as we progressed northwards; though south of Quito antiquities of any kind were rare, and in the Capital it was scarcely more use to look for them than to search for Chelsea ware in Chelsea, or for Caxtons

"*THIS* IS *VERY* OLD, SEÑOR!"

in Westminster. Still a few things were obtained, even there,— amongst others, the lance-point given on the next page,[1] which was found in an old wall that was being pulled down. Every one said, "Try Imbabura. Go to Ibarra, and to Carranqui the birthplace of Atahualpa."

[1] This was one of the two chipped objects which were obtained. The whole of the rest were polished.

So we went to Imbabura,[1] gradually acquiring things in stone as we rode along — accosting every person and enquiring at all the houses — sometimes spying them hanging as ornaments or charms around the necks of Indian women,[2] or used as weights by weavers on their looms, or as toys by children. Verity was a tolerably efficient assistant, and I found a more acute one presently at Otovalo in the person of the Yankee Jew who had anathematized the salt fish on Good Friday; and succeeded in enlisting the sympathies of several other persons who were not insensible to the value of the Almighty Dollar.

Time was becoming precious, for this northern journey had occupied longer than was intended; and it was arranged that Cotocachi should be disposed of first, and that I should pursue my quest for antiquities with Verity and Cevallos, whilst the Carrels returned southwards to make another attempt to ascend Illiniza. At Otovalo we were informed that our mountain was unapproach-

[1] Imbabura is bounded on the north by Colombia, and on the west, east, and south by the Provinces of Esmeraldas, Oriente, and Pichincha. It is divided into four cantons, Tulcan, Ibarra, Cotocachi and Otovalo, which are subdivided into twenty-nine parishes. Ibarra is the chief town. The mountain called Imbabura occupies a large part of the Province.

[2] See the illustration on page 237.

able from that direction, on account of earthquake fissures, and were advised to proceed to the village of Cotocachi, and seek the good offices of the Priest. On the 22nd of April we went there, and found him high up on a scaffolding, acting as master-builder for a new church, surrounded by scores of his parishioners, busy as bees. A good man was this Priest. He lodged and fed us, wrote a letter of recommendation to the owner of the highest property on the mountain, and got us off at 6.35 a.m. next morning, provided with a guide for the first part of the way.

From studying Cotocachi at a distance, it had been settled to make an ascent from the south or south-west. When sweeping the horizon on the top of the Pointe Jarrin, I found that it was much the most elevated and the only snow-clad mountain in the north of Ecuador, and had determined that the more southern of its two peaks was the loftier. The Chief of the Staff, on the contrary, maintained that the northern was the higher point. I overruled him, for on the cross-wire of the theodolite, when we were nearly on a level with the top of Cotocachi, there was a marked, though small, difference between the two peaks in favour of the southern one.

Our guide led westwards, through lanes whose banks and hedges were laden with ferns[1] (all different from those which had been met with before), and adhered to this course for about six miles, skirting the base of the mountain and apparently taking us away from the goal; moving parallel to an impassable quebrada, generally about seventy feet wide (which had been formed in 1868), until he came to a place where the walls had fallen in and choked the cleft. We crossed this natural bridge, and then steered north-north-west to Iltaqui (10,049 feet) — a very diminutive hacienda and the highest house upon the mountain — which was in charge of one old Indian.

[1] *Asplenium trichomanes*, L. (abundant); *Cheilanthes myriophylla*, Desv. (abundant); *Cystopteris fragilis*, Bernh.; *Notholæna sinuata*, Kaulf.; *Woodsia mollis*, J. Smith; and others.

When looking back from this place it was seen that there was good reason for bringing us by a circuitous route. The lower slopes of our mountain, and the comparatively flat ground at its base, were rent and riven in a most extreme manner. In no other part of Ecuador is there anything equalling this extraordinary assemblage of fissures, intersecting one another irregularly and forming a perfect maze of impassable clefts. The general appearance of the country between the villages of Cotocachi and Otovalo is not very unlike that of a biscuit which has been smashed by a blow of the fist. The cracks are all V shaped, and though seldom of great breadth are often very profound, and by general consent they are all *earthquake quebradas*. Several, at least, have been formed within the memory of man, while others are believed to be centuries old. It was not to be expected that any one would be found who had actually witnessed their formation,[1] or possessing certain knowledge of the immediate cause of their production. Some persons would probably have said with Shakespeare that

> "Oft the teeming earth
> Is with a kind of colic pinch'd and vex'd
> By the imprisoning of unruly wind
> Within her womb; which, for enlargement striving,
> Shakes the old beldame Earth, and topples down
> Steeples and moss-grown towers."

If, however, they had been caused by upheaval, there could scarcely have failed to have been some irregularities in the surface; and I imagine that they arise from a succession of *settlements* in this particular area. Whether they have been caused by upheavals or subsidences, it is clear that at the time they were produced the *surface* of the earth was *in a state of tension*.

After leaving Iltaqui, we were guided by the Indian up a small valley leading towards what may be termed the southern ridge of

[1] The quebrada we skirted was one of the largest, and was not less than six miles in length. It opened in the night. I am unable to give a view of this very remarkable scene. The photographic plates that were exposed at Iltaqui were smashed in the accident which occurred on the way back to Quito.

Cotocachi, and when this was struck turned sharply to the right, towards the summit. Cracks and fissures in the crest of this ridge again suggested that settlements were occurring. Our guide led well, and got us soon after mid-day up to the foot of the final peak, and more than 14,000 feet above the level of the sea. The ground then became too rugged for the mules, and we halted to consider.

From this direction, Cotocachi appears pyramidal rather than conical; and has a face on the east (fronting the basin of Imbabura) that is precipitous; and another less abrupt one on the west, largely covered with snow. This was to be our way; and catching sight of a small bit of flat ground a little higher, in the right direction, all hands set to work carrying baggage to it. The second trip upwards was being made when a transformation scene occurred. A clear sky became overclouded, the mountain was lost in mist; and, after the usual succession of rain, hail and sleet, a furious fall of snow took place, which rendered the air so thick that, although only a few yards apart, we could not see each other. The whole of the natives dropped their loads and fled, while Verity and the Carrels stuck to their work, and laboured to place the tent amid driving showers of snow, circling in a veritable *tourmente*. The gusts filled the tent and defied their efforts to install it. The wind tossed us about like playthings — neither the long arms of Louis nor the strong ones of Verity and Jean-Antoine availed anything. The whirling snow mocked our efforts, and for the only occasion on this journey we found it impossible to erect our habitation properly.

The tents taken to Ecuador, in general style, resembled that which is described in *Scrambles amongst the Alps*. The four poles, however, were divided.[1] Their upper halves were fixtures, and when the lower ones were withdrawn the tents could be *folded*,

[1] At the points where the poles crossed each other a little of the canvas was cut away, leaving a hole at each corner of the roof for ventilation (see illustration upon page 60). During snowy and rainy weather, it was frequently necessary to close these apertures, and this was done by covering them with the waterproof casings to our hats (see illustration upon page 144).

and made into packages of convenient size for mule-travelling. The wood was varnished to hinder it absorbing moisture; but on this northern journey some of my people thought to do a clever thing and scraped the poles to make them run in more easily, and thus made matters worse instead of better. The wood swelled, and did not slide in as freely as before; and in the hurry of the occasion some of the canvas became puckered, and prevented one of the lower halves from entering its socket. We struggled in vain to rectify it; and, when the tent was at last pitched, one or another had, for the next fourteen hours, to support the faulty corner to save the structure from collapsing.

In the morning six inches of new snow was lying around, and the mountain was loaded with it. Shall we proceed? If this had been dry, powdery snow I should have declined. There is no objection, beyond the labour involved, to traversing new-fallen snow upon mountain-slopes provided it will cohere, and adhere. Particles of granular snow coalesce slowly; and in cold weather, particularly, several days may elapse before they will *bind*. Happily, we never saw snow of this description in Ecuador, although it is common in most high regions. *Our* snow was generally *wet*. It may have been the product of intense cold; but, falling through atmosphere with temperatures considerably above the freezing-point, it arrived upon the ground in a thawing condition, and had not the tendency to slip upon slopes, which is a characteristic of the granular state.[1]

We therefore proceeded, after a preliminary inspection, and at 11.35 a.m., on the 24th of April, stood on the very highest point of Cotocachi. One hundred and ninety minutes were occupied in going from the camp (14,490 feet) to the summit (16,301 feet), and we consequently ascended 571 feet per hour, a rate much inferior to that attained on Antisana and Cayambe, which is to be attributed to the caution employed to avoid disturbance of

[1] During the whole time we were amongst the Great Andes of the Equator we neither saw a *snow-avalanche* nor the track of one.

the snow, and to the greater steepness of the ground.[1] I noticed that 657 steps were made without stopping, when between 15,000–16,000 feet high; and this compares favourably with the experiences of many practised mountaineers at a similar elevation (pressure) upon Mont Blanc. Though it must be admitted that the steps were short ones (as we were quite unable to do anything approaching this during the earlier part of the journey), there is reason to believe that we had, in the course of the last four months, become somewhat habituated to low pressures.

The true summit of Cotocachi is a pointed peak of lava,[2] broken up by frost, extremely steep at the finish, and upon that account bearing little snow. I estimate it to be 150 to 180 feet higher than the northern, or second summit. This mountain

COTOCACHI, FROM CARRANQUI.

---

[1] Left camp at 8.25 a.m., and went to the top without a halt. On the 24th of April, at 12 (noon), the Mercurial Barometer (reduced to 32° Faht.) read 16·661 inches, air temperature 36°·5 Faht. The 11 a.m. observation at Guayaquil (red. to 32°) was 29·869 inches, air temp. 81° Faht.

[2] "Purplish-grey rock, containing small whitish felspar crystals, with a good many minute vesicles... The ground mass appears to consist of a glassy base, containing minute crystallites, probably for the most part felspar, but perhaps also a pyroxenic mineral, with rods of opacite and with ferrite staining. In this occur crystals of plagioclastic felspar, not generally exceeding 0·3 inch, agreeing in general character with those already described, but perhaps more frequently containing enclosures, and 'dirty looking,' together with a pyroxenic mineral. The crystals of this are not very characteristic, but I think both augite and hypersthene can be identified... These rocks from Cotocachi appear to be hyperstheniferous augite-andesite."—Prof. T. G. Bonney, *Proc. Royal Soc.*, Nov. 27, 1884.

is probably the eleventh in rank of the Great Andes of the Equator. Tradition says that it was in eruption some centuries ago, and it is not unlikely that a crater lies buried beneath the glacier which at present occupies the depression between its two peaks.[1]

On the 25th of April we returned to Cotocachi. The lanes were thronged by troops of Indians, hurrying forward with unwonted alacrity to the village, where the streets and exits from the Plaza were barricaded, to prevent the escape of tormented cattle. Their eagerness was explained. What sweeter pastime is there than baiting a bull ? When can it be more fitly practised than upon a Sunday afternoon ?

The *élite* of Cotocachi were engaged at the Priest's house in perusing an account of the Ascent of Antisana, which had just been published by General Veintemilla in the Official Gazette. His Reverence insisted that it must be read in public, and told a satellite to inform the people that he had a communication to make to them. The news spread as if by magic. The populace followed us literally *en masse*, streamed into the building where the lecture was to be given until it was jammed tight with standing people, clambered on to the window-sills, and stood outside in thousands, craning their necks forward to catch the words of their Pastor; who from a slightly elevated desk, after a little introduction, read the whole of a very matter-of-fact relation, to

---

[1] There was abundance of the lichen *Stereocaulon turgescens*, Nyl., and of the moss *Grimmia ovata*, Web. & Mohr, amongst the summit rocks. Examples of these two genera were frequently seen closely against or surrounded by snow (15–16,600 feet), and it was not unusual to find them in such a position. Five species of *Grimmia* were found at 16,000 feet and *upwards*, elsewhere. Upon the very highest point of all there were two Grasses (*Trisetum Andinum*, Benth., and a *Deyeuxia* which is not yet determined), *only one root of each*, growing strongly ; two thousand feet above the upper limit of their ordinary range, in the most exposed position that could be selected, where during the greater part of the year temperature must be much below the freezing-point and the soil be hard frozen ;—yet growing strongly, evidently flourishing, and approaching maturity—the most remarkable instance of this kind that has ever come under my notice.

which they listened in the most perfect silence, and with a rapt attention that shewed their respect for their spiritual leader and gave evidence of thirst for information.[1]

When this was over we returned to Otovalo, and on the next day the Carrels went off to Quito, accompanied by David and the jovial arriero, leaving me with Verity and Cevallos. I was in very indifferent health, and received here, at a time when they were valuable, some attentions from the Yankee-Jew who had made himself conspicuous on Good Friday, by his wrath at the *table d'hôte*. The language of this hybrid Hebrew was often most unparliamentary; but he was a good-natured man, a trader before everything (he would either buy your hair or sell you a watch), and I endeavoured to requite his kindness when we met again at the Capital. Inducing him and an intelligent cobbler to work this locality in my absence, on the 28th of April I rode across Imbabura to Ibarra, passing through the villages of Hutantaqui and San Antonio.

A large part of the Province is occupied by the mountains Mojanda, Cotocachi, and Imbabura. The slopes of the latter extend from Carranqui almost to the Lake of San Pablo, and on the west commence to rise at the village of Iluman. The fertile and cultivated portion of the Province lies principally in the basin that is enclosed by the three mountains. The bottom of this is not so high as those which have been already mentioned, and it enjoys a happy mean between the chillness of the more elevated lands, and the sultry climate of the lower ground. To this higher temperature, more than to any difference in the soil, the fertility of Imbabura is to be ascribed; and the comparative

[1] Compulsory education was established by Garcia Moreno in Ecuador before it was introduced into Great Britain, and in 1880, in the interior, it was exceptional to find a person who could not read. They had little chance, however, of obtaining anything to read. There was no book-shop in Quito, nor, I believe, in the whole country. The people with whom we mixed (either Indians or half-whites) were always eager to have anything read to them. In this total absence of literature, and thirst for information, there was a great opportunity for a man of enterprize.

density of its population is a consequence of its fertility. Between the places which have been enumerated, the whole country is dotted with detached residences—Indian villas so to speak—each provided with its little plot of ground, where all and more than is necessary can be raised.[1] The daily wage of the people is said to be only a medio (two-pence), yet it appeared to be sufficient for their wants. They looked sleek and well-fed, and were rich enough to indulge in drunkenness.[2]

Notwithstanding this drawback, it is pleasant to ride across Imbabura. Foliage gives shadow, and the roads are well-beaten tracks, reasonably dry. Round about Hutantaqui and San Antonio in particular, there are a great number of artificial mounds, from twenty or thirty to two hundred or more feet in diameter (in form resembling the *panecillos* of the Volcanoes), which are universally considered to be *tumuli*. According to Father Velasco,[3] more than twelve thousand of these were erected after the defeat, on the Plain of Hutantaqui, of the tribes of Cayambe, Carranqui and Otovalo by the Inca monarch, Huayna-Capac. Though they are very numerous, it cannot be supposed for a moment that there are or ever have been 12,000 of these mounds in this locality. There are others in the neighbourhood of Carranqui which are said to have been investigated at various times by joint-stock companies, with disappointing results. They desired gold and silver, and found little except bones and pottery.

The villages which have just been mentioned, as well as the

[1] The following things were being grown in this small district—Maize, Wheat, Barley, Sugar-cane, Cotton; Peas, Lentils, French-beans, Potatoes, Yuca, Parsnips, Lettuce, Cabbages, and other ordinary vegetables; Bananas, Cherries, Strawberries, Chirimoya, Lemons, Oranges, and Grapes.

[2] Until our arrival in Imbabura, we had not seen half-a-dozen intoxicated persons in Ecuador; but when returning upon the 25th of April, in the little distance between Cotocachi and Otovalo, we passed three men who were dead drunk, a score of others badly inebriated, and many—including women—in a more or less advanced condition.

[3] *Histoire du Royaume de Quito*, par Don Juan de Velasco (translated by H. Ternaux-Compans), 8vo, Paris, 1840; vol. i, p. 53.

larger ones of the Province, were still in a very ruinous condition from the effects of the earthquake of August 16, 1868. This occurred at 1 a.m., and is generally believed to have originated in the space between Otovalo and Cotocachi (village), and to have been an affair of a few seconds. The havoc was confined to the basin of Imbabura. A shock appears to have travelled northwards, and to have *rebounded* upon Ibarra from the mountains of Colombia;[1] for the destruction at this place was more complete than in the towns closer to the great quebrada which opened in the night. I was told that not more than two dozen houses were left standing, and that lists were in existence shewing that 20,000 persons perished at Ibarra alone.[2] I imagine that the disturbance of the earth which caused the shock (or shocks) occurred at no great distance beneath the surface. If the focus of disturbance had been deep-seated, the area influenced would have been larger.

At Ibarra, I brought letters of introduction to Señor Teodoro Gomez de la Torre, the greatest landowner in the north of Ecuador, — a gentleman who was spoken of everywhere with respect. Amongst other things standing to his credit was that, when nominated for the Presidency upon the assassination of Garcia Moreno, he retired in favour of Borrero, rather than divide his party. "My house," he was accustomed to say, "is the

[1] The mountains of Colombia shut in the Province of Imbabura like a wall. Though their general elevation is very considerable, in the month of April they were without snow.

[2] If these lists were examined it would I expect be found that this number is a gross exaggeration. I think Ibarra never contained 20,000 persons. The place, however, was very badly wrecked. At the time of our visit, six churches, a convent, schools, and the hospital were in ruins.

In the earthquake of 1868 the Indians suffered less than the rest of the population, principally in consequence of the greater fragility and elasticity of their dwellings. Some may have been swallowed up by the opening of chasms, for in this rather thickly populated district a fissure several miles long could scarcely open anywhere without this happening.

In a Report from Mr. Alfred St. John to the Foreign Office, dated Quito, July 14, 1891, the entire population of the Province of Imbabura is said to be 67,940, and that of the town of Ibarra to be 6000 (see note to page 1).

only hotel at Ibarra," and he well sustained his reputation for hospitality.

On the 29th of April we went over to Carranqui, a village of 700 or 800 persons, about a mile and a quarter south of Ibarra, and a little above it; at this place proceeding as before, questioning every individual we met, exhibiting the things which had been already acquired, and enlisting Priest and Jefo-politico in the search, and speedily found that much was obtainable; but my increasing weakness, and inability to procure proper remedies, warned me that it was time to return, and after a second visit to Carranqui we went back to Otovalo, in possession of a collection that proved the existence of great numbers of implements in stone in Equatorial America, and raised a strong presumption that there was, at some remote period, a Stone Age. I give here all the remarks that will be offered upon this subject, although not a few of the examples to which reference will be made were procured at a later date.

I place first a class of objects to which, so far as I am aware, special attention has not hitherto been drawn by any traveller. Those included in the group figured upon page 269 all belong to a type which is numerous in Ecuador, and they should not perhaps be classed either as Ornaments, Weapons, or Implements. I call them Stars in Stone. They were found everywhere between Ibarra and Riobamba, and became embarrassing by their very quantity. The majority have six rays (and none have more), proceeding symmetrically from the centre, and the whole are fashioned alike upon each side. A certain number have only five rays, and occasional examples are irregular in shape (see the top figure, on the right). All are pierced by a hole, which has been drilled from the two sides, and the size of this varies considerably. In dimensions they range from three to five inches in diameter, and from three-quarters of an inch to two inches in thickness. Their weight is from five to twenty ounces. The larger part are

CHAP. XIV. *STARS IN STONE.* 269

made from basaltic rock and gabbro. Objects of this class were also cast in metal, but these are now rarely met with in Ecuador.[1]

Whilst they possess the general points of similarity that have been mentioned, scarcely any two are identical in form. Some are flat and thin, others are thick, or rise in the centre upon each

STARS IN STONE.

side into a shape like the hub of a wheel. The number of these objects that I collected was as much a matter of surprise to Ecuadorians as it was to myself. Though many persons were

[1] It is not unlikely that many examples in metal have perished in the melting-pot (like the axes and other implements and weapons), through the Ecuadorian mania for GOLD.

aware of the existence of these Stars in Stone, no one seemed to possess the least idea that they were so numerous, and so widely distributed.

In examining books upon the contiguous countries, I find several references to stars in stone and in metal. Yet no traveller appears to have been struck by their frequency. In the Report of *The U.S. Naval Astronomical Expedition to the Southern Hemisphere during the years* 1849–52,[1] in vol. ii, p. 138, figures are given of two stars in bronze (found at Cuzco, Peru), one having a sixth ray prolonged into a hatchet, which suggests that it must have been a war-club, or battle-axe. In Squier's book on Peru[2] (p. 177), there is a figure of a six-rayed object in bronze, said to have been one of several, which are designated by the Author (apparently following some earlier writer) *casse-têtes*, and he says that among the fractured skulls that were found "the larger part seemed to have been broken by blows from some such weapons." Mons. Wiener, in his book on Peru and Bolivia,[3] gives a figure of a star which was found at Ancon (near Lima), shewing a stick inserted in the central hole; and another figure of a somewhat similar form in bronze, also handled. Like Squier, he calls them *casse-têtes*.[4] Finally, the Doctors Reiss and Stübel remark, in their magnificent work upon the Peruvian Antiquities obtained at Ancon,[5] that "the few stone objects found here shew but slight

---

[1] By Lieut. J. M. Gilliss; 4to, Philadelphia, 1856.

[2] *Peru, Incidents of Travel and Exploration in the Land of the Incas*, by E. George Squier, M.A., F.S.A., late U.S. Commissioner to Peru; 8vo, New York, 1877. Squier says at the same page "if weapons of stone were ever found here, I failed to learn the fact." In this passage, he is speaking of Northern Peru, close to the frontiers of Ecuador.

[3] *Pérou et Bolivie*, Paris, 1880, p. 685. M. Wiener was sent in 1875–7 to Peru and Bolivia to collect antiquities, and he obtained a large number of objects. It is noticeable that in the hundreds of engravings in his book only about half-a-dozen things in stone are figured.

[4] This expression, freely translated, means '*nut-crackers*.'

[5] *The Necropolis of Ancon in Peru*, by W. Reiss & A. Stübel; London & Berlin, 3 vols., folio, 1880–1887.

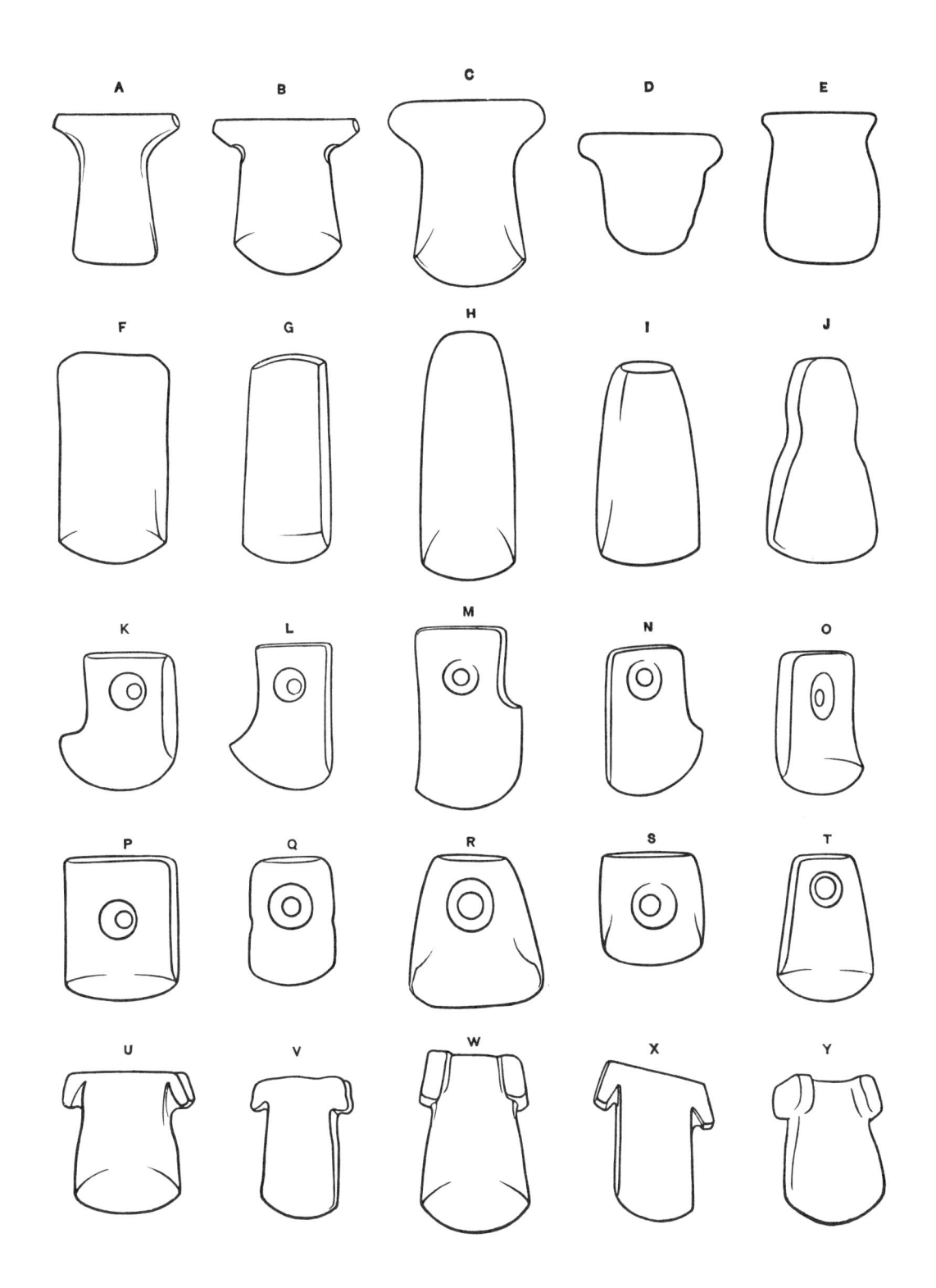

SOME TYPICAL STONE IMPLEMENTS COLLECTED BY THE AUTHOR IN ECUADOR.

traces of workmanship, an exception being . . . a stone weapon of the 'Morning Star' type. . . The six-rayed stone star, here found once only, is elsewhere in Peruvian graves by no means rare."

Though all these writers appear to regard these objects as a kind of battle-axe (and are probably correct so far as those having a ray prolonged into a hatchet are concerned), there are several considerations which make me hesitate to adopt the opinion that the Stars in Stone were habitually used as weapons. The Indians of this region were a quiet, inoffensive, unwarlike people. This is their nature still. Yet these objects were more numerous than any other kinds which were obtained, and are found everywhere. We should therefore be led to conclude that a great part of the population was provided with offensive weapons. The larger of the Stars (which are as heavy as a pound and a quarter) no doubt might be used effectively; but the smaller ones, weighing only a few ounces, would not be very formidable; and taking them as a whole they are less adapted either for offensive or defensive purposes than most of the implements which will presently be enumerated. To this may be added that many are uninjured, and do not seem to have been put to any use whatever. Francisco Campaña (a half-Indian who joined us during the latter part of the journey) had assisted in the examination of graves in Peru, and said these Stars in Stone were found there placed upon the breasts of corpses; and it seems to me more likely that they were to the Children of the Sun symbols of the luminary that they worshipped, than that they were employed by the natives for breaking each other's heads.

Out of the remainder of the objects in stone that were collected, a large number should undoubtedly be classed as Implements. Not a few others are Ornaments, and there is a residuum which may have been either ornamental or useful.

Upon the accompanying plate five different types of Implements are represented. In the series A—E, the whole of the edges are *rounded*, except the bottom ones. In the next line (F—J) all are of a chisel type. The tops and sides of these are sometimes flat or angular, and sometimes rounded ; and the lower, or cutting edges, are sharp. The examples in the next series (K—O) bear some resemblance to a bill-hook ; the top edges are flat ; and they are all pierced with holes drilled from the two sides. The specimens in the next row have similar holes — otherwise they approximate to the chisel type ; while the type represented in the series U—Y differs from all the others in having projecting shoulders, and (occasionally) in having a groove along the length of the top edge, apparently to facilitate handling.

All these five types were found in numbers, in many localities, and have evidently been amongst the most common and generally used implements during the Equatorial Stone Age. In minor respects they exhibit considerable variety, and there are large differences in their size, thickness, and weight. The type P—T was the most numerous, and I brought home more than fifty examples. The greater part have holes drilled from each side,[1] though in some the aperture is as broad internally as externally, that is to say, it passes straight through. The positions of the holes vary, — some being central, though most of them are nearest to the top. The lower edge is always the sharpest ; and, while many would not have cut butter, there are a few sharp enough to cut wood. Their weight ranges from $3\frac{1}{4}$ to 29 ozs., and like the Stars in Stone they have been fashioned from a diversity of rocks.

Besides many examples of these five types, a large number of undoubted Implements in stone were obtained, from which selections are given upon page 273. Those marked E, J, K, L, N—T are unique, and the other forms are more or less rare. The central one, marked M, was the only object for which the natives could assign a use, and it was pronounced to be a *corn-pounder*. This

---

[1] These are not strictly speaking 'countersunk' holes. They are less in diameter in the middle of the implements than they are on their surfaces.

CHAP. XIV. SOME UNUSUAL FORMS. 273

one weighs five and a quarter pounds, and I have another of eleven pounds. The form I, of which I have several examples, is con-

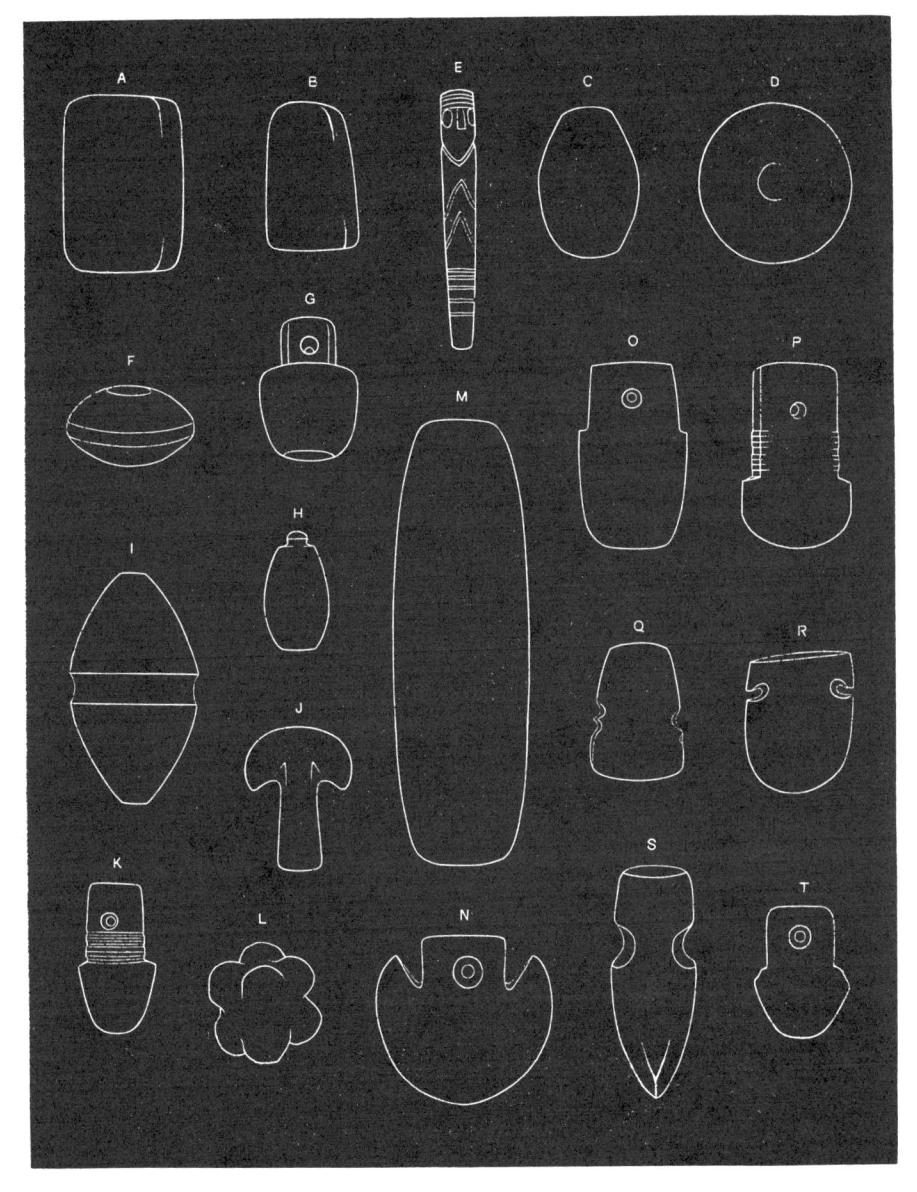

sidered by Mr. Thomas Ewbank[1] to be a "hollowing-hammer for metal," and it is possible that those marked A, B and C (and their

[1] At p. 137 of the Report by Lieut. Gilliss, already quoted, Mr. Ewbank says,— "The groove worked round the middle was the universal device by which

numerous varieties) were used for the same purpose. The objects D, F, G and H are more puzzling. The two latter somewhat resemble the two others represented upon this page, but differ from them in not having the circular cavities in the sides. The objects of this class are highly wrought, and fashioned out of hard stone. It seems not unlikely that they were used for sharpening tools, and that the examples G, H are new (that is, unused) specimens, belonging to the same class as those given upon this page. They have also been found by M. Wiener in Peru.

The smaller things that I obtained in stone are made from a greater variety of materials than the larger ones. Basaltic rock is used for about one third, and there are besides implements or objects in Glass, Jet, Jasper, Malachite, Saussurite, Serpentine, Porphyry, and Granite. While the larger implements and objects may weigh several pounds apiece, amongst these smaller matters there are many lighter than the eighth of an ounce, and I have two — a delicately carved cup with a handle, and a squatting figure — the united weight of which is less than *twenty-four grains!*

Amongst the distinctly ornamental objects in stone there are imitations of Maize-heads. These were particularly mentioned in Juan & Ulloa's work, nearly a century and a half ago, and seem

---

handles were secured to primeval stone axes, hammers, and chisels, namely, by bending a hazel or other pliable rod twice round the indentation, and then twisting or lashing the two ends together, to serve as a handle. Blacksmiths to this day everywhere thus handle their punches and chisels. They have discovered no mode superior to one which was in vogue before edge-tools of metal were known." The specimen to which he referred came from Cuzco, Peru.

M. Wiener, at p. 685 of his book, calls one of these a 'sling-stone,'— upon what ground is not clear. A few years ago implements of stone of this description were used by Indians on the coast of the North Pacific, handled in the manner described by Mr. Ewbank, and I suppose they are *still* used by them.

to have been better known at that time than they are at present. The Spanish writers say[1] :—

"The maize has ever been the delight of the Indians ; for, besides being their food, their favourite liquor chicha was made of it ; the Indian artists therefore used to shew their skill in making ears of it in a kind of very hard stone ; and so perfect was the resemblance that they could hardly be distinguished by the eye from nature ; especially as the colour was imitated to the greatest perfection ; some represented the yellow maize, some the white... The most surprizing circumstance of the whole is, the manner of

MAIZE-HEADS IN STONE.

their working, which, when we consider their want of instruments and the wretched form of those they had, appears an inexplicable mystery : for either they worked with copper tools, a metal little able to resist the hardness of stones ; or, to give the nice polish conspicuous on their works, other stones must have been used as tools."

Squier gives in his book on Peru (at p. 91) a bad representation of one of these stone maize-heads, and says that they were specially mentioned " by Padre Arriaga in his rare book on the *Extirpation of Idolatry in Peru* under the name *zaramama*," and were household gods of the ancient inhabitants. The examples engraved above came from Carranqui.

[1] *Relacion Historica del viaje a la Americana meridional*, 4to, Madrid, 1748, §§ 1047, 1048. The quotation is made from the fifth English edition, 8vo, London, 1807.

A number of other objects in stone in my collection are distinctly Ornaments, and in several instances were found still being worn by Indian women, who parted with them unwillingly. With others, in many instances, it is difficult to distinguish whether they were ornamental or useful. This is the case with the imitations of heads of animals which seemed to have been in favour in the basin of Riobamba, and with anvil-shaped objects which were very numerous throughout Imbabura.

That the principal part of these objects and implements in stone are of considerable or of *great* age is apparent from the fact that Garcilasso de la Vega scarcely mentions them. He says that the Indians

"knew not the invention of putting a handle of Wood to their Hammers, but worked with certain Instruments they had made of Copper, mixed with a sort of fine Brass. Neither did they know how to make Files or Graving-tools, or Bellows for Melting down Metals. . . But above all, their Carpenters seemed to be worst provided with Tools ; for though ours use many Instruments made of Iron, those of *Peru* had no other than a Hatchet, and a Pick-axe made of Copper ; they neither had Saw, nor Augre, nor Planer, nor any other Tool for the Carpenter's work, so that they could not make Arches or Portals for doors ; onely they hewed and cut their Timber, and whitened it, and then it was prepared for their Building : And for making their Hatchets and Pick-axes, and some few Rakes, they made use of the Silversmiths, for as yet they had not attained to the Art of Working in Iron. Nor did they know how to make Nails, or use them, but tied all their Timber with Cords of Hemp. Nor were their Hewers of Stone more artificial, for in cutting and shaping their Stones, they had no other Tool, than one made with some sharp Flints and Pebbles, with which they rather wore out the Stone by continual rubbing, than cutting."—*The Royal Commentaries of Peru*, pp. 52–3.

From this passage it appears that at the time of the Pizarros the Indians used tools of metal for most purposes. The concluding sentence evidently refers solely to fashioning stones for building. In the older writers in general I find nothing indicating that they had cognizance of a Stone Age; and modern travellers (so far as one can judge from casual references in their books) do not seem to have given serious attention to this matter. Such discoveries as may be made in the future, I anticipate, will confirm the opinion that the most part of these objects and implements in stone were already Antiquities at the time of the Spanish Conquest; and belong to an age long anterior to the times when the Inca Tupac conquered the 'Kingdom of Quitu,' and Huayna-Capac ravaged Imbabura.

In the course of enquiries for stone implements, many other things were brought, principally pieces of pottery. Metallic objects were rarely offered, and seldom seen. I heard of but a single little image in gold, and this could not be had. Silver articles were nearly as scarce. Even bronze and copper antiquities, when found, are often melted down, from the supposition that they are alloyed with gold. The annexed figure of the head of a silver pin is an example of a class which was formerly common and is now rare. The six-rayed star at the bottom of this page, and the two hatchets upon page 278 (which were part of a large 'find' at Cuenca) are nearly all that I obtained in bronze.

The popular idea of Peruvian (Ecuadorian) pottery is derived from the grotesque black ware that is found in most museums. Squier says of this that the greater part has been brought from the coast districts of *northern* Peru.[1] I saw little of it in Ecuador, and

[1] "It is safe to say that three-fourths of the pottery found in the museums of Europe and America, and called Peruvian, came from the coast or near it, and of this probably much the largest portion from the region ruled by the princes of Chimu" (near Truxillo).—*Peru*, pp. 177-8.

such examples as I collected (of black pottery) very likely came into the country from the south. The major part of that which was formerly used [1] by the Indians dwelling amongst the Great Andes of the Equator has a character of its own, and is distinguished by simplicity, and often by elegance of form. It is both glazed and unglazed; of various hues of Indian Red, and different degrees of fineness. Some of the older pieces are grey in colour. This old Indian pottery seems to have been neglected by other travellers, and I endeavoured to form such a collection as should convey an idea of the articles which were formerly in general use.

The shapes which seem to have been employed most extensively are given in the annexed outline. The bottoms of these vessels are flat, rounded, or pointed. The pointed and rounded forms were convenient for cooking, or for being warmed over fires. The Indians even now are little

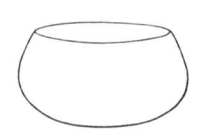

BRONZE HATCHETS FROM CUENCA.

provided with tables, and in the past were probably totally unacquainted with such luxuries. They squatted on the ground, and

---

[1] It is to be understood that all the utensils, &c., to which I am about to refer are now superseded by common modern pottery.

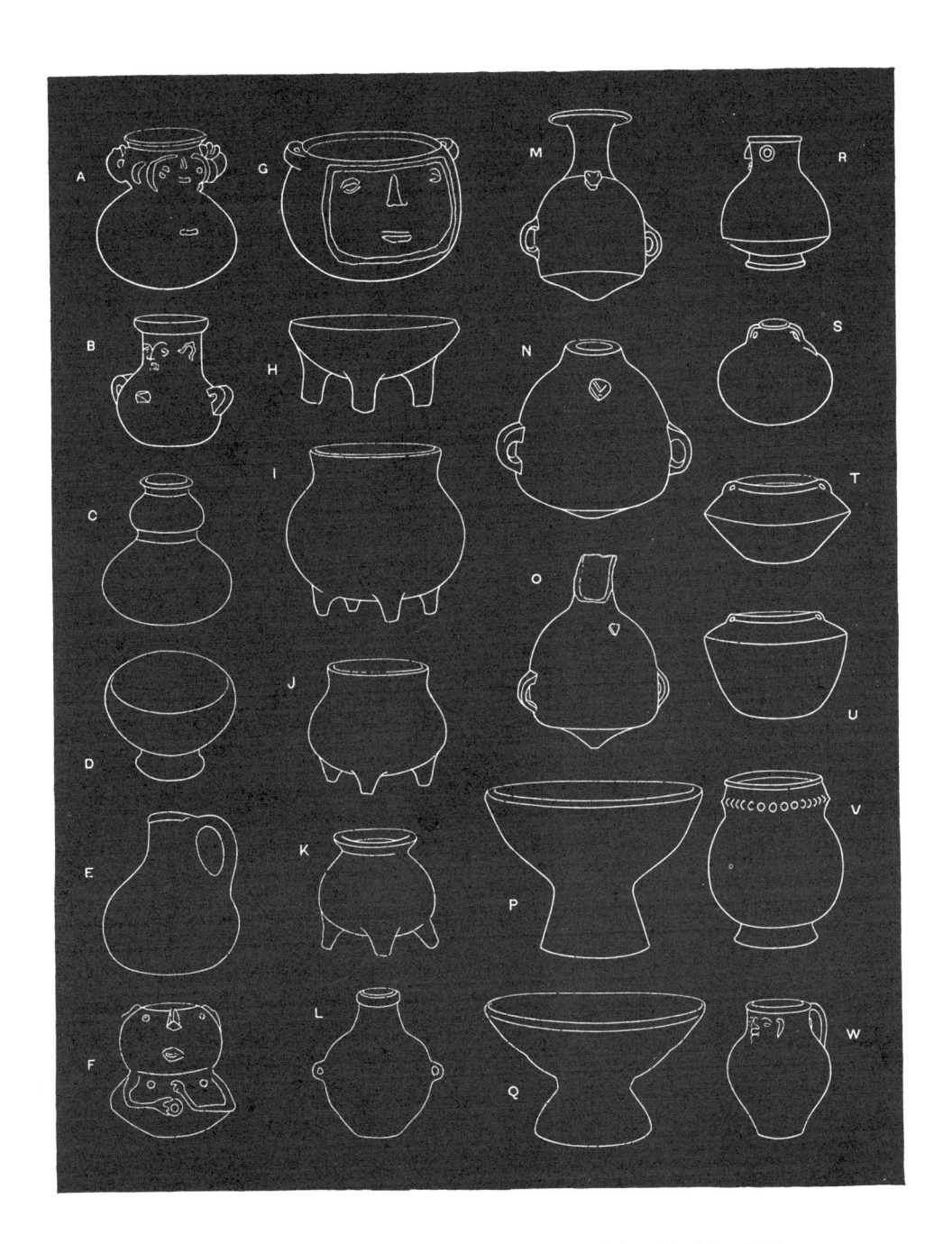

EXAMPLES OF OLD INDIAN POTTERY COLLECTED BY THE AUTHOR IN ECUADOR.

CHAP. XIV. *FORMS OF UTENSILS ORDINARILY EMPLOYED.* 279

cooked their food over wood fires; and these pointed and rounded bottoms to their utensils, though quite unsuited for placing upon smooth surfaces, would keep erect in the embers, or might be pressed into the earthen floor.

The natives did not depend exclusively upon these simple vessels. In the accompanying plate a number of the more ordi-

SOME OF THE LESS COMMON FORMS.

nary forms are grouped of their pots, bowls, jars, jugs, and bottles. The larger vessels, in which the more serious culinary operations would be performed, are provided with feet (see H—K), or even with legs (see figure at the bottom of the illustration on this page). Some have a pair of handles low down (B, M, N, O) that would be convenient to hold when pouring out liquids; others have very diminutive handles high up, by which the vessels were probably suspended. The ordinary single handle, seen in E and W, is less often found than the double ones.

ORNAMENTATION OF POTTERY.

Many of these vessels or utensils are without ornament, though some are embellished by crude representations of the human face (A, B, F, G, W). Ornamental details, incised, raised, or painted, occasionally occur; and a few of the more characteristic are brought together in the engraving above.

Amongst the less common forms there are *treble pots* like that represented on page 279. As the grouped parts are all connected internally, these can hardly have been family cruet-stands. They were apparently intended to hold liquids, and it is difficult to see what advantage can have been derived from this manner of construction. Double and treble pots were numerous in Imbabura; though I brought home few, for the reason which will appear presently.

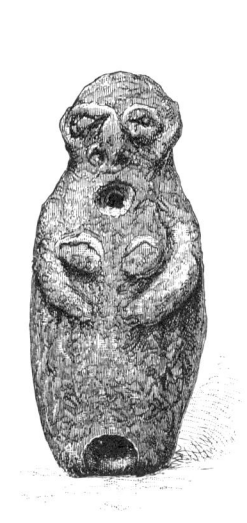

INDIAN MUSICAL WHISTLES.

Then there are the musical pottery whistles—delightfully ugly things, which are sometimes more useful to carry than letters of introduction. Simple airs can be got out of them, and on the homeward journey my people lightened the way by playing on these primitive instruments.

The most interesting, artistically, of all the objects in pottery which were obtained in Ecuador have been called 'vase-busts' by Mr. Ewbank. In the Report on *The U.S. Naval Astronomical Expedition*, from which I have already quoted, he gave a bad representation of an object of this class; saying (in 1856), "it is supposed there are not over two or three extant." The four examples which appear on the following pages are no doubt the work of four different artists; and, though all are old, they are by no means of equal age. The idea that any human being could have his face ornamented with a pointed beard or flowing moustache did not enter the brain of the Indian modeller until Spanish Dons invaded his continent. The oldest vases never give hair upon the lips or chin; and, if beards or moustaches are introduced, it is a certain indication that the works have been executed subsequently

THE DON POT.

to the Spanish Conquest. This was evidently the case in the piece that I term 'the Don pot.' All three of the other examples shew considerable power in portraying character, and very likely are portraits of eminent persons. The double-headed jar or vase is the finest specimen I have seen of Indian pottery, and I should have been happy to have obtained other examples modelled by the same hand.

The pottery which is represented on the previous pages was obtained in various ways, not a little of it coming from old graves, which were continually being disturbed. Señor Gomez de la Torre, hearing me lament that I was never able to be present at a find, very kindly offered to send the entire contents of a grave, and he was as good as his word. The case, however, did not even reach Guayaquil before my departure for Europe; and, upon arrival in London, its contents were found to have suffered severely

from Panama 'baggage-smashers' and other disturbing influences. Some rounded stones (presumably corn-pounders) had danced about and cannonaded the pottery. After much labour, most of the contents were 'restored,' and they are represented in the engraving upon page 284.[1]

[1] Dr. W. H. Flower has favoured me with the following note:—"The skull from Ibarra is evidently of considerable antiquity, as shewn by the dry and brittle

Somewhat elated by the success of the foray into Imbabura, we set out from Otovalo on the 2nd of May, to cross Mojanda to

THE CONTENTS OF A GRAVE.

Quito; intending to make the first day a short one, and to stop for the night at the little village Malchingi.[1] The pottery was carefully packed in straw, subdivided as much as possible; and, as there was little other luggage, our attention was almost solely given to the safety of our treasures.

condition of its bony tissue. How old, it is of course impossible to say, but there is nothing in its condition to forbid the supposition that it was buried before the time of the Spanish Conquest. It is, unfortunately, imperfect, the greater part of the cranial vault of the right side being broken away, probably in exhumation, as the fractures look recent, and the lower jaw and all the teeth are wanting. There is, however, enough to shew that it belonged to a man beyond middle age, and of considerable muscular development. The general ethnic characters are those frequently found in aboriginal American crania, though it is rather longer and narrower (the cephalic index being 76·6), and the orbits are lower and the nose wider than usual. On comparing it with a series of skulls of ancient Muiscas from graves in the neighbourhood of Bogota in the Museum of the Royal College of Surgeons, it is evidently of the same general type. Unlike most of the old skulls from the locality near which it was found it presents no sign of artificial deformation during infancy.

[1] There is a small inn at Malchingi, but between that place and Otovalo there is not, I believe, a single house. The nearest habitation farther west is the Hacienda of Alchipichi, a very large establishment, situated on the south-western slopes of Mojanda, about 1400 feet above the bottom of the Quebrada of Guallabamba. The descent to the bridge across the quebrada is exceedingly steep.

People of Imbabura Province with guitar and bells on the day of St. John, 24 June.

Cotacachi volcano rising beyond the town of Otavalo (*not* "Otovalo," as Whymper spells it). It has a terminal glacier inside the summit crater. The highest part was a hard climb for Whymper because of a hailstorm.

People of the town of Otavalo.

During McIntyre's 1966 climb of Cayambe, they relied upon animals and native guides to reach the edge of the snows, as did Whymper.

The north face of Cayambe. Whymper did not scale this risky side of the peak.

The route up Cayambe taken by Whymper and the Carrels.

McIntyre's guide José María Súpalo on the 1966 climb of Cayambe, at the Equatorial Line.

Sara Urca, from Cayambe Volcano, shot during McIntyre's 1966 Cayambe climb. At the time he found no record of any climb of Sara Urca since Whymper's feat in 1880.

"IT ROLLED OVER AND OVER DOWN THE SLOPE, AND DISAPPEARED."

It was getting late in the afternoon when we passed the lakes on Mojanda, and commenced the ascent of a long incline leading to the summit of the road. The worst of the way was over, and Verity and I pressed forward in advance of the rest, to reach our quarters in good time. Half an hour later, while stopping to get some angles, we heard shouts behind, and saw Cevallos running and gesticulating. "How it happened, Señor, cannot be said. I saw it falling. It has gone over a precipice. It is dead!" One of the mules had met with an accident a few minutes after we left them. Returning together, our arriero, pointing to the place where the fall had happened, said that the animal had rolled over and over down the slope and disappeared. We could see nothing of it; for the side of the mountain (a commonplace declivity of earth and boulders) was broken in some places by irregularities.

THE INCA VASE.

Cevallos and Verity descended to search, and reappeared with rueful faces, carrying a bundle of clothing saturated with slime, driving before them our unhappy, tottering beast, who after tumbling head over heels for a hundred feet had shot over a cliff about eighty feet high, and had been pulled up in a muddy pool underneath. Beyond knocking the breath out of its body, and losing the tip of one of its ears, it took no harm. But the packing-cases had burst; the family soup-tureens, the double and treble pots, and other precious relics of a past civilization, bounding down the declivity, had been hopelessly smashed into thousands of fragments, and we abandoned the wreck of our fragile treasures on the dreary paramo.

When night fell we were still some hours from Malchingi, stumbling and floundering among ruts and *camellones*. The others implored me to stop, and we dropped down and camped in a muddy ditch on the open moorland. I have reposed on better and cleaner couches; though, after all, a muddy ditch is not the worst of beds—one soon becomes attached to it. At Malchingi the dilapidated mule was left to recruit, and I pushed on to Quito — Cevallos following at his leisure; and arrived at the Capital at 10 p.m. on the 3rd of May, feeling more dead than alive, and looking, I was told, 'fit for the grave.'

THE MONEY-BOX.

LA CONDAMINE'S INSCRIBED STONE.

CHAPTER XV.

A VISIT TO THE PYRAMIDS OF QUITO.

A FEW days after our return, Jean-Antoine came in from Machachi, reporting that he and his cousin had ascended Illiniza from the north, in witness whereof he presented samples of the highest rock.[1] Louis remained behind, at the tambo of Antonio Racines,

[1] "Rough scoriaceous rock... In one specimen is an irregular branching tube or vein, coated with a dull greenish or brownish glass, which I suspect to be a fulgurite. I have only had a slice cut from the specimen broken from the rock *in situ*. It is not in a good condition for examination, but consists, so far as I can make out, of a ferrite-stained glass, containing crystals of the usual plagioclastic

keeping guard over stores, and enjoyed a quiet month alone, improving much in appearance and condition.

My stomach had gone all wrong,[1] as people say, and repose was necessary for restoration to health. During the next five weeks I went little out of doors, except for promenades in the city, and before we left it I had explored every street, lane, or alley in the place. Jean-Antoine and I turned out each evening to do a fresh section, walking warily in the centre of the thoroughfares, one a little in advance of the other. By ten o'clock nearly every one had gone to bed, and scarcely a sound would be heard except the voices of policemen bawling at the junctions of the streets, to announce their whereabouts.

In the middle of the month, when somewhat revived, I made an excursion to the Pyramids which should mark the ends of the long base-line that was measured in 1736 by La Condamine and his associates. In consequence of discussions which had arisen as to the figure of the Earth, the French Academy of Sciences, at the beginning of the last century, determined to send out two expeditions to measure arcs at a great distance apart. One of these went to the Gulf of Bothnia, and the other, composed of MM. Godin, Bouguer, and La Condamine, to Equatorial America. They commenced their work on a plain to the north-east of Quito, by measuring a very long base-line, and from its two ends carried a chain of triangles[2] (to the north beyond Ibarra, and to the south to Cuenca) over more than three degrees of latitude. Towards the end of their work they measured a base of verification near Cuenca, and found its length by direct measurement differed from the calculated length by less than *two feet!*

The toise that the French Academicians took out as an unit of

felspar, with a ferruginous mica, grains of hematite or magnetite. . . The rock is an andesite, but perhaps it is safest only to prefix the epithet micaceous."—Prof. T. G. Bonney, *Proc. Royal Soc.*, Nov. 27, 1884.

[1] This was started by exposure on March 31.

[2] A plan of these triangles is given in Pl. II. of La Condamine's work, *Mesure des trois premiers degrés du Méridien*, 4to, Paris, 1751, and also by Juan and Ulloa.

measure was a bar of iron, and it has ever since been known as 'the toise of Peru.' Guyot, in his valuable work *Tables Meteorological and Physical*, in a discussion of the various measures of length most generally used, says that "it may almost be called *the only common standard*, to which all the others are referred for comparison"; "the legal mètre is a legalised part of the toise of Peru, and this last remains the primitive standard."

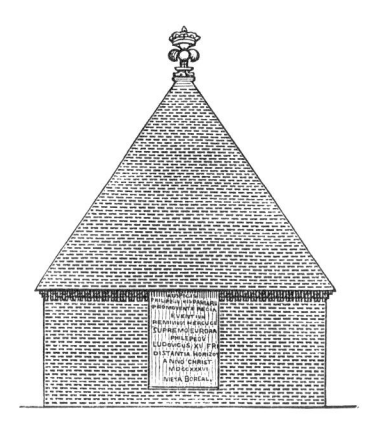

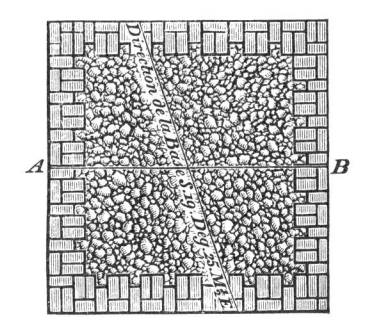

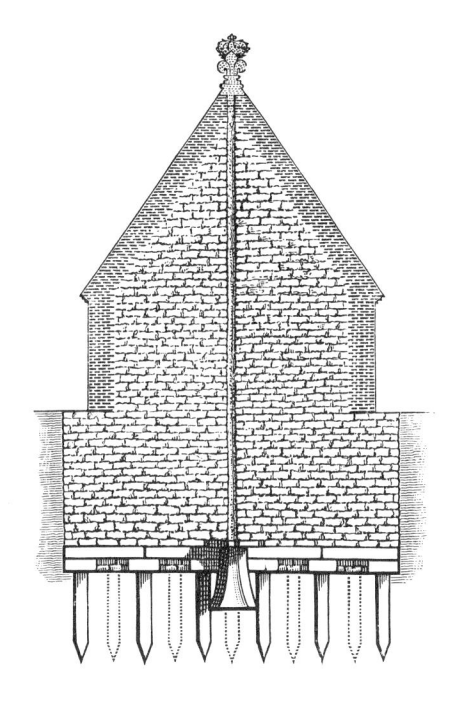

PLAN, SECTION, AND ELEVATION OF THE PYRAMIDS ERECTED BY THE ACADEMICIANS.
(From *Histoire des Pyramides de Quito.*)

As the measurement of the first base-line (upon which all the rest of the work depended) was intended to be, and apparently was, conducted with the greatest possible care, it was natural that the Academicians desired that its length should be preserved, and that the two ends should be marked by monuments of a permanent nature. This matter had, in fact, been discussed and settled before the observers left Paris, and upon the spot La Condamine specially charged himself with directing the erection of two pyramids, one at each end of the base.

In the section of the work [1] on his labours in Ecuador entitled *Histoire des Pyramides de Quito,* he recounts the difficulties that he experienced in this matter; how he fixed the centres of the pyramids most accurately over the two ends of the measurement; how he had to make his own bricks (which he took care should be of a size different from those usually employed, so that there might be no temptation to pull the monuments to pieces for the sake of their materials); how he had to construct a canal two leagues long to bring water for making mortar; and how stones had to be sought for and transported long distances on mule-back — this part of the business alone, he says, occupying several months, as a single stone often made a load. Then, in the case of the pyramid at the northern end, he found there was no solid foundation, and he had to create one by pile-driving, to search for wood fit for the piles, to bring workmen from Quito to fashion them, and to get them driven. But *the* thing above all others which gave him most trouble was finding, dressing, and transporting suitable stones for the Inscriptions. These stones were quarried in a ravine some hundreds of feet deep, and had to be hauled out by ropes, which had to be specially made; and then at the last moment the ropes broke, one of the stones was dashed to pieces, and they had to begin over again.

When at last all was complete, then there was infinite worry over the Inscriptions; for the French Academicians had associated with them two Spanish naval gentlemen, who took exception to the phraseology, for the sake of their Royal Master, and on their own account, &c., &c. At last all was settled and finished, and La Condamine returned to Paris, *via* the Amazons, arriving in 1745, after an absence of *ten years,* no doubt finding consolation in the thought that he had done a splendid piece of work, which could be referred to in generations to come, by means of these monuments.

[1] *Journal du Voyage fait par ordre du Roi,* &c., 4to, Paris, 1751.

Towards the end of 1747 he heard casually that orders had been given by the Court of Spain to erase the pyramids, and this order was carried out before he had time to interpose. In the pages to which I have referred he bemoans their fate, and recapitulates the details of their construction in a way which will almost raise a smile with those who do not know the country; but so little is this country changed that the account reads like a narration of operations which have just been conducted, rather than a relation of things which happened a century and a half ago. He especially laments the supposed destruction of the two great stones bearing the inscriptions, but concludes in the spirit of a true man by declaring that all such things are of no importance in comparison with the loss of the measure of the base,—"that length, which I had taken so much trouble to preserve, is now lost for ever."

La Condamine heard subsequently that orders were given for the reinstatement of the pyramids, though he probably never knew whether they were actually re-erected. When I was at Quito I felt a strong desire to learn what was their state, and to find out, if possible, whether they occupied the same positions as before. My friend, Señor Rafael Rebolledo, heard of my enquiries, and told me that there was on a farm at no great distance from one of his properties to the north-east of Quito a stone which he believed was part of the original pyramid of Oyambourou, and he invited me to go over to examine it. On the 15th of May, 1880, we rode over to his farm of Olalla, close to the little town of Pifo, and on the next day went to inspect the stone. It was about four feet long and six inches thick, placed in the middle of one side of the courtyard, and was used as a mounting-block. There had been an inscription upon it, but it was completely worn out in the centre through the use to which it had been put. At its two ends some letters could still be made out, and going down on hands and knees to compare them with the printed description that I carried, which gives the original inscription line by line, I found that it was the very great stone which La Condamine had taken so much trouble to procure, whose loss he had so pathetically lamented.

The pyramid (of Oyambara or Oyambourou) which now approximately marks the southern end of the base is about 1000

THE PYRAMID OF OYAMBARO, IN 1880.

feet distant from the place where the stone reposes, situated in a field of maize ; and is neither the original pyramid nor the one which was erected to replace it. I was informed on the spot that it was put up about thirty years earlier by a President of Ecuador, who so little appreciated the purpose for which it was originally designed that he moved it some hundreds of feet on one side, in order, he said, that *it might be better seen.* The traditional site of the original pyramids of Oyambourou was pointed out to me, but I found no trace of them.

The pyramid at the northern end of the base (Pyramid of Carabourou) was just visible as a speck of light, and on the next day I went to it, and found the structure there in just such a position as the original one is said to have occupied, at the very edge of the great ravine of Guallabamba, though whether it stands on the original site I am quite unable to say. The labours of the

Academicians are therefore, in a fashion, still commemorated; though the length of the base, as La Condamine feared, is now lost for ever.

The latter part of the month of May was principally occupied in arranging and despatching the collections. I re-examined, labelled, catalogued and packed more than 8000 separate objects, and succeeded in sending them to the coast, carriage *unpaid*. These were found awaiting me, while a few other cases which were forwarded some weeks later from Riobamba, carriage *paid*, were very tardy in making their appearance, and caused a fortnight's detention at Guayaquil. It is the usual habit in the country to pay for carriage in advance, and the carriers have their customers at their mercy. The establishment of a system of transit which shall be fair to both sides is a general want, that affords another great opportunity to persons of enterprize.

As our faces were now going to be set homewards, and a tolerably close estimate could be formed of the food and other matters that would be required, surplus stock was cleared out. I took a hundred Pounds over the counter in three days, and incurred no bad debts. The success of this (my first) essay at storekeeping was no doubt due to some lines that I saw on 'the Isthmus' (said to have been composed by a Californian miner of unusual literary ability), headed NO TRUST GIVEN, which in 1880 were exposed in a prominent position just outside the Railway Station at Panama, and probably remain there still, as they were looked upon with admiration, and were considered to embody a great truth, in extremely felicitous language.[1]

Some of these goods were purchased by the amiable Hebraic Yankee. In the interstices of the provision cases all sorts of things which it was supposed might be useful were stowed away,— amongst the rest, each tin contained a little pill-box, and each box

---

[1] The style of this composition may be inferred from the first line—
"To TRUST is to BUST."
The remaining lines are unfit for these pages.

held three little pills, and every unit was sufficient to effect its purpose. There were a hundred or so boxes to be got rid of, and the Jew was eager to trade for them. "Now Mr. ——," said I, as they were handed over, "Each of these little treasures is warranted to do its work." But he was suspicious; and, on going home, took the contents of a box, and subsequently took to his bed. I heard all about it, and went to see him, expecting to find him doleful. "Sorry to hear you are ill, Mr. ——. Have you tried those pills?" and found that he was delighted with his bargain. "Real fine medicine that! Mister," he exclaimed, almost rapturously, "there's no mistake about *that* medicine!"

These matters arranged, we were ready to start; before leaving paying another visit to the President of the Republic, this time under the care of H.E. the Chilian Minister, Señor J. Godoy.[1] General Veintemilla again enquired if there was anything he could do for me, and I asked for an Official statement of the Provinces and Chief Towns of Ecuador. The Minister of Haciendas, who was present, undertook to furnish this information, and did not do so. It has, however, quite recently been published by the Foreign Office, in the *Report* from Mr. Alfred St. John, dated Quito, July 14, 1891, and is given below.[2]

[1] I take this opportunity to acknowledge a number of civilities which were voluntarily and very cordially rendered by this accomplished Chilian, who almost immediately afterwards was appointed Prefect of Lima, on the occupation of that city by his countrymen.

[2]
Provinces.	Population.	Provinces.	Population.
Carchi	36,000	Loja	66,456
Imbabura	67,940	Bolivar	43,000
Pichincha	205,000	Rios	32,800
Leon	109,600	Oro	32,600
Tungurahua	103,033	Guayas	98,042
Chimborazo	122,300	Manabi	64,123
Cañar	64,014	Esmeraldas	14,553
Azuay	132,400	Oriente	80,000

Total . . . 1,271,861.

Mr. St. John says "the following list shows the population of the chief towns, which has been calculated approximately," and adds, "The taking of a census in

During the remainder of the journey we travelled under the auspices of a fresh interpreter-courier. Mr. Verity having left me, I engaged in his place a Quitonian, a half-Indian, Francisco Javier Campaña by name, who had tendered his services on several occasions. Verity, not long afterwards, was accidentally killed at Riobamba. Robberies were frequently occurring there, and some of the more decent inhabitants endeavoured to put them down by patrolling the place at night. Two of these parties met at the corner of a street, fired into each other, and Verity fell, mortally wounded.

Upon leaving Quito on June 7, it was understood that everything would be subordinated to a second ascent of Chimborazo, though if there was time and opportunity it was intended to give some attention to Illiniza, Altar, and Carihuairazo. A few miles on the road, we came upon a small knot of people who had assembled to bid our new interpreter farewell; including his wife, who cried, and screamed, and fell on his neck as if he were going to execution. I am told that amongst the Indians a display of grief upon the departure of a husband is quite the correct thing, but am unaware whether his *return* usually produces a corresponding amount of joy.

Ecuador is a matter of the greatest difficulty, owing to the fact that the Indians, who form a great part of the population, refuse to give the necessary particulars."

Quito, 50,000! Guayaquil, 45,000; Cuenca, 25,000; Riobamba, 12,000! Ambato, 10,000; Loja, 10,000; Latacunga, 10,000! Ibarra, 6000; Jipipapa, 5000; Otovalo, 5000; Porto-viejo, 5000; Guaranda, 4000; Tulcan, 3000.

In this list, Cotocachi (a larger place than Otovalo) is not mentioned. The Priest informed me in 1880 that there were 5000 Indians and 3000 whites in his *parish*. As the above is an Official statement, I only express my surprise at the increase in the population since 1880 by a few notes of admiration.

A STAMPEDE.

CHAPTER XVI.

UPON A WALK ON THE QUITO ROAD, AND A JOURNEY TO ALTAR.

OUR new courier was a little creature, who rode a diminutive animal, and so they were well matched; but the unhappy beast had also to carry a huge Mexican saddle which was as much as his master could lift—garnished as it was with many appendages, including the fashionable metal 'shoe-stirrups.' Campaña aspired to look *comme il faut*, and wore the orthodox buskins, with several ponchos one on top of the other, and tossed the tails of his comforter behind so that they might float in the wind, and shew his carved drinking-cup, which together with the macheta are outward and visible signs of respectability. Let it be said for the little man that under his auspices we travelled more rapidly, more pleasantly and economically than before. No unlawful gains went into his pockets, and he was an excellent interpreter.

We got away from Machachi on the 8th of June to make another attempt to scale Illiniza, proceeding south for about five miles along the high road, and then turning south-westwards (through the yards of a farm just past the Bridge of Jambeli) across some flat, open ground (which by Ecuadorians would be called *paramo* and in English Common or Moorland) steering towards the depression between the two peaks.[1] David Beltran had got a pet Llama, which was borrowed experimentally for this occasion, and it trotted alongside our party without giving trouble, wearing an expression of demure self-satisfaction on its face, as if perpetually saying to itself, "Gentlemen, see how well I go! Look how nicely I behave!" It was loaded with the photographic apparatus and other small matters, amounting in all to about 24 lbs., and carried that amount easily. Camped at 4 p.m. slightly lower than the Col between Great and Little Illiniza, against a large block of lava,[2] at a very bare and exposed spot (15,446 feet); and sent all, except the Carrels, 2000 feet lower, down to wood and water. Snow fell heavily during the night, and it blew hard from E.S.E. Min. temp. 26°·5 Faht.

In the morning, the first part of our way led over moderately inclined débris, and then up the rather ill-defined northern *arête*. At 8.30 a.m. we clearly overtopped Little Illiniza,[3] and about 9 came to the foot of the terminal cliff of glacier which crowns the summit of the main peak. Depositing here the mercurial barometer and other impedimenta, we quitted the *arête* and commenced a traverse of the eastern face, over ice-varnished ledges, beneath a canopy of icicles that garnished the crest of the ridge. "Let

---

[1] Immense numbers of the butterfly *Pieris xanthodice*, Lucas, were flying over this ground.

[2] "A moderately dark-grey, slightly vesicular, 'trachyte.' . . There are the usual granules of magnetite, and some minute colourless crystallites which may be apatite. . . The rock is a hornblendic augite-andesite, containing also some mica and hypersthene."—Prof. T. G. Bonney, *Proc. Royal Soc.*, Nov. 27, 1884.

[3] As the greatest height we reached on this day appeared to be 16,992 feet, I think the elevation assigned by Messrs. Reiss & Stübel to Little Illiniza (16,936 feet) is too much. See page 131.

Monsieur advance a little," said Jean-Antoine, and I crept up to him and looked over his shoulder. "We shall go there," he said, pointing to the declivity under the top of tops (surmounted by a cap of glacier and fringe of pendent icicles) where thickly-falling snow, unable to lodge, was frisking and gyrating, and sliding down in streams. "Carrel," I replied, "we will *not* go there"; and I went back to Machachi feeling very sore from this second repulse on Illiniza.[1]

As the nature of the work upon the two attempts to ascend this mountain was very similar (being a mixture of steep walking, actual climbing, and step-cutting in ice and snow), I was curious to compare our ascending rates upon these two occasions. I found that on the 9th of February one hundred and eighty-seven minutes were occupied in going from the camp (15,207 feet) to our highest point (17,023 feet). The rate of ascent therefore was 9·7 feet per minute. On the 9th of June, one hundred and fifty minutes were taken in ascending 1476 feet, and the rate, consequently, was 9·8 feet per minute. From this it appeared that there was no notable change in our condition, either in the way of amelioration or depreciation, in the four months that had elapsed between Feb. 9—June 9, during which time we had always been higher than 7000 feet above the level of the sea, and on several occasions

---

[1] Left camp 6.20 a.m. (temp. 32° Faht., blowing hard from N.E.), and took a general S.W. by S. course towards the highest point. Rocks glazed with ice, and unpleasant to touch. Followed the route taken by the Carrels at the beginning of May, but had they not well marked the route we should have been unable to advance. Seldom saw more than 200 yards in any direction. At 9.30 a.m. after reading barometer and collecting rocks, went back to camp, snow falling most of the way. Returned to Machachi by 7 p.m.

The Carrels said that their ascent was made in fine weather, and that they took an hour and a half over the last 200 feet. In the interval, the cornice at the summit, they said, had developed prodigiously. On the 9th of June it was composed of an enormous mass of icicles, fifty feet and upwards in length, which broke away from time to time, and fell over their line of ascent. There was more risk than I cared to encounter from the high wind, cold, and insecure footing on glazed rocks, raked by these falls from the overhanging cornice.

had experienced pressures *lower* than 16·5 inches (the pressure at the second camp on Chimborazo). It seemed probable that we had ascertained the worst that would happen to us, *provided we did not have to sustain still lower pressures.*

This does not, however, at all inform one whether our rate upon Illiniza was inferior to that which we should have attained upon the mountain if it had been placed at a lower level (that is to say, if a *higher* pressure had been experienced whilst ascending), and on this point there is very little enlightenment to be obtained by comparing the Illiniza rate with the rates of other persons upon equally elevated mountains in different parts of the world; for the difficulties presented upon mountain ascents vary so much as to make it nearly, or quite impossible to select any two upon which one might expect to attain precisely the same rate. The ascent of the Tetons, for example, cannot be compared with that of Pike's Peak, or the Aiguille du Dru with Altels. The natures of these mountains are dissimilar; and, in order to arrive at anything like just conclusions concerning the effects of diminished pressure, comparisons must be made between walks of a similar nature, taken under similar conditions. This brings me to what I consider one of the most interesting incidents of the journey, namely, a walk taken on the Quito road, at an elevation of about 10,000 feet, for comparison against a similar walk slightly above the sea-level.

Before starting for the Great Andes of the Equator, I had considered in what manner one might best determine whether diminution in atmospheric pressure weakened the bodily powers; and no method appeared so practicable as comparison, at different pressures, of the natural and habitual rate of walking. The simplicity of this idea may perhaps excite ridicule amongst those who are not aware of the regularity with which it is possible to walk, and of the precision with which a pedestrian may estimate his rate. Even amongst those who follow pedestrianism professionally, there are probably few who will admit the possibility of walking three miles without a greater difference than three seconds between any of the miles. Nevertheless it can be done, and by constant observation one may guess the rate, without reference to a watch, within a few seconds.

In 1879, my habitual pace when walking for exercise and in ordinary dress (not racing in airy costume) was well ascertained. I often walked a number of consecutive miles at about eleven minutes per mile. This was my natural and ordinary rate, and it was not necessary to go over a measured mile to learn it. But, in order that it might be verified, before leaving for Ecuador, I walked seven miles on the Lillie Bridge Grounds, Brompton, and had the time per mile noted by two attendants.

In Ecuador, I looked for the most level piece of road at a considerable elevation, and found nothing more suitable than the Quito road about two miles south of Machachi, where it was perfectly straight, and slightly descending towards the north. On this I measured a half-mile with Jean-Antoine, and placed the cousins at the two ends as witnesses and timekeepers. The same dress was used as before (ordinary walking dress, and heavy mountain boots). I found the time per mile was increased 54 seconds. This will be seen by comparing the statements given below.

	At Lillie Bridge Grounds, Brompton, Aug. 6, 1879.	On the Quito Road (9925 feet above sea-level), June 11, 1880.
	min. sec.	min. sec.
First Mile	10 45	11 13
Second ,,	11 0	12 32
Third ,,	10 58	12 3
Fourth ,,	10 59	12 13
Fifth ,,	11 14	12 11
Sixth ,,	11 18	11 35
Seventh ,,	11 11	. . .
Total time	77 25	71 47
Mean rate per mile	11 4 (nearly)	11 58 (nearly)
Max. temp. during walk	67°·5 Faht.	60°·5 Faht.
Min. ,, ,,	64°·0 ,,	49°·0 ,,
Mean ,, ,,	65°·75 ,,	54°·75 ,,
Wind	S.S.W. (force 3-5) gusty	S.S.E. (force 3-4)

On each of these occasions, the first mile was intentionally traversed at a quicker pace than the rest. Over the remainder (with the exception of the last mile at Machachi), at each place, I *endeavoured* to walk at exactly the same rate, mile per mile, and at Brompton did the next three miles in 11 min., 10.58 and 10.59 respectively. In the fifth and sixth miles heavy rain fell, and caused a marked diminution in the rate, which was improved in the last mile with better weather, and I left off feeling that another seven miles could *certainly* have been covered in *less* time.

Although endeavouring to accomplish the first mile on the Quito road at the same rate as in London, it took nearly half a minute longer, and the difference was larger on the second one.[1] The next three miles were walked at a tolerably regular pace, and I quickened up on the sixth, and left off feeling that I could scarcely improve the rate, and certainly could *not* walk another six miles in 71 min. 47 seconds.[2]

It is nearly impossible upon two such occasions to have the conditions exactly alike. At Machachi there were the *advantages* of being 10 lbs. lighter than in London and walking with temperature 11° Faht. cooler, and the *disadvantage* of being impeded by traffic. In London, though the track was kept clear, there was the disadvantage (during part of the time) of walking in dragging clothes, soaked with rain. All things considered, the conditions were pretty evenly balanced; and, as I am unable to assign the depreciation in my ordinary and habitual rate to any other cause,

[1] This was partly caused by having to pass three times through a large flock of sheep.

[2] Before this walk at Machachi my temperature was 98°·5 Faht., and 98°·4 35 minutes after it was over. Pulse before the walk 73, and 101 half an hour after it was over. [M. Paul Bert has shewn that, when sitting still, the rate of the pulse can be raised by reduction of pressure. See Appendix J.] Some years later, after walking six miles at a much faster rate, on a measured half-mile on a Surrey road with a gradient selected to correspond with that on the Quito road, I found that my pulse was only raised from 72·5 (mean of two minutes) to 96 (mean of four minutes).

Owing to the failure of a medical gentleman to keep his appointment, my pulse and temperature were not observed on Aug. 6, 1879.

I consider it was due to the fact that on the 11th of June, on the Quito Road, atmospheric pressure was a little over 21 inches, instead of the 29—30 inches to which I was accustomed.

Some persons[1] disbelieve in the reality of mountain-sickness, and seem reluctant to credit that human beings can be affected by diminution in atmospheric pressure, and to them, perhaps, this experiment will prove nothing. As regards myself, it appeared to me to be *conclusive* that a marked effect was produced, and an effect of a kind which I had never suspected at corresponding altitudes (pressures) in the Alps, where there was no possibility of applying a similar test.[2]

On the 12th of June we finally left Machachi, and marched (without change of animals) in three successive days to Latacunga,[3] Ambato, and Riobamba. The Jovial Man (who had sometimes been a cause of embarrassment) was replaced by a strong and very willing lad, named Domingo — otherwise the caravan was composed as before. The 15th was consumed in preparations for Altar, and in enquiries as to route. After balancing a number of opinions, it

[1] Including Men of Science. Prof. Piazzi Smyth, F.R.SS. L. & E., etc., etc., says in his *Teneriffe, an Astronomer's Experiment*, at pp. 381-2, "If a windlass or a treadmill were erected in London, and a gentleman in easy circumstances set some fine morning to perform at one of these ingenious machines an amount of work, equal to the mechanical task of raising his own weight up through the height of 10,000 feet perpendicular in seven hours,—I believe that, though breathing air, of a density of thirty mercurial inches, he would be distressed as much as the traveller who, by ascending a mountain, performs the same." The remainder of the passage should be read.

[2] It would be interesting if pedestrians, who have ascertained to a nicety the times within which they have frequently covered such distances as one hundred yards or a mile, would endeavour to repeat their performances on the flat pieces of road which can be found at the tops of some of the Alpine carriage passes.

[3] In returning from Machachi to Latacunga, we took the *old* road, past Mulalo, on the left bank of the Cutuchi, and visited the so-called Inca's house which is situated a short distance to the south of Callo. The small amount of the original structure still remaining has been embodied in some modern farm-buildings. The stones were finely dressed, and fitted without mortar or cement. I saw none measuring more than 18 × 12 × 12 inches.

was decided to proceed *via* Penipe, and we went to that place on June 16, leaving part of our animals at Riobamba to recruit.[1]

At Penipe, the Jefo-politico was also the village tailor. He administered the law and mended trousers alternately; and created a favourable impression on five minutes' acquaintance, after declaring, according to the manner of the country, that his house was ours, by adding with uncommon frankness, "but, Señor, I would recommend you *not* to go in-doors, for the fleas are numerous, and I think your Excellencies would be uncomfortable!"

Having obtained some information from him, we went on in the afternoon to a small hacienda called Candelaria, a miserably poor place, where nothing eatable could be had; and, being advised that mules could not be used much farther, negotiated transport with several young louts who were loafing about. For eighteen-pence each per day, and food, four of them agreed to go to the end of their world — that is to say, to the head of the Valley of Collanes.

The master of this ragged team could hardly be distinguished from his men. He was a young fellow of three or four and twenty, who wore a tattered billycock hat, and no shoes or stockings. His very sad countenance probably had some connection with his obvious poverty. The farm could scarcely have been more bare of food. There was general want of everything — of *yerba* for the beasts, who had to go back for forage; for ourselves there was nothing; and food for the porters had to be fetched from a distance and sent up after us. The master volunteered to come on the same terms as his men, and to this I consented, on condition that he *worked;* though feeling that it was somewhat out of place to have one of the great landed proprietors of the country in my train. This shoeless, stockingless, and almost *sans-culottian* youth

[1] Riobamba probably covers nearly as much ground as Quito. Its principal Plaza is large, and the streets are made of very unusual width, as a precaution in case of earthquakes. For the same reason the houses mostly consist of one floor only. It had an empty and deserted air, and in 1880 cannot, I think, have contained more than 7000 inhabitants.

claimed (I am informed, truly) to be the absolute owner of a princely domain. His land, he said, stretched from Candelaria to the Volcano Sangai. In the vicinity of the farm its boundaries were defined, "but elsewhere" (said with a grand sweep of the hand) "it extended as far as you could go to the east." At a moderate estimate, he owned three hundred square miles.

On the 17th of June, in two hours from the farm, we came to a patch of open ground in the middle of a forest, and the Master of Candelaria, who acted as guide, said mules could go no farther. Cevallos was left here with the animals, while we continued on foot, traversing at first a dense wood, which was impenetrable until three men with machetas had cleared a way, and then 800 very steep feet up the buttress of an alp.[1] This brought us to a track winding, at a high elevation, along the northern side of the Valley of Collanes. At the latter part of the day we crossed from the right to the left bank of the valley, and encamped (at 12,540 feet) in a little patch of trees, close to the foot of the highest peak of Altar.

This valley of Collanes was well watered. Rain fell all the way, and during nearly the whole of the succeeding four days. Its slopes were adapted for grazing, deep with luxuriant grass, yet without a house, or hut, or sign of life. "Why are there no cattle here?" "No money," replied the youth, gloomily. "Well," said Jean-Antoine, "if *I* had this valley I would make a fortune." When returning, we asked the Master if he would sell some of this land, pointing out a tract about six miles long by three or four broad — say twenty square miles, and he answered in the affirmative. "For how much?" He reflected a little, and said "one hundred pesos." "For three hundred and fifty francs, Carrel, the land is yours!" It was just one farthing per acre. As he was so moderate, I thought of buying Altar for myself, and asked what

---

[1] There were some very steep bits on this journey;—from the Bridge of Penipe to the village (about 350 feet); between Penipe and Candelaria, 950 feet in one continuous ascent; and then the 800 feet mentioned above. The track in the Valley of Collanes itself was more level and less undulating than usual.

CHAP. XVI.   AT CAMP IN THE VALLEY OF COLLANES.   305

he would take for the whole mountain. "No! no! he would not sell at any price." "Why not?" He was reluctant to answer. "Why will you not sell Altar?" *"Because there is much treasure there!"*

The treasures of Altar have yet to be discovered. The mountain is an extinct Volcano, having a crater in the form of a horse-shoe (larger than that of Cotopaxi), open towards the west;

AT CAMP IN THE VALLEY OF COLLANES.

with an irregular rim, carrying some of the finest rock peaks in Ecuador. The culminating point[1] is on the southern, and the second peak (which is only slightly inferior in elevation to the highest point) lies opposite to it on the northern side of the crater. The walls of the *cirque* are exceedingly rugged, with much snow, and the floor is occupied by a glacier, which is largely fed by falls from 'hanging-glaciers' on the surrounding slopes and cliffs. The

---

[1] According to La Condamine its height is 17,458 feet; Reiss & Stübel say 17,730 feet. It is probably the *fifth* in rank of the Great Andes of the Equator.

highest peak rises about 3500 feet above the *apparent* floor of the crater in cliffs as precipitous as the steepest part of the Eigher.

June 18. *In Camp in the Valley of Collanes.* Finding that we were nearly under the highest peak, and (from such glimpses as could be obtained through the clouds) that there was very little chance of an ascent being effected from the *inside* of the crater, I sent off J.-A. Carrel at 5.30 a.m., with two of the porters, to examine the *outside,* and Louis with another to the outside of the second peak. Soon after mid-day Jean-Antoine returned, and reported unfavourably; and at 4 p.m. Louis came back, saying he had no view of the second summit during the whole day, but thought we could go as far as he had seen.[1] Determined to shift camp to the north side of the mountain, outside the crater, if weather would permit. Min. temp. this night was 33°·5, and on the 17th, 29° Faht.

June 19. *In Camp in the Valley of Collanes.* High wind from the south-east nearly blew the tent over in the night, though it was well protected by trees. At daybreak there was a hard gale, and we were unable to move the camp. All the peaks of Altar were clouded, and much new snow had fallen on the lower crags.

[1] They brought back rock samples from the highest points which were reached. I judge, from the aneroids supplied to them, that Jean-Antoine's party got to about 15,500 feet on the south side of the highest point, and Louis' to about 14,500 feet on the north-west side of the second summit. In regard to the specimen broken by Jean-Antoine from rock *in situ* Prof. Bonney says (*Proc. Royal Soc.*, Nov. 27, 1884),— "A very dark compact rock, with fairly numerous specks of a greyish felspar, and with occasional minute vesicles. Under the microscope the ground-mass is found to be a glass, in itself almost colourless, but so crowded with opacite as to appear almost opaque with low powers; in fact its true structure can only be seen in very thin sections and with high powers. . . It is a little difficult to decide whether to retain this rock in the augite-andesites, or to term it a basalt." The rock from the northern peak of Altar is "a reddish-grey trachyte, studded with crystals of rather glassy white felspar, roughly about 1 inch diameter, and containing some minute vesicles. The ground-mass appears to be a clear glass, with numerous lath-like crystallites of felspar, but is so thickly crowded with ferrite and opacite, especially the former, as to be all but opaque except in the thinnest part of the section. . . The rock is an augite-andesite, probably containing some hypersthene."

Same state of things continued all day. Wind dropped at night. Min. temp. again 33°·5 Faht.

Watched for the peaks all day. Saw that the highest point near its summit was guarded by pinnacles as steep as the Aiguille du Dru. The face towards the north carried several hanging-glaciers. Frequently heard the roars of avalanches tumbling from them on to the glacier in the crater, the true bottom of which probably lies several hundred feet below the ice. This crater-glacier, in advancing, falls over a steep wall of rock at the head of the Valley of Collanes, in a manner somewhat similar to the Tschingel Glacier in the Gasteren Thal. Some of the ice breaks away in slices, and is re-compacted at the base of the cliff, while part maintains the continuity of the upper plateau with the fallen and smashed fragments. This connecting link of glacier (seen in front) appears to descend almost vertically.

June 20. *From Camp in the Valley of Collanes to Camp in the Valley of Naranjal.* Broke up camp and left at 7.25 a.m.; crossed a small ridge running out of the north-west end of the crater, and descended into the Valley of Naranjal. Spied a big rock surrounded by small trees, and camped against it (13,053 feet). The Valley of Naranjal skirts the outside of Altar on the north. Was told that in six hours it would bring one to the village of Utuñac. The second peak of Altar was almost exactly due East of camp.

In afternoon went with Jean-Antoine to the crest of the ridge on the north of our valley, to try to make out a route and for angles to fix our position. Descended after waiting two hours and seeing nothing. Great quantities of smoke rising from the bottom of our valley. Found camp nearly surrounded by flames—Louis Carrel having set fire to the grass to amuse himself. All hands had to work for an hour to beat out the flames and cut down bushes, and we narrowly escaped being burnt out. Continued windy and misty all night, and nothing could be seen. "This is going to be another Sara-urcu," groaned Jean-Antoine, whose thoughts were in the Val Tournanche. Min. temp. in night 34° Faht.

June 21. From Camp in Valley of Naranjal to Penipe. Settled overnight to return to Riobamba if there was no improvement in the weather. In morning, as before, fog right down to bottom of valley, with steady drizzle. Master of Candelaria said this was the regular thing, and gave no hope of improvement. Waited a little, and got occasional glimpses of second summit. Saw a hurricane was blowing near the top, the snow curling and eddying round in *tourmentes*. Broke up camp

THE BRIDGE OF PENIPE.

in despair, recrossed ridge at north-west end of Altar,[1] descended Valley of Collanes rapidly, and arrived at Penipe at 5.5 p.m. Remembering the advice of the worthy tailor, I endeavoured to

---

[1] Round about the summit of this pass between the two valleys, rather more than 13.000 feet above the level of the sea, on ground where snow had fallen every day during our stay, I collected twenty-six species of flowering plants in flower, including several Valerians and Geraniums, and five Gentians (*Gentiana cerastioides*, Griset; *G. cernua*, H.B.K.; *G. foliosa*, H.B.K.; *G. Rima Don*, Ruiz & Pavon; and *G. sedifolia*, H.B.K.) In the same neighbourhood the lichens *Usnea cornuta*, Koerb., and *Stereocaulon tomentosum*, Fries, and the moss *Grimmia amblyophylla*, C.M. were abundant.

sleep outside the house on a plank form—a thing with length and no breadth; and finding that this, through being near the ground, allowed the curs of Penipe to browse on my boots, shifted in the course of the night to the top of a table (which had breadth but no length), and curled myself up, as printers might say, into the shape of C, grotesque.

Little refreshed by slumber, we returned across the rickety bridge to Riobamba; without incident except a furious stampede of our animals, who took this way of shewing that they had benefited by their sojourn in the forest. As a general rule, Ecuadorian mules display no eagerness to get either onward or upward, and upon flat, open ground, where there is plenty of room, each one seems to wish to be *last;* while on approaching narrow places, and ruts in greasy earth where only one can pass at a time, suddenly galvanized into life, they dash forward with outstretched necks, racing to get through *first;* and deaf to command, persuasion or entreaty outstrip the arrieros, unheeding their shouts and "lado's," and rush at headlong speed, cannoning each other and dislodging their loads. Then arises Hullaballoo! while the corners of packing-cases are splintered and their sides stove in, to the future dismay of consignor and consignee. After six months' experience of the manners and customs of the Ecuadorian mule, one began to understand why glass was dear in Quito.

A THREATENED ATTACK.

CHAPTER XVII.

THE FIRST ASCENT OF CARIHUAIRAZO.

ALTHOUGH compelled by force of circumstances to leave Chimborazo for a while (see pp. 78-80), nothing had occurred to alter my determination to ascend that mountain again; and indeed it was strengthened, because I perceived that a repetition of barometric observations would have, for the measurements of pressure which had been made since the first ascent, much the same value as a 'base of verification' in a triangulation. There was no longer reluctance on the part of my assistants — they were my most willing and obedient servants — and we expected to have the company of Campaña and David, both of whom had shewn some aptitude in keeping on their legs. When preparations were completed at Riobamba, I proposed first to execute a measurement on the Quito road to get 'a scale' for Chimborazo; next to ascend Carihuairazo, to test the snow-going abilities of the aspirants; then to cross between the two mountains and to ascend Chimborazo by the long snow-slope which had been remarked from Guaranda (see p. 25); and lastly to complete the circuit of the mountain. Though little margin of time was left for the unforeseen, if everything went happily, it was possible to do this by the 8th of July, the date on which it would be necessary to leave, to catch the steamer going north from Guayaquil.

Before starting from the town, we took advantage of market-day to lay in additional stores; and as my people fancied the bread of the country, which was brought in for sale by Indian women, Jean-Antoine and I went to the Plaza, and bought a sackful. We then moved off to continue purchasing in another part, and presently found ourselves followed by one of the women, who talked glibly in some incomprehensible aboriginal dialect, proffering an armful of bread, which apparently she wanted to sell. We shook our heads and tried to get rid of her, but she would not be rebuffed, and became an annoyance by creating 'a scene.' It was at last explained by one of the bystanders that she wished us to take the bread *gratis*, that it was our due, she had not given enough for the money that had been paid; and nothing would induce that woman to go away until it was accepted, and her conscience was satisfied.

June 25.[1] *From Riobamba to Camp on lower slopes of Chimborazo.* Despatched the Carrels, David, Campaña, Cevallos, and Domingo at 9.15 a.m., with eleven beasts, and followed at 11.15. Made for the depression between Chimborazo and Carihuairazo, and camped about two and a half miles to the north-east of Chuquipoquio.[2] Rainy day. Min. temp. at night 30°·5 Faht.

June 26. *Measurement on road, &c.* Sent out Domingo to cut

[1] At the place marked Camp 7 on Map of Chimborazo.

[2] On the 24th, I received a letter from Mr. Chambers (Guayaquil), which had been written, and despatched by the ordinary post, on April 3. All letters in this country are liable to be opened and delayed. In 1880, it was said that the British Minister's letters were the only ones which were exempt from this treatment.

firewood; Campaña and David to Mocha and the neighbouring villages to collect antiquities and to buy food; and went with the Carrels to commence measurement on the high road, where it runs across the Paramo of Sanancajas. On return to camp found that Domingo had been assailed by two men, who took away his macheta, and would not restore it until he had given up all the money he possessed. At dusk a horseman rode up (who was recognized as one of the men attached to Chuquipoquio), and in a very insolent manner demanded payment for permission to camp, and for the grass our beasts were eating. Had it explained to him that he had better take himself off, and he rode away shouting that he would come back with others at night and steal our animals. About 9 p.m. Campaña and David came in, very excited, saying that a few miles off, on the high road, two men had spread a white cloth before their beasts, to try to frighten them, and had then rushed in. There was a tussle, and my men scampered off, with the loss of a few trifles.

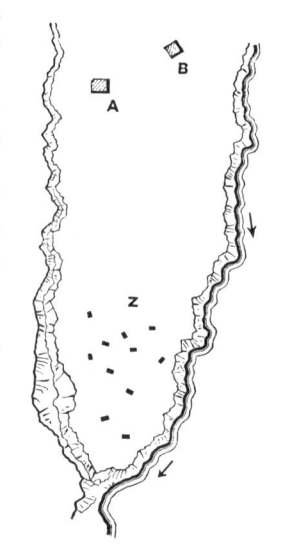

Putting these several things together, it seemed that Señor Chiriboga must have again come up from Riobamba "to watch over and care for us" (see p. 82), and it became necessary to avoid his attentions. The position of the camp was excellent for defence, though it had not been selected with any such view. There was a small torrent on the north side, and a narrow but deep earthquake fissure on the south. The two united towards the east, and our camp was placed on the west (at A, B). When the animals were driven into Z, no one could get at them without passing us. Kept watch until past midnight, and then roused Louis to take a turn for an hour, but before his time was half over he was snoring again. Continued to watch, and at 2 a.m. heard whistling, and low voices of persons approaching. Said nothing; took my whip and aroused the others; hung out the lanterns to shew them the way, and shouted defiance. Apparently, the thieves thought they might have a warm reception and went off. Night being very dark, we saw no one. After this my people considered that it might be as well to keep watch, and I went to sleep. A windy, rainy night.

June 27. From Camp near High Road to Camp on the south side of Carihuairazo. At 8.15 a.m. a muleteer from Machachi (known to Cevallos) came in and said that eleven beasts had been stolen from him last night, a few miles on the other side of the tambo. Even the loss of one animal would have caused us great inconvenience, — probably would have upset everything; and, as there were evidently cattle-stealers about, we abandoned the measurement, and moved upwards out of their reach, and beyond the attentions of the robber of Chuquipoquio. At 1.30 p.m. broke up camp, and proceeded by the valley between Chimborazo and Carihuairazo, called Yacu-larca, passing a number of half-wild cattle, with lashing tails and twitching heads, who could have made a very pretty mess of us if they had charged; and about 3.30 crossed the stream.

In the bed of this river (the Rio Blanco) there were quicksands, of which I became aware by being nearly shot over the head of my animal;[1] and the slopes on the farther side were found to be very swampy. Large thickets high up on the flanks of our mountain, with trees of considerable age, lead one to suppose that it was long since it was an active Volcano. We steered for a rather prominent clump, in a *vallon* running north and south, and camped at 13,377 feet on its western or right bank, nearly due south of the two principal summits of Carihuairazo. Violent wind at night from E. to N.E. Min. temp. 33° Faht.

[1] As the Rio Blanco was a trifling stream, we began to cross it in three or four places at once. Several of the animals passed over without trouble. My own refused to advance, until whipped, and in the very next step it plunged into a quicksand. All hands coming quickly, it was speedily extricated.

June 28. *In Camp.* Kept indoors. Had not got the bearing of the summit, and would not start. Clouds nearly down to our level all day, and from 12 to 8 p.m. rain, sleet or hail fell unceasingly. After that saw stars for a short time and got bearings. Prepared for an early start to-morrow. Cut bundles of branches and twigs to mark line of ascent. Rain and snow recommenced at 9 p.m., and continued to fall nearly all night.

June 29. *Ascent of the middle peak of Carihuairazo.* Left camp at 5.50 a.m. by lantern-light, with the Carrels, David, and Campaña,—the two latter being taken to test their snow-going abilities by a little preliminary exercise. Fitted them out in some of our old boots and socks, with gaiters extemporized out of coarse waterproof. Was also accompanied by a four-footed volunteer.

At the village of Penipe there were many dogs, and one of them followed our caravan, and could not be driven away. Possibly somebody had given it a bone, or shewn it a little kindness; and as the mongrel was grateful it became a pet, and then of course had to be named, and finding it answered to *Pedro* it was known thenceforward as Pedro de Penipe. When we left camp our dog insisted upon accompanying us, and it went to the top of the mountain.

From the reconnaissance on the 15th of January (see note to page 87) it was known that Carihuairazo had two principal peaks (lying not far to the north of the camp), and another minor one away to the west. The easternmost was the highest of the three, and we had marked a prominent ridge leading up to it, and observed that this ridge was on the west of our *vallon*. The ascent could not have been made without this previous knowledge. The summit was not seen until we were actually upon it, and during the day it was seldom possible to see more than one hundred and fifty feet in any direction. The leader was often invisible to the last man on the rope. Snow-spectacles frequently could not be used.

Commenced by steering N.W. up the hillside, and when the

crest of the ridge was reached changed the course to N.N.W., and followed the *arête*. Although this was only a little above 14,000 feet, every step was through deep, new snow.[1] About 7.30 entered on the glaciers surrounding the summits. Tied up, and placed David last on the rope, with the sticks to mark the route. Glacier soon steepened and required cutting. Small crevasses were snowed up, and the big ones looked immense, seen through the mist. Traversed several large snow-bridges, which drew exclamations of wonder from the Ecuadorians, who had never seen the like before. Snow steepened, and at last became a wall, nearly or quite as rapid as the final slope of the Wetterhorn.

At this stage Pedro wanted to give in, and sat down and whined. Handed him up from one to another. By a stroke of good fortune stumbled on a snow-bridge crossing the highest bergschrund. Then the wall became too steep to ascend directly. Made short zigzags, and presently saw a gigantic cornice looming through the fog—an indication that the summit was near. Consultation ended in going straight ahead, and we happily penetrated the most assailable point.

Temperature on the top of this mountain ranged from 38-40° Faht., and the mean of two readings of the Mercurial Barometer at 11 and 11.15 a.m. (reduced to 32° Faht.) was 16·519 inches.[2] This was not so low as I expected the barometer to fall, and while still on the summit I told the men that probably we were not on the highest point. Our peak terminated in a snow cone too small to stand upon, with a little patch of rock[3] peeping out a short

[1] In January this ridge was free from snow.

[2] The 11 a.m. observation at Guayaquil (reduced to 32° Faht.) was 29·928 inches, air temperature 74° Faht.

[3] "This rock breaks with a rather rough irregular fracture. The colour on this is a warm purplish-grey mottled with darker spots, and speckled with small rather light-coloured crystals of felspar with a rather satiny lustre. A few minute vesicles may be perceived under the microscope. . . Enclosures of glass or various microliths are occasionally seen, but the majority of the crystals are fairly clear, though a few are very dirty, and have a corroded look at the exterior. There is also present in the ground-mass a fair number of crystals of augite of a yellowish-green colour,

distance down upon the north side, bearing some lichens (*Lecidea* and *Lecanora*) and, for such a situation, a not inconsiderable quantity of a Moss which has been dubiously identified as *Grimmia apocarpa*, Hedw. This same species was found in the previous January near the second camp on Chimborazo, at the rather exceptional height (for a Moss) of 16,660 feet; but it was more remarkable to find it on the very apex of Carihuairazo (16,515 feet), completely surrounded as it was by permanent snow and ice upon all sides, as truly *insulated* as if it had been upon an island surrounded with water.

Carihuairazo forms the northern end of the *massif* of Chimborazo, and is separated from the greater mountain by a depression called Abraspungo.[1] Its northern slopes extend almost to the town of Ambato, and the Quito Road may be considered its boundary on the east. Historians say that it was formerly *loftier* than Chimborazo, and that a portion of its apex fell during a great earthquake which occurred at the end of the 17th century.[2] I cannot imagine that it was ever 4000 feet higher than it is at present. The ruins of such a peak would make a prodigious heap, yet we saw nothing indicating that a fall of great magnitude had occurred. The present summit-ridge *possibly* formed the southern and western sides of a crater, of which the northern and eastern sides may have fallen, and now lie buried under the glaciers at the summit. This, however, is pure conjecture.

not exceeding about ·03 inch in length, and two or three which in structure, dichroism, and parallel extinction agree with hypersthene. There are scattered crystals of hematite and scales of iron-glance. . . The ground-mass appears to be a clear glass thickly studded with dusty ferrite, and with minute crystallites in part, at least, felspar. The rock is, therefore, an augite-andesite."—Prof. T. G. Bonney, *Proc. Royal Soc.*, June 19, 1884.

[1] There is a rough track all the way up Yacu-larca to Abraspungo. As we did not descend by this path on the western side, I am not aware what direction it takes, after crossing the pass.

[2] It would be interesting if this tradition could be verified, as it might give a clue to the *age* of the glaciers which now completely envelop the top of the mountain.

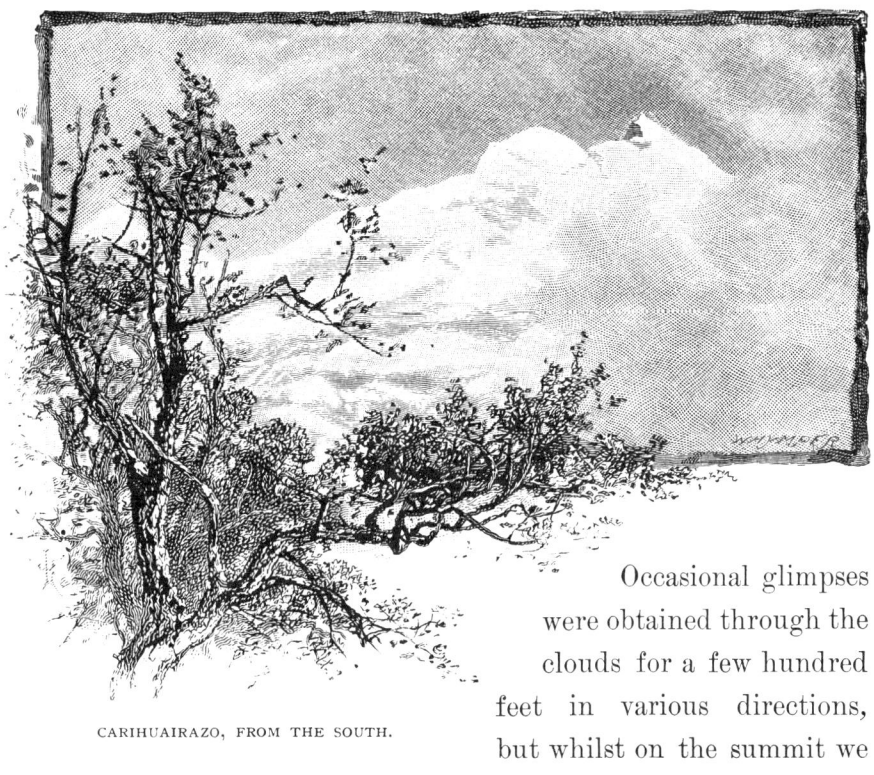

CARIHUAIRAZO, FROM THE SOUTH.

Occasional glimpses were obtained through the clouds for a few hundred feet in various directions, but whilst on the summit we neither saw Chimborazo nor the other peaks of Carihuairazo; and we returned to camp uncertain where we had been. At 4 p.m. the clouds opened, and shewed that we had stood on the western of the two principal peaks (that nearly in the middle of the engraving), which is distinctly, though slightly, lower than the eastern one.

The rate of ascent on this day was eleven feet per minute (3138 feet in 285 minutes).[1] Taking into consideration that this was their first experience upon steep snow, David and Campaña came out well, and they were greatly elated at the prospect of their promised ascent of Chimborazo. Presently their joy was turned into mourning. In a few hours the whole of us were

[1] Left camp 5.50 a.m. and arrived on summit 10.35 a.m. Left at 11.45 a.m.; came down fast; never lost sight of the sticks we had planted (though in some instances they were nearly covered by drifting snow), and got to camp at 2.5 p.m., without halting.

incapacitated by snow-blindness. Foreseeing what was coming, a brew of Sulphate of Zinc was made in our largest can, and served out wholesale. It was piteous to hear the Ecuadorians wailing under their little booth. Not knowing what had befallen them, they imagined they had lost their sight for ever. Pedro joined in the lamentations, and went moaning and staggering about, knocking his head unwittingly against the branches.

June 30. *At Camp on Carihuairazo.* All snow-blind, unable to move. Depended for assistance on Cevallos and Domingo.

FOURTH CAMP ON CHIMBORAZO (14,359 FEET).

July 1. *From Camp on Carihuairazo to Fourth Camp on Chimborazo, across Abraspungo.* Broke up camp at 10 a.m.; descended the *vallon*, and ascended Yacu-larca to Abraspungo, Jean-Antoine and Campaña travelling with bandaged eyes, and the rest wearing blue spectacles. Stopped on the summit of the pass to read the barometer, and found that the height (14,480 feet) was a little above that of the Great Arenal. After crossing it we kept for some time on a level,[1] and were then driven downwards to turn the end of a large stream of lava.[2] Rounding the base of this, we came upon an excellent place for camping, against a little rivulet, with plenty of firing, and made there our fourth camp on Chimborazo (14,359 feet). Min. temp. in night 30° Faht.

The fourth camp was not high enough for a starting-point, and on the 2nd of July we continued a few miles farther in a south-westerly direction, and established the fifth camp at the height of 15,811 feet, against a very large block of lava [3] (apparently, a loose mass imbedded in the soil, that had either been ejected or had fallen from the cliffs above) a little to the north of the ridge which hereafter will be termed the north-west ridge of Chimborazo.[4] I identified this as the long ridge seen from Guaranda, and knew that it led directly towards the summit. Jean-Antoine, however, maintained that I was mistaken. " I tell you what it is," said the Chief of the Staff, "*Monsieur deceives himself, prettily.*"

[1] A few hundred yards on the west of the pass, the swampy soil suddenly gives place to firm ground; and a little farther on the sandy slopes commence which stretch uninterruptedly round the north-west and western sides of the mountain.

[2] This prominent lava stream *appeared* to issue from the glaciers at the height of about 18,000 feet,—one could not see precisely where, owing to the large quantity of new-fallen snow.

[3] There was great difficulty in breaking specimens from this mass, which was unlike any other rock that I saw on the mountain. When broken, it crumbled somewhat in the manner of loaf-sugar. Prof. Bonney says:—"A rather crumbly rock of very irregular fracture, having a very dark grey ground-mass, in which crystals of glassy-white felspar, up to about ·2 inch long, are imbedded. When examined microscopically, it does not appear to differ materially from some of those already described . . . is different only in the colour of the ground-mass, and is best named a hypersthene-andesite."—*Proc. Royal Soc.*, June 19, 1884.

[4] The direction of this ridge is not strictly north-west. It is more nearly north-north-west.

CHIMBORAZO, FROM THE NORTH-NORTH-WEST.

CHAPTER XVIII.

ON THE SECOND ASCENT OF CHIMBORAZO.

THE aspect of Chimborazo from the north-north-west was quite unlike its appearance from any other direction. The two summits could not be seen,[1] and the mountain seemed to terminate in one very flat dome. I found that this *apparent* summit was actually at C on my map, and was part of the glacier which I have named Glacier de Reiss, after Dr. W. Reiss of Berlin. Under this great flat dome there were vertical sections of glacier, crowning precipices of rock, in a manner similar to those which are represented in the plate facing p. 76; and falls of ice occurred over these cliffs, as the glacier advanced, like those that are described upon page 78.[2] In order to be beyond the range of these ice-

[1] The highest of the two summits could be seen from the fourth camp, rising over the glacier that I have named Glacier de Spruce. The very highest point was, probably, concealed.

[2] The blocks of ice that fell from the faces of glacier marked E, E (on the inset *Sketch plan of part of the south side of Chimborazo*), over the cliffs B, C, sometimes rolled down the Glacier de Débris as far as Station 4.

avalanches, I kept the camp about three miles from the base of the cliffs.

The north-west ridge led up to the western end of 'the Northern Walls,'[1] and the tent might have been placed upon it even higher than the third camp on the south-west ridge (17,285 feet). To have done this would have cost much labour in porterage, and, balancing things, it seemed preferable to stop below, closer to things burnable; although the starting-point would be nearly fifteen hundred feet lower than upon the first occasion, and the ascent, consequently, would be that amount longer. We had come to our very last day. In one way and another all our margin of time had been dissipated, and unless the ascent was effected on the 3rd of July it could not be made at all. This was in no sense the fault of my people. Each man had his allotted tasks, knew them, and did them; and during these last days every one worked with a cheerfulness and alacrity beyond praise. Without bidding, Jean-Antoine now went to reconnoitre the ridge; Louis, David, and Campaña made things comfortable; Cevallos and Domingo drove away the animals to pasturage; and on the 3rd, while it was still night, all were in readiness, booted and gaitered, waiting for the signal to start.

Whilst chafing hands around the camp-fire,[2] Domingo and our four-footed friend appeared out of the darkness. The arriero-lad came to volunteer his services. I said "No; a couple of tyros are enough on a rope." Then a sudden idea seized us. Let us take Pedro. He was already entitled to bow-wows from all dogs who had stood on inferior eminences,—let us enable him to take precedence over the entire canine race. "Ha! Pedro; good dog, come here!" Pedro was sociable, and came willingly so long as we were round the fire; but moved away when we began to load, and

---

[1] I conjecture this was the ridge by which Dr. Stübel endeavoured to ascend Chimborazo. On the 3rd of July, from 17,000 feet upwards, it was entirely covered with snow, and down to 16,000 feet there were many patches upon it.

[2] The minimum this night was 25° Faht.

looked doubtfully. We took up the axes—he went farther off. Calls were in vain, and finally he put his tail between his legs and bolted down hill as hard as he could scamper. "No, my masters. *You may go up, but I shall go down—no more snow-blindness for me.*"

At 5.15 a.m., when tones began to change to detail, we left the camp; and this day, for once, the heavens seemed to smile upon us. The sky was bright—the air serene; and long before dawn, sixty miles away, we saw the cone of Cotopaxi clear cut against a cloudless horizon, and remarked how tranquil the great Volcano looked, and that not a sign of smoke was rising from its crater.[1] Soon a cold wind sprang up. I lingered behind, to beat my hands and feet, and whilst resting back against a rock, looking towards the north, saw the commencement of an eruption.

At 5.40 a.m. two puffs of steam were emitted, and then there was a pause. At 5.45 a column of inky blackness began to issue, and went up straight in the air with such prodigious velocity that in less than a minute it had risen 20,000 feet above the rim of the crater.[2] I could see the upper 10,000 feet of the volcano, and estimated the height of the column at double the height of the visible portion of the mountain. The top of the column, therefore, was nearly *forty thousand feet above the level of the sea.* At that elevation it encountered a powerful wind blowing from the east, and was rapidly borne towards the Pacific; remaining intensely black, seeming to spread very slightly, and presenting the appearance of a gigantic ⌐ drawn upon an otherwise perfectly clear sky. It was then caught by wind from the north, and, borne towards us, appeared to spread quickly.

Meanwhile the others progressed steadily over the snow-beds and stony débris on the crest of the ridge, and I did not catch them for nearly an hour. At 6.50 a.m. we tied up, as the snow

---

[1] This was the only occasion on which we saw the crater quite free from smoke and steam during the whole of our stay in Ecuador.

[2] I did not note the time it took to rise to this elevation. My impression is that it was an affair of a few *seconds*.

became continuous, and proceeded along the *arête* until it came to a termination at the extreme western end of 'the Northern Walls';[1] and then bore away horizontally to the right, to an islet of rock, and halted at 8.35 a.m. for breakfast.[2] The barometer said that we had risen 3000 feet in three hours and twenty minutes;—the mercury had sunk from 16·950 to 15·177 inches, while temperature had risen from 30° to 46° Faht. We were already 18,900 feet above the sea.

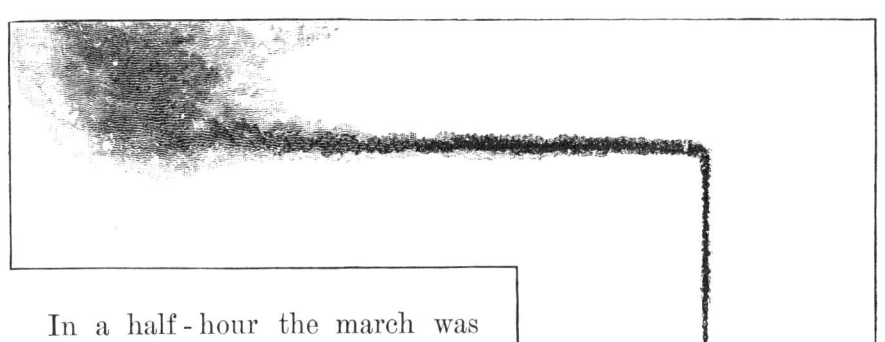

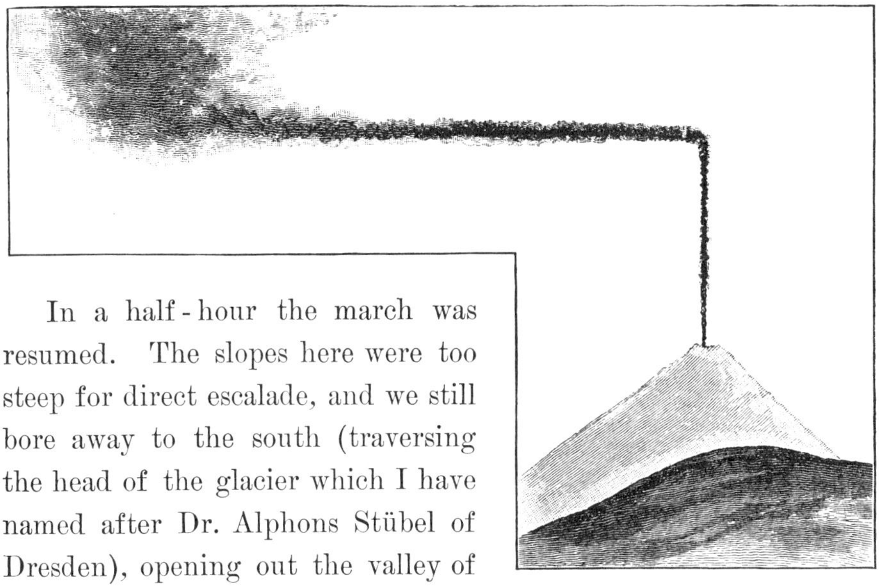

In a half-hour the march was resumed. The slopes here were too steep for direct escalade, and we still bore away to the south (traversing the head of the glacier which I have named after Dr. Alphons Stübel of Dresden), opening out the valley of the Chimbo, and an immense prospect beyond. "Hi! Carrel! what is that?" "Guaranda, Monsieur." "Guaranda! Monsieur deceives himself, does he?" but the man in front suddenly became deaf, and could not hear a word. At this time the view was magnificent. We could see to the bottom of the basin of the Chimbo, eleven thousand feet below, and overlooked the country on the west by four or five thousand feet. Between us and the sea, the whole expanse from north to south was filled by the Pacific Range of Ecuador, with countless peaks and ramifications—

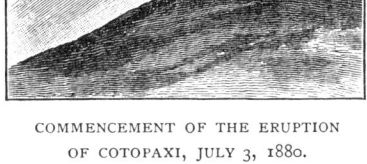

COMMENCEMENT OF THE ERUPTION OF COTOPAXI, JULY 3, 1880.

---

[1] This is just beyond the range of the engraving on p. 320, on the right.

[2] At the spot marked Z on the Map of Chimborazo.

valleys, vallons, dells and dales, backed by the Ocean,[1] rising above the haze which obscured the flat coast land.

Now we turned back to the north, and zigzagged to and fro to ease the ascent, getting into the direct rays of the sun, which was already more than fifty degrees high. The clouds from Cotopaxi were bearing down upon Chimborazo, seeming to rise higher and yet higher in the sky, although they were actually descending. For a full hour we saw the immense column still rising from the crater, and then the clouds which were drifting towards us shut it out.

When they commenced to intervene between the sun and ourselves the effects which were produced were truly amazing. We saw *a green sun*, and smears of colour something like verdigris green high up in the sky, which changed to equally extreme blood-reds, or to coarse brick-reds, and then passed in an instant to the colour of tarnished copper, or shining brass. No words can convey the faintest idea of the impressive appearance of these strange colours in the sky — seen one moment and gone the next — resembling nothing to which they can properly be compared, and surpassing in vivid intensity the wildest effects of the most gorgeous sunsets.

The terms that I have employed to designate the colours which were seen are both inadequate and inexact. Their most striking features were their extraordinary strength, their extreme coarseness, and their dissimilarity from any tints or tones ever seen in the sky, even during sunrises or sunsets of exceptional brilliancy. They were unlike colours for which there are recognized terms. They commenced to be seen when the clouds began to pass between the sun and ourselves, and were not seen previously. The changes from one hue to another had obvious connection with the varying densities of the clouds that passed; which were sometimes thick and sometimes light. No colours were seen when they moved overhead, and surrounded us on all sides.

---

[1] The part seen was probably distant 200 or more miles.

At 11 a.m., getting into the direct rays of the sun, the heat became oppressive, and David, exhausted by his flounderings in the snow, wished to return. "Impossible, David; it is now or never." Campaña, a light weight, sank in slightly, and shewed no signs of fatigue. At 11.30 a.m., we were again facing Guaranda; and striking the former route, made as before for the plateau between the two domes, bending round at first to the north, and subsequently to the east; avoiding the lowest part of the hollow, yet occasionally sinking up to the knees. At 1 p.m., when close to the very highest point, a great clamour and cackling broke out amongst the men, for the regular sweep of the dome was interrupted by some object. It was the top of our ten-foot pole sticking out of the snow, with a few tattered fragments of the red flag still attached.[1] Nature had built a wall of ice about six feet long on the eastern (or windward) side, and the flagstaff stood clear of it in front, with the frayed remnants of serge stiff frozen, pointing like fingers to the south-west, registering the direction of the wind that had prevailed![2]

During this time the clouds from Cotopaxi had been constantly approaching, and about mid-day they passed overhead.[3] The sun had become invisible, and temperature had fallen; and our first care was to dig a trench to leeward of the flagstaff to obtain protection, for the wind felt dangerously cold. Shortly after the barometer was hung up, it read 14·050 inches, with air temperature 20° Faht., and it continued to fall until 2 p.m., and then, with the thermometer at 15° Faht., the mercury stood at 14·028 inches, and *lower it would not go*.[4]

When the clouds from Cotopaxi first passed overhead, they

[1] All except the few scraps shewn in the engraving facing p. 326 had been blown away by the wind.

[2] We arrived on the summit at 1.20 p.m., having occupied four hours and a quarter over the ascent of the last sixteen hundred feet.

[3] They had taken six hours to travel about eighty miles.

[4] At 2 p.m., when the Mercurial Barometer (red. to 32° Faht.) was 14·044 inches, the Aneroid E read 12·990 inches.

were still, I think, not less than 5000 feet above us (or 25,000 to 26,000 feet above the sea), and they extended far to the south before the dust of which they were composed began to fall upon the summit of Chimborazo. It commenced to settle about ten minutes after our arrival, and in the course of an hour caused the snowy summit to look like a ploughed field. It filled our eyes and nostrils, rendered eating and drinking impossible,[1] and at last reduced us to breathing through handkerchiefs. The brass and glass of the mercurial barometer, like everything else, became coated with this all-pervading dust, but the vernier afforded protection to the portion of the tube which was behind it, and this protected part remained reasonably bright, while all the rest of the tube above and below was thickly encrusted. The height of the barometer on the summit of Chimborazo, on July 3, 1880, was registered in this manner by a volcanic eruption which occurred more than sixty miles away!

The surrounding country became obscured as soon as the falling dust reached our level, and thus our last ascent in Ecuador, like all the rest, rendered no view from the summit. By 2 o'clock in the afternoon even the Pointe Veintemilla could not be seen, and the darkness continued to increase so much that by 2.30 p.m. we thought it was best to depart. The last thing done, before leaving, was photographing the top of Chimborazo. The sky was dark with the clouds of ash, the people shivered under a temperature of 15° Faht., the wind fluttered everything that could move, the snow gave a poor foundation for the stand, and the gloom made focussing uncertain. All the conditions were favourable for the production of a bad photograph, and the result was just what might be expected. It is reproduced literally here, without embellishment, an authentic record of a memorable occasion.[2]

[1] My observed temperature on the summit of Chimborazo, on July 3, was 96°·3 Faht. See Appendix F.

[2] An 'instantaneous' plate was exposed for one minute, and it was necessary to keep wiping the lens during the whole of the operation. The engraving shews the dust commencing to settle among the ripples in the snow.

The surface of the snow had hardened under the increasing cold, and we slipped along quickly,— Louis first, followed by David ; then Campaña in my charge ; while Jean-Antoine came last, and acted as sheet-anchor. Though the little Interpreter tumbled about gloriously, he tugged no more than a good-sized fish at the end of a line ; and we descended boisterously, cutting the zigzags, and finding great advantage from sticks which had been planted to mark the route, in the same manner as upon Sara-urcu and Carihuairazo. About 4.45 a brief halt was made to get an observation of the mercurial barometer for the height of the snow-line (16,700 feet), and then, casting off the rope, we put on full steam, and arrived at camp at 5.10 p.m.[1]

By this time the coarser particles of the Volcanic Dust had fallen below our level, and were settling down into the valley of the Chimbo (the bottom of which was still 7000 feet beneath us), causing it to appear as if filled by thick smoke. The finest ones were still floating in the air like a light fog, and so it continued until night closed in. The tent was laden with the dust, and a large quantity had slipped and fallen down its sloping sides. I collected more than three ounces from the roof, and this was not the half of what remained upon it. Subsequently, I found that at the town of Ambato, between 11 and 11.15 a.m., upon a piece of paper one foot square, spread out to receive it, four ounces were

---

[1] I have felt it unnecessary to say much about the second ascent of Chimborazo, beyond indicating the direction that was followed. The north-west ridge (that referred to upon p. 25, and shewn on the left of the engraving facing p. 24) leads with remarkable directness towards the summit, and its crest or *arête* is unusually free from impediments. At the upper end, where it abuts against the Northern Walls (or, perhaps it should be said, where it issues from them, for I suspect that this is another lava-stream), one is already 18,900 feet above the sea, and so far as this point ice-axes are not required. It is then necessary to bear towards the south, and a certain amount of cutting is obligatory whilst traversing the head of the Glacier de Stübel. Crevasses there, though numerous, are easily avoided, and the steepest angles of the slopes do not exceed 35°. Beyond this, the route joins that described in Chapter III. Neither upon Jan. 4 nor July 3 were there any open crevasses in the plateau between the two domes.

collected; and that at Riobamba, upon paper similarly exposed, about as much fell per square foot as upon Chimborazo.

From these data I have calculated the minimum quantity which must have been ejected upon this occasion. Drawing two lines radiating from Cotopaxi, one leading to Riobamba, and the other to an equal distance west of the fifth camp (within which limits it is certain that the dust fell), and estimating that from our camp to Ambato only one-eighth of an ounce fell on each square foot, and that from Ambato to the Volcano four ounces fell on each square foot, I find that, at the least, *two millions of tons* must have been ejected during this eruption.[1] The quantity is underestimated in several ways. The amount is ignored that was carried beyond the limits which have been indicated, though it fell over many hundreds of square miles.[2] The quantity only is taken into account which was actually found *upon* the tent—not that which had fallen from it, nor that which had still to descend; and from Ambato northwards a fall of fifteen minutes only is reckoned, although it continued to settle for several hours.[3]

I have found it interesting to compare the dust deposited upon Chimborazo with that which fell upon our tent when we were encamped on the summit of Cotopaxi (see p. 153), which was

---

[1] This amount is equal to a column of solid lava (2·65 spec. grav.) 38 feet square and 18,600 feet high.

[2] And on ships upon the Pacific Ocean.

[3] As pure and undefiled Volcanic Dusts can seldom be procured, and are *desiderata* with students, I have placed the collections mentioned below in the hands of Mr. J. R. Gregory, 88 Charlotte Street, Fitzroy Square, from whom samples can be obtained.

1. Dust which fell at Quito (after an aerial voyage of 34 miles) from the great eruption of Cotopaxi in June, 1877 (see p. 125). 2. Dust which fell on the tent on Chimborazo (after an aerial voyage of 64 miles) from the eruption of Cotopaxi, July 3, 1880. 3. Lapilli and dust from the apex of the cone of Cotopaxi (19,500 feet). 4. Granular dust from sheltered places on Cotopaxi (see p. 141). 5. Lapilli from 15,000 feet on Cotopaxi. 6. Pumice lapilli from Ambato (see p. 94). 7. Fine dust from the ten-inch bed at Machachi (see p. 104). 8. Fine pumice-dust from the lowest bed at Machachi (see p. 104).

DAVID J.-A. CARREL CAMPANA

"THE SKY WAS DARK WITH THE CLOUDS OF ASH."

FROM A PHOTOGRAPH TAKEN ON THE SUMMIT OF CHIMBORAZO, JULY 3, 1880.

ejected during intermittent discharges of steam, and, presumably, was torn off by the violence of the blasts. It is reasonable to find that there is a considerable difference in the *weight* and *dimensions* of the particles of these two dusts. The larger and heavier atoms naturally settle soonest, and the smaller and lighter ones travel farthest. Upon several occasions I have endeavoured to count the number of particles in a grain of the Chimborazo deposit, and have found that the smaller ones do not weigh so much as $\frac{1}{25000}$ part of a grain, and that the finer atoms are lighter still.[1]

[1] Professor Bonney has examined the two dusts microscopically, and has favoured me with the following descriptions. No. I. (*Dust which fell on the tent at the summit of Cotopaxi, Feb.* 18-19, 1880). "The grains range from ·02 inch in diameter downwards, a considerable proportion varying between this and about ·01 inch. They may be thus distinguished:—(A) rock fragments, (B) mineral fragments. (A). These consist of (*a*) chips of colourless or nearly colourless glass, sometimes almost clear, sometimes clouded with ferrite or opacite, and containing microliths of felspar, &c.—chips, in short, of glassy lavas. (*b*) rough opaque, or nearly opaque grains, sometimes translucent at the edges, and including microliths of felspar and augite; these, when viewed with a dark background, have a scoriaceous exterior, and are greyish, blackish, or reddish-brown in colour; they are evidently minute lapilli of an andesitic lava. (B). Among these the following minerals may be recognized:—(*a*) felspar, showing occasionally plagioclastic twinning; (*b*) more rare, augite and perhaps hypersthene. I notice fragments both of glass and of minerals even among the finer dust, together with black specks, probably magnetite."

No. II. (*Dust which was ejected by Cotopaxi upon July* 3, 1880, *and fell upon the tent at the fifth camp on Chimborazo, distant sixty-four miles*). "The grains which make up this interesting deposit, as indicated by a glance at the slides with the unaided eye, are, as might be expected, decidedly smaller than those which characterise No. I, a very few only attain to a diameter of ·01 inch, and this is barely exceeded. Fragments measuring from ·003 to ·004 inch are common, and they vary from this size to the finest dust; the characteristic of the deposit, so far as I can ascertain, being the presence of grains ranging from about ·001 to ·003 inch. They consist, as before, of rock fragments and mineral fragments. Among the former (A) the rough dark lapilli are rare; the majority being translucent, and apparently smooth externally. These are chips of glass, commonly of a pale brownish colour, in which acicular microliths, probably of felspar, are frequent, with specks of ferrite. . . (B). The mineral fragments are felspar, as above, with a little augite, and there is one well-formed hypersthene crystal ·01 inch long, in which are enclosures of iron peroxide, &c., and, I think, minute cavities. Fragments of felspar and acicular crystallites are rather abundant among the finer dust."

The sole difference between this eruption and others which had been remarked of Cotopaxi, was, probably, only one of degree. If the pipe of the Volcano — its channel of communication with the depths below — had been filled with molten lava, a means of exit would have been afforded which would have prevented this great manifestation of energy. The outburst suggested explosion, — a violent deliverance of confined force; and I conjecture that the steam which was constantly welling up, instead of being permitted to escape freely, or by intermittent discharges, was more effectually imprisoned than usual [in the manner suggested upon pp. 153-4], and that thus the temporary quietude was produced which was noted in the early morning. During this time the subterranean forces were gathering strength, under constantly-increasing heat, due to augmented pressure; at last acquiring power sufficient to burst through the barrier, and then issued in a blast of inconceivable violence; rushing in a few seconds from depths with heat above the fusing-point of iron to cold beneath the freezing-point of mercury, rending the solid rock through which it passed into infinitesimal fragments, and driving millions of tons of this impalpable powder vertically in the air, twenty thousand feet above the lip of the crater.

The new readings of the barometer on the summit of Chimborazo, agreeing closely with those which were taken upon the first ascent, gave assurance, whilst still in the country, that there was no material error in the measurements of atmospheric pressure which had been made in the interior of Ecuador; and the altitude which has been deduced from them for Chimborazo, by nearly according with that which was obtained from the previous observations, renders it probable that the accepted height of that mountain is *too great by about* 927 *feet*.[1]

For a second time we saw the barometer standing nearly as low as 14 inches, without experiencing what I have ventured to term the *acute* symptoms of mountain-sickness; and, by a con-

[1] See Chapter XIX. for some further remarks upon the height of Chimborazo.

siderable improvement in our rate, had the opinion confirmed that man *can* become habituated to low pressures. The ascent from the fifth camp (15,811 feet) to the summit (20,498 feet), excluding halts, occupied 445 minutes, and was therefore executed at the rate of 632 feet per hour. The descent, excluding halts, was made in 145 minutes, or at the rate of 1939 feet per hour,—the mean of these being 1280 feet per hour ; a speed which, although comparing unfavourably with the superlative rates quoted upon pp. 31-2, was a distinct advance upon our first essay.

On the 4th of July we continued the circuit of the mountain by a high-level route, intending to stop for the night at the position of the First Camp ; and the march was made in a trifle over five hours (for most of the way at an elevation of 14,500 to 15,000 feet), without coming across any impediment worth mention ! The bearing of the First Camp was not known at starting, and I undertook to lead the caravan by the guidance of the barometer.

On the 26th of December, at the First Camp on Chimborazo, the barometer stood at 17·9 inches, and from daily observation of it I knew the great improbability that atmospheric pressure would be so much as one-tenth of an inch either higher or lower at the same spot. I proposed to intersect the Vallon de Carrel, a little higher than the First Camp, by keeping on a level with a pressure of 17·8 inches. For this purpose Aneroids were more useful than the Mercurials, inasmuch as they could be read on horseback while in movement, without checking the march of the caravan ; and I trusted to them alone, after having ascertained their Index-errors by comparison with the Mercurial.[1] Sometimes the nature of the ground drove us a little up or down, and pressure fell or rose as the case might be ; but at the earliest opportunity the level of 17·8 inches was resumed, and no other means were employed to find the desired place.

[1] It was indispensable to do this, in consequence of the large errors they had acquired. See *How to use the Aneroid Barometer*, § 66.

Upon leaving the fifth camp[1] we steered away from the summit for forty minutes, to turn the north-west ridge; and then bore round to the S.W., S.S.W., and for a long distance went nearly due South, below the Glacier de Stübel — the broadest glacier upon Chimborazo. After passing this, solely at the instigation of the aneroids, I changed the course to S.E. by E., and about 4 p.m. had the satisfaction of pointing out to my people (through a gap in the ridge on the north side of the Vallon de Carrel) the place where we had encamped on the 26th of December.

The part of Chimborazo traversed on this day was barren to the last degree, covered with beds of sand, extending upwards (as we had found in the Vallon de Carrel) nearly to the snow, and downwards farther than could be seen. All fissures and minor inequalities were entirely effaced.

These sandy slopes and plains are not perceived while crossing Chimborazo by the ordinary route, or from Guaranda, and they extend uninterruptedly from a little to the west of Tortorillas right round the western and north-western sides of the mountain, nearly to Abraspungo. The portion which at present is called 'The Great Arenal' is, in reality, only a small part of them. They are an important feature which has not hitherto been pointed out, produced by the same cause as the slope of ash on Cotopaxi [see pp. 146-8], namely, by the predominance of easterly winds, which scour the volcanic dusts from the eastern sides of the mountains, and deposit them on the leeward or western ones; and they form a most convenient highway, although sterile, infinitely more agreeable to travel over than the established route, through Chuquipoquio.

[1] We scoured the surroundings before departure, and discovered sixteen small beetles of six species, three of which (*Bembidium Andinum*, Bates, *Colpodes oreas*, Bates, and *Erirrhinoides distinctus*, Olliff) were obtained only at this locality. The others (*Helicorrhynchus vulsus*, Olliff, *Naupactus parvicollis*, Olliff, and *Macrops cœlorum*, Olliff) had previously been found at similar altitudes upon Pichincha and Cayambe. Descriptions of these beetles are given in the *Supplementary Appendix*.

FLORA OF CHIMBORAZO.

The stream was dried up in the Vallon de Carrel, and we continued onward towards Tortorillas until water was found, and made our Sixth Camp (13,353 feet) some distance short of the tambo, at the mouth of the Vallon de Débris, in a little nook, concealed from the view of persons crossing the Great Arenal. The 5th of July was occupied in completing collections[1] and other

[1] I give here a complete list of our Botanical gatherings upon Chimborazo, exclusive of species which were obtained lower than 14,000 feet.—Lichens. *Parmelia*, near *centrifuga*, south side (14–15,000 feet); *Umbilicaria sp.?* north-west side (15,800); *Neuropogon melaxanthus*, Nyl., second camp (16,660); *Alectoria divergens*, Ach., second camp (16,660); *A. ochroleuca*, Nyl., second camp (16,660); *Lecidea geographica*, Fr. var., second camp (16,660); *Stereocaulon sp.?* second camp (16,660); *Gyrophora* or perhaps *Endocarpon sp.?* third camp (17,285); *Lecanora* (section *Squamaria*), second camp (16,660); *Lecanora*, section *Placodium*, second camp (16,660); and *L. subfusca*, L., foot of the Southern Walls (18,400). Mosses. *Andreæa striata*, Mitt.; *Brachymenium fusiferum*, Jaeg.; *Grimmia consobrina*, Kunze; *G. apocarpa*, Hedw.?; *G. fusco-lutea*, Hook.; and *Mielichhoferia longiseta*, C.M., all from the immediate vicinity of the second camp (16,550–16,750). Fern. *Polypodium pycnolepis*, Kze., in Vallon de Carrel (14,900). Grasses. *Festuca mollis*, Kth., east side, above Chuquipoquio (14,000); and *Poa sp.?* south side (15,000–15,500). Flowering plants. Labiatæ:—*Stachys repens*, M. & G., above Chuquipoquio (14,000). Scrophulariaceæ:—*Bartsia gracilis*, Benth., north-east side (13–14,000); *Calceolaria rosmarinifolia*, Lam., above Chuquipoquio (14,000); *Castilleja fissifolia*, L., south side (14,000–15,000). Gentianaceæ:—*Gentiana cerastioides*, H.B.K., north side (13,000–14,000); *G. cernua*, H. & B., south side (14,000–16,000); *G. rupicola*, H.B.K., south side (15,500–16,300); *G. sedifolia*, H.B.K., south side (15,500–16,000); and *Halenia gracilis*, Griseb., north-east side (13,000–14,000). Ericaceæ:— *Vaccinium epacridifolium*, Benth., north side (13,000–14,000). Compositæ:—*Achyrophorus Quitensis*, Sz. Bip., south side (15,500–16,300); *Baccharis* (*Loricaria*) *ferruginea*, Pers., Vallon de Carrel (14,000–15,000); *Bidens humilis*, H.B.K., south side (13,000–16,500); *Chuquiragua insignis*, H. & B., south side (14,000–15,000); *Culcitium nivale*, H.B.K., near second camp (15,500–16,300); *C. reflexum*, Kth., Vallon de Carrel (14,000–15,000); and *Werneria sp.?* south side (14,000–15,000). Valerianeæ:—*Phyllactis latifolia*, Spruce, north side (13,000–14,000); *P. inconspicua*, Wedd.? second camp (16,600); *Valeriana alyssifolia*, Kth., Vallon de Carrel (14,000–15,000); *V. microphyllæ* aff., south side (13,000–14,000); *Valeriana sp.?* south side (15,500–16,500). Ribesiaceæ:— *Ribes glandulosum*, R. & P., north-east side (14,000). Leguminosæ:—*Astragalus geminiflorus*, H. & B., south side (14,000–15,000); *Lupinus humifusus*, Benth., north-east side (13,000–14,000); *Lupinus sp.?* (13,000–14,000); *Lupinus sp.?* south side

matters which had been cut short in January, and in the afternoon we transferred ourselves to Camp 7. On the next day the baggage was despatched to Riobamba under the care of Louis; whilst I with Jean-Antoine and Campaña resumed the measurement on the High Road for 'a scale for Chimborazo'; carrying it up to the Tambo of Chuquipoquio, and thus completing our work amongst the Great Andes of the Equator.

(14,000–15,000); and *Vicia setifolia*, H.B.K., near Chuquipoquio (12,000–14,000). Geraniaceæ :—*Geranium diffusum*, H.B.K., Vallon de Carrel (16,000). Malvaceæ :—*Malvastrum phyllanthos*, Asa Gray, south side (14,000–16,500). Caryophyllaceæ :—*Cerastium glutinosum*, Kth., south and north-east sides (13,000–14,000); *Cerastium sp.?* south side (13,000–14,000); *Stellaria leptopetala*, Benth., near second camp (15,500–16,000). Cruciferæ :—*Draba grandiflora*, Hook. & Arn., fourth camp (14,360); *D. obovata*, Benth., near second camp, etc. (15,500–16,660); *Draba sp.?* south side (14,000–15,000); *Draba sp.?* near second camp (15,500–16,000). Ranunculaceæ :—*Ranunculus Peruvianus*, Pers., north side (13,000–14,000); *R. præmorsus*, Kth., near second camp, etc. (15,500–16,500).

Humboldt says in the pamphlet entitled *Notice de deux tentatives d'ascension du Chimborazo*, dated Berlin, Sept. 1836 (pub. at Paris in 1838), " Les derniers végétaux cryptogames que je recueillis furent le *lecidea atrovirens* (*lichen geographicus*, Web.) et une nouvelle espèce de *gyrophora* d'Acharius (*gyrophora rugosa*), à peu près à 2820 toises d'altitude. La dernière mousse, le *grimmia longirostris* croissait à 400 toises plus bas." Reckoning the toise at 6·3945 English feet, it appears that his highest Lichens came from 18,032, and the Moss from 15,475 feet.

For the Zoological results, the reader is referred to the *Supplementary Appendix*. The last thing obtained on Chimborazo (near Tortorillas) was the *Hylodes* with which my name is associated. This was another of the species that recurred at similar altitudes. It had previously been captured upon Pichincha, Cotocachi, and Altar.

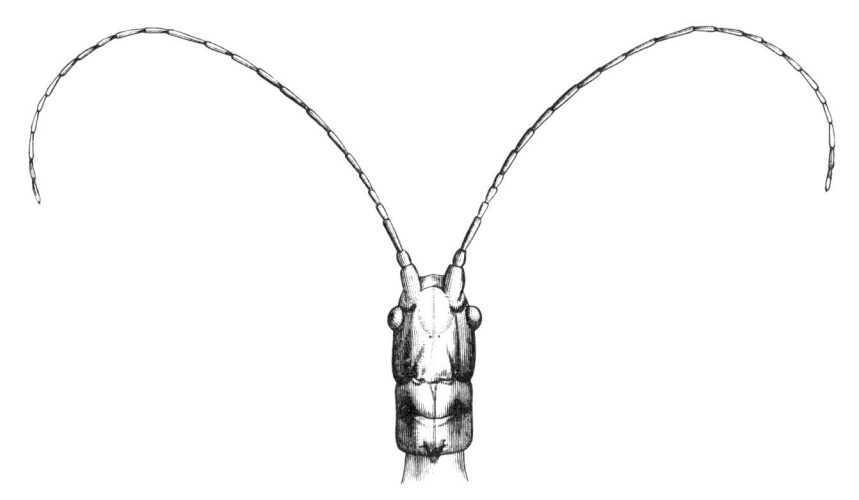

A PHASMA FROM LA DORMIDA, CAYAMBE.

CHAPTER XIX.

UPON SOME RESULTS OF THE JOURNEY.

In a very short time it was found that there were things to be *unlearned* as well as discovered in Ecuador. It had been supposed that the slopes of Chimborazo led continuously, without a break, down to the flat land bordering the shores of the Pacific [see p. 12]. I saw that this was not the case, and that an important range of mountains intervened between it and the Ocean. Next we ascertained that Chimborazo streamed with glaciers, although high authorities state that it has none; and in course of time it became apparent that the two "parallel Cordilleras," which according to geographers are the great feature of the country, do not exist.

The axis of the Andes of Ecuador, part of the backbone of South America, runs nearly north and south; and towards the western edge of the main chain there *is* a certain sequence of peaks more or less in a line with each other.[1] On the east of these summits there is a succession of basins,[2] of different dimensions

[1] See page 210, and my Route Map.
[2] See pages 85-6, 97, 105, 158-9, 167, 265, etc.

and at various elevations, and the nearest mountains on the eastern side occur at *irregular* distances. There is no such thing as one great valley in the interior of Ecuador. The mountains Pasochoa and Rumiñahui are the only two which lie *parallel* to the others on the western side.[1]

The main chain of the Andes was created by upheaval at some remote date, but no one can say when this movement occurred, or whether it was an affair of a year or was spread over thousands of years. All of the Great Andes of the Equator rise out of, or upon and above the main chain.[2] With the exception of Sara-urcu, they are all mountains of volcanic origin,[3] although they may not all have been active volcanoes. There will possibly be, for a long time to come, a diversity of opinions as to the manner of their formation. It seems to me probable that there were never many of these volcanoes in activity at any one moment. Some that are now extinct have evidently been alive; while others, like Pichincha and Tunguragua, are either dormant or are not perpetually in eruption. Cotopaxi and Sangai alone are in a state of constant activity, and these two mountains seem to be increasing their elevation.[4]

[1] The Pacific Range of Ecuador and the range running south from Chimborazo as far as the Rio Chanchan are, however, parallel to each other; and the course of the River Chimbo, from Guaranda to Chimbo, runs through a valley, speaking properly. I have already endeavoured to make it clear that this Pacific Range lies *outside* the main chain of the Andes. It has nothing to do with the "two parallel cordilleras."

[2] The elevation of the range in general, in Ecuador, although considerable, is not so great as it is farther to the south; and a railway might be carried there across the chain at a lower level than the Trans-Andean line which is at present being constructed to connect Buenos Ayres with Valparaiso.

[3] In Ecuador, the rocks that were previously at the surface are now almost entirely buried under lavas or volcanic-dusts, which have welled out of fissures or have been violently ejected.

[4] The excellent observers M. de la Condamine, and the Doctors Reiss & Stübel measured Cotopaxi and Sangai at an interval of 130 years. The former found the height of Cotopaxi was 18,865 feet, and Sangai 17,139 feet. The latter found the heights were 19,498 and 17,464 feet respectively.

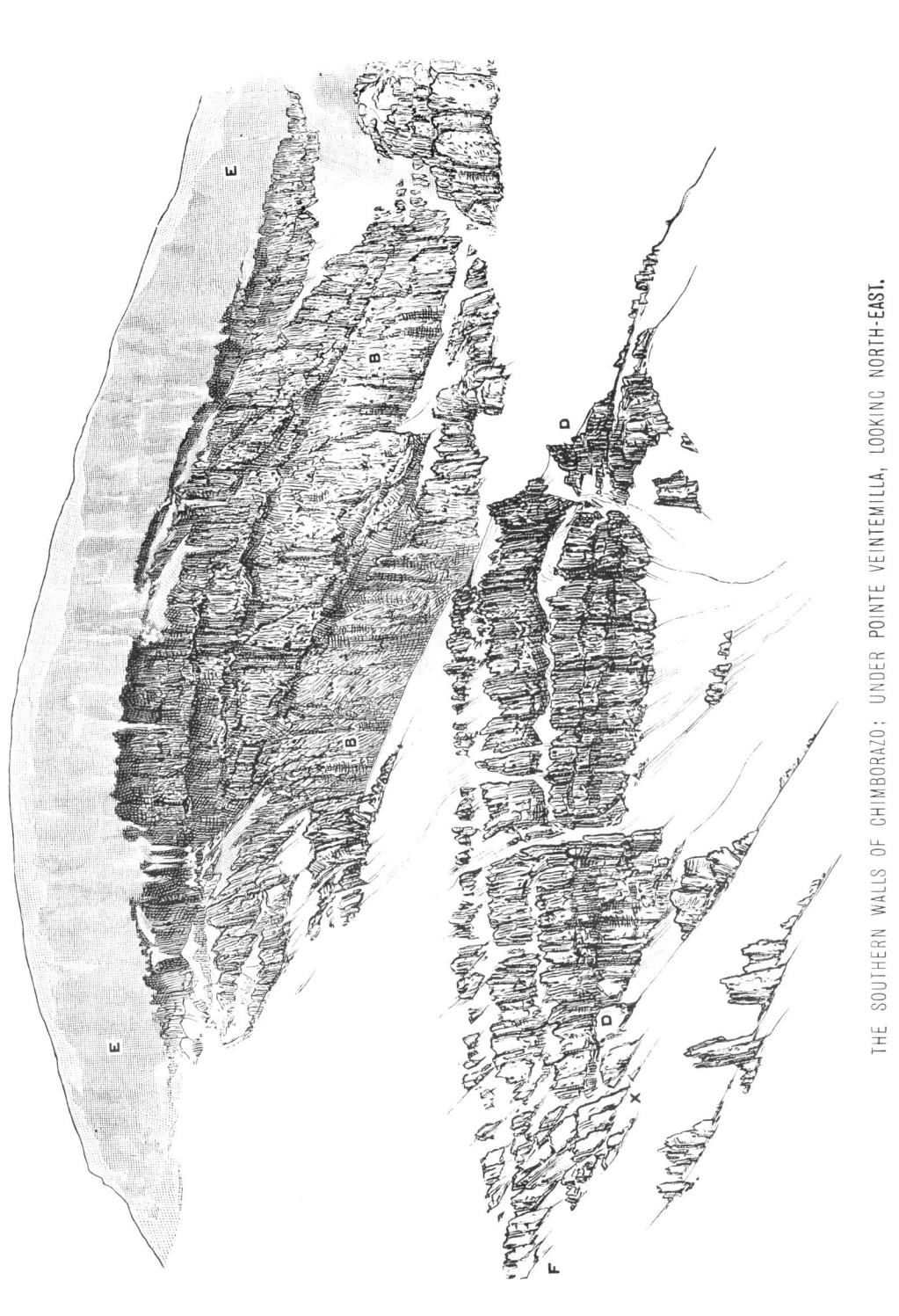

THE SOUTHERN WALLS OF CHIMBORAZO; UNDER POINTE VEINTEMILLA, LOOKING NORTH-EAST.

R. UPPER CLIFFS.   D. LOWER CLIFFS.   E. VERTICAL SECTION OF THE GLACIER ON THE SUMMIT.
F. HUMBOLDT AND BOUSSINGAULT'S HIGHEST?   X. LECANORA SUBFUSCA FOUND HERE.

CHAP. XIX. *CONFIGURATION OF THE ANDES OF ECUADOR.* 337

Of the extinct Volcanoes, Cayambe, Antisana and Chimborazo are the most important. There are lava-streams upon the flanks of all three mountains,[1] and I cannot doubt that they had craters of considerable size, though none can now be seen. The space at the summit of Antisana is sufficiently large to admit of one as great as that of Cotopaxi, and I think it may be assumed that under the snowy domes which now form the summits of Chimborazo there are rocky peaks which were formerly two of the highest points around the rim of a crater.

There are no records of eruptions of Chimborazo.[2] It must have been an extinct volcano for many ages. The complete burial of its crater, the thickness of the ice-cap at its summit and large size of its glaciers, the ruin and erosion of its lava-streams, and the height vegetation has attained upon its flanks are all indications that its activity ceased at a remote period. It is less regularly conical than Cotopaxi, Sangai or Tunguragua, and towards its summits has sheer cliffs,[3] that I have termed the Northern and Southern Walls, which it seems to me can only have been formed either by violent upheaval or by explosive blowing away of portions of the exterior of the cone. The Southern Walls are shewn in the illustrations facing pages 24, 64 and 76, and, more in detail, in the accompanying plate. They are in two series, B, B, and D, D.

[1] In the matter of lava-streams I differ from Boussingault, who says that none can be seen anywhere among the Volcanoes of Tropical America. "La masse du Chimborazo est formée par l'accumulation de débris trachytiques, amoncelés sans aucun ordre. Ces fragmens trachytiques, d'un volume souvent énorme, ont été soulevés à l'état solide; leurs angles sont toujours tranchans; rien n'indique qu'il y ait en fusion ou même un simple état de mollesse. *Nulle part, dans aucune des volcans de l'équateur, on n'observe rien qui puisse faire présumer une coulée de laves.*"—*Annales de Chimie et de Physique*, tome lviii, 2me série, p. 175, Paris, 1835.

I find this difficult to comprehend, as Boussingault visited Cotopaxi and the Hacienda of Antisana. See pages 138, 145, 187 and 189.

[2] "Chimboraço, Volcan (on ignore l'époque de son éruption)."—La Condamine in *Hist. de l'Acad. Royale des Sciences* (année 1746), Paris, 1751, pp. 650-1.

[3] There is some equally sheer cliff on the northern side of Cotopaxi, near the summit.

The latter stand in advance of the higher ones, and are passable at F ('the breach'), or may be skirted at the base. The upper cliffs B, B are unapproachable, on account of being crowned by glacier, which falls at intervals in tremendous avalanches, shaving the face of the rock. This ice-section (E, E), at the top of the cliffs, shews the thickness of the glacier on the summit of Chimborazo.

The faces of these precipices exhibit a large number of parallel bands (nearly horizontal in the lower series and distorted in the upper one) which are highly coloured, and upon the rare occasions that the cliffs are lighted by the sun they present a gay and attractive appearance. The highest strata of the upper series are black,[1] alternating with grey bands; warm grey, passing into strong red; black, changing into thin grey and yellow strata; warm grey again, passing into deep red; and, at the base, warm grey, alternating with thin strata of many colours, too numerous to recapitulate. The lower series commences at the top with a stratum of reddish-grey colour for about half the whole depth of the cliff; then a stratum of ashy grey, followed by a strong black band; indian red, succeeded by more black strata; and terminating at the base with a bed about 200 feet thick, of strongly reddish hue.

With the exception of the lowest rocks of the lower series, it is impossible to collect examples of these strata *in situ*, as the cliffs are well-nigh vertical; but specimens from all of the beds in the upper series (knocked off by the descent of the ice-avalanches) can be obtained on the surface of the Glacier de Débris, and they are found to be entirely volcanic products—principally andesitic lavas.[2] The colouring is superficial, the result of weathering, or decomposition. The natural colours of these rocks range from steel and iron-greys to purplish-black.

A great section of a somewhat similar nature was produced on

---

[1] It is not unlikely that this is the rock we obtained at 19,400 feet upon the first ascent. See pp. 67-8.

[2] Amongst these fragments on the glacier I found native sulphur.

the Island of Krakatoa by the blowing away of a portion of the cone during the convulsions which occurred in August, 1883;[1] and although it cannot be positively affirmed that the Southern Walls of Chimborazo have been fashioned in this way, one may go so far as to suggest that that which is known to have happened in the Straits of Sunda may also have occurred on the coast of the Pacific.

The relative situations of the Great Andes of the Equator will be seen by reference to the Route Map, where, for the first time, they are placed in the positions that they actually occupy. The Altitudes which were determined on my journey are arranged in a tabular form in Appendix A, in chronological order. The height of Chimborazo will probably possess more interest than any other for the majority of my readers. I give below the data which have been used in its computation, and a few remarks upon the previous determinations of its altitude by others. My *original* readings are given here (*not* reduced to 32° Faht.), and they were not taken until the attached thermometer had fallen to the temperature of the air. The Guayaquil barometer, it should be added, was 30 feet above the level of the sea.

Date.	Place.	Barometer.	Reading in inches.	Temp. of air and att. therm.
Jan. 4, 1880, 5.15 p.m.	Summit of Chimborazo	No. 558	14·100	21° Faht.
,, 6 p.m.	Guayaquil . . .	No. 554	29·892	85° ,,
Deduced altitude above the level of the sea, 20,545 feet.
July 3, ,, 1.40 p.m.	Summit of Chimborazo	No. 558	14·050	20° ,,
,, 2 p.m.	Summit of Chimborazo .	No. 558	14·028	15° ,,
,,	Mean of 11 a.m. & 6 p.m. Guayaquil	No. 554	30·021	75° ,,
Deduced altitude above the level of the sea, 20,461 feet.

Besides these two results (20,545 feet from the observations made on Jan. 4, and 20,461 feet from the 2 p.m. observations on July 3), Mr. Ellis has obtained a third one (20,489 feet) by

---

[1] A representation of this forms Plate 25 of the *Album* accompanying the interesting work *Krakatau*, by R. D. M. Verbeek, Brussels, 1885-6; and it has been reproduced in the *Report* of the Krakatoa Committee of the Royal Society, Lond. 1888, Pl. II.

employing the mean of the observations at 1.40 and 2 p.m. The altitude I adopt is the mean of his three results, namely 20,498 feet.

The height, however, which at the present time is accepted and quoted for Chimborazo is 21,425 feet. This altitude was deduced by J. Oltmanns (Professor of Astronomy at Berlin) from the observations of Alex. von Humboldt, who, after determining barometrically the elevation of Riobamba above the level of the sea, measured a base 1702 mètres long upon the outskirts of the town, and at one end of this base observed the angle of elevation of the apparent summit of the mountain. This measurement is referred to in Humboldt's *Recueil d'Observations Astronomiques*, etc., 4to, Paris, 1810, vol. 1, pp. lxxii-lxxiv of the *Introduction*, and the annexed diagram is projected from the data given in that work.[1] The line drawn from A to B represents his base, and *a* the position of the summit of Chimborazo. This figure shews more clearly than words the unsatisfactory nature of the data from which Prof. Oltmanns calculated the altitude.

Humboldt himself appeared to think it likely that there was some error in his observations; and he did so, doubtless, on account of the large difference that there was between the altitude which was deduced from his work and that which was obtained by La Condamine, who employed similar methods. The height of Chimborazo as determined by La Condamine was 3220 toises (= 20,592 feet). Juan and Ulloa (the Spanish officers who were associated with the French Academicians) in their book entitled *Observaciones Astronomicas y Phisicas hechas de orden de S. Mag. en los Reynos del Peru*, 4to, Madrid,

[1] The length of the base A B is stated to have been 1702·49 mètres; the angle A B *a*, 98° 34′ 50″; the angle *a* A B, 78° 16′ 20″; and the angle of elevation of the summit, seen from A, 6° 41′ 26″. This figure should be compared with fig. 6, Plate 1, in the *Recueil d'Observations Astronomiques*.

1748, p. 131, give 3380 toises (= 21,615 feet) as the height of Chimborazo. The French and Spanish observers, I believe, used the same data, and it is certain that either one or the other, or both, must have been in error in their calculations.[1]

The passage is given in the footnote in which Humboldt expresses a certain amount of doubt as to his own result.[2] In the various possible causes of error which he therein mentions, he omits to take into account:—1. The chance of error in the height of his base at Riobamba, and, 2. that neither the height nor the distance of a snowy dome can be determined with certainty unless a signal is placed upon it. The elevation he assigned to Riobamba was 9485 feet, which is 305 feet higher than the determination of Messrs. Reiss and Stübel, and 446 feet higher than my own.[3] It seems to me possible that there

[1] Although the height of Chimborazo deduced by Ulloa more nearly corresponded than La Condamine's with that obtained by Humboldt, the latter did not seem to put much confidence in it; for towards the end of his *Recueil d'Observations Astronomiques* (at p. 93 of the section entitled "*Nivellement barométrique*) there is the following amusing passage. "Lorsqu' Ulloa descendit dans les mines de Guanaxuato, il déduisit d'une mesure barométrique, que la mine de Valenciana avoit une profondeur de 1000 vares (838 mètres). L'inspecteur de la mine assura, et avec raison, que cette évaluation étoit du double trop forte ; le géomètre prétendit, de son côté, que son calcul barométrique ne laissoit pas de doute. Il est probable que le baromètre du savant voyageur s'étoit dérangé . . . On conçoit aisément que, depuis cette époque, les baromètres ne jouissent pas d'un grand crédit auprès du mineurs du Mexique."

[2] "Je n'ai pu, jusqu'à ce jour (1810), découvrir aucune cause d'erreur dans ma mesure du Chimborazo. Pour expliquer une différence de 100 toises de hauteur, il faudroit supposer ou que les angles des stations avec la cime a B A et a A B fussent faux de 10′·9, ou qu'on se fût trompé dans la mesure de la base de 91 mètres, ou que l'angle de hauteur pris en A fût trop grand de 21′ 58″. . . Je désire ardemment que, dans un pays où les lumières font des progrès si rapides, des hommes instruits répètent mes opérations sur le plateau de Tapia, pour qu'il ne reste aucun doute sur la véritable hauteur de la cime la plus élevée des Cordillères."—*Recueil d' Obs. Astron.*, vol. 1, p. lxxiv, *Introd.*

[3] The Ecuadorian altitudes which were deduced from the barometric observations of Humboldt are almost always *higher* (sometimes considerably higher) than those obtained from the barometric observations by Messrs. Reiss and Stübel, and by myself.

was a considerable initial error in the determination of the height of his base; and from simple inspection of the figure upon p. 340 it will be apparent that a very slight mistake in the identification of the true summit, at either of his stations A, B, would have produced a marked effect upon the distance of *a* from A B, and a serious error in the deduced value of the angle of elevation, which was calculated from the distance.

Humboldt's wish that his observations might be repeated has been fulfilled by his countrymen Messrs. Reiss and Stübel. In their *Alturas*, which were printed at Quito in 1873, the height of Chimborazo is stated to be (according to Dr. Reiss) 20,703 feet. By a private communication I know that these travellers adopted for this measurement similar methods to those which were employed by La Condamine and Humboldt.

There are therefore five different determinations of the height of Chimborazo, namely:—

La Condamine	20,592 feet.
Juan and Ulloa	21,615 ,,
Humboldt	21,425 ,,
Reiss and Stübel	20,703 ,,
Whymper	20,498 ,,

The first four of these were obtained by similar methods, and the fifth is derived from three observations of the mercurial barometer upon the summit of the mountain.

The order in which the Great Andes of the Equator should be placed (*so far as I am acquainted with them*) will be seen in the accompanying table. Several others, which are not included, should perhaps come before Pichincha. There was no opportunity of measuring the mountains of Llanganati [see pp. 97, 110], or the highest points in the range to the south of Chimborazo. Some of the loftiest peaks in the former group seemed to me to rise well *above* 16,000 feet, and the latter were not much inferior in elevation, although destitute of snow.

Name of Mountain.	ACADEMICIANS.		REISS & STÜBEL.		WHYMPER.	
	Toises.	Feet.	Mètres.	Feet.	Mètres.	Feet.
1. Chimborazo	3220	20,592	6310	20,703	6247	20,498
2. Cotopaxi	2950	18,865	5943	19,498	5978	19,613
3. Antisana	3020	19,313	5756	18,885	5893	19,335
4. Cayambe	3030	19,377	5840	19,161	5848	19,186
5. Altar	2730	17,458	5404	17,730	...	...
6. Sangai	2680	17,139	5323	17,464	...	...
7. Illiniza	2717	17,375	5305	17,405	...	...
8. Tunguragua	2620	16,755	5087	16,690	...	...
9. Carihuairazo	2450	15,668	5106	16,752	5034	16,515[1]
10. Sincholagua	2570	16,435	4988	16,365	...	...
11. Cotocachi	2570	16,435	4966	16,293	4968	16,301
12. Guagua-Pichincha	...	...	4787	15,706	4851	15,918
Rucu-Pichincha	2430	15,540	4737	15,542	...	...
13. Corazon	2470	15,796	4816	15,801	4838	15,871
14. Rumiñahui	...	...	4757	15,607	...	...
15. Sara-urcu	...	...	4800	15,749	4725	15,502

[1] Height of the middle peak of Carihuairazo.

The determinations of the Academicians are quoted from *Histoire de l'Académie Royale des Sciences* (année 1746), Paris, 1751, pp. 650-651; and those of Messrs. Reiss and Stübel are taken from their *Alturas tomadas en la Republica del Ecuador*, Quito, 1873.

The heights that are quoted for these mountains, as well as the other altitudes which are given in Appendix A, depend exclusively upon observations of Mercurial Barometers. The two 'Fortin's' which were used in the interior [see p. 33] were preserved intact to the end of the journey. The precautions that were taken to ensure their safety which have been mentioned upon pp. 54-5 would have been of little avail if they had not been supplemented by unceasing care on the part of Jean-Antoine Carrel, who took charge of them during the whole of the time we were amongst the mountains. When travelling over roads, or lower slopes where porterage could be obtained, he carried his 'babies' and nothing besides. Above the snow-line he was always encumbered with one, and sometimes with both of them, *in addition* to the matters which it was his proper business to transport; and the fact that he was always laden with 12½ or 25 lbs. *additional* weight must be taken into account if comparisons are instituted with his rates. The conservation of these instruments occupied the first place in the thoughts of every one during the whole of the time we were in the interior, as they were the Standards upon which everything depended.

The comparisons of the Aneroid Barometers which were made against the Mercurials whilst in the field are given in Appendix C; but the account of the subsequent investigations into the behaviour of Aneroids in general extends to too great length to be included in this volume, and is rendered in the pamphlet *How to use the Aneroid Barometer*.[1]

JEAN-ANTOINE AND THE BABIES.

---

[1] The following is a recapitulation of the principal points which have come out in the course of this enquiry.

1. All aneroids lose upon the mercurial barometer when submitted to diminished pressure. When diminished pressure is maintained continuously, the loss commonly continues to augment during several weeks, and sometimes grows to a very important amount. The most important part of any loss that will occur will take place in the first week. The loss which takes place in the first week is greater than in any subsequent one. A considerable part of the loss which takes place in the first week occurs in the first day. The loss may be traced in a single hour, and in successive hours upon aneroids with expanded scales. The amount of the loss which occurs is different in different instruments. The amount of the loss in any aneroid depends (*a*) upon the duration of time it may experience diminished pressure, and (*b*) upon the extent of the reduction in pressure.

2. When pressure is restored, all aneroids recover a portion of the loss which has previously occurred; and some, in course of recovery, gain more than they have

In Appendix E, a few remarks are made upon TEMPERATURES in Ecuador, and I refer here only to those which were experienced on Summits. If there had been a constant diminution of 1° Faht. for every 300 feet of ascent from the level of the sea, temperatures at the tops even of the *lowest* of the peaks we ascended would always

Date.	Mountain.	Height in Feet.	Temperature on Summit.	Temperature at Guayaquil.
1880.			Faht.	Faht.
Jan. 4 (5.15 p.m)	Chimborazo	20,498	21°	85° (6 p.m.)
Feb. 2 (1.15 ,,)	Corazon	15,871	37° – 43°	79° (11 a.m.)
,, 18 (6.20 a.m.)	Cotopaxi	19,613	21°	82° (,,)
Mar. 10 (10 – 11.40 a.m.)	Antisana	19,335	44° – 60°	80° (,,)
,, 23 (11.15 a.m.)	Pichincha	15,918	46°	80° (,,)
April 4 (10.45 – 11 a.m.)	Cayambe	19,186	32° – 41°	79° (,,)
,, 17 (1.30 – 2.40 p.m.)	Sara-urcu	15,502	43°·5 – 55°	80° (,,)
,, 24 (12 noon)	Cotocachi	16,301	36°	81° (,,)
June 29 (11 – 11.15 a.m.)	Carihuairazo	16,515	38° – 42°	74° (,,)
July 3 (1.40 – 2 p.m.)	Chimborazo	20,498	15° – 20°	74° (,,)

have been found well below the freezing-point. The above Table of Temperatures, 'in the shade,' shews those which were actually experienced.

previously lost. Minus index-errors are sometimes lessened, and plus index-errors are sometimes increased. The recovery is gradual, and commonly extends over a greater length of time than the period during which diminished pressure has been experienced. In aneroids which have been kept at diminished pressures for a considerable space of time [a week or upwards] the most important part of the amount that will be recovered will be regained in the first week. The greater part of the recovery of the first week is usually accomplished in the first day. The recovery in the first hour is almost always larger than that in any subsequent hour.

3. The errors which will probably be exhibited by aneroids during natural variations of pressure may be learned approximately by submitting them to artificially-produced variations of pressure; but the one-hour test which has heretofore been commonly applied for 'verification' is of little value except for determining errors of graduation, and the errors which will be exhibited at similar pressures *in a similar length of time*.

4. Comparisons of travellers' aneroids against the mercurial barometer at natural pressure, upon return to the level of the sea, after prolonged journeys in elevated regions, have not the value which is at present assigned to them.

5. Large reductions will have to be made in the heights of many positions which have been determined by aneroids.

In all cases they were higher than might have been expected. The excess is most marked in the three mountains which are situated farthest to the East, namely, Sara-urcu, Cayambe and Antisana; and this, it seems to me, can only be accounted for by supposing that the warm currents borne from the heated Amazonian basin, by the nearly constant easterly winds, are deflected rather abruptly upwards from their natural level, on approaching these mountain-barriers.

Upon a number of occasions, abrupt transitions of temperature occurred at our high camps, or whilst ascending still higher. Equally rapid changes are, however, unknown on the lower ground, and it is therefore obvious that the amount of ascent equivalent to a fall of 1° Faht. would have been found very variable if a number of *simultaneous* observations of temperature had been made at spots no great distance apart, placed on different levels.[1]

THE SNOW-LINE.—Those who are most conversant with snow-mountains generally speak with hesitation upon this subject. The difficulty consists in determining what 'the snow-line' really is, or should be considered. If it should be the very lowest point at which any large masses of snow are found permanently, many mountains would have to be classed as entering the snow-line which are not generally admitted to be within it. The quantity

---

[1] Thus, on July 3, 1880, at 5 p.m., on the north-western side of Chimborazo, at an elevation of 16,700 feet, temperature in the shade was 26°·5 Faht. At the same time, at Riobamba (9039 feet) it was 50° Faht. This gives a fall of 1° Faht. for every 326 feet of elevation.

On July 3, 1880, at 2 p.m., on the Summit of Chimborazo (20,498 feet), temperature was 15° Faht. On the same day, at 2.30 p.m., at Riobamba, it was 54°·72 Faht. (11° R.). This gives a fall of 1° Faht. for every 288 feet.

On this day (July 3, 1880), upon leaving camp (15,811 feet), at 5.15 a.m., temperature was 30° Faht. By 8.45 a.m. (at 18,900 feet), temperature in the shade had risen to 46° Faht. The sun had not at that time struck the western side of the mountain. Two hours later, when in the direct rays of the sun, the heat felt oppressive; and in another two hours there was a fall of at least 35° Faht. (from 50° to 15°). This abrupt drop was caused by the clouds of Volcanic Dust intercepting the rays of, and absorbing the heat radiated from the sun!

that should be found permanently upon any mountain to entitle it to be considered within the snow-line cannot be determined, and I see little utility in retaining a phrase which is incapable of definition, and is interpreted so variously. The following information is given from personal observation.

Range south of Chimborazo (15-16,000 feet). No permanent snow.

Chimborazo (20,498 feet). In January, little snow below 16,600 feet on the south side, but at that time it extended nearly one thousand feet lower on the E. and N. sides. In June-July there was deep snow as low as 15,600 feet on all these sides. At the same time, there was little snow below 16,700 feet upon the W. side.

Carihuairazo (16,515 feet). Very little snow below 15,000 feet in January, and much in June-July as low as 14,300 feet.

Corazon (15,871 feet). Much snow fell almost daily upon this mountain down to 14,500 feet, but there were no permanent snow-beds on the E. side, although there were some upon the W. side.

Atacatzo (14,892 feet). No permanent snow.

Pichincha (15,918 feet). The snow-beds were quite trifling in extent.

Cotocachi (16,301 feet). Permanent snow, in large beds, as low as 14,500 feet.

Imbabura (15,033 feet). No permanent snow.

Cayambe (19,186 feet). Scarcely any snow below 16,000 feet on the west side. Covered with snow at 15,000 feet on the eastern side.

Sara-urcu (15,502 feet). Snow fell daily upon this mountain lower than 14,000 feet, and was remaining permanently at about that elevation.

Antisana (19,335 feet). Permanently covered with snow at 16,000 feet on the western side. I am not able to speak about the eastern side.

Sincholagua (16,365 feet). Large beds of permanent snow as low as 15,300 feet.

Rumiñahui (15,607 feet). There was a small amount of permanent snow on the E., and none on the W. side.

Cotopaxi (19,613 feet). Snow fell frequently on Cotopaxi in February quite one thousand feet lower than it fell upon Chimborazo in January. It was remaining permanently on the western side at about 15,500 feet.

Llanganati group. Much snow below 16,000 feet.

Altar (17,730 feet). Many large snow-beds below 14,000 feet.

From examination of the above list, it will be seen that snow is in greater abundance upon the more easterly of the Great Andes of the Equator than upon the western ones; and is commonly found at lower levels upon the eastern than upon the western sides of the same mountains.

Previous travellers have said little or nothing about the GLACIERS of Ecuador,—in some cases, it may be, because they were unable to recognize glaciers when they saw them; or, in others, through not actually having seen any, owing to the prevalence of bad weather. Humboldt, in the passage that is given in the foot-note,[1] says that he did not see in the Tropics anything resembling the Glaciers of Switzerland; and Boussingault states that the *only* glacier he saw in Tropical America was upon the mountain Tunguragua. I have been somewhat exercised to account for these statements; and, from certain points of view, I still find them quite incomprehensible.[2]

Glaciers of large dimensions exist upon the Andes of the

[1] "Je n'ai rien vu sous les tropiques, ni à Quito, ni au Mexique, qui ressemble aux *glaciers* de la Suisse. J'avais pensé 1° que des causes météorologiques s'opposaient au changement des *névés* ou *glaciers* par l'absorption de l'eau qui pénètre et cimente les grains incohérents de grésil et les cristaux de neige ; 2° que les *coulées de neige*, source primitive de tout glacier, n'avaient pas lieu, lors même que la forme et la pente des vallées pouvaient favoriser leur descente, à cause du manque de volume et de poids de la neige *surincombante*. * * * M. Boussingault, que j'ai consulté sur l'existence des petits amas de neige et de grésil que les Indiens de Calpi m'avaient dit se trouver couverts de sables, bien au-dessous de la limite actuelle des neiges du Chimborazo, m'écrit : 'Je ne sais rien des *neiges* souterraines du Chimborazo, et je doute fort de leur existence ; mais au volcan de Tungurahua, nous avons rencontré, le colonel Hall et moi, à la hauteur de la ville de Quito (donc à peu près à 1500 toises de hauteur absolue) une masse énorme de neige endurcie, un véritable glacier comme ceux de la Suisse. C'est le seul *glacier* que j'aie vu en Amérique entre les tropiques.' "—*Asie Centrale*, par A. de Humboldt, vol. iii. pp. 264-266.

The above passage quoted from *Asie Centrale* (published in 1843) does not appear to harmonise with the following extract quoted from an article contributed by Boussingault to the *Annales de Chimie et de Physique*, published in 1835. "Je voulais contempler à mon aise, rassasier pour ainsi dire ma vue de ces *glaciers* majestueux qui m'avaient procuré si souvent les émotions de la science, et auxquels je devais bientôt dire un éternel adieu" (p. 151). Boussingault makes frequent reference to the *glaciers* in subsequent pages of the same article.

[2] See pp. 24, 32, and 77.

Equator. They attain their greatest size upon Antisana, Cayambe, and Chimborazo, and there are considerable ones upon Altar, Carihuairazo, Cotocachi, Illiniza, Sara-urcu, and Sincholagua.[1] The glaciers upon Antisana were thicker and the crevasses in them were larger than any we saw elsewhere. Upon Cayambe I counted twelve,[2] flowing from the central reservoir, all of which, according to the prevailing custom, might have had names bestowed upon them; and when making the circuit of Chimborazo in June-July, 1880, I noted the bearings of and named eleven which were entitled to be distinguished.[3] The one marked A is called Abraspungo; the next is dedicated to Mr. R. Spruce, whose admirable work in Ecuador (which, unfortunately, has permanently disabled him) has been very inadequately recognized; and the two following are named after the Doctors Reiss and Stübel. These are succeeded by the Glacier de Thielmann and the Glacier de Débris. The next one (G), named Tortorillas, is rather ill-defined; H and I are the Glaciers of Humboldt and Boussingault, and the most eastern one is consecrated to the assassinated President, Garcia Moreno.

In essential features the Glaciers of Ecuador do not differ from the Glaciers of the Alps, and in minor points they present little novelty. One has been noticed upon p. 198. Another was seen in the middle of the Glacier de Débris, namely, a *moulin*[4] in which the water flowed upwards instead of downwards; and not far from this I came upon a 'glacier-table,' a slab of rock three or four feet in diameter, which had attained an unusual height upon a slender

---

[1] There is also some very obscured glacier upon Cotopaxi. My glimpses of Quilindaña and Tunguragua were too slight to permit me to speak with certainty, but I *believe* that there are also glaciers upon those mountains.

[2] There are no doubt others upon Cayambe. I did not see its north and north-east sides.

[3] Of the northern side, through constant prevalence of bad weather, a clear view was not obtained.

[4] "Moulins are formed by deep cracks" (crevasses) "intersecting glacier rivulets. The water in descending such cracks scoops out for itself a shaft, sometimes many feet wide, and some hundreds of feet deep, into which the cataract plunges."—Tyndall's *Glaciers of the Alps*, 8vo, London, 1860, p. 424.

stem of ice, and then, instead of slipping off as is ordinarily the case, had gradually declined towards the west, bending the shaft which had formerly supported it into the form of a reversed ㄱ. The rock was touching the surface of the glacier, still adhering to the ice-pedestal; and this, although it had undergone crushing on the inner curve and *tension* on the outer side, *shewed no signs of fracture*.

BOTANY. — The collections which were formed were undertaken with the view of contributing to the knowledge of the Range in Altitude of species, and the remarks which follow have solely reference to the extreme upper range of species in Equatorial South America.

Examples of twenty Botanical *Orders* were obtained at 15,000 feet above the level of the sea and upwards, and twelve of these touched or exceeded the height of 16,000 feet. In the Tables upon pp. 352, 353 the altitudes are given, and the names of the species so far as they have been identified, of the representatives which attained the very greatest heights. These Tables, and the Zoological ones which follow, include only such species as were actually collected.

Species of fifteen *genera* of Lichens were collected in the interior of Ecuador,[1] out of which eight (those marked by asterisks in the footnote) were obtained at 15,000 feet or higher: examples of twenty-six *genera* of Mosses were collected,[2] twelve of which were found at 15,000 feet and upwards: while out of fifty-eight *genera* of Flowering Plants (collected exclusively in the interior), fifty-nine *species* came from 14,000 feet or higher, and of these thirty-five species reached or surpassed 15,000 feet, and twenty

---

[1] * *Alectoria, Bæomyces, Cladonia,* * *Gyrophora,* * *Lecanora,* * *Lecidea, Leptogium,* * *Neuropogon,* * *Parmelia, Physcia, Ramalina,* * *Stereocaulon, Sticta,* * *Umbilicaria,* and *Usnea.*

[2] * *Andreæa, Aneura,* * *Bartramia,* * *Brachymenium,* * *Brentelia,* * *Cryptopodium, Daltonia, Dicranum,* * *Didymodon,* * *Grimmia, Hypnum, Lejeunia, Macromitium, Metzgeria,* * *Mielichhoferia, Mnium, Neckera,* * *Orthotrichum, Plagiochila, Porotrichum,* * *Racomitrium, Rhizogonium, Sematophyllum,* * *Splachnobryum, Thuidium,* and * *Webera.*

species 16,000 feet, above the level of the sea. Including all Orders, forty-two *species* were taken at 16,000 feet or higher,[1] and almost all of these came either from Antisana or Chimborazo,[2] principally from the latter mountain, which even at the height of 17,000 feet has a large amount of soil free from snow.

One looks vainly amongst this flora for the brilliant clusters of gem-like flowers which are so conspicuous near the snow-line of the Alps. Yellows predominate in it, and they, like the other hues, are wanting in purity. The highest species, with few exceptions, were also found at considerably lower levels; and the plants which were taken at the greatest altitudes were generally solitary individuals, separated by long distances from their nearest relatives.

ZOOLOGY. — The Zoological collections also which were made in Ecuador were formed with the view of bringing together the species which range highest; but they were not so strictly limited as the Botanical ones, and, if time and opportunity had permitted, I should have endeavoured to have worked in a more comprehensive manner.

ANNELIDA. — Earthworms were not numerous anywhere at great elevations. The highest positions at which they were found were in the neighbourhood of our camp on Cayambe (14,760 feet), and upon the summit of Corazon (15,871 feet).[3]

[1] So far as I am aware, nothing has hitherto been obtained from the height of 16,000 feet in Equatorial America, except the Lichens mentioned in the note at the foot of p. 334, and, perhaps, the Moss to which reference is made at p. 76. The Saxifrage which was discovered by Boussingault upon his attempt to ascend Chimborazo in 1831, Humboldt says (*Aspects of Nature*, vol. 2, pp. 35-6), was found at 15,770 feet. "On the declivity of the Chimborazo the *Saxifraga Boussingaulti*, described by Adolph Brongniart, grows beyond the limit of perpetual snow on loose boulders of rock at 15,770 feet above the level of the sea, not at 17,000 as stated in two estimable English journals. The Saxifrage discovered by Boussingault is certainly, up to the present time, the highest known phænogamous plant on the surface of the earth."

[2] These will be found enumerated upon pages 199 and 333-4.

[3] *Rhinodrilus Ecuadoriensis* [see p. 112] will shortly be described by Dr. Benham in the *Annals and Magazine of Natural History*.

Order.	Name of Species.	Locality.	Altitude in feet.	By whom identified or described.
LICHENES	Lecanora subfusca, L.	Chimborazo (south side)	18,400	Prof. D. Oliver.
FUNGI	Cantharellus Whymperi	Pichincha (south-west side)	15,300	Messrs. Massee & Murray.
MUSCI	Grimmia ovata, Web. & Mohr.	Cotocachi (summit of)	16,300	Mr. Antony Gepp.
Do.	G. apocarpa, Hedw. ?	Carihuairazo (summit of)	16,515	Do.
Do.	G. consobrina, Kunze	Chimborazo (south side)	16,660	Do.
Do.	G. fusco-lutea, Hook.	Do. do.	16,660	Mr. G. Mitten.
Do.	Brachymenium fusiferum, Jaeg.	Do. do.	16,660	Mr. Antony Gepp.
Do.	Andreæa striata, Mitt.	Do. do.	16,660	Do.
Do.	Mielichhoferia longiseta, C. M.	Do. do.	16,660	Mr. G. Mitten.
LYCOPODIACEÆ	Lycopodium Saururus, L.	Antisana (15-16,000), Corazon	15,871	Mr. William Carruthers.
FILICES	Polypodium pycnolepis, Kze.	Chimborazo (south side)	14,900	Do.
GRAMINEÆ	Trisetum Andinum, Benth.	Cotocachi (summit of)	16,300	Mr. A. B. Rendle.
Do.	Deyeuxia ?	Do. do.	16,300	Do.
CYPERACEÆ	Carex Jamesoni, Boott, var.	Sincholagua (west side)	14,500	Do.
LABIATÆ	Stachys repens, M. & G.	Chimborazo (south-east side)	14,000	Mr. James Britten.
SCROPHULARIACEÆ	Castilleja fissifolia, L.	Do. (south side)	15,000	Do.
GENTIANACEÆ	Gentiana rupicola, H. B. K.	Do. do.	16,300	Do.
Do.	G. cernua, H. & B.	Do. do.	16,000	Do.
Do.	G. sedifolia, H. B. K.	Do. do.	16,000	Do.
ERICACEÆ	Vaccinium penæoides, H. B. K.	Antisana (west side)	15,800	Do.
COMPOSITÆ	Achyrophorus, near setosus, Wedd.	Do. do.	16,000	Do.
Do.	A. Quitensis, Sz. Bip.	Chimborazo (south side)	16,300	Do.
Do.	Culcitium reflexum, Kth.	Antisana (west side)	15,800	Do.
Do.	C. nivale, H. B. K.	Chimborazo (south side)	16,300	Do.

CHAP. XIX.   BOTANICAL HIGHEST-POINT TABLE.

Order.	Name of Species.	Locality.	Altitude in feet.	By whom identified.
COMPOSITÆ	*Loricaria ferruginea*, Pers.	Antisana (west side)	15,800	Mr. Jas. Britten.
Do.	*Werneria sp.*	Corazon (summit of)	15,871	Do.
VALERIANEÆ	*Valeriana Bonplandiana*, Wedd.	Cotopaxi (west-north-west side)	14,500	Do.
Do.	*V. alyssifolia*, Kth.	Chimborazo (south side)	14,700	Do.
Do.	*Phyllactis inconspicua*, Wedd.	Do. do. (north-east side)	16,600	Do.
RIBESIACEÆ	*Ribes glandulosum*, R. & P.	Do. (north-east side)	14,000	
ONAGRACEÆ	*Fuchsia Loxensis*, H.B.K.	Corredor Machai	12,779	
LEGUMINOSÆ	*Lupinus microphyllus*, Desv.	Antisana (west side)	14,500	
Do.	*Astragalus geminiflorus*, H.B.K.	Chimborazo (14-15,000) and Antisana	14,800	
Do.	*Lupinus nubigenus*, H. & B.	Antisana (west side)	15,000	
GERANIACEÆ	*Geranium diffusum*, H.B.K.	Chimborazo (south side)	16,000	
MALVACEÆ	*Malvastrum phyllanthos*, Asa Gray	Antisana (15,500), Chimborazo	16,500	⎫
Do.	*M. Pinchinchense*, Asa Gray	Antisana (west side)	16,000	⎬ Mr. E. G. Baker.
HYPERICINEÆ	*Hypericum* (*Brathys*) *strutheolæfolium*, Juss.	Road to the Great Arenal	12,000	⎭
CAROPHYLLACEÆ	*Cerastium glutinosum*, Kunth.	Chimborazo (north-east side)	14,000	
Do.	*Cerastium ?*	Antisana (west side)	15,000	
Do.	*Arenaria dicranoides*, H.B.K.	Corazon (summit of)	15,871	
Do.	*Stellaria leptopetala*, Benth.	Altar (13,000), Chimborazo	16,600	
CRUCIFERÆ	*Draba grandiflora*, Hook. & Arn.	Chimborazo (north-west side)	14,360	
Do.	*D. imbricata*, C. A. Mey.	Corazon (summit of)	15,871	
Do.	*D. arctioides*, H.B.K.	Antisana (west side)	16,000	
Do.	*D. obovata*, Benth.	Corazon (15,871), Chimborazo	16,660	
RANUNCULACEÆ	*Ranunculus Peruvianus*, Pers.	Chimborazo (14,000), Antisana	15,000	
Do.	*R. præmorsus*, Kth.	Chimborazo (south side)	16,500	

MYRIOPODA.—Amongst the species of Centipedes which were obtained in Ecuador, two, belonging to the genus *Newportia*, are considered new by Mr. R. I. Pocock; and have been described by him under the names *N. monticola* and *N. dentata* in the *Annals and Magazine of Natural History* for August, 1890. The former of these came from La Dormida, Cayambe (11,800 feet), and the latter from the Seventh Camp on Chimborazo (12,000 feet). Two of the others, namely, *Otistigma scabricauda* (Humb. & Sauss.), and *Scolopocryptops Mexicanus*, Humb. & Sauss., have a rather wide range. The first-named was obtained at various localities between 8500-12,000 feet, and the other was found nearly everywhere *in the interior* up to 13,300 feet. It was taken at Tortorillas (Chimborazo), at the Hacienda of Antisana, and at many intermediate points.[1] Only one species of Millipede was seen in the interior, namely, *Spirobolus spinipodex*, Karsch, and this was found as high as 12,000 feet on Pichincha, and from 12,000 to 13,000 feet on the south side of Chimborazo. Another Millipede, *? Spirostreptus æquatorialis*, Porath, was taken on the banks of the Guayas, at Guayaquil.

COLEOPTERA.—Descriptions of 104 new species, by Messrs. H. W. Bates, D. Sharp, H. S. Gorham, A. S. Olliff and M. Jacoby will be found at pp. 7-88 in the *Supplementary Appendix*. The number of beetles obtained on this journey which, thus far, have been identified or described amounts to two hundred and six.

ORTHOPTERA.—The whole of this collection remains undescribed. Leaping Orthoptera were found very numerous up to the height of 12-13,000 feet, and upon Chimborazo were obtained in the Vallon de Carrel at 16,000 feet. Earwigs were not generally abundant in the

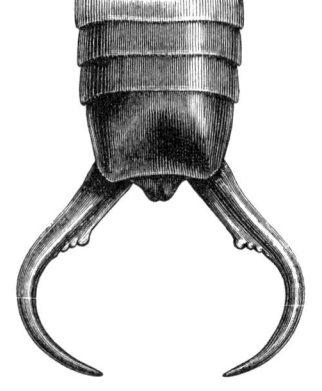

FORCEPS OF AN EARWIG FROM CAYAMBE, ENLARGED FOUR DIAMETERS.

[1] I understand from Mr. Pocock that this is a Mexican species, and is common in the West Indies and in Brazil.

interior, and it was a surprise to find them ranging so high as the Sixth Camp on Chimborazo (13,353 feet), and up to 14,000 feet on Cayambe. The species on the former mountain was just under one-half of an inch in length, and an enlarged Figure of it is given herewith, to assist in its future identification. The Cayambe species was one inch in length, with unusually large forceps. From the low country I have a species one inch and a half in length.

Examples of the very curious insects called *Phasmas* were taken on the Plain of Tumbaco, in the basin of Machachi, at La Dormida, Cayambe, and as high as 13,000 feet (in the woods) on Pichincha. Their close resemblance to sticks and twigs causes them to be readily overlooked, and many natives in the interior had never seen them. They have, however, the local name *Caballo de palo*.

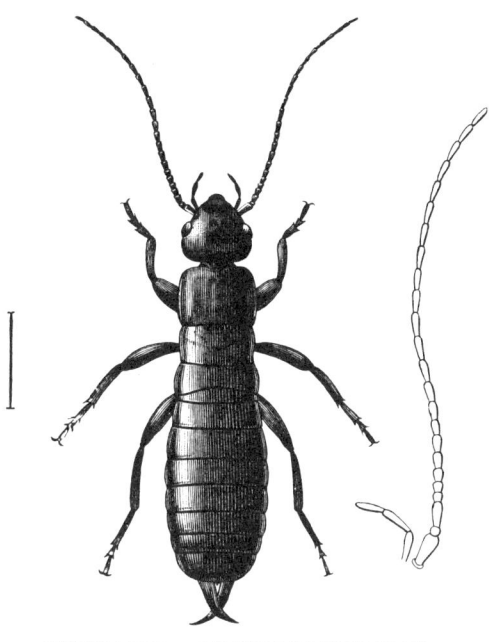

EARWIG FROM 13,353 FEET ON CHIMBORAZO.

NEUROPTERA.—Dragon-flies and May-flies were numerous in some parts of the interior, especially in the basin of Machachi. The greatest elevation at which they were *obtained* was on the track from Machachi to Pedregal (the pass between Pasochoa and Rumiñahui). Dragon-flies were *seen* higher than 12,000 feet on Pichincha and Cotocachi.

HYMENOPTERA.—The Ants alone have been worked out,—by Mr. Peter Cameron; whose contribution will be found at pp. 89-98 of the *Supplementary Appendix*. The 'set' specimens of the remainder, have been compared with the collections in the British (Natural History) Museum, and it is found that the following families and genera are included amongst them.

The *Tenthredinidæ* are represented by a species of *Strongylogaster*.

There are several species of *Ichneumonidæ*, apparently belonging to the genera *Ichneumon, Mesostenus, Ophion, Hemiteles, Cryptus, Echthrus*, and *Lissonota* (?).

There is a single small species belonging to the family *Chrysididæ*.

The *Dorylidæ* are represented by a single species, apparently belonging to *Labidus*.

In *Scoliidæ* there are three handsome species of *Dielis*.

In *Pompilidæ* several species belonging to the genera *Pompilus* and *Pepsis* were obtained.

In *Sphegidæ* there are two species of *Sphex*.

The *Vespidæ* are represented by species of *Polistes* and *Polybia*.

The greater part of the collection, however, consists of *Apidæ* (Bees), and the species obtained appear to belong to the following genera: *Megacilissa, Halictus, Ceratina, Melissodes* (?), *Eucera* (?), *Anthophora, Megachile, Xylocopa, Euglossa, Eulema, Bombus, Tetrapedia*, and *Trigona*. Among these, a black and white *Bombus*, closely resembling a Chilian species, is particularly common.

The species that are believed to come under *Dielis* include the formidable insect which is figured upon p. 96 under the nickname of "the Bishop." This seemed to be very widely distributed. It was obtained at various places between 7500 - 11,000 feet, and was seen as high as 12,000 feet. Another large and equally stinging *Dielis* was taken by myself on the Plain of Tumbaco, but was seen there only. Two large and beautiful species which are believed to come under *Pepsis* were captured between 11-12,000 feet on Pichincha, at 12,000 feet on Illiniza, and at a similar altitude upon Cotocachi. These four above-mentioned insects were the largest of the Hymenoptera taken anywhere in Ecuador. Several other species were obtained as high as 12,000 feet, and two at greater elevations, namely, an *Ichneumon* in the neighbourhood of the Hacienda of Antisana (13,300 feet), and an *Ophion* near Tortorillas, Chimborazo (13,300 feet). None of the Hymenopterous insects made themselves objectionable. We were stung by them only when their liberty was interfered with.

LEPIDOPTERA. — I am greatly indebted to Messrs. Godman & Salvin for having examined the BUTTERFLIES [see *Supp. App.* pp. 96-110]. Twenty-nine species were obtained from 7300 feet upwards. Two of these, namely, *Colias dimera*, Doubl. & Hew., and *Pieris xanthodice*, Lucas, are exceedingly numerous in the interior of Ecuador, and the latter species attains a greater range in altitude [from below 9000 feet to above 15,000 feet] than I observed in the case of any other Butterfly.[1]

PIERIS XANTHODICE, LUCAS.

The MOTHS have undergone a preliminary examination at the hands of Mr. H. Druce, who recognizes the following 23 genera.

Agrotis (7 - 11,800 feet).
Arctia (9800).
Azelina (1500).
Castina (3 - 4000).
Cidaria (12,500 - 13,300).
Charidea (3 - 4,000).
Crambus (9 - 10,000).
Dariza (13,300).
Dolecta (9000).
Endrobia (9200).
Epiolus (11,800).

Erebus (0 - 9800).
Eupyra (3 - 8500).
Eurimene (11,800).
Halsidota (10,000 - 11,800).
Leptosphetta (3 - 4000).
Lophocampa (8500).
[2] *Margaronia* (level of sea).
[2] *Opisogonia* (11,500 - 12,000).
Sangala (3 - 8500).
[2] *Scordylia* (12,350 - 13,300).
[2] *Scotosia* (8000 - 8500).

Semeopus (9200).

There are probably species of not fewer than 13 other genera in the collection.

[1] This Butterfly, I am informed by Messrs. Godman & Salvin, has a wide range *in latitude* in the Andes. [2] Caught in the daytime.

Thirty-five species were captured at or above 8500 feet. The largest of the whole has been identified by Mr. Druce as *Erebus odora*, Lin. Of the three examples which were obtained, two—a male and a female—were brought in alive by my young friends at Machachi (9800). The third was secured upon the homeward voyage, on the Pacific Steam Navigation Company's SS. *Ilo*, about 100 miles south of Panama. I noticed this moth, careering about the ship, twenty-four hours before it was taken. Some of the crew said that it flew on board while we were at sea, but it seems to me more probable that it came to us while the *Ilo* was lying in the Guayaquil river. One of the Machachi specimens measures $7\frac{1}{4}$ inches across the wings. All three examples were powerful and tenacious of life, and this moth is also exceptional in its great range in altitude,—having been taken, as I have stated above, at the level of the sea, and nearly 10,000 feet higher.

The species which were secured at the greatest heights have not been determined—even generically. Amongst others may be noted a beautiful pure white moth, with wings of satin-like texture, which was taken at about 12,000 feet, in the daytime, on the eastern slopes of Pichincha. A Figure of this is annexed, of the natural size. Another, at first sight not very dissimilar in appearance, but of smaller size, and having a suspicion of golden colour on the otherwise pure white upper wings, was captured at our camp on Cotocachi (14,500 feet), in the dusk. The loftiest position at which we actually obtained moths was on the very highest point of Guagua Pichincha (15,918 feet). A rather numerous

MOTH FROM 12,000 FEET ON PICHINCHA.

company was fluttering about the summit ridge. This, the highest moth obtained, was also the smallest taken anywhere in Ecuador.

DIPTERA.—The Diptera as a whole have not been examined, but I have had the advantage of submitting some sections to Baron C. R. Osten Sacken, who has recognised amongst them species of the following genera.

MOTHS FROM 14,500 FEET ON COTOCACHI, AND SUMMIT OF PICHINCHA.

Sciara, a broad-winged species of a South-American and Mexican type, like *Sc. Americana*, Wied.

Plecia, a small black species. Another larger and more slender species (Cotocachi, 11-13,000 feet) may perhaps belong to the genus *Spodius*, Lw. (*Hesperinus*, Walk.) which has been found in the British possessions of North America, in the higher regions of the Rocky Mountains, and also in Eastern Europe.

Dilophus, a single specimen of a small species of very ordinary appearance.

Bibio, male specimens of a black species of ordinary appearance.

Pachyrrhina, a couple of specimens.

Tipula, four or five species; one of them from La Dormida, Cayambe (11,800 feet), with the knot-like swellings on the joints of the antennæ, peculiar to some South-American and Mexican species.

Dicranomyia, a male specimen, camp on Cayambe (15,000 feet).

Rhyphus, a single specimen, with pretty variegated wings.

Tabanus, a single specimen of a small, inconspicuous species.

Chrysopila, a single specimen of the usual type, with the golden pubescence.

Odontomyia, ordinary type.

Empis, several specimens of a small black species from Antisana, and La Dormida, Cayambe.

Asilus, a small gray species, represented by a couple of specimens.

Eristalis. I could distinguish three species,—one with a gray transverse band on the thorax, not unlike the *E. albiceps*, Macq., from the southern United States, or the *E. seniculus* from Cuba.

Mesograpta (an exclusively American genus), a couple of species of ordinary appearance.

Allograpta, a single specimen may belong to this genus.

Volucella, two specimens of medium size, the body dark brownish violet.

Tachinidæ, abundantly represented, as might be expected from an American mountain-fauna; among them several *Dejeaniæ*, with black or rufous hairs and spines, the latter very like the species common in the Rocky Mountains.

Rather numerous *Muscidæ* and *Anthomyidæ*, some of them resembling European species, and among them the genuine *Musca domestica*.

A small *Ortalid* (*Euxesta ?*), some *Drosophilæ*, a *Sapromyza*, a *Calobata*, and a *Tæniaptera* conclude the series.

Some of the Diptera were the only insects in the interior that were aggressive. There were several species of Flies on the Quito Road that assailed us wantonly and pertinaciously. Above 7000 feet, Musquitoes were found only at one place (and not in a situation where there seemed to be any special reason for their location, though there must have been one), namely, upon the road between Penipe and the Hacienda of Candelaria, a little below the latter place, at about 9000 feet. The members of this colony were energetic, and attacked us with spirit and determination. Musquito nets were not *necessary* anywhere in Ecuador, although at some places (Bodegas de Babahoyo, for example) they would have been useful.

ARACHNIDA.—The Scorpions have been identified by Prof. E. Ray Lankester and Mr. R. I. Pocock, but the major part of this collection has not been worked out. Spiders were found on the summits of Corazon and Pichincha, and at many other nearly equally elevated positions. The legions which swarmed upon the slopes below indicate that entomological food was in abundance; and I do not doubt that there were, even in the close vicinity of perpetual snow, multitudes of very minute insects that gave them sustenance.

CRUSTACEA. — References to the few species which were met with in Ecuador will be found at pp. 121-127 of the *Supplementary Appendix*. The Amphipod (*Hyalella inermis*, S. I. Smith) to which I was introduced at Machachi [see p. 118] was subsequently taken in pools round about the Hacienda of Antisana (13,300 feet), and no Amphipod appears to have been obtained hitherto elsewhere at so considerable an elevation. The annexed Figure is magnified ten diameters.

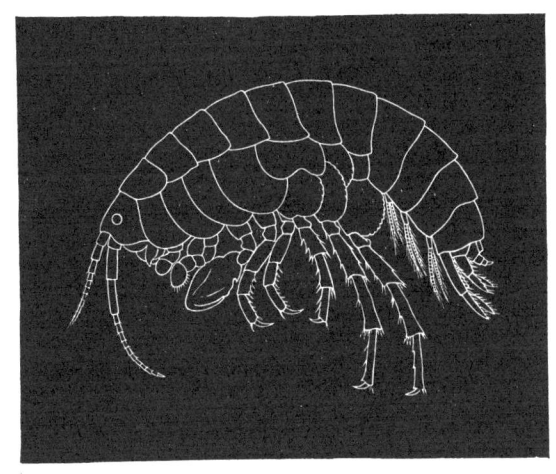

HYALELLA INERMIS, S. I. SMITH (9800-13,300 FEET).

In the Tables upon pp. 362, 363, a first attempt is made to shew at a glance the highest points which are attained in Ecuador by various forms of animal life. They include two 'stragglers,' namely, the small Bug that has been referred to the genus *Emesa* [p. 134], which was captured on the *southern* side of Illiniza, on snow at 16,500 feet; and a Fly, that Baron Osten Sacken identifies as belonging to the genus *Tanypus*, which was taken, on snow, at 16,200 feet on the *northern* side of the same mountain. These insects, doubtless, had been carried by wind away from their usual haunts. The situations where they were found could not have been their natural dwelling-places.

While forming these collections I was led to remark the frequency with which closely similar forms *recurred* at similar altitudes, upon mountains often long distances apart. This was observed in regard to things living *in* the soil, as well as in respect to winged insects of roving habits. It was not unusual to see Butterflies, apparently of the same species, at closely similar altitudes upon widely separated mountains. This was the case with a *Lycæna*

	Name of Species.		Locality.	Altitude in feet.	By whom identified or described.
ANNELIDA (Earthworm)	*Rhinodrilus Ecuadoriensis*	n. sp.	Cayambe (south-west side)	14,760	Dr. W. B. Benham.
MYRIOPODA (Centipede)	*Scolopocryptops Mexicanus*, Humb. & Sauss.		Chimborazo (south side)	13,300	Mr. R. I. Pocock.
COLEOPTERA (Carabidæ)	*Colpodes megacephalus*	n. sp.	Pichincha (on summit-ridge)	15,600	Mr H. W. Bates.
Do. do.	*C. diopsis*	n. sp.	Corazon (on actual summit)	15,871	Do.
Do. do.	*C. oreas*	n. sp.	Chimborazo (west side)	15,800	Do.
Do. do.	*Bembidium Andinum*	n. sp.	Do. do.	15,800	Do.
Do. (Otiorrhynchidæ)	*Helicorrhynchus vulsus*	n. gen.	Do. do.	16,000	Mr. A. Sidney Olliff.
Do. do.	*Naupactus parvicollis*	n. sp.	Do. do.	15,800	Do.
Do. (Curculionidæ)	*Amathynetes alticola*	n. gen.	Do. do.	15,800	Do.
Do. do.	*Macrops cœlorum*	n. sp.	Do. do.	16,000	Do.
Do. do.	*Erirrhinoides distinctus*	n. sp.	Do. do.	15,800	Do.
ORTHOPTERA (Forficula)	Not identified		Cayambe (south-west side)	14,000	
Do. (Blatta)	Do.		Valley of Collanes, Altar	12,500	
Do. (Saltatoria)	Do.		Chimborazo (west side)	16,000	
Do. (Phasma)	Do.		Pichincha (south side)	13,000	
NEUROPTERA (Dragonflies)	Do.		Between Machachi & Pedregal	11,500	
HYMENOPTERA (Formicidæ)	*Pheidole monticola*	n. sp.	Panecillo (top of), Quito	10,000	Mr. Peter Cameron.
Do. (Ichneumonidæ)	*Ichneumon* ? sp.		Hacienda of Antisana	13,300	Mr. W. F. Kirby.
Do. do.	*Ophion* ? sp.		Tortorillas, Chimborazo	13,200	Do.

ZOOLOGICAL HIGHEST-POINT TABLE.

	Name of Species.	Locality.	Altitude in feet.	By whom identified or described.
LEPIDOPTERA (Butterflies)	*Colias alticola* . . . n. sp.	Antisana (west side)	16,000	Messrs. Godman & Salvin.
Do. (Moths)	Not identified	Pichincha (on actual summit)	15,918	
RHYNCHOTA	*Emesa ? sp.*	Illiniza (south side)	16,500	Mr. W. L. Distant.
Do.	*Neomiris præcelsus* . . n. gen.	Hacienda of Antisana	13,300	Do.
DIPTERA	*Tanypus ? sp.*	Illiniza (north side)	16,200	Baron C. R. Osten Sacken.
Do.	Not identified	Carihuairazo (south-west side)	15,800	
Do.	Do.	Corazon (on actual summit)	15,871	
ARACHNIDA (Scorpions)	*Teuthraustes atramentarius*, Simon	Do. (east side)	12,000	Mr. R. I. Pocock.
Do. (Spiders)	Not identified	Do. (on the actual summit)	15,871	
Do. do.	Do.	Chimborazo (west side)	15,811	
Do. do.	Do.	Do. (south side)	15,000	
Do. do.	Do.	Pichincha (on actual summit)	15,918	
CRUSTACEA (Isopoda)	*Metoponorthus pruinosus*, Brandt	Hacienda of Antisana	13,300	Rev. A. E. Eaton.
Do. (Amphipoda)	*Hyalella inermis*, S. I. Smith	Do.	13,300	Rev. T. R. R. Stebbing.
REPTILIA (Lacertilia)	*Liocephalus trachycephalus* (A. Dum.)	La Dormida, Cayambe	11,805	Mr. G. A. Boulenger.
Do. (Ophidia)	*Liophis alticola* (Cope)	Plain of Tumbaco	8,500	Do.
BATRACHIA	*Hylodes Whymperi* . . n. sp.	Tortorillas, Chimborazo	13,200	Do.
Do.	*Nototrema marsupiatum* (Dum. & Bibr.)	Hacienda of Antisana	13,300	Do.
FISH	*Cyclopium cyclopum*, Humboldt	Machachi (neighbourhood of)	9,800	Dr. F. Day (the late).

that has not been described, which was taken at 11-12,500 feet on Pichincha and thirty-six miles away at 12,000 feet on Cotocachi, and was not seen elsewhere. But, for the most part, butterflies which were taken at considerable elevations were also found on the connecting, lower ground. Thus, *Pieris xanthodice*, Lucas, though captured so high as 14,000 and 15,000 feet, was found everywhere in the intervening basins; and as, even had this not been so, it would need little effort for them to pass from one mountain to another, and further as they may sometimes suffer involuntary transportation, no particular stress can be laid upon such instances of *occasional* recurrence at similar elevations.

One Butterfly, however, was exceptional in being found upon nearly all the mountains we visited, in numbers, and seemed to be established between the elevations 12,000-16,000 feet. This is described by Messrs. Godman & Salvin, at p. 107 of the *Supplementary Appendix*, as *Colias alticola*. It was first obtained near Tortorillas, Chimborazo (13,300 feet), and was seen in the Vallon de Carrel as high as 16,000 feet. When we were encamped upon Antisana it attracted attention by the great elevation above the level of the sea at which it was flying (16,000 feet). It was seen subsequently upon all the mountains we visited (except Sara-urcu) between the elevations of 12-15,000 feet, and was captured at 12,000 feet on Pichincha, at 13,000 feet on Cayambe, and at 15,000 feet on the western side of Chimborazo, and was never either taken or seen in the basins between these mountains.

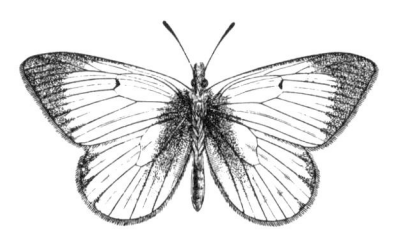

COLIAS ALTICOLA, GODMAN & SALVIN.

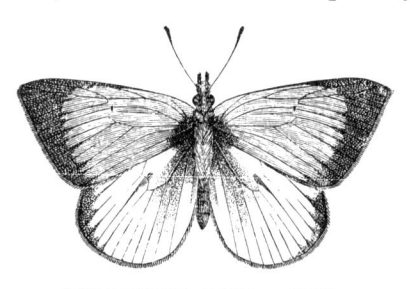

COLIAS DIMERA, DOUBL. & HEW.

The only other species with which this could have been confused is represented in the annexed Figure. This, the most common butterfly in the interior of Ecuador, is found from 7200-11,000 feet, and is sometimes met with so high as 12-13,000 feet. The range in altitude of *Colias dimera* therefore overlaps that of *C. alticola* ; but while the former species is distributed nearly everywhere in the interior and *occasionally* reaches a considerable height, the latter affects great elevations and is not seen on the lower ground. Inasmuch as *Colias alticola* is well established on the upper slopes of the Great Andes of the Equator, and is the only one ranging up to perpetual snow, it seems probable that it was 'the yellow butterfly' which was observed by Bonpland on Chimborazo, in 1802 [see p. 114]. So far as is known, it attains a higher elevation than any other Butterfly on either of the two American Continents.

The recurrence of species whose habits are in-terranean, at great heights, long distances apart, is perhaps more noteworthy than the case which has just been given of a butterfly domiciled in insular situations. The following beetles were found at the localities which are mentioned, and only at those places.

Species.	Localities.	Approximate distance apart in miles.
Colpodes diopsis, Bates	Summit of Corazon 15,870 Pichincha . . 14-15,000	24
C. megacephalus, Bates	Hac. of Antisana 13,300 Cayambe . . . 12-14,000 Pichincha . . 15,600	36
C. orthomus, Bates	Hac. of Antisana 13,300 Cayambe . . . 12-15,000	40
C. steno, Bates	Pichincha . . 14-15,500 Cayambe . . . 15,000	42
Helicorrhynchus vulsus, Olliff	Pichincha . . 15,500 Chimborazo . . 15,800-16,000	94
Macrops coelorum, Olliff	Pichincha . . 15,500 Chimborazo . . 16,000	94
Naupactus parvicollis, Olliff	Cayambe . . . 15,000 Chimborazo . . 15,800	120
Pelmatellus Andium, Bates	Cotocachi . . 11,000-13,500 Chimborazo . . 12-13,300	140

The fact that none of these species were seen at lower elevations cannot be regarded as evidence that they are restricted to the lofty positions at which they were discovered; though it is unlikely that insects which obviously found themselves 'at home' under the conditions that were mentioned at pages 113 and 237 will be found at *much* lower levels, enjoying much higher mean temperatures.

Upon the whole, it appeared that most individual species had a comparatively small range in altitude in Ecuador. One of the most prominent exceptions to the general rule was the Moth (*Erebus odora*, Lin.) which was referred to upon p. 358, that was taken at the level of the sea and nearly ten thousand feet above it. This was exceeded only by one other species, namely, by a Wood-louse which has been identified by the Rev. A. E. Eaton as *Metoponorthus pruinosus*, Brandt; and this little Crustacean seems entitled to consideration, for it must possess in a most unusual degree the power of accommodating itself to circumstances.[1]

It now remains to summarize our experiences at low pressures; and, before recapitulating them, to offer a few general remarks upon the affections, pains and disorders which are so often called *Mal de montagne* or Mountain-sickness.

This term has been in use throughout the nineteenth century. It was originally adopted because it was observed that men and other animals were affected in various unpleasant ways upon reaching great elevations on mountains; and, as it was unknown that the same effects could be produced in mid-air, in balloon, or at the level of the sea by artificial reduction in pressure, it was concluded that they were *peculiar* to mountains. To the present time, amongst ignorant persons, they are often supposed to arise from purely local causes.

[1] It was obtained among roots of trees on the banks of the Guayas, just outside Guayaquil; in the garden of Señor Gomez de la Torre at Ibarra (7200 feet); at the back of the Hacienda of Guachala (9200 feet); on the track between Antisanilla and Piñantura (11,000 feet); in the woods on Pichincha (12,000 feet); and close to the Hacienda of Antisana (13,300 feet).

While there is not the least doubt that they are directly or indirectly produced by diminution in atmospheric pressure, many writers (even amongst those who are well convinced that this is the true cause) continue to speak, when discussing mountain-sickness, solely of elevation above the level of the sea and ignore pressure; and in this way help to perpetuate the false idea that it is an effect of *altitude*. In the remarks that follow, less prominence will be given to the heights which were reached than to the pressures which were experienced; though, as it is more usual to *think in feet* than in barometric inches, the approximately equivalent elevations will be given with the pressures that are mentioned.

Notwithstanding the large number of allusions which had been made in print to Mountain-sickness, I was unable, prior to my journey amongst the Great Andes of the Equator, to tell at what pressure it was probable that we might or should be affected. I found, also, that I could not distinguish with certainty the effects which were due to diminution in pressure from those which might have arisen from other causes; or, further, say which (if any) of the effects that might be certainly due to diminution in pressure would remain permanently if one should continue constantly at a low pressure. These three points were those upon which I sought for information.—Firstly, *at what pressure* shall we commence to be affected? Secondly, *in what way* shall we be affected? Thirdly, can one become *habituated to low pressures?*

The answer to the first question came sooner than was expected. At a pressure of 16·500 inches (16,664 feet) we were incapacitated for work [pp. 48-53], and found ourselves preoccupied by the paramount necessity of obtaining air. All pains had been taken to eliminate the possibility of complications from other causes, and I repeat [see p. 52] "that our 'incapacity' at this time was neither due to exhaustion nor to deficiency of bodily strength, nor to weakness from want of food, but was caused by the whole of our attention being taken up in efforts to get air."

Three things were especially noticeable—(*a*) the suddenness with which we were vanquished; and (*b*) the simultaneous collapse of the Carrels and myself; although (*c*) Mr. Perring remained unaffected.

Before being overcome in this way, no symptoms were remarked in ourselves,[1] and during the attack the only external indication that we were affected was given by laboured respiration, accompanied by spasmodic gasps or gulps; but conjoined there was intense headache, and (what others have termed) an indescribable feeling of illness, pervading almost the whole body.

This attack, which came upon us so suddenly, passed away very gradually, by such infinitesimal degrees that I am unable to say when we entirely recovered from it. It seemed to arrive at a maximum quickly, to remain equally intense for several hours, and it then died away imperceptibly. While it lasted, there was feverishness, marked acceleration in the rate of the pulse, and rise in body temperature [pp. 49, 52]. Twenty-four hours after its commencement there was a distinct improvement in the condition of the Carrels; the intensity of their headaches had diminished, and the 'indescribable feeling of illness' had disappeared. Twelve hours earlier than this it was possible to satisfy our wants for air by breathing through the nostrils alone. At 1 p.m. on Dec. 28, I was able to keep my mouth shut during the ten minutes requisite for taking my temperature.

Thirty-six hours after the commencement of the attack, the Carrels were much better, and became eager to continue exploration. Anticipating that they might be adversely affected upon sustaining further diminution in pressure, I directed them not to endeavour to reach a great elevation [p. 53], but gave no reasons

---

[1] Our animals, however, shewed decided signs of exhaustion before pressure had fallen to 17 inches [see p. 46], and they were nearly dead beat by the time they arrived at the Second Camp (16·500 inches).

If more attention had been paid to ourselves, I do not doubt that premonitory symptoms would have been noticed. My excuse, or explanation, is given on pp. 44, 51. I was taken unawares, not expecting to be affected so soon.

for the instruction; and they, imagining that the ascent of the mountain was the first consideration, made a push for the summit [p. 59]. They were away nearly twelve hours, and during this time experienced reduction in pressure from 16·500 to about 15·100 inches, while ascending from 16,664 to 19,300 feet. Upon return, their condition closely approached complete exhaustion. They staggered like men in an advanced state of intoxication, and threw themselves down and went to sleep without either eating or drinking [p. 59].[1]

During the time they had been absent, my own condition had materially improved; and thus it appeared that although there was a likelihood we should become habituated to a pressure of 16·500 inches, there was a probability that we should be further affected at still lower pressures. This determined the position of the Third Camp (16·000 inches; 17,285 feet). While transport was being effected between the two posts, it seemed that we had grown weaker, and we certainly were [p. 61] "comparatively lifeless and feeble, and had a strong disposition to sit down." By January 2, headaches had nearly departed, feverishness had disappeared (my temperature had fallen to 97°·9 Faht.), and the circulation had gone back to the normal rate; but *respiration* continued to be affected, and it was found that we could not satisfy our wants for air, *while in movement*, except by breathing through nostrils *and* mouths.

Under the further fall in pressure which occurred when ascending on January 3 to the foot of the Southern Walls of Chimborazo (16·000 to 15·290 inches) it was remarked that the rate of travelling was unusually slow; and this was more distinctly seen on the following day when mounting to the summit (pressure declining from 16·000 to 14·100 inches). At a little above 19,000 feet, I noticed that "our paces got shorter and shorter, until at last the

---

[1] At the time of their return, no opinion could be formed as to their *rate*. If two hours were occupied in halts, and ten hours in movement, the mean of their ascending and descending rates would be only 526 feet per hour.

toe of one step almost touched the heel of the next one." Our rate on this day was deplorable, partly owing to exceptional softness of the snow [p. 71].

Circumstances then compelled me to leave Chimborazo [pp. 78-80] and to descend to lower levels. Between Jan. 12 and Feb. 17, the highest pressure observed was 22·156, at Ambato, and the lowest was 16·348 inches, on Illiniza [p. 133]. Upon February 18-19, we stayed at or close to the summit of Cotopaxi (19,500 to 19,613 feet) for twenty-six consecutive hours, with the barometer standing at 14·750 inches, without any serious inconvenience [p. 150]. This was the greatest length of time we remained continuously at so low pressure.

As we were not 'incapacitated' upon Cotopaxi, it was not likely that we should be very acutely affected upon Antisana or Cayambe. Headache did not occur at all, while ascending these considerable mountains; and nothing was noted that could be attributed to 'rarefaction of the air' except the feeling of lassitude and want of bodily strength, which always manifested itself at the lower and lowest pressures [pp. 61, 70, 150, 235]. The spirit indeed was willing but the flesh was weak. Upon Cayambe there was convincing evidence that my two assistants were less vigorous than usual [p. 235].

After quitting Cayambe, the barometer was not again seen standing below 16 inches until the second ascent of Chimborazo; and upon this occasion our experiences did not differ from those last mentioned. No one had headache; but, while in movement, all found it was necessary to breathe through the mouth as well as through the nostrils. When at rest, sufficient air could be obtained through the nostrils alone; and on the summit I was able to keep my mouth shut for ten minutes while observing my temperature.

Excluding the time passed on the flat coast land, we were 212 days in Ecuador, and the nights were passed at the pressures and elevations mentioned upon the next page.

Number of nights.	Atmospheric pressure experienced.	Height above level of sea.
4	29·000 – 28·500 inches	Less than 6000 feet.
4	23·600 – 22·540 ,,	Between 6000 - 8000 feet.
30	22·510 – 21·900 ,,	do. 8000 - 9000 ,,
90	21·720 – 21·110 ,,	do. 9000 - 10,000 ,,
6	20·920 – 20·200 ,,	do. 10,000 - 11,000 ,,
15	19·800 – 19·500 ,,	do. 11,000 - 12,000 ,,
14	19·270 – 18·900 ,,	do. 12,000 - 13,000 ,,
13	18·755 – 18·280 ,,	do. 13,000 - 14,000 ,,
4	18·080 – 17·780 ,,	do. 14,000 - 14,500 ,,
4	17·730 ,,	At 14,762 ,,
1	17·410 ,,	do. 14,992 ,,
5	17·430 ,,	do. 15,139 ,,
1	17·250 ,,	do. 15,207 ,,
1	17·220 ,,	do. 15,446 ,,
2	16·950 ,,	do. 15,811 ,,
1	16·840 ,,	do. 15,984 ,,
10	16·500 ,,	do. 16,664 ,,
6	16·000 ,,	do. 17,285 ,,
1	14·750 ,,	do. 19,500 ,,

Having recapitulated the various ways in which we were affected whilst among the Great Andes, I now pass on to the question, Can one become habituated to low pressures? and in connection with this bring together in a tabular form upon page 372 a few examples of the rates of speed that were attained over the longer courses; selecting them only from instances in which the times occupied were exactly noted and the differences of level were well ascertained, and taking them from those in which we started unexhausted by previous work, from places where atmospheric pressure was already low.

Without a few words of explanation, not much edification can be obtained from this table. A reader may compare the entry at January 7 with that of June 9 and conclude from the apparent falling-off that there is evidence of deterioration rather than of improvement. This conclusion would be erroneous. The dissimilarity of the work sufficiently accounts for the difference between

RATES OF SPEED (ASCENDING).

Date. 1880.	Mountain.	References to Pages.	Approximate pressure experienced, in inches.	Height above the level of the sea, in feet.	Time occupied, ex. halts in minutes.	Height ascended, in feet.	Rate of ascent per min. in feet.
	CHIMBORAZO.						
Jan. 3	Third camp to foot of S. Walls	63	16·000 – 15·290	17,285 – 18,528	115	1243	10·8
,, 4	Third camp to summit	71	16·000 – 14·100	17,285 – 20,498	630	3213	5·1
,, 6	Third camp to foot of S. Walls	75	16·000 – 15·290	17,285 – 18,528	88	1243	14·1
,, 7	Do. do	79	Do.	Do.	85	Do.	14·6
	ILLINIZA.						
Feb. 9	Camp to highest point attained	132	17·250 – 16·300	15,207 – 17,023	187	1816	9·7
	COTOPAXI.						
,, 18	First camp to summit	145	17·400 – 14·770	15,139 – 19,613	360	4474	12·1
	ANTISANA.						
Mar. 7	Camp to highest point attained	191	16·830 – 15·940	15,984 – 17,623	190	1639	8·6
,, 10	Camp to summit	198	16·830 – 15·140	15,984 – 19,335	252	3351	13·0
	CAYAMBE.						
April 4	Camp to summit	234	17·730 – 14·980	14,762 – 19,186	320	4424	13·8
	COTOCACHI.						
,, 24	Camp to summit	263	17·780 – 16·660	14,490 – 16,301	190	1811	9·5
	ILLINIZA.						
June 9	Camp to highest point attained	298	17·220 – 16·200	15,446 – 16,922	150	1476	9·8
	CARIHUAIRAZO.						
,, 29	Camp to summit	317	18·550 – 16·520	13,377 – 16,515	285	3138	11·0
	CHIMBORAZO.						
July 3	Fifth camp to summit	331	16·950 – 14·050	15,811 – 20,498	445	4687	10·5

the rates. Few of these examples can properly be compared with each other; for, besides the reason given upon p. 299, on some occasions the party was larger or smaller (and this always exerts an influence); and sometimes we were laden and at others unencumbered. The condition of the weather has also to be taken into account.

Upon the whole these observations afford indications that we became *somewhat* habituated to low pressures. If the entries at January 3, 6 and 7 are compared, a continuous advance will be noted. This, however, was partly due to increasing familiarity with the ground which was traversed. There is stronger evidence of improvement on Feb. 18, when over a much longer course the mean rate was faster than on the shorter one of January 3; and this was exceeded upon March 10 and April 4 when we were unembarrassed by natives. The nature of the work upon Illiniza and Cotocachi was similar, and through absorption of time by step-cutting the rates upon those mountains were slower than upon Cotopaxi, Antisana or Cayambe. Comparison of the entries at Feb. 9, April 24 and June 9 shews no deterioration, although there is little sign of progress. There is a more marked contrast between the rates of January 4 and July 3, but this is modified if due allowance is made in the first case for the exceptional softness of the snow, in the second one for the greater simplicity of the route.

But although it seemed that we *did* become somewhat habituated to low pressures, and that this was shewn amongst other ways by improvement in speed, it appeared to me that the best of our rates were inferior to those which we should have attained over the same ground at higher pressures; and I brought this point to the test related upon pp. 300-301, and obtained from that experiment evidence that I was materially affected by, and weakened at, a pressure of 21 inches (9850 feet). It need scarcely be remarked that this observation has a very wide interest; for, if it is really the case that the bodily powers are lessened under prolonged diminution in pressure, the fact must affect all calculations which may be made on the basis of higher pressures either in respect to the marching of troops, transport by animals, the labour of the navvy, or any other description of work dependent upon muscular exertion.

In reviewing the whole of our experiences, two different sets of effects could be distinguished; namely, those which were transitory, and those which were permanent,—that is to say, permanent so long as we remained at low pressures.

The transitory effects were acceleration of the circulation of the blood, increase in the temperature of the body, and pressure on the blood-vessels. The permanent ones were augmentation of the rate of breathing and disturbance of the habitual manner of respiration, indisposition to take food, and lessening of muscular power. The whole of these, doubtless, were due to diminution in pressure, but the transitory ones, presumably, *were produced by some cause which was itself only temporary*.[1] There are strong grounds for believing that they are due to the expansion (under diminution of *external* pressure) of gaseous matter within the body; which seeks to be liberated, and causes an *internal* pressure that strongly affects the blood-vessels. While equilibrium was being restored between the internal and external pressure, the 'indescribable feeling of illness' gradually disappeared, and headache died away; and it may be reasonably expected that these 'acute' troubles can be escaped by taking pains to avoid abrupt diminution of pressure.[2]

[1] During the whole time we were in Ecuador, neither with ourselves nor among the people who were employed, was there anything observed of the nature of hemorrhage, vomiting, or nausea (although among our *viandes* there was something that would have strained the stomach of an ostrich [see pp. 61 and 207]); and it thus appears that these unpleasant features are not indispensable accompaniments of life at great elevations.

[2] Or, on the contrary, suffocation may be expected, probably accompanied by hemorrhage, by persons who submit themselves to a very rapid reduction in pressure (either in balloon, or artificially), if they have previously been living for some length of time with the barometer at 29 to 30 inches.

From the 'permanent' effects there is no escape. The large increase in the rate of respiration and the compulsory breathing through open mouths were caused by involuntary efforts to make up for the decrease in the *density* of the air by imbibing a greater *volume*. It was possible, without any great effort, at a pressure of 14·750 inches (19,600 feet), to sustain life, *while at rest*, by increasing the volume of air inspired, and thus in some measure to compensate for the reduction in its density (which was then half that of air at the level of the sea). But *when in movement* it became difficult to enlarge the breathing capacity to the extent necessary to meet the *further* demand for air which was the result of muscular exertion;[1] and, notwithstanding the increased efforts which were put forth to meet this demand, there was, in all probability, a *considerable* deficiency in the weight and value of the amount which was imbibed.

When the effects consequent upon experiencing diminution in atmospheric pressure were first noticed, it was guessed that they were in some way due to a peculiarity in the air. Father Joseph de Acosta was amongst the earliest to mention the subject, and in Book III of his *Natural & Moral History* he devotes a Chapter to "Some mervellous effects of the windes, which are in some partes of the Indies," giving first a few prefatory remarks upon sea-sickness, which he says "it be true that the motion of the shippe helpes much, in that it moves more or less, and likewise the infections and ill-savours of things in the shippe; yet the proper and naturall cause is the aire and the vapors of the sea. . . It is proved by many experiences, that the aire of the sea is the chiefe cause of this strange indisposition"; and, having settled to his own satisfaction that the air of the

The immunity from headache of Mr. Perring and others who accompanied us I consider was due to their having lived for a considerable length of time at lower pressures than ourselves.

[1] In ascending a mountain, the respiration is quickened by two causes—(1) by muscular exertion, and (2) by diminution in pressure. These act independently of each other.

sea is the principal cause of sea-sickness, he goes on to express his belief that the air at great heights is the cause of mountain-sickness.

"I thought good," he says, "to speake this, to shew a strange effect, which happens in some partes of the Indies, where the ayre and the wind that rains makes men dazie, not lesse, but more than at sea. Some hold it for a fable, others say that it is an addition ; for my parte I will speak what I have tried. There is in Peru a high mountaine which they call Pariacaca, and having heard speake of the alteration it bred, I went as well prepared as I could . . . but notwithstanding all my provision, when I came to mount the stairs, as they call them, which is the top of this mountaine, I was suddenly surprized with so mortall and strange a pang that I was ready to fall from my beast to the ground ; and although we were many in company, yet every one made haste (without any tarrying for his companion) to free himselfe speedily from this ill passage. Being then alone with one Indian, whom I intreated to keep me on my beast, I was surprised with such pangs of straining and casting as I thought to cast vp my soul too ; for having cast vp meate, fleugme, and choller, both yellow and greene, in the end I cast vp blood, with the straining of my stomacke. To conclude, if this had continued, I should vndoubtedly have died ; but this lasted not above three or four houres, that we were come into a more convenient and naturall temperature. . . Some in the passage demaunded confession, thinking verily to die ; others got off their beasts, beeing overcome with casting . . . and it was tolde me that some have lost their lives there with this accident. . . But commonly it dooth no important harme, onely this, paine and troublesome distaste while it endures : and not onely the passage of Pariacaca hath this propertie, but also all this ridge of the mountaine, which runnes above five hundred leagues long, and in what place soever you passe, you shall find strange intemperatures, yet more in some partes than in other, and rather to those which mount from the sea than from the plaines.[1] . . And no doubt but the winde is the cause of this intemperature and strange alteration, or the aire that raignes there. . . I therefore perswade my selfe, that the element of the aire is there so subtile and delicate, as it is not proportionable with the breathing of man, which requires a more grosse and temperate aire, and I beleeve it is the cause that doth so much alter the stomacke and trouble all the disposition."

---

[1] The reason of this being that the Andean slopes on the side of the Pacific are usually steeper than those upon the east of the chain. A more abrupt reduction in pressure is consequently experienced.

At the end of this highly interesting passage, by some process of reasoning that is not manifested, Father Acosta shrewdly guesses that the air is 'delicate' at great heights,[1] and "is not proportionable with the breathing of man, which requires a more grosse aire."

Subsequently, when diminution in atmospheric pressure was demonstrated by means of the barometer, men spoke of the effects of 'rarefaction of the air,' though without having a distinct idea how it operated; and after the discovery of oxygen they began to lay all the troubles to want of oxygen, which it seems to have been thought settled in the atmosphere like sediment in muddy water.

Latterly, Professor Paul Bert endeavoured to shew that no troubles would occur through diminution in pressure (or rarefaction of the air) if one imbibed sufficient oxygen; and he carried on a long series of laboratory experiments with the ultimate aim of offering practical suggestions for the guidance of mountain-travellers and aeronauts. His two final experiments, with the conclusions at which he arrived from them, are related in his own words at the end of this volume.

It will be seen by reference to Appendix **J** (where these experiments are given at full length), that Prof. Bert observed the rate of the pulse was accelerated when pressure was reduced, that it fell again when pressure was restored, and that he noticed it was temporarily reduced upon imbibing oxygen. He considered that in the inhalation of oxygen he had discovered a panacea for all ills arising from diminution in pressure, and at the conclusion of his book (*La Pression Barométrique*) gave various 'practical hints' for the guidance of mountain-travellers and aeronauts.

At p. 1103 he suggests that the former class might carry metal cylinders, weighing $28\frac{1}{2}$ lbs., holding 330 litres of oxygen compressed to one-thirtieth of its ordinary bulk, an amount which he calculates would suffice for one man for more than an hour (at what elevation or pressure is not stated); and at p. 1061 he

---

[1] The Barometer had not been invented when Acosta's *Natural & Moral History* was first printed (1590).

mentions twenty litres per minute as the *least* quantity that a party of three persons would require at an elevation approximately corresponding to the upper 5000 feet of Mount Everest. Thus, if a trio should encamp upon Mount Everest at the height of 24,000 feet, and pass an entire day in ascending and descending the final 5000 feet, and a second night at the camp (say thirty-five hours in all at 24,000 feet or higher), the *least* quantity that would be required (according to Prof. Paul Bert) would be 20 litres × 2100, say 200 hogsheads of oxygen. Feeling, no doubt, that there might be difficulty in transporting and installing this amount, he adds (p. 1104) that "it would certainly be preferable to produce the oxygen on the spot," and says that "scientific expeditions of long duration to the highlands of Tibet, Ladak, and the Pamir could perfectly well carry the necessary apparatus." The recent voyagers in these regions do not, however, appear to have adopted Prof. Bert's suggestions, and so far as I am aware they have not been followed by a single mountain-traveller.

Amongst the practical hints offered by Prof. Bert for the guidance of aeronauts, who may aspire to reach great elevations, there are to be found the recommendations to make "un repas d'aliments substantiels" before departure; to eat frequently while ascending; to go slowly at great heights (that is to say, to mount gradually); and, especially, "in order to be completely safe," to inhale oxygen—doing so *continuously* when higher than 5 to 6000 mètres (16,405-19,686 feet).[1] "If these precautions," he says, "had been taken with the *Zenith*, there would have been no catastrophe to deplore."

This is a reference to the fate that befell two aeronauts (Crocé-Spinelli and Sivel) who were experimented upon by Prof. Bert on March 9, 1874. He shut them up in his metal cylinder and reduced pressure to about the equivalent of 24,000 feet above the sea. They imbibed oxygen; noticed that the rate of their pulses

---

[1] Want of space obliges me to compress these directions. They will be found at pp. 1094-96 of *La Pression Barométrique*.

fell temporarily, and seemed fascinated by the experiment. They received, however, several very emphatic indications of the danger attendant upon *rapid* diminution of pressure,[1] which were confirmed upon an actual balloon ascent made thirteen days later. Taking no warning from these premonitory symptoms, on April 15, 1875, they left the earth at 11.35 a.m., and in two hours rose to the height of about 26,000 feet, and for two hours more hovered about 26-28,000 feet. At the end of this time both were found suffocated, with their mouths full of blood; but neither the time nor the elevation at which they died is known exactly, as M. Tissandier, the sole survivor of the party, was rendered insensible, and thus was unable to give a complete account of the affair.

Various suggestions were made as to the immediate cause of their death, and upon these Prof. Bert remarks (p. 1075) that none deserve to be reproduced, they are " old ideas, already condemned "; and to the end of his volume (which was published three years after the catastrophe—allowing him ample time to reconsider his position) he maintains (1) that deficiency of oxygen was the cause of the death of these aeronauts and of all the evils that are produced by diminution in pressure, and (2) that artificial inhalation of oxygen is the sovereign remedy. It does not appear that he took the practical course of remaining in his cylinder for a length of time, at a pressure corresponding to that which proved fatal to his pupils.[2] If he had done this, and had emerged alive, he would have made out a strong case.

Prof. Bert omits to state what effect is produced on Respiration

[1] Notwithstanding the draughts of oxygen, their pulses rose to 132 and 135. They experienced a sort of drunken sensation and could neither see nor hear clearly. One of them commenced to eat and soon stopped; "and when I made," says M. Bert, "a sign to him to continue, he answered me with a gesture of disgust." Upon their balloon ascent on Mar. 22, 1874, they experienced strong pressure in the head.

[2] Whose death seems to have exercised a deterrent effect upon aeronauts. There has not been, I believe, any subsequent attempt to reach the elevation at which they perished, and I have not heard that any one, since 1875, has even soared so high as twenty thousand feet.

when his method is adopted; he ignores the influence of Time, and argues as if the effect produced in a minute is similar to that which would be caused in an hour, a day, or a week; and he sets an inordinate value upon the apparent checking of the rate of the pulse, which in itself, apart from other considerations, is of little moment. He assumes that the rate of the pulse is permanently accelerated while experiencing low pressures, and bases his recommendations upon that supposition. From the absence in his two final experiments (the crown of his work) of all reference to the effect of inhalation of oxygen upon respiration, and there being but one solitary observation of the temperature of the body (at the end of Exp. 257), one naturally enquires whether the rate of respiration and the temperature of the body were observed; and, if they were, whether a satisfactory result was noted?

Professor Bert's attention, presumably, was first directed to acceleration in the circulation upon reduction of pressure through the frequent references which had been made to the subject by aeronauts and mountain-travellers. De Saussure was amongst the first to remark it on land,[1] and Gay-Lussac and Biot in balloon.[2]

[1] "Mais de tous nos organes, celui est le plus affecté par la rareté de l'air, c'est celui de la respiration. On sait que pour entretenir la vie, sur-tout celle des animaux à sang chaud, il faut qu'une quantité déterminé d'air traverse leurs poumons dans un tems donné. Si donc l'air qu'ils respirent est le double plus rare, il faudra que leurs inspirations soient le double plus fréquentes, afin que la rareté soit compensée par le volume. C'est cette accélération forcée de la respiration qui est la cause de la fatigue et des angoisses que l'on éprouve à ces grandes hauteurs. Car en même tems que la respiration s'accélere, la circulation s'accélere aussi. Je m'en étois souvent apperçu sur de hautes cimes, mais je voulois en faire une épreuve exacte sur le Mont-Blanc; et pour que l'action du mouvement du voyage ne pût pas se confondre avec celle de la rareté de l'air, je ne fis mon épreuve qu'après que nous fûmes restés tranquilles, ou à peu près tranquilles pendant 4 heures sur la cime de la montagne. Alors le pouls de Pierre Balmat se trouva battre 98 pulsations par minute; celui de Têtu, mon domestique 112, et le mien 100. A Chamouni, également après le repos, les mêmes, dans le même ordre battirent 49, 60, 72. Nous étions donc tous là dans un état de fièvre."—*Voyages dans les Alpes*, § 2021, Vol. 4, 1796.

[2] In 1804, in balloon, when no higher than 8600 feet, they observed that their respective pulses rose from 62 to 80, and from 89 to 111.

Aeronauts never remain a sufficiently long time at considerable elevations to be able to say whether the acceleration is temporary or permanent. De Saussure and others seem to have been under the impression that it always accompanies increase in the rate of respiration. In the passage given on p. 380 from *Voyages dans les Alpes*, he states as a fact that "at the same time the respiration is accelerated" [under diminution of pressure] "the circulation is also quickened"; and from the general tenour of the passage it is evident he considered that the joint increase in the rate of the respiration and circulation was continuous, when remaining in a state of rest at great elevations, at one constant pressure.

This was not our experience amongst the Great Andes of the Equator. *At the first,* following the general (and probably the *invariable*) rule with those who sustain a considerable diminution in pressure in a comparatively short time, there was a large and very unpleasant increase in the rate of my pulse, accompanied by a considerable rise in body temperature; and (although they would not permit any observations to be made on their persons) I do not doubt that the same occurred with Jean-Antoine and Louis Carrel, as they spoke of strong feverishness. But while continuing to live with the barometer standing at 16·500 inches the pulse slowed down and ultimately fell to its normal rate; the temperature of the body also fell until it got to its normal degree; and the subsequent fluctuations which occurred in the rate of the pulse and in the temperature of the body,[1] even whilst sustaining further diminution of pressure, were only such as could be assigned to common causes. The righting of our condition occurred in the ordinary course of nature, without having recourse to artificial use of oxygen;[2] and I ask (1) If the unpleasant effects which were experienced upon Chimborazo [gaspings, feverishness, intense headache, and an indescribable feeling of illness pervading almost the

[1] See Appendix F.

[2] During the whole journey I did not, personally, consume so much as an ounce of Chlorate of Potash.

whole body] were directly due to want of oxygen, why did they not continue while we remained at a pressure of 16·500 inches? and (2) In what way should I have benefited my circulation and temperature (when both became normal) by taking draughts of oxygen?

It is clear, as regards the pressures [elevations] we dealt with (which it is interesting to observe embraced those at which Prof. Bert urged *continuous inhalation*, namely, 5 to 6,000 mètres above the sea), that the artificial use of oxygen was not *necessary;* and, further, that the temporary increase in the rate of the circulation and in the temperature of the body, and the other conjoined disagreeables, could not have been *directly* due to rarefaction of the air or want of oxygen (although they occurred under diminution of pressure), and that they must have been produced, as it is suggested on p. 374, by some cause which was itself only temporary.

In a discussion that took place in Paris, at the Académie de Médecine, after the death of Crocé-Spinelli and Sivel, M. Colin remarked that the gas in the human body must needs have a tendency to expand under diminution of external pressure. This was pointed out a century earlier by Haller and others. Prof. Bert, however, refused to believe that this expansion could produce an important effect, although he could not deny that it occurred. During his Experiments 256 and 257, there were evidences that it did occur,[1] and he made the following observations upon them. "Amongst other phenomena which persisted, *notwithstanding the inspiration of oxygen,* because they depend entirely upon the diminution in the density of the air, I mention the gaseous evacuations . . . respecting which neither aeronauts nor mountain-travellers have spoken."[2] They are, no doubt, caused by expansion of internal gas, consequent upon diminution in external pressure.

[1] In Experiment 256 there are the following records. "11.25; gaz s'échappant par en haut et par en bas." "11.31; gaz s'échappent, et cependant le ventre reste un peu gonflé." "11.47; des gaz s'échappent par la bouche et l'anus." "11.48; encore gaz." "11.52; encore gaz."

[2] This has not been due to non-familiarity with the 'phenomena.'

Prof. Bert, in mentioning them, got close *au fond du sujet*, and then skipped away from an unpleasant topic. Was this because the facts did not agree with his theory? He seemed to fail to perceive that the released gas was only that which found a ready outlet, and to take no note of that which remained in the body, without the possibility of immediate escape.

There are strong grounds for believing that the sudden dizziness and headaches, the slight hemorrhages, the 'mortal pangs' and 'drunken sensation,' of which so many have had experience either on land, in balloon, or when sustaining artificial diminution in pressure, and the insensibility and fatal hemorrhages which have occurred in the most extreme cases, have all been caused by internal pressure; and that the degree of intensity of the effects, and their earlier or later appearance, depend upon the *extent* of the diminution in pressure, the *rate at which it is reduced*, and *the length of time it is experienced*. An unlimited number of combinations can be produced when to these are added the complications arising from the effect on respiration of rarefaction of the air, and differences in individual constitutions.

The various affections which have been classed together, confused and confounded, under the single term Mountain-sickness, are fundamentally caused, as I see the matter, by diminution in atmospheric pressure, which operates in at least two ways; namely, (A), by lessening the value of the air that can be inspired in any given time, and (B) by causing the air or gas within the body to expand, and to press upon the internal organs. The results which ensue from A are permanent (*i.e.* so long as the cause exists), and are aggravated the more pressure is reduced. The effects produced by B may be temporary and pass away when equilibrium has been restored between the internal and external pressure; or they may be fatal, under very large and rapid reduction in pressure.[1]

[1] Of nausea and vomiting I have no experience. They did not happen in the Andes, and they have never occurred either to myself, or to men in my employment,

It follows, if the facts have not been misinterpreted, that the evils coming under B will be minimized (in mountain-travellers) by gradual ascent, and may even be entirely avoided by keeping a constant watch over the rate of the pulse and the temperature of the body. But from the effects on respiration none can escape. In every country, and at all times, they will impose limitations upon the range of man; and those persons in the future, who, either in pursuit of knowledge or in quest of fame, may strive to reach the loftiest summits on the earth, will find themselves confronted by augmenting difficulties which they will have to meet with constantly diminishing powers.

or in people with whom we have been casually associated, on any mountain, in any part of the world. I imagine that these unpleasant features (though undoubtedly occurring in a certain percentage of men and other animals under diminution in pressure) must be principally due to peculiarities of individual constitutions, or to want of judgment. Our indisposition to eat at great elevations (low pressures) has been noticed. It is not impossible, if we had done violence to our inclinations, that we should have paid a penalty.

A TROPICAL DREAM.

CHAPTER XX.

RETURN TO GUAYAQUIL—CONCLUSION.

ALTHOUGH our work amongst the Great Andes of the Equator was completed upon arrival at Chuquipoquio, a Public Duty still remained to be performed. It had been concluded from the tameness of my attitude on the 17th of January [see p. 89] that travellers could be defrauded with impunity, and be kept prisoners without fear of consequences. In the Public interest, it was desirable to correct this idea. The road-measuring was a slow operation, and when the people attached to the Tambo, out of curiosity came to inspect us, they afforded a convenient opportunity for a discourse to them upon the iniquity of their ways; and I emphasized my remarks in a manner which I trust left such an abiding *impression* as will render it less likely in the future that an Englishman will be robbed in this neighbourhood.

We departed from Riobamba on the 8th of July, intending to take what is termed the Railway Route to Guayaquil; and, mounting the slopes that enclose the basin on the south, arrived at dusk at the village of Nanti (10,669 feet). The next place being a good distance away, we stopped at the highest house or hut, which was occupied by some half-Indians. In the night there were wailings and lamentations, and Campaña came to ask if I would *sell a candle*, as the mother was dying, and there was not a light of any sort to be found in the whole village!

Next morning, five and a half hours of hard going brought us to the village of Guamote, and here we struck the southern continuation of the Moreno (or Quito) Road.[1] At this part, and until we diverged from it in the afternoon of July 10, it was mostly in excellent condition,—a fine, broad highway, more than sufficient for the wants of a thickly-populated district, though passing over bleak, uncultivated moorland (*paramo*), which it would be too complimentary to term a howling wilderness. From Guamote to the end of this day's journey, we neither met nor passed either man or beast, and the natural repulsiveness of the surroundings was heightened by skulls and skeletons lying on each side of the road, of unburied men who had perished in one of the revolutionary combats.[2] At 5 p.m. we came to a large (apparently deserted) Hacienda, called Galti, and a little farther south halted for the night at a hut (11,772 feet) about three hundred feet above the road.

On the 10th, we travelled without seeing a house or person until we caught sight of the village of Alausi on the other side of a

[1] I could not learn what direction the road takes between Guamote and Chuquipoquio, or even whether that section was completed. On the Route Map it is not laid down to the south of Guamote, as we moved too quickly to observe its numerous changes of direction; but it is to be understood that we travelled over the high road between Guamote and the place where it was quitted, opposite to Alausi. South of Guamote it rises to a considerable elevation. I stopped at what appeared to be the highest point for a reading of the mercurial barometer, and found there that it was about 11,362 feet above the sea. It descended upon Galti, and rose again to about 11,500 feet.

[2] Through this tract of country (Sibambe to Riobamba) it is proposed to carry the Railway which is to be a joy to holders of Ecuadorian bonds!

deep valley, and then stopped perplexed, not knowing how to get to it, or where to go. A casual man, who turned up at the right moment, said that by breaking away to the west we could make a short cut to the Bridge of Chimbo (the terminus of the Railway). We followed his advice, and, after many windings through a wild, wooded country, found ourselves at dusk at the commencement of the descent towards the Pacific; plunged down the forest-covered slopes, and at 7 p.m. were brought to a stand by darkness when about 9000 feet above the sea. Not a soul had been seen since the casual man. All of us went to bed supperless, as the food was nearly exhausted. Off again soon after sunrise, we descended 4400 feet without a break, and then came to a diminutive Hacienda, called Cayandeli, where a solitary man in possession declared there was nothing to eat.

During the last two days, the route had skirted the eastern side of the Range of Chimborazo. The slopes which we had now to descend were at its extreme southern end. Since leaving Riobamba, views had been confined either to the immediate surroundings or to a few miles away, and Chimborazo and its allies were invisible. The same, too, was the case with the country on the east. We passed Sangai without seeing it, or any of the mountains in its vicinity. On entering the forest, the range of vision became even more circumscribed by the tortuous bends of the ever-winding track. Sometimes it was ill-marked, overgrown and readily lost.[1] We went astray, and at night on the 11th were still in the jungle, and retired to rest, supperless, on the top of the packing-cases.

Except for the pangs of hunger, and a growing apprehension that the steamer at Guayaquil would be missed, this descent through the forest would have been enjoyable. In the course of a day, the nakedness of the Interior changed to the luxuriance of the Tropics; the increasing warmth was grateful; and presently

[1] The descent commenced at about 11,160 feet above the sea, and continued without intermission for more than 9000 feet. We saw the barometer rise six inches and three-quarters upon the 11th of July.

we came again into the Land of Butterflies, and saw the great *Morphos* sailing to and fro, with myriads of attendant satellites in chrome, carmine and vermilion. The last part of the march, on the morning of the 12th, passed through forest-trees rising 150 feet high, mast-like, without a branch, laden with a parasitic growth. Then the sky began to be seen, a vista opened out—we had arrived at the Valley of the Chimbo.

The Bridge was a wooden structure, spanning the River just before it turned abruptly to the west. The Railway was hidden away in jungle, and had to be *discovered*. There was no station or train; nor house or hut; nor person or means of procuring information. The right bank of the river formed the Terminus. The line ran up to the edge of the stream, without stops to prevent the train running into the water, and looked as if it had been cut in half by the torrent. The only indication of civilization was a contractor's shed, mounted on wheels.[1] Campaña went down the rails in search of life, and learnt that a train *might* arrive to-day, or *perhaps* it would come *mañana*. We waited in hungry expectation (paying off the arrieros in the meanwhile), and about twelve o'clock *the* train hove in sight, bringing three persons and nothing more.

Shortly before leaving Quito, General Veintemilla spontaneously favoured me with a letter to the Railway authorities, directing them to afford every attention, assistance, etcetera. This letter was shewn to the persons in charge of the train, and they were informed that we were famished, and ready to purchase any food that could be spared. The President's letter bore fruit. The Conductor brought out two small pine-apples,[2] and presented them with many polite phrases,—the pine-apples were mine; he himself and all that he had was mine, and so forth. I tried to *buy*, but he would not hear of it; and, as there was no time to waste, the

[1] On this journey we were victims of the pleasantry of a person at Riobamba, who informed us that it would take two days to get to the Bridge of Chimbo, where there was a *capital hotel;* and that we should find plenty of food on the way. Seeing no reason to doubt the information, surplus provisions were cleared out at Riobamba, and we started with only a day's supply. Potatoes were obtained at Nanti, Guamote and Galti, but after the latter place nothing whatever could be procured.

[2] Local products, worth perhaps ten cents apiece.

pine-apples were cut up forthwith into five portions—the donor consuming a share.

The train ran as far as the first station smoothly, and there the engine went off the track. While affairs were being rectified, I sent into the village, and having acquired the materials for a good, square meal, entertained the Conductor as my guest. "Now," thought I, "that pine-apple account is balanced."

At Yaguachi, after again expressing my obligations, I was about to leave, when the Conductor put his hand on my shoulder and stopped me. "The fares!" General Veintemilla's letter was comprehensive, and might have covered anything from special trains downwards, and I remarked that it seemed to imply free transit. "No," was the reply, made with admirable readiness, "it embraces everything *except* that." "How much?" "Three pesos and a half apiece." I paid the amount like a lamb, and was going off, when the Conductor again stopped me. "There is the baggage." "How much?" I paid his charge, but there still seemed to be something on his mind. "Is there anything else?" "Yes, Señor; *your Excellency has forgotten to pay for the pine-apples!*"[1]

[1] The Ecuadorian Railway was commenced under the auspices of the Government. It is now in the hands of a Company, and its construction, I am informed, is being pushed on actively. In 1888, the section was opened from Duran (opposite to Guayaquil) to Yaguachi, and it is said that several kilomètres are finished beyond the Bridge of Chimbo (now called Chimbo). From this latter point to Sibambe is only 15 miles in a direct line, but the distance by the railroad (as laid out) will be 50 miles, and upon this section there will be a rise of 7727 feet.

I have no information as to the direction in which it is proposed to carry this line (after passing Sibambe) beyond that which is furnished in the *Report* from Mr. Alfred St. John (Quito, July 14, 1891), where it is stated that "a French syndicate has obtained a concession from the Equatorian Congress for the purpose of carrying the railway from Chimbo *to Riobamba*, and eventually to Quito, but thus far the French financiers have been unable to raise the necessary funds. Should a satisfactory arrangement be made by the Equatorian Government with the bondholders for the settlement of the foreign debt, British capitalists might inquire into the feasibility and probable profitableness of such an undertaking, but before embarking into it very sound guarantees should be exacted."

The line has not yet arrived at Sibambe; and, should it ever do so, it will come

E. WILSON, DEL.

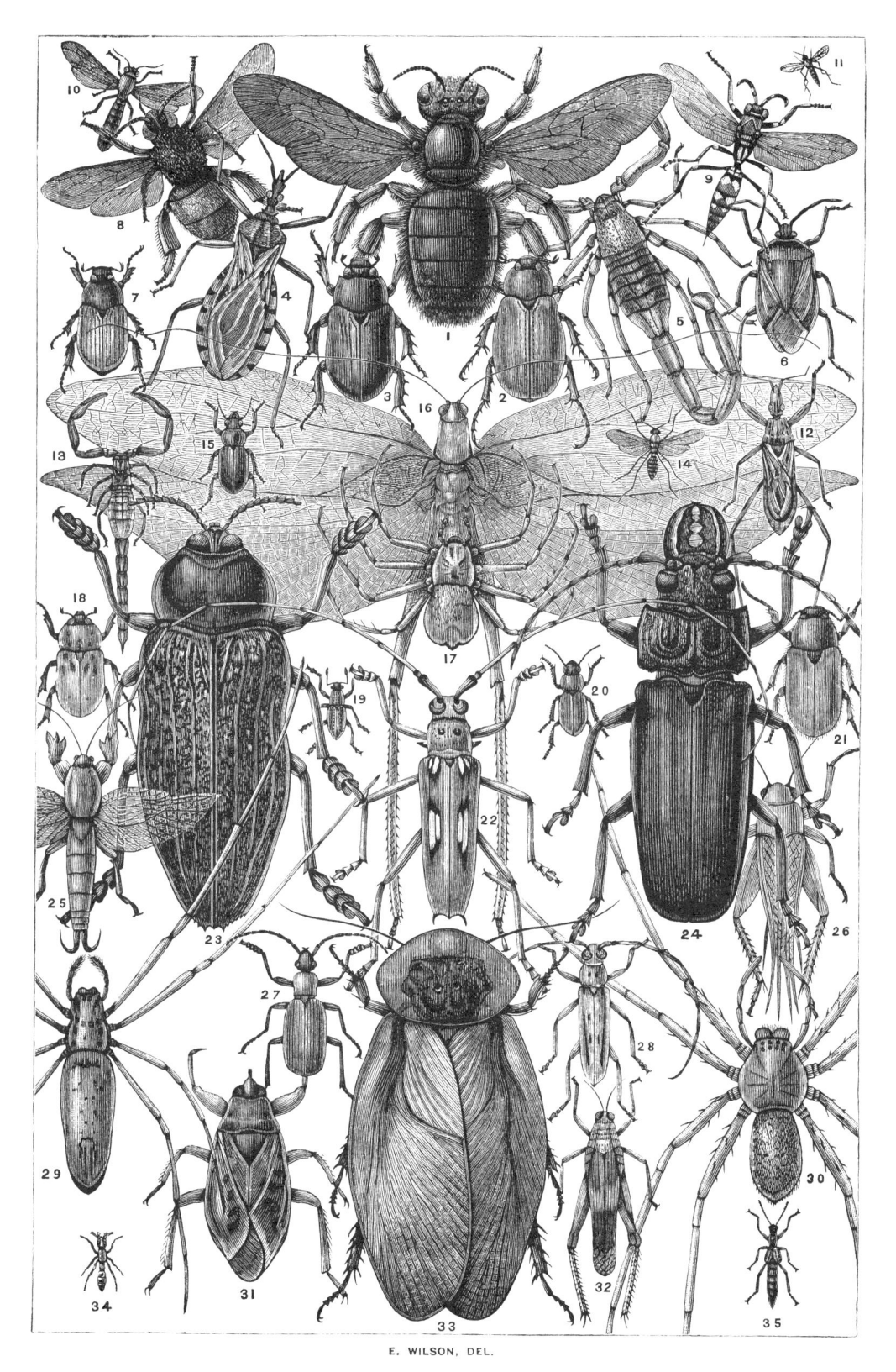

SELECTIONS FROM THE AUTHOR'S BEDROOM COLLECTION AT GUAYAQUIL.

We went by steam-launch from Yaguachi to Guayaquil and there separated,—Campaña returning to Quito *via* Bodegas, and the Carrels going by steamer to Panama. During the next fortnight, I lived principally in the hotel called *The Ninth of October;* where, although in a certain sense solitary, I was never without company. The wonderful exuberance of life chased away drowsiness, and, when sleep came, one's very dreams were tropical. Droves of mice galloped about at night, and swarms of minute ants pervaded everything. The harsh gnawings of voracious rats were subdued by the softer music of the tender mosquito. These, the indigenous inhabitants, were supplemented by a large floating population; and, in all, I collected fifty species of vermin in a single room. A few selections are given in the accompanying plate from 'my bedfellows at Guayaquil.'[1]

Eleven years have elapsed since our return to Europe. Due regard to my ordinary avocations, and various inevitable delays

to the edge of a tract of country without traffic or population. The Bridge of Chimbo is 1132 and Sibambe is 8859 feet above the level of the sea. Throughout the course of the fifty miles of line between these two places there will therefore be an *average* gradient of 1 in 34; but, as it will be impossible to construct the whole with one uniform grade, some parts will necessarily be steeper. Those who propose to lay out money on this line might enquire (I adopt the words of Mr. St. John) into "the feasibility and probable profitableness" of *working* a line with an average gradient of 1 in 34 during the occurrence of torrential tropical rain, and into the effect of swiftly running water on loose soil.

From this interesting though brief *Report* I find that [in 1891] the trade with the interior is conducted in just the same manner as in 1880. "Goods," it is said, "are carried on mules, horses, and donkeys. Very heavy loads are carried by gangs of Indians. All the merchandize transported to and from the northern and central provinces of the Andean region passes through Babahoyo and Chimbo, *but mostly through the former place*... The railway is little used for the conveyance of goods for the highlands, as but few animals can be procured at Chimbo, the present terminus of the line."

[1] COLEOPTERA (2, 3, 7, 15, 18-24, 27, 28, 35). ORTHOPTERA (16, 25, 26, 32, 33). HYMENOPTERA (1, 8-10, 14, 34). HEMIPTERA (4, 6, 12, 31). DIPTERA (11). SCORPIONS and SPIDERS (5, 13, 17, 29, 30). These are given upon the scale of nature. The larger species have been omitted on account of their size, and the smallest ones from the difficulty of representing them.

have prevented this volume from appearing earlier; and I much regret that its publication comes too late to benefit my right-hand man and trusted assistant, Jean-Antoine Carrel. In the higher regions, we were at constant war with the elements; and, in comparison with what he and his cousin endured, hard-labour on a treadmill would have been pleasurable, and rest in a casual ward would have been luxury. They derived no advantage from the journey except their hard-earned pay, and I had hoped that this relation of it might have procured for them some recognition of their indefatigable industry in the service of science. Men of their class are indispensable to a worker in elevated regions. They have been so in the past, and they will be in the future; and, if it cannot be done as an act of justice, upon the lower ground of policy it would be expedient sometimes to acknowledge their exceptional, unrewarded services.[1]

No commiseration need be entertained for myself. The enterprize was my own seeking, and a traveller should be prepared to take the sours with the sweets. More than twenty years have passed since I drew out the plan of a journey amongst the Great Andes of the Equator. Engrossed by my work, the time has fled; and now that the toil is over the labour is forgotten,—an instant bridges the interval; and it seems less like a project which has been accomplished than a Dream that has yet to be realized.

[1] Through the sudden death of Jean-Antoine Carrel in 1890, some of the members of his family were left in straitened circumstances. Upon this being brought to the notice of the Royal Geographical Society by Mr. Douglas W. Freshfield, the Council granted the sum of £21 towards a Fund which was being raised by the *Daily Graphic* for the relief of those who were in need; and enhanced the value of the donation by a letter, from which the following paragraph is extracted. "The Council do not, as a rule, consider it within their province to contribute to Funds of this nature. But they have resolved to make an exception in the present case in order emphatically to mark their appreciation of the high services rendered to geographical science by the late J.-A. Carrel. . . by transporting delicate instruments to great heights with such care that on your return to England they proved to have suffered no injury whatever."

APPENDIX

A.—ALTITUDES DETERMINED IN ECUADOR.

The heights entered in the tables at pp. 399–401, have been calculated [1] from observations of Mercurial Barometers, unless the contrary is pointed out. Three mercurials were taken to Ecuador, and were made for the journey by Mr. J. J. Hicks, of Hatton Garden, London. Two of these (marked No. 550 and No. 558) were Mountain Barometers on Fortin's principle, and were intended for use in the interior, No. 550 being graduated from 32·5 to 10 inches, and No. 558 from 32·5 to 12 inches. The third barometer (No. 554) of the Kew pattern, was intended for employment at the level of the sea, and was graduated from 32 to 27 inches. All three read to $\frac{1}{500}$ of an inch (0·002).

After having been under examination by myself for some time, they were sent to Kew Observatory for verification, and the certificates which were given stated that the error of No. 550 was + 0·004, of No. 558 − 0·005, and that No. 554 was free from error. These barometers remained in my hands under constant examination and comparison until our departure.

We arrived at Guayaquil on December 9th, 1879, and upon the 10th, 11th, and 12th I took two readings daily of the three mercurials for comparison against each other. The mean of the greatest differences between the three instruments on these six occasions amounted to one-hundredth of an inch (0·010).

Mr. George Chambers, British Consul at Guayaquil, very kindly volunteered to read No. 554 during our absence in the interior ; and he did so at 11 a.m. and at 6 p.m., from December 1879 to July 1880.[2] These hours were considered by us to be the most likely ones at which we should be able to observe simultaneously.

Nos. 550 and 558 travelled in company as far as the Third Camp on Chimborazo ; but after that time, as a general rule, I took No. 558 alone to the greater heights, and left the other below, in reserve. No. 558 accompanied us everywhere, and consequently travelled more than No. 550, and the latter more than No. 554 (left at Guayaquil).

During our stay in the interior I compared the two mercurials against each other upon all convenient occasions, and perceived a slight increase in the difference of their readings.

Upon return to Guayaquil, the increase was found to amount to 0·003 of an inch, having been 0·006 at the start, and 0·009 on return. These two barometers were also compared (upon return to Guayaquil) against No.

---

[1] By Mr. William Ellis, F.R.A.S., of Greenwich Observatory.
[2] Mr. Chambers also read Aneroid No. 580 (which was left with him in case of accident to the mercurial barometer) throughout the same period.

554 upon seventeen occasions, and the mean of the extreme differences between the three instruments was now found to amount to 0·022 of an inch. From comparison of the readings as a whole, I concluded that No. 554 had taken in some air, but I was unable to determine which of the other two was most in error.

It seemed desirable, upon return to London, to have all three barometers verified by reference to some acknowledged standard other than Kew; and by the kind permission of Mr. Robert H. Scott, F.R.S., they were compared, in September 1880, against the standard of the Meteorological Office. The certificates given by Mr. Strachan [1] stated that at 30 inches the error of No. 550 was + 0·017, of No. 554 + 0·030, and of No. 558 − 0·004 of an inch. Hence it appeared that, since the verification at Kew, No. 554 had *acquired* an error of 0·030 of an inch, that No. 550 had *increased* its error by 0·013 of an inch, and that No. 558 had *decreased* its error by 0·001 of an inch. But as one can read on the verniers of these barometers only to $\frac{1}{500}$ of an inch, the certificate for No. 558 really amounted to saying that there was no alteration in the error; and this was the more satisfactory inasmuch as No. 558 was the barometer which had travelled everywhere, which had been employed upon all the summits, and against which the comparisons had been made that are recorded in the subsequent sections of this appendix. My indefatigable assistant, Jean-Antoine Carrel, carried this instrument throughout the entire journey in the interior; and to have preserved it intact, without alteration of error, whilst executing the severe labour incident upon our ascents, is, I believe, an unprecedented performance.[2] I give herewith reduced facsimiles of the certificate of Kew Observatory and of the Meteorological Office relating to No. 558.

The altitudes which have been deduced by Mr. Ellis from my observations of mercurial barometer have been calculated by Guyot's Tables (*Smithsonian Meteorological and Physical Tables*); and, as he has used the corresponding observations made by Mr. Chambers at Guayaquil, they generally differ to some extent from the results of my rough computations on the spot, where the 'corresponding observations' were unknown to me.

The determinations which are most deserving of confidence are those which are obtained from the means of a number of observations, and those which are least reliable are naturally those which depend upon one observation only. In several instances, the exceptionally high temperature which was observed at great elevations has caused me some perplexity. The most extreme case was upon the summit of Antisana. At this great elevation, surrounded by snow and ice in every direction for several miles, the temperature fluctuated during our stay from 44° to 60° Faht., though the sun was con-

---

[1] Who was neither acquainted with my recent comparisons nor with the certificates previously given at Kew.
[2] The manner of packing, transporting, and suspending the two barometers which were used in the field has been already mentioned. It may be added here that throughout the whole time they were employed, whilst being moved from one place to another, they were invariably carried reversed, *i.e.* with cisterns uppermost. Before they were reversed, and packed in their cases, the mercury was driven to the tops of the tubes by means of the cistern screws; and, after reversal, the cistern screws were turned back about half a turn, to allow a little play to the mercury.

APPENDIX. *ALTITUDES DETERMINED IN ECUADOR.* 397

Bar Form B.

KEW OBSERVATORY.—Certificate of Examination.

Barometer by _Hicks, London_
Mountain No. 558

Compared with the Standard Barometer of the Kew Observatory.

CORRECTION (including capillary action) = −0·005 in. inch

Scale of inches examined and found _Satisfactory_

CORRECTIONS TO ATTACHED THERMOMETER. No. 60185 K.O. 1925

At 32°	At 42°	At 52°	At 62°	At 72°	At 82°	At 92°
−0·0	+0·2	+0·2	+0·2	+0·1	+0·1	+0·1

Note.—I.—When the sign of the Correction is +, the quantity is to be *added* to the observed scale reading, and when − to be *subtracted* from it.

II.—Mercurial Thermometers are liable, through age, to read too high; the Thermometer ought, therefore, at some future date, to be again tested at the melting point of ice, and if its reading at that point be found different from the one now given, an appropriate correction should be applied to all the above points.

Kew Observatory,
May 1879

G. M. Whipple
Superintendent.

K. 250-1-78.

Fortin's mountain

| CORRECTIONS to SCALE READINGS of BAROMETER. ||||
by _Hicks 558_	at 29·5	at 30·0	at 30·5	att^d ther^r
		−·004		+0·4

When the sign of the correction is +, the quantity is to be *added* to the observed reading; and when − to be *subtracted* from it. The corrections given above include those for Index-error, Capacity, and Capillarity.

Meteorological Office. _September_ 1880. _R. Strachan_

cealed during the whole time, and we were more or less in a cloud. At the Hacienda of Antisana, which is surrounded by extensive grassy slopes, and is about 6000 feet below the summit, during our three days' stay, I noted no higher temperature than 49° Faht. In the calculations for the height of Antisana the *observed* air temperature, namely 55° Faht., has been employed; and in almost all other cases the *observed* temperatures have been employed, and have not been *assumed*. Yet I cannot but feel that a closer approximation to the truth might have been obtained (especially in the case of Antisana) if assumed (and very much lower) air temperatures had sometimes been used.[1]

My immediate predecessors in Ecuador, Messrs. Reiss and Stübel, printed a list at Quito in 1871 of many hundreds of altitudes which had been determined by them by mercurial barometer.[2] There is a fair agreement between their altitudes and my own, and generally a close accordance in cases where the determinations are from the mean of a number of observations by each observer. Amongst towns, villages, and farms, the following may be quoted:—

	WHYMPER.	REISS & STÜBEL.
Quito	9,343 feet.	9,350 feet.
Latacunga	9,141 ,,	9,190 ,,
Machachi	9,839 ,,	9,629 ,,
Ambato	8,606 ,,	8,556 ,,
Riobamba	9,039 ,,	9,180 ,,
Cotocachi	7,970 ,,	8,048 ,,
Guaranda	8,894 ,,	8,753 ,,
Penipe	8,100 ,,	8,104 ,,
Cayambe	9,323 ,,	9,357 ,,
Mocha	10,708 ,,	10,774 ,,
Hac. Antisana	13,306 ,,	13,370 ,,
,, Pedregal	11,629 ,,	11,585 ,,
,, Candelaria	9,400 ,,	9,491 ,,
,, Guachala	9,217 ,,	9,190 ,,
La Dormida, Cayambe	11,805 ,,	11,749 ,,
Pass of Abraspungo	14,480 ,,	14,410 ,,

[1] In *Nature*, February 5, 1880, it is said, on the authority of Professor Plantamour, "it happens every year that the temperature on the St. Bernard, during several hours, or even during several days, of December, is higher than that of Geneva. During December 1879, this anomaly lasted for a longer period of time than usual; the average temperature of December on the St. Bernard (2070 mètres above Geneva) was 8°·4 C. higher than that at Geneva. . . . Professor Plantamour observes how difficult it is in such cases to determine the mean temperature of the stratum of air between the two stations, and how great the error of the barometrical levelling and of the reduction of the observed pressure to the sea-level would be if we applied the barometrical formula to such cases."

[2] This list, which will be invaluable to future travellers in Ecuador, is more likely to be procured at Dresden or Berlin than in Quito.

APPENDIX. ALTITUDES DETERMINED IN ECUADOR.

No.	Date.	Place of Observation.	Altitude.	No. of Observations.
1.	Dec. 16, 1879	Muñapamba	1,337 feet	2
2.	,, 16-17, ,,	Tambo Loma	6,700 ,,	*
3.	,, 17, ,,	Tambo Gobierno	10,417 ,,	2
4.	,, 18-25, ,,	Guaranda, level of Plaza	8,894 ,,	14
5.	,, 26-7, ,,	Chimborazo, First Camp	14,375 ,,	2
6.	,, 28-30, ,,	Do. Second do.	16,664 ,,	4
7.	Jan. 2-3, 1880	Do. Third do.	17,285 ,,	3
8.	,, 4, ,,	Do. Summit (see ch. xix)	20,545 ,,	1
9.	,, 3, 6, ,,	Do., foot of Southern Walls	18,528 ,,	2
10.	,, 14-15, ,,	Tambo of Chuquipoquio	11,704 ,,	4
11.	,, 18-22, ,,	Ambato, level of Plaza	8,606 ,,	10
12.	,, 25, ,,	Latacunga, do. do.	9,141 ,,	2
13.	,, ,, ,,	Summit of Tiupullo ridge	11,559 ,,	3
14.	Jan., Feb., and June	Machachi, level of high road	9,839 ,,	36
15.	Feb. 2, ,,	Corazon, highest reached W. side	15,131 ,,	1
16.	,, ,, ,,	Do. Summit	15,871 ,,	1
17.	,, 8, 10, ,,	Hacienda de la Rosario	10,356 ,,	4
18.	,, 9, ,,	Illiniza, Camp on S. side	15,207 ,,	1
19.	,, ,, ,,	Do. Highest reached S. side	17,023 ,,	1
20.	,, 14, ,,	Hacienda of Pedregal	11,629 ,,	2
21.	,, 15, ,,	Cotopaxi, foot of Yanasache lava	13,455 ,,	2
22.	,, 16, ,,	Do. First Camp	15,139 ,,	1
23.	,, 18, 19, ,,	Do. Second do.	19,500 ,,	*
24.	,, ,, ,,	Do. Summit	19,613 ,,	5
25.	Mar., May, and June	Quito, level of chief Plaza	9,343 ,,	22
26.	Mar. 19, ,,	Do. The Panecillo	2,985 ,,	*

* From observations of Aneroid Barometers.

No.	Date.	Place of Observation.	Altitude.	No. of Observations.
27.	Mar. 5, 1880	Hacienda of Antisanilla	12,342 feet	1
28.	" 6-9, "	Do. Antisana	13,306 ,,	6
29.	7, ,,	Antisana, highest point attained	17,623 ,,	1
30.	,, ,, ,,	Do. foot of glacier, W. side	15,295 ,,	1
31.	,, 9-10, ,,	Do. Camp on	15,984 ,,	2
32.	,, 10, ,,	Do. Summit	19,335 ,,	2
33.	,, 22, ,,	Pichincha, First Camp	14,007 ,,	1
34.	,, 22-3, ,,	Do. Second do.	14,992 ,,	2
35.	,, 23, ,,	Do. Summit	15,918 ,,	1
36.	,, 27, ,,	Quebrada of Guallabamba (top)	9,306 ,,	1
37.	,, ,, ,,	Do. do. (bottom)	6,472 ,,	1
38.	,, ,, ,,	Village of Guallabamba	7,133 ,,	1
39.	,, 28-9, ,,	Hacienda of Guachala	9,217 ,,	2
40.	,, 30, ,,	Do. Chuarpongo	9,665 ,,	1
41.	Apr. 2-5, ,,	Cayambe, Camp on	14,762 ,,	4
42.	,, 3, ,,	Do. Pointe Jarrin	16,164 ,,	1
43.	,, 4, ,,	Do. Summit	19,186 ,,	2
44.	,, 8, ,,	Do. La Dormida	11,805 ,,	1
45.	,, 12, ,,	Sara-urcu, Camp on	13,754 ,,	1
46.	,, 17, ,,	Do. Summit	15,502 ,,	1
47.	,, 20, ,,	Village of Cayambe	9,323 ,,	1
48.	,, 22, ,,	Hacienda of Ocampo	8,192 ,,	1
49.	,, ,, ,,	Village of Cotocachi	7,970 ,,	1
50.	,, 24, ,,	Cotocachi, Camp on	14,490 ,,	1
51.	,, ,, ,,	Do. Summit	16,301 ,,	1
52.	,, 25, ,,	Do. Hut called Iltaqui	10,049 ,,	1

APPENDIX. *ALTITUDES DETERMINED IN ECUADOR.* 401

No.	Date.	Place of Observation.	Altitude.	No. of Observations.
53.	June 8, 1880	Illiniza, Camp on N. side	15,446 feet	1
54.	,, 9, ,,	Do. Highest reached N. side	16,922 ,,	1
55.	,, 14, ,,	Village of Mocha	10,708 ,,	2
56.	,, ,, ,,	Highest point of the Paramo between Mocha and Riobamba	11,879 ,,	1
57.	June-July ,,	Riobamba	9,039 ,,	12
58.	June 16, ,,	Village of Penipe	8,100 ,,	1
59.	,, ,, ,,	Hacienda of Candelaria	9,400 ,,	1
60.	,, 17-18, ,,	Camp in Valley of Collanes	12,540 ,,	4
61.	,, 20, ,,	Do. Valley of Naranjal	13,053 ,,	2
62.	,, 28, ,,	Carihuairazo, Camp on	13,377 ,,	5
63.	,, 29, ,,	Do. Summit of W. peak	16,515 ,,	2
64.	July 1, ,,	Pass of Abraspungo	14,480 ,,	1
65.	,, ,, ,,	Chimborazo, Fourth Camp	14,359 ,,	1
66.	,, 2, ,,	Do. Fifth do.	15,811 ,,	2
67.	,, 3, ,,	Do. Summit (see ch. xix)	20,475 ,,	2
68.	,, ,, ,,	Do. Halt for snow-line	16,703 ,,	1
69.	,, 5, ,,	Do. Sixth Camp	13,353 ,,	1
70.	,, 9, ,,	Village of Nanti	10,669 ,,	1
71.	,, ,, ,,	Road between Guamote and Galti	11,362 ,,	1
72.	,, 10, ,,	Camp above Hacienda of Galti	11,772 ,,	1
73.	,, ,, ,,	Commencement of the descent towards the Pacific	11,160 ,,	*
74.	,, ,, ,,	Camp in forest	9,000 ,,	*
75.	,, 11, ,,	Hacienda of Cayandeli	4,600 ,,	*
76.	,, ,, ,,	Last camp, near Bridge of Chimbo	1,430 ,,	*

* From observations of Aneroid Barometers.

B.—THE RANGE OF THE BAROMETER IN ECUADOR.

The remarkable stability of the barometer in Ecuador has been frequently noticed. It seems to have been first publicly pointed out by La Condamine, who said that, at Quito, he found the greatest difference (during a year ?) hardly exceeded a line and a half.[1] This amount is equal to 0·133 of an English inch.

Shortly before my departure for Ecuador, M. Boussingault presented a Memoir to the French Academy of Sciences[2] dealing with this subject, and quoted 2·11 millimètres as the (mean?) *diurnal* variation at Quito. My movements were too rapid to permit of a series of observations at any one point to determine the daily range, or the periodical variations, and circumstances did not allow me even upon a single occasion to read the barometer for twenty-four consecutive hours. But so far as my observations extended they supported or confirmed previous reports respecting the small range of the barometer in this country. The greatest difference I observed in any one day in the interior was 0·134 of an inch, at Riobamba, on June 24, 1880 ; and the greatest at the level of the sea was 0·092 of an inch, at Guayaquil, on July 18, 1880. The violent storms which often raged seemed to affect the barometer scarcely, if at all, and the variations in the height of the mercurial column were as much due to differences in the air temperature as to any alterations in pressure.

The highest readings recorded by Mr. Chambers at Guayaquil (30 feet above sea level) were :—

    In Dec. 1879 (max. of obs. on 16 days) 29·970 inches.
    ,, Jan. 1880 (,,   ,,   22   ,,) 29·910   ,,
    ,, Feb. ,, (,,   ,,   20   ,,) 29·971   ,,
    ,, Mar. ,, (,,   ,,   23   ,,) 29·921   ,,
    ,, April ,, (,,   ,,   30   ,,) 29·959   ,,
    ,, June ,, (,,   ,,   11   ,,) 29·943   ,,
    ,, July ,, (,,   ,,   10   ,,) 29·925   ,,

The above readings are reduced to 32° Faht.

---

[1] "Nous avons éprouvé à Quito pendant des années entières, que sa plus grande différence ne passe guère une ligne et demie. M. Godin a le premier remarqué que ses variations, qui sont à peu près d'une ligne en vingt-quatre heures, ont des alternatives assez régulières, ce qui étant une fois connu, donne lieu de juger de la hauteur moyenne du Mercure, par une seule expérience."—*Relation abrégée d'un Voyage fait dans l'Interieur de l'Amérique méridionale*, par M. de la Condamine ; Paris, 8vo, 1745, pp. 21-22. See also *Journal du Voyage*, etc., par M. de la Condamine ; Paris, 4to, 1751, p. 109.

[2] A résumé of this was printed in the *Comptes Rendus*, vol. 88, Nos. 23, 24 ; pp. 1158-1165, 1240-1243, June 9 and 16, 1879, under the title *Détermination de la hauteur du mercure dans le baromètre sous l'équateur ; amplitude des variations diurnes barométriques à diverses stations dans les Cordillères*, par M. Boussingault.

APPENDIX. RANGE OF THE BAROMETER IN ECUADOR.

April was the only month upon which he observed *every day* at 11 A.M. and 6 P.M., and the extreme difference between his readings in that month amounted to 0·197 of an inch.[1]

An Astronomical and Meteorological Observatory was established at Quito while Garcia Moreno was President of the Republic, and in October 1878 this institution commenced to publish a Bulletin,[2] containing barometric observations, made daily at 6 A.M., 2 P.M., and 10 P.M. I was informed at Quito, in 1880, that the barometer employed was not at the Observatory, and was at a much lower level, at the extreme opposite (southern) end of the city; but since then its position appears to have been changed.[3] From this publication I have constructed the following table, embracing the period between September 1879–August 1880 inclusive :—

	Max. reading in the Month at			Min. reading in the Month at		
	6 A.M.	2 P.M.	10 P.M.	6 A.M.	2 P.M.	10 P.M.
1879, Sept.	548·41	548·40	548·47	546·84	546·72	546·84
,, Oct.	548·38	548·12	548·41	546·73	546·69	546·39
,, Nov.	547·82	548·28	548·36	546·79	545·63	546·63
,, Dec.	548·66	549·30	549·12	545·82	545·82	545·84
1880, Jan.	548·43	548·40	548·40	547·88	547·74	548·07
,, Feb.	547·87	547·44	547·77	547·00	546·54	547·08
,, March	548·81	547·58	547·80	547·19	546·47	546·30
,, April	547·70	547·05	547·86	545·86	544·54	545·95
,, May	547·93	548·02	548·98	545·90	545·41	546·20
,, June	547·96	547·91	548·53	545·60	545·09	546·14
,, July	548·56	547·74	548·61	545·84	546·81	547·00
,, Aug.	547·78	546·93	547·88	546·76	545·08	546·88

The readings are in millimètres reduced to 32° Faht.

The highest recorded reading in the twelve months is 549·30 mm., on December 1, 1879, and the lowest 544·54 mm., on April 14, 1880; and the difference of these two, or the extreme range recorded in the Bulletin for this period is 4·76 mm., which is equal to 2·1 Paris lines, or nearly half as much again as the amount named by La Condamine. As, however, the observations published in the Bulletin are only for 6 A.M., 2 P.M., and 10 P.M., they do not give the extreme range of the barometer at Quito.

La Condamine said that the barometer at Quito attained its greatest height at about 9 A.M., and dropped to its minimum about 3 P.M. Boussingault says in *Comptes Rendus*, 1879, pp. 1158-9, "On sait en effet que, dans les régions équinoxiales, le mercure, dans le baromètre, atteint le maximum

---

[1] In the same month the greatest difference between the readings at Quito (as recorded in the Bulletin, which is referred to in the next paragraph) was 0·157 of an inch.

[2] Under the title *Boletin del Observatorio Astronomico de Quito, publicado por Juan B. Menten, Director del mismo Observatorio.* Quito. Imprenta nacional.

[3] The following note occurs at p. 66 of the Bulletin, dated October 1880: "Desde el 1° de setiembre se ha variado la colocacion del Barómetro lo que explica la diferencia con los meses anteriores."

de hauteur entre 8 et 10 heures du matin ; qu'il descend ensuite jusque vers 4 heures de l'après-midi ; qu'il est à la hauteur minima entre 3 et 4 heures, pour remonter jusqu'à 11 heures du soir, sans arriver toutefois à la hauteur à laquelle il était à 9 heures du matin ; qu'il s'abaisse enfin jusqu'à 4 heures du matin, sans tomber aussi bas qu' à 4 heures du soir ; qu'il recommence alors son évolution. C'est là, du moins, ce qui a lieu généralement."

The observations published in the Quito Bulletin do not always accord with this statement. In some months, the means of the 2 P.M. observations are higher instead of lower than the means of those at 6 A.M. and 10 P.M., and it will be seen from the table at p. 000 that the very highest reading of the entire year is one at 2 P.M. The following observations, however, made by myself at Machachi, so far as they go, follow the law as stated by Boussingault.

At MACHACHI. Bar. No. 558 (reduced to 32° Faht.).

1880.	10 A.M.	11 A.M.	2 P.M.	6 P.M.	7.20 P.M.
	Inches.	Inches.	Inches.	Inches.	Inches.
Jan. 26	...	...	...	...	21·135
,, 28	...	...	...	...	21·147
,, 29	...	21·114	...	...	...
,, 29	...	...	...	...	21·108
,, 30	...	21·163	...	...	...
,, 30	...	..	...	21·114	...
,, 31	...	21·159	...	...	...
Feb. 1	...	...	...	21·096	...
,, 4	...	...	...	21·092	...
,, 5	...	...	...	21·120	...
,, 11	...	...	...	21·134	...
,, 27	...	21·099	...	...	...
,, 28	...	21·127	...	...	...
,, 29	21·179	...	...	...	...
June 7	...	...	...	...	21·167
,, 10	..	...	21·131	...	...
Means	21·179	21·165	21·131	21·111	21·139

The smallness of the differences in pressure in Ecuador, and the regularity of the variations, render that country particularly suitable for carrying out such experiments as it is still desirable to make with the barometer ; and there is probably no other region on or near to the Equator where observations can be made with such facility between the heights of 7000 to 16,000 feet.

C.—COMPARISONS OF THE ANEROID AGAINST THE MERCURIAL BAROMETER.

Aneroids were carried to Ecuador to endeavour to ascertain whether the *means* of the readings of several, or of a number, would or would not accord with the mercurial barometer at low pressures.

It has long been known that the indications afforded by a *single* aneroid are apt to be of a very deceiving nature, even at moderate elevations; but it seemed to me *possible* if several, or if a number were employed, that one might, by inter-comparison, discriminate between those which went most astray and those which held closely together; and that, by adoption of the means of the readings of the latter, a decent approximation might be obtained to the truth, possibly even at great altitudes. It may be added that I wished this might prove to be the case; for the portability of aneroids, the facility with which they can be read, and the quickness of their action, would render them valuable for many purposes, if their indications could be relied upon.

Eight aneroids were taken. One of these, by Casella, marked No. 580, had been made for an earlier journey; and, through being only graduated to 20 inches, was of no service for comparison at great heights.[1] The seven remaining aneroids were constructed expressly for the expedition, and were under trial and examination for nearly twelve months before our departure. They were selected from picked instruments, and only those were taken such as were, so far as one could tell, in all respects as perfect as could be produced.[2] These seven aneroids were marked A–G. A, B, and C were graduated from 31 down to 15 inches, and D, E, F, G were graduated from 31 down to 13 inches,—a range which I thought would be sufficient for my purposes.[3]

It became apparent at an early stage of the journey, *a.* that the whole of the aneroids had acquired considerable errors; *b.* that they differed amongst each other to a very large extent; and *c.* that neither means of the whole, nor means of those which held closest together, nor means of any combination, would give decent approximations to the truth. The more evident this became the greater importance I attached to the preservation of the mercurials. Comparisons of the aneroids against the mercurials were neverthe-

---

[1] This was left with Mr. Chambers at Guayaquil, as a reserve for him, in case accident befell the Standard Mercurial; and he read both instruments during the whole of our absence in the interior.

[2] I abstain, however, from mentioning the names of the makers (to whom I am much indebted), lest the remarks which follow should be construed to their disadvantage.

[3] It proved to be inadequate.

less continued until the end of the journey;[1] and after two months' experience in the interior the behaviour of the aneroids in ascending and descending was so well ascertained that one might, I think, have made use of their indications to determine differences of level without committing very great mistakes.

In the following pages, I propose first to give some of my experiences, and then to draw such conclusions as appear to be warranted.[2]

§ 1. Shortly before my departure from London, I made (on October 25, 1879) a final comparison of the aneroids against the mercurial barometer. Only one of the aneroids corresponded exactly, and of the others some were too high and some were too low, the greatest difference between them amounting to 0·225 of an inch, and the mean of the whole showing an error of + 0·148 of an inch.

§ 2. Our ship stopped a clear day (November 20, 1879) at Jamaica, and I took the opportunity to carry the aneroids to the top of the Blue Mountains,[3] comparing them against the mercurial before starting and upon return, and comparing them against each other at the highest point attained. The following is the complete record, and it will be seen from it that the mean

No. of Barometer.	At start.	At top.	On return.
Aneroid 580	29·980	25·430	29·975
,, A	29·850	25·500	29·850
,, B	29·800	25·250	29·800
,, C	29·700	25·120	29·650
,, D	29·850	25·400	29·880
,, E	29·800	25·300	29·750
,, F	29·750	25·350	29·700
,, G	29·800	25·310	29·700
Extreme differences	0·280	0·380	0·325
Mean of aneroids	29·816	25·332	29·788
Merc. bar. No. 554	29·876	. . .	29·854
Mean error of aneroids	− 0·060	. . .	− 0·066

error of the aneroids (which in London was + 0·148) had changed on arrival at Kingston to − 0·060, and upon return in the evening of November 20 it was still further increased to − 0·066.

[1] In all the comparisons which are made throughout this paper the readings of the mercurial barometer are reduced to 32° Faht.

[2] Paragraphs 1–10 should be read in connection with the tables at pp. 412, 413.

[3] Drove to Gordonstown, walked thence to Newcastle, and on until we came to a notch in the mountains commanding a view of the northern side of the island. Read the aneroids at this place.

APPENDIX. COMPARISONS OF THE ANEROID BAROMETER. 407

§ 3. Comparisons were again made at Colon and Guayaquil, and at neither of these places (at the level of the sea) was there any further increase in the mean error of the aneroids; but at Muñapamba (where we commenced to mount the Pacific range of Ecuador) their difference amongst each other had risen to 0·500 of an inch, and the mean error was increased to − 0·098 of an inch.

§ 4. At Tambo Gobierno (the culminating point of the road over the Pacific range of Ecuador), 10,417 feet above the sea, the mean error of the aneroids had risen to − 0·487 of an inch, and the extreme difference of their readings amounted to 0·715.

§ 5. With the descent on the other side the aneroids came more closely together, but their mean error continued to augment,—being upon arrival at Guaranda[2] (8894 feet) − 0·520, and it rose in one week to − 0·655. The 'greatest difference' also continued to increase, and it stood on Christmas Day at 0·800 of an inch. The following record showing the continual increases in the errors, will be found interesting.

No. of Barometer.	Dec. 18, 1879.	Dec. 20, 1879.	Dec. 23, 1879.	Dec. 25, 1879.
Aneroid A	21·700	21·700	21·700	21·600
,, B	21·170	20·960	20·940	20·870
,, D	21·460	21·430	21·450	21·390
,, E	21·500	21·500	21·500	21·440
,, F	21·220	21·030	20·950	20·800
,, G	21·400	21·380	21·300	21·300
Extreme differences	0·530	0·740	0·760	0·800
Mean of aneroids	21·408	21·333	21·321	21·233
Mean Merc. bar.	21·928	21·912	21·934	21·888
Mean errors of aneroids	− 0·520	− 0·579	− 0·613	− 0·655

§ 6. Upon December 26, 1879, we encamped on the Arenal (14,375 feet), at the foot of Chimborazo, and on the morning of the 27th the mean error of the aneroids was found to be − 0·737, and their greatest difference 0·880.

§ 7. We then moved up to the Second Camp on Chimborazo (16,664 feet, the mean error continuing to rise, and amounting upon December 30 to − 0·903.

§ 8. Upon arrival at the Third Camp (17,285 feet) I found that comparisons at greater heights would have to be made between five aneroids

[1] As aneroid 580 was left at Guayaquil, the comparisons are now between the seven remaining instruments.
[2] Aneroid C was lost or stolen shortly before arrival at Guaranda, thus reducing the number under comparison to six.

only, as the error which B had acquired was so large that we had already got *beyond its range*. The mean error of the aneroids at this point amounted to -0.974, and their greatest difference to 1.120 inches.

§ 9. The aneroids D and E were alone taken to the summit of Chimborazo on the first ascent, January 4, 1880, and these two were taken because they were working better than the others. The readings on the summit are instructive.

Merc. bar. No. 558 .	14·110 inches.
Aneroid D	13·050 ,,
do. E	12·900 (by estimation).

The mean of the two aneroids is seen to be 12.975 inches, and the error of this upon the mercurial -1.135 inches. I defer comment to a later point.

§ 10. Their prolonged residence upon Chimborazo seriously affected the constitutions of aneroids F and G. The index of the latter instrument became immovable, and the former was afflicted with a quivering action which set observation at defiance. Comparisons for the remainder of the journey were thus restricted to A, B, D, E only, and they are given in the tables upon pp. 21–23 so far as is necessary to support the statements,—*a.* that the aneroids acquired considerable errors ; *b.* that they differed amongst each other to a very large extent ; and *c.* that their means were far from the truth.

§ 11. After we had been three to four weeks in the interior, the aneroids A, B, D, E were found to hold pretty constantly together (or, speaking more correctly, their movements were harmonious), and they seemed to have acquired their maximum errors for the pressures at which they were used.[1] Of the above four instruments B had the largest index-error, and the following table shows that it remained tolerably constant. It then became interesting

Date.	Place of Observation.	Merc. bar. 558.	Aneroid B.	Error of B.
Jan. 14, 1880	Chuquipoquio	19·683 inch	17·820 inch	− 1·863 inch
Feb. 8, ,,	Hac. de la Rosario	20·805 ,,	19·100 ,,	− 1·705 ,,
,, 9, ,,	Illiniza (S. side) .	17·239 ,,	15·400 ,,	− 1·839 ,,
,, 16, ,,	On Cotopaxi .	17·431 ,,	15·650 ,,	− 1·781 ,,
,, 26, ,,	Machachi . .	21·142 ,,	19·360 ,,	− 1·782 ,,
Mar. 28, ,,	Hac. Guachala	21·618 ,,	19·950 ,,	− 1·668 ,,
May 15, ,,	Quito . . .	21·631 ,,	19·990 ,,	− 1·641 ,,
June 8, ,,	Illiniza (N. side) .	17·222 ,,	15·400 ,,	− 1·822 ,,

to observe whether aneroids which had acquired such large index-errors could be usefully employed for the determination of differences of level.

[1] See the last column of the table at p. 413.

§ 12. Upon the journey to the north of Quito I carried merc. bar. No. 558 and aneroids A and B, and upon arrival at the top of the great ravine of Guallabamba took simultaneous observations of the mercurial and the aneroids. At the bottom of the ravine, two hours and a half later, readings of all three were repeated with the following result :—

Date.	Barometer.	Read at top.	Read at bottom.
Mar. 27, 1880	Merc. bar. 558 (red. to 32° Faht.)	21·692	23·929
do.	Aneroid A	21·140	23·400
do.	do. B	19·940	22·200

The rise of the Mercurial Barometer was 2·237 inches.
    do.   do.   Aneroid A   ,,   2·260   ,,
    do.   do.   ,,   B   ,,   2·260   ,,

§ 13. The foregoing experiment is a *descending* one employing two aneroids, and the next is an *ascending* one in which three were observed. Upon the occasion of the attempt to ascend Illiniza from the north, I read the three aneroids A, B, D before departure from Machachi (9839 feet), and did the same at our camp (15,446 feet).

Date.	Barometer.	At Machachi (9 a. m.)	At Camp (6 p. m.)
June 8, 1880	Merc. bar. 558	21·176 inches	17·222 inches.
do.	Aneroid A	20·650 ,,	16·810 ,,
do.	do. B	19·530 ,,	15·400 ,,
do.	do. D	20·290 ,,	16·380 ,,

The fall of the Mercurial Barometer was 3·954 inches.
The mean fall of the three aneroids was 3·960 ,,

§ 14. Upon the second ascent of Chimborazo I carried aneroids A and E to the summit, reading them at the fifth camp and at the top. Aneroid A became much out of range, and I therefore cannot give its reading.

Date.	Barometer.	Fifth Camp (4 a. m.)	Summit (2 p. m.)
July 3, 1880	Merc. bar. 558	16·931 inches	14·044 inches.
do.	Aneroid E	16·060 ,,	12·990 ,,

The fall of the Mercurial Barometer was 2·887 inches.
    do.   Aneroid E   ,,   3·070   ,,

§ 15. The examples which are quoted in §§ 12, 13, 14 give the closest coincidences that I can mention from amongst experiments of this order. Upon the whole, it appeared to me that better values could be obtained from aneroids by taking the *mean* of ascending and descending observations,[1] than by taking the means of either ascending or descending ones alone, and I now give an example in which this method of treatment was adopted.

On March 19, 1880, I carried the aneroids A, B, D, E from our lodging

---

[1] When ascent and descent are only a short space of time apart.

410 COMPARISONS OF THE ANEROID BAROMETER. APPENDIX.

at Quito to the top of the hill called the Panecillo, on this occasion reading the 'scales of feet' upon them before departure, and again upon return to Quito. From the means of the ascending and descending readings, the summit of the Panecillo appears to be 651·25 feet above the level of the principal Plaza of Quito, which from the mean of twenty-two observations of mercurial barometer by myself is found to be 9343·3 feet above the sea. I have no observation of mercurial barometer on the Panecillo; and, if I had, should still quote by preference the independent observations of Messrs. Reiss and Stübel, who, from the mean of a large number of observations of mercurial barometer, give for the height of Quito 9350 feet, and for the Panecillo (two observations of m. b.) 10,007 feet. Their *difference of level* therefore is 657 feet, or 5 feet 9 inches more than the height indicated by the aneroids.

Barometer.	At Quito, in Hotel.	Summit of Panecillo.	= a rise of	On return to Quito.	= a fall of
Aneroid A	10,680 feet	11,325 feet	645 feet	10,760 feet	565 feet
do. B	12,310 ,,	13,050 ,,	740 ,,	12,390 ,,	660 ,,
do. D	11,260 ,,	11,950 ,,	690 ,,	11,340 ,,	610 ,,
do. E	11,000 ,,	11,680 ,,	680 ,,	11,060 ,,	620 ,,

Mean of ascending readings 688·75 feet.
Mean of descending do. 613·75 feet.
Mean of ascending and descending 651·25 feet.

§ 16. As the journey approached its termination, I became curious to observe how the aneroids would read against the mercurials upon return to the level of the sea. We arrived at Guayaquil again on July 13, 1880, and the barometers were compared against each other from the 16th to the 27th.[1] The error of aneroid A upon the 16th was − 0·361 of an inch, and of E − 0·321, but by the 27th their respective errors diminished to − 0·341 and − 0·291. I have not allowed the index of either to be altered. They continued to recover in the course of time; and I found, upon January 9, 1885, that aneroid E possessed an index-error of + 0·160, which was very nearly its error upon the last comparison in 1879 before our start, when it was seen to be + 0·182. Aneroid A did not recover with the same rapidity. Upon January 9, 1885, its error had diminished to − 0·200, and in five years more it recovered another tenth of an inch.

§ 17. In the tables at pp. 414, 415, the comparisons of the aneroids A and E are presented separated from the others. These two instruments were those which were most consistent in their behaviour, and were those which were most frequently employed. From inspection of the tables it will be immediately apparent that 'a good return' is of little value as a test of working.

[1] See the tables at pp. 414, 415, for this and for the succeeding paragraph.

Upon the last comparison before departure, these two aneroids possessed almost exactly similar index-errors ($+0\cdot172$ and $+0\cdot182$), and upon return to Guayaquil their index-errors were not far apart ($-0\cdot341$ and $-0\cdot291$). It would have appeared legitimate to conclude that their working had closely corresponded, but inspection of the last two columns of the table shows that such a conclusion would have been extremely erroneous. The case of E, taken by itself, is still stronger. This, in course of time, 'returned' almost perfectly; and inasmuch as this instrument (like all the others) was tested before departure, inch by inch, against the mercurial barometer under the air-pump, and corresponded almost perfectly, it would have seemed right to conclude that its readings in the interim must have been nearly free from error. Yet this instrument, at the greatest height at which it was compared, was found to possess a minus error of an inch and a fifth, the value of which, at the elevation in question, exceeds *two thousand feet* (see § 9).

§ 18. Some of the more important conclusions which must be arrived at from consideration of the results of these comparisons of the aneroid against the mercurial barometer are so obvious that I consider it unnecessary even to point them out; and, in the remarks which follow, I endeavour more to indicate the ways in which the aneroid may be advantageously used, than to emphasize the objections which might be urged against its employment.

A. It seems possible, without reference to a standard, by intercomparison of a number of aneroids, to discriminate between them, and to select those in which most confidence should be placed.

B. That, with aneroids of the present construction, it is unlikely that decent approximations to the truth will be obtained at low pressures, even when employing a large number of instruments. The errors of the whole series (A — G) were invariably minus ones, and in the worst cases amounted to as much as *two inches* upon the mercurial barometer.

C. That differences of level at great heights (low pressures) may be determined with considerable accuracy with aneroids, even when they have acquired very large index-errors.

D. That in observations of this description a nearer approach to the truth is generally obtained by employing the mean of ascending and descending readings than by taking ascending or descending readings separately.

E. That the test which is commonly applied of comparing for brief periods (minutes or hours) aneroids against mercurial barometers under the air-pump is of little or no value in determining the errors which will appear in aneroids used at low pressures for long periods (weeks or months).

F. That, similarly, comparisons of aneroids against mercurial barometers in balloon for a brief space of time afford little or no clue to the errors which will be exhibited by the former when subjected to low pressures for

412 COMPARISONS OF THE ANEROID BAROMETER. APPENDIX.

No.	Date.	Place of Observation.	No. of Aneroids observed.	Greatest difference between Aneroids.	Mean of Aneroids.	Mercurial Barometer (red. to 32° Faht.)	Mean error of Aneroids.
1.	Oct. 25, 1879	London	8	0·225 inch.	29·916 inch.	29·768 inch.	+ 0·148 inch.
2.	Nov. 18, ,,	Off S. Domingo (at sea)	8	0·260 ,,	29·886 ,,	29·985 ,,	− 0·099 ,,
3.	,, 20, ,,	Kingston, Jamaica	8	0·280 ,,	29·816 ,,	29·876 ,,	− 0·060 ,,
4.	,, ,, ,,	Above Newcastle, Jamaica	8	0·380 ,,	25·332 ,,	.	.
5.	,, ,, ,,	Kingston, do.	8	0·325 ,,	29·788 ,,	29·854 ,,	− 0·066 ,,
6.	Dec. 2, ,,	Colon, Isthmus of Panama	8	0·360 ,,	29·790 ,,	29·845 ,,	− 0·055 ,,
7.	,, 10-12, ,,	Guayaquil, Ecuador	8	0·346 ,,	29·769 ,,	29·824 ,,	− 0·055 ,,
8.	,, 16, ,,	Muñapamba, do.	7	0·500 ,,	28·510 ,,	28·608 ,,	− 0·098 ,,
9.	,, 17, ,,	Tambo Gobierno, Ecuador	7	0·715 ,,	20·272 ,,	20·759 ,,	− 0·487 ,,
10.	,, ,, ,,	San José de Chimbo, do.	7	0·660 ,,	21·955 ,,	.	.
11.	,, 18, ,,	Guaranda, do.	6	0·530 ,,	21·408 ,,	21·928 ,,	− 0·520 ,,
12.	,, 20, ,,	Do. do.	6	0·740 ,,	21·333 ,,	21·912 ,,	− 0·579 ,,
13.	,, 23, ,,	Do. do.	6	0·760 ,,	21·321 ,,	21·934 ,,	− 0·613 ,,
14.	,, 25, ,,	Do. do.	6	0·800 ,,	21·233 ,,	21·888 ,,	− 0·655 ,,
15.	,, 27, ,,	Chimborazo, First Camp	6	0·880 ,,	17·135 ,,	17·872 ,,	− 0·737 ,,
16.	,, 28, ,,	Do. Second do.	6	0·780 ,,	15·643 ,,	16·476 ,,	− 0·833 ,,
17.	,, 29, ,,	Do. do. do.	6	0·830 ,,	15·611 ,,	16·488 ,,	− 0·877 ,,

APPENDIX.   COMPARISONS OF THE ANEROID BAROMETER. 413

No.	Date.	Place of Observation.	No. of Aneroids observed.	Greatest difference between Aneroids.	Mean of Aneroids.	Mercurial Barometer (red. to 32° Faht.)	Mean error of Aneroids.
18.	Dec. 30, 1879	Chimborazo, Second Camp	6	0·825 inch.	15·577 inch.	16·480 inch.	− 0·903 inch.
19.	Jan. 4-5, 1880	Do. Third do.	4	1·120 ,,	15·045 ,,	16.019 ,,	− 0·974 ,,
20.	,, 4, ,,	Do. Summit of	2	0·150 ,,	12·975 ,,	14·110 ,,	− 1·135 ,,
21.	,, 9, ,,	Do. Second Camp	4	1·180 ,,	15·372 ,,	16·468 ,,	− 1·096 ,,
22.	,, 14, ,,	Tambo of Chuquipoquio	4	1·305 ,,	18·575 ,,	19·670 ,,	− 1·095 ,,
23.	,, 22, ,,	Ambato	4	1·160 ,,	21·172 ,,	22·094 ,,	− 0·922 ,,
24.	,, 29, ,,	Machachi	4	1·150 ,,	20·121 ,,	21·117 ,,	− 0·996 ,,
25.	Feb. 8, ,,	Hacienda de la Rosario	4	1·200 ,,	19·810 ,,	20·785 ,,	− 0·975 ,,
26.	,, 9, ,,	Illiniza, Camp on S. side	4	1·340 ,,	16·217 ,,	17·239 ,,	− 1·022 ,,
27.	,, 16, ,,	Cotopaxi, do.	4	1·310 ,,	16·440 ,,	17·431 ,,	− 0·991 ,,
28.	,, 26, ,,	Machachi	4	1·190 ,,	20·075 ,,	21·121 ,,	− 1·046 ,,
29.	Mar. 20, ,,	Quito	4	1·175 ,,	20·556 ,,	21·565 ,,	− 1·009 ,,
30.	,, 27, ,,	Quebrada of Guallabamba (top)	2	1·200 ,,	20·540 ,,	21·692 ,,	− 1·152 ,,
31.	,, ,, ,,	Do. do. (bottom)	2	1·200 ,,	22·800 ,,	23·929 ,,	− 1·129 ,,
32.	May 15, ,,	Quito	4	1·080 ,,	20·655 ,,	21·624 ,,	− 0·969 ,,
33.	June 8, ,,	Illiniza, Camp on N. side	3	1·410 ,,	16·197 ,,	17·222 ,,	− 1·025 ,,
34.	,, 11, ,,	Machachi	4	1·210 ,,	20·142 ,,	. .	. .

414 COMPARISONS OF THE ANEROID BAROMETER. APPENDIX.

No.	Date.	Place of Observation.	Mercurial Barometer, No. 558 (red. to 32° Faht.)	Aneroid A.	Aneroid E.	Error of A.	Error of E.
1.	Oct. 25, 1879	London	29·768 inch.	29·940 inch.	29·950 inch.	+ 0·172 inch.	+ 0·182 inch.
2.	Dec. 2, ,,	Colon, Isthmus of Panama	29·854 ,,	29·810 ,,	29·800 ,,	− 0·044 ,,	− 0·054 ,,
3.	,, 10, ,,	Guayaquil, Ecuador	29·767 ,,	29·750 ,,	29·750 ,,	− 0·017 ,,	− 0·017 ,,
4.	,, 16, ,,	Muñapamba, do.	28·611 ,,	28·525 ,,	28·500 ,,	− 0·086 ,,	− 0·111 ,,
5.	,, 17, ,,	Tambo Gobierno, Ecuador	20·777 ,,	20·640 ,,	20·400 ,,	− 0·137 ,,	− 0·377 ,,
6.	,, 18, ,,	Guaranda, do.	21·938 ,,	21·700 ,,	21·500 ,,	− 0·238 ,,	− 0·438 ,,
7.	,, 25, ,,	Do. do.	21·901 ,,	21·600 ,,	21·440 ,,	− 0·301 ,,	− 0·461 ,,
8.	,, 27, ,,	Chimborazo, First Camp	17·872 ,,	17·600 ,,	17·220 ,,	− 0·272 ,,	− 0·652 ,,
9.	,, 28, ,,	Do. Second do.	16·476 ,,	16·030 ,,	15·760 ,,	− 0·446 ,,	− 0·716 ,,
10.	,, 30, ,,	Do. do. do.	16·480 ,,	15·975 ,,	15·700 ,,	− 0·505 ,,	− 0·780 ,,
11.	Jan. 4-5, 1880	Do. Third do.	16·019 ,,	15·435 ,,	15·265 ,,	− 0·584 ,,	− 0·754 ,,
12.	,, 4, ,,	Do. Summit of	14·110 ,,	. .	12·900 ,,	. .	− 1·210 ,,
13.	,, 9, ,,	Do. Second Camp	16·468 ,,	15·880 ,,	15·460 ,,	− 0·588 ,,	− 1·008 ,,
14.	,, 14, ,,	Tambo of Chuquipoquio	19·683 ,,	19·125 ,,	18·775 ,,	− 0·558 ,,	− 0·908 ,,
15.	,, 22, ,,	Ambato	22·091 ,,	21·640 ,,	21·400 ,,	− 0·451 ,,	− 0·691 ,,
16.	,, 29, ,,	Machachi	21·114 ,,	20·580 ,,	20·325 ,,	− 0·534 ,,	− 0·789 ,,
17.	Feb. 8, ,,	Hacienda de la Rosario	20·805 ,,	20·300 ,,	20·000 ,,	− 0·505 ,,	− 0·805 ,,
18.	,, 9, ,,	Illiniza, Camp on S. side	17·239 ,,	16·740 ,,	16·380 ,,	− 0·499 ,,	− 0·859 ,,

APPENDIX. *COMPARISONS OF THE ANEROID BAROMETER.* 415

No.	Date.	Place of Observation.	Mercurial Barometer, No. 558 (red. to 32° Faht.)	Aneroid A.	Aneroid E.	Error of A.	Error of E.
19.	Feb. 16, 1880	Cotopaxi, Camp on	17·431 inch.	16·960 inch.	16·600 inch.	− 0·471 inch.	− 0·831 inch.
20.	,, 26, ,,	Machachi	21·142 ,,	20·550 ,,	20·290 ,,	− 0·592 ,,	− 0·852 ,,
21.	Mar. 20, ,,	Quito	21·577 ,,	21·000 ,,	20·800 ,,	− 0·577 ,,	− 0·777 ,,
22.	May 15, ,,	Do.	21·631 ,,	21·070 ,,	20·890 ,,	− 0·561 ,,	− 0·741 ,,
23.	,, 20, ,,	Do.	21·612 ,,	21·050 ,,	20·880 ,,	− 0·562 ,,	− 0·732 ,,
24.	June 8, ,,	Illiniza, Camp on N. side	17·222 ,,	16·810 ,,	. .	− 0·412 ,,	. .
25.	,, 28, ,,	Carihuairazo, Camp on	18·545 ,,	18·030 ,,	17·690 ,,	− 0·515 ,,	− 0·855 ,,
26.	,, 29, ,,	Do. Summit of	16·514 ,,	16·035 ,,	15·700 ,,	− 0·479 ,,	− 0·814 ,,
27.	July 3, ,,	Chimborazo, Fifth Camp	16·931 ,,	16·300 ,,	16·060 ,,	− 0·631 ,,	− 0·871 ,,
28.	,, ,, ,,	Do. Summit of	14·044 ,,	beyond its range	12·990 ,,	. .	− 1·054 ,,
29.	,, 10, ,,	Commencement of descent towards Pacific Ocean	. .	19·600 ,,	19·380 ,,	. .	. .
30.	,, ,, ,,	Camp in forest	. .	21·250 ,,	21·200 ,,	. .	. .
31.	,, 11, ,,	Hacienda of Cayandeli	. .	24·850 ,,	24·770 ,,	. .	. .
32.	,, ,, ,,	Camp near Bridge of Chimbo	. .	27·930 ,,	27·910 ,,	. .	. .
33.	,, 16, ,,	Guayaquil	29·911 ,,	29·550 ,,	29·590 ,,	− 0·361 ,,	− 0·321 ,,
34.	,, 27, ,,	Do.	29·941 ,,	29·600 ,,	29·650 ,,	− 0·341 ,,	− 0·291 ,,
35.	Jan. 9, 1885	London	29·740 ,,	29·540 ,,	29·900 ,,	− 0·200 ,,	+ 0·160 ,,

prolonged periods. [The balloon test is only a repetition of the air-pump test. In the former case the instruments are exposed to a natural, and in the latter case to an artificial diminution of pressure; and if the duration of time is equal in each case the results ought to correspond exactly.]

G. That very material errors may be fallen into by regarding 'a good return' at the level of the sea as a proof of correct working, at low pressures, of aneroids of the present construction.

H. That for the detection of such errors as aneroids (of the present construction) will exhibit when subjected to low pressures for a length of time, aneroids should be subjected artificially to similar pressures for a long period.

D.—UPON BOILING-POINT OBSERVATIONS.

Henderson's boiling-point apparatus, and nine boiling-point thermometers, were taken lest accidents might occur to the barometers. The thermometers were self-registering; they were constructed in two series, in order that the scales might not be too finely divided; and they were verified in the customary manner.

As the barometers were not injured, it was unnecessary to depend for altitude upon the indications afforded by the boiling-point of water. Observations of the boiling-point were, however, made at seventeen different stations from 8400 to 19,500 feet above the sea, for the purpose of *comparison against the barometers*. These observations have been worked out for altitude by Mr. W. Ellis, F.R.A.S., but are not quoted in this volume. As a general rule, three or more thermometers were boiled at each station, and in the calculations for altitude the *means* have been used of the observations which were made on each occasion.

It was found, in all cases, that the mean boiling-point at every station was higher than the corresponding barometer would lead one to expect,[1] from the tables which are generally accepted as authoritative, namely, Regnault's, as given in the *Smithsonian Tables, Meteorological and Physical*, third edition, Washington, 1859. The divergencies became more pronounced the higher we ascended, and this leads to the opinion that the tables are not perfect.

I venture to take the opportunity to make a few general remarks upon the method of attempting to determine altitudes by observations of the boiling-point of water; but I offer them with great diffidence, as they will be found somewhat opposed to the expressed opinions of eminent travellers, and of persons in authority.

Of late years, the practice of deducing altitudes from observations of the boiling-point of water has to a considerable extent superseded the older method of obtaining them by observation of the mercurial barometer: and it has been assumed (I think, erroneously) that the former method is but slightly inferior to the latter in accuracy, and is superior to it in facility. I think that any person who will, even at the level of the sea, take the trouble to examine the matter for himself, will speedily be convinced that the boiling-point method is one which must always be liable to considerable errors *upon* the mercurial barometer; that mountain-travellers who have had experience of the two methods—more especially those who have experimented upon the summits of lofty peaks—will concur with me in saying that the occasions are very rare indeed upon which observations of the mercurial barometer cannot be made, even upon those on which high wind and severe cold are experienced at inconvenient situations; and that, upon the other hand, occa-

---

[1] The heights deduced from the boiling-point observations are consequently lower than the truth.

sions are numerous on which, from one cause or another, it is impossible to make observations of the boiling-point of water under such conditions as will allow the observations to be of value.

The experimentalist, when at considerable elevations, will soon learn to distrust single readings or the use of single thermometers, through noticing how seldom his observed boiling-points accord with the 'corresponding barometric pressure,' or agree with each other; and will consider it necessary to employ at least several thermometers and to repeat his observations. I find, in practice, that to do this out of doors, under *favourable* conditions, occupies as great a length of time, or greater, than to take two careful observations of the mercurial barometer, a quarter of an hour apart.[1] So far as convenience and rapidity of observation are concerned, the balance appears to be in favour of the mercurial barometer when the conditions are favourable, and more distinctly so when the conditions are adverse.

Assuming that the thermometers which are employed are boiled in the correct manner,[2] and with the utmost care, there yet remain several possible causes of error,[3] and with thermometers of the kind usually employed, in which a degree of Fahrenheit's scale seldom extends over more than the eighth of an inch, I think an error of half a degree and upwards is probable in a single observation of one thermometer.[4] To obtain a more extended scale (to lessen the probability of error) the traveller must either carry an embarrassing number of thermometers, or else employ instruments of unusual and inconvenient length.

Near the level of the sea, the value of one degree of the Fahrenheit scale is about 0·590 of an inch on a barometer, and one inch of the barometer is

---

[1] The amount of time actually consumed in making a series of observations of the boiling-point is *longer* than is necessary for several observations of mercurial barometer; as in the former case undivided attention must be given to the operations, while in the latter it is only necessary to inspect the instrument at intervals, other things being done in the meanwhile. As it is seldom possible to remain more than an hour upon a very elevated summit, every minute is of importance.

[2] They should not be boiled in open vessels, nor immersed in the water. This, however, is not unfrequently done. See *A note on an alleged ascent of Chimborazo in 1856, by Messrs. Remy and Brenchley*, in the *Alpine Journal*, vol. x. pp. 226-31, 1881. Also see Livingstone's *Last Journals*, vol. ii. p. 198, 1874. Livingstone enters in his Journal, less than eleven months before his death, that "there is a full degree of difference between boiling in an open pot and in Casella's apparatus." It may, I think, be taken as certain that Dr. Livingstone would not have made this entry at such a time if he had been previously acquainted with the fact.

[3] Amongst others, the liability of mercurial thermometers to read too high by age. See the Kew certificate at p. 397 (of the attached thermometer), and compare the error therein stated with the error on return as stated in the Meteorological Office certificate.

Also see S. W. Baker's *Albert N'Yanza*, vol. ii. pp. 362-3, 8vo, 1866, for an instance of a boiling-point thermometer acquiring an error of $+0\cdot8$ of a degree Faht. in $4\frac{3}{4}$ years. This thermometer was made by Casella, and was supplied by the Royal Geographical Society.

See also Sir S. W. Baker's *Ismailia*, vol. ii. p. 562, 8vo, 1874, for an example of a boiling-point thermometer apparently changing its index-error from $+0\cdot20$ to $-0\cdot10$ Faht.

[4] Much larger differences than half a degree Fahrenheit may be observed between thermometers which are sent out by makers of the best repute, accompanied by 'verifications' stating only infinitesimal errors.

about equal to 900 feet of altitude. The value of a degree of the Fahrenheit scale is therefore equal to about 531 feet.

At the height of the summit of Mont Blanc the value of one degree of the Fahrenheit scale is about equal to 0·375 of an inch on a barometer, and at this elevation the value of one inch on a barometer is about equal to 1600 feet. In this case, the value of a degree of the Fahrenheit scale is therefore about 600 feet.

From comparison of the means of a number of observations of the boiling-point of water, made by myself in Ecuador, against the mercurial barometer, when the latter was standing at 16·522 to 17·427 inches, the value of a degree of a Fahrenheit scale, at that pressure, appears to be 613 feet.

From the previous paragraphs it is seen that the value of each degree of a thermometric scale is greater the higher we ascend. It is consequently necessary, in order to obtain as good proportional results at a high level as at the level of the sea, that personal errors, and errors arising from method or instrumental defects must be *lessened*. This, in practice, will not, I think, be found possible. The higher we ascend the greater are the difficulties of observation.

Should it, however, be found possible to obtain absolutely perfect instruments, and to observe without introducing personal errors, it remains to be seen whether the observations will accord with the 'corresponding barometric pressure.'[1]

Few observations for comparison have hitherto been made of the boiling-point of water against the mercurial barometer at great heights, and I am not acquainted with any which have been made at greater elevations than those by Dr. (now Sir Joseph) Hooker in 1848-50, by the brothers Schlagintweit in 1855-56, and by M. Wisse in Ecuador in 1844-49. Dr. Hooker quotes[2] observations for comparison at seventeen stations above 13,000 feet, his loftiest being the Donkia Pass, 18,466 feet. The brothers Schlagintweit record[3] observations at five stations above 13,000 feet, their most elevated point of observation being their camp on Ibi Gamin, 19,323 feet.[4] M. Wisse[5] observed at only two stations above 13,000 feet. My own series

---

[1] The remarks which accompany the section in the *Smithsonian Tables* (Section iv. p. 96') upon the thermometrical measurement of heights well deserve attention. "It may be seen that the heights determined by the means of the temperature of boiling-water are less reliable than those deduced from barometrical observations. Both derive the difference of altitude from the difference of atmospheric pressure. But the temperature of boiling-water gives only *indirectly* the atmospheric pressure, which is given *directly* by the barometer. This method is thus liable to all the chances of error which may affect the measurements by means of the barometer, besides adding to them new ones peculiar to itself, the principal of which, not to speak of the differences exhibited in the various tables of the force of vapour, is the difficulty of ascertaining with the necessary accuracy the true temperature of boiling-water."

[2] In *Himalayan Journals*, vol. ii. p. 458; 8vo, London, 1854.

[3] In their *Results of a Scientific Mission to India and High Asia*, vol. ii, p. 28; 4to, London and Leipzig, 1862.

[4] At p. 336 of the same volume, the height of this camp is said to be 19,094 feet. I am not aware which determination is the more correct one.

[5] The observations are given by Regnault in *Annales de Chimie et de Physique*, vol. 28, p. 123, 1850.

includes thirteen stations at greater heights than 13,000 feet, the loftiest being the camp close to the summit of Cotopaxi (19,478 feet), the summit of Antisana (19,335 feet), and the summit of Cayambe (19,186 feet). The mean height of these three positions as deduced from observations of mercurial barometer is 19,333 feet. Five, four, and two thermometers respectively were boiled at them, and the mean error of the final results as deduced from the boiling-points at the three grouped stations is — 513 feet.

In comparing this unsatisfactory record with the observations made by Dr. Hooker, I find that the majority of his boiling-point results showed considerable minus errors; and that at his loftiest station (18,466 feet) the error was — 600 feet.

Upon examining the observations of the brothers Schlagintweit,[1] I find that their boiling-points were always higher than the simultaneously-observed barometers would lead one to expect (and, so far, they are in harmony with the observations by Dr. Hooker and myself). Their errors were, however, small as compared with ours, and their results as a whole are, I think, more harmonious than it is reasonable to expect can be obtained by a method which includes so many possibilities of error.

The information afforded by M. Wisse is not so copious as one could desire. The observations which are quoted in *Annales de Chimie et de Physique* were made by him at twenty-six different places between June 1844 and May 1849, but only five of his stations were higher than 10,000 feet above the sea, and only two of these reached 15,000 feet. It is not said whether the recorded boiling-points were single observations or the means of several; nor is it stated whether the recorded observations are the *whole* which were made, or are only *selected* instances in which the boiling-point observations closely accorded with the barometric ones. From their remarkable accordance with each other it seems not improbable that this was the case.

From examination and comparison of these observations as a whole it would seem by no means certain that the barometric pressure corresponding to any given boiling-point has been well ascertained; and it would appear desirable that more comprehensive and thorough investigations in this direction should be made, if it should continue to be the practice to attempt to determine the heights of lofty positions by observation of the boiling-point of water.

But should such observations be made as would determine absolutely the boiling-point of water corresponding to every inch of the barometer, the fundamental objection to the use of this method would not be overcome, namely, that it is a cumbrous procedure, a method built up upon another, which must always (as is stated in the remarks already quoted from the *Smithsonian Tables*) be "*liable* to all the chances of error which may affect measurements by means of the barometer, *besides adding to them new ones peculiar to itself.*" This objection applies (although not with equal force) to all observations made by this method, in every region and at any height.

---

[1] It should be noted that the Schlagintweits employed thermometers 21 inches long. This probably permitted greater refinement of observation.

E.—TEMPERATURES IN ECUADOR.

The temperatures experienced in Ecuador were moderate both as regards heat and cold. During our stay at Guayaquil in December 1879, the highest temperature observed in the shade was 85° Faht., at 1.30 P.M., on the 10th; and on our return in July 1880, 79° at 3 P.M. on the 21st. The highest recorded by Mr. Chambers during our absence in the interior occurred on December 21, 23, 25, 1879, on each of which days he observed 87·5 at 6 P.M. Although these figures do not represent the maximum in the shade at Guayaquil, they are not, I believe, far beneath it. Temperature at this place appears to have a very small range; so far as I could learn, seldom rising to 90°, and not generally falling much below 65° at night. The lowest temperature I noted during our stay was 70° at 7.30 A.M., on July 27, 1880. From Mr. Chambers's observations it would appear that the months December and January are distinctly warmer than June and July.[1]

Moving, as we did in the interior, from one place to another, at continually varying elevations, it was not easy to tell whether one month was or was not notably warmer than another; but from the Bulletin which is printed by the Observatory at Quito[2] I am able to form the following table,

Date.	Maximum observed on any Day of the Month.	Minimum observed on any Day of the Month.
December 1879	22·8 (8th)	4·8 (1st)
January 1880	23·7 (2nd)	7·4 (2nd)
February ,,	24·0 (27th)	7·0 (12th, 13th, 22nd)
March ,,	22·9 (3rd)	5 6 (24th)
April ,,	22.5 (14th)	7·0 (20th)
May ,,	22·3 (3rd)	8·0 (2nd, 20th, 21st)
June ,,	22·8 (17th)	6·5 (3rd, 30th)
July ,,	22.6 (19th)	6·7 (6th)
August ,,	22·6 (2nd and 5th)	3·5 (12th)
September ,,	23·4 (23rd)	4·1 (10th)
October ,,	20.2 (9th)	5·6 (5th, 6th, 7th, 11th)
November ,,	20·3 (29th)	6·8 (14th, 22nd)

[1] The head-coverings worn by Ecuadorians show that the sun's rays are seldom so powerful as to be dangerous. In Guayaquil the Panama straw hat is very generally used, and at Quito and other towns in the interior tall black hats are not unfrequently seen on well-to-do people, while the lower orders use ordinary felt wideawakes and straw hats. I did not see any persons in the whole country wearing helmets and protective devices such as are commonly employed in tropical or hot countries. In the interior the sun is not often perfectly clear at mid-day, and only on one occasion did I feel that its rays were sufficiently fierce to be dangerous, namely, at Guachala (9217), in March 1880, at 8 A.M.

[2] *Boletin del Observatorio Astronomico de Quito.* Inprenta nacional. The temperatures are given in the centigrade scale.

from which it appears that the highest maximum (24°·0) of the entire twelve months December 1879–November 1880, inclusive, occurred upon February 27th, and the lowest (20°·2) upon October 9th, the difference between the highest and lowest maxima of the twelve months thus being only 3°·8 centigrade (=6°·84 Faht.).

The Bulletin does not record a single occasion on which the freezing-point was touched at Quito. The lowest minimum (3°.5) of the entire twelve months occurred on the 12th of August, and the highest (8°·0) upon three days in May, their difference amounting to only 4°·5 C. (= 8°·1 Faht.).

From inspection of the whole of the observations printed in the Bulletin, it appears that October was the coldest and January was the warmest month at Quito; and that the difference of the *means* of these two months amounted to less than 4° Faht.![1]

The range of the entire year, that is to say, the difference between the lowest minimum and the highest maximum, amounted at Quito to only 20°·5 C. (= 36°·9 Faht.).

Temperature at several of the towns at which we stopped in the interior appeared to be influenced by position as well as by altitude. Thus, Machachi (9839), although scarcely 500 feet higher than Quito, was found by us to be a chilly place as compared with the capital. At the former place it was seldom as warm as 60° Faht. at mid-day, while at Quito I noted a higher temperature than this upon several occasions at 10 P.M. Ambato (8606) though only 433 feet lower than Riobamba (9039), seemed to possess a cheerful degree of warmth; and the latter place, although less elevated, appeared to be colder than Quito. At Ambato temperature ranged from 65-70° Faht. at mid-day during our stay; and our impression agreed with the opinion current in the country that it is a warm place. Upon this account Ecuadorians come here from various parts when holiday-making.[2]

The *highest* temperature in the shade that we experienced anywhere in the *interior*, out of doors, was at the bottom of the ravine of Guallabamba (6472) on March 27, 1880. This was 75°·5 Faht. The *lowest* recorded during the whole journey was the minimum of the night of February 18, 1880, near the summit of Cotopaxi, namely, 13° Faht. Upon several occasions rapid changes of temperature occurred in a short space of time, the most remarkable experience of this description being that which was referred to in the chapter upon Antisana. This, as well as the temperatures observed at other summits, has been dealt with elsewhere.

Temperatures which will possess a wider interest are the nocturnal minima observed at our camping-places, from their being the only recorded observations of this nature made at high elevations near the Equator. They are brought together in the annexed table, arranged according to altitude, and

---

[1] The thermometric observations are made at Quito at 6 A.M., 2 P.M., and 10 P.M. The means referred to in the above paragraph are those of these three sets of observations. I have reason to believe that the observations were not made at the Observatory, but at a lower and more sheltered position at the extreme opposite end of the city.

[2] The temperatures quoted in this paragraph are indoor ones, but owing to the ill-fitting windows and to the doors opening directly into the air they differ little from shade temperatures out of doors.

TABLE OF NOCTURNAL MINIMA.

Date.	Place of Observation.	Altitude.	Temp. Faht.
April 7, 1880	La Dormida, Cayambe	11,805 feet	38°·5
,, 8, ,,	Do. do.	,, ,,	40·5
June 25, ,,	Camp near Chuquipoquio	11,850 ,,	33·5
,, 17, ,,	Do. in Valley of Collanes	12,540 ,,	29°
,, 18, ,,	Do. do. do.	,, ,,	33°
,, 19, ,,	Do. do. do.	,, ,,	33·5
April 15, ,,	Do. at Corredor Machai	12,779 ,,	39·5
June 20, ,,	Do. in Valley of Naranjal	13,053 ,,	34°
Mar. 6, ,,	Hacienda of Antisana	13,306 ,,	34°
,, 7, ,,	Do. do.	,, ,,	36·5
,, 8, ,,	Do. do.	,, ,,	33·5
June 27, ,,	Camp on Carihuairazo	13,377 ,,	33°
April 12, ,,	Do. Sara-urcu	13,754 ,,	35°
July 2, ,,	Fourth Camp, Chimborazo	14,359 ,,	30°
Dec. 26, 1879	First do. do.	14,375 ,,	21°
April 2, 1880	Camp on Cayambe	14,762 ,,	27°
,, 3, ,,	Do. do.	,, ,,	31°
,, 4, ,,	Do. do.	,, ,,	24·5
,, 5, ,,	Do. do.	,, ,,	24°
Mar. 22, ,,	Second Camp on Pichincha	14,992 ,,	29°
Feb. 16, ,,	First Camp on Cotopaxi	15,139 ,,	25°
,, 19, ,,	Do. do. do.	,, ,,	28°
,, 20, ,,	Do. do. do.	,, ,,	24°
June 8, ,,	Camp on N. side of Illiniza	15,446 ,,	26·5
July 2, ,,	Fifth Camp, Chimborazo	15,811 ,,	25°
Dec. 28, 1879	Second do. do.	16,664 ,,	21°
,, 30, ,,	Do. do. do.	,, ,,	20·5
,, 31, ,,	Do. do. do.	,, ,,	20·5
Jan. 5, 1880	Third do. do.	17,285 ,,	17°
,, 7, ,,	Do. do. do.	,, ,,	20°
Feb. 18, ,,	Camp at summit of Cotopaxi	19,500 ,,	13°

were observed with a registering spirit minimum thermometer, by Casella, which, as a rule, was placed about four feet on the windward side of the tent, in free air, 3 feet 6 inches to 4 feet from the ground. The most discordant of the readings is the minimum of the night of December 26, 1879. [See pp. 40, 41.]

If the difference of altitude of the extremes of the series is divided by the difference of the observed minima it will be found that the diminution of temperature is at the rate of one degree Fahrenheit per 296 feet.[1] If the observation near the summit of Cotopaxi should be rejected (on account of the possibility that it was considerably influenced by radiation),[2] and the remainder alone accepted, it will be seen that the diminution is at the rate of one degree for about 267 feet.[3] It would seem probable that the observation near the summit of Cotopaxi was *not* greatly affected by the warmth of the cone.

It cannot, however, be doubted that the circumjacent air is often considerably affected by radiation from heated rock-surfaces rising high above the line of perpetual congelation. Bare rock, much above the snow-line, when exposed to sunshine, often becomes heated to such an extent as to be almost painful to the touch. This warmth is subsequently parted with, and must affect the temperature of the neighbouring air to a material extent,— in calm weather, I imagine, to a much greater distance than four feet, the recognised distance for placing thermometers from the soil. As the object, when observing for minimum temperatures, is to register the lowest temperatures that occur, the end in view is most likely to be attained by placing the thermometer to windward, and as far as possible from the earth; and should this be done on high and isolated summits the observations will not perhaps be much influenced by terrestrial radiation, though they can scarcely fail to be affected by it to some small extent. I acted upon this supposition, and hence the thermometer was not placed in one invariable position.

[1] "We possess a great accumulation of observations of mountain temperature, but the results are only loosely accordant, and appear to indicate that the rate of increase depends in some considerable degree on the season of the year and the local situation of the place of observation. If we assemble the most accordant, and especially those cases where the heights ascended have been considerable, and trigonometrically determined, we find an average decrement of 1° of Fahrenheit's thermometer for every 100 yards of ascent. . . . As a general average deduced from balloon ascents, 400 feet per degree of Fahrenheit would seem to be preferable to 300." *Meteorology*, by Sir John F. W. Herschell, pp. 22-3, 2nd ed., Edinburgh, 1862.

[2] See the chapter upon Cotopaxi.

[3] This is a considerably less value per degree than has been found by Mr. Glaisher upon his balloon ascents (where the observations have not been affected by terrestrial radiation). See the *Reports of the British Association for the Advancement of Science*, 1862-66.

F.—UPON BODY TEMPERATURE.

The temperatures given in the following table were taken at the suggestion of Dr. W. Marcet, F.R.S., with a Hicks' patent clinical registering thermometer, graduated to fifths of degrees, of the kind which is now almost invariably employed; and the observations were made exclusively upon myself, by placing the bulb of the thermometer as far back under the tongue as was convenient, and allowing it to remain there (the mouth being closed) for ten to twelve minutes. In most cases the observations were repeated, though I find in practice that the highest obtainable temperature is registered within ten minutes.

My temperature is slightly lower than that which is considered the standard (namely 98°·4 Faht.), and the mean of a large number of observations taken midway between meals would probably be close to 98°·3 (provided the observations were made at the same part of the body). The extremes of the temperatures given in the table are both higher and lower than I have remarked (upon myself) on any other occasions.

After the first experiences upon Chimborazo were over, no effect was observed that could be attributed to diminished pressure, and the most severe cold that we experienced seemed scarcely to exert any influence. The low readings on the summits of Cayambe (97°·1) and Chimborazo (96°·3) must be ascribed to exertion and to abstinence from food, and principally to the latter cause. The following details, given in chronological order, will render any further remarks unnecessary :—

Nov. 21, 28; Dec. 10, 23, 1879 (98·05–98·4).—The readings at Kingston, Colon, Guayaquil, and Guaranda were all taken indoors, before breakfast. With air temperature ranging from 57° to 80°, and barometer 21·990 to 30·000 inches, bodily temperature varied only one-third of a degree Faht.

Dec. 27 (98·4).—In tent, first camp on Chimborazo. After breakfast, and before active exertion.

Dec. 28 (100·4).—In tent, second camp on Chimborazo. The recorded temperature is probably considerably lower than that which was experienced in the previous night. In the next six days I ate much less than usual; and by

Jan. 2, 1880, temperature was reduced to 97·9, at the second camp.

Jan. 8 (98·4).—In tent. Four days after the first ascent of Chimborazo, temperature had returned to its ordinary level, and deviated very slightly from it during the next three months.

Jan. 29 (98·45).—Indoors, two hours after dinner.

Feb. 9 (98·65).—Open air, in shade, at the highest point attained on the south side of Illiniza. Exertion had been severe and continuous since 8 A.M.

Feb. 18 (98·2).—In tent, close to the summit of Cotopaxi. Taken after ascending from the first camp (a rise of about 4400 feet). Barometer stood at 14·798 inches. Experienced headache and gasping for breath on the 18th, but no headache on the 19th. Bodily temperature did not seem affected at all.

Feb. 20, in tent ; Mar. 6, indoors, do not require mention.

Mar. 10 (98·6).—Open air, on the summit of Antisana. The reading was taken after a meal. Exertion had been severe and continuous since 6 A.M.

Mar. 22, in cave ; Mar. 25, indoors, do not require mention.

April 3 (99·1).—In tent, camp on Cayambe. Felt feverish, and could only attribute it to exposure on March 31.

April 4 (97·1).—Open air, on the summit of Cayambe. The reading was taken one hour after arrival at the summit. Exertion had been considerable, and nothing had been eaten since 4 A.M.

June 8 (97·9).—In tent, camp on north side of Illiniza. In the months of April and May I was almost continuously unwell, and frequently feverish, but by the commencement of June bodily temperature had fallen to its usual level.

June 28, 29 ; July 1 (97·7–98·4).—On Carihuairazo. The differences recorded on these days are accounted for by the readings having sometimes been taken before and sometimes after meals.

July 2 (97·8).—In tent. Does not require mention.

July 3 (96·3).—Open air, on the summit of Chimborazo. There was a moderately strong and cold wind. Air temperature was 15° Faht. Had eaten scarcely anything since 5 A.M. This was the lowest record on the journey.

July 5 (98·25).—In tent. Bodily temperature had by this time risen again to its ordinary level, and it fluctuated very slightly until return to Panama.

Aug. 3 (99·2).—Indoors, at Panama. The increase is to be attributed to the hospitality of the residents on the Isthmus more than to the deadly nature of its climate. On August 7 the maximum was attained (101°), but from that time temperature commenced to diminish, and on

Aug. 14, at St. Thomas, with almost the highest air temperature which was noted on the entire journey (84°), it had again fallen to its ordinary level.

APPENDIX. TABLE OF BLOOD TEMPERATURES.

Date.	Hour.	Place of Observation.	Altitude in feet.	Blood Temp.	Shade temp. of air.
1879.				Fahr.	Fahr.
Nov. 21.	8 a.m.	Kingston, Jamaica	...	98·05	79°
,, 28.	7 ,,	Colon, Isthmus of Panama	...	98·4	80°
Dec. 10.	7 ,,	Guayaquil, Ecuador	30	98·2	76°
,, 23.	7.30 ,,	Guaranda, do.	8,894	98·2	57°
,, 27.	10.30 ,,	Chimborazo, First Camp	14,375	98·4	51°·5
,, 28.	1 p.m.	Do. Second do.	16,664	100·4	49°
1880.					
Jan. 2.	7 a.m.	Do. do. do.	,,	97·9	34·5
,, 8.	11.30 ,,	Do. Third do.	17,285	98·4	51°
,, 29.	4.30 p.m.	Machachi	9,839	98·45	60°
Feb. 9.	1.25 ,,	Illiniza, South side	17,023	98·65	49·5
,, 18.	4 ,,	Cotopaxi, Second Camp	19,500	98·2	55°
,, 20.	12.30 ,,	Do. First do.	15,139	98·	41°
Mar. 6.	8.15 ,,	Hacienda of Antisana	13,306	98·	41°
,, 10.	11.10 a.m.	Antisana, Summit	19,335	98·6	47°
,, 22.	10 p.m.	Pichincha, Second Camp	14,992	98·1	39°
,, 25.	8 a.m.	Quito	9,343	98·	57°
Apr. 3.	4.30 p.m.	Cayambe, Camp on	14,762	99·1	42°
,, 4.	11.15 a.m.	Do. Summit	19,186	97·1	38°
June 8.	8 p.m.	Illiniza, Camp N. side	15,446	97·9	45°
,, 11.	4 ,,	Machachi	9,839	98·5	60°
,, ,,	6.15 ,,	Do.	,,	98·4	55°
,, 28.	4 ,,	Carihuairazo, Camp on	13,377	98·	51°
,, ,,	5.40 ,,	Do. do.	,,	98·1	48°
,, 29.	11 a.m.	Do. Summit	16,515	98·4	40°
July 1.	8.30 ,,	Do. Camp	13,377	97·7	44·5
,, 2.	9.15 p.m.	Chimborazo, Fifth Camp	15,811	97·8	36°
,, 3.	2 ,,	Do. Summit	20,498	96·3	15°
,, 5.	9 a.m.	Do. Sixth Camp	13,353	98·25	52·5
,, 17.	9 p.m.	Guayaquil	30	98·5	74·5
Aug. 3.	6.45 a.m.	Panama	60	99·2	78°
,, 6.	9.45 ,,	Colon	20	100·6	80°
,, 7.	9 a.m.	Between Colon and Jamaica	...	101·	81°–83°
,, 8.	7.30 ,,	Do. do.	...	99·	83°
,, 9.	8.30 ,,	Kingston, Jamaica	...	98·9	83·5
,, 14.	8 ,,	St. Thomas	...	98·2	84°

G.—HUMBOLDT'S ATTEMPT TO ASCEND CHIMBORAZO.

"On June 9, 1802, the travellers left Quito for Chimborazo, and on June 23 they climbed almost to the summit of the giant mountain, at that time regarded as the highest in the world, and attained the height never before reached by any human being of 18,096 feet.[1] Upon reaching an elevation of 15,600 feet, the path, relates Humboldt, became every moment narrower and steeper. The natives, with one exception, refused to accompany us farther, and were deaf to entreaties and threatenings, maintaining they suffered more than we did from the rarity of the air. We were left alone—Bonpland, our estimable friend Carlos Montufar, a half-caste Indian from the neighbouring village of San Juan, and myself.

"By dint of great exertion and considerable patience, we reached a greater height than we had dared to hope for, seeing we had been almost constantly enveloped in mist. In many places the ridge was not wider than from eight to ten inches! To our left a precipice covered with snow, the surface of which shone like glass from the effects of frost. This thin sheet of ice was at an inclination of about 30°. On the right was a fearful abyss, from 800 to 1000 feet deep, from the sides of which projected huge masses of naked rock. We leant over rather more to this side than the other, for it seemed less to be dreaded than the precipice on our left, where the smooth sides afforded no opportunity of checking a fall by catching hold of projecting pieces of rock, and where the thin crust of ice furnished no security against being precipitated into the loose snow beneath.[2]

"The sloping surface of snow extended to such a distance that light pieces of dolerite (the only substance at hand), when rolled down the incline, were lost sight of before reaching any resting-place.

"The rock became more friable, and the ascent increasingly difficult and dangerous. At certain places where it was very steep, we were obliged to use both hands and feet, and the edges of the rock were so sharp that we were painfully cut, especially on our hands. . . . The loose position of the stones upon the narrow ridge necessitated extreme caution, since many masses that appeared to be firmly attached proved to be only embedded in sand.

"We advanced all the more slowly, as every place that seemed insecure had first to be tested. Fortunately, the attempt to reach the summit of

---

[1] It will be seen at a later point there is a claim to have reached the height of 19,286 feet.—*E. W.*

[2] At p. 308, vol. i., of K. Bruhns' *Life of Humboldt* the following significant sentence occurs: "We feared nothing so much as the half-frozen snow." This is said in connection with an ascent of Pichincha.—*E. W.*

Chimborazo had been reserved for our last enterprise among the mountains of South America, so that we had gained some experience, and knew how far we could rely on our own powers. It is a peculiar characteristic of all excursions on the Andes, that beyond the line of perpetual snow Europeans are always left without guides just at the point where, from their complete ignorance of the locality, help is most needed. In everything Europeans are left to take the lead.

"We could no longer see the summit, even by glimpses, and were therefore doubly anxious to ascertain how much of the ascent had still to be accomplished. We opened the tube barometer at a spot where the ridge was wide enough to allow two persons to stand side by side in safety. We were only at an elevation of 17,300 feet, therefore scarcely 200 feet higher than we had attained three months previously upon the Antisana.

"After an hour's cautious climbing, the ridge of rock became less steep, but the mist unfortunately remained as thick as ever. One after another we all began to feel indisposed, and experienced a feeling of nausea accompanied by giddiness, which was far more distressing than the difficulty of breathing. . . . Blood exuded from the lips and gums, and the eyes became bloodshot. There was nothing particularly alarming to us in these symptoms, with which we had grown familiar by experience. Once when upon the Pichincha, though bleeding did not occur, I was seized with such violent pain in the stomach and overpowering giddiness, that I sank upon the ground in a state of insensibility, in which condition I was found by my companions, from whom I had withdrawn for the sake of making some experiments in electricity. The elevation then was not so great, being less than 13,800 feet. On the Antisana, however, at a height of 17,022 feet, our young travelling companion, Don Carlos Montufar, had suffered severely from bleeding of the lips. All these phenomena vary greatly in different individuals according to age, constitution, tenderness of the skin, and previous exertion of muscular power; yet in the same individual they constitute a kind of gauge for the amount of rarefaction of the atmosphere and for the absolute height that has been attained.

"The stratum of mist which had hidden every distant object from our view began, notwithstanding the perfect calm, suddenly to dissipate—an effect probably due to the action of electricity. We recognized once more the dome-shaped summit of Chimborazo, now in close proximity. It was a grand and solemn spectacle, and the hope of attaining the object of all our efforts animated us with renewed strength. The ridge of rock, only here and there covered with a thin sprinkling of snow, became somewhat wider; and we were hurrying forward with assured footsteps, when our further progress was suddenly stopped by a ravine, some 400 feet deep and 60 feet wide, which presented an insurmountable barrier to our undertaking. We could see clearly that the ridge on which we stood continued in the same direction on the other side of the ravine; but I was doubtful whether, after all, it really led to the summit. There was no means of getting round the cleft. On Antisana, after a night of severe frost, Bonpland had been able to travel a considerable distance upon the frozen surface of snow; but here the softness of the snowy mass prohibited such an attempt, and the nature of the declivity rendered it equally impossible to scale the sides.

"It was now one o'clock in the day. We fixed up the barometer with great care, and found it stood at thirteen inches $11\frac{2}{10}$ lines. The temperature of the air was only three degrees below the freezing-point; but from our long residence in the tropics even this amount of cold seemed quite benumbing. Our boots were wet through with snow-water, for the sand, which here and there lay on the mountain ridge, was mixed with the remains of former snow-drifts. According to the barometric formula given by Laplace, we had now reached an elevation of 19,286 English feet.

"We remained but a short time in this dreary waste, for we were soon again enveloped in mist, which hung about us motionless. We saw nothing more of the summit of Chimborazo, nor of the neighbouring snow mountains, far less of the elevated plain of Quito. We were isolated as in a balloon; a few rock lichens were to be observed above the line of perpetual snow, at a height of 16,920 feet; the last green moss we noticed was growing about 2600 feet lower. A butterfly was captured by M. Bonpland, at a height of 15,000 feet, and a fly was observed 1600 feet higher; both had been carried up into the higher regions of the atmosphere by the currents of air originating in the warmer plains below.

"As the weather became increasingly threatening, we hurried down along the ridge of rock, and from the insecurity of our footing found that greater caution even was necessary than during the ascent. We delayed no longer than sufficed for collecting fragments of rock as specimens of the mountain structure. We foresaw that in Europe we should frequently be asked for '*a fragment from Chimborazo.*'

"When we were at a height of about 17,400 feet, we encountered a violent hailstorm, which gave place to snow twenty minutes before passing the limit of perpetual snow, and the flakes were so thick that the ridge was soon covered several inches deep. The danger would indeed have been great had the snow overtaken us at a height of 18,000 feet. At a few minutes past two we reached the spot where we had left the mules."—*Life of Humboldt*, by Karl Bruhns, vol. i. pp. 311–315. London, 1873.

H.—BOUSSINGAULT'S ATTEMPTS TO ASCEND CHIMBORAZO.

[Ascension au Chimborazo exécutée le 16 décembre, 1831, par M. Boussingault.]

"Je ne pouvais mieux terminer mes recherches sur les trachytes des Cordillières, que par une étude spéciale du Chimborazo. . . . J'expose ainsi les raisons qui m'ont conduit sur le Chimborazo, parce que je blâme hautement les excursions périlleuses sur les montagnes, quand elles ne sont pas entreprises dans l'intérêt de la science.

"De Riobamba, le Chimborazo présente deux pentes d'une inclinaison très différente. L'une, celle qui regarde l'Arenal, est très abrupte ; et l'on voit sortir de dessous la glace de nombreux pics de trachyte. L'autre qui descend vers le site appelé *Chillapullu*, non loin de Mocha, est au contraire peu inclinée, mais d'une étendue considérable. Après avoir bien examiné les environs de la montagne, ce fut par cette pente que nous résolûmes de l'attaquer. Le 14 décembre, 1831, nous allâmes prendre gîte dans la métairie du Chimborazo. . . . La métairie se trouve à 3800 mètres de hauteur.

"Le 15 à sept heures du matin, nous nous mîmes en route guidés par un Indien de la métairie. . . . Nous suivîmes en le remontant un ruisseau encaissé entre deux murs de trachyte, dont les eaux descendent du glacier ; bientôt nous quittâmes cette crevasse pour nous diriger vers Mocha, en longeant la base du Chimborazo. Nous nous élevions insensiblement ; nos mulets marchaient avec peine et difficulté, au milieu des débris de roche qui sont accumulés au pied de la montagne. La pente devenait très rapide, le sol était meuble et les mulets s'arrêtaient presque à chaque pas pour faire une longue pause, ils n'obéissaient plus à l'éperon. La respiration de ces animaux était précipitée, haletante. Nous étions alors précisément à la hauteur du Mont Blanc, car le baromètre indiqua une élévation de 4808 mètres au dessus du niveau de la mer.

"Après nous être couvert le visage avec des masques de taffetas léger, afin de nous préserver des accidens que nous avions ressentis sur l'Antisana, nous commençâmes à gravir une arête que aboutit à un point déjà très élevé du glacier. Il était midi. Nous montions lentement, et, à mesure que nous nous engagions sur la neige, la difficulté de respirer en marchant se faisait de plus en plus sentir, nous rétablissions aisément nos forces en nous arrêtant, sans toutefois nous asseoir, tous les huit ou dix pas. . . . Nous atteignîmes bientôt un rocher noir qui s'élevait au dessus de l'arête que nous suivions. Nous continuâmes encore à nous élever pendant quelque temps, mais non sans éprouver beaucoup de fatigue occasionée par le peu de consistance d'un sol neigeux qui s'affaissait sans cesse sous nos pas, et dans lequel nous enfoncions quelquefois jusqu'à la ceinture. Malgré tous nos efforts, nous fûmes bientôt convaincus de l'impossibilité de passer en avant ; en effet, un peu au delà de la roche noire, la neige meuble avait plus de quatre pieds de profondeur. Nous allâmes nous reposer sur un bloc de trachyte qui ressemblait à une île au milieu d'une mer de neige. Nous étions à 5115 mètres d'élévation. Il était une heure et demie. Ainsi après beaucoup de fatigues, nous nous étions seulement élevés de 307 mètres au dessus du point où nous avions mis pied à terre.

"En quelques instans nous étions descendus là où nous avions laissé nos mulets. J'employai quelques momens à examiner cette partie de la montagne en géologue, et à recueillir une suite de roches. A trois heures et demie nous nous mîmes en route. A six heures nous étions rendus à la métairie.

"Le temps avait été magnifique, jamais le Chimborazo ne nous parut aussi majestueux, mais après notre course infructueuse, nous ne pouvions le regarder sans éprouver un sentiment de dépit. Nous résolûmes de tenter l'ascension par le côté abrupte, c'est-à-dire par la pente qui regarde l'Arenal. Nous savions que c'était par ce côté que M. de Humboldt s'était élevé sur cette montagne ; on nous avait bien montré de Rio-Bamba le point où il était parvenu, mais il nous fut impossible d'obtenir des renseignemens exacts sur la route qu'il avait suivie pour y arriver. Les Indiens qui avaient accompagné cet intrépide voyageur n'existaient plus.

"Il était sept heures quand, le lendemain, nous prenions la route de l'Arenal. . . . A mesure que nous avancions, le terrain s'élevait d'une manière sensible. En général, les plateaux trachytiques qui supportent les pics isolés dont les Andes sont comme hérissées, se relèvent peu à peu vers la base de ces mêmes pics. Les crevasses nombreuses et profondes qui sillonnent ces plateaux, semblent toutes diverger d'un centre commun ; elles se rétrécissent en même temps qu'elles s'éloignent de ce centre. On ne saurait mieux les comparer qu'à ces fentes que l'on remarque à la surface d'un verre étoilé. A neuf heures, nous fîmes halte pour déjeuner à l'ombre d'un énorme bloc de trachyte auquel nous donnâmes le nom de Pedron del Almuerzo. Je fis là une observation barométrique, parce que j'avais l'espoir d'y observer également vers quatre heures après midi, afin de connaître, à cette élévation, la variation diurne du baromètre. Le Pedron est élevé de 4335 mètres. Nous dépassâmes sur nos mulets la limite des neiges. Nous étions à 4945 mètres de hauteur quand nous mîmes pied à terre. Le terrain devint alors tout à fait impracticable aux mulets ; ces animaux cherchaient d'ailleurs à nous faire comprendre avec leur instinct vraiment extraordinaire, la lassitude qu'ils éprouvaient ; leurs oreilles ordinairement si droites et si attentives, étaient entièrement abattues, et pendant des haltes fréquentes qu'ils faisaient pour respirer, ils ne cessaient de regarder vers la plaine. Peu d'écuyers ont probablement conduit leur monture à une semblable élévation ; et pour arriver à dos de mulets, sur un sol mouvant au delà de la limite des neiges, il fallait peut-être avoir fait plusieurs années d'équitation dans les Andes.

"Après avoir examiné la localité dans laquelle nous nous étions placés, nous reconnûmes que pour gagner une arête qui montait vers le sommet du Chimborazo, nous devions d'abord gravir une pente excessivement rapide, qui se présentait devant nous. Elle était formée en grande partie de blocs de roche de toutes grosseurs disposés en talus ; çà et là ces fragmens trachytiques étaient recouverts par des nappes de glace plus ou moins étendues ; et sur plusieurs points, on pouvait clairement apercevoir que ces débris de roche reposaient sur de la neige endurcie.

" Il était dix heures trois quarts quand nous avions laissé nos mulets ; tant que nous marchions sur les rochers, nous n'éprouvions pas de grande difficulté, on aurait dit que nous montions un escalier en mauvais état ; ce qu'il y avait de plus pénible, c'était l'attention soutenue qu'il fallait avoir pour choisir la pierre sur laquelle on pût poser le pied avec quelque sécurité. Nous reprenions haleine tous les six ou huit pas, mais sans nous asseoir, et souvent même ce repos était utilisé à tailler pour ma collection des échantillons géologiques. Mais aussitôt que nous atteignions une surface neigeuse, la chaleur du soleil devenait suffocante, notre respiration pénible, et par conséquent nos repos plus fréquens, plus nécessaires.

"A 11 heures ¾, nous achevions de traverser une nappe de glace assez étendue, sur laquelle il nous avait fallu faire des entailles pour assurer nos pas. Ce passage ne s'était pas fait sans danger, une glissade eût coûté la vie. Nous entrâmes de nouveau sur des débris de trachyte, c'était pour nous la terre ferme, et dès lors il nous fut permis de nous élever un peu plus rapidement. Nous marchions en file, moi d'abord, puis le colonel Hall, mon nègre venait ensuite ; il suivait exactement nos pas, afin de ne pas compromettre la sûreté des instrumens qui lui étaient confiés.

" Bientôt nous eûmes atteint l'arête que nous devions suivre. Cette arête n'était pas telle que nous l'avions jugée dans le lointain ; elle ne portait, à la vérité, que très peu de neige, mais elle présentait des escarpemens difficiles à escalader. Il fallut faire des efforts inouïs ; et la gymnastique est pénible dans ces régions aériennes. Enfin, nous arrivâmes au pied d'un mur de trachyte, coupé à pic, qui avait plusieurs centaines de mètres de hauteur. Il y eut un moment visible de découragement dans l'expédition, quand le baromètre nous eut appris que nous étions seulement à 5680 mètres d'élévation. C'était peu pour nous, car ce n'était pas même la hauteur à laquelle nous nous étions placés sur le Cotopaxi. D'ailleurs, M. de Humboldt avait gravi plus haut sur le Chimborazo, et nous voulions au moins atteindre la station à laquelle s'était arrêté ce savant voyageur. Les explorateurs de montagne, lorsqu'ils sont découragés, sont toujours fort disposés à s'asseoir : c'est ce que nous fîmes à la station de la Peña-Colorada (Rocher-Rouge). C'était le premier repos assis que nous nous permettions ; nous avions tous une soif excessive, aussi notre première occupation fut-elle de sucer des glaçons pour nous désaltérer.

" Il était midi trois quarts, et cependant nous ressentions un froid assez vif ; le thermomètre s'était abaissé à 0°, 4. Nous nous trouvions alors enveloppés dans un nuage.

  * * * * * *

" Lorsque le nuage dans lequel nous étions plongés fut dissipé, nous examinâmes notre situation ; en regardant le Rocher Rouge, nous avions à notre droite un abîme épouvantable ; à gauche, vers l'Arenal, on distinguait une roche avancée qui ressemblait à un belvédère ; il était important d'y parvenir, afin de reconnaître s'il était possible de tourner le Rocher Rouge, et de voir en même temps s'il était permis de monter encore. L'accès de ce belvédère était scabreux, j'y parvins cependant avec l'aide de mes deux compagnons. Je reconnus alors que si nous pouvions gravir une surface de neige très inclinée, qui s'appuyait sur une face du Rocher Rouge opposée au côté par lequel nous l'avions abordé, nous pourrions atteindre une élévation plus considérable. Pour se faire une idée assez nette de la topographie du Chimborazo, qu'on se figure un immense rocher soutenu de tous côtés par des arcs-boutans. Les arêtes sont les arcs-boutans qui, de la plaine, semblent s'appuyer sur cet énorme bloc pour l'étayer.

"Avant d'entreprendre ce passage dangereux, j'ordonnai à mon nègre d'aller *essayer la neige;* elle était d'une consistance convenable. Hall et le nègre réussirent à tourner le pied de la position que j'occupais, je me réunis à eux lorsqu'ils furent assez solidement établis pour me recevoir, car pour les rejoindre, il fallut descendre en glissant environ 25 pieds de glace. . . .

"Nous avancions avec précaution; à droite nous pouvions nous appuyer sur le rocher; à gauche la pente était effrayante, et avant de nous engager en avant, nous commençâmes par bien nous familiariser avec le précipice. . . .

"Nous commencions déjà à ressentir plus que nous ne l'avions jamais éprouvé, l'effet de la raréfaction de l'air; nous étions forcés de nous arrêter tous les deux ou trois pas, et souvent même de nous coucher pendant quelques secondes. Une fois assis, nous nous remettions à l'instant même; notre souffrance n'avait lieu que pendant le mouvement. La neige présenta bientôt une circonstance qui rendit notre marche aussi lente que dangereuse; il n'y avait guère que trois ou quatre pouces de neige molle; au dessous se trouvait une glace très dure et glissante; nous fûmes obligés de faire des entailles dans cette glace afin d'assurer nos pas. . . . La neige devint plus favorable, nous fîmes un dernier effort, et à une heure trois quarts nous étions sur l'arête si désirée. Là, nous fûmes convaincus qu'il était impossible de faire plus, nous nous trouvions au pied d'un prisme de trachyte dont la base supérieure, recouverte d'une coupole de neige, forme le sommet du Chimborazo.

"L'arête sur laquelle nous étions parvenus avait seulement quelques pieds de largeur. De toutes parts nous étions environnés de précipices, nos alentours offraient les accidens les plus bizarres. La couleur foncée de la roche contrastait de la manière la plus tranchée avec la blancheur éblouissante de la neige. De longues stalagmites de glace paraissaient suspendues sur nos têtes; on eût dit une magnifique cascade qui venait de se geler.

"Nous étions à 6004 mètres de hauteur absolue; c'est, je crois, la plus grande élévation à laquelle les hommes se soient encore élevés sur les montagnes.

"A 2 heures, le mercure se soutenait dans le baromètre à 371 mm. 1 (13 pouces 8 lig. $\frac{1}{2}$), le thermomètre du baromètre était à 7°, 8 C. A l'ombre d'un rocher, le thermomètre libre indiqua également 7°, 8.

*   *   *   *   *   *

"Pendant tout le temps que nous étions occupés à faire nos observations sur le Chimborazo, le temps s'était maintenu de toute beauté; le soleil était assez chaud pour nous incommoder légèrement. Vers trois heures, nous aperçûmes quelques nuages qui se formaient en bas, dans la plaine; le tonnerre gronda bientôt, au dessous de notre station; le bruit était peu intense, mais il était prolongé ; nous pensâmes d'abord que c'était un bramido, un rugissement souterrain. Des nuages obscurs ne tardèrent pas à entourer la base de la montagne ; ils s'élevaient vers nous avec lenteur : nous n'avions pas de temps à perdre, car il fallait passer les mauvais pas avant d'être envahis, autrement nous eussions couru les plus grands dangers. Une chute abondante de neige, ou une gelée qui eût rendu le chemin glissant, suffisait pour empêcher notre retour, et nous n'avions aucune provision pour séjourner sur le glacier.

"La descente fut pénible. Après nous être abaissés de 300 à 400 mètres, nous pénétrâmes dans les nuages, en y entrant par la partie supérieure ; un peu plus bas, il commença à tomber du grésil, qui refroidit considérablement l'air, et au moment où nous retrouvâmes l'Indien qui gardait nos mulets, le nuage lança sur nous une grêle assez grosse pour nous faire éprouver une sensation douloureuse, lorsqu'elle nous atteignait sur les mains ou dans la figure.

"A quatre heures trois quarts j'ouvris mon baromètre au Pedron del Almuerzo. . . . A mesure que nous descendions, une pluie glaciale se mêlait à la grêle. La nuit nous surprit en chemin ; il était huit heures quand nous entrâmes dans la métairie du Chimborazo."—*Annales de Chimie et de Physique*, par MM. Gay-Lussac et Arago, tome lviii, 2me serie, pp. 156–175. Paris, 1835.

I.—DECLARATION OF FRANCISCO J. CAMPAÑA.

Upon our return to Guayaquil I caused Campaña to make a declaration before the British Consul touching what he knew relating to the second ascent of Chimborazo. A translation of this document is appended.

[TRANSLATION.]

"I, Javier Campaña of Quito, hereby declare that upon July 3, 1880, I accompanied Mr. Edward Whymper to the very highest point of the summit of Chimborazo. We were also accompanied by Jean-Antoine Carrel and by Louis Carrel (Mr. Whymper's two Italian mountaineers), and by David Beltran of Machachi.

"Mr. Whymper placed his tent on July 2, 1880, on the north-west side of Chimborazo, at a height, so he tells me, of about 16,000 feet, and he provided for the use of myself and of David the things which were necessary for an ascent, namely, good strong boots with large nails, warm gloves, and spectacles to protect the eyes against the glare of the snow, and ice-axes to help us along.

"We started from the tent at 5·15 on the morning of July 3, 1880, and at once commenced to ascend towards the summit. The way at first was over loose stones, but after we had ascended for about 1000 feet we came to snow, and the remainder of the ascent was entirely over snow, with the exception of one or two little places where rocks came through the snow. We stopped to eat on one of these little patches of rock at 8.35 A.M., and after Mr. Whymper had examined his mercurial barometer he encouraged us to proceed by telling us that we had already got more than half-way up from the tent. From this place we saw the sea.

"We went on again at 9.5 A.M. and found the snow get steeper and steeper. We were all tied together with a good strong rope, in case any one should slip, and except for this and for the things with which we had been provided I should not have been able to get along at all. Sometimes it was very cold, and there was much wind, but when we were in the sun it was very hot. Whether in the sun or in the shade the snow was very soft, and we sank in deeply, often up to the knees. This was very fatiguing, and it was owing to this that we took so much longer time in ascending the upper than the lower part of the mountain.

"To break the ascent we zigzagged about, and at one time came round to the side fronting Guaranda, and then came back to above the place where the tent was pitched. At last we got on to the top, and could see the two summits. The snow was very soft indeed here, and we went along very slowly, and had often to stop to get breath. The highest of the two summits was on our left hand, that is, upon the north side of the mountain, and we went to it, without going upon the lower one. As we approached the very highest point we saw that there was something strange upon it, and when we got up we found the pole of the flag which Mr. Whymper had put up on January 4, 1880. It stood up about $1\frac{1}{2}$ varas above the snow, and very little of the flag remained, as it had been torn to pieces by the wind. I took a small piece of the flag to show to my friends below, and was filled with joy at being the first Ecuadorian to reach the summit of the great Chimborazo!

"We arrived on the very highest point of the summit at 1.20 P.M., and about the same time ashes from Cotopaxi began to fall. They filled our eyes, noses, mouths, and ears, and made the snow quite black. Mr. Whymper, however, prepared his instruments, and was at work during the whole time we were on the summit. He did not once sit down to rest from the time we left the tent in the morning until the time that we returned to it in the evening. He took the height of the mountain with his barometers, and told us that the observations he now made agreed very well with those which he made upon the first ascent of Chimborazo on January 4, 1880.

"At 2.30 P.M. we left the summit, and came down as fast as we could, only stopping a little from time to time to allow Mr. Whymper to collect rocks at various places. We arrived again at the tent at 5.10 P.M., and found it covered with the ashes from Cotopaxi, which were still falling, and filled the whole valleys with a thick cloud. On the 4th July we continued the tour of the mountain and arrived at night close to Tortorillas, and on the 6th we returned to Riobamba, having had a most successful journey, without accidents of any sort whatever—not only having made the tour and the second ascent of Chimborazo, but having also made *en route*, on the 29th of June, the ascent of Carihuairazo.

"GUAYAQUIL, *July* 19, 1880.

(Signed) "FRANCO. JR. CAMPAÑA."

Declared and subscribed at
Guayaquil this twentieth day
of July 1880, Before me

GEO. CHAMBERS,
H.B.M.'s Consul, Guayaquil.

J.—EXPERIMENTS BY M. PAUL BERT.

The book entitled *La Pression Barométrique*, by Mons. P. Bert, was published in 1878, but I refrained from reading or procuring it until after my return from Ecuador. It did not appear to me likely that the points which I desired to investigate could be settled by laboratory experiments, and this seems also to have been the opinion of M. Bert.[1]

The general conclusions which are given at the close of the book (pp. 1153-55) in respect to the effects of diminished pressure [2] are :—

1. La diminution de la pression barométrique n'agit sur les êtres vivants qu'en diminuant la tension de l'oxygène dans l'air qu'ils respirent, dans le sang qui anime leurs tissus, et en les exposant ainsi à des menaces d'asphyxie (p. 1153).

2. Les effets fâcheux de la diminution de pression peuvent être efficacement combattus par la respiration d'un air suffisamment riche en oxygène pour maintenir à la valeur normale la tension de ce gaz (p. 1154).

3. Les êtres actuellement existants à l'état sauvage sur la surface du globe sont accommodés au degré de tension oxygénée sous laquelle ils vivent: toute diminution, toute augmentation paraît leur être défavorable quand ils sont dans l'état de santé (p. 1155).

These conclusions were arrived at after a very long series of experiments of various kinds had been made upon birds, dogs, cats, rabbits, etc., from which it clearly appeared that death can be brought about in these animals if pressure is reduced rapidly to a low point. Sparrows, for example, were killed before pressure had been reduced so low as that which reigns at the summit of Mount Everest. Dogs, it was found, were harder to kill than cats (p. 738). The various animals exhibited much the same symptoms at these artificially produced low pressures as human beings at the natural low pressures which are experienced at great heights ; and, like them, they recovered very rapidly (even when apparently dying) when pressure was restored.

In further experiments with sparrows, pressure was lowered very rapidly, and the birds operated upon were reduced to a dying state ; oxygen was then let in, and the birds revived ; pressure was then still further reduced and the birds were again made extremely ill, but recovered by a further introduction of oxygen ; and the experiments were continued until the atmosphere in which the birds were confined contained 91 per cent of oxygen, and in that mixture they lived at a pressure of 75 millimètres, which is less than a *third*

---

[1] He says in his Preface, "j'ai dû laisser systématiquement de côté trois ordres de questions qui ne pouvaient être attaquées dans le laboratoire, et pour lesquelles, par suite, les conditions certaines de la preuve ne pouvaient être rassemblées ; c'est à savoir : les oscillations quotidiennes du baromètre, les applications thérapeutiques, *l'acclimatement sur les hauts lieux.*"

[2] Numerous experiments at augmented pressures were also made.

of that which would be experienced at the top of Mount Everest, and about one *tenth* of atmospheric pressure at the level of the sea.

These experiments upon animals were followed by others upon himself. M. Bert says (p. 749):—

"Je ne pouvais évidemment me borner, au moment d'émettre des préceptes pratiques destinés aux voyageurs en montagne et aux aéronautes, à des expériences faites sur des animaux, si convaincantes qu'elles fussent.

"Je résolus de commencer par expérimenter sur moi-même. J'avais déjà, dans mes grands cylindres en tôle, subi l'influence d'assez notables dépressions, jusqu'à éprouver certains malaises. Je pensai alors à m'y soumettre de nouveau, pour faire disparaître les accidents en respirant un air suroxygéné.

"Je plaçais alors à côté de moi, dans l'appareil, un grand sac de caoutchouc, contenant un air d'autant plus riche en oxygène, que la dépression devait être plus forte."

The first experiment of this nature was made by M. Bert upon himself on February 20, 1874. He shut himself up in a metal cylinder, with his bag of oxygen, and had pressure reduced in 35 minutes to 450 millimètres, and remained at that pressure, or a little lower, during 68 minutes. After this, air was gradually let in, and in 25 minutes more he returned, so to speak, to the level of the sea. The lowest pressure to which M. Bert was subjected on this occasion was about equal to that which reigns at the summit of Mont Blanc, and before this point was reached he experienced both nausea and dizziness, and his pulse rose from 64 to 100. He refreshed himself with oxygen from time to time with beneficial effects, and found that he could reduce the rate of his pulse, in *two minutes*, from 90 to 69. This experiment, from first to last, extended over 128 minutes.

Upon March 9, 1874, a second experiment of this nature was made in M. Bert's apparatus by MM. Crocé-Spinelli and Sivel, and upon this occasion pressure was reduced in 37 minutes to 304 mm., which is about equal to that which would be experienced at a height of 24,000 feet above the sea. The experimenters remained, however, only a very short time under this pressure. In 7 minutes they returned below what is the equivalent of the height of Mont Blanc, and in 59 minutes from the commencement of the experiment returned to the level of the sea. Like M. Bert, they refreshed themselves with oxygen, but their pulses nevertheless rose to 132 and 135; and, at the lowest pressure, they experienced a sort of drunken sensation, and could neither see nor hear clearly.

In these two experiments, said M. Bert (p. 758),

"l'oxygène n'avait été employé que d'une manière intermittente, pour diminuer pendant quelques instants la gravité des accidents de la décompression. Je voulus opérer un peu différemment, laisser arriver les malaises jusqu'à un certain degré, pour respirer alors d'une manière continue l'air suroxygéné, tout en continuant à diminuer encore la pression barométrique, et voir ce qui adviendrait."

Before these further laboratory experiments were made, MM. Crocé-Spinelli and Sivel repeated their experiences, this time in balloon, and upon March 22, 1874, rose until they attained a height of about 24,000 feet. As before, they took occasional draughts of oxygen; but they remained a much greater length of time above the height of Mont Blanc, and were more perceptibly affected, especially M. Crocé-Spinelli, who endeavoured to eat at the greatest elevation. His pulse rose to 140.

APPENDIX. EXPERIMENTS BY M. PAUL BERT.

Four and six days later M. Paul Bert made his experiments, Nos. 256 and 257, in which he reduced himself successively to pressures about equivalent to the heights of Chimborazo and of Mount Everest. I am much indebted to the courtesy of Mons. G. Masson, the publisher of *La Pression Barométrique*, for permitting the details of these two experiments to be reprinted here at full length.

EXPÉRIENCE CCLVI.—28 mars.—J'entre dans l'appareil à $10^h 55^m$; la porte est fermée à $11^h 4^m$; j'ai alors 58 pulsations à la minute. Pression barométrique, 761^{mm} ;
$11^h 10^m$; pression 715^{mm} ; pouls, 62 ;
$11^h 20^m$; 580^{mm} ; pouls, 63 ;
$11^h 23^m$; 535^{mm} ; pouls, 63 ; quelques sensations nauséeuses ;
$11^h 25^m$; 510^{mm} ; gaz s'échappant par en haut et par en bas ;
$11^h 27^m$; 495^{mm} ; pouls, 66 ;
$11^h 31^m$; 455^{mm} ; pouls, 64 ; sensation nauséeuse ; gaz s'échappent, et cependant le ventre reste un peu gonflé ;
$11^h 33^m$; 435^{mm} ; pouls, 70 ; l'acte de siffler, que j'exécutais très-bien à la pression normale, qui était devenu assez difficile dès 520^{mm}, est complétement impossible ;
$11^h 35^m$; 425^{mm} ; pouls, 72 ; un peu de trouble de la vue, qui est moins nette ;
$11^h 37^m$; 412^{mm} ; pouls, 76 ; je suis assez mal à mon aise, avec l'œil un peu trouble.

Je commence alors à inspirer d'une manière continue dans le sac plein d'air suroxygéné que j'ai à côté de moi ; l'expiration se fait au dehors. Quelques éblouissements surviennent, puis tout accident disparait, et je me trouve, jusqu'à la fin de l'expérience, dans un état de bien-être parfait.

Le pouls, qui était tombé instantanément à 63, s'abaisse encore, quoique la décompression aille en augmentant.

$11^h 41^m$; pression, 408^{mm} ; 60 pulsations.
$11^h 46^m$; 382^{mm} ; pouls, 63 ;
$11^h 47^m$; 380^{mm} ; des gaz s'échappent par la bouche et l'anus ; bien-être parfait ;
$11^h 48^m$; 369^{mm} ; 58 pulsations ; encore gaz ;
$11^h 51^m$; 355^{mm} ; 59 pulsations ;
$11^h 52^m$; 350^{mm} ; encore gaz ;
$11^h 55^m$; 338^{mm} ; je fais quelques efforts pour ouvrir et fermer un flacon ; le pouls monte à 63 ; la pression commence à remonter ;
$11^h 59^m$; 400^{mm} ; 60 pulsations ;
Midi ; 440^{mm} ; impossible de siffler ;
Midi 2^m ; 490^{mm} ; 60 pulsations ; impossible de siffler ; je cesse de respirer l'air suroxygéné ;
Midi 3^m ; 520^{mm} ; impossible de siffler ; 56 pulsations ;
Midi 5^m ; 540^{mm} ; je commence à pouvoir siffler ;
Midi 7^m ; 570^{mm} ; je siffle très-bien ; 59 pulsations ;
Midi 10^m ; revenu à la pression normale ; 52 pulsations.

Cette expérience montre de la manière la plus nette que les inspirations continues d'oxygène, après avoir fait cesser les symptômes fâcheux, les empêchent de reparaître, quoique la pression barométrique continue à diminuer. Il n'est rien de plus probant. La dépression atteinte a été de 338 millimètres, correspondante à la hauteur de 6500^m environ, c'est-à-dire un peu plus que celle du Chimborazo.

Entre autres phénomènes qui ont persisté nonobstant l'inspiration d'oxygène, parce qu'ils dépendent exclusivement de la diminution de densité de l'air, je citerai les évacuations gazeuses et l'impossibilité de siffler, qui avait été notée déjà dans l'expérience précédente, et dont ne parlent ni les aéronautes ni les ascensionnistes ; elle a été observée au-dessous de 500 millimètres.

L'expérience suivante, conduite de la même manière, est encore plus frappante à cause de l'énorme dépression à laquelle je me suis impunément soumis :

EXPÉRIENCE CCLVII.—30 mars.—J'entre à 10ʰ 15ᵐ dans l'appareil; pression barométrique 759ᵐᵐ. J'ai avec moi un moineau, dont la température rectale est 41°, 9, un rat et une bougie.

10ʰ 22ᵐ; on ferme la porte; j'ai 60 pulsations;
10ʰ 29ᵐ; pression 710ᵐᵐ; 63 pulsations;
10ʰ 34ᵐ; 665ᵐᵐ; pouls, 64;
10ʰ 40ᵐ; 640ᵐᵐ; pouls, 65; je vois apparaître des bulles de gaz dans l'eau que j'ai à côté de moi dans un verre;
10ʰ 43ᵐ; 605ᵐᵐ;
10ʰ 46ᵐ; 580ᵐᵐ; pouls, 66;
555ᵐᵐ; je siffle assez facilement; la flamme de la bougie bleuit un peu, la mèche s'allonge; elle est à peu près la moitié de la longueur de la flamme;
510ᵐᵐ; impossible de siffler dans les notes hautes;
10ʰ 53ᵐ; 480ᵐᵐ; 70 pulsations; un peu de malaise;
10ʰ 53ᵐ; 455ᵐᵐ; 78 pulsations; sentiment de congestion à la tête; gaz s'échappant par en haut et par en bas;
10ʰ 58ᵐ; 430ᵐᵐ; pouls, 80 : l'oiseau vomit, paraît assez malade, mais reste perché; le rat semble fort tranquille;
11ʰ 410ᵐᵐ; pouls, 86; je place devant ma bouche le tube du sac à oxygène, que la dépression a gonflé, et je respire ainsi un mélange très-suroxygéné; j'ai quelques éblouissements;
11ʰ 2ᵐ; 400ᵐᵐ; le pouls est tombé à 64; l'oiseau vomit de nouveau; le rat paraît fort anxieux;
11ʰ 5ᵐ; 378ᵐᵐ; 66 pulsations; impossibilité de siffler;
11ʰ 9ᵐ; 360ᵐᵐ; 72 pulsations; un peu de malaise, bien que j'aie respiré l'oxygène d'une manière continue, mais à distance, il est vrai. Je prends alors le tube de dégagement dans la bouche, sans fermer les narines, et le garde ainsi jusqu'à la fin de l'expérience. Le malaise disparaît aussitôt;
11ʰ 11ᵐ; 348ᵐᵐ; 66 pulsations; le moineau a 126 respirations à la minute;
11ʰ 14ᵐ; 323ᵐᵐ; 64 pulsations; le moineau, qui vomit très-fort, reste cependant perché;
11ʰ 17ᵐ; 310ᵐᵐ; j'ai un peu de malaise, avec pouls à 75;
11ʰ 19ᵐ; 300ᵐᵐ; le moineau est fort malade;
11ʰ 22ᵐ; 295ᵐᵐ; 64 pulsations; mon malaise a complétement disparu;
11ʰ 24ᵐ; 288ᵐᵐ;
11ʰ 27ᵐ; 280ᵐᵐ; pulsations, 66; la flamme de la bougie est très-bleue; la mèche a environ ⅔ de la longueur de la flamme;
11ʰ 33ᵐ; 258ᵐᵐ; 70 pulsations; l'oiseau vomit et semble extrêmement malade, mais il reste toujours perché;
11ʰ 34ᵐ; 255ᵐᵐ;
11ʰ 36ᵐ; 248ᵐᵐ; 64 pulsations; je laisse augmenter la pression;
11ʰ 38ᵐ; 290ᵐᵐ; pouls, 63;
11ʰ 40ᵐ; 340ᵐᵐ; la température rectale du moineau n'est plus que de 36°, 4;
11ʰ 43ᵐ; 390ᵐᵐ; pouls, 54; je cesse de respirer l'oxygène;
11ʰ 44ᵐ; 420ᵐᵐ; impossible de siffler; l'oiseau est toujours bien malade, accroupi sur son perchoir;
11ʰ 46ᵐ; 480ᵐᵐ; impossible de siffler;
11ʰ 47ᵐ; 550ᵐᵐ; id.; 66 pulsations;
11ʰ 48ᵐ; 580ᵐᵐ; je puis siffler les notes basses, mais non les hautes;
11ʰ 49ᵐ; 630ᵐᵐ; je siffle très-bien;
11ʰ 51ᵐ; revenu à la pression normale; j'ai seulement 52 pulsations. La température rectale du moineau est 36°, 1; celle du rat 34°; la mienne, sous la langue, 36°, 5. A 3ʰ 30ᵐ, le moineau n'a encore que 38°, 7 dans le rectum.

Voici donc une expérience dans laquelle je suis arrivé en une heure un quart à une pression minima de 248 millimètres, c'est-à-dire à moins d'un tiers de la pression normale, pendant laquelle je suis resté 45 minutes au-dessous de 400 millimètres, sans avoir éprouvé de malaise à partir du moment où j'ai commencé à respirer régulièrement l'air suroxygéné. Mon pouls est resté dès lors à son chiffre normal; il s'est même abaissé vers la fin, soit à cause du long repos dans la station assise, soit sous l'influence de la respiration d'un air suroxygéné. A côté de moi, un moineau et un rat se trouvaient fort malades, et leur température s'abaissait de plusieurs degrés. Quant à moi, bien loin de courir un danger, je ne ressentais aucun des inconvénients légers de la décompression, ni l'état nauséeux, ni le mal de tête, ni la congestion à la tête, et je n'en éprouvai pas davantage après être sorti de l'appareil. Il me semblait même que j'eusse pu aller beaucoup plus bas encore, sans nul encombre, et j'y étais parfaitement disposé, si mes pompes à vapeur, fatiguées du travail, n'eussent refusé d'épuiser davantage l'air des cylindres. Peut-être dois-je en accuser la complicité des personnes présentes à l'expérience, qui venaient fréquemment me regarder à travers les hublots et, malgré l'aspect tout à fait naturel de ma physionomie, semblaient fort effrayées de me voir exposé à cette énorme diminution de pression. Elle correspondait, en effet, à plus de 8800 mètres, c'est-à-dire à une hauteur supérieure à celle que les voyageurs en montagne et les aéronautes, hormis MM. Coxwel et Glaisher, aient pu atteindre encore. Je n'éprouvais aucun malaise à cette pression qui avait failli être si funeste aux deux intrépides Anglais, et à laquelle devaient périr peu de mois plus tard MM. Crocé-Spinelli et Sivel.

These experiments, as a whole, demonstrated that artificially-produced diminution of pressure caused effects similar to those which are experienced by travellers on the earth, or in balloon, at great elevations; and that the appearance of some of these effects may be retarded, or if they appear that they may be *temporarily* driven away, by inspiring oxygen. They also proved that one may descend with extreme rapidity from great heights without injurious effects appearing immediately. In his experiment No. 256, M. Bert made a descent, so to speak, of 15,000 feet in ten minutes; and in No. 257 he came down 17,400 feet in nine minutes, in each case, it seemed, without taking any harm.

Emboldened by the impunity which apparently could be enjoyed by the use of this simple means, MM. Crocé-Spinelli and Sivel, accompanied by M. Gaston Tissandier, upon April 15, 1875, started upon another aerial voyage. The two former died at or about 28,000 feet above the sea, and M. Tissandier narrowly escaped. In discussing what was the cause of the death of these two unfortunates, M. Bert says (p. 1061) that the quantity of oxygen they carried was insufficient for so high an ascent,[1] and this may have been the case; but it is certain that the immediate cause of the catastrophe was not due to exhaustion of their supply, inasmuch as, when the balloon reached earth again, there was a quantity of oxygen still remaining in the *ballonnets* in which it was carried.

The opinion of M. Bert was that no harm would have been taken if these voyagers had imbibed more oxygen, and he appears to have imagined that this was proved by the fact that he himself (while inhaling the gas) had been able to sustain a pressure of 248 mm. ($= 9.057$ inches) for *one or two minutes*. This experiment, however, proved no more than that he was able to live for one or two minutes in air of about one-third the density of that to which we are accustomed; and there seems every likelihood, if he had

---

[1] "J'étais alors absent de Paris, et prévenu par une lettre de Crocé-Spinelli de leur prochain voyage, lettre dans laquelle il m'indiquait la quantité d'oxygène qu'ils allaient emporter (elle devait être, je crois, de 150 litres), je lui fis remarquer l'insuffisance. 'Dans les hauts lieux où cette respiration artificielle vous sera indispensable, lui disais-je, vous devez compter, pour trois hommes, sur une consommation d'au moins 20 litres par minute; voyez comment votre provision sera vite épuisée.'"

continued for an hour or two at a pressure of 248 mm., he would have met with the same fate as his pupils. I contend that no certain conclusions can be drawn, in regard to this subject, as to the effects which will be produced in *hours* from experiments extending over *minutes*.

Although it has been pointed out that the artificial inhalation of oxygen was not found *necessary* at the pressures which are dealt with in this volume, I by no means decry its use, or entertain the opinion that it is undesirable. Mischief is unlikely to result from any quantity that a mountain-traveller will be able to imbibe, but it will always be found difficult to take such an amount as can yield substantial benefit. The most that can be expected from its employment is that it may "mitigate the distressing symptoms," or, possibly, slightly retard their appearance. And, although differing from the conclusions drawn by M. Bert, I take this opportunity to express admiration for the courage and perseverance with which he prosecuted his experiments; and terminate this inadequate reference to his labours by recommending *La Pression Barométrique* as a storehouse of interesting facts.

CHIMBORAZO, FROM GUAYAQUIL.

INDEX

INDEX.

ABRASPUNGO, 86, 316, 318-19, 332, 349, 398, 401.
Academicians, 16, 107, 288-93.
Accident to a mule, 285-6.
Acosta, Father Joseph de, 192-3, 375-7.
Aeronauts, Introd., v-vii, 377-80, 382, 438-42.
Agua Clara, 14.
Aguirre family, 127, 159, 184, 205, 217.
Aiguille du Dru, 299, 307.
—— du Géant, 58.
—— du Gouter, 229.
—— du Midi, 58.
Air (see Rarefaction of Air).
Alausi, Village of, 386.
Alchipichi, Hacienda of, 284.
Alcohol, 10.
Alligators, 4.
Aloasi, Village of, 108.
Alpargatas, 143.
Alpine Club, Introd., xii.
Altar, 85-6, 96, 235-6, 296, 302, 304-8, 334, 343, 347, 349, 353, 362-4.
Altitudes (see Greatest Altitudes).
—— determined in Ecuador, 339, 395-401.
Amazons, River, 25, 92, 193, 195, 201, 239, 290.
Ambato, basin of, 90, 97, 110.
—— Bishop of, 96, 116, 356.
—— Governor of, 87, 91.
—— population of, 93, 295.
—— town of, 82-3, 86, 89-97, 104, 178, 302, 316, 327-8, 370, 398, 399, 413-14, 422.
Amphipoda, 117, 361, 363.
Aña, tambo S., 122, 124, 138.
Ancon, 270.
Aneroid Barometers, 33, 38, 56-7, 67, 70, 72, 219-21, 325, 331-2, 344-5, 399, 401, 405-16.
Annelida (see Earth-worms).

Antiquities, 256-8, 268-84.
Antisana, 101, 121, 133, 145, 156, 159, 165, 184-205, 210-15, 224, 228, 230-1, 240, 245, 255, 262, 343, 345-7, 349, 351-3, 359, 363, 370, 372-3, 396, 400, 420, 422, 426-7, 429, 431.
—— Hacienda of, 41, 184, 186, 188-91, 194, 196, 198-200, 204, 354, 357, 361-3, 365-6, 398, 400, 423.
Antisanilla, Hacienda of, 159, 185, 188-9, 201, 204, 366, 400.
—— Lava-stream of, 187-9, 199.
Antonio, Village of S., 265-6.
Ants, 10, 355, 362.
Arachnida (see Scorpions and Spiders).
Arenal, the Great, 20, 21, 24, 26, 30-1, 33, 40-3, 76-8, 86, 93, 319, 332-3.
Arriaga, Padre, 275.
Arrieros, 6, 9, 21, 39-40, 159, 208, 309.
Arriero-courier, 47, 60, 62-3, 73.
Ascents, rate of, 32, 66, 70-1, 75, 79, 149, 162, 164, 191, 198, 234-5, 262-3, 298, 317, 331.
Ash, Volcanic (see Volcanic dust).
Atacatzo, 105-6, 108-9, 167, 170, 210, 231, 347.
Atahualpa, 257.
Atlantic Ocean, 239.
Atmospheric pressure (see Pressure).
Avalanches, ice-, 78, 307, 320-1, 338.
—— snow-, 195, 262.
Azuay, Province of, 294.

BAKER, Mr. E. G., 115, 353.
—— Sir S. W., 418.
Balsabamba, Village of, 11, 15.
Banks in Ecuador, 181-3.
Baños, Village of, 97, 193.
Baquero's Hotel, 98.
Barometer, Aneroid (see Aneroid).

INDEX.

Barometer, Mercurial, Introd., x, xii, 33-6, 53-7, 66-7, 69-72, 134, 157, 186, 195-6, 212, 219-21, 230, 232, 244, 249-50, 263, 297-8, 315, 319, 323, 325-7, 330-1, 339, 341, 343-4, 377, 395-8, 402-20.
—— range of, in Ecuador, 402-4.
Barona, Dr. Abel, 91.
Barraganetal, 14.
Base-line of the Academicians, 288-93.
Bass' Ale, 83, 178.
Bates, Mr. H. W., 10, 112, 116, 137-8, 200, 222, 236-7, 332, 354, 362, 365.
Batrachia, 116, 144, 334, 363.
Battle-axes, 270-1.
Bees (see Hymenoptera).
Beetles (see Coleoptera).
Bellew, Dr., 49.
Bellows, utility of, 51.
Beltran, David (of Machachi), 165, 218, 236, 241, 246, 297, 310-12, 314-15, 317-18, 321, 325, 327, 435.
Benham, Prof. W. B., 112, 351, 362.
Bert, Mons. Paul, Introd., viii, 301, 377–80, 382–3, 437-42.
Biot, Mons., 380.
Bishop of Ambato, 96, 116.
—— of Rochester, Introd., viii.
Blaine, Mr., 90, 168, 175.
Blanco, Rio, 313.
Bodegas de Babahoyo, 2-6, 15, 360, 391.
Body temperature, 52, 150, 301, 326, 368, 425-7.
Bogota, 284.
Bogs, 160.
Boiling-point observations, 33-4, 253, 417-20.
Bolivar, Province of, 294.
Bolivia, Introd., xi, 270.
Bombs, Volcanic, 138.
Bonds, Ecuadorian, 177.
Bonney, Prof. T. G., 65, 68, 94, 104, 111, 125, 140-1, 164, 189, 194, 212, 234, 242, 249, 263, 288, 297, 306, 316, 319, 329.
Bonpland, Mons. A., 27, 113-14, 365, 428-30.
Borrero, Dr., 174, 267.
Botanical Tables, 352-3.

Botany (see Ferns, Flowering plants, Fungi, Grasses, Lichens, Mosses).
Bothnia, Gulf of, 288.
Bouguer, Mons., 107, 111, 288.
Boulenger, Mr. G. A., 363.
Boussingault, Mons. J.-D., Introd., xiii, 23, 25, 27, 29-32, 41, 76-7, 185-6, 192, 236, 348, 351, 402-4, 431-5.
—— Glacier de, 349.
Brenchley, Mr., 211, 418.
Brévent, 33.
British Minister at Quito, Introd., xiii, 166, 172-3.
Britten, Mr. James, 352-3.
Brocklehurst, Mr. T. U., Introd., viii.
Bronze, 277-8.
Browning, E. Barrett, 33.
Bruhns, Karl (Life of Humboldt), 28-9, 77, 428-30.
Buckley, Mr., 10.
Buenos Ayres, 336.
Bugs (see Rhynchota).
Butterflies (see Lepidoptera).

CAAMAÑO, Senor, 175.
Callo, 99, 124, 127, 302.
Camellones, 8, 21, 286.
Cameron, Mr. Peter, 355, 362.
Campaña, F. J. (interpreter), 271, 295-6, 310-12, 314, 317-18, 321, 325, 327, 334, 386, 389, 391, 435-6.
Cañar, Province of, 294.
Candelaria, Hacienda of, 303-4, 308, 360, 398, 401.
Canzacoto, 214-15.
Carabourou, Pyramid of, 218, 292.
Carchi, Province of, 294.
Carihuairazo, 23, 85-7, 90, 97, 131, 158, 252, 295, 310-18, 327, 343, 345, 347, 349, 352, 363, 372, 401, 415, 423, 426-7, 436.
Carranqui, Village of, 256-7, 265-6, 268, 275.
Carrel, Jean-Antoine, Introd., xii, 6, 26, 34, 50-3, 59, 62, 67, 69, 71, 78-80, 107, 109, 116, 132, 136, 143, 145, 147, 150-1, 155, 164, 177, 190, 194-5, 197-8, 205, 207, 209-11, 224-5, 227, 235-6, 241, 244-5, 259, 261,

287-8, 297-8, 300, 304, 306-7, 311, 314, 318-19, 321, 323, 327, 334, 343-4, 381, 392, 396, 435.

Carrel, Louis, Introd., xii, 6, 26, 42, 50, 59, 68, 71, 73, 79, 81-2, 101, 122, 130, 132, 134, 136, 145, 150, 155, 159-60, 165, 209, 211-12, 225, 235, 236, 241, 244, 248, 261, 287, 297-8, 306-7, 311-12, 314, 321, 327, 334, 381, 435.

Carrel, Vallon de, 43, 58, 62, 331-3, 354, 364.

Carrion, Señor J., 173.

Carruthers, Mr. William, 21, 352.

Casella, Mr. Louis, 405, 418, 424.

Catarama, Village of, 86.

Cattle, 198, 202, 204, 244-5, 313.

Cayambe (mountain), 112, 121, 133, 145, 154, 156, 169, 215-16, 217-37, 238-40, 249, 251, 262, 332, 343, 345-7, 349, 351, 354-5, 359, 362-5, 370, 372-3, 400, 420, 423, 425-7.

—— Village of, 180, 218, 222-3, 227-8, 241, 245, 250, 255-6, 266, 398, 400.

Cayandeli, Hacienda of, 387, 401, 415.

Census, 1, 168, 294-5.

Centipedes, 354, 362.

Cevallos (arriero), 160, 164, 218, 241, 258, 265, 285-6, 304, 311, 313, 318, 321.

Chambers, Mr. G., Introd., xiv, 2-4, 13, 33-4, 38, 56, 66, 72, 97, 196, 311, 395-6, 402, 405, 421, 436.

Chambo, River, 85, 97.

Chanchan, River, 5, 336.

Chaupi, Hills of, 99, 170.

Chicago, ox-check of, 61-2, 83, 207.

Childers, Rt. Hon. H. C., Introd., xiv.

Chili, Introd., x, xi, 2

Chilian Minister, 294.

Chillapullu, 431.

Chillo, 124, 127, 159, 184-5, 205, 215, 255.

Chillogallo, Village of, 208.

Chimbo, 14, 86, 336, 390-1.

—— Bridge of, 14, 387, 389-90, 401, 415.

—— River, 4, 5, 13, 20, 86, 105, 323, 327, 336.

Chimbo, Village of S. José de, 15, 34, 412.

Chimborazo, 2, 5, 12-14, 20-33, 40-80, 82-7, 90, 93, 110, 114, 121, 131, 156, 158, 172, 193, 198, 200-2, 213, 215, 219, 230, 295, 299, 310-13, 316-43, 345-9, 351-5, 357, 362-5, 367-70, 372, 381, 387, 407-9, 425-36.

—— the breach, 25-6, 64, 66-7, 77, 338.

—— first Camp on, 40-2, 331, 399, 412, 414, 423, 425, 427.

—— second Camp on, 47-59, 76-80, 86, 193, 202, 299, 333-4, 368, 399, 407, 412-14, 423, 425, 427.

—— third Camp on, 59-60, 63, 66-7, 70, 73-5, 78-9, 193, 321, 333, 369, 372, 395, 399, 407, 413, 414, 423.

—— fourth Camp on, 318-19, 334, 401, 423.

—— fifth Camp on, 319, 321-2, 327-8, 332, 401, 415, 423.

—— sixth Camp on, 333, 401, 427.

—— seventh Camp on, 311-12, 334.

—— Arenals of, 20, 21, 24, 26, 30-1, 33, 40-3, 76-8, 86, 93, 319, 332-3.

—— crevasses on, 24, 26, 33, 58, 67-8, 327.

—— flora of, 333-4.

—— from the Pacific, 2, 20.

—— glaciers of, 23-5, 30, 58, 67-8, 75-8, 86-7, 319-20, 323, 327, 332, 335, 338.

—— height of, Introd., xi, 32-3, 71-2, 330, 339-43, 399, 401.

—— lava-streams of, 47, 57, 59, 64, 319.

—— Map of, 17, 80, 323, 334.

—— Marquis of, 82, 89, 91.

—— Northern Walls of, 320-1, 323, 327.

—— Pacific Ocean seen from, 68, 324.

—— North-west ridge of, 319, 321-3, 327, 332.

—— Province of, 294.

—— Southern Walls of, 25, 64-7, 75-9, 333, 337-8, 369, 372, 399.

—— Summits of, 23-4, 57, 64, 68-70, 78, 320, 325-9, 337, 339-42, 399, 408, 413-15.

Chimborazo, South-west ridge, 25, 46, 53, 58-60, 64-7, 75, 77, 321.
—— vallons of, 22, 40, 42-3, 46, 58, 62, 76, 331-3, 354, 364.
Chimu, 277.
Chinchona bark, 13, 243.
Chiribogas of Riobamba, 82, 89, 91, 312.
Chlorate of potash, 49-50, 381.
Chota, Valley of, 214-15.
Christian names, 103.
Chuarpongo, Hacienda of, 223, 400.
Chuquipoquio, Tambo of, 29, 79-90, 120, 311-13, 332-4, 385-6, 399, 408, 413-14, 423.
Church, Mr. G. E., 90, 168, 175-6.
Cloud, cumulus, 74-5, 145.
Cock-fighting, 222-3.
Col du Géant, Introd., x.
Colegio, Hacienda of, 186, 204-5.
Coleoptera, 10, 112, 116-17, 137-8, 169, 176, 200, 213, 222, 236-7, 246, 332, 354, 362, 365-6, 391.
Colias alticola, 200, 363-5.
—— *dimera*, 357, 364-5.
Colin, Mons., 382.
Collanes, Valley of, 303-8, 362, 401, 423.
Colombia, Introd., xiii, 246, 258, 267.
Colon, 407, 412, 414, 427.
Condamine, Mons. de la, 12, 15-17, 33, 107, 110-11, 128-9, 154, 158, 164, 196, 212, 218, 235-6, 287-93, 305, 340-3, 402-3.
Condor, 78, 200-5, 224.
Coral snake, 3.
Corazon, 105, 107-12, 116, 134, 158, 170, 210, 213, 215, 230-1, 343, 345, 347, 351-3, 360, 362-3, 365, 399.
Cordilleras, Parallel, 335-6.
Cornices, tufted, 120, 133-4, 191, 232.
Corredor Machai, 241-50, 353.
Cotocachi (mountain), 99, 133, 169, 231, 256, 258-65, 334, 343, 345, 347, 349, 352, 355-6, 358-9, 364-5, 372-3, 400.
—— Village of, 178, 259-60, 264-7, 295, 398, 400.
Cotopaxi, 73, 96, 98-9, 110, 121-30, 135-59, 162, 170, 210, 231, 252-5, 322-30, 332, 336-7, 343, 345, 347, 349, 353, 370, 372-3, 399, 408, 413, 415, 420, 422-4, 426-7, 433, 436.
Cotopaxi, angles of slopes, 123, 147.
—— crater of, 121-2, 125-7, 128, 130, 146-54, 210, 252, 322, 324, 330.
—— dust ejected by, 125, 138, 140-2, 146-7, 153, 326-30.
—— eruptions of, 125-9, 138, 147, 153-5, 322-30.
—— fish ejected by ? 252-4.
—— flames from, 128, 152-3.
—— glaciers on, 146, 349.
—— height of, 154-5, 399.
Couloir, 109.
Cousobamba, Village of, 222.
Cowper, W. (quotations from), 117, 246.
Crania, 284.
Crater of Altar, 305-7.
—— Antisana, 197.
—— Carihuairazo, 316.
—— Chimborazo, 337.
—— Cotocachi, 264.
—— Cotopaxi, 121-2, 125-7, 128, 130, 146-54, 210, 252.
—— Pichincha, 209-11.
—— Sangai, 74.
Crevasses on Antisana, 190-1, 194-5, 197-8, 349.
—— Carihuairazo, 315.
—— Cayambe, 231-3.
—— Chimborazo, 24, 26, 33, 67-8, 327.
—— Illiniza, 132-3.
—— Sara-urcu, 248-9.
Crickets, 116.
Crocé-Spinelli (aeronaut), 378-9, 382, 438, 441.
Crosse & Blackwell, Messrs., 62.
Crustacea, 117, 361, 363, 366.
Cuenca, Town of, 174, 277, 288, 295.
Currant-bushes, 87, 250, 333.
Cutuchi, River, 97-9, 124, 127, 137, 302.
Cuzco, 270, 274.
Cyclopium cyclopum, 117, 251-5, 363.

DARWIN, Dr., Introd., x.
Daule, River, 4.
David (see Beltran).
Day, the late Dr. F., 255, 363.

INDEX.

Débris, Glacier de, 17, 58, 73, 76-8, 80, 320, 338.
—— Vallon de, 43, 58, 76, 333.
Declaration of F. J. Campaña, 435-6.
Deer, 115, 160, 225.
Demerara, 112.
Depôt on Chimborazo, 43.
Diptera, 112, 114, 116, 130, 176, 200, 250, 359-61, 363, 391, 430.
Distant, Mr. W. L., 134, 363.
Dixon, Mr. George, Introd., xiii.
Dogs on Cayambe, 224-7.
—— of Machachi, 118-19.
—— Pedro de Penipe, 314-15, 318, 321-2.
Domingo (arriero), 302, 311-12, 318, 321.
—— S. de los Colorados, 214-15.
Donkeys, 9, 106-7.
Dormida, la, 238-41, 243, 250, 354-5, 359, 363, 398, 400, 423.
Dragon-flies, 115, 355, 362.
Dress, 148-9.
Dru, Aiguille du, 299, 307.
Druce, Mr. H., 357-8.
Drunkenness, 266.
Duprat, Señor J. G., 91, 94.
Duran, Village of, 390.
Dykes, 110, 132.
Dysentery, 50, 79.

Earrings, 167, 183.
Earthquakes, 260, 267, 303.
Earthworms, 111-12, 351, 362.
Earwigs, 354-5, 362.
Eaton, Rev. A. E., 363, 366.
Ecuador, President of, Introd., xiii, 172-5, 264, 294.
—— bonds, 177, 386, 390.
—— banks in, 181-3.
Ecuadorian loan, Introd., xii.
Eigher, 306.
Ellis, Mr. W., 196, 339, 395-6, 417.
Ensillada, 21, 209-11.
Entomology, 113-17, 134, 137-8, 169, 187, 200-1, 213, 215, 222, 236-7, 239, 246, 297, 332, 354-66, 391.
Equator, 124, 156, 162, 169, 186, 201, 228, 240.
Eruptions of Cotopaxi, 125-9, 138, 147, 153-5, 322-30.

Eruptions of Sangai, 73-5.
—— Tunguragua, 96-7.
Esmeraldas, 105, 126, 159.
—— Province of, 16, 258, 294.
—— River, 124, 228.
Espinosa, Señor Javier, 173.
—— Señor Jarrin de, 222-4, 227, 229, 231, 236.
Everest, Mount, Introd., viii., 378, 437, 439.
Ewbank, Mr. Thomas, 273, 281.

Falcons, 224.
Ferns, 62, 115, 187, 199, 250, 259, 333, 352.
Fish, 117, 251-5, 363.
Fleas, 98, 100, 303.
Flies (see Diptera).
Flores, Señor Antonio (Pres. of Ecuador), 175.
Flower, Dr. W. H., 283.
Flowering plants, 21, 87, 111, 115, 144, 199-200, 213, 308, 333-4, 350-3.
Food, Introd., xi, 45, 185.
Forsyth, Sir T. D., 49, 84.
Fossilized bones, 65.
Foxes, 115.
Freshfield, Mr. Douglas, Introd., xiii., 392.
Frogs, 103, 116.
—— tree-, 116, 334.
Frost-bite, 71, 81-2, 91.
Fuchsias, 115, 250, 353.
Fungi, 199, 209, 352.

Gaiters, 71, 81.
Galti, Hacienda of, 386, 389, 401.
Garcilasso de la Vega, 239-40, 276.
Gasteren Thal, 307.
Gay-Lussac, Mons., 380.
Geneva, 398.
Gepp, Mr. Antony, 352.
Giacometti (maître d'hôtel), 170-1, 216.
—— hotel, 166.
Gilliss, Lieut. J. M., 270, 273.
Glacier de Boussingault, 349.
—— de Débris, 58, 73, 77-8, 80, 320, 338, 349.
—— de Humboldt, 349.
—— de Moreno, 87, 349.

Glacier de Reiss, 320, 349.
—— de Spruce, 320, 349.
—— de Stübel, 323, 327, 332, 349.
—— de Thielmann, 58, 62, 67, 349.
—— de Tortorillas, 349.
—— Espinosa, 231.
—— Tschingel, 307.
Glaciers, 348-50.
—— on Altar, 305, 307, 349.
—— Antisana, 190-1, 194-5, 197-8, 349.
—— Carihuairazo, 315-16, 349.
—— Cayambe, 228-9, 231-3, 349.
—— Chimborazo, 24-5, 58, 67-8, 75-8, 86-7, 319-20, 323, 327, 332, 349-50.
—— Cotocachi, 264, 349.
—— Cotopaxi, 146, 349.
—— Illiniza, 132-3, 297-8, 349.
—— Sara-urcu, 244, 247-9, 349.
—— Sincholagua, 160-2, 349.
Glaisher, Mr. J., Introd., vii, 35, 424, 441.
Gobierno (tambo), 13-15, 38, 187, 399, 407, 412, 414.
Godin, Mons., 288, 402.
Godman & Salvin, Messrs., 200, 357, 363-4.
Godoy, Señor J. (Chilian Minister), 294.
Gold, 92, 155, 181, 240, 266, 269, 277.
Gordonstown (Jamaica), 406.
Gorham, Rev. H. S., 116, 213, 222, 246, 354, 362.
Gosset, Mr. P. C., 195.
Gouter, Aiguille du, 229.
Graham, Mr. W. W., Introd., viii.
Grande, Rio, 105, 158, 160, 185.
Grasses, 87, 160, 198-9, 242, 244, 246, 248, 264, 333, 352.
Graves, 282-4.
Greatest altitudes for Batrachia, 363.
—— Beetles, 213, 332, 362, 365-6.
—— Butterflies, 200, 357, 363-5.
—— Centipedes, 354, 362.
—— Crustacea, 361, 363, 366.
—— Cumulus cloud, 145.
—— Earthworms, 112, 351, 362.
—— Ferns, 62, 333, 352.
—— Flies, 361, 363.
—— Flowering plants, 111, 144, 199, 250, 333-4, 350-3.
—— Fuchsias, 250, 353.

Greatest altitudes for Fungi, 209, 352.
—— Grasses, 264, 352.
—— Hymenoptera, 356-7, 362.
—— Lichens, 76, 333, 350, 352.
—— Mosses, 264, 316, 333, 350-2.
—— Moths, 358-9, 363.
—— night passed at, 157.
—— Phasmas, 355, 362.
—— position determined on the spot by instruments, Introd., x.
—— Reptiles, 363.
—— Rhynchota, 134, 361, 363.
—— Scorpions, 107, 363.
—— Spiders, 360, 363.
Gregorio (of Machachi), 142, 165.
Gregory, Mr. J. R., 328.
Gringos, 92, 99, 100, 173, 221, 227.
Guachala, Hacienda of, 217, 222-3, 366, 398, 400, 408, 421.
Gualea, 214-15.
Guallabamba, Ravine of, 127, 218-21, 400, 409, 413, 422.
—— Rio de, 185, 228.
—— Village of, 221-2, 400.
Guamani, 185.
Guamote, Village of, 86, 386, 389, 401.
Guanaxuato, Mines of, 341.
Guaranda, 12-15, 18-39, 46-7, 51-2, 60, 62-3, 73, 79, 83, 105, 178, 295, 311, 319, 323, 325, 332, 336, 398, 399, 407, 412, 414, 427, 436.
Guard, 60, 62-3.
Guayaquil, Introd., xiv, 1-4, 12-14, 16-18, 20, 22, 33-4, 36, 38, 56, 66, 71-2, 97, 125, 129, 173-5, 178, 180-2, 203, 221, 230, 232, 244, 250, 263, 283, 293, 295, 311, 339, 354, 366, 385, 387, 390-1, 395-6, 402, 405, 407, 410-12, 414-15, 421, 425, 427, 436.
Guayas, Province of, 294.
—— River, 3-5, 354, 358, 366.
Gunzberg, Baron Gabriel de, 203.
Guyot, Dr. Arnold, 289, 396.

HACIENDA, 82.
Hail, 29, 84, 112, 134, 143-4, 162, 194, 261.
Hall, Colonel, 29, 76, 348, 433.
Hamilton, Mr. Douglas-, Introd., xiii, 166, 172-3, 180.

Hassaurek, Mr. F., 176, 218.
Headache, 49, 52, 61, 150, 368-70, 374.
Hebrides, 249.
Henderson, Dr., 49.
Herschell, Sir John F. W., 424.
Heuer, Mr. Edmund, Introd., xiii.
Hicks, Mr. J. J., 395, 397, 425.
Highest-point tables, 112, 352-3, 362-3.
Himalayas, Introd., viii, x, xi.
Hooker, Sir Joseph, 419-20.
Hotels, 11, 98, 170-1, 268, 391.
Huayna-Capac (Inca monarch), 266, 277.
Humboldt, Alex. von, Introd., x, xi, 23, 25, 27, 33, 72, 76-7, 113-14, 123, 129, 189, 201, 205, 212, 236, 251-5, 334, 340-2, 348, 351, 428-30, 432-3.
—— Glacier de, 349.
Humming-birds, 214-15.
Hutantaqui, Village of, 265-6.
Hymenoptera, 96, 116, 200, 355-7, 362, 391.

IBARRA, Town of, 257-8, 265, 267-8, 283, 288, 295, 366.
Ibi Gamin (Kamet), Introd., x, 419.
Ice-axes, 163-4, 322, 327.
Ice-traffic, 22.
Icicles, 75, 297-8.
Illiniza, 99, 105, 107-8, 130-4, 162, 210, 231, 233, 235-6, 258, 287, 295, 297-9, 343, 347, 349, 356, 361-3, 370, 372-3, 399-401, 408-9, 413-15, 423, 426-7.
Iltaqui, Hacienda of, 259-60, 400.
Iluman, Village of, 265.
Imbabura, Province of, 256-8, 265-7, 276-7, 281, 284, 294.
—— (mountain), 228, 231, 252, 256, 258, 265, 347.
Incas, 237, 257, 266, 270, 277.
Inca's house, 302.
Indians, 9, 39-40, 60-2, 83, 87, 98, 177-8, 205, 214, 227, 239-40, 264-7, 271, 274-6, 278-9, 282, 295, 311.
Inscribed stones, 287, 290-2.
Insects (see Entomology).
Isco, River, 187-8.

JACOBY, Mr. M., 117, 354, 362.
Jamaica, 406, 412, 427.
Jambeli, bridge of, 105, 297.
Jameson, Dr. W., 112, 168, 230.
Jarrin, Pointe, 231-4, 259.
Jefo-politico, 22, 60, 119, 222-3, 227, 245, 255, 268, 303.
Jipipapa, Town of, 295.
Jones, Mr. (of Quito), 180.
José, S. de Chimbo, 15.
Juan & Ulloa, 33, 128, 274-5, 288, 290, 340-2.

KAMET (Ibi Gamin), Introd., x.
Karakorum range, 49.
Kirby, Mr. W. F., 362.
Krakatoa, 154, 339.

LACE made by Indians, 178.
Ladak, 378.
Land, value in Ecuador, 304-5.
Latacunga, 97-8, 105, 124-7, 129, 178, 295, 302, 398, 399.
—— ladies of, 98, 101.
Lava, 43, 47, 57, 64, 65, 67, 78, 110, 111, 123, 126, 138, 140, 145, 146, 148, 153, 189, 194, 263, 319, 336-8.
Lava-streams, 64-5, 187, 189, 194, 319, 327, 337.
Leon, Province of, 294.
Lepidoptera, 10, 113-15, 117, 200-1, 239, 297, 357-9, 361, 363-5, 388, 430.
Lice-eating, 10, 98, 101.
Lichens, 76, 111, 144, 169, 189, 199, 213, 250, 264, 308, 316.
Lightning, 144, 147, 162-4, 170.
Lima, 270, 294.
Limpiopongo, Plain of, 124, 137.
Litter, 87-8, 90.
Livingstone's Last Journals, 418.
Lizards, 103, 115, 176, 218.
Llamas, 96, 297.
Llanganati, mountains of, 97, 106, 110, 342, 347.
Lloa, Village of, 208, 215.
Loads, 6, 47, 132.
Loja, Town of, 295.
—— Province of, 294.
Loma, tambo, 11, 12, 15, 399.

Lopez, Señor, 135.
Lorenzo (of Machachi), 108-9, 165.

MACHACHI, 95, 97, 99-119, 124-5, 130, 134, 136, 138-9, 141-2, 155, 158, 160, 165, 218, 254-5, 257, 287, 296, 298, 300-2, 313, 328, 358, 361-3, 398, 399, 404, 408, 409, 413-15, 422, 427.
—— basin of, 99, 101, 105, 114, 185, 207, 355.
Machangara, River, 207.
Macheta, 182, 304, 312.
Magdalena, Village of, 208.
Maize-heads in stone, 274-5.
Malchingi, Village, 284, 286.
Maldonado, Don Pedro, 12, 15-17.
—— map, 12, 15-17, 158, 240.
Manabi, Province of, 173, 294.
Maps of Ecuador, 12, 15-18, 339.
Marcet, Dr. W., 49.
Massee & Murray, Messrs., 209, 352.
Masson, Mons. G., Introd., viii. 439.
Mathews, Mr. C. E., Introd., xii.
Maximum temperatures (see Temperatures).
Medios, 181.
Menten, Father J. B., 93, 168, 403.
Mera, Señor J. L., 173.
Mexico, Introd., viii, 341, 348, 354.
Miguel, S. (village), 15.
Millipedes, 354.
Mindo, 214-15.
Minimum temperatures (see Temperatures).
Minister, British, Introd., xiii, 166, 311.
—— Chilian, 294.
—— for Foreign Affairs, 91-2.
Mitten, Mr. G., 352.
Mocha, Village of, 30, 83, 87, 90-1, 312, 398, 401, 431.
Mojanda, 169, 218, 228, 231, 255-6, 265, 284-5.
Mona, la (Village of), 7, 10, 11, 15.
Money, 181-2.
Monk's Valley, 224, 229-30.
Mont Blanc, Introd., ix, 33, 58, 263, 380, 419, 431, 438.

Montenegro, Lieut.-Col., 22.
Montufar, Señor Carlos, 27, 114, 428-9.
Moraines, 191, 194, 229, 249.
Moreno, Garcia (Pres. of Ecuador), 90, 173-4, 265, 267, 403.
—— Assassination of, 174.
—— Glacier de, 87, 349.
Morphos, 10, 388.
Mosses, 76, 111, 134, 145, 169, 230, 239, 250, 308, 316, 333-4, 350-2, 430.
Moths (see Lepidoptera).
Mountain-sickness, Introd., v-xi, 26, 43-4, 48-53, 59, 61, 67, 70, 84-5, 120-1, 157, 330-1, 366-84, 429, 431, 434, 437-42.
Muiscas, 284.
Mulalo, Village of, 126-7, 129-30, 302.
Mules, 6, 42, 46-7, 76, 79, 159-60, 208, 285-6, 309.
Muñapamba, Village of, 10-12, 15, 38, 187, 399, 407, 412, 414.
Musquitoes, 360, 391.
Myriopoda, 354, 362.

NANEGAL, 214-15.
Nanti, Village of, 85, 386, 389, 401.
Napo, River, 124, 193, 215.
Naranjal, Valley of, 307-8, 401, 423.
Neuroptera, 115, 355, 362.
Newcastle (Jamaica), 406.
Nocturnal Minima (see Temperatures).
Nono, 18, 214-15.
Northern Walls of Chimborazo, 320-1, 323, 327.

OBERTI, Paul, 93.
Ocampo, Hacienda of, 400.
Olalla, Hacienda of, 291.
Oliver, Prof. D., 242, 352.
Olliff, Mr. A. S., 116-17, 213, 236, 332, 354, 362, 365.
Oltmanns, Prof. J., 340.
Opossums, 115.
Orellana, 239-40.
Oriente, Province of, 258, 294.
Ornamentation of Pottery, 280.
Oro, Province of, 294.
Orthoptera, 354, 362, 391.
Orton, Prof. J., 117, 201, 205.

INDEX. 453

Osten Sacken, Baron C. R., 359, 363.
Otovalo, 178, 180, 218, 256, 258, 260, 265-6, 268, 284, 295.
Outfit, 46.
Owen, Sir Richard, 65.
Ox-cheek of Chicago, 61-2, 83, 207.
Oxygen, Introd., viii, 49, 377-80, 382, 437-42.
Oyambaro, Pyramid of, 291-2.

PABLO, Lake S., 265.
Pacific Ocean, 2, 12, 20, 68, 105, 124-5, 201, 239, 322, 324, 328.
—— Range of Ecuador, 5, 12-14, 21, 86, 106, 323, 335-6, 407.
Pamir, 378.
Panama, 1, 10, 17, 125, 293, 391, 426-7.
—— baggage-smashers, 283.
—— hats, 101, 421.
Panecillos, 99, 117, 134, 169, 208, 266.
Papallacta, 193, 217, 239, 251.
Paraffin-oil, 243.
Paramos, 90, 99, 297, 312, 386.
Pasochoa, 101, 105-6, 158, 170, 185, 205, 231, 336, 355.
Passports, Introd., xiv.
Pastassa, River, 85, 97, 193.
Patate, River, 97.
Pazmiño, Señor, 22, 37, 39.
Pedregal, Hacienda of, 105, 136, 155, 158-9, 164, 355, 362, 398, 399.
—— Rio, 159.
Penipe, Village of, 85, 303-4, 308-9, 360, 398, 401.
—— Pedro de, 314-15, 321-2.
Perring, Mr., 2, 51, 58, 60, 62, 70, 73, 79, 80, 98, 136, 184, 257, 368.
Peru, Introd., xi, 2, 239-40, 270-1, 274-77, 289, 376.
Peso, 181.
Phasmas, 116, 335, 355, 362.
Photography, 37, 189, 246, 326.
Pichincha, 94, 106-7, 112, 156, 164, 166-7, 170, 201, 207-15, 230-1, 332, 334, 336, 342-3, 345, 347, 352, 354-6, 358-60, 362-6, 400, 423, 427-9.
—— Province of, 258, 294.
Pifo, Village of, 185, 217, 291.
Pike's Peak, 299.

Pilalo, 215.
Pills, 294.
Pimelodus cyclopum, 251-5.
Piñantura, Hacienda of, 185, 187-8, 201, 204, 366.
Pintac, Village of, 186-7, 204.
Pita, Rio, 124, 136-7, 159, 164, 185-6.
Pizarro, Gonzalo, 239-40, 250.
Pizarros, 276.
Plagemann, Dr. A., Introd., viii.
Plantamour, Prof., 398.
Platt, of Oldham, 205.
Playas, Hacienda of, 9, 11, 15.
Pocock, Mr. R. I., 354, 360, 362-3.
Police, Commissary of, 22, 37, 39.
Ponchos, 102, 241.
Population in Provinces of Ecuador, 294.
—— in Towns of Ecuador, 295.
Portillo Pass, Introd., x.
Porto-viejo, 295.
Potash, chlorate of, 49-50, 381.
Pottery, 266, 277-86.
Prescott on Chimborazo, 20.
Presidents of Ecuador, 172-5, 267, 292.
Pressure, Atmospheric, Introd., v-xii, 33-6, 38, 44-5, 51-3, 57, 70, 84-5, 149-50, 330-1, 344-5, 367-84.
Prices, 39, 83, 178-80.
Priests, 22, 175, 259, 264, 268, 295.
Provinces of Ecuador, 294.
Provisions, 45-6.
Puela, 215.
Puengasi ridge, 105, 167, 184-5.
Pulse, rate of, 301, 368-9, 374, 377-82, 438-40.
Pumas, 115, 229, 243.
Pumice, 94-5, 104, 212.
Putnam, Dr., 254-5.
Pyramids of Quito, 287-93.
Pyrenean mastiffs, 119.

QUARTZ, 245, 249.
Quebradas, 108, 168, 218-19, 259-60.
Quicksand, 313.
Quinine, 22, 180, 243.
Quito, 5, 15-17, 24, 99, 107, 112, 124-5, 165-85, 187, 203, 205-9, 214, 216-19, 220-1, 236, 239, 251, 257, 265-7, 286, 288, 290-1, 295, 309, 328, 342-

INDEX.

3, 348, 389, 391, 398, 399, 402-4, 408-10, 413, 415, 421-2, 427-8, 430.
Quito, Bank of, 181-3.
—— Basin of, 105, 167.
—— Hotel at, 166, 170-1.
—— lighting of, 206.
—— Observatory at, 217, 403, 421-2.
—— Omnibus, 97.
—— Panecillo of, 169-70, 217, 362, 399, 410.
—— population of, 167-8, 295.
—— Road, 2, 6, 7, 8, 20, 90, 97-9, 105, 173-4, 187, 296, 299-302, 311-12, 316, 334, 360, 386.
—— water-carrier at, 168-9.
Quitu, 239-40, 277.
Quixos, 239-40.

RACINES, ANTONIO (of Machachi), 100, 117-18, 141, 165, 254, 287.
Railway, the Ecuadorian, 135, 385, 387, 389-91.
—— Trans-Andean, 336.
Raisin, Miss C., 94, 104.
Range in altitude, 112-13, 350, 357-8, 364-6.
Rarefaction of air, Introd., vi, viii, 44, 46-53, 66, 70, 121, 149-50, 370, 377, 380-3.
Rates of speed, 27, 31-2, 66, 70-1, 75, 79, 149, 155, 162, 164, 191, 198, 234-5, 262-3, 298-301, 317, 325, 331, 344, 369-74.
Reals, 181.
Rebolledo, Señor Rafael, 188-9, 204, 291.
Recurring species, 112, 213, 361, 364-6.
Reed-pipes, 116, 119.
Regnault's Tables, 417.
Reiss, Dr. W., 186.
Reiss, Glacier de, 320.
Reiss & Stübel, Doctors, Introd., xiii, 33, 73, 96, 110, 129, 131, 154, 158, 186, 196-7, 212, 230, 235, 270, 297, 305, 321, 341-3, 349, 398, 410.
Remy, Mons. Jules, 210-11, 418.
Rendle, Mr. A. B., 352.
Reptilia, 3-4, 103, 115, 176, 218, 363.
Respiration, 30, 31, 49, 52, 150, 367-70, 374-5, 379-84, 431, 433.

Revolutions in Ecuador, 173-5, 180.
Rhynchota, 10, 112, 134, 176, 200, 361, 363, 391.
Riobamba, 30, 82, 85-7, 91, 105-6, 166, 255, 268, 276, 293, 295, 302-3, 308-12, 328, 340-1, 346, 385-7, 389-90, 398, 401-2, 422, 431-2, 436.
Rios, Province of, 294.
River Amazons, 25, 92, 193, 195, 201, 239, 290.
—— Blanco, 313.
—— Chambo, 85, 97.
—— Chimbo, 4, 5, 13, 20, 86, 105, 323, 327.
—— Daule, 4.
—— Esmeraldas, 124, 228.
—— Grande, 105, 158, 160, 185.
—— Guallabamba, 185, 228.
—— Guayas, 3-5, 354, 366.
—— Isco, 187-8.
—— Jorge, S., 10.
—— Machangara, 207.
—— Napo, 124, 193, 215.
—— Pastassa, 85, 97, 193.
—— Patate, 97.
—— Pedregal, 159.
—— Pita, 124, 136-7, 159, 164, 185-6.
—— Yaguachi, 4-5.
Roads, 89-90, 97-9, 187.
—— the Royal, 8-12, 187.
Rochester, Bishop of, Introd., viii.
Rocks, descriptions of, 65, 67-8, 164, 189, 194, 212, 230, 234, 242, 249, 263, 286-7, 297, 306, 315-16, 319.
Rosa, farm of S., 93.
Rosario, Hacienda de la, 122-4, 130-1, 134, 153, 399, 408, 413-14.
Rumiñahui, 99, 101, 105, 110, 116, 136, 145, 158, 170, 231, 336, 343, 347, 355.
Rycaut, Sir Paul, 239.

SALISBURY, Marquis of, Introd., xiii.
Salvias, 115.
Sanancajas, Paramo of, 90, 312.
Sand, Volcanic, 43, 140.
Sangai, 73-5, 96, 131, 153, 156, 235-6, 252, 304, 336-7, 383, 387.
Sara-urcu, 236, 242-51, 307, 327, 343, 345-7, 349, 400, 423.
Saussure, Mons. H. B. de, Introd., ix, x, 380-1.

INDEX.

Savaneta, Village of, 9, 11, 15.
Schlagintweits (the Travellers), Introd., x, xi, 419-20.
Sclater, Dr. P. L., 214.
Scorpions, 107, 176, 360, 363, 391.
Scott, Mr. R. H., 396.
Shakespeare, quotation from, 260.
Sharp, Dr. D., 116, 354, 362.
Sherry, Dry, 93.
Shoes, 39-40, 143.
Sibambe, Village of, 386, 390-1.
Sincholagua, 101, 124, 145, 157-64, 170, 185, 231, 233, 343, 347, 349, 352.
Sivel, Mons. (aeronaut), 378-9, 382, 438, 441.
Slater, Mr. Daniel, 206.
Smyth, Prof. Piazzi, 302.
Snakes, 3-4.
Snow, 29, 30, 58, 64-5, 68-70, 73, 109, 132-3, 142, 146, 160, 162, 190-2, 194-5, 213, 228, 248-9, 261-2, 298, 305, 308, 315, 321-2, 325-7, 342, 346-8.
Snow-blindness, 59, 71, 192-3, 318.
Snow-cornices, 120, 133-4, 191, 232, 298, 315.
Snow-line, 86, 110, 327, 346-8.
Snow-spectacles, 192, 206, 314.
Snow-storms, 84, 225, 243, 261, 298.
Sol, 181.
Southern Walls of Chimborazo, 25, 64-7, 75-9, 333, 337-8, 369, 372.
Spiders, 112, 115-16, 169, 243, 360, 363, 391.
Springs, 160.
Spruce, Mr. R., 12-13, 73, 349.
—— Glacier de, 320, 349.
Spurs, 102.
Spy, the, 240-1, 243, 246.
Squier, Mr. E. George, 270, 275.
Stars in stone, 268-71.
Steam-blasts, 74-5, 147, 150, 153-4, 330.
Stebbing, Rev. T. R. R., 118, 363.
Stevenson, Mr. W. B., 18.
St. Bernard, 398.
St. John, Mr. Alfred, Report by, 267, 294, 390-1.
St. Thomas, 426-7.
Stone Age, 256, 268.
Stone implements, 256, 258, 268-77.

Strachan, Mr. R., 396-7.
Stragglers, 113-14, 134.
Stübel, Glacier de, 323, 327, 332, 349.
Sucre, 181.
Sulphur, 338.
Sunda, Straits of, 339.
Surinam, 112.

Tambillo ridge, 101, 105, 166-7.
Tambos, 10-11, 193.
—— keeper at Machachi, 99, 100, 117-18, 141, 165, 254, 287.
Tambo of S. Aña, 122, 124, 138.
—— Balsabamba, 11.
—— Chuquipoquio, 29, 79-80, 120, 311-13, 332-4, 385, 399.
—— Gobierno, 13-15, 38, 187, 399, 407, 412, 414.
—— Loma, 11, 12, 15, 399.
—— Machachi (see Machachi).
—— Muñapamba, 11.
—— Playas, 11.
—— Savaneta, 11.
—— Tortorillas, 21, 24, 31, 40, 83, 86, 332-4.
Tapia, Plateau of, 341.
Teall, Mr. J. J. H., 189.
Temperatures, 15, 22, 41, 66, 70-1, 134, 142-3, 148, 160, 170, 186, 194, 196, 212, 221, 230, 232-3, 238, 244-6, 249-50, 253, 263, 297-8, 300-1, 313, 315, 319, 321, 323, 325-6, 346, 396-8, 421-4.
—— body, 52, 150, 301, 326, 425-7.
—— highest observed in the interior, 221, 422.
—— lowest observed, 149, 422.
—— maxima, 84, 221, 300, 421.
—— minima, 40, 41, 52, 59, 61, 84, 149, 194, 210, 237, 297, 300, 306-8, 311, 313, 319, 321, 421.
—— Table of Nocturnal Minima, 423.
—— on summits, 70, 110, 149, 196, 212, 233, 249, 263, 315, 325, 345-6.
Teneriffe, 302.
Tent, 59, 261-2, 327-8.
Tetons, 299.
Theakston, Mr. J., 6.
Theodolite, 24, 110, 259.
—— stand, 55-6.

INDEX.

Thielmann, Freiherr von, Introd., xiii, 130, 138-9, 349.
—— Glacier de, 58, 62, 67, 349.
Thermometers, boiling-point, 33-4.
Thunderstorms, 78, 84, 101, 116, 134, 136, 143, 162-4, 170, 186.
Tibet, 378.
Tissandier, Mons. Gaston (aeronaut), 379, 441.
Tiupullo ridge, 97, 99,105,122,170, 399.
Torre, Señor T. Gomez de la, 267-8, 283, 366.
Tortorillas, Glacier de, 349.
—— Tambo of, 21, 24, 31, 40, 41, 43, 83, 86, 332-4, 354, 357, 362-4, 436.
—— Vallon of, 43, 76.
Towns in Ecuador, 295.
Trans-Andean Railway, 336.
Treasures, 23, 92, 155, 240, 305.
Trotter, Col. H., 84.
Truxillo, 277.
Tschingel Glacier, 307.
Tulcan, 258, 295.
Tumbaco, Plain of, 106, 167, 185, 215, 217-18, 355-6, 363.
Tumuli, 266.
Tunguragua, 24, 30, 85, 96-7, 126, 156, 215, 252, 336-7, 343, 348-9.
—— Province of, 294.
Tupac (Inca monarch), 277.

Utuñac, Village of, 307.

Val Tournanche, Introd., xii, 308.
Valenciana, Mine of, 341.
Valparaiso, 336.
Vase-busts, 281.
Veintemilla, President of Ecuador, Introd., xiii, 172-5, 264, 294, 389-90.
—— Pointe, 172, 326.
Velasco, Don Juan de, 251, 266.
Ventanas, Village of, 86.
Venezuela, 112.
Verbenas, 115.
Verbeek, Mr. R. D. M., 339.
Verity, Mr. (interpreter), 180, 184, 188, 192, 205-6, 209, 218, 227, 229, 236, 241, 245-6, 258, 261, 265, 285, 294-5.
Vertical range, 113.

Villavicencio, Dr. Manuel, 12, 193, 209, 236, 251.
Volcanic dust, 43, 94-5, 103-4, 111, 125, 140-2, 146-8, 153, 230, 326-30, 336, 346.
Volcanic eruptions, 73-5, 94-5, 96-7, 103-4, 122-9, 138, 147, 153-4, 251, 264, 322-30.
Volcanoes, 74-5, 94-6, 121-30, 136-55, 164, 197, 210, 263-4, 266, 304-5, 313, 322-30, 336-9.

Wagner, Dr., 93.
Water, 14, 168.
Water-carrier at Quito, 168-9.
Waterhouse, Mr., 10.
Weasels, 115.
Weather, 10-11, 25, 29, 32, 45, 63, 66, 78, 84, 112, 116, 130-1, 134-5, 136, 143, 155, 186-7, 194, 208, 216, 225, 244-6, 298, 306-8, 314.
Wetterhorn, 315.
Whistles, Indian musical, 281.
White, Mr. Adam, 10.
White Valley, 229-30.
Wiener, Mons. C., 270, 274.
Wilson, Mr. J. S., 203.
Wind, 66, 69, 75, 78, 123, 146, 148, 233, 261, 297-8, 300, 306, 308, 322, 325.
Wine, virtues of, 50, 207.
Wisse, M., Boiling-point obs. by, 419-20.
Wolf, Dr., 127, 129, 130.
Wood-lice, 363, 366.

Yacu-larca, 313, 318.
Yaguachi, River, 4, 5.
—— Village, 390-1.
Yambo, Village, 97.
Yanasache lava, 138, 145.
Yana-urcu, 218.
Yarkund, 49, 84.
Yarouqui, Plain of, 218.

Zamborondon, 5.
Zinc, Sulphate of, 59, 192, 318.
Zoology (see Arachnida, Batrachia, Coleoptera, Crustacea, Diptera, Earthworms, Fish, Frogs, Hymenoptera, Lepidoptera, Reptilia, Rhynchota, Spiders, etc.)